T H E CLASSIC FRENCH CINEMA, 1930-1960

Indiana University Press
BLOOMINGTON AND INDIANAPOLIS

I.B. Tauris Publishers
LONDON AND NEW YORK

THE CLASSIC FRENCH CINEMA, 1930-1960

COLIN CRISP

Published in 1997 by

Indiana University Press
601 North Morton Street
Bloomington, Indiana 47404-3797   USA

and

I. B. Tauris and Co. Ltd.
Victoria House
Bloomsbury Square
London WC1B 4DZ

© 1993 by Colin Crisp
First paperback edition 1997

The paper used in this publication meets the minimum requirements of American
National Standard for Information Sciences—Permanence of Paper for Printed
Library Materials, ANSI Z39.48-1984.

Manufactured in the United States of America

Library of Congress Cataloging-in-Publication Data

Crisp, C. G.
    The classic French cinema, 1930–1960 / Colin Crisp.
        p.   cm.
    Includes bibliographical references. (p.   ) and index.
ISBN 0-253-31550-6 (cloth : alk. paper) — ISBN 0-253-21115-8 (pbk.)
    1. Motion pictures—France—History.   I. Title.
PN1993.5.F7C78   1993
791.43'0944'0904—dc20   92-21657

A full British CIP record is available from the British Library

ISBN 1-86064-165-2

1 2 3 4 5 01 00 99 98 97

For Jane

C O N T E N T S

Photo Section follows page 325

LIST OF FIGURES

ACKNOWLEDGMENTS

I would like to thank Griffith University for the support that it provided, both in time and in funding, while I was researching this material.

I would also like to thank, once more, the director and staff of the IDHEC library, without whom and without which this book would not have been possible.

I am most grateful to Marcel Carné for his kind permission to reproduce stills from *Le Jour se lève*, *Les Portes de la nuit*, *Les Enfants du paradis*, *Les Visiteurs du soir*, and *Juliette ou la clé des songes*, and also for permission to reproduce the poster for *Les Enfants du paradis* on the cover of this book.

My sincere thanks also to Melvyn A. Siblini of Les Editions Veyrier for permission to reproduce illustrations 15, 16, 27, 46, 47, and 48 from J. Siclier, *La France de Pétain et son cinéma*, and to Michel Rachline of Les Editions Albin Michel for permission to reproduce illustrations 4, 12, 31, and 35 from *Jacques Prévert: drôle de vie*, which appeared under the imprint of Les Editions Ramsay.

The following illustrations are reproduced by permission of *La Cinémathèque Française*: numbers 7, 18, 22, 34, 36, 39, 40, 41, 42, 43.

The following are reproduced from J.-L. Passek, *D'un cinéma l'autre*, published by the Centre Georges Pompidou, by permission of the author: 20, 50, 51, 52, 53.

All rights reserved on the following illustrations: 3, 8, 11, 13, 21, 23, 25, 26, 28, 29, 30, 32, 33, 37, 45, 54, 55, and 57, reproduced from C. Brieu, L. Ikor, and J. M. Viguier, *Joinville: Le Cinéma*, published by Les Editions Ramsay; 1, 14, 49 from F. Courtade, *Les Malédictions du cinéma français*, published by Alain Moreau; 17, reproduced from *La France de Pétain et son cinéma*, copyright held by J.-C. Sabria.

INTRODUCTION

This book proposes to investigate one of the most exciting and inventive of all national cinemas, the classic French cinema. For most purposes the classic period can be thought of as lasting from the introduction of sound in 1929 to the end of the fifties—a period of approximately thirty years.

For several decades—ever since in fact those New Wave critics such as Truffaut and Godard who later became directors successfully outlawed it as convention-ridden, literary, and unimaginative—the classic French cinema has not been well regarded even within France, and its visibility outside France has been severely limited. The technical and stylistic achievements of the French silent cinema which preceded it have never ceased to be respected, however infrequently the films themselves may be viewed; while the technical and stylistic achievements of the New Wave which displaced it have been canonized by a generation of critics as the rebirth of a cinema of sincerity, of creativity, and of commitment. But the three decades of filmmaking that separate these internationally acclaimed schools are usually thought of as having produced at best a scattering of fine films, which are fine either because they were made outside the industrial structures of the age or because they somehow transcended the constraints of those industrial structures.

Among the twenty or thirty films of the period which are widely recognized as impressive, most people interested in the cinema would have seen some or all of the following: *Zéro de conduite* and *L'Atalante; Sous les toits de Paris* and *A nous la liberté; Marius* and *Fanny; Boudu sauvé des eaux, Le Crime de M Lange, La Grande Illusion,* and *La Règle du jeu; La Kermesse héroïque; Le Jour se lève* and *Quai des brumes; Les Visiteurs du soir* and *Les Enfants du paradis; Pépé le Moko; Remorques; Orphée; Le Salaire de la peur; Les Dames du Bois de Boulogne;* and the Hulot films.

This list is already impressive and could easily be extended to a hundred films which must be considered fine by any standards; yet the usual explanation for the high quality of such films involves an appeal to the creative genius of certain specific directors—Jean Renoir, René Clair, Jacques Feyder, Robert Bresson, Jean Vigo, Jean Cocteau, Jean Grémillon, perhaps Henri-Georges Clouzot, Marcel Carné, Jacques Tati, Julien Duvivier, perhaps even the poet-scriptwriter Jacques Prévert. These individuals are usually seen as endowing the films with an expressive intensity that permits them to transcend the "classic" or routine production of the age. The possibility that such films are good not *despite* being borne of the classic production system, but rather because of it, that their quality and diversity were in fact a logical outcome of that system, is rarely contemplated. Yet this is the inevitable conclusion of any detailed study of the film industry of the time. It was precisely the structure of the production system which permitted René Clair to write and direct *Sous les toits de Paris, Le Million, A nous la liberté, Quatorze Juillet,* and *Le Dernier Milliardaire* at the same time as innumerable long-forgotten directors were transferring to the screen popular plays and operettas; that permitted Cocteau to write and direct *Orphée* and *Le Testament d'Orphée* at the same time as innumerable long-forgotten directors were filming Franco-Italian megaproductions. It was precisely the structure of the production system which allowed the ready absorption of those Russian and German filmmakers whose money and techniques generated the poetic realist movement with such films as *Quai des brumes* and *Le Jour se lève.* It was within the classic French production system that Jean Renoir and René Clair could produce such films as *Elena et les hommes, Le Testament du Dr Cordelier, Le Silence est d'or, Les Belles-de-nuit,* and *Les Grandes Manoeuvres* after a largely sterile period in America. It was precisely in France, where cultural traditions and institutions resisted the moral strictures of a censorship system, that sexuality and deviance could be freely explored at a time when the Hays Code and its analogues were inhibiting the representation of such themes elsewhere; that the class conflicts and social distress of the age could be explored at a time when such social realism was anathema elsewhere; that the injustices of the legal and political systems could be explored at a time when the Cold War was inhibiting such national self-criticism elsewhere.

It might be claimed that this extraordinary diversity casts doubt on the very existence of a French classic cinema as a distinct and definable entity. Did a French classic cinema ever exist in the sense that its classic Hollywood counterpart did? The study by Bordwell, Staiger, and Thompson of this latter cinema,[1] itself a classic, describes a reasonably coherent and integrated set of filmmaking practices growing out of a reasonably stable set of industrial conditions, resembling in certain key respects the industrial conditions applying throughout all large-scale economic undertakings in America at the time and tending to produce a detailed division of labor under a hierarchical management structure. But even without such an account, one would have been in little doubt about the existence of a classic Hollywood cinema, however inadequately its characteristics and conditions of existence might hitherto have been articulated.

The same is not so true of France. It is not so easy to identify recurrent stylistic and technical factors in the films listed earlier, and made in France between 1929 and 1958, as it is to identify them in Hollywood productions of that period. Yet the French film establishment of the time harbored no such doubts: at the beginning of the period and at its end there was a clear consensus to the effect that a classic cinema with distinctive stylistic traits deriving from a distinctive commercial and industrial base did in fact exist. In the thirties this was attributed to the advent of sound technology, which pressured producers toward studio production, artifice, and an ever greater dependence on technology. It was attributed to the sudden importance of dialogues, which pressured producers to call on theatrical and literary scriptwriters and to transcribe popular successes from other media. It was attributed to the dependence on a mass public to recoup the significantly greater production costs and to the fact that that public had been fatally conditioned long since by the cultural colonization of France by the Hollywood cinema. In these circumstances, the classic French cinema must inevitably be doomed to replicate the industrial classicism of Hollywood, with its stultifying realism and its stultifying thematics of the individual.

At the end of the period under discussion, French commentators were equally convinced that there was a classic French product, readily recognizable by a series of recurrent traits. They labelled these traits "psychological realism," or (sardonically) "the quality tradition," and were violently critical of their every manifestation. For them, the classic French cinema was a servile cinema, produced by employees working mechanically and unimaginatively to rigidly prescribed but indefensible principles. Its figureheads—actors like Edwige Feuillère and Pierre Fresnay, scriptwriters like Aurenche and Bost, directors like Autant-Lara and Delannoy—were betraying and debasing the cinema. The industrial division of labor had led to a fragmented work process marked by specialization; no single person concerned could have any overall appreciation, let alone directive control, of that process. In these circumstances, films were produced to formulas fossilized by overuse, authorial self-expression had no place, and the cinema could never aspire to be an artform.

These two moments—the moment when a new set of practices was developing and was being greeted with painful apprehension and the moment when it was being contested as a set of outdated routines—serve to define the periodization of the classic cinema to be discussed in this book. It is a cinema which emerged from and which was displaced by an "art cinema," yet as is apparent from the films already listed it cannot readily be defined *against* an art cinema. Indeed, it provided the conditions for the existence of such an art cinema, while requiring simultaneously the production of a majority of more commercial films. This very diversity is precisely what must be explained, since it is one of the factors which most clearly distinguished the classic French cinema from its American, British, and German counterparts.

The present study proposes to do just that; but it also proposes to explore the limits to that diversity. As cultural critics have repeatedly observed, not all things are possible at all times. The conditions of production circumscribe more or less tightly and determine more or less precisely what can and cannot be done, what is likely or not likely to be thought at a given moment and in a given society. The debris of endless unrealized projects which litter the careers of all classic French filmmakers is sufficient in itself to demonstrate that the system's diversity and flexibility had its limits. We will never know what Prévert's complete version of *Une partie de campagne* would have looked like, with Michel Simon as a pederast baker; and we will never see *Les Caves du Vatican*, which he was scripting with Gide for Yves Allégret. Among the numerous doomed projects launched by Grémillon in the postwar years we will never see *Le Massacre des innocents* or *La Commune* and can at best read the published script of his epic on the 1848 revolution, *Le Printemps de la liberté*. We will never see Carné's science fiction project, *Les Evadés de l'an 2000*; nor will we see *La Fleur de l'age*, which he was directing to a script by Prévert with the well-tried team of Trauner, Kosma, Arletty, and Carette—it had to be abandoned when bad weather caused cost overruns after three months of shooting. Nor will we see *L'Air pur*, with which René Clair intended to mark his triumphal return to French production, but which was abandoned on the outbreak of war. The number of projects that Bresson was unable to realize far exceeds those he did realize. In particular, we will never know what his film on Loyola would have looked like. In the period from 1945 to 1950 he was unable to find a producer for any of his projects; in the same five-year period, Feyder participated at best marginally in one last film, and most of the other leading directors of the day—Carné, Grémillon, Becker, Autant-Lara—were able to make no more than a single film.

Such instances of unrealized projects and limited output serve as a constant reminder that a set of constraints existed quite independent of the will of any of the individuals involved in the filmmaking process, which served to condition the final array of films produced. Clearly these constraints will always have an important economic constituent in the case of such a heavily technologized medium as the cinema, but there will also be a political constituent, if only because of the political potential of any medium of representation. Alongside these political and economic factors, though not by any means totally distinct from them, the inherited cultural forms and traditions of a society will carry over in a variety of ways into filmic forms and practices. Thus a film-production system within a market economy will exist alongside other cultural media of representation—the theater, painting, music hall and vaudeville, opera and operetta, etc.— themselves more or less integrated into that market economy; and the processes of training, both formal and informal, that have been institutionalized for those media will interact with the processes of training, both formal and informal, which the film industry has itself developed, producing personnel trained to see certain ways of behavior, certain ways of using the available technology, as normal, natural, and right. It is the technical practices that arise from this interplay of determinants—particularly the practices of producers, of scriptwriters, of directors, of actors, of set designers, of cinematographers, of editors, and of film composers—that will structure the resultant films. It is these technical practices that will produce what is globally, if vaguely, referred to as the "style" of a film, of a film movement, of a national cinema. To the degree that they are institutionalized and recurrent, they will tend to produce generic regularities in style and in content.

These, then, are the general categories that will be used to understand and explain, first, the substance and style of the films produced within the classic French cinema and, second, the nature and evolution of that cinema itself. They will thus serve as categories to structure the sections of this book, both internally and in their relation one to another. Consideration of the economic and political conditions operative over the relevant period in France might well reinforce the suspicion that there could be no coherent body of classic films, if only because the broad conditions of production would seem to have varied so dramatically between 1930 and 1960. World War II, the four-year German occupation of France, and the difficult period succeeding the Liberation bisect our thirty-year period, creating two distinct decades separated by an interregnum during which conditions of existence in all spheres of French society were so radically aberrant that no continuity of production practice could be expected. The two decades themselves—the thirties and the fifties—are sufficiently distinctive: on the one hand a decade of social and economic crisis beginning with the Depression and including the Popular Front coalition and the preparations for war, and on the other hand a period of cold war associated with the early development of consumer capitalism, youth culture, and the generation gap. Inevitably these factors must affect the cinema as a culture industry and as a form of mediation of social existence. Moreover, during the interregnum of occupation not only was production heavily regulated and monitored, but many noteworthy producers, directors, and set designers were obliged, because of their politics or their race, to go underground and/or leave the country. Into this gap, conventional wisdom has it, a large body of new filmmakers stepped. Surely this transformation of personnel within the production sector might be expected to transform production practices and thus film style?

But this partial renewal of personnel was itself only one of many waves of immigration and of emigration effecting large-scale interchanges among the filmmaking communities of France, Eastern Europe, Germany, Italy, and America. Such interchanges must raise questions about the specificity of national production systems. If filmmakers were able to move so fluently between production systems, was it not because those systems were largely indistinguishable one from another? If they were not so at the beginning, surely they must in a very short while have become so, as a result of the interchange of ideas and of techniques. If the French cinema was not already largely Americanized in the thirties, surely it must have become largely Germanized in the forties or largely Italianized in the fifties when coproductions began to pave the way to a common cultural market. Did the people involved in these exchanges and migrations themselves feel that different national systems had distinctive features, and if so did they feel that those features were inherently valuable and to be preserved, or irritants inhibiting efficient production? Is there evidence to suggest that certain distinctive characteristics persisted despite the exchange of personnel and practices, such as might suggest that they were determined not by any "superficial" causes (the experience and intentions of the filmmakers), but by a more fundamental causation (for instance, long-standing national cultural, industrial, and economic traditions)?

One such distinctive characteristic was repeatedly remarked upon by all those with international experience—the atomized and relatively artisanal nature of the film "industry" in France compared to the oligarchical blocks of America and the monolithic Rank and UFA conglomerates of the British and German industries, and the lack of vertical integration of production, distribution, and exhibition sectors. Neither the long-established Pathé and Gaumont firms nor the wartime Continental company established by the Germans significantly modified this fragmented proliferation of production companies. The effects of this distinctive and persistent industrial structure were dramatic in the extreme: the constant sense of economic peril threatening each of the constituent production companies, the recurrent crises and collapses within the industry, the reluctance to undertake long-term investment in technology, all can be traced back to this original cause. The pathetic inadequacy of the technology available for long periods to French filmmakers, the lack of any reliable studio base for production companies, and the lack of continuity in employment for key personnel in turn affected in major ways the filmmaking process and thus the type of film produced.

An investigation of the political economy and industrial structure of the cinema can thus begin to explain what technology was available, how it was used, and why. It needs to be supplemented, however, by an account of the cultural traditions introduced into the film industry from adjacent media by personnel already adapted to work habits considered normal in those arenas. Were the scriptwriters, for instance, who had for the most part been accustomed to working within the theatrical structures of acts and scenes, inclined to structure their narratives differently from those with a literary background, or from those with neither, such as Prévert, whose poetic career developed in parallel to his scriptwriting career? Were these narrative structures compatible with the norms imported by musicians, who brought to the cinema notions of symphonic form, of counterpoint, or of a vaudeville-like sequencing of items? Was continuity considered as much a virtue within the classic French cinema as it was in Hollywood, and if not, why not?

Such questions are especially important to an understanding of the work practices of the classic filmmakers because no formal mechanisms for recruiting and training a body of filmmakers in specifically cinematic routines developed until the end of the war. Nor were trade unions or professional organizations a significant organizational element until after the war.

Subsequently, however, the expectation (and even in some cases formal requirement) of a professional qualification became widespread, and the regulatory mechanism of unionization became insistent. What importance had this move from the informal and even anarchic to the formal and even doctrinaire? Do formally trained editors, directors, and cameramen act differently from those trained in the loose master/apprentice system of the thirties? Do they represent their work and their output to themselves in the same way? How did classic French filmmakers see their job?

This question points in three directions: first, toward the critical debates current during those thirty years concerning the nature of film and of filmmaking; second, toward the reflections of the filmmakers themselves on the nature of their work, in autobiography, treatise, and interview; and third, toward those filmmaking courses which were developed in the latter half of the period and which were for the most part established and taught by key industrial personnel. All provide valuable information on the ideology and work practices of the personnel, particularly the critical debates in journals and reviews, not just as statements of belief, but also as an index of the jockeying for dominance of the principal critical discourses—those of truth, of pleasure, of art, of politics, of morality, and of understanding. It is a chapter devoted to these journals and those discourses that closes the analysis of the classic French cinema as a system.

The final chapters explore that system in its day-to-day operation. They attempt, that is, to answer the question "How did the classic French filmmakers go about their job; how did they accommodate themselves to the constraints of the system and exploit its possibilities?" Who was employed by whom, at what point in the production process, how did they use the available plant and technology, and why? How did editors understand their job; what forms of editing practice did they use? How did cinematographers light a shot, and what was the degree of their control over framing and camera movement? What styles of acting did the cast draw on, were scripts written around actors or around milieus, and who determined the degree of stylization of the sets and costumes? In sum, by whom did the crucial decisions get made, what were those decisions, and on what criteria were they made—what mode of production did the industrial structure generate, and what filmmaking practices resulted?

This is not, of course, an entirely original ambition. A vast number of articles and several dozen books have been written, primarily in French, about specific periods or aspects of the classic French cinema. Much of the present study is based on these, selectively summarizing, synthesizing, and qualifying them. Certain aspects of the period have been more fully dealt with than others: Paul Léglise has done an admirably exhaustive job in recording the political history of the French cinema from its origins to 1946;[2] an early comparative study of the economic history of the industry by Bächlin[3] has been reused by many commentators since; two very useful histories by Courtade[4] and Jeancolas[5] are slightly incoherent precisely because they provide a vast but relatively unsystematized wealth of information; and Sadoul's brief narrative history[6] of the classic cinema provides an invaluable baseline. Much valuable archival research has been done by Raymond Chirat[7] and Vincent Pinel[8] to identify and catalogue the actual output of the French film industry over this period. Innumerable articles have been written on such aspects of the industry as the ciné-club movement, the cinémathèque, the Cannes Film Festival, and the critical reviews of the period. As many books have been written about, or by, the key figures of the industry, especially the directors.

In English, the task of describing and accounting for the first seventy years of the French cinema has been left to a small but active group of researchers. Dudley Andrews and Roy Armes have over the years done extremely valuable work, and Richard Abel, after having chronicled the silent French cinema, has gone on to provide a splendid anthology of French film criticism in the decades preceding World War II.

I have not tried to do justice to all this material, but merely to extract from it those elements that could contribute to my broader argument about the defining characteristics of the classic cinema and their origins. Certain other areas have been less well treated by researchers—no equivalent of Barry Salt's work[9] has been done detailing the available technology, nor is there any convenient history of the studios in France. Whereas much has been done on exchanges of personnel with America, perhaps for political reasons practically nothing exists on the equivalent exchanges with Germany. Most of the material on specific categories of worker and their work —directors and actors, scriptwriters, set designers and cinematographers— is lacking in distance and needs to be used with caution. Little serious work has been devoted to editors and editing, largely because of the low status they endured for most of this period.

More particularly, no attempt has been made to pull all this together so as to recognize the coherences and the tensions between work practices in different fields and to see their relationship to the filmmakers' backgrounds and cultural traditions, to available technology, and to economic and political determinants. There exists, that is, no adequate overview with a rigorous methodological basis. It was to rectify this omission that the present work was undertaken. While it does attempt such an overview, however, there are some things it does not do. As an initial decision of principle, priority was given to feature-length fiction films rather than to shorts, newsreels, or documentaries, and to production rather than to distribution or exhibition. The latter are dealt with only when, and insofar as, they impinge significantly on the former.

Within those limits, however—and they are still embarrassingly broad —this study aims to provide a sufficient understanding of the classic French cinema to explain such specificities of the resultant films as the degree of generic conventionalization, the degree of validity that can be accorded to claims of authorial expressivity, and the degree of stylistic coherence and evolution that this cinema achieved. It aims, that is, to describe and explain the French classic cinema in sufficient detail to allow its output of films to be themselves described and explained.

In doing so it not only summarizes and synthesizes a great deal of work, most of it published only in French, but it radically rewrites certain aspects of the industrial history of the classic French cinema. For instance, new light is shed on the periodization of the classic cinema and of the stylistic evolution that occurred within it. The extent and duration of German influence on the postwar industrial organization is reevaluated. Perhaps most importantly, the mythic state of crisis which the French cinema continually seemed to be experiencing is both called into question and explained. Finally, the New Wave of French filmmakers who saw themselves as breaking decisively with the classic French cinema are seen rather as a logical consequence of institutional and technological changes which had their roots at least as far back as the war years; consequently, rather than marking a complete break with the classic French cinema, they can be seen as one of its own more successful products.

THE CLASSIC FRENCH CINEMA, 1930-1960

ONE

POLITICAL ECONOMY AND
INDUSTRIAL STRUCTURE 1930–1940

> You are all anti-interventionists; but as soon as one of your activities is threatened, you call for the State to step in.
>
> Tardieu, government minister, in a speech to the Congress on the Economy, 1930

> If we want the French cinema to survive, international commerce in film must be regulated.
>
> René Jeanne, *Lectures pour tous*, January 1931

> It is impossible for a government that aspires to create a new social order to allow a means of propaganda as powerful as the cinema to remain in the hands of groups who may well have interests opposed to its own.
>
> Paul Faure, confidant of Léon Blum, April 1936

THE POLITICAL ECONOMY OF THE LEISURE
INDUSTRIES IN THE DEPRESSION

French historians of the cinema have been tempted into romantic attitudes when describing the conditions under which the French sound cinema developed and operated, such that it can seem that the French cinema, lurching from crisis to crisis, was unduly unfortunate among national cinemas. All these crises are represented as fundamentally economic in nature, and all can be traced back to two founding conditions, one international and one national. Internationally, of course, the Depression radically disrupted all industrial undertakings, not just in the cinema and not just in France; it was compounded at the national levels, however, by the unfortunate fact that the French did not develop their own sound system but had to buy into foreign patents—American and German—at great and continuing cost to the industry.

The consequences of these two factors are multiple. Technologically, and therefore technically, stylistically, the center of cinematic developments could seem to be elsewhere, with the French cinema constantly bringing up the rear, and with French film personnel constantly being drained off to the active centers of Hollywood and UFA, whence they returned starry-eyed at the possibilities opened up for them by the new technologies. Industrially, the production units of the French system were so small that they were chronically unable to generate the capital needed to update the studios, the laboratories, or the manufacturing industries in order to compete on an even footing with foreign film industries. Those few companies which had some semblance of industrial muscle through the vertical integration of production, distribution, and exhibition, either never survived into the talkie era or, having survived, crashed catastrophically. Scandals, bankruptcies, and embezzlements litter the history of the industry. Aware of the anarchic state of the industry, the government seemed as incapable of coping with it as it was of coping with the Depression as a whole. It called repeatedly for reports, then failed to act on them.

When the industry is portrayed thus lurching from economic crisis to economic crisis under the constant threat of total disintegration, and lacking the political will to redress the situation, it is difficult to understand how it could have survived, let alone flourished. Yet flourish it did, at least in a limited sense: the quantity, quality, and diversity of the industrial output of the French film industry is markedly superior to that of any other European film industry of the time. It is the only one of those national film industries to survive the aggressive cultural colonialism of Hollywood throughout the thirty years from 1930 to 1960 with a vitality sufficient to regenerate itself on three separate occasions: during the war, while under German occupation, after the liberation, when the Blum-Byrnes accords might have been expected to doom it, and in 1960, when the "New Wave" of French filmmakers were among the first to exploit the possibilities of new film technologies.

Despite the crises, then, the French film industry was by no means as persecuted as these standard representations would have it. An underlying vitality existed, which needs to be accounted for. It is not that the standard accounts are incorrect, but they need reinterpreting so as to recognize that the conditions under which films were made in France, not just in the thirties but throughout the "classic" period, opened up possibilities not available in other countries, at the same time as they closed off many of those possibilities which were exploited in America, in Britain, and in Germany.

In other words it is important to identify the distinctive features of the French industrial structure and to attempt to see in what way that structure was a logical (though not necessarily the only logical) outcome of the economic and political conditions of existence under which it developed. This will be the aim of the present section. It will require a brief account of the distinctive way in which the Depression affected the French economy, of the reaction of the leisure industries in general and of the cinema in particular to this economic context, of the problems thus posed for the transition to sound, involving as it did a vast injection of capital into the industry in order to update production facilities and exhibition outlets, and of the way in which the industry responded to these pressures, resulting in a distinctive industrial structure which, however many disadvantages it may have had, nevertheless allowed for one major advantage: the development of a set of practices appropriate to artisanal low-budget productions which could ensure the survival of a sufficient number of production houses despite relatively low returns on investment.

It must have seemed to the French of 1930–1931 that they had escaped all the worst effects of the Depression which had by then ravaged all other Western economies. By 1935–1936, however, it had become apparent to them that on the contrary they had been affected at least as severely as any other Western country and indeed that their economy was the only one of these where there was as yet no sign of a return toward prosperity. It is this which is the most distinctive feature of the French situation: a delay in the worst impact of the Depression, such that its effects only become apparent in 1932 and only reach crisis point in 1934, followed by a particularly severe period of economic stagnation lasting several years, at precisely the time when the economies of neighboring countries were showing signs of a definitive recovery. This induced an impression first of all that France was uniquely favored, such that nothing *need* be done, and subsequently that France was uniquely disfavored, such that nothing *could* be done.[1]

After eight years of progressive and seemingly irresistible monetary fluctuations following World War I, the French economy had experienced a significant stabilization in 1926, which was to last through 1930. The election of the Poincaré government in 1926 and the firm measures that it introduced, coinciding with the favorable effects of the Dawes plan and a reduction in public debt, induced a remarkable recovery, such that the franc became one of the most reliable of currencies, and extremely attractive to foreign investors. Moreover, the Poincaré government resisted the temptation to revalue it, thus favoring exports and producing a series of positive balances of payments. By 1929, France had outdistanced both Britain and America in its recovery with respect to its prewar situation. Unemployment was largely eliminated. In 1929, there were already 1.3 million unemployed in Britain and 1.8 million in Germany; in France, by 1930 there were still no more than 13,000. An influx of foreign workers was attracted by the employment prospects, and productivity per worker and per hour worked represented enormous gains over the prewar situation. These improvements were reflected in a higher standard of living, which was most marked in the case of industrialists but was significant for public servants and even for salaried workers.

Between 1930 and 1935, however, through a series of gradual recessions interspersed with marginal recoveries, the economy deteriorated to a point where industrial production was 25% below that of 1930 and was showing no sign of recovery. Exports were 44% below in quantity and 82% in value. Production in all other Western countries had already reached its low point toward 1932 and was well on the way to recovery by 1935. That of Britain, for instance, had already exceeded its 1929 level, and the recovery of the German economy was almost as strong. The cause of this discrepancy would seem to lie in the devaluations forced on those other countries by the early severity of the Depression,[2] whereas in France an unconditional commitment to the defense of the franc, encouraged by the impression of having escaped the Depression, led to the currency's becoming progressively over-valued with respect to other countries. From the end of 1931 onward, exports began to suffer, unemployment to rise, productivity to decrease. From then on there was a persistent deficit in the balance of payments throughout the thirties, despite an elaborate system of quotas which by 1936 extended to 65% of all imported goods.

Government responses to this situation were ad hoc and inadequate. In fact, successive governments seemed impotent. The Depression had the effect of aggravating the chronic ministerial instability of the third Republic. Only in 1935 did a political program develop which was founded on a global analysis of the conditions necessary for recovery—the deflationary policy of the Laval government. That particularly controversial policy was largely responsible for the defeat of the right in the elections of 1936, leading to the victory of the Popular Front in the elections of May 1936.[3]

The Popular Front came to office with a set of policies which reversed the conservative program of preceding years: instead of giving priority to the economic sector and attempting to balance the budget by reducing expenditure, the Popular Front proposed a series of social reforms involving significant public sector expenditure—the dole, public works, agricultural subsidies, and above all the reduction of the work week to 40 hours—intending that these social measures should in turn trigger an economic recovery.

It was left little leisure to implement these reforms, however. Widespread strikes greeted its first months in power. The government hurriedly introduced paid holidays, the 40-hour week, and subsequently, almost by accident, the nationalization of the railways; but its reforming period was brief, and the results fell below expectations. Tentative signs of a recovery were followed by a further recession in 1938. The Popular Front government under Blum, grouping socialist, Communist, and radical tendencies, fell, and fell apart, with radical tendencies dominating the remaining governments of the decade.

While the general atmosphere of economic instability, crisis, and social upheaval which marked this succession of political and economic phenomena inevitably affected the cinema, both as an industry and as a signifying system employed in the representation of social phenomena, certain elements in the mix deserve to be isolated for the more direct impact they had on leisure industries such as the cinema.

The reduction in available work had a number of consequences: unemployment increased particularly in those sectors of the economy, such as the cinema, that were experiencing direct competition with foreign products. The threat of unemployment introduced a fear among those privileged workers still in possession of a full-time or nearly full-time job: they would work under any conditions rather than lose that job. Protests about conditions or about levels of technology thus became less likely. Large numbers of workers simply opted out into retirement, especially women and foreign workers. People with transferable skills moved to countries with a healthier economy and more attractive working conditions. Thus large numbers of film workers spent part or all of the period 1933–1939 in Germany or America. Counterbalancing this tendency, however, we might note that political or economic conditions in other countries were often even more unfavorable, inducing large numbers of workers to emigrate from those countries to (or through) France.

Perhaps more important, however, was the move away from investment in new technology which resulted from these conditions. Living standards overall did not suffer a significant lowering during the decade—indeed, food consumption actually increased by some 5% between 1930 and 1935—but this maintenance of living standards occurred at the expense of investment. As Asselain puts it, "the proportion of the national revenue allocated to investment and to consumption was considerably modified: investment, to be precise, collapsed. . . . In other words, the maintenance of consumption took place essentially to the detriment of future growth."[4] One of the constant complaints of those working on the cinema at the time was precisely the absence of capital for updating French production facilities such that French films might acquire the same technical finish that German, American, and British films enjoyed. Not only did this contribute to a general air of clumsiness and amateurishness that attaches to many of the films of the thirties, particularly of the period 1930–1935, but it undercut any future improvement in the level of technical finish. The French product would not for the foreseeable future match the American product in this respect, as its critics never ceased pointing out; and much of the postwar obsession with producing "a quality product" can best be understood in the light of this longstanding "humiliation." Effectively, this means that the French cinema did not exploit the window of opportunity opened up by the few years of prosperity in the early thirties during which the French economy was performing, or at least could seem to be performing, better than those of the other developed countries.

In another sense it did exploit that opportunity, since production increased dramatically between 1928 and 1931. Estimates of the extent of that increase (fig. 1.1) vary greatly, because of continuing debate concerning the definition of "a French film." Certain commentators limit their use of that

FIGURE 1.1 Classic French Film Production 1924–1959

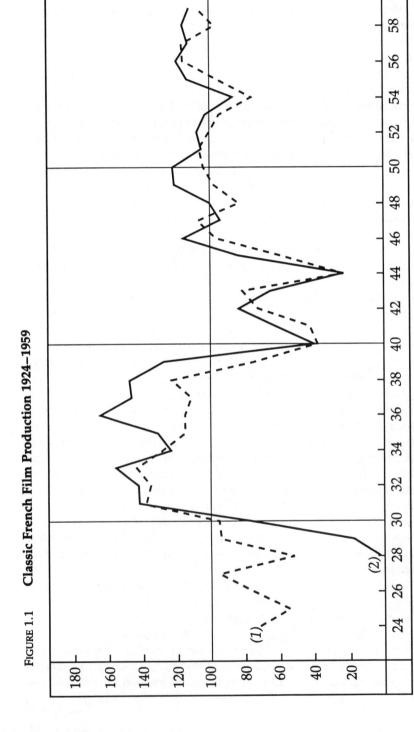

(1) Georges Sadoul, *Le Cinéma Français* (1962): French films distributed (excluding versions).
(2) From Vincent Pinel, *Filmographie* (1985): French sound films produced. See also *Le Film Français* 869/870, which gives another marginally different set of figures.

term to French-language films made in France by French production companies using primarily French personnel, while others recognize as French
those French-language versions made by foreign companies in France
and/or those exclusively French-language films made in Germany and elsewhere. Estimates also vary according to whether production dates or
screening dates are privileged. Finally, new data for the thirties have come
to hand over recent decades.

Nevertheless, certain trends are clear. From a basis of around 60–70
films a year in the mid-twenties, and a low of about 52 in 1928, French film
production rose rapidly, experiencing boom years in 1931–1933. Production
slumped slightly in 1934, when the Depression was affecting most severely
the French economy, but the recovery was almost immediate and quite at
odds with the enduring crisis that affected the economy in general. Production continued high in the years 1936–1938 but retreated to a low of 39 in
1940, during the German invasion and occupation.

To a certain extent, the general economic trends of attendance patterns
and returns on investments, which thus encourage or discourage production, could have been predicted from the broader economic and political
patterns of the day. In his most useful study of the viability of the various
theatrical spectacles of France, Professor Leroy provides graphs which indicate clearly the intimate relationship between these two spheres.[5] His data
provide an index of the dramatic drop in receipts for all forms of spectacle
in times of war, contrasting with the boom in attendance during periods of
social anxiety such as recessions and, most specifically, the Depression. Attendance both for theater and for cinema climbs steadily in the years following World War I and remains high in the twenties, generating increasing
receipts; but toward 1930, as the receipts for theatrical performances begin
the decline that was to continue till World War II, those of cinema leave
them behind and continue strong till the war (fig. 1.2).

Thus, between 1928 and 1934, the number of theatrical performances
(including touring companies) in France fell from 38,792 to 25,588, the number of working actors fell from 1,498 to 648, and the number of cabarets
and music halls fell from 101 to 69. Between 1925 and 1935 the number of
musical concerts fell from 1,850 to 1,134.

Equally vivid is the breakdown of receipts of the various forms of spectacle in Paris, given by Durand in his study of the cinema-going public (fig.
1.3).[6] From constituting 30% of the receipts in the twenties, the cinema
rapidly expanded to constitute two-thirds of them in the thirties. In real
terms, theatrical receipts fell by almost 50% in the decade, as did other spectacles. This was not caused simply by a displacement of other spectacles
by the cinema, however, since the same drop in attendance and receipts is
apparent for nonaudiovisual spectacles, such as concerts. It would seem
that the money to fund the relatively large cost of attending spectacles such
as live theater, opera, and concerts, was simply less readily available. Cinema benefited primarily from the simple fact that it was a particularly cheap

FIGURE 1.2   **Returns for Theatre and Cinema 1895–1940**

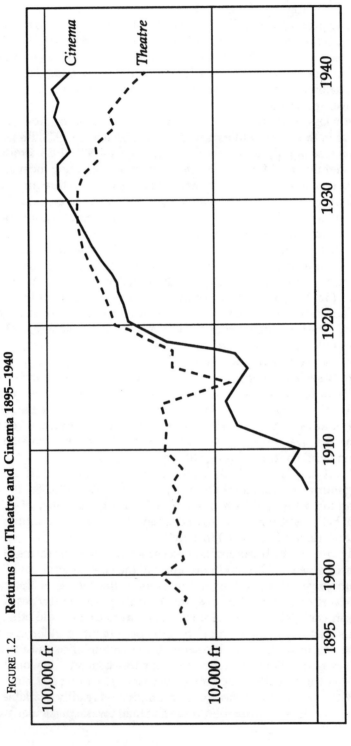

Source: D. Leroy, *Economie des arts du spectacle vivant*, p. 303.

FIGURE 1.3 **Returns for Various Media 1922–1952**
(in 1938 francs, and corrected for the cost of living)

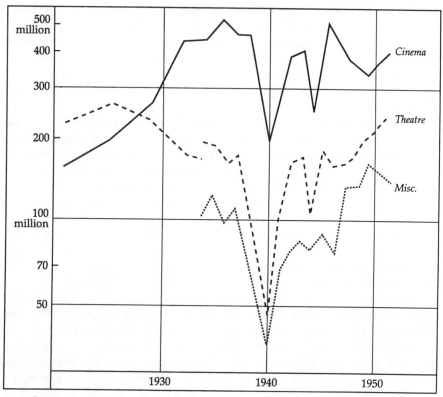

Source: J. Durand, *Le Cinéma et son public,* 1958, p. 92.

form of entertainment. In 1937, for example, when the average price of a cinema seat was six francs, a boxing match cost 25 francs, while theater and music hall cost between 35 and 45 francs.[7] Not only were entry prices markedly cheaper in the cinema, but they increased less rapidly than the entry prices to other spectacles.

Most crucially, when all due allowance is made for the cost of living, the cinema receipts for all of France increased rapidly in real terms from 600 million francs in 1929 to 1,000 million francs in 1932 and remained healthy at around 180% of 1929 levels. Parisian receipts, for which data go back further, confirm this trend, showing that between 1925 and 1935 receipts rose in real terms by 280%. This far outweighs any increase in the cost of production caused by the move to sound.

This economic boom that the early sound cinema enjoyed was certainly in part due to the novelty value of the talkie, which at least momentarily must have benefited cinema attendances in 1930 and 1931. It must also have been due in part to the fact that, in its new dialogued form, cinema resembled legitimate theater to an extent that it never had before. Producers were quick to exploit the existing theatrical repertoire as a quarry for cinematic scenarios. Going to the cinema, or at least to a certain cinema, could constitute a cultural experience which directly substituted for those "legitimate theatre" experiences that were rapidly becoming more difficult for the middle classes to afford. Thus some of the increase in the cinema audiences around 1930 can be attributed to the appeal of a theatrical cinema to a class of audience that would have disdained to be seen at a film in the twenties. Effectively, the class profile of the audiences was slightly modified. Alongside this, one can place the continuing spread of the cinema circuits to more and more remote areas of France. In the thirties, many regions were still served, at best if at all, only by travelling projectionists. In the years immediately following the introduction of sound, the number of cinemas in France increased from just over three thousand in 1930 to just over four thousand in 1933, after which point it increased only gradually throughout the thirties.[8] As these established cinema circuits spread in the early thirties, a wider rural audience was made available for exploitation, though attendance patterns continued to be dominated by Paris, where one-third of all entries were regularly recorded.[9]

But more than any of these factors favoring the increase of French film production in the thirties is the language factor. The relative fluidity with which silent films could move across international frontiers had made the world a single market, subject to ready domination by the larger and more efficient producers. France had ceased to be such a country during World War I, and the export earnings of the film industry were small during the twenties. The major trusts of America had been able to acquire something approaching a stranglehold on the national markets of Europe, dictating the terms on which their products could be exploited. France had not been exempt from this situation: within its total market of some six hundred to seven hundred films per year, America had provided over half and sometimes three-quarters, while the powerful German industry had likewise often outperformed the French industry in France.

With the development of the talkie, linguistic frontiers suddenly acquired the status of major economic barriers to industrial exploitation—barriers which in the short term were total, but which even in the long term radically modified the power relations of the national production systems. In a sense, these linguistic barriers merely exaggerated the effects of an industrial compartmentalization which was one of the incidental effects of the Depression on the world economy. International exchange networks were disrupted, and national economies everywhere tended to contract within their own boundaries. On the whole, given that French film industry had had no significant external market to lose, but a large internal market to gain, the effects were distinctly beneficial. Figure 1.4, outlining the trans-

FIGURE 1.4   **The French Market for Feature Films 1924–1938**
(including films in the original language)

ORIGIN	1924	1925	1926	1927	1928	1929	1930	1931	1932	1933	1934	1935	1936	1937	1938
France	68	73	55	74	94	52	94	139	157	149	126	115	116	111	122
Semi-French				7	2					9					
USA	589	577	444	368	313	211	237	220	208	230	220	248	231	230	239
Germany	20	29	33	91	122	130	111	60	99	113	45	60	41	31	26
Italy	9	13	14	10	7	3	2	8	4	17	4	10	3	5	5
England		7	2	8	23	23	16	8	7	34	29	19	32	29	21
Austria		2	4	2	1		2	1	1				1		
Russia	6		1	10	4	9	2	8	6	2	5	6	14	14	1
Denmark	1		6	5	1	3	2			1	2				
Sweden		2	5	2	4	1	2					1			
Spain		1		2	4		1	1	1	5	1	2			
Belgium			1		3	1	1	1	4	1	1		1	3	1
Poland					2	1	1		4	4	1	1			1
Czechoslovakia					1	1	3		2	6	1	1	6		2
Other				2	2	3	4	7	3	1	1	3	3	1	8
TOTAL	693	704	565	581	583	437	478	453	496	572	436	466	448	424	426
French as % of Total Market	9.8	10.4	9.7	12.7	16.1	11.9	19.6	30.7	31.7	26.0	28.9	24.7	25.9	26.2	28.6
U.S. as % of Total Market	85	82	79	63	54	48	50	49	42	40	50	53	52	54	56

Source: P. Léglise, vol. 2, p. 214; from *La Cinématographie Française*.

formation which the French market underwent at this point, is particularly enlightening: although the data are incomplete and drawn from a variety of sources, they clearly demonstrate the positive effects on the economics of French production within the national market. From occupying on the average 10% of that market in the twenties, French films came to occupy a steady 30% and more throughout the thirties.

Moreover, this increased numerical prominence was undoubtedly multiplied by a factor difficult to estimate, but no less real, due to the confirmed preference on the part of French people for French language films; consequently, attendance figures at the screenings of French films, whenever they have been measured, have proved significantly higher than at screenings of films of other nationalities dubbed into French.[10] At the Renaitour enquiry in 1937 the American delegates produced figures which demonstrated this preference conclusively: in 1936, of the 75 most popular films in France the top six were French; only 15 of the 75 were American, against 56 French.[11] In surveys conducted between 1945 and 1947, between 69% and 85% of French people claimed to prefer French films over American,[12] and detailed analyses of postwar attendance patterns confirm that this preference affected their filmgoing habits. Audience records for the years from 1950 to 1952, for instance, show French films consistently outperforming American, with all other nations further behind again. Indeed, at that time, when the market was again being swamped by a backlog of American films such that the number of French films on the market had again retreated to 25–30%, the total audience attracted to those French films was never lower than 43%, and more normally 50%.[13] There is no reason to doubt that this phenomenon dates at least from the development of the sound film. Indeed Sadoul quotes an estimate of 70% of the share of receipts going to French rather than dubbed films in 1935.[14]

In several respects, therefore, conventional French histories of their national cinema are simply not justified in the somewhat apocalyptic approach they take to conditions facing that cinema as it moved into the sound era: attendances at the cinema as at spectacles overall increased significantly; indeed, they increased particularly dramatically in the case of the cinema, which overtook and displaced other forms of popular entertainment; linguistic barriers dramatically favored the national product over its long-term American rival, as did local audience preferences; the number of films produced increased, as did the real value of receipts of the French cinema and the proportion of those receipts going to the French producer. It was of course far from being a period of unalloyed industrial bliss, but neither was it the catastrophic disaster it is often described as—and, indeed, was sometimes claimed to be at the time.

As a first corrective to this positive image, we might note that despite the increase in spectators and in receipts during the period when sound was being introduced, the French filmgoing public was still grotesquely small by international standards and incomparably small for a major film-producing country. Figure 1.5 compares attendance figures for various European film-producing countries of similar size. For most years France is well below all other countries. Moreover, having increased to a level of something over 200 million with the advent of sound, attendance remained stable in France for the rest of the decade, whereas in all other countries attendance figures increased dramatically from 1932 onward. Indeed, the average cinema attendance for each member of the population had historically been low in France—about 3.6 attendances per year in 1919. It rose above 5 per year with the advent of sound and remained stable at between 5.5 and 6 per year throughout the thirties, whereas that of England in 1937 was 30 per year, and that of America 40 per year.

While discrepancies in the overall scale of attendance are clearly due to different attitudes toward filmgoing in the different countries, established well before the thirties, economic and demographic factors may help to account for the failure of the French cinema to attract wider audiences after 1932. On the one hand, the retarded effect of the Depression on France meant that the amount of disposable income available to them for leisure activities did not increase after 1933 as it did in most other countries. Given that there was in all countries of Europe a close relationship throughout the thirties between the gross national product, the consumption budget available to families, and the amount spent on the cinema,[15] this in itself would be sufficient explanation. In addition, however, the birthrate may well have played a significant part. Various studies have shown the importance of specific age-groups in the profile of film spectators.[16] In all cases, the key age-group is from 10–25 years of age: their attendance rate is twice to three times the national norm. But the size of that 10–25-year-old cohort has varied widely in the twentieth century as birthrates have been affected both directly and indirectly by wars, and indeed by the Depression. In France, the 1930s saw a significant reduction of the relevant age-group because of the reduced birthrate during World War I, whereas the forties were to benefit from the increased birthrate of the 1920s. Overall, however, the remarkable stability ("stagnation") of the French population, which numbered 41.7 million in 1913 and 41.9 million in 1938, meant that there was no "natural" growth in the overall potential audience. Indeed the gross number of 10–25-year-olds in 1936 was smaller than it had been in 1911, and from 1935 onward, deaths exceeded births and the population temporarily decreased. In 1933, Gael Fain was already predicting a dramatic decrease in cinema attendance arising from the demographic distribution of age groups, unless something radical was done to attract new audiences.[17]

These factors may well account for the failure of French audiences to grow in the thirties. That lack of growth in turn certainly deprived the French cinema of the major injection of funds which British, German, and Italian film industries experienced throughout the thirties. It was compounded by other economic factors which drained off a significant percentage of the receipts, right at the time when the production and exhibition

FIGURE 1.5   **Audience Size in Various European Nations**

	1929	1930	1931	1932	1933	1934	1935	1936	1937	1938	1939	1940	1941	1942	1943	1944
Britain							907	917	946	987	990	1027	1309	1494	1541	1575
Germany	328	290	273	238	247	280	317				624					
Italy								253	301	335	346	356	408	459		
France	150	200	234	233	219	208	231			220			225	281	304	245
Per head	3.9	5.3	6.1	6.1	5.7	5.4	5.9			5.6			5.6	6.8	7.4	6.0

Source: J. Durand, *Le Cinéma et son public*, 1958, p. 209.

sectors were in dire need of an injection of funds in order to update their facilities. One continuing drain on receipts was the failure of the French industry to develop and patent its own sound technology. After 1930, every user of sound film equipment in France had to pay royalties to the relevant German or American firm for the right to use that format. Courtade cites the normal cost as 40–50% of receipts.[18] Among other problems which such a system inevitably raised, we might here simply note two: the economic effect of massive amounts of funds being diverted out of the country; and the implications for national control of the cinema, when foreign firms could so dictate the programming of the exhibition circuits. These two problems—the financial viability of the national film industry and the extent of foreign control of the national film industry—were the central preoccupations of the period.

PROFITABILITY

As far as the financial viability of the industry was concerned, there were three main preoccupations not already mentioned: the increased cost of production of sound films, the cost of re-equipping studios and cinemas in order to make and screen those films, and the extent to which government taxes ate away at whatever margin might remain to producers after these factors were taken into account. The overall cost of production during the period 1920–1940 is given in figure 1.6. While the estimates of actual costs come from Sadoul, who does not cite his source, the figures do correspond very closely for the sound period to estimates of other historians and economists. The economist Gael Fain in 1933 gives a figure for production costs between September 1927 and September 1928 of 67 films costing 80 million francs, which corresponds exactly to the costs given by Coissac for production from 1 January to 31 December 1927.[19] This is probably more accurate than Sadoul's figures for the same period and suggests a 66% increase in the real cost of sound production or, taking into account the decrease in purchasing power, a real increase of some 55%. This can be compared with another estimate given by political economist Peter Bächlin in 1945, who puts the increased cost of sound production at 25–35% per film.[20] The principal increases in cost were in studio hire (up from between two and five thousand francs per day to about twenty thousand francs per day), in filmstock (up 50%, because of the higher speed), and in the extra technical staff (cost of labor doubled).

The increased cost of screening the resultant products can best be estimated by considering the cost of installing the available equipment in a given cinema. American firms were regularly charging a quarter to a half million francs, sometimes 800,000 francs, to install their sound projection equipment in a single cinema.[21] The Madeleine and the Aubert Palace cost respectively 450,000 and 600,000 francs. Although installation of German

FIGURE 1.6   Average Cost of Production of French Feature Films

	Actual Cost	"Real" Cost*		Actual Cost	"Real" Cost*
1923	250,000	416,000	1939	2,500,000	2,066,000
1927	500,000	600,000	1945	10,000,000	2,347,000
	1,200,000**	1,440,000	1947	21,000,000	
1931	2,000,000	2,222,000	1950	47,400,000	
1934	1,500,000	1,923,000	1955	109,000,000	
1937	2,250,000	2,319,000	1960	173,000,000†	3,840,000

*Base 1929 = 100   **Contradictory estimate from G. Fain
†Including coproductions; 100% French films = 101,000,000 actual cost (or
in "real" costs still 2,240,000)
Source: G. Sadoul, Le Cinéma Français

equipment was much less expensive, perhaps only half as costly, the finance capital needed to convert the existing cinemas, which numbered some four thousand by 1934, would have been of the order of one billion francs; and this takes no account of the conversion of the production studios or the construction of one thousand new cinemas. It was precisely at this time that American cinemas were converting to sound, and the cost to them was an estimated 300 million dollars, with an additional 24 million dollars spent on refitting studios.[22] The scale of the investment required in America was such as to deliver the industry definitively into the hands of the electrical firms and financial institutions behind the conversion. In France, likewise, financial institutions such as Bauer and Marchal, Kohan-Corniglion-Molinier, and the BNC were to become dominant at this time, with unfortunate consequences when the depression hit in later years.

Various factors were conspiring throughout the thirties to ensure that the production arm of the industry did not itself have at its disposal the funds necessary to undertake these major tasks. Although the entry price and the overall receipts remained stable over this period, what the public was offered for its money increased dramatically; and it increased in such a way as to reduce the returns to the producer. The most obvious way in which this happened was through the generalization of the double program. Under intense competition, exhibitors (and critically the Pathé-Natan chain in July 1933) sought to gain an advantage over rival cinemas by offering two films for the price of one. Of necessity, their rivals came to do likewise. The effect of this was to halve the profits accruing to each film on the program. In 1936 a study showed that France was the country which offered the longest programs in Europe, with a norm of 4,200–5,000 meters, followed by Luxembourg, Belgium, and then Germany with 3,200–3,500 meters.[23] In many cases competition generated even further bonuses for the public, with three or even four films for the one entry price. An extreme instance cited by Courtade is a large Marseilles cinema which by 1939 was offering six full-length feature films for a single entry price.[24] The effects of such practices on the viability of the industry are obvious: on the one hand, production of large numbers of films is necessary to fulfill the demand; but, on the other, returns are proportionately smaller, and production companies are under pressure to produce cheap, rapidly made films. The margin for error is minimal, and companies making errors of judgment will go under.

But it was not only double and triple programs that were offered to customers: the silent film custom of surrounding a projection with floorshows, music-hall acts, and a cafe concert atmosphere in which the consumption of food was included in the overall price of the night's entertainment—a custom which had died out at the end of the twenties, now returned in the form of added inducements to attend a particular cinema. As an example, an advertisement appeared in one paper of the time for a Thursday screening of a double program which included a bock and a snack (chips or sandwich), all for 2,75 fr. In the *Est républicain*, an advertisement for a children's program costing 1 fr invited the public to bargain over the entry price, which included two full-length films.

While exhibitors felt pressured into these practices and defended them time and again during the thirties, distributors and producers, in France as in America, where in 1941 10,349 out of the 17,919 regular cinemas were still screening double (or triple) programs, repeatedly attempted to induce the government to legislate against them. It did not, though by December 1937 the pressure was such that Raymond Lussiez, speaking on behalf of the powerful exhibitors' lobby, agreed to ensure that screenings did not extend beyond midnight and did not exceed 5,200 meters.[25] It was an assurance which was inadequate and which, as the Marseilles example mentioned earlier demonstrates, was not to be implemented. Costly exhibition practices continued, and this had a significant impact on production not only directly and in the short term, through the diminution of returns on investment per film, but indirectly and in the long term, in that it tended to eliminate from the screens of France for the whole decade those short films and documentaries which had been the training ground for that generation of filmmakers and which were again in the postwar period to be the training ground for the New Wave. If there is one central factor responsible for the sparsity of talent available to take over during and after the war, it is this lack of any logical means of acquiring quasi-professional technical competences during the thirties. In fact, during that decade, only the first-run cinemas preserved the single-film program, since it was in their interest to prolong their exclusive rights over films for as many screenings as possible. They thus became the sole remaining refuge of the short film and the documentary.

A final difficulty facing the production sector in its aspiration for economic stability was the heavy tax burden placed on it by the state. The

FIGURE 1.7   Taxes on Various Spectacles 1920–1940

1	Theaters, concerts, circuses, etc.	I 10%	II 6%	III 3%	= 19%
2	Music halls, bike races, billiards, duelling	10	10	5	25%
3	Cinema (i) up to 15,000 fr per month	10	10	5	25%
	(ii) up to 50,000 fr per month	10	15	75	32.5%
	(iii) up to 100,000 fr per month	10	20	10	40%
	(iv) over 100,000 fr per month	10	25	12.5	47.5%
4	Dances, bullfights, supper concerts, etc.	25	25	12.5	62.5%

Source: P. Léglise, *Histoire de la politique du cinéma français*, vol. 1, p. 58.
The percentages given are maxima, and varied over the 20 years.

"poor tax," first applied to spectacles in 1407, cancelled at the revolution, then restored in 1809, was still in existence at this time, when it amounted to 10% of all receipts. To this the state had added during World War I a tax intended to fund treatment of the war wounded, which privileged the theater and other high-culture spectacles over the cinema for fear of turning the public toward inferior spectacles ("to encourage spectators to see and listen to the beauties of certain works of art, and discourage them from others").[26] The state tax was a graded tax, increasing with monthly receipts and varying from a minimum of 10% to a maximum of 25%. Finally, the law permitted municipalities to tax cinema receipts as well, to a graded maximum of between 5% and 12.5%.

Figure 1.7, taken from Léglise's admirable account of the legislative context in which the cinema industry functioned, summarizes the situation of the early cinema with respect to other spectacles.

On top of these indirect taxes, the cinema was subject to the same general direct taxes as any other commercial operation. Despite modifications in these taxes, the cinema was regularly paying 35% of receipts in taxes during the early thirties, with Parisian cinemas taxed at a rate 50% higher than provincial ones and thus paying the bulk of the taxes (nearly 3/4).[27]

The reduction of this tax burden, during the Depression, and at a time of aggressive intraprofessional competition and price wars, was the subject of much lobbying. There were threats of strikes, threats to eliminate all mention of antagonistic politicians from film news, editorials in all trade papers describing the situation as critical. For the *Cinématographie Française*, "the *vital* problem for our industry is the abolition of the tax on spectacles, unjust and unjustified taxes which weigh heavily not only on exhibitors but indirectly on all branches of our industry. . . . We might note moreoever that, out of the share coming to French producers and out of distributors' costs, significant amounts are expatriated, particularly through the importation of negative and positive filmstock made abroad and the payment of recording fees to German and American radioelectric corporations."[28] Some success was achieved by the campaign: a law of 25 July 1935 reduced the state tax rates to 2%, 10%, 15%, and 20% (though they reduced the tax on music halls by twice as much) and allowed municipalities to vary the poor tax. Nevertheless, the problem remained a critical one; in a further editorial in its number 1000[29] entitled "The French cinema—the most heavily taxed in the world," the *Cinématographie Française* listed the taxes, customs duties, patent rights, and other duties still imposed on the French cinema and calculated that in 1936, out of total receipts of 1 billion francs in France and North Africa, the industry had paid over 400 million to various administrative instrumentalities.

The year 1937 saw, however, a further increase in the tax on the cinema. A total transformation of all state taxes, rationalizing them to 6% on sales and 2% on other operations, affected the cinema extremely disadvantageously. Oddly enough, cinema managements could gain significant reductions in tax if they included an orchestral or music-hall performance with their screening, so anxious was the state to protect live performances over recorded media. Thus it was for detax purposes that cinemas such as the 6,000-seat Gaumont Palace included a full orchestra, singing stars, and dancers in the prewar film programs. Even when, at the end of 1937, the state revised its tax scale, the film industry was still dissatisfied, and all Paris cinemas closed from 4 January 1938; there was talk of closing the studios as well. Finally, a state-appointed commission reported in favor of the film industry, noting that

(1) The progressive nature of the state tax hit large cinemas more severely than medium-size ones.
(2) Cinemas were more severely hit than other categories of spectacle.
(3) The imposition of a municipal tax in addition exacerbated this inequality.
(4) An extremely severe discriminatory régime disadvantaged Parisian cinemas over provincial ones, even before the Parisian municipal tax was applied.[30]

The result was a reform of the tax system in February 1939 as it applied to cinemas, giving full satisfaction to the industry. But the fact remains that throughout the thirties it had been systematically disadvantaged by tax laws which were specifically designed to penalize it with respect to other "superior" forms of entertainment. Moreover, the relief gained in 1939 was, of course, extremely short lived: a further total transformation of the economic context within which film production took place would follow the German occupation.

To this summary of factors detrimental to the economics of the French cinema we might add the continuing inability of the industry to open up an export market. Exports had been relatively small throughout the twenties, contributing to the massively unfavorable economic conditions of the time, and though the introduction of sound in some ways favored the French industry, it did not favor its export potential. Even Chevanne, promoting in 1933 the attempts by Pathé-Natan and Osso to open up export markets by creating distribution networks in foreign countries (20% and 17% of their turnover, respectively), acknowledges that the overall industrial results are disappointing. Not only was the linguistic barrier a problem, but the overvaluation of the franc made French films uncompetitive on world markets: the costs of production in France were proportionately higher than in other countries. Indeed, this unavailability of export markets, together with the increased cost of production, had been one factor behind the double program, intended to generate a greater internal audience. Only after the devaluation of the franc, from 1935 on, did a small but growing export sector develop, until the war eliminated it.

The preceding outline of the main economic pressures on the industry during the thirties bears out some aspects of the recurrent complaints about the need for economic relief within a hard-pressed industry. It does not, however, invalidate the earlier observations to the effect that to some extent the French cinema experienced a boom in the earlier thirties and resisted the depression conditions of the late thirties to a degree that singled it out at the time as one of the few remaining attractive sectors of the economy. The questions that arise, then, are, first, in any overall accounting of these advantages and disadvantages was the industry viable and in some sense healthy, and, second, was it sufficiently viable and healthy to invest the immense sums of money needed not just to transform the studios and the cinemas for sound recording and reproduction, but to update plant that was widely recognized as outdated and to match its foreign competitors in such fields as color cinematography, already well advanced in America by the end of the thirties.

It was not only interested parties within the industry who came to the conclusion that the French cinema of the thirties faced a chronic deficit, suggesting an underlying structural inadequacy. Picking up on an analysis of the silent film industry, Gael Fain in 1933 quotes two fellow economists, each of whom have concluded that the French film industry was running at a global deficit.[31] Depending on the factors taken into account, they estimate the deficit at 150–200 million francs per year (M. Girardeau) or 1,390 million francs (M. Cousinet). Other estimates put the chronic annual deficit rather lower at 50 million francs,[32] and Guy de Carmoy in his official report presented to the Conseil National Economique in July 1936, while less pessimistic than some about the overall industrial situation, estimated it as 100 million francs per year, about 60–70% of which affected the production houses, and estimated that one in three productions each year failed to cover its production costs.[33] Perhaps the most coherent and persuasive argument for an ongoing deficit was put forward by M. Weill, administrator of Pathé after its crash, to the Interparliamentary Group for the Defence of

Cinema in December 1937. He lists the receipts, taxes, and foreign producers' percentages, to reveal that French producers earned 144 million francs in 1932, 137 in 1933, and 130 in 1934, against outgoings of 235, 233, and 189 million francs, respectively. This constitutes a continuing deficit of 30–40%.

This may seem convincingly precise; but of course it was meant to seem so: it was a plea for tax relief to government authorities as part of an appeal from a company in straitened circumstances, itself part of the industry's ongoing campaign for tax relief. Another "balance sheet" drawn up in 1938 by Pierre Cheret for the *Cinématographie Française* attributed the current crisis to an 80% increase in production costs over the previous three years, whereas receipts had only increased by 40%. But he does not indicate whether the initial 1935 situation was favorable or not. Moreover, when one relates the figures he provides for 1938 to those provided by Durand for surrounding years, both costs and receipts had improved at a relatively similar rate, such that in real terms 1938 was an above average year for the decade.

As an alternative index of this continuing deficit, historians and economists alike have been inclined to cite the bankruptcy rate within the film industry. From a positive situation in 1933 in which 58 production firms go bankrupt or into liquidation to be replaced by 228 others, with a net credit balance of 47 million francs, the situation deteriorates from year to year with greater deficits and an ever greater proliferation of new companies entering the market with ever smaller capital resources.

In addition, 86 cinemas went bankrupt in 1933 and a further 95 in 1934, with another 254 closing down. In themselves, however, these figures do not prove anything, except perhaps the ruthless nature of an unregulated free-market capitalism. Certainly the suggestion of a steadily falling capital base to the production industry and a rapidly increasing fragmentation of the production system are valuable indexes of trends to be picked up later; but in the malthusian competitiveness of a sector of a capitalist economy in which the State steadfastly refused to intervene, and where small undercapitalized firms took large risks on credit, it was inevitable that large numbers would fail. One flop must destroy their financial base and their credit rating. This proves nothing about the overall viability of the industry. What is interesting is that so many new firms continued to appear; for this is a powerful index of the continuing attractiveness of a sector which, contrary to most others, still held prospects for those able to assemble the funding. It is hard to see how the additional costs of sound production could have eaten significantly into the additional profits to French producers. In the absence of conclusive data, available information is compatible with the hypothesis that allowing for the increased cost of production caused by sound, the increase in returns to producers in the thirties was comparable to the increase in the number of films produced. One could reasonably conclude that, in unregulated conditions, market factors regulated production and maintained a relatively unchanged margin of profitability and of risk from the twenties through the thirties. Perhaps one-third of films might fail to meet costs, and in a fragmented industry up to a third of the production companies would crash; but the industry as a whole was more likely in profit than the contrary.

PROTECTIONISM

If the reality of a crisis remains unproven, however, there can be no doubt about the continuing belief that such a crisis existed among the personnel in the industry. This crisis was not only economic, but also political: it involved a struggle for control of the industry, both between nations and between classes. The struggle between nations was most intense in the first years of the decade and involved a French commitment to defending the national cinema against German and, particularly, American cultural colonization. The struggle within the nation focused on the later years of the decade and involved a commitment to using the cinema for the promotion and defense of the Popular Front.

Fears about foreign control were not new to the French cinema. The massive dominance of the national market by American and other foreign films had been a prime factor in the sense of an ongoing "crisis of the cinema" in the twenties. That the whole of sound cinema should effectively be obligated and in hock to German and American technology merely exacerbated this existing situation. When Kodak had taken over the Pathé firm producing negative filmstock in 1926, there had been widely voiced fears that it was a step by the U.S. trusts to buy into and take over, step by step, the various elements of the French film industry,[34] or simply to buy up competing firms in order to wind down their production. Certainly, from that time on, the French film industry had been reliant on foreign firms for its supplies of raw film. Loss of national autonomy was a continuing preoccupation, not just for economic reasons, but because foreign appropriation of a prime system of representation was seen as a threat, given the conventional use that American interests had made of those means to represent France, the French, and their institutions.[35]

These fears were inflamed once again by the massive move by Paramount into the French production system in 1930. It was a move which could easily seem to foreshadow a takeover of the entire cinema by the American majors. Reacting rapidly—indeed over-rapidly as it was to prove—to the linguistic barriers erected by sound cinema, Paramount in April 1930 bought up the Gaumont-St. Maurice studios at Joinville and within a fortnight had equipped them for sound production. Eight months before, on his way through Paris, Jesse Lassky, the Paramount vice-president, had foreshadowed his intentions in terms not calculated to reassure the French: "I'll buy the rights of a book, a play or a script that I think suited to the French temperament yet which has the potential to succeed with the American public too. Our various departments will undertake the detailed work associated with the production of a talkie. The film is shot in America. The basic costs (of costumes, models, decoupage, etc.) being established for the American film, I have a copy of it filmed in France with an entirely French cast, according to the original outline which the French producer need only follow to the letter."[36]

Immense amounts of money were poured into the project, the number of studios was increased, ultra-modern laboratories were installed, and within a year of opening, the output of films exceeded the production of any other company in France (24 films in 1932). But Lassky's plans had expanded in the intervening months: St. Maurice was to be the site of production for a multitude of European linguistic communities, with different crews filming the same scenario in three, five, or ten different languages. In many cases, for economy's sake, only the closer shots were re-taken in different language versions, then interpersed with the more distant shots from the original American version. Overawed by the dynamism, the scale of spending, and the output, the *Cinématographie Française* for 18 April 1931 had difficulty in finding words to describe the phenomenon. After eulogizing the equipment, it went on: "But what makes you feel you're dreaming is the thought that simultaneously, as the studios were being built amid great noise and bustle, 150 films in 14 different languages (French, Swedish, Spanish, Italian, German, Portuguese, Czech, Danish, Hungarian, Romanian, Yugoslav, Polish, Norwegian, and even Russian), including 100 feature films and some 50 shorts, have been produced in the space of a year . . . ; compared to the 60 or 70 silent films put out annually by the Hollywood majors in recent years, the record established by the Paramount Joinville Studios speaks for itself. . . . Thus one can see French films shot in Joinville not only in French cinemas, but in Belgium, Switzerland, North Africa, Canada, New York, Louisiana, Florida, California . . . , Poland, Romania, Portugal, and even China. . . . Half this production will be given over to French language films."[37]

Retrospectively, all French critics have labelled these Paramount productions as banal and pedestrian, and some contemporary accounts suggest they were seen in the same light then.[38] No figures exist on the exact economic status of their output, so it is uncertain whether the undertaking would have flourished or not. Two factors extraneous to its operations terminated it as abruptly as it had begun. First, in America, Paramount was facing liquidation because of the effects of the Depression; extremely profitable in 1930, it had just broken even in 1931 and had registered an enormous deficit for 1932. Foreign productions had to be cut back. Second, the development of an effective and cheap method of dubbing different languages over a single acted version allowed them to cater to different linguistic communities much more cheaply. From then on, at one-sixth the cost, they could produce multiple-language versions from a single American version. The Joinville operation became superfluous and was wound down.

Nevertheless, the practice of producing multiple-language versions was one that did not cease so quickly. The other American majors, and notably MGM, had produced them in Hollywood, and in 1931 Britain was producing 15 French-language versions of its films and 25 German versions. The practice was therefore extremely widespread and contributed to early anxiety about the definition of "a French film." When the French market was being inundated in one year by some 30 French versions, all of which had been made in other countries with different but relatively low levels of French technical and artistic participation, and by 25 French versions of American films produced in Joinville by Paramount, it was hard to know what constituted a French film. What was certain was that, financed abroad, they resulted in the expatriation of a large percentage of the receipts.

Most of these went to Germany, for after America it was Germany that produced most such versions. Moreover when dubbing became widespread and other countries ceased the practice, Germany continued producing French-language films at its Neubabelsburg studios in Berlin. A few such films are more authentically French in that, though made in Berlin, they were from French scenarios, rather than being versions of prior German scripts. Chirat calculates these German-made French films, recognized officially as French when screened in France, as constituting some 11% of the 1,305 films which he lists in his catalogue of French films 1929–1939.[39] The extent of the funds siphoned out of the French film industry by these practices was cause for some protest as the prospect of war approached: Jeancolas quotes an article by Henri Jeanson, protesting at *L'Etrange M. Victor*, "a strange production by this strange UFA in Berlin which for some time has been undertaking strange activities—activities which permit Germany to procure in France the foreign funding necessary for the extensive production in its war factories."[40]

Within France, as early as February 1929, Tobis had bought and equipped the Epinay Studios for sound production. More cautious than Paramount, the German firm mounted a lower-profile operation which aimed at a higher aesthetic level than that achieved by Paramount. It produced René Clair's four sound films between 1930 and 1932, as well as Duvivier's *Allô Berlin, ici Paris* and Feyder's famous pair, *Pension Mimosas* and *La Kermesse héroïque*. Precisely because it was such an evident success, the German enterprise was almost more unnerving than the briefer fireworks of Paramount. The artistic level was high, the commercial success undeniable, for ten years large sections of the French film community were influenced by it to work in Berlin where they made other French-language films, large sums of money were flowing out of the country, and yet the films produced by Tobis were nominally French. Nationalist susceptibilities combined with economic concern to heighten a sense of injustice, which translated into an ever more intense conviction that the French cinema was under threat.

Even the retreat of some nations from 1932 onward to the practice of dubbing was not reassuring. In "pretending" to speak French, the foreign actors were intruding unfairly on a linguistic market which the French themselves should be allowed to exploit alone. The Union des Artistes spoke of dubbing as the "spoliation of the actor's personality" and forbade its members to participate;[41] the Gaumont house journal, defending its production interests, spoke darkly of "A terrible change [which] menaces not only the industry and commerce of the French film, but above all the French soul," likening it to the insidious threat of Communism;[42] and René Jeanne asked rhetorically, "Can we accept, even if they aren't presented explicitly as French, films . . . whose artistic value, whatever precautions one might take, will remain inferior to those made in an exclusively national fashion?"[43]

Even when the government ruled in September 1932 that "all dubbing into French must be done in France with French personnel," nationalist fears were not appeased, and critics voiced the fear that authorizing dubbing merely ensured that American cultural colonialism of the world could proceed unimpeded and French screens would be flooded with foreign imports.

> Are we to resign ourselves to allowing French influence in all the lands where it still exists to diminish, to the benefit of American influence? This humiliation is being inflicted on us by the American films flooding onto French screens, and we aren't doing anything to stop it. . . . If we want the French cinema to survive, international commerce in relation to the film industry must be regulated.[44]

The same anti-Americanism is apparent in Yvan Noë's harangue, published in 1933:

> There is a deadly danger that our film industry will become a mere distributor of American films in France and will little by little cease to produce. . . . Dubbing a supposedly "psychological" American comedy can only have one result—flooding our screens with insidious tomfooleries and warping the tastes of the French public. . . . The American cinema tends to stultify us, to destroy through its childishness and its admirably turned out idiocies our judgment, our good sense, and our critical appreciation, in short, to induce mental paralysis.[45]

It is not that these apprehensions concerning economic viability and national autonomy were in bad faith; but it is worth recapitulating the evidence against them. Audiences for the cinema had increased, receipts had increased, production had increased; the cinema industry resisted better than most the belated but persistent effects of the Depression in France; the proportion of foreign films on the French market had decreased dramatically, and the proportion of funds accruing to producers of French-language films had increased from about 35–40% in the mid-twenties to about 65–70% in the mid-thirties. The sense of crisis was partly a transfer from the more general sense of a social and economic crisis; it was motivated by chauvinist attitudes toward Anglo-Saxon nations and more particularly toward the current Nazi régime in Germany; it was certainly in part an attempt to capitalize, consciously or unconsciously, on these and other fears to ensure the retention and if possible the expansion of the French share of its national market; and most importantly it arose from a sense of living in a totally unregulated world, where no framework of industrial legislation existed to establish a pattern of routines and expectations. Anyone could set up a company, without capital, and claim to be a filmmaker. They need demonstrate no competences, professional, industrial, financial, or moral to any authority. It is not to be wondered at that in these circumstances many crashed, or that the possibility of easy money might attract crooks and con men. The sense of anarchy engendered by this free-floating situation is attested by all participants, though not all found it uniformly unacceptable. Those that did so called for four main sorts of reforms—(1) a reduction in the tax levels, and/or (2) quotas on foreign imports to protect the national product, and/or (3) the establishment of a national funding body, able to provide an adequate capital base to guarantee a viable national program of production and modernization, and/or (4) the development of large national trusts, on the model of UFA, Rank, and the American majors, able by their size and the capital resources they could mobilize to compete on equal terms with the foreign corporations. Central to the first three of these was active government intervention in the affairs of the industry, perhaps even a willingness to subsidize it directly or indirectly; central to the fourth was the establishment, again possibly with government backing, of at least one entrepreneurial firm able to integrate production, distribution, and exhibition on a large scale. Neither of these options was to eventuate, and the history of the French film industry in the thirties was to demonstrate that neither was necessary: an unregulated, fragmented, and heavily taxed industry—totally exposed to foreign competition and without any adequate capital base—went on to produce large numbers of films of the highest artistic quality throughout the thirties.

THE COLLAPSE OF PATHÉ AND OF GAUMONT

That no sizable trust eventuated is one of the more surprising aspects of this industrial situation. It is a fact that cannot be deduced from the prevailing conditions, which might, on the evidence of other countries' film industries, have been expected to generate an oligopoly, or even a single monolithic national production house. It is one of the key factors distinguishing the French film industry from others, in this prewar period, and it had a determining effect on the financial strength of the industry, on the state of industrial plant and technology, on the industrial practices of all groups involved in the filmmaking process, from producer through to editor, and thus on the nature of the films themselves.

The contrast with other countries is revealing. In America, in Britain, and in Germany, the film industry evolved rapidly from being an artisanal craft-oriented industry constituted by a set of owner-managed firms into being a subsidiary of state or private corporations dominated by a few massive horizontally and/or vertically integrated firms. It moved, in short, from a capitalist to an advanced capitalist phase; and the financial demands of the change to sound film technology were often crucial in this development.

This model of industrial conglomerate emerging from a period of rapid economic expansion combined with abrupt contraction of the market has the appeal of linking the emergent industrial structure intimately and indeed causally with the conditions of production.

Explanations as to why this causality did not operate in France are mostly sketchy and unconvincing. There were several firms at the end of the twenties positioned to exploit the economic crises of sound and the Depression—Gaumont and Pathé, most clearly, but also a number of slightly less prominent but entrepreneurial firms, such as Franco-Film, run by Robert Hurel, Aubert Film, run by Louis Aubert, and the Société des Cinéromans, run by Jean Sapène. In one way or another, the fate of all of these became involved in that of the Gaumont and Pathé organizations such that an account of the fate of those two enterprises necessarily summarizes the fate of all French moves toward the formation of large-scale trusts on the foreign model.

Early in the twenties, capitulating to the American onslaught, Léon Gaumont had retreated from large-scale production to concentrate on distribution and on his extensive exhibition circuit. A 1925 agreement with MGM made of his firm Gaumont Metro Goldwyn (GMG!), and for three years he thus drew profit from the ailing state of French film production, acting as little more than a local branch office for the American firm while hiring out his studio as a rental concern. This link was broken in 1928, when Gaumont decided to develop its own sound system. With the failure of that enterprise, and faced with the need to raise vast capital sums to fund transformation of his studios and cinemas to sound, Léon Gaumont decided to retire from control, saying "my old age is approaching fast and I don't feel capable of undertaking so intense a struggle as that which is on the horizon."[46] He granted the financial group Kohan-Corniglion-Molinier (KCM) an option on his shares, which they subsequently took up.

But the KCM group had at that stage already acquired control of both Aubert and Franco Film. Franco Film had been born of the gap left in production by Gaumont's withdrawal, when Hurel, a producer for Paramount, had resigned to found it out of a consortium of small production firms. By the summer of 1928 it was so successful that it bought out the La Victorine Studios. Right from the beginning, Hurel's financial backup had been Edouard Corniglion-Molinier of KCM. In 1929, Hurel, like Gaumont, hesitated at the scale of investment needed to move into sound film and ceased production to concentrate on exhibition: he expanded his circuit by acquiring the MGM circuit, at the expense of going deeply into debt with the Banque Nationale de Crédit. When KCM took up the Gaumont options, then, it was already in financial control of Franco Film and already indebted to the BNC.

Aubert had been in the production business for much longer: he had established his first production company in 1909, and during the twenties his firm was a major producer and distributor, with a circuit of 30 cinemas as well. In the early twenties, Aubert through his distribution initiatives was, with Pathé, a key figure in defending the French cinema from total American control, but after a disastrous production year in 1925–1926 cut back on activities and began to withdraw from personal involvement in the firm.[47] Finally he abandoned the industry for a political career as deputy for the Vendée. Franco-Film had acquired options on Aubert's firm, which it took up in the summer of 1929, thus creating an ephemeral group called Franco-Film-Aubert, under the financial auspices of the group KCM and the BNC. When KCM took over Gaumont, it brought to the merger not just these two, but the Joinville studios, another significant production firm (the Société Générale des Films), and a film equipment firm called Continsouza. The resultant conglomerate, Gaumont-Franco-Film-Aubert (GFFA), looked very strong, with a number of affiliates integrating the whole range of cinematic activities: several factories manufacturing film equipment (the "Cité Elgé" at la Villette and the Continsouza works in the rue des Pyrénées), numerous film studios (five in the Cité Elgé, two at Joinville St. Maurice, four in Nice), two laboratories (in the Cité Elgé and Nice), a major cinema circuit both in Paris (21 cinemas, notably the 6,000-seat Gaumont Palace) and in the provinces (23 cinemas in Lyon, Bordeaux, Marseilles, Lille, Toulouse, etc.), a network of foreign agencies (Barcelona, Berlin, Vienna, Budapest, Prague, Milan . . .) and a sizable collection of silent and sound films (from the Gaumont, Franco-Film, Aubert and SGF catalogues).[48] But the cost to KCM of engineering this merger was to leave GFFA a net debtor to the Banque Nationale de Crédit, to the extent of some 98 million francs, which was to prove a double handicap. First, it was an undesirable burden at a time when all its cinemas needed modernizing. The renovation and sonorization in 1931 of the Gaumont Palace alone cost over 41 million francs—like many others it cost far more than expected because of the difficult acoustics in the barn-like cinemas of the silent period, which had been designed with quite other criteria in mind. The Studio La Victorine was totally sonorized in the same year and la Villette extended by the addition of two further studios. But if the conglomerate had been soundly financed in the first place, raising the extra finance in a relatively benign period would not have been disastrous. What triggered GFFA's real problem was the banking crisis which followed almost immediately on the group's formation, and which brought about the collapse of the Banque Nationale de Crédit. A run of withdrawals, caused by a crisis of confidence, bankrupted the BNC, which had too much of its capital tied up in Gaumont and had loaned too heavily elsewhere. The state became involved in trying to refloat the BNC and thus became involved in the GFFA problem when it and other creditors called in the BNC's debts. Already in 1931, therefore, GFFA not only had no credit, but its debts to the BNC were being called in. The firm was obliged to limit its activities severely, selling off most of its foreign agencies, selling off its equipment factories, renting out its various studios (notably Joinville St. Maurice to Paramount), and concentrating its attention on its extensive cinema circuit. Despite these economies, and for reasons that have never been made entirely clear, GFFA was forced into liquidation in July 1934. As late as 1933 it had felt able to extend its circuit by the large-scale takeover of the failing Haïk cinemas, which made GFFA's circuit the most extensive in France, but it may have been this very takeover that produced critical financial conditions for the company once again. As far as production was concerned, in the period 1930–1933, Gaumont had produced overall no more than a dozen films and 20 coproductions. Some of these were of importance, notably Vigo's *Zéro de conduite* and *L'Atalante*; yet the discrepancy between the promise of 1930 and actual achievement four years later was such as to awaken not only expressions of regret from Léon Gaumont but the suspicion of scandal in a nation where such major collapses of apparently sound firms were becoming alarmingly frequent.

The trajectory followed by the Pathé firm shares certain features with that of Gaumont but is distinct in that a single individual, Bernard Natan, to whom Pathé ceded control in 1929, is often seen as being personally responsible for the company's downfall. In 1920, Pathé had reorganized Pathé Cinema into two sections: Pathé Cinema itself was to focus on the rapidly growing amateur filmmaking business, organized around the enormously popular Pathé Baby 9.5 mm camera; while Pathé-Consortium was to focus on commercial film production—producing raw filmstock, renting out studios in Vincennes and Nice, producing a few films itself, but concentrating more on the distribution and exhibition sectors. Control of the Pathé-Consortium was early wrested from Pathé by his financial backers, notably the Banque Bauer et Marchal, which over-extended the firm in some costly super-productions. For the rest of the twenties, Pathé-Consortium was primarily a distribution/exhibition company, but affiliated to some semi-independent production companies which stepped in, as had Aubert, to profit from this cutback by Pathé and Gaumont.

Jean Sapène's Société des Cinéromans was the most important of these. Indeed, with the Banque Bauer et Marchal's support he had effectively taken control of Pathé in 1923, and his Société became the central production element in a powerful vertically integrated corporation under his management. By 1927 Pathé-Consortium's production arm had again begun to falter. Commentators have suggested that this may have been because of Sapène's increasing intrusion into the daily routine of filmmaking; a competent and enterprising manager, he seems to have been less than reliable in the aesthetic and commercial evaluation of scripts.[49] Progressively he took over all critical decision making from his executive producer, Louis Nalpas, to whom the firm's production success was largely due. In particular, he failed in his attempt to make a star of his wife. His disillusionment, the resignation of Louis Nalpas to found his own firm, and the fact that Pathé's own position was now tenuous in the extreme produced a leadership crisis in the corporation, which was exacerbated by Pathé's decision that old age and the problems of transition to sound were sufficient motive for resignation. Bernard Natan took over on 1 March 1929.

Natan, long associated with the film business, had entered film production in 1926 from a base of film processing and film publicity. Rapidly successful, he bought up the Epinay Studio and constructed a new one on rue Francoeur. By the time he bid for Pathé, he was being hailed as one of the most important figures in film production. With the support of the Banque Bauer et Marchal, he merged his interests with Pathé. The concern which he then controlled, despite Pathé's having disposed of its filmstock factory to Eastman Kodak, was a major corporation capable of competing on even terms with foreign trusts. It owned 55 cinemas and controlled the programs of many more (69 in Paris, 35 in Greater Paris, 91 in the provinces, and two in Brussels),[50] Natan's studios in Epinay and Francoeur, his Rapid-Film processing and publicity concerns, the Sapène-created production facilities of Pathé-Consortium, the Joinville Studios and laboratories, and a vast stock of films.

Yet by 1936, Pathé too was in liquidation. There is disagreement as to whether its collapse was due to Natan's systematic embezzlement of the funds, to extensive bribery payments to which he was reputedly subject, to his overly grandiose projects at a time of economic constriction, or simply to "mismanagement." The belief was widespread that he saw himself as the French equivalent of a great American producer and tried to live and act out that megalomanic role before having created the solid financial basis that would have justified his act. To an extent, all these factors may have contributed. Certainly he brought with him to the merger some problems of which Pathé-Cinéma was not aware at the time. His Rapid-Films was significantly overextended and in debt; when he merged with Pathé, the debt was transferred to Pathé. Moreover, several of the films made during his early production years around 1910 seem to have been intensely pornographic in nature. One of them was commercialized under the evocative title of *Soeur Vaseline*. In addition, he had once been convicted on a morals charge. Cleynen claims that the now respectable Natan, associate of politicians and of the social élite, was constantly having to buy up old prints of these, and silence former associates, at exorbitant cost. For some years, indeed until 1934, no public doubts were raised concerning Pathé's viability. Natan was a consummate publicist, devoting much of his energy to writing eulogistic publicity for Pathé-Natan and himself. The Pathé studios were turning out more films than any other French company—20 in 1931 alone. They matched American practices in attracting prestigious directors and stars to "long-term" contracts, including Maurice Tourneur, Baroncelli, Jean Grémillon, Marcel L'Herbier; Gaby Morlay, Arletty, and Renée de St. Cyr (though French contracts seldom exceeded two or three films, so the actors never became "the property" of a company as they did in America). His films featured Vanel, Jean Marchat, Victor Francen, René Lefèvre, Fernandel, and Raimu. Even in 1934 Pathé was still signing exclusive contracts, for instance with Charles Boyer and Annabelle.[51] Meanwhile, however, Natan's finances were becoming progressively more shady and unsound. For one thing, he had been living high, paying vast personal commissions to himself and to his friends. Again, the Banque Bauer et Marchal, which had all along been his principal financial support, was caught up in the banking crisis. Worse, and arguably in collusion with that bank,[52] Natan seems to have been systematically defrauding the company by setting up affiliates alongside Pathé Cinéma and siphoning off its assets into them. According to this view, having taken over a firm with 400 million francs in assets, Natan stripped it clean and took it into a debt of at least 200 million francs. Surprised at receiving no dividends in 1935, shareholders protested. The company went into liquidation in February 1936, Natan was charged in September of that year and, as a result of a judicial enquiry, was finally condemned to prison at the end of 1938.[53] He was still there when the Germans invaded; being a Jew, he was deported and died in a concentration camp.

While details are less clear than in the Pathé case, the Gaumont collapse may well have involved similar instances of large-scale corruption. Jeancolas notes the particular care of various officials and politicians to distance themselves from the subsequent report and to prevent any reliable investigation. A suggestive remark concerning the Gaumont collapse by the deputy Doussain, to the effect that "we must put an end to certain forms of blackmail, to certain scandalous appointments handed out to people who do nothing . . . "[54] could have applied equally well to Pathé-Natan. A similar remark had been made in 1933 by the minister for national education: "The cinema is currently surrounded by a very dubious environment. I'm not thinking of that form of immorality that is so to speak traditional and even classic in it, but certain procedures born of competitiveness."[55]

To sum up: Gaumont effectively ceased operations in 1934 and Pathé in 1935. The two major vertically integrated corporations on the trust model had both collapsed within five years of the departure of the key figures who had built up their various elements—Pathé, Gaumont, Aubert, Hurel, Sapène, and Nalpas. The fact that numerous details are known concerning the Pathé collapse which are not known concerning Gaumont has served to personalize the former and thus to conceal certain nonpersonal features which both collapses have in common and which may help us understand why the French experience, with all it entailed for later production practices and textual characteristics, was so distinct from the American, German, and British. These have to do with the scale of investment needed, the practices and resources of the banks involved in funding that investment, and the lack of expertise of those called on to oversee the resulting crisis—a lack of expertise which at least possibly in both cases involved collusion in corrupt practices between bankers and managers.

Neither firm was in a position to fund the transition to sound by itself, Gaumont being effectively in debt from the start and Pathé encumbered by Natan's debt of uncertain proportions; the problem was that the private banks and financial firms with which they were associated were not large enough to withstand the pressures placed on them in the crisis period of 1931–1932 while still funding the film industry's re-equipping. Perhaps also, French banks were overly cautious by comparison with their American counterparts which at this point seized control of the industry and reorganized it to suit their own purposes. At the heart of the problem, however, is the fact that, deceived by the relative boom in audiences of those years, at this crucial moment both Gaumont and Pathé launched into a buying spree, picking up large cinema circuits from other failing companies. These, in turn, needed investment for modernization, precisely at a moment when investment funds were drying up rapidly, as the French modified their economic behavior in favor of immediate consumption.

That these general circumstances were widespread in France at the time is attested by the large number of crashes in which some form of fraud was known to have taken place, associated with abuse of positions of authority and the selling of favors. The Stavisky case, festering precisely at this time, is just the best-known of a series of them; there was also Marthe Hanau, Oustric, and the Lévy Brothers.[56] In fact, the Pathé crash, involving the embezzlement or squandering of some six hundred million francs, was twice as large as the more notorious Stavisky deficit. Such crashes seem to have been merely the sensational extremes of a fairly general problem of maladministration common to most areas of French business at the time and related to a reluctance to move out of the era of the personalized owner-managed firm with its basically artisanal approach to production. But the absence of any strong political guidelines or intervention in the industrial world such as would have provided the required framework was probably also an important factor. Essentially, Western governments were incapable of comprehending and coping with the novel transformations which capitalism was undergoing in that period, and this inability was exacerbated in France by the intense instability of the political institutions themselves.

GOVERNMENTAL INACTION

The state itself seemed to recognize that it should intervene in July 1934 when, having inherited and called in GFFA's debts to the Banque Nationale de Crédit and thus been directly involved in its bankruptcy, it decided to set up a commission under Maurice Petsch to report not just on the problems specific to Gaumont, but on the problems of the French cinema in general. It was an action that economists and some elements of the industry had been suggesting since the twenties, but which others (notably the exhibitors) had been resisting with equal intensity. For the former, the state needed to intervene in order to rationalize funding, possibly by the creation of a State Film Bank such as existed in Germany funded from a percentage of entry receipts, possibly by a nationalized production system which would provide a unified corporation able to compete with foreign trusts. Among the anti-interventionists, certain producers saw a state production system as usurping their function and their profits, while exhibitors feared that any new tax would cause an increase in entry prices, which would reduce receipts and make them de facto tax collectors. Unquestionably, others were apprehensive that business practices of an uncertain propriety would be brought to light. Essentially, the industry's aspirations can be summarized as seeking government subsidy and protection without government monitoring or control. As Tardieu, the responsible minister, had said impatiently in 1930, "You are all anti-interventionists; but as soon as one of your activities begins to suffer, you call on the state for help."[57] In fact the last time the state had attempted to provide concrete help to the industry was in 1928, when Herriot had introduced a form of import quota by way of export incentives which allocated to each French film seven import licenses to be conveyed to other nations that would distribute it. The system might have theoretically allowed the French cinema to supply the national market with at least one-eighth of the film it needed, but it was subverted by American retaliation: Will Hays threatened a total ban on U.S. film imports if it was enforced, which would have destroyed the exhibitors, and in the face of this threat the government backed down.[58] As well as demonstrating the reluctance of the state to take strong stands on the legislation of the cinema, this incident is symptomatic of the divided nature of the industry in France, each branch preoccupied with its own immediate problems and lacking not just an interest in the industry as a whole but even a common forum in which such an interest might have been developed. The German industry had by that time developed its single powerful central Film Council, the Filmkammer, to debate problems of general interest to the industry, and when in April/May 1935 at the Congress of Berlin the German delegation proposed extending this model to the international level, through the creation of similar councils in all countries, with an international council assembling delegates from all nations, there was wide agreement among those present. The French alone seemed to lack a national voice. In his editorial of 11 May 1935 P.-A. Harlé noted that none of the thirty French delegates could speak in the name of all, and that this lack of a common purpose and united will surprised the delegates of other countries.[59] When the state called for a report on the French cinema with a view to a total reorganization of the industry, it finally looked as if such a forum for formulating industry-wide policy might be created and a "more rational" industrial structure instituted.

Maurice Petsch submitted his report a year later, in June 1935. Its analysis of the situation was exhaustive and its proposals radical.[60] Organizationally and financially, he saw the industry as deplorably incoherent. Production was entrusted to hundreds of small undercapitalized firms, a large percentage of which went bankrupt each year; the few large firms which had seemed on the way to a coherent structure had likewise just collapsed; work conditions were intolerable in the outdated facilities; the French-language market was too small to ensure an adequate return on the cost of production; credit terms to fund production were onerous, and the distributors who had become de facto bankers of the industry tended to determine production policy and (through block booking) exhibition programs, to the detriment of both.

Essentially, he proposed two reforms which would have transformed the financial and industrial structure of the industry: first, a national credit organization, funded from a variety of taxes (on foreign films, royalties, cinema licenses, and entrance fees), whose task would be to foster film production by funding it at a controlled and reasonable interest rate; and second, a "technical committee" composed of 25 representatives of all branches of the industry and of the related public service departments, to advise on the disbursement of those funds, using criteria of technical competence, financial reputation, and the reputation of the industry and the nation abroad. Amid a flood of subsidiary and complementary recommendations, a few others stand out. First, the state should refloat GFFA, over which it now had effective control, and should use it as a pilot firm to test the effects of its policy. In effect a public sector element would be used as a model and trigger for private sector recovery. Second, the state should reform its own administration of the industry, assembling all public services that had to do with the cinema under a single ministry. As Paul Léglise says, these proposals were too radical for the period. They offended all sectors of the industry in one way or another, either by regulating their activities or by usurping their funding control, their decision-making powers, or a percentage of their profit. In addition, they offended the Americans by assuming total control over the import and distribution of foreign films in France. Moreover, they looked remarkably like that move toward nationalization of the economy which many had feared. When government legislation based on the report was foreshadowed in October 1935, a number of interested parties unleashed industrial activity aimed at undermining it. They were successful, and the projected law never eventuated. The various elements of Petsch's report that were to have found expression in it, however, were to recur in other proposals over the coming years, some of them finally forming the basis of the wartime legislation introduced by the Germans and perpetuated in the postwar period.

The state had a second opportunity to intervene in the film industry in 1936, when Guy de Carmoy's report on the cinema, commissioned by the Conseil National Economique, was presented. But in the intervening year, and perhaps under the impulse of debates surrounding the Petsch report, much had changed. Notably, the industry had organized itself into a series of federations grouping the various industrial sectors, the Fédération des Chambres Syndicales de la Cinématographie Française. The chambers' main focus of concern was that the cinema should take in hand its own industrial destiny and thus forestall state intervention: self-regulation was preferable to state regulation. The strategy of de Carmoy was to recognize in his recommendations this newfound corporative purposefulness and to exploit it in achieving the solution to the industrial weaknesses identified by Petsch.

Essentially his analysis was analogous to that of Petsch, though it focused also on industrial relations and the need to modernize industrial plant. It was strengthened by a survey of the procedures whereby other countries had coped with similar problems. America, he noted, had introduced self-regulation and had restructured itself under the influence of the banks, which had acquired a controlling interest in the industry. The economy, though severely affected by the Depression, had emerged from it more rapidly than had the French economy, and the film industry had not had to cope with such strong competition from foreign films. In England, a quota system introduced in 1927 had required at least 5% of the films distributed to be British, and this percentage had been steadily increased to 20%. This protection, complemented by heavy duty on foreign films, had been successful in encouraging the national film industry. Italy had likewise introduced a quota, progressive over the years from 10% to 25%, and a tax on foreign films, but had in addition improved the procedures for funding production by introducing a subsidy based on the producers' past performance. Perhaps even more importantly, it had taken over an important production firm, *L'Unione cinematographica educative* (LUCE) and a distribution firm with an exhibition network of seventy cinemas under its control. It had thus moved toward the partly nationalized industrial organization suggested for GFFA. In Germany, the professions had been regulated through the registration of all film personnel and their incorporation into a Filmkammer, production had been regulated through the need to obtain official authorization to proceed with the production of a film, and exhibition had been regulated through control over the development of cinema circuits. A Film Credit Bank had been instituted as a subsidiary of four large banks in Berlin to provide credit on favorable terms; and the double program had been prohibited, thus creating better conditions for the recovery of costs on individual films.

In one way or another, therefore, all those mechanisms proposed over the last decade for France had been tried elsewhere: quotas, public sector production, a film bank, and program regulation. The authority for these measures had come from the industry itself in one case, and from the state in another. For Guy de Carmoy, the German situation was closest to the French, and he recommended elements from it, especially in the economic sphere. But rather than attributing authority to the state for the monitoring and approval of the system, with a "Filmkammer" as perhaps no more than a discussion forum, he recommended a federation of professional groups as the executive authority, under the nominal supervision of the state, which would only intervene if the profession so requested. It was this professional federation which would supervise and administer the centralized credit available for production.[61]

It was a solution calculated to delight the new industrial leadership. Ironically, however, the volatile political situation disadvantaged it: the report came out in July 1936, just after the election of a Popular Front government which had for some time been foreshadowing massive state intervention if elected. In April, the socialist Paul Faure, a close confidante of Léon Blum, had declared that "if one day our party acquires total political control, it will make of the cinema a state institution. For it is impossible for a government that aspires to inaugurate a new social order to allow a means of propaganda as powerful as the cinema to remain in the hands of groups who may well have interests opposed to its own."[62]

A state-controlled GFFA was the ideal mechanism to begin this program of nationalization and thus was what the more moderate elements on the political left were advocating. The more radical left, however, would settle for nothing less than the total nationalization of the film industry. As outlined by Jarville, secretary-general of the film workers union, this was to consist of

(1) the nationalization of the means of production, the state progressively buying up the laboratories and studios;
(2) state funding of production, to produce films expressing the aspirations of the people;
(3) control of any private production through precensorship of scripts;
(4) state control of distribution and export;
(5) state control of exhibition, programming and promotion;
(6) the establishment of a state organization for training film personnel, supported by a scholarship system.[63]

Jarville's proposal first appeared in Le Peuple in February 1937 and was spelled out in elaborate detail to the Renaitour commission of inquiry into the film industry at its sitting on 24 March 1937.[64] The aim was to put the industry under the control of a tripartite council consisting of representatives of film personnel, of consumers, and of "the collectivity," leading to a cinema that would *"be at the service of the people, and under the control of the people"*[65] and that would therefore express "the real aspirations of the people."

The private sector response was immediate. The extent of its anxiety can be measured in P-A Harlé's editorial of 26 April:

> What is in question here is *the freedom of the cinema*—the commercial freedom of exhibitors, the creative freedom of producers, the independence of the film news. What's proposed, let's be clear, is the appropriation by two or three big firms supported by the state and under the orders of the state, of all the commercial activity of the French cinema. Up till now the development of an industry has been based on competition between independent firms on independent initiative, freely decided. The small-scale programming maneuvers undertaken by rival firms competing in a given town are as nothing compared to the heavy hand of the state, crushing the independent exhibitors in order to favor municipal screenings. . . . What is proposed is a *state institution*, along Soviet lines.[66]

As it happened, the industry's fears were not to be realized. The corporate sector mobilized most effectively, developing its own Confédération générale along the lines recommended by de Carmoy; and the government, which had after all many other problems on its plate at that time, and in areas much more economically problematic than a film industry which was, despite everything, relatively buoyant, made no decisive moves at all. Its fears of state control allayed, the private sector's unity again gave way before the internal divisions which had long beset it, and the institutional self-regulation which it had promised did not eventuate either.

Lacking either a legislative framework or any strong internal professional regulation, the industry settled into the institutional structure which had seemed inevitable with the collapse of the major firms—a patchwork of production, distribution, and exhibition companies, lacking any coherent legislative framework within which to operate, lacking any large-scale organizations capable of dominating and driving the industry, and lacking any assured funding for production, let alone for modernization of facilities. It settled, that is, back into the pattern of the late twenties. That nothing had changed between the late twenties and the late thirties can be recognized in the similarity between the following two observations—first, an analysis provided by Gael Fain and Louis Pommery in 1928, and second, a series of comments by Jean Zay in 1936. Fain and Pommery noted that

> In the face of foreign firms, powerfully equipped, strongly concentrated, we see in France an industry divided into three branches, each preoccupied with trying to impose its own divergent interest, debating like Byzan-

tine theologians, at a time when the city walls are already under siege. We see a mass of cinemas crushed by taxes yet incapable of working toward common goals. We see besides one or two large societies a great number of independent producers struggling to make films with whatever financial resources they happen to be able to put together.[67]

In 1936 Jean Zay, minister for education (therefore responsible for the cinema) under the Popular Front government, was still talking of the "mire," the "incoherence" and the "quasi-general collapse" of an industry: "there is no large production company left in France . . . there are only two companies of any size and they are foreign,[68] mostly concentrating on non-French production: most of our films emerge from small companies created specifically for the production of that one film, and having no permanent place in the cinema industry."[69] Instances of this latter practice are provided by Jeancolas:[70] "L'Amour veille (1937, Henry Roussell) was produced by the "Société du film L'Amour veille"; Vidocq (1938, Jacques Daroy) was produced by the "Société de production du film Vidocq"; Brazza (1939, Léon Poirier) was produced by the "Société de production du film Brazza." "In these conditions," said Zay, "I don't think anyone can expect that the classic principles of a liberal market can continue to operate pure and simply, or that the state can continue to preserve a totally noninterventionist stance." He spent the next year elaborating a proposed legislative framework for the industry.[71] That framework was announced in October 1937, but an unexplained silence fell and it was only in March 1939 that it came before the Chamber of Deputies. By then, however, war was threatening, and the legislation never became effective.

This sorry tale of well-intentioned but ineffectual state inactivity seems to have been typical of the time. Of the interwar period, Asselain says "it can be characterized by the absence of any systematic effort on the part of the state to exercise in any coherent way the new responsibilities conferred on it by its economic power. Its interventionism in the energy and transport sector . . . do not conform to any overall program. . . . The state has neither the means nor the will to prosecute a genuine economic policy. . . . There is no real attempt by the State to take over the investment role of the collapsing private sector."[72]

The years 1935–1939 can be summed up therefore as a period when both state and industry recognized the need for a set of routinized working practices, incorporated either in legislation or in an agreed professional code, but when neither state nor industry could manage to agree on them or to mobilize the energy to develop and impose them. As P.-A. Harlé noted when Jean Zay's legislation finally came before the Chamber, "This statute has been established by representatives of the state because the industry demanded it without itself being capable of formulating it. We are good at destroying but not at creating. We'll have a fine time pulling this statute to bits. Each will try to get the juiciest morsel for himself."[73]

INDUSTRIAL STRUCTURE

In sum, the industrial structure, as it emerged from the transition to sound, was marked first of all by a tendency toward dominance by fewer and fewer large firms with some form of vertical integration, but after 1933 it became clear that none of these firms had the financial resources to withstand a crisis which lasted unconscionably long in France and which deprived the financial banking sector of the ability to provide the credit on which all production depended. The predominance of small owner-managed production companies divorced from both production facilities and exhibition circuits is confirmed by 1935.

At its most "rationalized," in 1931–1932, there were some four French firms and two foreign firms dominating production. Of about 70 films produced in France by French companies and in the French language that year, 20 were produced by Pathé-Natan, 12 by Osso, 9 by Haïk, about 9 by Braunberger and perhaps 4 by Gaumont. To them, one can add the French Paramount subsidiary, with 25 French-language films filmed in its St Maurice studios, and the Tobis Epinay production. Aside from the Gaumont, Pathé, and Paramount cases already mentioned, Braunberger was forced to severely restrict his activities in 1932 by cash-flow problems, and (at least in his own account) because his backer turned out to be a con man who had been juggling accounts between banks till his bubble burst.[74] Jacques Haïk likewise seems to have suffered financial problems in 1933–1934 which effectively terminated his production career. After producing 24 films between 1929 and 1933, his firm was declared bankrupt in 1934. Osso, who produced numerous films in the twenties for Paramount, before founding his own company, was also forced into receivership in 1934, apparently through investing too heavily in an attempted super-production (*La Bataille*, Farkas, 1933). Of the six companies, only Braunberger survived beyond 1935, and his production for the period 1932–1939 totalled a mere five films.

In 1931 the larger production firms had been tending toward integration; by 1935 all of them had been obliged to renounce it. For instance, Haïk had built and sonorized a studio at Courbevoie, had acquired a significant cinema circuit, and had built several large cinemas in Paris. Braunberger had taken over and sonorized the Billancourt studio, had bought the Panthéon as an art cinema, and had associated with Richebé, who had a cinema circuit in the South. The scale of the Pathé and Gaumont enterprises at this stage has already been mentioned.

By 1934 only Gaumont and Braunberger had studios, the latter in name only; Gaumont's had been mostly rented out since 1925 because its own production was not adequate, and Braunberger did likewise till 1938 when he sold it. At the beginning of the thirties, Pathé and Gaumont had dominated the exhibition sector with circuits involving over half the main city cinemas; with Pathé's crash, the two that remained in the late thirties were the Haïk circuit, taken over and enlarged by Siritzky, and the refloated Gaumont's circuit, taken over and expanded by Havas but maintaining the Gaumont name for prestige reasons. Neither had connections to the production sector. Perhaps the only residue of coherent production-distribution-exhibition concerns were in the South where Pagnol's and Richebé's companies both owned studios in which they made their own films for screening in their own cinemas. Neither moved into the Paris market, however, which alone would have been large enough to provide the cashflow to generate a large corporation on the foreign model. The small scale of the resulting companies confirmed the French film industry in its artisanal tendencies. In this it was not untypical of French industry as a whole. Although there is a consistent trend away from small businesses in France between 1900 and 1939, that trend is much less pronounced than in other Western countries. The number of automobile producers in France, for instance, passes from 155 in 1914 to 60 in 1932 to 31 in 1939; but this is still a lot of relatively small firms. Only Citroen had at that stage really moved into large-scale production; the consequence had been a rapid increase in its share of the market, over-extension, and bankruptcy in 1934.

But the small scale of the production units also had the effect of ensuring that the French cinema could never be self-sufficient as far as funding was concerned. Had a strong financial establishment been integrated into the industry as the funding source for a few large firms, the production sector would have been able to plan long-term production schedules without being dependent on the week-by-week receipts from its most recent productions. As it was, the production sector was confirmed in its reliance on ad hoc funding for each project, and each individual firm risked bankruptcy with every project. While the sector itself was, as we have seen, in some senses flourishing, no individual element of the sector could be said to be flourishing; and it was this omnipresent local sense of crisis which was being expressed when representatives spoke of "the crisis of the French cinema." To make matters worse, the industry as a whole depended on outside sources for 60% of its funding, and that was by far the highest percentage of credit required by any French industry of the day. One in three films failed to break even; at times, over a third of the active companies were going bankrupt each year. Credit agencies, themselves in crisis, could scarcely be expected to rejoice at the thought of committing their funds to such an uncertain form of investment. Each project thus became harder to fund. Had a larger corporate organization existed, able to balance losses on one film against profits on two others, and thus capitalize on the real long-term possibility of a continuing if marginal profitability, there would have been no sense of crisis, financial or psychological.

In the circumstances, however, the distributor and/or the exhibitor were a much more attractive element for banks than was the producer: a distributor dealing with several producers, and a circuit dealing with several distributors and with a regular clientele, could spread the effects of successful and unsuccessful films across a year's earnings in a way that small production firms could not. Distributors, with guarantees from exhibitors to take specific films, thus became the de facto bankers of the system, each providing a number of production firms with credits for specific projects in return for the right to distribute them.

Again, because the so-called production units in fact did not themselves own the means of production, but had to rent studios and material, and because the long delays in getting returns on a film meant that they could seldom pay on the spot for such services, studios and laboratories mostly expected to do the work on long-term credit, in return for a share of future profits on their work. They thus became a second major "informal" source of credit-funding for production. The production company itself provided no more than 20% on average of the funding for a film and at times paid the bulk of that 20% to itself in "fees."

This is not an unusual situation for an artisanal film production system; it had existed in Germany until the creation of the Film Credit Bank in 1933, which within two years was funding 70% of German production to an extent of 68% of costs.[75] A minority of American production had also functioned in this way, mostly concentrating on the B film market. Wherever it happened, however, what it meant was that a prime preoccupation of the production sector was the organization of an adequate minimal funding package. It also meant that, in obtaining it, the producer had necessarily to guarantee that his creditors would get the first slice of any receipts, thus ensuring that his own share of receipts was at once most at risk and most remote in time. This further reinforced the funding problems for succeeding projects in a circular manner.

The fragmentation of production among a myriad of small production companies, mostly inactive or at best sporadically active, also had decisive effects upon the nature of the films produced. Briefly, three areas deserve particular mention: the technical finish of the films, the scale on which they could be produced, and the degree of generic conventionalization which could be expected to occur.

The lack of investment in modernization led to a constant problem of technical inadequacy in most areas of the industry but particularly in studio equipment, where the facilities for sound, lighting, and editing were often inadequate. Technicians were constantly having to make do with out-of-date machinery, and this tended to limit the degree of technical finish that they could achieve, especially by comparison with the American or German product. Exacerbating this situation, the production system imposed upon all major technical contributors a chaotic work pattern. Hired one month for a given film by a given company to work in a given studio with given collaborators, they could not be sure when they next would work, but it would almost certainly be with different collaborators and different equipment. Such a situation militated against achieving levels of technical confidence and technical competence such as the technicians in other countries knew, who were salaried on a continuing basis to work with the same collaborators and equipment.

In more direct ways, the undercapitalization of these firms tended to inhibit large-scale undertakings. Credit was not readily available, especially for companies with little or no industrial record by which they could demonstrate their competence, and no state subsidies or cheap loans were available as they were in other countries. Funding packages were scraped together and kept to a minimum. In these circumstances, the normal film product of the thirties came to be a small- to medium-sized initiative, and few films after Gance's super-productions bear comparison with the epics and the historical reconstructions of the American cinema. It was an area where the French cinema was not able to compete until international co-productions became the norm, in the fifties, except for isolated wartime projects such as *Les Enfants du paradis*, generated by unrepeatable circumstances.

Finally, the lack of continuity in production and the lack of any recurrent collaboration between teams of workers militated against the formation of genres. It was not readily possible for a production company to exploit a success, since the chances were fairly high that by the time the film turned out to be a success the production company would no longer exist. If it did exist, or if another arose, tempted to repeat the success, it would inevitably have to begin anew with largely different personnel. In particular, the collapse of those few firms which offered contracts to recognized actors militated in a variety of ways against the construction of those mythic stereotypes which serve as one of the more potent sets of generic conventions. This is not to say that genres did not arise, and even less to say that the resultant films were free of conventions. But simply those conventions were exploited less systematically and less rapidly than in, say, America, so they tended not to cohere into those *arrays* of *recurrent* conventions which characterized the classic American cinema of this period.

TWO

POLITICAL ECONOMY AND INDUSTRIAL STRUCTURE 1940–1960

The idea of a free market in the film industry can seem seductive; the problem is how to avoid its becoming a case of the free fox in the free fowlyard.

Jean Néry, *La Technique Cinématographique* 131, April 1953

What the French need is frivolous films—empty, and even a little stupid; and it's our job to see that they get them.

Goebbels, in his diary, 15 May 1942

WARTIME REGULATION OF THE INDUSTRY

It is normal for French historians to define 1944–1945 as a radical break in the evolution of the French cinema as in so many other aspects of their society. Sadoul, providing data on the French cinema's economic viability, takes it for granted that the relevant periodization is 1930–1945 and 1945–1961.[1] Jeancolas, as the title of his book proclaims, sees the 1930s as having lasted for fifteen years, from 1929 to 1944,[2] and in this he is recapitulating the views of the very first French historian of the war years, Roger Regént, who in 1948 was already preoccupied with demonstrating that the French cinema of 1940–44 represented a survival and continuation of the cinema of the thirties. That 1945 saw a clean break with the past is equally implicit in René Bonnell's economic history of the cinema since that date,[3] and in Charles Ford's more conventional *Histoire du cinéma français contemporain, 1945–1977*.[4] That the war's end is more crucial than its beginning as a historical marker is also implicit in François Garçon's *De Blum à Pétain: cinéma et société française, 1936–1944*.[5] Even Jacques Siclier, treating the wartime cinema as an autonomous area of study, feels able to assert that "it was quite simply the continuation of the French cinema of the thirties."[6] In fact, when they don't isolate it as a totally distinct moment,[7] French historians of the cinema always link it to the past rather than to the future. There is a good deal of evidence that points in the other direction—evidence relating to the establishment of a legislative framework in 1941–1942 that was to provide for the first time a reliable organizational framework for the activities of the industry, and which was to act as the basis for all postwar legislation relating to the cinema; evidence relating to the establishment of funding schemes which were for the first time to provide a reliable financial basis for production and which were to be perpetuated in postwar financial legislation; evidence relating to the administrative structure of the wartime cinema, which proved particularly effective, and on which the postwar industrial administration was to be modelled. In all these ways, the early occupation years provided a clear break with the thirties and inaugurated systems which, with strategic redefinitions and renamings to preserve national pride, were to continue on through the supposed break of the liberation and reconstruction. It is understandable that, in their general sensitivity to their own wartime past and their recurrent representation of the liberation as the purging of an unfortunate and totally irredeemable experience, French writers on the cinema should be inclined to minimize such continuities in favor of a rhetoric of new beginnings. It is also understandable that historians aware of the political logic that represents the war as a consequence of German humiliations in the twenties and territorial conflicts that date back even further should see it as an endpoint rather than a beginning. It is even understandable that, focusing purely on the personnel involved in filmmaking and their attempts to recapture the "typically French style" of the thirties, such critics as Siclier should emphasize links with the thirties, though an argument can equally well be made that the war brought about a radical transformation in personnel, due to the forced absence of many leftwing and most Jewish workers. Within the narrower logic of a history of French film, even the liberation saw no new beginnings; and the rest of this chapter will attempt to substantiate the argument that the industrial conditions established during the war served as the foundation of postwar classic French cinema. For fairly obvious reasons, the point of departure for this argument that targets 1940 as the beginning of the postwar French cinema will not be the general economic conditions within which production took place, as it was in the initial section, with political responses or lack of response to them as a secondary consideration, but rather the prevailing political conditions themselves; for if in some very general way the primacy of the economic over the political can still be argued here—the war, say, as the last of a series of violent national and international convulsions caused by the unstable conditions of a rapidly evolving monopoly capitalism—it is clear that, as far as the cinema was concerned, the primacy of the political over the economic was unquestionable. The economics of film production, distribution, and exhibition were not just caused, but systematically determined, by political considerations extending far beyond them.

That the occupying German forces should wish to monitor and control any cinematic production that took place in France is natural enough. For any totalitarian régime, the control of the principal systems of signification and representation seems a logical and inevitable step in the sanitizing of social consciousness. The views expressed by Goebbels on this matter are not significantly different from those of Stalin or Faure, and the history of the German cinema under the fascist régime was one of progressive unification with a view to nationalization. It is probable that the same progression would have taken place in France, in time—indeed, it had arguably already begun to take place, given that Continental Films, the German-controlled production agency in France, through privileged access to funding and materials, was achieving by 1944 a major share of the market. As in Germany, however, the fascist régime did not impose this unified system from above, but simply introduced mechanisms which would ensure that the industry evolved toward it in time.

Their principal preoccupation was to ensure that they knew what was happening in the film industry and that they could monitor and, if necessary, direct the nature of all production. No such monitoring and control had been possible in the thirties. Very soon after the Germans seized operational control, they introduced the necessary approval, monitoring, and reporting procedures, and they ensured that an organizational structure was in place which would implement these determinations efficiently.

It was on 17 June 1940 that Marshal Pétain announced that the French forces had ceased fighting, and the armistice he requested was signed on 22 June. The German high command agreed to a notional division of France into two sectors, one under direct German command, the other—the southern two-fifths of France—under the formal control of a French government willing to cooperate with them. The German army of occupation was to control the northern sector from its headquarters in Paris. By 1 July, the French government, which had retreated to Bordeaux in the face of the invading army, had installed itself at Vichy, which was to be its permanent location. On 10–11 July the Etat Français came into existence, and Marshal Pétain was named as head of state. The division into two zones began to collapse in November 1942, following the American and British invasion of North Africa; German troops were no longer confined to the northern zone, but occupied the whole of France. The occupation effectively ended in August 1944. Retreating before the Anglo-American troops which had landed in Normandy on 6 June, the Germans abandoned Paris on 18 August, and a liberated Paris was ruled by a provincial government headed by de Gaulle from 24 August 1944.

One of the first laws passed by the German occupational forces was the law of 16 August 1940, establishing a general organizational model for all forms of industrial production in France. All workers' and employers' organizations were disbanded and replaced by a Comité d'Organisation, composed of members proposed by the various branches of that industry for the minister's consideration and headed by a government-appointed commissioner. These committees were to produce statistical data, production programs, lists of material needed to fulfil these production programs, legislative frameworks for the firms working within that industry, and proposals concerning the price of goods and services. All the recommendations of the organizational committees were to be subject to ministerial approval. Although attached to the information services of the vice-president of the council, the cinema was included under this industrial legislation.[8]

The greater part of the restructuring of the film industry, including the introduction of a legislative framework within which it could conduct its business, took place within this framework and had been completed by 1942. The restructuring is best discussed under three headings—institutional, financial, and political—though the last of these relates mainly to Jewish influence in the cinema and was not of lasting legislative impact as were the others.

In institutional terms, the administration of the cinema during the war years was to devolve, in accordance with the overall industrial legislation, onto the Comité d'Organisation des Industries Cinématographiques (COIC, or "Couac" as it was known in the trade), which was an organ of the Vichy government. This can give the impression that the restructuring measures which were introduced under the aegis of COIC were largely French-initiated and -controlled. While not entirely false, this was by no means the simple truth. A high degree of monitoring and "consultation" was maintained by the German administration, such that the French authorities knew what was expected of them on occasion (for instance in relation to Jews) and indeed introduced legislation which retrospectively was to seem embarrassingly in advance of German requests.

Already in July 1940 representatives of the film industry present in Paris were "invited" to found corporative groupings for each branch of the film industry.[9] Simultaneously, the Germans were establishing their control over the industry in a number of ways, summed up by Siclier as follows: renting the big Paris studios, provisionally banning all French production, founding a German production company named Continental Films to produce French-language films under German administration, creating two distribution firms to rent and screen dubbed German films, and establishing a censorship body.[10]

Cumulatively, these measures could readily be interpreted as introducing the "Germanization" of production, distribution, and exhibition, and equally importantly as establishing direct German control over administration and decision making in the industry. Perhaps hastened by the pressure of these developments, the Vichy government, protesting its right to formal authority over the cinema, hastily created the Service du Cinéma on 16 August 1940. The Service du Cinéma was organized into three sections, one of which dealt with the various industrial sectors (technical industries, production, distribution, exhibition, import, and export), one with censorship and propaganda, one with legal and financial questions, including the Jewish question. It was the Service du Cinéma which established the Organizational Committee (COIC) as an executive body with the function of "overall administration of the film industry and of personnel involved in filmmaking." To this end COIC was requested "to take all measures that it sees as necessary in technical, economic or social matters."[11] COIC itself was made up of a consultative committee of 20 members representing the profession and subdivided into five subcommissions (technical industries, producers, artistic and technical personnel, distributors, exhibitors). Effectively, these corporative groupings fulfilled the initial program requested of the industry by the Germans. Moreover, the seat of the Service du Cinéma and of its executive committee was not in Vichy, but in Paris, at rue de Babylone and 92 Champs-Elysées respectively. Here they were constantly in consultation with the Propagandaabteilung in Frankreich, and according to Brasillach (briefly director of the Service) "were reduced to discussing all those matters of the greatest significance for the French cinema with [that body],"[12] which in turn was constantly "posing obstacles in the way of its activities." The organization of the cinema in the nonoccupied zone was delegated to a subsection of the Service du Cinéma, which merely communicated decisions and directives to agents in the main provincial towns of the South.

It is clear then that COIC was far from totally autonomous in its control of restructuring the industry. As Léglise remarks, the same measures that constituted a rationalization of professional procedures for the French industry could constitute a form of political intervention, monitoring, and control for the occupier. As a specific but perhaps isolated instance of direct intervention by German authorities over the Service du Cinéma and COIC, we can note Jeancolas's account of the distribution and exhibition of *Face au bolchevisme*.[13] This German propaganda film was distributed and promoted under the auspices of COIC and the Vichy information ministry. It is unlikely either that they themselves could have refused that authorization or that the many cinema-owners who publicized and screened it (and others like it) could have chosen to do otherwise, had they wished to. In these circumstances it is not surprising that Brasillach should at the time have seen the process as inducing the French to implement a series of procedures which gave to the Germans the effective control of the industry: "it is obvious that the Germans had, when they first invaded France, and have perfected since, a *plan* for taking over the French cinema. . . . What they intended to obtain was

a monopoly on exports
a dominant position in distribution
control of exhibition
control of the commercial sector of production."[14]

Some have argued that their aim was as much to exploit the industry for much-needed financial gain as to control a crucial informational medium. The evidence suggests, however, that Brasillach's fears about "a *plan*" are probably excessive and due to the paranoia of a defeated nation. Had Germany had a systematic plan for the domination and exploitation of the French cinema, it could have implemented it immediately and effortlessly. French historians are inclined to quote as evidence for such a plan the entry which Goebbels made in his diary after viewing *La Symphonie fantastique*, produced by Continental: "Greven is going about this in entirely the wrong way. He seems to think it's his job to raise the quality of the French cinema. But it's not for us to provide the French with good films, and especially not to give them films with a nationalist flavor. What the French need are frivolous films, empty, and even a little stupid, and it's our job to see they get them. It's not our business to develop their nationalism." And a few days later: "We'd be mad to set up in rivalry with ourselves. Our policy must be the same as that of the Americans with respect to the American continent: we must become the dominant power of the European continent. Insofar as films are produced in other countries, they must retain a purely local flavor. We must prevent as far as possible the creation of any other national cinema industry."[15]

On the basis of this entry, Siclier claims that the Germans were reluctant to see the French cinema getting on its feet again, since they would have preferred to absorb it.[16] But had they wished to do that, they could have done so by a single act of legislation. Goebbels's diary entry was made in May 1942, and no effort was made to change the broad lines of the policy toward the French cinema after that point. During the succeeding two years, several very large and prestigious national film projects were undertaken, such as *Le Ciel est à vous* and *Les Enfants du paradis*, which a word from Greven, let alone Goebbels, would at any time have halted. It is easier to see the diary entry as little more than the jeu d'esprit of a clever, cultured, and witty man, getting off a private crack at the American "empire," and perhaps even indirectly proud of the quality of a French cinema which after all was part of his own and Germany's currently expanding "empire."

It is probable, then, that no systematic plan existed; the French cinema was administered within a general schema devised to renovate all French industry along lines acceptable to Germany and designed to make it an efficient source of goods and wealth to support the future German empire. This involved the creation of hierarchical structures without significant consultation, such that orders and policy priorities would be generated in Germany and transmitted down, not always necessarily in the form of explicit order, to be implemented at grass-roots level. Such a hierarchical system allowed the uncontested introduction of certain of the policies which had been talked of, in vain, in the French film industry for at least a decade, and it allowed the introduction of those policies in a political context where the professionals could not protest, delay, or subvert their implementation as they so effectively had throughout the thirties, and as they certainly would have continued to do, given half a chance. But such a hierarchical and relatively (for France) authoritarian system puts a lot of power in the hands of the individuals at the summit of each institutional structure, and it is the good fortune of the French cinema that in the first 18 months or so following the occupation, the three individuals appointed to those institutional positions combined a wide knowledge of the needs of the French cinema with a desire not just to get it on its feet again, but to make it an industry producing high-quality films. Nor can this be put down solely to a desire for commercial productivity on the Germans' part, such as would have helped to fund their own war effort. It was not, as Brasillach implies, solely the commercial sector of film production that Continental or its national German masters devoted themselves to developing. The list of films produced by Continental and the list of directors that it employed to shoot them would alone be enough to give the lie to this claim. The French cinema was not then the object of any particular policy on Goebbels's part, vindictive or not, nor was it even the object of any systematic policy, let alone a systematically exploitative policy. It was a minor industry within an occupied territory, subject to the general principles of all such industries, and with the same very general aims underlying those principles. Within that rather vaguer political context than is usually outlined, the structures favored authoritarian state control for the first time in the French cinema's history, and enlightened policy saw to it that the three people in positions to exercise that control were well versed in the problems and their possible solutions and therefore exercised it both to the immediate and to the long-term benefit of the French cinema. This account does not pander, as do most, to myths of the French cinema as the embattled underdog, fighting for survival against the malevolent intentions of the occupier and subverting those intentions by cunning wherever possible. It takes rather as its starting point the organizational structures and legislation introduced, the authorities which approved that legislation, the films made within the legislation, and the authorities who approved the making and screening of those films. The crucial approval at all stages was German, and the results were almost invariably favorable. It is not, as many French accounts would have it,[17] "paradoxical" that the French cinema should have flourished under these circumstances, but perfectly logical.

The three key players were Greven, de Carmoy and Raoul Ploquin. Greven had been a producer for UFA during the thirties, when it was making multilanguage versions with visiting actors and technicians, and had therefore already acquired extensive contacts in the French film industry. In 1939 he became head of production and seems to have met with approval from Max Winckler, Goebbels's appointment to oversee the economic aspects of the German cinema. In October 1940 Winckler appointed Greven to the equivalent role in France. As well as this overseer role as Propagandastaffel official responsible for all matters related to the cinema, he had the specific role of manager of Continental Films, with its extensive distribution and exhibition circuits confiscated from Jewish businessmen (notably the Haïk and Siritzky circuits, which were among the best equipped in France) and its multitude of associated activities—laboratories, studios, and export monopoly. His position gave him powers that justify the title "grand master of cinema in France."[18]

What is surprising is the tact and discretion with which this extensive German authority over French cinematic activity was exercised. French testimony from the period suggests that the cinema-going public was totally unaware of it, regarding the films of the time, including those produced by the German company, as purely and simply "French."[19] Winckler instructed that no German presence was to be apparent in any of the French industrial elements they controlled, "to respect French law and psychology."[20] The front men used by the Germans seem in most cases to have been respectable French legal firms. Greven in turn exercised his role with such discretion that both at the time and retrospectively it was and is impossible to identify any element of pro-German propaganda in the thirty films produced by Continental. Certainly, Greven did not in any way exercise his unlimited authority to impose a direction on French production, not even the direction of "light-hearted entertainment." As Raoul Ploquin was to say many years later,

> as soon as I was nominated to direct COIC, on 15 October 1940, I made contact with [Greven] and asked of him his intentions. To hear him speak, they were perfectly pure: he wanted to help me get the film industry working again. Continental and its production, together with the circuits he had requisitioned, would serve as building blocks in this task. . . . He assured me formally that none of Continental's films would have the faintest political color and that all form of propaganda would be radically excluded. He mentioned the names of Christian-Jacque, Clouzot, Decoin, Carné, and a few other directors whom he proposed to hire, and this list reassured me considerably. . . . I must say that on these two points he kept his word. . . . I might add that the quality of the films produced by that society was, overall, most satisfying.[21]

A francophile, who lived apparently exclusively for his work, Greven seems to have had as his sole aim the successful development of an industry to which he had devoted his life and which allowed him to mix with intellectual and artistic figures whom he admired. He respected the directors he hired to the point of allowing them considerable independence and even went so far as not to notice that one of his scriptwriters was a Jew and a Communist.[22] His benevolence ensured that the reforms proposed by the Service du Cinéma and COIC, which fell within the guidelines required of French industries, were approved and implemented without problems.

Guy de Carmoy was appointed founding director of the Service du Cinéma in the Autumn of 1940, and though he only held the position for about a year till September 1941, he was able to begin implementing certain aspects of those reforms recommended in his report of five years previously. Inevitably, however, these were modified away from the professional orientation which they had originally had and away from the liberal political framework within which they had originally been designed, toward a more dirigiste and corporative set of policies. It was de Carmoy also who recommended Raoul Ploquin as director of COIC, set up in December 1940. Ploquin was a particularly appropriate choice since he had been director of production for Tobis's German production of French-language films throughout the thirties, and in this capacity had an extensive acquaintance with Greven as a respected colleague. He also had an appreciation of the advantages of certain of the production practices and funding mechanisms of the German industry and an awareness of the extent of modernization needed within the French industry. If his relations with Greven gradually deteriorated (due apparently to his desire to impose the legislation already applying to French companies on Greven's Continental as well) such that he resigned in May 1942; nevertheless by that time the job he had been assigned was largely completed.

No better informed or more committed group could have been appointed to such key positions, and they used their authority to good effect. A flood of legislation provided the necessary conditions to resuscitate a shell-shocked industry. Totally paralyzed by the invasion and defeat, film production had already started up before the end of 1940 in the unoccupied zone to which the greater part of the producers, directors, technicians, and actors had retreated. It took off in the North as well as soon as the German authorities approved it in April 1941. In the South, seven films were made in late 1940, 15 in 1941; in the North 43 were produced in 1941. Within a year of collapse, then, the French cinema was producing again, and at the maximum rate permitted by the limited supply of raw materials available.

The legislation introduced by COIC which regulated the conditions under which this wartime production took place is of the utmost importance. Its most enduring effect was to institute a reliable system of mechanisms for modifying and monitoring the financial base of the industry. An incidental effect of this financial regularization and of the general corporative orientation of the industrial structure was to ensure the exclusion from the industry both of the "undesirable elements" which had caused the scandals of the thirties and of the sense of incipient anarchy which had been a major factor in the sense of an ongoing crisis during the thirties.

First of all, membership in any branch of the film industry became dependent on the acquisition of a "professional card," a workcard delivered by COIC on the recommendation of a body made up of members of that branch. The general criteria (aside from not being a Jew) were commercial probity and professional recognition. As an instance of the effect that such a simple mechanism could have, the founding of a production company was now no longer open to anyone, regardless of financial status or criminal background, but dependent on professional standing and the ability to demonstrate financial resources of five million francs. The immediate effect was to decimate the number of practicing producers for the duration of the war. This measure was reinforced by the lack of material: filmstock was at a premium, relatively few film projects could be approved at first, and only those producers with very high credentials had a chance of acquiring approval. Faced in 1941–1942 with proposals for 150–200 films and only enough filmstock for 50, COIC was obliged to institute annual "production programs"; ultimately, 57 films were approved for 1941–1942 and 72 for 1942–1943. In the latter case 44 production companies were given approval (in addition to Continental, which acted outside the regulations), selected because they were "financially and technically well equipped."[23]

Second, detailed records now began to be kept concerning cinema receipts, such that the ongoing "health" of the industry could be constantly monitored. COIC itself had to authorize all cinema tickets for an invariable range of entry prices, and exhibitors became accountable for the sale of them and for keeping records of receipts for each screening of each program on a pro forma supplied by COIC. Precise, consistent, and reliable knowledge concerning the success or failure of particular films, genres, cinemas, regions, and the industry as a whole became available from this time onward.

Third, the double program was suppressed, with an overall limit of first 4300 meters per program, later reducing to 3,800 meters and finally (partly because of shortage of filmstock) to 3,300 meters (of which only one film was to exceed 1,300 meters in length). The single-film program was not at all popular with audiences, and not least because exhibitors initially attempted to disguise it by advertising a short in such a way as to suggest it was a second major film; but for producers, the returns per entry immediately increased, and the temptation/pressure to supply low-budget quickies was reduced.

Fourth, a law of 19 May 1941 introduced the principle of advances to producers, providing them henceforth with a more assured financial base on which to undertake their production and thus a greater ability to provide it with the "technical finish" of a quality product.

The funding was provided by the Crédit National, to a maximum of 50 million francs or 65% of the cost of production, whichever was lowest. To obtain it, a producer had to submit to COIC a dossier relating to the projected film; on approval COIC would forward its recommendation to the Crédit National, and agreement as to the scale of the loan and the terms of repayment would be established by a committee of COIC and the Crédit National. It was no longer necessary to await the returns of the previous film before adequate funding for the next became available.

Fifth, the production of short films, and notably documentaries, was identified for special budgetary support. Given the abolition of the double feature, many more shorts were now needed, and they became an invaluable training ground for a new generation of professional personnel.

Sixth, the complex tax régime which had plagued the cinema in the thirties was simplified by a radical move: the suppression of the three existing forms of taxation (one of which dated back to 1407) and their replacement by a single graduated tax. The fact that tax rates were calculated now on weekly rather than on monthly takes also seems to have had incidental benefits.[24] Unfortunately, this tax reform did not extend to the 1% armament tax instituted at the outbreak of war and was later largely undercut by a nationwide 18% luxury tax introduced in October 1942, applicable to the cinema.

Nevertheless, altogether this package of financial reforms was extremely beneficial to the industry and was complemented by a factor for which the industrial reformers could scarcely claim total credit: a largely protected market. Just as the introduction of sound had established linguistic barriers which incidentally favored the local industry, so the occupation established political barriers which had the same effect. All foreign films other than German and Italian were immediately excluded from the northern zone, and eighteen months later from the unoccupied zone as well. It was American films that had always provided the keenest competition for the local product. With these out of the way, the French industry's percentage of receipts rose to 85%. By comparison, except in the Alsace-Lorraine area, where there had always been a strong demand for German-language films, German and Italian imports provided no real challenge. French historians of the cinema, understandably, have tended to interpret this as a rejection of the occupiers' culture, cultural traditions, and cultural values. Sadoul was perhaps the first to talk of a wartime French population "spontaneously boycotting German programs," such that exhibitors, "tired of screening their films to empty houses . . . refused to rent them."[25] Sadoul, of course, was politically of the extreme left, but his partisan observations have since acquired a certain authority. They need to be questioned. German films dubbed into French had never rated very highly in France in the thirties even when there was no reason to reject them on nationalist grounds, as Durand's figures demonstrate. Nor were they to do so in the postwar years.

Their performance during the war was neither significantly better nor significantly worse than before or after. From occupying 10–15% of the market, and about 5% of receipts, they came to occupy in 1941 43% of the market and about 20% of receipts.[26] Siclier provides a useful counter to the prevailing French myth of an "audience of résistants" when he says,

a widespread view has it that the public coldshouldered these films out of patriotism. Actually, no! They didn't attract as many spectators as

French films, but they were seen by lots of people. . . . German melodramas, comedies, psychological dramas, costume dramas, musicals, adventures, cop shows, all attracted a French public in need of distraction. Zarah Leander, whose popularity was established in 1938–1939 . . . was seen as a substitute for Greta Garbo and much appreciated, as was Marike Rokk, the singing, dancing star of Georg Jacoby. . . . The ghost of Hollywood haunted these productions, which are far from having left unpleasant memories, even if in the immediate postwar period few French people dared admit to having enjoyed them.[27]

Indeed, anti-Semitic films such as Le Juif Süss enjoyed respectable runs in many regions and returned handsome profits.[28] Jeancolas notes its success even in the unoccupied zone where exhibitors were free to select their own programs and (while recognizing the source as not entirely reliable) quotes a Lyon correspondent as follows:

At the La Scala, the success of Le Juif Süss became the focus of a real craze. That film, in two weeks, brought in well over 200,000 francs. At each screening and repeatedly, applause broke out; and that had never happened before in our city.[29]

Nevertheless, freed from all other competition in the occupied zone, and from 15 October 1942 throughout France, enjoying rapidly rising attendances in 1942 and 1943, the French cinema could for the first and perhaps only time since before World War I hope, even expect, to recoup costs and show a profit on nearly all films solely on the basis of the national market. Another crucial reason for this success was that there was little alternative entertainment for the public. Dances had been banned after the collapse, and a curfew of 10 P.M. was placed on all cafés, which anyway had not much in the way of alcoholic beverages to serve, even when permitted.[30] Also, all memoirs of the period underline the importance of the cinema as a refuge from the unpleasant realities of everyday life.[31] As André Cayatte said, "The occupation was a period when all films were successful because the cinema replaced everything else: meeting place, heated area, means of escape, weekend outings."[32] But the main reason for this sudden profitability was the fact that the receipts, running at about 90% of prewar levels in real terms, were spread now among far fewer films, because of the reduction in foreign imports and the restriction of French production. The total market in 1941–1944 averaged only 100–130 films instead of the 450–580 films that disputed the prewar market. The average take which each film could expect, in real terms, was therefore nearly four times what it could expect before the war. This slightly overstates the case since the prewar market included many films in the original language, not dubbed into French, and these earned far lower receipts. Even excluding them, however, French films cannot have averaged less than 2.5 times the take of prewar years. Thus the rationing of production on the basis of limited supplies of primary material was of enormous benefit to those producers fortunate enough to receive approval to actually make a film. Those who didn't, of course, simply ceased to be active film producers, since there was no alternative to the formal channels for approval; no amount of initiative and no amount of influence in financial circles could circumvent the necessity for COIC approval.

Financial regulation therefore introduced a fairly rigorous form of control over production, with a concomitant potential for indirect forms of control over expression. Political regulation introduced further controls, both over production, in the form of censorship, and over personnel, in the form of anti-Semitic legislation. The cinema was specifically mentioned in the general legislation regulating the status of Jews that was promulgated in October of 1940 by Marshal Pétain. That legislation prohibited them from any position of responsibility, elective or otherwise, in a political, cultural, legal, or military organization. Article 5 of it read as follows:

> Jews may not under any condition exercise any of the following professions:
> Directors, managers, editors of newspapers, magazines, agencies, or periodicals, except those of a strictly scientific nature. Directors, administrators, managers of enterprises having as their object the production, impression, distribution, or exhibition of films; directors and cameramen, administrators, managers of theaters or cinemas, theatrical entrepreneurs; directors, administrators, managers of all enterprises related to radio broadcasting . . .[33]

Research seems to indicate that this legislation was not explicitly forced on the French state by the Germans. Jeancolas summarizes the evidence as demonstrating that the various anti-Semitic laws promulgated from the autumn of 1940 on were primarily of French inspiration.[34] Unquestionably the Germans would have acted had this not been forthcoming, but the long tradition of anti-Semitism in France was sufficient to generate its own spontaneous legislation.

On 26 November 1940, a German regulation reinforced this requirement with specific application to the cinema:

> Whoever collaborates in film production in any way, whether intellectual or technical, in the distribution, maintenance, and projection of films and in the construction, sale, and rental of cameras, projectors, or other elements used in film production must obtain the approval of the Militärbefehlshaber for France . . .
>
> Approval will be accorded only if
> (a) a necessity can be demonstrated
> (b) there is no objection to the person requesting it.[35]

Several subsequent modifications only served to make the exclusion of Jews from all aspects of film production more explicit. Summarizing them, the law of 6 June 1942 stated that Jews could not hold positions of an artistic nature in the theater, the cinema, or any other form of entertainment, except in certain limited circumstances. These laws were enforced at government level by a Commissaire Général aux Questions Juives and at industrial level by a subsection of the Service du Cinéma. Xavier Vallat, the inaugural commissioner, saw the task facing him in the cinema as particularly onerous, since he estimated that 85% of the personnel were Jewish.[36] Reporting on his first six months of activity, he "could claim to have purged 3,000 public servants and to have got rid of the same number proportionately from positions in the press, radio, cinema, and all areas where their role gave them power . . . over the minds of the public."[37]

The loss of film personnel was double in that Communists as well as Jews were subject to exclusion. Not the subject of explicit legislation of the sort directed at the Jews, those who had been overtly allied with the prewar leftwing governments of the Popular Front had nevertheless seen the danger signals and in many cases left the country. Those who had not went into hiding, working if at all from clandestinity. Indeed, many of the more politically committed were active in the resistance and would have had little or no time to devote to their former profession even had they been able.

Where they did manage to continue working in the industry, their activity was of necessity severely circumscribed by the formal censorship procedures which were introduced during the occupation. Initially there were separate censorship bodies for the occupied and unoccupied zones, with the Propagandaabteilung in Paris performing the task for the former while the Service du Cinéma nearby performed the task for the latter. In fact, however, the Propagandaabteilung had a watching brief over the decisions of the Service du Cinéma and was the effective final authority in all matters of censorship. COIC managed to unify France as a single market from February 1941, on condition that films shot in the unoccupied zone were subject to a second censorship by the Germans. Vichy exercised no such role in regard to films shot in the North, or dubbed German films.

Wherever undertaken, films were subject to three successive controls, each of which was formalized by a visa. There was a production visa, an exhibition visa and an export visa. The first of these was granted on the advice of a consultative committee, which checked the subject matter by way of first a synopsis of the storyline and second a detailed technical découpage. The finished film was again subject to examination, with the normal possibilities of cuts or total bans if aspects of it not apparent in the synopsis and découpage were found to be undesirable. An export visa, likewise, was only to be delivered "where the finished film was in total conformity to the spirit of the synopsis and on all important points with the detailed technical découpage."[38]

As the formal legislation itself noted in its advice to producers, these visas would only be delivered subject to the film's conforming to appropriate ideological values, and the widespread discourses of moral rigorism and regeneration pervading official, and indeed popular, declarations about not just the cinema but all French society at the time made it perfectly clear that there were a multitude of largely unspecified prohibitions on subject matter. What resulted was inevitably a high degree of self-censorship. It would not have occurred to French producers of the time that there was any real point in considering a script proposal which directly, or indeed indirectly, questioned the rights of the occupier or the direction of his policies, or which continued in matters of style or subject matter the dominant directions of prewar French cinema, now condemned as morbid and decadent.

EFFECTS OF THE REGULATION

As this last example makes clear, these organizational, financial, and political developments had far-reaching effects both on the way in which films were made and on the sort of films that were made. Cumulatively, they changed dramatically such crucial factors as

- who was involved in filmmaking
- where those people came from
- what forms of experience and training were normal for filmmakers
- what sorts of film were made, in terms of scale, of technical finish, and of subject matter.

For a start, most of those who were known to have Jewish or Communist backgrounds were now excluded from the industry.

The magazine *Ciné Mondial* helpfully listed some of those concerned, in that they were Jews and had been active in the French cinema during the previous decade. "In a country like ours," it said, "which has always been associated with the qualities of clarity, harmony, and balance, the cinema has been becoming little by little under Jewish influence, the insidious expression of the worst instincts of humanity. No need to cite titles, only remember those films—the more dangerous for being sometimes of quality—which promoted the virtues of the urban scum of our cosmopolitan capitals."[39] The number and importance of the figures mentioned gives some indication of the impact such legislation must necessarily have on the industry. Among 16 producers and distributors it mentions Pierre Braunberger, Adolph Osso, Bernard Natan of Pathé-Natan, Jacques Haïk, and the Hakim brothers; among directors, Raymond Bernard, Robert Siodmak, Pierre Chenal, and Henri Diamant-Berger; among actors, Dalio and J.-P. Aumont; among scriptwriters, Jacques Natanson and Charles Delac. Many of these had of course already gone into exile or hiding long before the promulgation of the legislation. Cumulatively, as Jeancolas notes, French anti-Semitism mutilated the French cinema.[40] Perhaps exaggerating the extent of this, Garçon claims that "by comparison with prewar years, 47 professional filmmakers ceased all activity following the collapse and the intolerance which then beset the country. This includes no less than 46% of all directors who had filmed two or more films between 1936 and 1940. Among the most prolific, we might note Maurice de Cannonge who had made 10 films, Raymond Bernard (6), Pierre Colombier (8), Julien Duvivier (7), René Pujol (7). . . . If we can believe Claude Autant-Lara in a wartime interview (*Je Suis Partout*, 3 September 1943), the French cinema had been deprived of 50% of its directors and 80% of its producers."[41]

The most active publicist of this anti-Semitic purge was Lucien Rebatet, who wrote under the name of François Vinneuil. Critic with *Action Française* from 1930 till the war, and with the even more rightwing *Je Suis Partout* from 1933 until its disappearance in 1944, he is nevertheless usually credited with speaking out for an artistic cinema in the prewar years rather than employing a political terminology. Extremely conservative, he nevertheless admired Renoir and didn't entirely retract that approval even during the intensely Communist period of *La Marseillaise*,[42] while roundly condemning the production of such rightwing filmmakers as Gance and L'Herbier. In the "bleak period" that the years 1933–1940 represented for French criticism, he could seem the one bright light, such that Nino Frank could speak of him as "the prince of film critics." Nevertheless, even before the war, when he spoke of Renoir's films he was inclined to qualify his praise in sinisterly political terms: "Henceforth, concerning the political films of Jean Renoir, if I find myself praising 'the artist' I will not forget to mention in every line that this 'citizen' would be fodder for the concentration camp in any authentic French state."[43]

Under the occupation, these rightwing political views found overt and forceful expression in *Action Française* and *Je Suis Partout*. The following extract from Rebatet's 1941 book is typical:

> Whatever is done about the French cinema, our prime concern must be to eliminate the Jews from it. . . . We must sooner or later expel from our land several hundred thousand Jews, beginning with those Jews whose papers are not in order, the non-naturalized, the most recently arrived, those whose political and financial evildoing is most manifest, that's to say the totality of Jews in the cinema."[44]

He speaks of Chaplin as "a demi-Jew":

> Noone has ever denied a Jew could have a degree of genius, especially when a little Christian blood flows in his veins, correcting—rarely, it's true—the heredity of his race. [Julien Duvivier and others] are married to Jews and secured by them within the clutches of Israel. . . . Marcel Carné is aryan. But he has become impregnated with Jewish influences, he

owes his success exclusively to Jews, he has been cultivated by them, and his works filmed under their trademark. . . . Carné and his Jews have mired the French cinema in a fatalism, a determinism that have degraded it.[45]

Of course, Rebatet's line conformed to the Nazi proclamations of the previous year (1940) excluding all Jews, without exception or qualification, from all position of influence in the cinema, and those of late 1941 banning them from all artistic activity. But it would be unjust to imply that this rightwing political discourse was limited to a single film critic: it was general in the French wartime press and a commonplace in film publications of all categories. *Le Film*, the sole trade weekly to be published during the war years, proclaims the necessity to

> learn to stand tall again, we people of the cinema who have been deformed by 20 years of cohabitation with Jews . . . mostly foreign Jews, recently emerged from ghettos, with dubious commercial practices. . . . We have lost our sense of what is right and wrong, which is particularly serious since we have people's souls entrusted to us. Most of us screened to our spectators anything at all, provided it made money. These films, which we must have realized were ignoble, dangerous not only for young French people individually but for the mentality of the country as a whole, we were so weak-minded as to buy them, screen them, project them, and proclaim them artistic with much advertising hoo-hah. We must see things as they are. If we want our country to forgive us, let's first of all unreservedly confess our faults. Let's "purge" our own selves. Expelling unhealthy elements from the country is the job of the authorities. Our job, as men of the trade, is to adopt a proper attitude once again. Those who don't feel up to it should get out of the trade, into jobs where they can't contaminate anyone.[46]

Consequently, as film production began to boom in 1942 and 1943, openings appeared in all technical and artistic areas, and an influx of new filmmakers appeared. On the whole, this new group was made up of people trained in the industry, since a crucial criterion for practicing the profession, in the critical conditions created by lack of material, was experience in the industry and recognition by colleagues. The war therefore represented a significant moment in the transformation of attitudes toward the cinema. The previous generation had mostly approached the cinema from outside it—from classical music, the theater, literature, or more generally from the complexity of cultural movement of the twenties. For them, cinema had been one among a multitude of cultural passions, and one to which frequently no more than a happy accident led them to commit themselves. For the new generation, cinema was their life, their career, and their principal cultural experience. They were formed in the cinema and their training, however informal, fitted them for no other career. The establish-

ment of IDHEC—the Institut des Hautes Etudes Cinématographiques—
which was to become the main film school and prime source of professional
qualifications over the next twenty years, was a natural concomitant of this
tendency and was itself to reinforce the move toward a professionalization
of the industry. From now on, formal training and recognized qualifications
were to be a normal expectation in the industry, complementing that regulation of personnel represented by the professional work card and that regulation of production represented by the various "visas." The formalization
of all aspects of the industry contrasts markedly with accounts of the "anarchic" prewar conditions.

Once admitted to the profession, this personnel was inevitably constrained in the type of films it could make, first of all by the censorship
limitations on subject and style already mentioned. The "poetic realist"
films of the prewar years were condemned and banned under legislation
relating to the cleansing and regulation of the film market. In November
1940, 65 such films were excluded from exhibition, together with 45 foreign
films. These included war films, films relating to poverty or to criminality,
and films on French colonial subjects. More generally they included all
films expressive of either a defeatist or a triumphalist France and all films
which criticized explicitly or implicitly those institutions of the state now
considered essential to its moral regeneration—church, family and state.
By implication, these criteria for exclusion operated on new productions as
well, and, when joined to the prohibition of any critical reflection on existing conditions of occupied life, constituted a fairly dramatic limitation of
style and of subject matter. As Courtade notes when discussing the production of these four years, "you would look in vain for any allusion to
ration cards, electricity cuts, or pedicabs. As for youth camps, obligatory
work service, "terrorism" and collaboration, not a chance. Ultimately, the
war itself is absent from the films, as are newspapers and calendars: the
Vichy cinema achieved the remarkable tour de force of being pretty well
timeless."[47]

Those films that were made, however, had a better chance of being made
from a sound financial base. Both because of the rapid increase in receipts
and because of advances from the Crédit National, producers could begin
to think on a scale that had not been possible in the thirties. Films of the
scope of Les Visiteurs du soir, let alone Les Enfants du paradis, could not have
emerged from the French film industry of the thirties. Potentially, also, the
technical finish of these films could be more studied than previously,
though this was counterbalanced by the technical problems resulting from
the cinema's low priority in the scheme for national renovation and from
the failure and destruction of technology as a byproduct of wartime activities. The tendency toward fewer films of a larger, more finished quality
was furthered by the elimination of the double program, which favored
them at the expense of the shorter B grade quickies produced in the thirties
to satisfy the demand for quantity. Finally, the single program also favored

the development of large-scale production of those shorts and documentaries at which the state's funding was directed, and which were to provide a useful apprenticeship for the next generation of filmmakers, then being trained formally in IDHEC or informally as assistants in the profession. An urgent demand existed for such short subjects, and over 400 were produced during the four years of occupation, compared to 220 feature films.[48]

The procedures by which these films were made were also now significantly different from prewar years. It was no longer possible to leave details of story, treatment, or style vague, relying on the competence of the personnel to make them good at the time of shooting. Censorship regulations required a detailed treatment in advance of approval to shoot and required also that this foreshadowed treatment be adhered to in all crucial details. Spontaneity, improvization, and last minute changes of mind were rendered difficult if not impossible. This tendency was furthered by rationing of filmstock forced on COIC by the shortage of supply. For a feature film of 2500 meters, a film crew had at its disposal a maximum of 30,000 meters of film and 20,000 meters of negative sound film. Multiple takes became a thing to fear and avoid, as did any tendency to explore and experiment on the set, and ingenuity was applied rather to achieving what was planned than to evolving it in new and unpredictable directions. Preplanning, rehearsal, and the regimentation of shooting procedures were effectively forced on an industry which had never taken them very seriously heretofore.

Cumulatively, these modifications of existing forms of administration and practices of production are sufficiently significant to justify seeing the occupation as a time of radical new beginnings for the French cinema rather than as the twilight of the thirties. Nevertheless, there is one fundamental continuity which must be underlined: the characteristic industrial structure which had evolved out of the collapse of the larger companies in the thirties survived the crises of 1940 and the subsequent renovation of the industry.

In some respects, Continental bid fair to repeat, but from a position of exemplary political and financial dominance, the abortive attempts by Gaumont and Pathé to constitute a major force within the industry and over time. Funded amply and directly from its parent firm in Germany, owning its own studios and laboratories, secure in the control of its own distribution, linked to major circuits in the North and East, endowed by government fiat with a total monopoly over the export of French films, Greven's firm set about developing a stable of personnel—directors, actors, technicians—on long-term contracts, whose name and products would in the long run cast a favorable light on the firm. On the basis of the thirty films produced by the firm in the three years from February 1941 to February 1944, there is no reason to believe they would not have succeeded. Gradually, over the forties, the French film industry might have developed toward a monopoly situation just as had the German industries in the thirties, leading in due course to nationalization.

Whether or not this would have happened is a topic for speculation; what in fact happened is that, despite several contrary pressures, the industry developed once again toward a fragmented structure in which small-scale production firms with a relatively small capital base, with no plant of their own and no long-term production program, put together one-off packages for sale to circuits which they did not own. With the disappearance of Continental in 1944, it was this "tolerated" after-echo of an earlier industrial structure which survived to continue into the postwar years.

One reason that the structure survived was that not only the market but also the production system had been fragmented by the division of France into occupied and unoccupied zones, with different conditions of production, distribution, and exhibition applying to them at different points in time. Thus Pagnol and Richebé, in the unoccupied zone, found it much easier to re-launch production in the later months of 1940 than did the bulk of the industry, in occupied Paris, partly because they produced their own films, and in their own studios, but also because most of the Paris film personnel had retreated with a large percentage of the rest of the population, army, and government, to the South.

Once production was authorized in the North, however, the available materials were allocated among a reasonably large number of French production firms, which all therefore began production once again on a (numerically) small scale much as in the thirties. This was undoubtedly part of a deliberate COIC policy to regenerate the industry on a broad front. It was also due to the financial inability of these firms in the initial years to undertake quantitatively larger-scale production. Moreover, they were all firms that had produced in the thirties and which saw themselves as recommencing on a similar basis and scale. The result was that, excluding the Continental production, wartime French film production was once again undertaken largely on a one-off basis by a host of small production firms. In 1941 the 47 films (excluding Continental's) are produced by 31 firms; in 1942, the 70 are produced by 41 firms; in 1943, the 49 by 34 firms. Relatively few of these firms have any continuous active existence over three or more years—only 19 out of 61—and of these only 12 produce as many as five films in those years.[49] Over half the firms do not manage to produce more than two films. While it is therefore technically accurate to claim that we see a *concentration* of French interests around a reduced number of production/distribution groups, this concentration never went very far and was countered by a number of other factors which in the long run proved the more significant. Sixty-one active firms does not in any way resemble, as Courtade would have it do, "the gigantic concentration under-

ι in Germany only a year before."[50]

loreover, the fragmented production situation remained similar to pre-
years in that very few of these firms had their own studios, and the
that did so had no aspiration at all to link them in an integrated and

closed system with an exhibition circuit. Gaumont had lost its studios at la Victorine and la Cité Elgé but still had St. Maurice at Joinville; it also acquired Pagnol's studios at Marseilles. These studios, however, were not used by Gaumont for its own productions. Instead, it merely invested financially in other productions for which it acted as distributor and exhibitor. Forced reluctantly into production in 1942, it remained content to act on a small scale, while focusing primarily on exhibition.[51] It was a period of relative lethargy for the company: cut loose from its funding parent Havas, which had been nationalized by the Vichy government, Gaumont did not have the financial clout to work toward a monopoly position.

Pathé, reconstituted by financial groups in 1939 and once again functioning as Pathé Cinéma in 1940, looked sufficiently strong once again to establish a vertically integrated and autonomous company of a sort to dominate the French sector of the industry and redefine its structure. It is a little fatuous, however, to explore these possibilities, since to do so assumes that the free play of market forces might have produced conditions which one or the other company could have exploited in order to acquire something approaching the market dominance of Rank, UFA, or an American major. In fact, however, no such free play existed: it is most unlikely that the Germans would have tolerated the growth of a French company to the point where it could challenge Continental's dominance, and it is equally unlikely that COIC would have allocated resources and funding in such a way as to permit this. Indeed, various members of COIC themselves aspired to found or resuscitate their own production companies, within a structure analogous to the prewar industrial structure. In the year 1943–1944, six of the French groups formally authorized by COIC are directed by members of COIC: aside from the Pathé group (Borderie) and Gaumont (Pagnol), we find Richebé Films (Richebé was by this time president of COIC), Regina (O'Connell), CCFC (Harispuru), and Synops-Minerva Films (Roland Tual). A seventh, Les Films Raoul Ploquin, was directed by the founding president of COIC. This seems clear evidence of a COIC policy (based to a degree on vested interest but also on a common assumption that the future French film industry should resemble in its basic structure the past industry) directed toward the recreation of a "fragmented" industry, but this time within a regulated framework and on a sound financial basis.

Altogether, it is hard to see how this evidence can be interpreted, as does Luigi Freddi, the Italian director-general for the cinema at the time, as a subtly camouflaged Germanization of the infrastructure of the French film industry.[52] Freddi's exaggeration of the extent to which the industry was Germanized is clearly calculated to substantiate his claim to have altruistically saved from the grasping Germans all that could be saved of the French industry[53]—a claim which is hard to reconcile with wartime alliances but is admittedly in line with certain longstanding Franco-Italian alliances in the cinema.

THE POSTWAR REGENERATION OF THE FRENCH FILM INDUSTRY

From September 1943, when the English landed in Calabria and the Americans in Salerno, through to August 1944, when de Gaulle took over in a liberated Paris, the conditions under which this wartime industry operated, never easy in material terms, became more and more onerous. Personnel with a known Nazi background (such as Le Vigan) abandoned films in mid-shoot, studios and cinemas were damaged by wartime actions (to the extent of 1.5 billion francs, according to the War Damages Commission, including 12% of all cinemas), electricity cuts and transport problems increased (the latter often through resistance action), inflation rates rocketed, and attendance figures drastically decreased, partly due to lack of transport. In one way or another, production, distribution, and exhibition were all dramatically affected by these factors, and the French film industry once again ground to a halt. Nevertheless, it now had in place a set of organizations and mechanisms which were capable of regenerating it relatively rapidly—which had, indeed, been developed precisely to that effect. It is not surprising, therefore, to find that these organizations and mechanisms are reactivated, in slightly modified forms, and that they do manage once again to regenerate the French film industry with surprising rapidity.

Stéphane Lévy-Klein, speaking of COIC's enduring importance to the industry, is one of the few to acknowledge the extent of the postwar cinema's debt to the occupation. "Certain of these measures were taken up again after the liberation—the law of 26 October 1940 requiring a formal authorization for entry to the profession, the banning of the double program . . . , the monitoring of cinema entries and receipts, . . . the requirement of a visa before filming could begin, the regulation of financing, etc. A large block of our current legislation in cinematic matters is inherited from Vichy."[54] To this list we can add the fact that various tax concessions beneficial to the artistic personnel of the industry were perpetuated, that the censorship classification system introduced during the occupation was reproduced in the postwar legislation and, most importantly, that COIC itself, which had produced this legislation, was reborn in the postwar period, first as the Office Professionel du Cinéma (OPC), then as the Centre National de la Cinématographie (CNC), a government authority administering the film industry in permanent consultation with the profession. Most commentators oppose the CNC to the COIC. While recognizing that the OPC had "resembled COIC like a brother," in that it had had the same form, the same lines of command, and the same responsibilities, Léglise sees the CNC as an entirely different sort of organization, pointing away from the direct government control of the occupation years toward professional self-regulation: "The period of Vichy and of its corporatist dirigisme are about to disappear forever."[55] Taking precisely the opposite stance (which is not surprising since under the last years of the occupation he had been director-general of COIC), Richebé sees the tripartite professional committee of 1942–1944 as having acquired autonomy in its self-regulation of the industry, whereas the postwar modifications of the industry "[saw] the profession lose its independence and its powers to the exclusive benefit of the director-general, and thus of the state."[56] If Richebé's interest is evident, the more general French interest in seeing the postwar industry as purged of its German-imposed characteristics is no less evident. It is clearly true that a central organism such as the CNC, focusing the interests of all elements of the profession and with lines of communication direct to government, is much closer to the COIC than either is to the totally unfocused prewar situation. The functions of the CNC—to produce legislative proposals, to coordinate, rationalize, and develop industrial procedures, to monitor the financing and profitability of the industry, to dispense government funding for production, and to organize the technical and artistic training of film personnel—are all-embracing and remarkably similar to those of COIC. Like COIC, moreover, it was not to be autonomous but rather (1) the source of proposals which were subject to political considerations at government level and (2) the executive, implementing those proposals passed into law by the government. Neither of the two opposing stances seems adequate, therefore: rather, professional autonomy was at no time after 1941 a real possibility, and the postwar interventionism of the French state merely replaced, though with less authoritarian potential, that of the German occupation.

A measure of the extent to which the COIC/CNC regulations had transformed postwar filmmaking in France by comparison with the prewar situation is the astonishment experienced by French filmmakers returning from exile in America. René Clair, attempting to make his first postwar film in France contrasted "the atmosphere one breathes in our country with the freer air of America. . . . For someone who has not seen France for five years, there can be no doubt that Nazism has left its mark on it. Yes, a country cannot live through fascist rule for so long without suffering in some way. For instance, I'm struck by the artificial barriers placed in the way of any activity. I can't accept that someone wanting to make a film should have to submit requests to so many authorities, who will refuse if he can't prove he's conformed to various arbitrary regulations."[57]

But if there is a high degree of continuity between wartime and postwar conditions, there is, nevertheless, one change that occurs: the move back toward market forces rather than a preconceived political program as a principal determinant of the industry's development.

This move was never total, since the postwar governments were consistently more interventionist than the prewar governments, and the survival of the national film industry became a part, if a minor part, of the systematic regeneration and promotion of French culture which was a main task of that intervention. Nevertheless, it could only proceed within limits determined by overall economic considerations. For this reason, it is useful to have an overview of the performance of that economy, and particularly of those aspects relevant to the economic viability of the film industry. On the whole, the postwar performance of the French economy was good—better than that of Britain or the United States, but not as good as that of Japan or Germany. A steady increase in gross domestic product of about 5% per year was recorded over a period of 25 years, which far exceeded any previous period of growth and which knew only one minor setback around 1953. Two periods of fairly severe inflation, around 1951 and 1956–1957, were related to the Korean War and the Algerian War, respectively.

This growth in the economy was primarily due to large-scale public sector intervention in the postwar years. The consequences of six years of war, if not as severe as World War I in terms of human losses, were far worse in terms of material destruction[58]—one quarter of the national wealth compared to one tenth in World War I. Support was general across party lines for a concerted national effort of reconstruction and for the widespread nationalizations which were a central element of it. It was at this time (1945–1948) that the state took over Renault, Les Charbonnages du Nord, and Crédit Lyonnais, nationalizing energy (gas, electricity, and oil) and transport (sea and air). As Asselain says, due largely to her prewar experience which suggested that the capitalist system and the governing elites had both proved a failure, "France at the time of the liberation was infused far beyond the leftwing parties, by a spirit of anticapitalism, the intensity of which is hard to conceive nowadays."[59] In the five years after the war's end, the state's share of investment was never less than 50% and as much as 66%. Toward the end of the fifties, the private sector, encouraged by public sector funding of various sorts, gradually took over the primary role in this process.

Complementing these nationalizations, long-term national economic planning became a standard feature of the political process, with a series of five-year plans to coordinate and orient public sector activity. Rapid recovery, steady growth, low unemployment, and a rapid return to monetary stability led to a climate of confidence in which increasing investment and continued growth were assured. Rationing ended in 1949; by 1950 the national budget was in balance and external trade was healthy. This was largely due to Marshall Plan aid and a devaluation of the franc, but it was also related to a relaxing of the "compartmentalization" of national economies which had been a feature of prewar years. The most dramatic symptom of this was the negotiations leading to the Common Market. In 1951 a treaty had been signed instituting a common European program in matters of coal and steel, which came into force in 1953. This was seen as the forerunner of much wider cooperation which would benefit European economies through advantages of scale and allow them to compete effectively with the United States, and later Japan.

A periodization of this growth would see 1958 as a logical break point for a variety of reasons. It was the year in which the leftwing government, discredited by a sudden financial crisis, was forced out, allowing de Gaulle's return to power. It therefore marks the transition from "fourth republic" to "fifth republic." It was marked by a further devaluation which allowed a rapid economic recovery, both internally and externally. Moreover, it was at the end of 1958 (1 January 1959) that the Common Market officially came into existence. In terms of the French cinema, too, there was a logical break point here: the last months of 1958 saw the screening of Chabrol's first films, *Le Beau Serge* and *Les Cousins*, and the beginning of 1959, *Les 400 Coups* and *A bout de souffle*; largely because of the promotional discourse surrounding them, these films were to seem a significant new departure in filmmaking practice. By the end of 1959, no one involved in the French film industry could doubt that dramatic changes had taken place in their industrial environment.

There is another related sense in which the years 1958–1959 constituted a radical break for the French film industry. This can best be measured by looking at attendance figures for the postwar years (fig. 2.1). Essentially they show that, after the low figures for the crisis year of 1944, attendances rise rapidly to maxima in 1947 of 424 million and in 1957 of 411 million before declining rapidly throughout the sixties. Again, these figures can be conceived of in terms of three plateaus—of around 220 million entries throughout the thirties, 390 million throughout the period 1945–1958, and 180 million from 1969 onward, the two intervening periods being made up respectively of the wartime crisis and of the steady but rapid decline between 1958 and 1969. The years from 1945 to 1958–1959 represent, therefore, a boom period such as the French cinema had never known before and has never known since. In effect, the average attendance rate per head of population had risen from 5.5–6.0 during the thirties to a level of 9.0 during the fifties.

Explanations as to why this happened and why the rate subsequently dropped off to about 4.0 attendances per year focus naturally enough on the categories of the populace who attend, the amount of disposable income available to them for leisure activities, and the forms of leisure activity competing with the cinema for that "leisure income."

One relevant factor is the birthrate. The crucial 15–24-year-old group, which regularly visits the cinema 2.5 times as often as other groups, increased from 5.5 million in 1941 to 6.5 million in 1946. This increase, resulting from high postwar birthrates in the twenties, shifted the proportions of age-groups within a basically stable population in a way that would be expected to increase filmgoing by about 10–12%. Since, however, it increased by about 80%, other factors must be presumed to dominate. One of these is psychological. The cinema was an extremely cheap way of providing oneself with a night's entertainment in the late forties when there were few other forms of popular entertainment available and when various forms of rationing were still making daily existence difficult. Moreover, the bulk of the population had been prevented from seeing the output of the

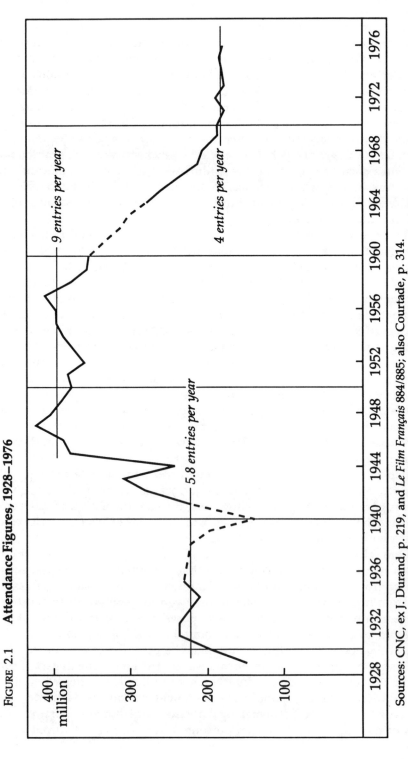

FIGURE 2.1   **Attendance Figures, 1928–1976**

9 entries per year

5.8 entries per year

4 entries per year

400 million

300

200

100

1928 1932 1936 1940 1944 1948 1952 1956 1960 1964 1968 1972 1976

Sources: CNC, ex J. Durand, p. 219, and *Le Film Français* 884/885; also Courtade, p. 314.
Dotted line: extrapolation from receipts (1936–37, 1939–40) and from Bonnell, p. 24.

American and British cinemas for four years, and all of the population had missed out on the last two years. There was a lot of catching up to do, of a sort that constituted a concrete externalization of newfound liberty. These factors were reinforced by the fact that several dramatic transformations had been happening in the relevant cinemas, manifested in such films as David Lean's *Brief Encounter* and Orson Welles's *Citizen Kane*. The sense of exhilaration which this process of "catching up" produced is evident in all writing on the cinema at the time. The advent of the first neorealist films from Italy only served to increase the sense that the cinema had been and still was going through an exciting period.

This postwar commitment of the French public to the cinema as the logical object of their leisure expenditure peaked in 1947 and again in 1957 at over 400 million spectators. In view of the statistics produced by Leroy,[60] this relative stability during the fifties can seem a form of defeat. Gross national product, disposable income, consumer spending, and in particular spending on leisure and culture all rose markedly throughout the fifties. One area within the field of culture and leisure that benefited particularly powerfully from this increase was the area of TV/radio/gramophones; the volume of spending on the cinema, however (like that on the theater and other attractions and on books and newspapers), remained stable or fell. This tendency for cinema, along with other spectacles, to form a smaller and smaller percentage of an increasing culture and leisure budget was to be confirmed in the 1960s, when leisure spending doubled, to form an even more significant part of consumer spending than in the fifties, while the volume of spending on the cinema plummeted dramatically, and the value of it was only maintained because of rising entry prices.[61] A different breakdown of leisure spending in the fifties provided by Gallais-Hamonno confirms that the spending on cinema (and various other spectacles) diminishes as a percentage of the leisure budget and that it is spending on TV and on "physical leisures" such as travel, camping, and sports that replaces it.

During the sixties the share of the leisure budget occupied by sport and camping was to increase from 5.5% to 8.8%, while that of theaters and concerts was to decrease from 15.2% to 11%. Overall, these figures suggest a long-term tendency operating between 1950 and 1970 for cinema and live spectacles to be displaced as leisure activities by TV and the group of physical leisures. Certain aspects of the latter, such as camping or weekend drives in the country, relate to the progressive motorization of the population during this period. In this sense, spending on motor cars can be seen as part of the leisure budget, and a part which displaces cinema both directly, in that there is less disposable income remaining to be spent on it, and indirectly, in that there is less time available to attend the cinema. There is also less need to attend it, since the notion of "escape" can be realized in new ways, through greater physical mobility and through contact with a "natural" world that contrasts dramatically with the weekday work environment.

The extent to which these two factors—TV and the increase in motorization—might be interpreted as displacing cinema as a leisure activity is illustrated by figure 2.2.

Confirmation of these trends is provided by comparable data from other Western nations. In the United States, the graph of cinema attendance is remarkably close to the inverse of motorization. During the war, as spending on motorization decreased, cinema attendances increased. From 1943 on, as motorization began to increase again, cinema attendances fell. Only the introduction of drive-ins, capitalizing on this mobility, is thought to have prevented an even more severe reduction in entries.[62]

That these two factors are causally related has, however, been called into question by other studies, which suggest that the motorization of the population, in France at least, where a large section of the rural population had always been out of ready reach of the cinema circuits, had had unexpected side-benefits. In 1956, 82% of cinema entries were recorded from the seven major cities, with only 18% from rural areas. Several rural departments had no more than a dozen cinemas to cater to their widely dispersed population. An indication of the higher attendance rates that might have been achieved if the rural areas had been more fully colonized by cinemas is provided by the figures for average attendance in those areas where a cinema was available: the average for such areas was 15 visits to the cinema in 1952 and 1953, against a national average of about nine. So if more city people were diverted by motorization from the cinema as a leisure activity, more country people were brought within reach of it. Overall, a study by the CNC showed no correspondence between those times when motorization affects leisure (weekends, holidays, fine weather) and the decrease in cinema attendance, which was homogeneous throughout the week and year.[63] A more local study in the outer Parisian suburb of Massy-Anthony in 1963 revealed similar findings.

It would seem, then, that in France at least, television was a more direct competitor with the cinema than was motorized leisure. This is certainly compatible with the fact that cinema entries maintained a high level throughout the fifties in France, since television was particularly slow to develop in France, with only 13% of households equipped by April 1960. By comparison, in Britain and America the spread of television receivers was much more rapid, and the fall-off in cinema entries began earlier than in France. One important factor here is availability: by 1958 it was still available in only 70% of the territory, as against 90% in Britain, Germany, and Italy. In 1960 the relative availability was 80% in France, 95% in the other countries,[64] and there was only one channel, state-run with a very poor level of program by comparison with British or even American channels.

It has often been suggested that this replacement of cinema by television was partly due to the dependence of television on films for a large percentage of its programming time. When films are available in the home, inde-

FIGURE 2.2   **Cinema, Television, and Motorization**

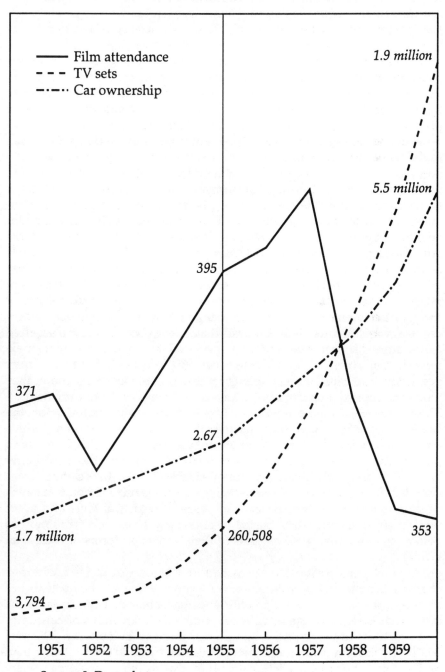

Source: J. Durand

pendently of weather problems and at no extra cost, there is less incentive to go out to the cinema. Thus the dramatic fall-off in cinema entries corresponds not only with the period when television receivers began to penetrate French households, but with a dramatic increase in the number of films screened on television.

That television was indeed an important factor in the reduction of cinema audiences is demonstrated by a study of the region of Lille where television penetrated more households earlier than elsewhere in France. Between 1956 and 1961 there was an increase in receivers of 312%, to the point where with 8% of the French population it had 15% of the television receivers. Cinema attendances reduced much faster in the Lille region than in the rest of France, particularly after 1957—in all, by 29% between 1949 and 1961, as against 10% for the whole of France. The same phenomenon was recorded in the Ruhr area of Germany. But, as the excellent study of these factors in the *Film Français* suggests, there is a more global relationship between disposable income and leisure patterns. Rather than look for specific competing activities which might account for the patterns of cinema attendance, it might be more valid simply to acknowledge that as disposable income increases and a population becomes more wealthy, forms of leisure which might be seen as providing escape from the unpalatable aspects of poverty no longer have the attraction they once had. A detailed study of the disparate patterns of leisure activities and relative wealth in Italy, where regional variations are large, suggests that, as the poor of Calabria acquired a little more disposable income, they increased disproportionately their expenditure on cinema (by 127.5% between 1950 and 1957). When wealthier populations acquired corresponding increases in disposable income, they tended to expend it on activities which took them away from the cinema.[65] These observations are compatible with those concerning motorization: the late forties were still affected by postwar deprivations and rationing, which corresponds with the all-time high in cinema attendance. The fifties was a period when increasing incomes saw a balance between those in poorer areas attending the cinema more frequently and those in wealthier areas attending less. The year 1957 seems to have been the turning point, at which time the majority of the society had passed the critical level of relative wealth: consequently, they ceased to attend the cinema as frequently as before, spending progressively less of their budget on forms of fantasized escape.

An analogous conclusion is reached by Claude Degand.[66] Looking at changes in consumer spending over the period 1950–1963, he notes that of all categories of consumer expenditure, cinema and other spectacles is the only category to decrease in volume, while other categories of consumption, such as furniture and white goods, increase by between 50% and 300%, and camping and gramophones increase by up to 600%. Rather than an imaginary escape into fictional worlds, the evolving consumer society was inclined to spend its new wealth on improving the existing world, escaping to nature, or on gambling. The latter activity, with its promise of limitless wealth for the randomly lucky few, provided the form of expenditure that offered most to the postwar generation by comparison with the previous generation, helped greatly by the introduction of the tiercé which more than doubled the sums invested in gambling between 1961 and 1964.[67] A further observation based on these statistics is that the period of the fifties saw a dramatic increase in all forms of consumer spending related to the individual and to the home and that it was those forms of spending related to public or community activities which showed decreases. This move away from a population that expects to go out for its services and entertainment, and toward a population which expects services and entertainment to be delivered to the home has been documented in a multitude of ways. It was one of the essential factors in the steadily growing pressure on cinema throughout this period to transform itself from a popular community activity toward a more private and elitist artform, such as would appeal to that bourgeois audience still willing to "go out to the cinema," as it expected to go out to the opera, to a concert, or to a play. It was a pressure, that is, that was to require the transformation of discourses on the cinema from entertainment toward art and to favor the development of a "New Wave" of "artistic" films. In this light the New Wave can be classed with the rise of hard and soft pornography and with the widescreen stereophonic sound epic as a necessary response to changing consumer and leisure routines, since these were the three genres which TV, for one reason or another, was unable to provide. Insofar as it is valid to set up an opposition between the classic French cinema and the New Wave, these statistics are a powerful index of the moment when the classic French cinema ceases to be the dominant film mode; and they have the inestimable advantage of providing a clear indication of a central reason why it ceased so to be.

POSTWAR TRANSFORMATIONS OF THE FRENCH CINEMA

It is clear that the socioeconomic environment within which the postwar film industry worked was evolving rapidly and in the process was inevitably to produce powerful strains within the industry which would require it in turn to evolve. There were three critical moments which were to determine the conditions under which the industry functioned for the rest of the period: 28 May 1946, which saw the Blum-Byrnes agreement between France and America, in which the French cinema became a pawn in negotiations to secure a loan and which resulted in a long-term debate concerning the international trade in films and, in particular, concerning import quotas; 23 September 1948, when at the insistent demand of the industry, a government committed to large-scale intervention with a view to revitalizing production agreed to a "temporary" law subsidizing production by means of a surtax on entries; and 19 October 1949, when an agreement formalizing the principle of international coproductions—in this first instance, between France and Italy—was signed in Rome.

The Blum-Byrnes agreement mobilized the French film industry in a concerted political campaign as no other cause was to do in the postwar era. Anxiety within the industry had been great in the period immediately following the liberation because the percentage of foreign films, primarily American, on the French market seemed disproportionately large—60% in early 1945—to an industry that had become used to the protected market environment of the war when foreign imports had occupied only 35% of the market numerically, and much less by value. This disproportion was largely due to the backlog of several years of foreign films being introduced into France, combined with the collapse of French production in the chaos at war's end; but French producers were quick to call attention to the need for control, and the cinema's governing body acknowledged "the danger posed to our national production by foreign competition."[68]

In these circumstances, it was an explosive move for Léon Blum to sign an agreement with James F. Byrnes, U.S. Secretary of State for Commerce and future counsellor for the major Hollywood companies, to the effect that "no restriction of any sort whatever would be imposed on the import of American films into France."[69] As for screening them, the only limitation was a complex regulation that imposed an expectation that exhibitors would screen on average four weeks of French films each three months (= 30% of screen-time). Moreover, as an American spokesman said, "The U.S. government notes with satisfaction that in taking these measures the French government envisages the total elimination of all protection from the moment when the French film industry has recovered its competitive power."[70]

In fact, however, the Blum-Byrnes agreement seemed to the French industry to be deliberately establishing conditions under which it never could recover its competitiveness. Raymond Bernard, for the Association of Directors, spoke of "treachery"; Henry Jeanson, for screenwriters, spoke of the French government "selling its soul"; Grémillon, for technicians, spoke of the agreement as suppressing French culture's right to freedom of expression; Jouvet evoked the cultural colonization which must inevitably result; all were in favor of organizing a Committee for the Defense of the French Cinema.[71] Léon Blum, explaining to them his motives, noted that in exchange France had acquired a significant and indeed essential concession: America had cancelled 1.8 billion dollars worth of debts and had opened a further credit of 500 million dollars. "I admit," he said, "that if it had been necessary in the superior interests of France as a whole to sacrifice the French film industry, I wouldn't have hesitated. . . . The basis suggested by the French industry, namely seven weeks set aside for French films . . . proved impossible, since our American friends wanted a system based on the principle of free competition."[72]

As another element in its defense, the French government could point to the large exhibition circuits it now held, which were free to concentrate largely on French films. Indeed, the Continental holdings which had originated as prewar Jewish-owned circuits had been nationalized at the liberation, as one minor element of the vast nationalization process already mentioned. They were thenceforth known as the UGC—Union Générale du Cinéma. Moreover, as Blum pointed out, the quota allocated to French films was higher than that allocated by the British government to its films in the prewar period (22%) and even more so than Italy (17%)—both of which had at the time received envious comment in France. Objectively, the result was that during the period 1946–1947 American imports experienced rapid growth from 77 out of 186 films in general exhibition (41%) to 175 out of 323 (54%), while French production remained stable in the eighties. The French Communist party was quick to capitalize on the anti-American reaction, pointing out that Hollywood's films had already been amortized before reaching France, so could be "dumped" at prices that undercut the local product. Thorez, secretary-general of the PCF, protested that "The American film invading our screens thanks to Léon Blum is not only depriving our artists, our musicians, our workers, and our technicians, of their daily crust, it's literally poisoning the soul of our children, our young men and women, who are being turned into docile slaves of the American millionaires rather than French citizens, attached to the moral and intellectual values which constituted the grandeur and the glory of our native land."[73]

The Committee for the Defense of the French Cinema—a national movement from December 1947, presided over by the long-time Communist campaigner for the French cinema, Léon Moussinac—organized in January 1948 a demonstration by 10,000 actors, directors, and technicians from the Madeleine to the Place de la République. Manifestos were published and public meetings were organized. Well-known members of the profession toured cinemas, speaking during the intermission about the iniquitous effects of the agreement.[74] Only the exhibitors were silent, since the proliferation of films on the market played into their hands.

Finally, the government felt constrained by this pressure to modify the terms of the agreement, increasing the quota from four to five weeks every three months (38% of screen-time) and reintroducing a quota of 121 visas per year for dubbed American films and 65 for other countries (except where those countries made demonstrable efforts to import and distribute French films). Needless to say, this unilateral revision of the terms of an international agreement was not calculated to please the Americans, but they seem to have accepted it. One reason was that the quota was not strictly observed—indeed, it was only in 1955 that the screening time of French films finally passed the 20 weeks per year level—but despite this, as figure 2.3 indicates, these measures were effective in reducing the total number of dubbed films on the market to a low of 150 in 1952.

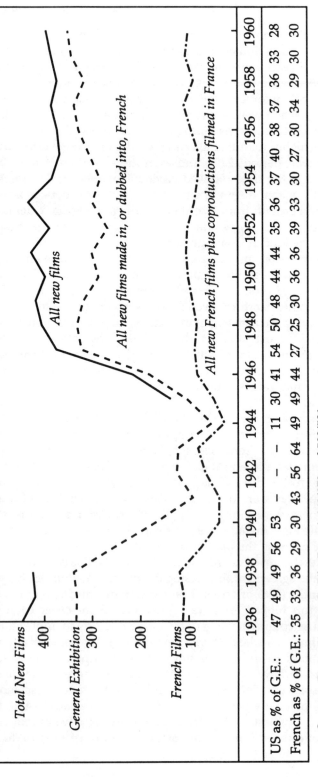

FIGURE 2.3   The French Market 1936–1960

	1936	1938	1940	1942	1944	1946	1948	1950	1952	1954	1956	1958	1960
US as % of G.E.:	47	49 49	56 53	– –	11 30	41 54	50 48	44 44	35 36	37 40	38 37	36 33	28
French as % of G.E.:	35	33 36	29 30	43 56	64 49	44 27	25 30	36 36	33 39	30 27	30 34	30 29	30

Total New Films — All new films

General Exhibition — All new films made in, or dubbed into, French

French Films — All new French films plus coproductions filmed in France

Sources: Pierre Autré in *Le Film Français* 869/870 and 500/501.

The revision of the Blum-Byrnes accords would not, however, in itself have been sufficient to ensure the revitalization of French national production. As a second and more positive measure, therefore, the government introduced simultaneously the first of its postwar aid-programs targeted on the production and exhibition sectors. The law of 23 September 1948 introduced an additional tax on ticket prices and a tax on all films imposed at the time they received their exhibition visa, graduated according to their length. The funds from this tax were managed by the CNC and were available to subsidize the various claimants within the profession.[75] As it proved, the two main beneficiaries were feature film producers and exhibitors, each group receiving approximately six billion francs over the six years in which the scheme operated, with smaller sums being allocated to news programs, export promotion, etc. The first moneys from the fund were distributed in January 1949. Inevitably they proved a more attractive proposition than the Crédit National, which, though it had been providing funds for production for years, was still operating basically as a bank: the funds which it provided had to be repaid from receipts before producers themselves began to receive returns from their production, whereas the funds from the aid legislation were simple handouts based on a percentage of receipts and requiring no repayment (though they had necessarily to be reinvested in another film). Consequently, the Crédit National funding tended to reduce from its previous level of 25–30% of the total cost of production to a negligible level by 1953. Over the same period, the aid funding replaced it almost exactly, accounting for 21% of the total cost of production.

Outrageously protectionist in nature and calculated both to encourage a crucial cultural industry and to ensure full employment in the industry, the measures found few opponents in a postwar period of material deprivation. An inquiry undertaken when their projected term expired in 1953 suggested that the dubious practices of certain financiers and producers of the thirties had not entirely disappeared in the more regulated postwar industry. The minister for industry and commerce, M. Lacoste, advised the film industry to clean up its act, saying the government was not going to provide a free ride for just any wild-eyed producer, "There's no law that says the nation must make sacrifices to support industries that don't deserve it"; and his aide pointed out that "the law had been intended to provide a period of relief during which the industry could discipline and organize itself. Not only has it not seized this opportunity, but it has even exploited the chance to set up dubious new deals. . . . The law has not ended the risky balancing acts typical of the industry—it has merely facilitated them."[76]

Nevertheless, despite such doubts and despite the general economic recovery, the aid legislation was confirmed in 1954 under a new title (the Fonds de Développement de l'Industrie Cinématographique or FDIC) and continued in force till 1959. At that point, though the fact of subsidizing the cinema was not called into question, the automatic nature of the funding no longer seemed so logical.

The evidence suggests that in the early years the effects on production were positive. Statistics published by the various sources (fig. 1.1) show that the level of production increased in 1949 and 1950. On the other hand it would probably have done so anyway, as a knock-on effect of the increases in cinema attendance in 1946 and 1947 fed into the producers' coffers. Indeed, it is interesting to note how the production figures for the fifties reproduce the graph of entries, with about a year's delay, with the setback to entries in 1953 coinciding with the recession of that year, and having as one effect a reduced production of films in 1954.

But an aspect of the aid which came to be considered more ambivalent in its effects was its tendency to generate and then perpetuate a particular array of producers within the industry.[77] In a sense this was a side effect of its rationalizing of the financial basis of film production. The newfound stability and confidence of those firms initially benefiting from it led to their progressive reinvestment of the "profits" and their progressive dominance of the market. It is an interesting fact that this tendency, which might have registered as healthy in any other country's film industry, was seen as having its dangerous aspect in France: it registered as a potential fossilization, preventing new blood and new ideas from revitalizing the industry.

Moreover, in the economic climate of the day, with state stimulation of the economy giving way to private investment, it began to seem inexcusable that tax moneys should be handed over automatically to all production firms, including those that were flourishing. The 1959 revision of the system therefore introduced the notion of *selective* aid, based on quality. Already the 1954 law had specified the desirability of subsidizing "films of a nature to serve the cause of the French cinema and to open new perspectives in filmic art or to promote the great themes and problems of the French Union."[78] Now, this was strengthened: anyone wishing to obtain the funding could submit a découpage to the CNC, and the funding would be decided according to merit and need. Rather than reinvesting profits on previous films, the system now provided an advance on prospective receipts; and rather than a subsidy, the funding was a loan to be repaid if the film made a profit. This system proved extraordinarily effective in introducing new blood into the industry, and must be considered a key factor in the development of a Nouvelle Vague of young filmmakers. It also proved amazingly effective in maintaining and even increasing production in the face of rapidly declining cinema audiences, though here it was complemented by new technologies and by the new production procedures associated with them which dramatically reduced the average cost of production. It is improbable, however, that the transformation of the production sector would have happened without them.

During the fifties, however, at least half of the aid funding went to the exhibition sector. Basically, this funding was destined to upgrade and extend the exhibition sector's cinemas, and it was supplemented in the FDIC period by additional funding to modernize the technical industries associated with film production. Particular attention was given to "small" exhibitors, as against the big circuit-owners. Probably as a partial consequence of this aid (but also of course because of the generally high level of attendances), the number of cinemas in France expanded during the late fifties to its maximum of just under six thousand. One effect of the 1959 modification to the aid law was to exclude the exhibition sector from the program, concentrating instead on filling the seats in those cinemas that already existed.

The whole question of state aid is extremely controversial in any capitalist or even mixed economy, but in a fascinating and provocative study of the nature of film as a culture industry, J.-C. Batz has made a good case for its being essential to the viability of the industry in any nation with a relatively small linguistic market. Arguing from the nature of film as a product and from current practices of film consumption, he concludes that some "denaturization" of the free market is inherent in the system and can only be redressed by quotas, by state subsidies, or by some combination of the two.[79] Novalaise, in his study of fifties profitability, came to the same conclusion. "The state aid is a determining factor in this question of profitability. . . . Suppress that aid to the cinema, and French production must collapse."

The third of the major transformations of the postwar film industry was the development of a system of international coproductions. It too can be seen in the light of an "aid program," since one central motive in the government's sponsoring of the system was the desire to counter the superproductions of the American cinema, with their high technology and quality finish. Only a massive injection of capital could produce an industry capable of matching such productions, and the solution was to think in terms of a transnational, and even European, film industry, able to call on the capital and on the technical and artistic personnel of several nations. Yet because officially a product of each of these nations, the films so produced were guaranteed not just a transnational distribution and exhibition but also whatever financial privileges each nation provided its national output. In this respect, the film industry through its system of coproductions already in 1949 foreshadowed the principles of the Common Market to be established a decade later.

The idea was of course not entirely new. Setting aside the European coproductions of the twenties and the multiple-language productions of the thirties, the producer André Paulvé had already established the principle of Franco-Italian coproductions in 1939 and continued to produce them during and after the war.[80] Indeed, all three Italian companies active in France before the war (Lux-Zenith, Francinex, and la Scalera) had been able to pursue their activities after 1940. A Franco-Italian agreement had ensured the participation of Cinecitta in the CIMEX operation run by André Paulvé at Nice which managed the La Victorine and St Laurent-du-Var Studios and two prestigious Nice cinemas. Italian participation had therefore supported the production of such French films as *Lumière d'été*, *Les Visiteurs du soir*, *L'Eternel Retour*, and *Les Enfants du paradis*.

A postwar agreement resuscitating this system of coproductions was signed and in existence in October 1946 and came into effect in February 1947, but complications caused by the Blum-Byrnes law, the aid law, and incompatible national legislation negated them. Effectively, the system came into existence in February 1949 with the signing of a new Franco-Italian agreement, to be followed by a Franco-German agreement in March 1953, a Franco-Spanish agreement in November 1953, and about ten quantitatively less important ones (Poland, Czechoslovakia, Yugoslavia, Austria, Argentina, Belgium, etc.). Films could be and were made outside these agreements, by producers from two or more countries, under much the same conditions ("coparticipations"); but the set of formally recognized regulations governing the financing and distribution of coproductions was reassuring for funding agencies.

Figure 2.4 indicates the importance which these coproductions assumed as a major percentage of French production in the fifties. They introduced once again the problem of nomenclature into the discussion of "the French cinema," in much the same way as had the multiple-language versions of the thirties—a problem which several times threatened to spill over into defensive chauvinist discourse about the fall-off in 100% French films. A convention developed according to which, although for commercial purposes all such films ("the Quota Films") had double nationality, only those films in which French producers had provided more than 50% of the funding would be recognized as "French films" for statistical purposes. The normal pattern was for a majority producer to provide 70–80% of the funding and a minority producer 30% or 20% and for the film to be made in the country and language of the majority producer. To protect the interests of participating film industries, these coproductions were initially realized under terms which required the twinning of two productions, one made in each of the participating countries; but the administrative complexities involved in matching the financial, artistic, and material provisions of one film with those of a subsequent twinned film soon led to a notion of "global equivalence."

The different technical standards of participating countries led to several difficult moments as did their different emphasis on moral values; but the system expanded at a rate even greater than the raw data suggests, since the coproductions had significantly larger budgets than other films—between 2 and 2.5 times larger throughout the decade, on average. By the end of 1959, French producers had participated in the production of 382 coproductions and 27 coparticipations, which in 1953 and 1954, then again from 1957 onward, represented about 50% of all their involvement in production by volume, and well over 50% by value. As an index of their success, the percentage of receipts coming to French film producers from these coproductions rose rapidly from 22% in 1952 to 32% in 1953 and about 40%

FIGURE 2.4 **Coproductions**

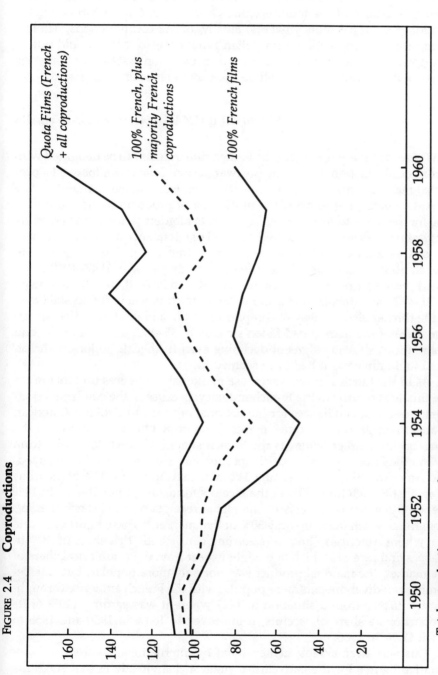

Quota Films (French + all coproductions)

100% French, plus majority French coproductions

100% French films

160
140
120
100
80
60
40
20

1950   1952   1954   1956   1958   1960

Total coproductions = area between solid lines
Source: *Le Film Français* 884/885.

in 1954. Of the 1955 production of 106 films, 15 films had after three years earned one-third of the total receipts. Of those 15, 6 were coproductions including the top 3 moneymakers. Finally, of 382 coproductions, 325 had been made in conjunction with Italian producers, so that it would not be exaggerating to say that the two national production systems by that stage were totally "twinned" and well on the way to becoming integrated.

PROFITABILITY IN THE POSTWAR YEARS

There was every reason for the French film industry to be delighted with its financial situation during the postwar period. It had won for itself a protected market, with a quota on imports; it had won for itself a massive state subsidy, amounting to over 20% of the cost of production and more than that for the renovation and extension of its exhibition sector; it was enjoying (at least until 1958) by far the highest level of attendance it had ever known; national economic conditions were steadily improving. The percentage of French films on the market after the threatening period of 1947–1948 when it had reduced from its wartime high of 64% to 28%, then 25%, had risen to 30–39% and stabilized at around 30%, which is where it had stabilized in the thirties also. By way of comparison, from a high of 54%, the American share of the market had fallen steadily to 35–40% and was at the end of the fifties showing signs of declining even further. It no longer threatened to dominate as it had once seemed to.

As in the thirties, moreover, these market-share figures underestimate the financial returns to the French industry, because of the confirmed preference of French audiences for the national product. In 1947 the American share of receipts on the French market had jumped to 53% from 54% of the films on the market, whereas the French share had fallen to 37.8%, from 27% of the films. By 1955–1956 the proportions had been steadily reversed, and American films were earning 34% of the receipts from 38% of the films as against French films 50% of the receipts from 30% of the films.[81] In 1960 French films earned 53.12% of the global receipts on the French market, from films which made up only 30% of that market.[82] These figures indicate that where American films were earning consistently that share of the audiences and receipts which one might expect from their numerical share of the market, the national product was not only more popular, but was becoming rapidly more and more popular with the French audience throughout the fifties: from a situation in 1947 where it was earning 140% of its proportionate share of receipts, it improved to 160% in 1955 and 1956 to reach 177% in 1960.

This was a remarkable achievement by international standards. Comparative figures for the early fifties suggest that already at that stage the French national film industry was unique in Western countries for its ability to resist the inroads of the American product on its local market. When

America was still attracting 43% of receipts in France, it was attracting 75% of them in Australia, 75% in Belgium, 70% in Holland, 70% in Italy, 80% in Canada, 60% in Sweden, 70% in Brazil, 80% in South Africa, and 70% in Britain.[83]

Another index of the national preference for the local product is the extent to which the "best sellers" of the decade were French or at least quota films: of the 60 most successful films of the fifties, 19 were American, which is in proportion to their market share or a little lower; 36 were quota films (of which 31 were French or Franco-Italian with a French majority), which is 55% of the total at a time when their market share was 30%.[84] This dominance of French over American films was progressive: between 1946 and 1951 all records for Parisian releases were held by American Films. In 1955–1956 the top film (*Les Grandes Manoeuvres*) was French but followed by three foreign films. By 1956–1957 the top four "best sellers" were French.[85]

Perhaps the most intensive analysis of this relative preference for local films was undertaken by the CNC over the period 1955–1960. The statistical branch analyzed over a five-year period the receipts for the 459 films, French and foreign, first screened on the French market in 1955.[86] Of the 459 films investigated, 107 were French (23%), and 352 foreign (77%). Receipts were split approximately evenly between the two groups, indicating that the French public went to French films approximately three times more often than to the foreign films (specifically, 1,726,000 spectators for French films, on average, as against 556,000 spectators for each foreign film). Of foreign films, American and Italian were by far the most popular, averaging just under half the entries and returns for each French film. It must be remembered, however, that with a raw cost (of dubbing) at *one-twentieth* that required to produce a French film, American films were still making a handsome profit with *one-third* the receipts of a French film. By the late fifties, only in the Alsace-Lorraine area, where the German language and culture were still particularly strong, did foreign films offer a significant threat to the local product. When the pro-European minister, Robert Schuman, opened up the French market to virtually free entry of German-language films, the share of receipts going to French language films dropped in that region dramatically to 12.8%, against a national average at the time of 48%.[87]

Of course this market which the French industry had managed to retain and even to recapture was still small by international standards—at its strongest in the late forties, it was less than two-thirds that of Italy and less than a quarter that of Britain—but it was supplemented to some extent by an expanding export market, which grew steadily from 1.2 billion francs in 1950 to 2.8 billion in 1954, 4.8 billion in 1957,[88] and 7.8 billion in 1960.[89] This increase in export earnings was partly due to the development of co-production agreements which guaranteed French producers an entry to certain foreign markets. Cumulatively, in the course of six years, export earnings had supplemented national market earnings by an amount rising from 4.6% in 1950 to 6.1% in 1954, 8.8% in 1957, and 11.9% in 1960. These figures are probably still gross underestimates, since, though based on official data for repatriated earnings, they do not include the large but unspecified sums invested abroad in other films or repatriated in other forms. Sadoul indeed considers that they underestimate real export earnings by 50%.[90] Whichever is the case, the figures indicate the success of the export incentives included in the aid laws, designed specifically to stimulate such growth. By 1960 French films had appropriated 11% of the German market and 20% of its receipts and along with Italian and Franco-Italian productions were making significant inroads on the American market for the first time.

It is clear from these figures alone that the postwar period from 1947–1960 saw a particularly favorable conjunction of circumstances for the French film industry, of a sort to produce substantial financial benefits. The exact scale of the profits accruing to the industry is not clear, since no global figures concerning its profitability were published. This in itself is significant, considering the flurry of (often misleading) statistics which flourished in the thirties in order to demonstrate its lack of profitability.

Where they are available, however, the figures are reasonably favorable throughout the decade and explain why Claude Degand in *Le Cinéma . . . cette industrie* could entitle his chapter on this period "*Les Belles Années.*" Quoting CNC figures, *Arts* claimed that in 1958 global profits to producers on their investment were 32%. An interesting index of the confidence of the industry as a whole in its ongoing profitability is the decreasing extent to which it felt obliged to advertise its products during this period. From a norm of 1.3% of the budget of a film in 1939, publicity spending dropped to 0.3% in 1958. At that time American films were devoting 2% of their budget to it. This would seem to suggest that the industry as a whole was fairly confident of automatic profitability of its products.

This extremely optimistic evaluation of the situation needs to be qualified in a number of ways. First, although inflation was more moderate than in the immediate postwar years, it nevertheless still existed; when the earnings came in one or two years after production, they had depreciated with respect to the initial investment. Second, those earnings were not "pure" profit: the producers and distributors had to pay tax on them, administer their businesses out of them, pay for the cost of the copies of each film, pay for publicity, and transport the films about the country.

These costs were negligible for the production sector, however, not just because the firms consisted for the most part of no more than a desk, a secretary, and a director of production, but because the production sector had developed the habit of incorporating these running costs into the cost of the film, as "incidental costs." Commonly, 5–7% of the money borrowed to fund the film was used by the producer for this purpose. Many commentators on the industry saw this as an unethical business practice, but it seems to have continued unchecked; and as a consequence of it, running costs did not have to come out of profits.

Finally, the factor that prevented the industry from profiting as it might have from the conjunction of favorable circumstances was the CNC's rigid control of entry prices. In real terms the price of entry had remained at about 4fr50 (1937 base) throughout the war—a little higher in 1943 which, in conjunction with the increase in spectators and the monopoly of the market enjoyed by French films, produced a boom year which everyone looked back on nostalgically. After the boom of 1945, which was largely to the benefit of American films, entry prices fell steadily with respect to inflation, so that as the number of spectators doubled, entry prices halved. It was this that made filmgoing a particularly cheap form of entertainment around 1947–1952 and filled the cinemas; but it did not fill the pockets of producers or exhibitors. The latter in particular were constantly lobbying for the right to set their own prices, but they only achieved this in a very limited form— for certain first-run cinemas—in 1958. In the course of the fifties, however, the entry price gradually returned to its wartime level, and this (in conjunction with the increased market share of French films) favored producers as it favored exhibitors. By 1960, profits were as high as during the war. They were, however, shared among more films, and those films were costing more because the coproductions increased in cost at a rate significantly greater than inflation. The returns per film were never again as favorable as during the war, when every film might hope to triple its investment.

Despite these qualifications, it is not possible to take too seriously the sporadic protests of the industry, which continued throughout this period, as throughout every other period, to the effect that it was in a state of "crisis" and permanent structural deficit. On the other hand, however positive the global profitability of the industry, it would be unwise to minimize the risk factor involved in investing in the production of films: because the production companies themselves still had for the most part a minimal financial base, nearly all the 78% of a film's funding outside the state aid had to be borrowed at interest. As a typical instance indicating the scale of the risk capital involved, in 1951 the global total of credit accorded by financial firms for film production was 3.5 billion francs, out of a total production cost of 5 billion. Over two-thirds of production was still being undertaken on credit in 1958, which, as in earlier decades, was far higher than any other industry's risk levels (4% in the clothing industry, for instance, 12% in champagne, 37% in iron and steel).[91] Given that in any one year a significant percentage of the production would lose money and that the vast majority of production firms were investing in a single film and had not the financial resources to withstand significant losses, it is not surprising that, even in these benign circumstances, quite large numbers of firms continued to go bankrupt throughout the fifties.[92] As in the thirties, they were replaced by ever larger numbers eager to enter the marketplace, but unlike the thirties, this situation no longer attracted general concern from within the industry. As a measure of the continuing atomization of the industry, from a base of 61 registered production companies during the war years (of which about 40 were active in any given year), by 1947 there were already 250 registered production houses, in a year when 75 films were produced. These numbers rose steadily throughout the following decade by about 20–30 per year to reach 300 in 1952 and 463 in 1958. The maximum of 698 registered production companies was reached in 1964, at which time the regulations were tightened to limit the proliferation; the requisite financial base of 5 million francs which had been established during the war by COIC, when it represented a sum larger than the cost of producing a film, had by then become ridiculously low. Because of inflation and the increase of coproductions, the average cost of producing a film had risen to about 150 million francs in 1959, with coproductions regularly costing over 250 million. A regulation requiring a minimum financial base of 30 million francs[93] dramatically reduced the number of registered production companies, at least temporarily.

Nevertheless it is clear that the "fragmented" industrial structure, arrived at in the mid-thirties and reaffirmed to some extent even during the war, was confirmed in this period as a fundamental and ongoing characteristic of the French film industry, surviving economic and political changes of the most dramatic kind. Often called "artisanal," its essential characteristics were and are

(1) a large number of production companies, each involved in relatively few productions per year.
(2) a divorce between production companies and production facilities, which must usually be rented on credit.
(3) a lack of any large-scale vertical integration between production, distribution, exhibition, and manufacturing sectors.
(4) an unreliable funding base for production, which must often be renegotiated for each film.
(5) the personalization of the production system, such that specific individuals are both the focus for production activities and the guarantee (or otherwise) of funding reliability.
(6) the absence of any ongoing contractual basis for most of the intellectual and technical personnel.

During the fifties, the production of quota films fluctuated in the range 100–130, and the number of production firms active in funding them varied in the range 100–180, reaching a maximum of 198 in 1961 and stabilizing in the region of 130 during the sixties. These figures clearly indicate that it was not only in the international sphere that coproductions were becoming common: "internal" coproductions in which two or more small production firms combined to assemble the necessary capital were progressively more common. In 1954, when a film cost on average just over 100 million francs to make, some 290 of the 300 registered production firms had a capital base of less than 20 million francs.[94] In these circumstances it is not surprising that well over two-thirds of the firms in any one year were confined to producing a maximum of one film per year, and most of the others produced two. In 1956, the proportion producing only one film had increased to 63% (106 out of 163), and those producing no more than two had increased to 86% (131 out of 163), while 252 companies were totally inactive. In 1959, a year of booming production, only four firms produced more than two films: Filmsonor (6 films), Pathé (4 films), Sirius (4 films) and Gaumont (3 films); and for Filmsonor this was an atypical year. Most of these "more prolific" production firms produced or coproduced three or four films per year throughout the decade.

Among them, only three had sufficient financial clout, based on extensive exhibition circuits, to transform this situation, had they been so inclined—Gaumont, Pathé, and the UGC. At no stage did they attempt to do so. UGC was a nationalized circuit without any real interest in production; it funded a number of productions in favorable circumstances but several times announced that it was retiring entirely from that sector, notably in 1961.[95] Again, therefore, it is the two reconstituted French exhibition/distribution majors, private enterprises and once again prosperous, that might have been expected to move toward the vertical integration that had evaded them in the thirties. It is hard in the abstract to see any significant economic impediments to such an expansion.

On the one hand, however, the vertical integration of the American industry had itself recently been denounced as oligopolistic and detrimental to a liberal market economy: antitrust laws had effectively dismantled it, and the industry was moved toward a radically different set of production practices somewhat nearer to the French system. For the French to move in the reverse direction at such a time would have been perverse in the extreme. Moreover, the advantages of the "fragmented" system, especially as moderated by a clear regulatory framework and a massive government subsidy, had by this time become apparent to the French industry. Finally, the industry had come to erect as a positive value the "artisanal," "personalized" system of film production and would have reacted violently against any attempt to transform it. Since such an attempt would have had to attract the approval of the CNC, which monitored and approved submissions for film production, and since that body, partly composed of industry representatives, was intensely responsive to the industry's lobbying, it would not have been easy for the two majors to overcome practical barriers to their ambitions, had they ever harbored such ambitions.

For a variety of reasons, then, perhaps predominantly ideological, neither Pathé nor Gaumont made such a move in the fifties; and the crisis of declining spectators at the end of the fifties pressured them into concentrating their attention even more exclusively on the distribution and exhibition sectors—especially distribution, which was of all the sectors the

FIGURE 2.5   **Distribution Firms: Numbers and Market Share**

	1957		1960		1964	
Nationwide	8	30%	6	32.4%	3	15.75%
Multiregional	7	10%	10	10.4%	8	13.75%
Uniregional	128	} 25%	111	} 25.2%	122	} 30.5%
Art film	20		20		22	
American	8	35%	7	32%	7	40%
Total Active Firms	171		154		162	

Source: R. Bonnell, *Le Cinéma exploité*, 1978, p. 212.

most profitable and the most stable. Its financial stability had long made it the focus for much of the financing of production either directly or indirectly. Effectively, it continued to act as the banker for the production sector, either providing funds or standing as guarantor. In return it received first cut of returns and charged a healthy commission of 35–50%. This position of economic dominance ensured that it acquired a considerable influence over the types of film that were made, and this in turn forced many producers, if they were to preserve their independence, to act as their own distributors. Inevitably, however, this still involved negotiating sooner or later with those major distributors who controlled access to first-run Parisian cinemas. In general, throughout the classic period, the distribution sector was relatively fragmented: a multitude of small distribution companies, each dealing with few films (and perhaps only those one or two which their parent production company had produced) were complemented by some twenty-five middle-sized firms with a nationwide or international orientation (figure 2.5). Eighty percent of the distribution firms confined their activity to a specific region, mostly supplying small local cinemas; the third of the market supplied by American films devolved on a relatively few large distribution companies; and in between these, some fifteen French firms (mainly Parisian) supplied 40% of the market's films. Although about 3,500 different films were distributed each year, only three firms in 1957 were distributing over 200 of these.[96] Only after 1960 did power gradually begin to concentrate in the hands of three or four major French distribution companies.

The exhibition sector throughout this period was even more atomized than the other two sectors. In the fifties, 4,000 of the 5,500 cinemas in France were owned "privately" and were dependent on local or regional distributors. Only 2% of the cinemas were owned by the big chains, mostly in big cities. The rural areas of France had in fact not yet been "developed" by the cinema at the end of the fifties, at which time the crisis of failing entry numbers ensured that they never would be. Yet, although small in the number of cinemas they owned, the major chains occupied a crucial position in the industry because of the intense concentration of spectators in first-run urban cinemas. In 1955 there were six leading exhibition circuits in Paris sharing 19 first-run cinemas. Between them, these 19 cinemas recorded one-third of all Parisian entries, and one-tenth of the total French audience.[97] In 1960 75% of receipts was obtained from 25% of the cinemas, notably those owned by Pathé, Gaumont, and UGC. Although these receipts were roughly steady in real terms, the exhibition sector enjoyed a steadily greater percentage of them as tax was reduced. In addition, until 1959 the state aid package provided an enormous injection of nonrepayable funding to the exhibition sector intended to encourage it to extend and modernize its facilities. The number of cinemas increased steadily from 5,007 in 1950 to a maximum of 5,834 in 1959, at which time it began gradually to reduce under the impact of falling entries. The number of seats which had been stable at 1 for every 18 people from 1937 to 1950 likewise rose under the influence of large audiences to 1 for every 14 in 1959.[98]

Within this relatively prosperous and expansionary environment, however, the exhibition sector faced a novel problem caused by the changing viewing habits of the population. In the wartime, all French films attracted good audiences; in the postwar period, audiences were still relatively dispersed across the range of films offered; but as the fifties progressed they showed a tendency to concentrate on fewer and fewer productions. By the end of the fifties, fewer and fewer films were achieving an audience of 100,000 spectators in first-run Parisian cinemas, but those that did so attracted larger and larger numbers of spectators. This can be interpreted as the beginning of that tendency toward a different audience, exercising greater selectivity, which was to see the cinema as a social institution totally transformed in the 1960s, away from a mass and routinized habit oriented around local cinema attendance, toward an elitist and criterion-based activity. In this new environment, the exhibition sector was to acquire an industrial importance which it had never had in the classic period and which was to allow it to displace the distribution sector as the focus of decision making in matters of financing and programming. Likewise, in the changed circumstances, exacerbated by the removal of state aid in 1959, Gaumont and Pathé, which had fused their exhibition activities, were able to dominate the sector and extend their influence into the provinces in a way that they never had in the classic period.

THREE

PLANT AND TECHNOLOGY

> The real disaster for the French cinema was that not one teensy weensy bomb ever fell on Joinville, Courbevoie, or Boulogne-Billancourt.
>
> René Gilson, *Film Français* 567/8, Spring 1955

> We're always more than willing to rake in the profits, but we're unwilling to spend even five centimes more than we need to, that's the plain truth of it.
>
> Doublon, *La Cinématographie Française* 531, January 1929

> I'm currently shooting a film in Cinemascope; it's a French film, yet I'm obliged if I want to get the necessary precision to use a Mitchell camera (from America), a Moy panning platform (from England), a Fearless foot elevator (from America), a small crane (from Italy) and a larger crane (from England).
>
> Alain Douarinou, *Le Technicien du Film* 5, April 1955

> Talkies and sonorized films are something entirely new. They're interesting inventions but I can't see them remaining fashionable very long.
>
> Louis Lumière

OVERVIEW

The factors discussed in the first two chapters—the prevailing economic conditions, the place of the cinema within the French economy, government policy toward the cinema, and the industrial structure which arose out of these conditions—are so inextricably intertwined that it would have been impossible to understand the latter without considering simultaneously the others. They demanded to be treated as a coherent whole. In a sense, the same is true of the industrial plant and the technology available to that industry. It is self-evident that those economic and industrial factors constructed a set of limiting conditions which largely determined what form the studios took, how they were equipped, how they were used, what form the service facilities such as laboratories and manufacturing industries took, who owned them, and what possibility there was for renovation and modernization in the course of the period 1930–1960, as the "new technologies" of color, wide screen, stereophonic sound, and 3D competed for introduction. And this in turn is clearly important because the filmmakers' work practices, which cumulatively constitute what is here defined as the various "styles" of the resultant films, were themselves constrained and in certain ways determined by the plant and technology available to those filmmakers. At the very least, some ways of making films must seem more feasible, more "natural," than others; and where the technology and its management was different from elsewhere, was distinctively French, the possibility existed that a distinctively French style would appear.

But if all these factors are intertwined, it is nevertheless a little easier to isolate plant and technology in a provisionally separate discussion, if only because of its material physical existence. It could be, and often was, described in detail by those who had to work with it. It loomed large in those people's everyday calculations; it constituted the tools of their trade, the wall against which they battered their head in frustration year after year. For it is beyond doubt that the permanent sense of an industry in crisis which emerges from contemporary representations of the French cinema was in part due to the everyday reality of working with plant and technology which was from the beginning barely adequate and which after the war was visibly deteriorating from year to year. The industry must be in crisis, it must be in need of restructuring and of state aid, if these working conditions were the best that could be achieved without them. Such an attitude was particularly likely to be voiced by those who had experienced working conditions in other countries, when and if they returned.

The following are typical of innumerable such observations voiced over the thirty years from 1930 to 1960:

1. Ever since 1928 there's been talk of our grandiose studios, our myriad projectors, the blinding illumination of our studios, the colossal décors we're going to film there, the impressive size of casts, and so forth. Rubbish. Mere publicity. . . . The truth is enough to make you die of shame: we have no real studios. . . . Let me list all we *don't* have:

   • studios 120 m × 30 m, equipped with 10,000 amps, and 20,000 for arcs
   • labs capable of providing positive prints by the following morning
   • a workshop capable of producing four high-quality sets per day

- 200 young men to replace the 200 useless slobs who keep saying, "I've been making films for 20 years," and haven't yet realized they ought to have been doing something else for at least the last 18.

2. . . . the English studios offered a level of luxury and comfort which the French studios couldn't match. People working there were treated as lords. For Lazare (Meerson), it was like a promotion: he had a lot of assistants, he worked in greater luxury.

3. There is a lack of tooling in the French cinema, such that everything has to be reinvented anew for each film.

4. We've heard over and over again how cramped our French studios are, heard of their inadequacy, their disgusting filth, the faulty soundproofing that leaves technicians at the mercy of the slightest exterior noise. . . . Need I add to this list the archaic sound and electrical equipment, worn threadbare, cables that are daily held together with bits of string, short-circuits it takes a whole morning to hunt down, rails for the dollies that are twisted, good only for the scrapheap.
In such conditions, to make a film of any ambition in France today is to take on a stubborn, exhausting, and unremitting struggle. . . .
I know: the war. But believe me, that excuse is only partly valid. Already before the war the equipment in our studios, not to mention the studios themselves, was distinctly dated and not at all appropriate to the needs of contemporary technicians.

5. We lack studios, our equipment is 15 years behind that of other countries, we depend on foreign sources for color and sound, we have only one filmstock factory, and that's in the hands of the American capitalists.

6. In 1945, the French cinema was turning out masterpieces using only ends of string and sardine cans. . . . They are still in general at the level of "making do" and ingenuity. We have the finest technicians. . . . We find them working with equipment that sends shivers down the spine of foreign filmmakers.[1]

Admittedly, there are claims to the contrary, though far fewer: French studios and equipment are the best, largest, and the most modern in the world. Such claims usually prove to have been making the trivial point that some relatively minor modifications to a given studio are the most recent, therefore the studio is the "most modern." Mostly they emerge directly or indirectly from studio owners engaged in self-promotion.

It is also true, however, that downplaying the available technology became an essential element in the prevailing aesthetic discourse within French filmmaking circles: their films were made without visible material advantages, by sheer force of will, directly out of the stuff of the imagination. And this discourse had its heroic side: French filmmakers were the underdogs, despised and marginalized in the twenties, apparently overwhelmed by the technological supremacy of the Americans, but fighting back against all odds and astonishing the world by their flair and ingenuity.

Nevertheless, a simple description of the state of plant and material at various points in time makes it clear that there is an objective basis for this aesthetic myth. That there should be such an objectively inadequate technology is not surprising. There were very few periods when the economic situation and the industrial structure of the French film industry were such as to induce or allow industrialists to modernize their facilities. There was the period of two to three years just after the introduction of sound, and there was the period of two to three years during the war. Aside from the inherent improbability of the industry's investing on the occupiers' behalf at that time, the subsequent collapse and lean period at war's end would have undermined any such project—as indeed would the 1932–1934 crash have done in the earlier case.

But if there is any validity in the calculations of the first chapter, they demonstrate however tentatively that the industry was never or seldom in such a financial crisis as it so persistently claimed. Industry-wide profitability was a regular phenomenon, but several factors in the industrial structure ensured that those profits did not get reinvested to modernize the facilities. First, of course, the fragmented nature of the production system meant that no one company was secure enough financially for long enough to make such an investment. If the industry had been unified as were the similarly-scaled industries in England and Germany, profits and losses would have evened out in a year, and over the years a moderate profitability would have accumulated to allow reinvestment. This never happened in France, where most companies were subject at any moment to bankruptcy if a single film failed badly. Moreover, the disjunction in management between these production companies and the studios, which for the most part the companies merely rented, rendered any reinvestment of profits in studio facilities less likely. Certain production companies, for greater or lesser periods, did have a proprietorial relationship with one or another studio facility, but since they themselves did not use that facility for any significant proportion of the year, their attitude toward it was as a rental company to its plant: the aim was to charge other producers as much as possible while spending as little as possible on the plant itself. The nature of sound film production more or less obliged their clients to rent those facilities rather than film entirely on location, however outdated the facilities might be. The renting companies in turn, for whom studio and equipment hire was a major budget item, were always anxious to minimize that expenditure by reducing rental periods as far as possible. Moreover, their renting was done on a credit basis, with the studios and labs providing services and facilities in return for a slice of the hypothetical profits that the film would earn. While that slice had priority over the producers' own returns, it was uncertain and it was in the future. It did not constitute a reliable basis on which to undertake present renovations. As Quéval put it, "This form of credit (to producers for services provided) covers about 8% of the cost of a film.

Extremely advantageous to the producer, these advances have, however, the concomitant disadvantage of holding up the renewal and modernization of technical equipment, which as a result of these practices is deferred again and again, from film to film."[2]

Cumulatively, the result of these industrial practices was that no one in a managerial position had any compelling financial motive for upgrading and renovating the facilities, and even if they did, the wherewithal was lacking. While these generalities do not hold true in all cases, they are sufficiently valid to account in global terms for the technological difficulties facing filmmakers throughout this period; and, because those filmmakers and their practices are the focus of the argument in the later part of the book, most attention will be focused on those aspects of plant and technology which affected them: notably studios and their equipment. Nevertheless, other aspects of plant and technology, more or less directly related to these, were also conditioned by the prevailing economic and industrial circumstances: manufacturers of filmstock, of cameras, lenses, lighting, editing tables, and endless other items of everyday use were equally affected by the lack of capital base both for production companies and for studio proprietors. They survived or disappeared as independent firms according as French studios were able to update their facilities, or as foreign firms were induced to recognize the superiority of the French product. Very few survived. In the field of manufacturing, the camera firms (Debrie and Eclair) are outstanding exceptions.

Finally, the exhibition sector was affected, though to a lesser extent and with fewer implications for the industry and its products, by the lack of capital funding. Cinemas were slow to spread to the more rural areas of France and slow to be renovated in the more urban areas. In particular, they were slow to re-equip for cinemascope, which involved an exorbitant charge for the lenses and in many cases extensive modification of the cinema itself. Producers were no more ready than exhibitors to move into the newer technologies of cinemascope, of 3D, and even of color film. Modernization was deferred from year to year. Indeed, whereas in the immediate postwar years all these technological developments could still be seen as inevitable advances which were destined to be generalized across the industry sooner or later, as funding permitted, by the end of the fifties even color film and the large-screen format had made little impact, such that at that time they might have appeared rather as a momentary fad of the past rather than as an industrial norm of the future.

It is this complex thirty-year relationship with technology and with industrial renewal that the present chapter intends to explore.

CONVERSION TO SOUND

At the point where they were faced with conversion to sound, French film studios were not in good shape. For a start, many of them were already very old. The first studios dated from 1897–1902, and by 1907 there were already ten in the Paris region.[3] Of those that were to be converted to sound and to form the basis of classic film production, the Eclair studios at Epinay had been built in 1902, the Cité Elgé at Buttes-Chaumont in 1905, and the Menchen studio at Epinay in 1914. Several others had been built in the early twenties—la Victorine in 1921, Joinville and Billancourt in 1923. Only one was recent (Francoeur, 1927). Rather than recognize that sound film production imposed conditions which required a radically different design, French firms preferred to modify as best they could existing studios which in several cases would have been better scrapped.

To make matters worse, these studios had sometimes been designed for quite other purposes (early ones were often modified photographic studios, and Billancourt began life as a workshop) and were often poorly sited for their future purpose. For silent film purposes, the noise of a nearby road, railway, or airport was of no importance, but it rendered the adaptation to sound difficult or impossible. Most had been built in the proprietor's backyard or on randomly acquired land. Several in inner Paris were built on land that was already, or was soon to become, too expensive to justify such use and impossible to extend; at the very least, terrain for exteriors was limited. As late as 1935, the studio François I was to be sited close to the Champs-Elysées which, while convenient to production houses, rendered it especially subject to these difficulties.

More generally, all early studios were (naturally enough) sited around Paris. But it rapidly became apparent that the Paris region was far from ideal for film production. The weather was unpredictable, the number of days of continuous bright sunlight was restricted, and in winter the days were short. Even before World War I; therefore, Pathé and Gaumont had subsidiary studios in the Côte d'Azur region, where these limitations were to some extent made good and where the variety of mountain, coast, and seascape provided a wealth of settings for exteriors. Postwar shortages of coal in Paris provided a further incentive to locate production in the South, and in 1920 the construction of la Victorine near Nice seemed to indicate that the Côte d'Azur was to become the Hollywood of French filmmaking. Reputedly, in constructing la Victorine, Nalpas saw it as a reply to American studio construction in California, which had largely taken place in 1911–1915 and which had already come to symbolize America's displacement of France as the leading film-producing nation. The number of films produced in the many Nice studios of the twenties was sufficiently large to suggest that Nalpas's vision might be realized—twenty-five films a year from 1923 to 1929,[4] when total French production averaged only 55–60—but the advent of fully electrified studios, then of sound, largely negated the area's advantages by rendering the film studio an autonomous and hermetic world, which might as well be located in the Arctic or at the Equator. During the thirties, only 34 films were made in the Nice region, and the focus of activity reverted to the Paris studios.

These were not only aging, but they had already been subject in most cases to ad hoc extensions and modifications. Expansion in the prewar period had seen new stages added to studios of whatever size and in whatever orientation the site allowed. Then when electrification finally saw arc lights replacing the dependence on sun, around 1924, the "glasshouse" roofs and sides of older studios had to be blacked out and generators and cabling introduced as best possible. In many cases, the timing of studio construction was extremely unfortunate. La Victorine, built in 1921, was designed as an enormous glasshouse on the prewar model and was therefore outdated as soon as built; it had to be converted at great cost to electricity in late 1924. Joinville, newly built in 1923, had to be totally remodelled for electrification when Pathé took it over later that year.

This bad timing extended to the Francoeur studio, built in 1927 but without the requirements of sound in mind. Within two years of its construction, it was outmoded and Pathé-Natan had to begin remodelling it. Not one of these French studios was specifically designed, from the ground up, for sound production. By contrast, when Paramount leased the St. Maurice site as a base for its European operations, it totally dismantled the outdated Aubert studios already on the site, leaving only the manager's residence and gatehouse, and replacing them with an entirely new purpose-designed studio on the American model. The contrast says a lot for national differences in the conversion process and in industrialization in general, but it is also of course related to the different levels of finance available to firms from the two nations. It also relates to different attitudes toward the studio as a property. Paramount had no doubt about its own ability to produce films in sufficient quantity to justify an investment of that magnitude. Since about 1920, however, both Pathé and Eclair had regarded their studios not as production lines for their own films, but primarily as rental properties; and in 1925 with the death of Feuillade and the lack of other ongoing in-house projects, Gaumont similarly turned to renting out the Cité Elgé.

Faced with the conversion to sound, therefore, French studio proprietors engaged in quite different calculations from their American counterparts. They had just been through a process of conversion—to electrification—and needed a respite before facing further large-scale investment. Their problems were further exacerbated by the fact that they had no corporate connections to any of the sound patent-holders. Any conversion involved a choice among foreign vendors, without any certainty that the chosen format would capture enough of the exhibition market to justify their investment. It is understandable, therefore, that the process of conversion was slow and occasionally adventurist in nature, undertaken by individual production companies momentarily flush with funds from some lucky coup.

That it should have been American firms that made the running in introducing talkies was perhaps inevitable given the degree of dominance they exercised in the world marketplace during the twenties and the degree of competition that existed between them. Several French firms had experimented before the war with the synchronizing of disk and film, notably Gaumont, which had developed a rudimentary form of sound film based on this principle before the turn of the century. Indeed, at the Paris Exhibition of 1900, three different sound-on-disk systems were presented by French manufacturers—the Phonorama, the Phono-Cinéma-Théâtre, and Gaumont's Chronophone. Richebé remembers his father installing a sound system in their Marseilles cinema in about 1912, which was when the 6,000-seat Gaumont Palace in Paris first advertised its Filmparlants Gaumont.[5] The problems of synchrony and of record-length were discouraging,[6] but Gaumont continued work on the format, taking out patents in July 1918 and presenting a reasonably effective sound-on-disk filmscreening on 15 June 1922. This was in effect the identical format to that which Warner Brothers first exploited commercially as Vitaphone, the format used for *The Jazz Singer*, yet Gaumont does not seem to have proceeded further with his exploration of it. Instead, in 1925–1926 he began discussions with Electrical Fono-Film of Denmark for use of the Petersen-Poulsen system, which used optical sound recorded on film. He founded the Société Française des Films Parlants to develop the system, but there does not seem to have been any sense of urgency behind the company's work. Progress was slow, and it was not until October 1928 that Gaumont felt able to demonstrate publicly his Cinéphone. One reason for the lack of urgency has been suggested by Courtade, who quotes several authoritative articles from the 1920s in which French filmmakers speculate complacently about the possibilities of sound film. Their unanimous view is that any sound production will be confined to music, song, vaudeville. No production system would be so foolish as to produce talking films that were restricted to a specific language community. Noise and spectacle will be added to the "silent" film, but not spoken language, or its universality will be lost.[7]

Gaumont's 1928 demonstration program included a silent feature film (*L'Eau du Nil*) sonorized by the Cinéphone method. It drew favorable publicity, notably from the influential *Cinématographie Française*, where P.-A. Harlé described the impact of sound as being equivalent to that of the first screenings by Lumière.

> Now it's up to the artists to work out how to use this discovery, with its new and spectacular possibilities. We should get a move on, if we don't want to see a replay of "the French film held back by the war." The Americans, seizing on the possibilities, have been making talkies for a year already, and real ones at that. Unless . . . we manage to exploit rapidly the Gaumont "Cinéphone" . . . we will find ourselves once more invaded, and our wails of dismay will be quite simply ridiculous.[8]

Arguably, however, it was already too late. The Cinéphone system suffered from a major disadvantage, compared to other optical sound systems, in that the sound was recorded on a second, separate band of film, passing through the projector at a different rate from the image band. The quality of the recording might be finer, but the problems of synchrony and the cumbrous nature of the system were major drawbacks to exhibitors. Gaumont had to turn down Epstein's request to use the system in the production of *Finis terrae*, saying the equipment was not yet up to the job. He presented his system to the Conservatoire des Arts et Métiers in February 1929, defending his decision not to market it yet and acknowledging that research still needed to be done to perfect a single-band system. He even predicted one in which the sound would use the infrared and ultraviolet range, while the image used the visible color range. Already, however, in February 1929 the foreign systems were beginning to be exploited in France, backed up by readily available equipment. Although development continued and some cinemas were fitted out for the Cinéphone system, and although some films (e.g., Gance's *La Fin du monde*) were eventually filmed using it, French industry was simply unable to compete at that late stage with foreign concerns already producing in quantity. France had no conglomerates like Western Electric or General Electric (parent company of the Radio Corporation of America) which might tool up rapidly and mass-produce the required equipment, and French producers, however ambivalent they were toward sound, could not afford to delay indefinitely once they saw how popular the first imported sound films were. The French had definitively lost the battle to obtain a share in the sonorization of the industry; American and German firms would share the French market between them as they were to share out the whole cinematic world.

The aggressiveness and arrogance with which the American industry approached this economic and cultural colonization of the rest of the world, and more specifically of Europe, is exemplified by an irresistibly sinister article appearing in the *Film Mercury* of 1930, which notes complacently the willingness of foreign industrialists "to flog their film industries to Uncle Sam," and which foresees "the imminent extermination of what little remains of what used to be called the European film."[9]

Among European nations, Germany alone recognized in time the potential dangers and the potential profits of sound film and had the means to respond to the American invasion of Europe. In 1919 three German inventors[10] had patented the triergon sound-on-film system, and between 1922 and 1926 they tried to interest the German film industry in it. Like the French industry, however, the German cinema at first saw no need to introduce an expensive novelty, involving a limitless cost in converting cinemas, and the risk that it might be a passing fad. Indeed, Hollywood itself had resisted sound film, available to it in commercializable form since 1923, for similar reasons. Both Laemmle of Universal and Zukor of Paramount had rejected at that time de Forest's Phonophone system, which was to form the basis of Fox Movietone newsreels, until the Warners/Fox performances demonstrated that it was a viable commercial proposition—indeed, that to ignore it was an *unviable* commercial stance. The German industry came to this conclusion in 1928; Tobis acquired the triergon patent and began to install sound equipment in German cinemas. By early 1929 they had merged with a potential rival system developed by Siemans and AEG ("Klangfilm") to form Tobis Klangfilm and had, not without difficulty, acquired extensive financial backing from Dutch and Swiss sources. They now felt strong enough to challenge American patents in Europe and were successful in Germany, Holland, Czechoslovakia, Hungary, Switzerland, and Austria. Throughout 1929, the German firm used litigation as a strategy for delaying or denying the American firms' entry to European markets. Its patents position was strong and strengthened still further by an agreement with the British Talking Picture Company. Hollywood responded with a boycott on the exhibition of its films. When these were undermined by Warners and RKO, which began to rent films to exhibitors in the disputed markets, and by RCA's buying into the Tobis Klangfilm corporation, it became apparent that a larger cartel involving the existing cartels of both countries and covering all three sound-on-film systems would be more profitable than the current battle. As the *Revue du Cinéma* sardonically observed, just as the two American rivals had seen the light and come to an agreement, so now were the American association and its German rivals: "although [they] continue to snarl at one another like china dogs and seem to say 'Just let me get at them and you'll see fur fly,' no one seriously doubts that they'll end up forming an alliance."[11]

They did so. Representatives of Tobis Klangfilm, RCA, Western Electric, and the U.S. film industry began exploratory talks in the spring of 1929; they finally met in Paris in June 1930 to establish an "understanding" about spheres of interest. The way in which this "Paris Agreement" divided up the world market is well known: Tobis Klangfilm was allocated exclusive rights for most of Europe, including Scandinavia, while Western Electric and RCA were allocated the United States, Canada, Australia, New Zealand, India, and the Soviet Union. Returns from the British market were to go three-quarters to Western Electric and RCA, one-quarter to Tobis Klangfilm; the rest of the world was to be open to competition between systems. France became the major European nation within this latter category, of countries in which the various competing systems were to vie for supremacy.

This "Paris Agreement" was never formally ratified because of a dispute between the parties, and at a second conference in February 1932 further disputes about payments, rights, and spheres of interest surfaced which effectively negated the agreement. In the following years, as Hollywood opportunistically negotiated with individual countries and companies, the electrical firms stood to lose out on those royalties which they had hoped to guarantee by the Paris Agreement. Finally, in 1935, the interested parties met and negotiated a second "Paris Agreement" which, while less rewarding to them than the first, had the benefit of assuring them a constant level of royalties without competition. The agreement lasted till World War II.

Having early lost any opportunity to profit from patent royalties, French producers and exhibitors were obliged to maneuver throughout the thirties as best they could within a situation that offered only degrees of disadvantage. They could represent their case at the conferences, they could attempt to exploit the uncertain and shifting cartel structure within and between American and German firms, but whatever the outcome it had to involve a heavy financial drain on the minimal capital available for conversion to sound. Moreover, the electrical firms' public battles about patents, coupled with the ongoing uncertainty as to which system would emerge as dominant, inevitably led to anxieties and delays within the French industry. The conversion to sound both of studios and of cinemas began later in France than in other leading film-producing nations and was more drawn out than in other such nations.

An additional complication was the fact that the cost of sound-on-disk systems was markedly lower than optical sound systems, costing perhaps only 10% as much; and this may have been one powerful factor in their retention in France. In April of 1930, when the *Revue du Cinéma* was attempting to summarize the state of play for its readers, it said that conversion to optical sound cost 200,000 francs, whereas conversion to disk cost only 45,000 francs. Other sources indicate that it might have cost as little as 20,000 francs for the French Synchrophone sound-on-disk system.[12] Noting that rumor in the industry had it that disks were to be superseded, the *Revue du Cinéma* observed that "facts at the moment seem to prove that this is an error, and the formula which is becoming more and more generalized is a mixed one, in which optical sound is used for film production in the studio, whereas disk sound is used in the cinemas." Editing problems, of course, rendered disk sound unsuitable for production, but for exhibition purposes the *Revue*'s commentator could still see transfer of the soundtrack to disks as a viable and indeed desirable long-term proposition. Indeed, sound-on-disk on the Vitaphone model was dominant throughout 1930 and 1931, and the final phasing out of disk sound from French cinemas did not happen till 1934, perhaps in some areas later. But of course in those many cinemas which had equipped for disk sound, a double conversion process had by then been necessary—from silent to disk, then from disk to optical sound. The cheaper conversion had proved the dearer in the long run.

The conversion of French cinemas therefore began in early 1929 and did not end till late 1934. The first year saw a proliferation of opportunistic firms attempting to market sound systems under a variety of imaginative names—Courtade lists some of the 37 different systems available in late 1929 as Boma, Cinénor, Cinéphone, Electrovox, Survox, Synchronista, Syntok, Tona, and l'Idéal Sonore, soon to be followed by the Synchrophone and the Fullvox.[13] But the three earliest systems—the RCA Photophone, Western Electric Movietone, and Tobis Klangfilm—with the power of crucial patents behind them and the financial clout of large corporations backed by banks, emerged quite rapidly as market leaders. After Gaumont's October 1928 demonstration in the Caméo, the first cinemas to convert were the Madeleine Cinema, converted by Western Electric in November in order to demonstrate the Movietone system, and the Paramount Cinema. In January 1929 *The Jazz Singer* was screened in Vitaphone in the Aubert Palace, and by February Tobis had converted the Rialto for its own demonstration performance. By the end of August 1929, 16 cinemas had been equipped in Paris and two in the provinces[14] (by Aubert and by Richebé, in Lyon and Marseilles respectively).

Jeancolas cites the Chambre Syndicale's figures for the subsequent conversion process as follows: March 1930, 194 cinemas; May, 250; September, 450; December, 552; March 1931, 703; October 1931, 1,027. Thus, even at the end of 1930, the year in which the French industry acknowledged the inevitability of the conversion process, only 552 of about 4,000 French cinemas were equipped. It is hard to agree with Jeancolas that the conversion has "proceeded apace."[15] Already in July 1929, America had converted a greater percentage of cinemas than had France over two years later, in October 1931; and in December 1929 Germany also had outpaced France, with over 200 cinemas converted. Of all European countries, however, Britain was fastest to convert its cinemas to sound (22% in 1929, 63% by the end of 1930, according to Douglas Gomery).[16] Consequently it was used as a showplace for America's equipment and a bridgehead for Continental expansion. One thing all these countries had in common, however, was that larger circuits in the capital cities began the process, and they began it by equipping their most prestigious cinemas. Thereafter the flow on to regional and rural areas was slow. In France by late 1932, 95% of Parisian cinemas had been sonorized, but less than 50% of those nationwide.

The slow rate of the conversion process was not just due to economics, it was partially a consequence of the relative unavailability of sound films. The number of films needed to feed the French market had been approximately 600 in the twenties; when the conversion to sound had been effected, it was to stabilize at around 450. Had all cinemas converted rapidly to sound, the films needed to feed the screens would not have been available. Silent films were of necessity dominant still in regional centers and rural areas, but even in urban centers the sonorized cinemas had to screen silent films for some of the time. Indeed, for some years strong distributors such as ACE imposed on such cinemas packages including a number of silent films in return for the opportunity to screen a potentially profitable talkie.[17] As the production of silent films ceased, this practice died out, and by 1932 the opposite problem had arisen: some two thousand non-Parisian cinemas could still only screen silent films, but scarcely a single silent film had been produced for two years. Anxiety about resuscitating the flow of silent films was frequently expressed in the industrial press, and a large section of the industry still saw the silent as a viable artistic and commercial prospect till about 1935. Lacking new films, however, the pressure on smaller regional and rural cinemas became progressively more acute. Some eight hundred to one thousand of them disappeared at this stage, largely because they were incapable of conversion to sound, or because the cost couldn't be justified given the size of the clientele.

For those that did convert, the profits to be made in the early months were very large indeed. Richebé, who had spent a half million francs equipping the Capitole in Marseilles in anticipation of the coming of sound, and a further 800,000 francs for the rights to one of the first French sound films, *La Route est belle*—a total of 1,300,000 francs on speculation—recorded a quarter of a million francs in receipts in the first week of screening. The previous record had been Chaplin's *Goldrush* at 165,000 francs for the first week and 130,000 the second. After five weeks, houses were still packed and Richebé had taken in 1,250,000 francs on one film in one house. Conveniently setting aside questions of tax, he asserts with some truth that he had effectively paid off his total investment in that time.[18] René Clair, likewise, talks of enormous profits from his first sound film for Tobis, *Sous les toits de Paris*, such that the not inconsiderable cost of the film was covered by returns from a single cinema.[19]

The cost of conversion to small regional cinemas was effective in altering the balance of cinema ownership toward large circuits, since it pushed Gaumont, Pathé, Haïk, and others toward buying up attractive properties in regional centers which were failing or where the proprietor preferred to opt out rather than face the transformed commercial and technological future. Other effects were equally important. Alongside numerous cinemas that failed and disappeared, an enormous building program was undertaken by the prosperous circuits to renew and extend those circuits. Jeancolas talks of "an uncontrolled frenzy" of cinema construction.[20] On the one hand, the Depression had not yet struck France, and on the other the acoustic requirements of sound film often made total reconstruction a preferable financial alternative to the extensive remodelling that was almost essential. The enormous Gaumont Palace was renovated and sonorized, as was the Pathé-Montparnasse, "and dozens of other cinemas were renovated or built, anchored along the outer boulevards, as close as possible to the working-class suburbs that furnished the main batallions of spectators."[21]

The same feverish construction had been going on in provincial capitals as in Paris. Demand from this expanding exhibition network put pressure on production companies to tool up French studios for sound production. Because this was typically slow in happening, early sound films screened in France were mostly subtitled American films. To cater to the demand while tooling up, French producers "sonorized" large numbers of existing silent films and produced music tracks for those that, conceived as silents, were currently in production. Additionally, the more entrepreneurial of them contracted with the British studios or with Tobis in Germany, which had converted earlier, to make French-language films. It was thus that Braunberger produced *La Route est belle* (Florey, 1929, GB) and Pathé produced *Les Trois Masques* (Hugon, 1929).

Tobis seems to have been the first firm to actually equip a French studio for regular production. Its Epinay studio was ready for use in February 1929.[22] In the course of 1929, Braunberger had bought the Billancourt studio and converted it with Western Electric equipment. Natan bought the other Epinay studio and equipped it with Tobis equipment like its neighbor. His Francoeur studio he equipped with RCA. Haïk built the Courbevoie studio and installed Tobis equipment, and by December of 1929 Gaumont had equipped the enormous Cité Elgé studios. As soon as Natan's bid for Pathé was successful, he sonorized the Joinville studios; and by April 1930, Paramount had begun production of sound films on its St. Maurice site. Its purpose-designed studios were completed two months later. Except for la Victorine in Nice, the conversion of which dragged on till the end of 1931, the process had taken some fifteen months.

In the course of conversion, an unofficial competition arose among certain producers as to who would present to the French public the first authentic French talkie. Historians are still not agreed on the result, partly because it depends on definition of "French" and of "talkie." *L'Eau du Nil* (Vandal, 1928), used by Gaumont to promote their never-to-be-industrialized system, was screened on 18 October 1928, but it was a film shot as a silent and sonorized with a music track. Even the American films presented over the next few months—*White Shadows in the South Seas* (Flaherty and Van Dyke, 1928) in November 1928 and *The Jazz Singer* (Crosland, 1927) in January 1929—resembled silent films with musical items inserted; there were only snatches of dialogue.

It was late in 1929 before French producers managed to present French-language films to the public; and in the meantime several further American talkies subtitled into French had been screened, notably *Broadway Melody* and *Weary River*. On 22 October 1929, Aubert Franco-Film[23] premièred *Le Collier de la reine* (Ravel, 1929); but this resembled *L'Eau du Nil* in that it was initially designed as a silent film, then sonorized by a musical accompaniment with a single extended section of dialogue. It was somewhat less of a "talkie" even than *The Jazz Singer*. The film usually cited as the first 100% French talkie is *Les Trois Masques* (Hugon, 1929), presented by Pathé-Natan on 31 October 1929. It was certainly the first to be conceived as a talkie and presented as such, but because the French studios were as yet inadequately equipped, it was filmed in Britain. The same is true of the Braunberger productions of *La Route est belle* (Florey, 1929) and of *L'Amour chante* (Florey, 1930), filmed in Germany, and the Tobis production of *La Nuit est à nous* (Roussell, 1929, with a German version by Carl Froelich), filmed in Germany.

Meanwhile, a whole range of films which had begun production as silent films were being partially or wholly recast and sonorized in different ways. L'Herbier incorporated a sonorized Bourse sequence in *L'Argent* (1928); *La Petite Marchande d'allumettes* (Renoir), finished January 1928, was not issued till December 1929 when it had been equipped with a music track; and the screening of *Au bonheur des dames* (Duvivier, 1929) was delayed till 1930 in order to sonorize sections of it. Gance's *La Fin du monde* (1930) had been conceived as a silent film, and he hurriedly but reluctantly remodelled it as a sound film, considering it ruined in the process. It may be the case that the first authentically 100% French talkie, conceived and filmed as such in French studios, was the Tobis production of *Le Requin* (Chomette, 1929), though there is some doubt here, too, as to whether it warrants the title of 100% talkie. A final claimant is *Le Mystère de la Villa Rosa* (Hervil and Mercanton, 1929), produced by Haïk in his new Courbevoie studio and equipped with a distinctly superior soundtrack. Certainly it was not until late 1930 that French studios were producing in quantity French-language films that were more than sonorized silents; and even then a very great proportion of them were produced by Paramount and Tobis as French-language versions of German- or English-language films. Pathé-Natan, however, produced 12 talkies in that year, beginning with *L'Enfant de l'amour* (L'Herbier, 1929–1930) and following up with *Mon gosse de père* (de Limur, 1930) and *Accusé, levez-vous* (Tourneur, 1930);[24] Tobis, with René Clair under contract, produced the first of his great series *Sous les toits de Paris* (Clair, 1930) and *Le Million* (Clair, 1930–1931);[25] and Braunberger began his two prolific years of production that were to see 13 films screened, including Renoir's first two sound films.

THE AESTHETICS OF SOUND: REALISM AND MODERNISM

If French production can be considered to have become "regularized" from 1930 onward—that is, some two years after it did so in America—the technology of sound recording nevertheless imposed severe constraints in these early years which were to have both short-term and long-term effects on the classic cinema, of France as of other countries. To some degree, sound can be considered responsible for shifting filmmaking toward studio production rather than location and toward realism rather than toward modernism. This was a more significant move for French film production than it was for American film production, since both location work and modernist stylistics had been common components of twenties filmmaking in France. It is therefore worth recalling the characteristics of early sound recording.

First, the microphones used were omnidirectional. They picked up sound coming from all directions, not just that most desired. For speech, therefore, they had to be placed as close to the speakers as possible to minimize other ambient noise. For the silent film, such vagrant noise had been unimportant; now it had to be eliminated where possible. Studios had to be isolated from exterior noises of cars, planes, trains, and construction work. Internally, floors, walls, and walkways had to be silenced, and sets had to be both of acoustically appropriate materials and acoustically appropriate volumes. Standing screens of a reflective or absorbent nature became standard items of studio equipment. The noise of the camera had to be minimized, and this involved both modifying its construction to eliminate rattles and enclosing it in a hood, or "mattressing." Occasionally the whole machine, together with its operator, was put inside a sound-booth fitted with a window to film through. In either case, cameras became less mobile, and in the latter case, panning was significantly restricted. Even where partially mobile, the cameras were linked by a flexible cable to a motor, itself enclosed in soundproofing. The fixed microphones also inhibited movement, though experiments proceeded with moving them as the actors moved. Because of their relative insensitivity, however, the actors had to force their voices. They also had to maintain a relatively constant volume; and the limited range of the microphone's response meant that the voices of many actors would not reproduce at all well. Other actors, such as Mosjoukine, with a foreign accent, were now relegated from being the romantic lead to playing the quaint foreigner.

Perhaps the greatest transformation took place with respect to film music. Hitherto, in the extreme instance, the accompaniment to a film was produced by a local pianist from a repertoire of generic pieces strung together in an ad hoc arrangement on the night; it could now be a calculated structural element, fitted with precision to the needs of the specific film by a professional musician with a full orchestra on call—could perhaps even be incorporated in the initial conceptualization of the narrative. However, in the first few years, any music track had to be recorded at the same time as the speech track, which further restricted the conditions under which recording could take place. Cumulatively, these restrictions, together with the elaborate and cumbrous nature of the recording equipment itself, made location shooting highly impractical. Only in the studio could an adequate clarity and control of sound quality be obtained.[26]

Within the studios, lighting techniques had to be significantly modified. The arc lamps, which had been standard equipment, were noisy and had to be replaced wherever possible—certainly close to the actors and camera—with tungsten lamps. These generated a greater heat, which in turn required better ventilation; but ventilation tended to be noisy, and in turn required isolation. The tungsten lights were also at the red end of the spectrum, so the orthochromatic film which had been standard equipment during the twenties, but which was insensitive to red, had to be replaced by panchromatic film. This affected the look of films quite considerably, since orthochromatic film had been strong on contrast effects, whereas panchromatic film lent itself to gradations of shadings. It also affected the practices of set decorators, in that it allowed them to paint their sets in a range of soft colors; before, they had had to keep them colorless because orthochromatic film distorted any colors used.[27] Wahkevitch recalls using panchro for the first time on *Daïnah la métisse* (Grémillon, 1931).

> The first sound camera that I saw at Epinay looked like . . . a piece of furniture some 60 cm wide by 70–80 cm high and long. . . . It was acoustically deadened by a series of little air-cushions spaced out around it, resembling the pear-shaped air-triggers on old cameras. These little rubber bladders would deflate after a while and the sound assistant would have to pump them all up with a bicycle pump. Indeed, as they deflated, the whole machine began to vibrate, which wasn't good for the sound. . . . In addition, there was a Reis microphone that was an alabaster (or marble) cube with sides of 7–8 cm containing fragments of carbon, sorts of granules which compressed more or less according to the density of the sound. . . . After some use, these granules clustered together and became too compact to fulfill their function . . . ; the same assistant would take a wooden hammer and belt the microphone to free up the carbon particles. . . . Focusing was a frightful task, because we had to work through a complicated system of levers; to change the lens, you had to open the box with infinite caution, and to reload the film it took at least 20 minutes. . . . For travelling, this whole enormous machine had to be loaded onto rails; everyone called it "the donkey" because it was stubborn and moved only when it felt like it. . . . [There was also a sort of camera] in which the cameraman was enclosed in a little lair . . . ; the cabin was insulated with acoustic material, very tiny, and with the smallest of windows . . . sometimes double glass. For travelling, it had to be all loaded onto rails and trundled, cabin and all, about the studio.[28]

Such was the eccentricity of the sound technology that those who claimed to understand its ways could exercise tyrannical control in the studios. Numerous anecdotes from the early thirties indicate the degree to which this new category of workers, the sound technicians, acquired rights of decision over filmmaking practices, determining what could and could not be done, which takes were acceptable and which were not.

But possibly the most important effect of conversion to sound was to increase the cost of filmmaking. There were certain respects in which cost savings were recorded, especially for the exhibitor who felt less and less obliged as the thirties proceeded to hire live acts as a preliminary to the screening. Moreover, the pianists and groups of musicians, or sometimes even sizable orchestras, which had been hired to provide aural accompaniment to the so-called "silent" film, were no longer necessary. For producers, however, costs were adversely affected first by the studio proprietors' need to impose steeper hire charges in order to service their loans, and second, if more banally, by the fact that sound film was designed for 24 frames a second compared to the silent film rate of 16 frames, which significantly increased the consumption of filmstock (though Brounlow and Salt have both demonstrated that recording and projecting speeds in the late twenties were already approaching 24 fps).

The effects of these cost increases were many and varied. Producers became more conscious of the need to reduce studio hire. This could best be achieved by increasing preplanning. Scripting became the opportunity for a meticulous programming of the period of studio hire, so that details of camerawork, lighting, and acting were worked out in advance. The découpage of the script came to supplant the editing of the filmed takes as the moment of most intense creative intervention. Scriptwriters themselves became a crucial link in the creative chain, whereas they had been almost nonexistent in France in the twenties. For lack of sufficient trained scriptwriters in the early thirties, existing theatrical scripts became a principal source of cinematic productions. This suited producers, anxious to maximize profits, since the purchase of a theatrical script whose popularity had been guaranteed on the boulevards was a safer investment than an unknown property.

The actors who had proved popular on the boulevards, in vaudeville, and in music hall, were purchased along with the scripts, and for similar reasons. But they brought with them a different style of acting from that which had been standard in the "silent" film—not naturalistic, by any means, but not as melodramatic as that of the silent cinema. With the adjunction of words, the process of signification was no longer dependent on gesture and facial expression: these could be reduced in scale. In the same way, the foregrounding of signification that subtitles had effected was eliminated. But the script, being the property that the producer was counting on for profitability, had to be respected. The sentences of the theatrical script and the narrative blocks of the theatrical scenes and acts had to be retained, thus inhibiting the editor's ability to generate the rapid montages often found in twenties films. Shots became on average longer. The indifferent quality of early sound prompted the use of close-ups both to offer redundant confirmation of the words being spoken and to allow microphones to be closer to the speakers. The director of photography was therefore required to modify his assumptions about camera distance and framing. Not least, the increased importance of verbal interplay changed the nature of the scripts being selected for filming. Static theatrical tableaus based on wit and on "telling" dominated over dynamic narratives focusing on the "showing" of action. Moreover, while those scripts were being filmed, a religious silence now had to be preserved by all those not involved. No more could the director prompt, coach, and exhort his actors and technicians during the filming. All had to be word- and movement-perfect in advance. Finally, as Alexander Walker has reminded us, the introduction of sound changed the nature of the aural address of the cinema, and thus changed the nature of the contract between spectator and text.

Silent movies had enabled the casual spectator to drop in, and within a minute or two to be locked into the story and characters. Mime acting made the characters' predicaments easily intelligible: subtitles gave people emotional cues to follow rather than narrative points to recall. But dialogue altered all this: it demanded attention, it enforced silence on the audience who had hitherto been able to swap comments on the movie below the music of the pianist and pit orchestra. Now one had to shut up, sit up, and pay attention to a plot that more and more was conveyed in words, not pictures.[29]

All aspects of filmmaking were affected, then, either directly or indirectly, by the introduction of sound—scriptwriting, acting, camerawork, set decoration, editing, the composition of film music, and, as a consequence of these, directing itself. Sound was not simply an element that could be added to the preexisting filmmaking practices, like a new ingredient, a splendid bit of decoration on the filmmakers' cake. It resembled rather a new chemical which interacted violently with preexisting practices, transforming them totally to produce a new and distinct array of practices. This must be a central factor in any claim that a classic French cinema was coming into existence at this point in time, distinct in kind from the cinema of the twenties that it displaced.

It is not clear, however, that the various tendencies—toward preproduction rather than postproduction, studio production rather than location work, word rather than action—were necessarily mutually reinforcing. In particular it is not clear that they must necessarily produce that realism which is characteristic of all classic cinemas, but particularly of the French classic cinema by comparison with the extensive avant-garde modernism of much of the twenties cinema. It is not clear, that is, that the introduction of sound can be identified as the single central and necessary cause of that realism typical of classic French cinema. It is only clear that, once sound was introduced, the cinema did move closer to that form of realism which Hollywood had established as "classic."

The difficulty is well illustrated by Steve Neale's excellent discussion of the relation between technological change in the cinema and technical aesthetic practices, where his crucial link section is marked by necessarily weak verbs:

The introduction of sound allowed [sic] the synchronization of dialogue with the image of the actor. . . . It contributed [sic] both to a decisive orientation of space, time, and narrative around individualized characters and to a rigid codification of cinematic story-telling according to the conventions of . . . classical découpage. . . . It was in part the development of these conventions that was to be taken as a hallmark of the cinema's new capacity for realism. Films were now closer in the way they told their stories to the novels of the nineteenth century, the very touchstones of realist art. Added to this, and as part and parcel of it, was the simple fact that with the addition of sound, mechanically or electronically reproduced, the cinema could [*sic*] now reflect more of the world as experienced through our two basic senses . . . realism doubly guaranteed by approximation to the conventions of the novel and by the technological reproduction of sounds as well as sights.[30]

Sound *allowed* such a realism, but it allowed many other things too, much closer to the modernist visual and temporal structuring of twenties films. The move toward greater studio work, for instance, might rather have favored the stylizations, distortions, and other artifices inherent in modernist representations of reality. Set decorators made a plausible case for location work in the silent French cinema being the principal filmic pressure toward realism in set decoration, claiming that the need for stylistic coherence required them to integrate their sets with the "natural" exteriors. It was in wholly studio-made productions, where even "nature" was reconstructed and stylized on stage, that the German expressionist cinema had developed, and the same was true of French films of the twenties. In forcing filmmakers into the studio, sound technology might have favored the cubist, surrealist, abstract, and impressionist set designs of the twenties created for directors like L'Herbier, Chomette, Dulac, Epstein, and Clair. On the contrary, it destroyed them. As Neale goes on to note, "Mechanically and electronically reproduced and synchronized sound introduced, in theory, a wide range of aesthetic possibilities and practices. Given the aesthetic, economic, and industrial contexts in which sound was introduced, however, these possibilities, in practice, were rapidly curtailed."[31]

He is speaking primarily of the American context. It is scarcely possible to make a similar sweeping statement concerning the French context. Aesthetically, the weight of twenties filmmaking pointed in quite different directions, and the aesthetic background of most key personnel of the French classic cinema, especially directors, scriptwriters, set decorators, and musicians, was heavily modernist and avant-garde. A very large proportion of them had had training in fine arts or in a conservatorium, which led them in their work outside the cinema to adopt a modernist tradition.

Similarly, as we have seen, the industrial context was so radically different in France from America, Britain, or Germany, that it is hardly possible even to contemplate applying to it the term "industrial." Most commentators use the term "artisanal"; and it was marked only sporadically and locally by that routinization of work practices which goes with regular daily employment on repetitive and specialized tasks. This context can be used to explain the *relative* diversity of French filmmaking practice, its *relative* indifference to some practices which became in America signs of a quality finished product, such that American commentators looking at French thirties films were and are inclined to talk of incompetence, clumsiness, or backwardness. But beyond such relatively distinctive characteristics, the French cinema of the sound period did quite rapidly reject nine-tenths of the aesthetic possibilities open to it and regularly practiced in the twenties, in favor of a certain realism in which sounds are sourced in the image or at best heavily motivated by events in the image, and in which a coherent and largely naturalistic diegesis is constructed.

If it is not aesthetic or industrial factors that were the prime constraints in this process, it seems reasonable to see economic factors as central in determining the general limitations of usage of sound technology. The logic of this economic pressure is implicit in certain characteristics of early sound film mentioned previously. Sound had increased the risk to producers; producers were anxious to exploit proven successes; these were available in the Boulevard theater; the lack of scriptwriters meant that producers had to rely on the existing theatrical repertoire; the theater gave primacy to speech, to dialogue, to psychological motivation, to a certain realism. Sound-image matches were normal. By adopting this realism, producers increased cinema attendance among the audiences previously oriented toward the theater; the sound cinema decisively displaced the theater and other spectacles as an entertainment form, moving from a 40% share of audiences in 1929 to a 64% share in 1932; and it did it by moving toward more realistic practices. An added factor was the advent of Paramount's St. Maurice production studio, which, turning out vast numbers of American-style light entertainment films based on the realist format and on technical procedures that had already become confirmed as the norm in that country, helped to determine audience expectations in those early years. But as important as was the American model, it was the opportunity to *counter* American influence that was important to producers at this time. The language barrier offered the French industry a chance to recapture at least some of that audience which it had lost to American films around 1920. It was an economic incentive not to be refused.

It was not that French filmmakers ceased abruptly trying to make more exploratory films at that stage, but rather that contingent circumstances of a primarily economic nature forced on the early sound cinema in France an alternative film format which swamped their explorations and which proved so successful with the public that it became more and more difficult to find producers or patrons willing to undertake productions that would clearly alienate that new public. Even when the first feverish transcription of theatrical works was beginning to die down, the importance given to the word and to dialogue remained. Consequently, it was to previously demonstrated successes in related fields (the novel and the short story) that producers turned for further filmscripts; and the new category of worker, the scriptwriter, whom they employed to transpose those texts, was almost inevitably drawn from literary circles; in general scriptwriters had literary training which predisposed them to reproducing in their filmscripts the literary realism of their originals.

The introduction of sound, then, saw an aesthetic revolution of a fundamentally conservative nature take place in the French cinema, and a large percentage of those involved protested at the banality of synchronizing sound and image track. To resign oneself to "showing lips moving" whenever speech was heard seemed the depths of aesthetic degradation. Disappointment and outrage at the banality of "realistic" sourced sound inspire many of the articles by the music critic Vuillermoz—who proposed an ideal of "transposing" sound rather than reproducing it along with its source. "Every time science provides our industrialists of the filmworld with a new potential to take a step forward, they exploit it to take three backward. . . . Everything they are given which might allow an escape into the unknown, they instinctively use to produce the most servile of copies. But the cinema cannot achieve the dignity of an art unless it *transposes*. Three-dimensional film, color, and sound could theoretically provide an ever more powerful means of transposition: in practice, they will make it ever more difficult. They will provide unimaginative drudges with new ways to copy reality."[32] Quoting him approvingly, René Clair notes that "it is not the invention of the talkie that frightens one, it's the deplorable use that industrialists will undoubtedly make of it. The sound film, or more exactly, synchronous reproduction of images and sounds might at best be useful for musical accompaniments, for news films, for educational films, etc. . . . "[33]

Jeancolas cites several prominent film people who were of the same view, notably Abel Gance: "The talkie? Yes, for documentaries, for embalming alive great orators, great tragedians, great singers. But not for the rest, please! The cinema may be dying, but it doesn't need ceaseless chatter about its deathbed."

Jean-Paul Sartre, noting the abysmal quality of early talkies, recounted Aesop's fable of the fox who, envious of the (silent and beautiful) peacock, tempted it to speak. Its voice was horrible. "But what Aesop doesn't tell us is that without any doubt after such an experience the peacock returned voluntarily to its silence. I think the cinema is likewise in the process of acquiring the right to be silent."[34]

Obliged ultimately to acknowledge that the talkie was here to stay and that its initial impact had been to undermine all the hard-won artistic conquests of the twenties, such filmmakers not uncommonly bemoaned the passing of the silent for its malleability and its universality. As René Clair said, "First, we had the impression we were inventing an entirely original means of expression . . . and second, we saw it as becoming a means of communication with a universal appeal—without the language barrier getting in the way. . . . One of the most telling criticisms that has been made against the talkie is that it requires a dialogue comprehensible to spectators of all intellectual levels—that's to say, let's be frank, of the simplest intellect."[35]

Marcel L'Herbier: "[In] the silent film we thought we had attained a maximum of expressive power thanks to our cameras, thanks to our understanding of the laws of the image and the laws of silence."[36] "The talkie as it is today doesn't interest me much. The faithful reproduction of the words of an actor or the arrival at the station of a locomotive has no real artistic value, any more than an exact color photograph has. For the moment, the color film and the talkie have no more than curiosity value. They will give the impression of being 'an art' the day when, far from reproducing colors and sounds 'as they are,' color, noise, and sound are used to produce stylized effects, calculated, artificial, having a specific emotive value. . . . The cinema has become—at what cost—an original independent art form. . . . It would be disastrous if it seized on a technological development to backpedal, artistically speaking. From this point of view, the recording of words will have regrettable consequences."[37]

Rather than collaborate in the "degradation" of cinema represented by realism, such filmmakers initiated a debate as to the proper usage of the new technology. If not realistic sound, motivated by or sourced in the image and modelled on the lip synch of dialogue, then what? The two most common responses were counterpoint and symphonic sound.

The contrapuntal school, drawing on montage experiments of the twenties, echoed the Russian manifesto of Alexandrov, Eisenstein, and Pudovkin in seeing the soundtrack as simply another filmic element subject to montage treatment. It might consist of many levels of sound—dialogues, noises, musics—all working with or against one another, and with or against the image track, and with or against preceding and succeeding elements of the film. Clair looked to cartoons as the sole genre where sound was being used inventively. Perhaps they might provide a lead for the other genres. And he underlined everywhere he saw it those rare uses of non-correspondence—even praising *Broadway Melody* for a few tentative uses of sound "off." "It is often more interesting to see the face of the listener than that of the speaker . . . [Such examples] indicate that in the talkie the first age is over, when it was a question simply of showing, with a puerile insistence, that the actor's mouth opened exactly at the moment when the sound was heard and that, so to speak, the technology was working well. It's the *alternate* use of the image and of the sound it produces—and not their *simultaneous* use—which creates the best effects in the sound and talkie film. It could be that this primary rule emerging from the chaos of a nascent technology will become one of the technical laws of tomorrow."[38]

Such calls for "transposition," dislocation, and counterpoint came primarily from the musical world and from the art-film directors of the twenties. To these would soon be added the voices of film scenarists, deploring the "filmed theater" of the early cinema and opening a debate about the distinctive form for the filmscript.[39]

The only French filmmaker to pursue the ideals implicit in them with any popular success was René Clair himself. His first sound films explore what can seem perverse disjunctions of sound and image. Sometimes taken as indicative of Clair's *rejection* of sound film, and analogous to the notorious toilet-flushing anecdote which Renoir loved to recount, such disjunctions can better be seen as attempts, consonant with his "musical" items and abrupt pan-punctuations, to explore the potential for an alternative *nonrealistic* sound film—a project he never renounced, as witness the astonishing *Belles-de-nuit*. Perhaps the only other extended usage of nonsynchronous techniques was in *L'Age d'or*, which was, however, unlike Clair's films, not a commercially funded production but the consequence of a typically eighteenth-century act of artistic patronage. Occasional tentative explorations of such techniques by Grémillon within a commercial context were catastrophic; Natan, who had produced Grémillon's *La Petite Lise* (1930), was so outraged by the use of an unsourced voice and a little counterpoint between sound and image tracks that he swore Grémillon would never make another film for him. Admittedly, the public had been equally disconcerted by it, and this, rather than offended aesthetic sensibilities, was probably at the origin of Natan's outrage.[40]

Grémillon, as a musician, was particularly sensitive to the potential for contrapuntal uses of sound, and to some extent he composed his films as symphonies, using a musical format to organize the découpage. He was one of those most outspoken concerning the potential for sound to be used not contrapuntally so much as in symphonic ways as an alternative to realistic narrative. Instead of motivated sound and tight causal links, he saw films, or at least segments of films, as potentially organized like symphonic movements in which, while not openly contrapuntal, the various sonorous elements interwove in the manner of musical lines of melody.

For the symphonist, speech is not important so much for its communicative potential as for its sonic contribution to a chorale-like soundtrack. This notion was repeatedly and forcefully promoted by Gance: "The spoken film and the sonorized film, in my view," he said, "are precisely the same sort of thing, since a person speaking doesn't interest me any more than a motor, a siren, etc."[41] "I exclude categorically from the cinema to come any such thing as the dialogued film, but I appeal passionately for the great visual and sonorous symphony which, thanks to synchronism, will have captured those universal sounds and movements, to offer them to our amazed eyes and ears like a magnificent, indeed divine, gift."[42] "[I have devised] for *Le Vaisseau fantôme* . . . various techniques which substitute their suggestiveness for the normal meanings of words. For example, I will show the old port at Concarneau. You'll hear a child's voice; then that voice will blend in with the sound of the boats rocked gently by the wind. And those sounds in turn will modulate into words. My boats will speak. . . . And this conversation will imperceptibly become music, and the music will suffice to convey the sense of the scene."[43] Jean Epstein put forward similar views: "Imagine, with your eyes closed, passing through a village at festival time, or Yvetot on a market day. The sound of life breaks like waves on your ears. The black and white film has achieved its real place, has fulfilled its role: to oppose, to combine very simple images according to rhythms, intersections which are meaningful. The role of the sound film seems to me likewise to be the writing of such sonorous events, their meaningful groupings, their compositions and relationships, their breaks and connections."[44] Germaine Dulac was of the same opinion: "Speech and sound in the cinema may, in the manner of an orchestration, accompany the image, but on no account may they replace it. . . . The cinema must remain cinema, that's to say harmony and rhythm of images, despite the advent of speech."[45]

Poirier, Kirsanoff, and Chomette also promoted the contrapuntal use of sound. As Kirsanoff said: "I don't wish to imply that we should banish speech, but rather that it can, in my opinion, play a role as just one constitutive element, of the same order as any other noise, as music, as sound in general, thus forming part of the new potential that sound reproduction offers us."[46] Kirsanoff's *Rapt* was an attempt to realize this potential, but it was poorly received. The notion of the film symphony generated a small number of works in early years of sound, notably Ruttman's *Melody of the World*, but only rarely did segments of French sound films recall these passionate assertions; the storm sequence in *Remorques* (Grémillon, 1939-1941) is perhaps the only extended experiment with such a technique in a commercial narrative film.

The inclusion of counterpoint and/or symphonic form in the standard fictional narrative did not prove commercially viable, and by 1935 the twenties modernist movement had to acknowledge the supremacy of realistic sound, (re)synchronized with the image track. But if the defeat was decisive, it was never total; and the equilibrium between realism and modernism reached in France after the advent of sound was not the same as that reached in America. Any history of the French classic cinema must acknowledge the recurrent surfacing of modernist tendencies such as expressionist figures, locations and lighting, surrealist juxtapositions and hallucinatory effects, and formalist experiments, as the basically ambitious and aesthetically committed personnel in key positions in the industry explored the extent to which a fundamentally realist narrative could be inflected by technical practices borrowed from more elitist art forms. This exploration of the limits of realism and of the potential for "transposition" must be taken into account in any attempt to define and account for that best-known of classic French styles, poetic realism.

THE STUDIO SYSTEM 1930-1948

The studio, established by sound as an essential condition of production, continued to dominate production methods in France long after it ceased to be essential. Studio production was the norm until the end of the war, with a constantly increasing number of stages and of new studios being built to cope with demand; but the period 1945-1950 saw a transition toward greater use of exteriors, and over the following decade a decreasing emphasis on set design in favor of "natural" locations led to a steady decline in demand for studios and a steady decrease in the number of available stages. After 1960 this decline was to become more marked than ever, such that the New Wave has tended to be associated with the renunciation of studio work in favor of the "authenticity" of natural locations; yet they in fact only capitalized on possibilities which had existed since 1933 and which had been thoroughly explored at different times during the classical period.

During the years 1929–1932 it was difficult to record sound live outside. Newsreel productions did so, but the transport of cumbrous equipment inhibited the mobility which is usually considered intrinsic to that genre, and the quality of sound was not good. In 1932, when postsynchronization became widely available, it became possible to film on location (or in the studio, of course) silent, and to add voices and/or musictrack at a later point. The quality of cinematography in exteriors improved enormously as, relieved of its encumbering padding and sound equipment, the camera recovered its mobility, its ability to reach awkward spots and film from difficult angles. But the quality of postsynchronized sound was still generally reckoned to be poor, if only because it lacked the "authenticity" of location recordings. *La Technique Cinématographique* of July/August 1934 sums up a common complaint when it says that "exteriors demand a quite specific ambiance and resonance, impossible to recreate in the hermetic situation of a sound studio."[47]

The consequent tendency toward location shooting was further encouraged by the fact that French camera design and manufacture remained a leader in the international field, surviving the transformation to sound technology and solving technical problems related to location shooting at least as rapidly as did American manufacturers. Where in America the blimped Mitchell cameras continued to be used throughout the thirties—first with ad hoc blimping, then after 1934 with a factory-designed blimp, largely because studio production was the standard and location mobility not a crucial criterion—Debrie had by 1934 developed their famous Parvo silent camera, first produced in 1908, into a Super Parvo sound camera of very modest dimensions, allowing far greater mobility.[48] The unit needed no shielding to reduce noise, so measured only 50 cm × 35 cm × 27 cm, only one-third the size of the blimped version of the Parvo. Like its predecessor, it rapidly established itself as a valuable professional tool in film production around the world, and large numbers were exported or fabricated abroad under license.

Perhaps equally interesting was the Caméréclair-Radio developed by J. Méry for the Eclair company and first marketed at about the beginning of 1933. Designed specifically as a light and relatively portable camera for location shooting, it allowed simultaneous recording of sound and image on two separate reels of film. It was small, maneuverable, and able to record sound at great distances. A 1934 technical report[49] spoke of its being able to record a conversation at 30 meters, an orator at 50 meters, and background noises at several hundred meters. It was widely used for exterior image-sound location shooting from the moment of its introduction. Of the many firms using them, Les Enregistrements Sonores Marcel Petiot did so for work on *Mireille* (Gaveau and Servaës, 1933–1934), *Primerose* (Guissart, 1933–1934), *Le Grand Jeu* (Feyder, 1933–1934), *Poliche* (Gance, 1934), *Chansons de Paris* (de Baroncelli, 1934), and some 25 other films in the first 18 months after their introduction. This included work on board the Paris-Le Havre express train and on the decks and in the engine room of the S.S. *Ile de France*, a successful experiment with the aid of a "telemicrophone" to record from the shore a dialogue being conducted on a dinghy in the middle of the Seine (for *Poliche*) and a scene requiring the simultaneous recording by a single camera-mounted microphone of a compère (at 5 meters), the public (at 12 meters), the orchestra (at 30 meters), and the chorus (at 25 meters and to one side).

In view of this, the fact that location shooting became an essential if quantitatively minor part of most thirties films should not seem surprising. Producers were able to contemplate sending the crew on location to some appropriately atmospheric region of France precisely because the equipment available to them had been designed with that in mind. Indeed, as early as 1933 several films had been shot entirely on location. Marcel Pagnol, flush with funds from the success of *Marius* and *Fanny*, bought his own Philips sound truck complete with technician and filmed *Jofroi* (1933–1934) and *Angèle* (1934) on location in Provence. While this undertaking did require a certain initiative, descriptions of it as radically innovative and foreshadowing the New Wave[50] are clearly excessive. Silent filmmakers had regularly filmed on location thus until three years previously, and the technology necessary to return to such practices was then becoming widely available. Vigo was shooting location work for *L'Atalante* (1933–1934) at that time, and Renoir's *Toni* (1934–1935) is largely filmed in natural settings.[51]

From this point onward, therefore, the studio was no longer a technologically-determined necessity, and if demand for studio-space was such that the number of stages increased over the next decade, it was because of a range of other factors. One of these was "quality." Studio production allowed control over environmental factors and over the profilmic reality to a degree that location shooting never could. Another factor was aesthetics. It was not just a professional finish that studio production could offer, but an ability to mold the representation of reality in ways not attainable on location. The poeticization of reality which was a prime aim of set designers was only possible under studio conditions. A final factor was cost. No detailed comparison between location and studio production was ever undertaken, but it was widely believed and repeated in interested circles during the whole thirty years of the classic cinema that incidental costs relating to location shooting—transport of equipment, technicians, and actors, together with insurance and weather-caused delays—significantly exceeded the cost of studio hire and set construction, especially if the criteria of quality and of poetics were of importance. Whether true or not, this myth was effective in perpetuating studio usage.

The French industry entered the sound era with two studio complexes that, with a little chauvinist enthusiasm helping, could be said to stand up to international comparison—Joinville and La Victorine; to these the Americans added St. Maurice. Over the period from 1930 to 1947, four new studio complexes were developed and several old ones extended. In 1932, M. Rampillon had the Neuilly studios built, remodelling them from a former panel-beating workshop. Equipped with Tobis sound and Debrie cameras, they were well used throughout the next 20 years, averaging seven films a year from their three stages in the postwar years, with a maximum of ten in a year. Never figuring as one of the major studios, they were nevertheless used for some of the most prestigious films of these years: *Un Carnet de bal* (Duvivier, 1937), *La Symphonie pastorale* (Delannoy, 1946), *Le Diable au corps* (Autant-Lara, 1946–1947), *Quai des orfèvres* (Clouzot, 1947), *Jeux interdits* (Clément, 1951–1952), and *Thérèse Raquin* (Carné, 1953). One disadvantage was a rather limited back lot for exteriors, of 100 m × 50 m.

In 1934 Pagnol moved from location shooting to studio production by the simple expedient of building himself a studio in the Eastern suburb of Marseilles, with RCA sound and Debrie cameras. It was not by any means fully occupied by his own productions, and he rented it to others when possible, but without quite the same insistent financial pressures as other studio proprietors experienced. In 1941, pretexting anxieties about the Germans taking it over, he leased it to Gaumont.

At almost the same time as Pagnol was building his Marseilles studios, a new studio complex was built in the heart of Paris's most prestigious 8th arrondissement, alongside the Champs-Elysées. Operative in January 1935, the François I had the advantage of being centrally located to a number of production houses, but its design was unusual because of the constraints of geography, and it had no back lot for exteriors.

The last major studio complex to be constructed in the classical period was the Boulogne studio built in 1941 but prevented by the German occupying authorities from undertaking production. Effective only from 1944, the Boulogne studio was equipped with Western Electric sound. In May 1948 two new groups of stages were brought into production on adjacent land, making a total of seven stages in three clusters.

This steady increase in studio capacity received setbacks in 1940, when a fire at Joinville knocked out most of the stages, leaving a large vacant lot for exteriors throughout most of the forties, and in 1945 at La Victorine when a fire knocked out two stages, of which only one had been rebuilt twelve years later. Again in 1944 allied bombardments of Nice and of Bordeaux definitively destroyed the small St Laurent du Var studio and temporarily destroyed the Côte d'Argent studio. The latter was reconstructed at the liberation, with Western Electric sound and Debrie cameras, but was mostly used for short film production. The Joinville destruction was partially made good in 1946–1947, when one of its stages was rebuilt. At its moment of greatest capacity, between 1948 and 1953, the industry had 67 stages at its disposal[52] and was using them to produce about 115 feature films per year. In fact, two films per year per stage came to be seen as a normal rate of production within the industry between 1930 and 1960. This is not an imposing rate of productivity. In part it can be explained by the relative idleness of the southern studios in the thirties. Those at Nice, with seven stages equipped for production, produced only 34 films or parts of films in ten years; and again in postwar years La Victorine was at best sporadically in production. The war years saw a displacement of film personnel and consequently film production from Paris to Nice, providing the southern studios with full employment for the first and only time during the thirty years of the classic cinema.

But there are two more important factors which help to explain the relatively poor productivity of the French studio system—the disjunction between ownership of the studios and production of the films, and the small and decreasing area of back lots and of construction workshops. A firm which is mass-producing films in its own studios (such as only Paramount ever did in France, and that for only 18 months) can program their usage in detail. The technicians and workers, used to coordinating with one another on a regular basis, know what to expect of one another. The same technicians and workers, faced with a range of different production companies moving through the premises or hired by a succession of different production companies at irregular intervals, to work in conjunction with different colleagues each time, can never hope to achieve the efficiencies of a routinized set of procedures. And when to this is added a lack of construction and storage space such that sets often have to be built from scratch on the stage where filming is to take place, then dismantled in situ after shooting, the stages are occupied by each set for far longer than would be the case in a better equipped and better designed studio. Moreover when, as was often the case, laboratories which are part of a different organization do the developing, and delays occur, the sets have to remain on stage until the developed film confirms that the takes are acceptable. In an American studio, such viewing of rushes would always happen on the following morning, not days or a week later. A 1937 estimate to the Renaitour commission of inquiry into the cinema put at 180–200 days per year the actual usage of studio stages, because of 40-hour-week regulations and inefficiencies of renting.[53] Each French film at that time was therefore requiring 90–100 days of stage time, usually as a result of occupying an array of two to three stages for a period of 30–45 working days. This sort of inefficiency increased production costs to a degree that alarmed the industry.

On the whole, however, once the conversion to sound had been achieved, there was a decade from 1935 to 1945 during which complaints about technological backwardness were fewer and were more moderately expressed. Incited by the Renaitour inquiry to expound on all aspects of the industry that needed government intervention, representatives of the various trades and interest groups identified the industrial structure, financial chaos, the organization of credit, taxes, and censorship as requiring immediate action (which of course, they were not to get). Little mention is made of the level of equipment, and those few references that exist tend to suggest that it was seen as tolerable at that time. German, American, and English studios are acknowledged as bigger and better equipped, but the difference is no longer seen as critical to the quality of the product.[54] An air of confidence in the technical competence of French workers and technicians surrounds these statements, and for a decade after this it is primarily financial considerations and then political considerations which are seen as hindering the French cinema from acceding to its place in the sun.

This confidence expressed itself in a renewed aspiration to found a central site of film production equivalent to Hollywood and capable of competing with American productions on their own terms. La Victorine in Nice had been originally conceived as such a center, not least because of climatic considerations; Paramount had looked for a suitable area of land there from 1923 on; in October 1931 the engineer Paulet spoke of building such a complex at La Californie; a month later the Cannes City Films concern briefly flourished. The construction of the Paramount St. Maurice studio had in 1930 been surrounded by a similar promotional discourse: in alliance with Pathé's Joinville studios less than a kilometer away, they would constitute the hub of a vast and vital film-production center.[55] But by 1935, La Victorine was largely out of production, and St. Maurice was used more for dubbing foreign imports than for producing French films. Still the dream persisted, especially in the South where production was languishing—indeed, the dream persisted there precisely because of a need to find some formula to regenerate film production in the South, to recreate the golden age of the twenties. By constructing a superb complex of studios, they hoped to retain production companies there for the whole year, instead of seeing filmmakers desert Nice as soon as the sun ceased to be the exclusive privilege of the Coast.[56]

Perhaps the most detailed and concrete set of proposals for a French Hollywood appeared in *Architecture d'Aujourd'hui*, number 4, April 1938. Alongside a set of prescriptions for the ideal studio complex, a three-page "prospectus" announced that a syndicate had bought up 45 hectares of land adjacent to the Cannes Country Club and bordering the route Napoléon, with a view to realizing on that site such an "ideal studio." Architect's plans, produced by the architect-engineer O. Bauer, accompanied the prospectus, indicating that the complex would incorporate nine stages (1 of 60 × 40 m, 4 of 45 × 25 m, and 4 of 30 × 18 m) together with elaborate dependencies, housing for an extensive community, and a luxury hotel overlooking the Country Club's land. Within this complex specific mention is made of avoiding the wastage of rental time occasioned by constructing and dismantling sets on the stage itself by focusing all set construction in a "great hall," around which the stages would be arranged in a gigantic fan shape.

The scheme had the advantage of being timely: the Gaumont and Pathé collapses had provided the government with an ideal opportunity to intervene in the industry, to nationalize the two bankrupt empires, rationalize them, and then concentrate production in a single location. This was certainly what the CGT (union) representative to the Renaitour inquiry had proposed the year before. Ultimately, the scheme came to nothing because of the war; but the concept remained alive in the film community. The course on studios written in 1944 by Yvan Noë for the Ecole Technique du Cinéma par Correspondance reproduces in some detail the same specifications for an ideal studio in an ideal location and foreshadows its imminent realization in the vicinity of Nice. "You only have to look around the Côte d'Azur and you'll find such an ideal location with ease; and it's clear that France will soon acquire this complete instrument of film production so earnestly desired by all filmmakers. It will attract to the French cinema that recognition appropriate to it from the international film community."[57]

This was again a timely moment, when such a project had a real chance of being realized as a national project within the framework of postwar reconstruction and nationalization. The unified national administrative structure of the cinema set up during the war was to be maintained, extensive elements of the industry tainted by managerial collaboration with the Nazis were to be nationalized, and there was a widespread consensus within the industry in favor of concentrating the industry's activities in order the better to compete with a renewed American "invasion." It is perhaps in this light that the Pathé-Gaumont merger of studio and laboratory facilities in early 1947 should be viewed, though industrial relations related to unionization of the workforce also played a part, as did the desire to forestall nationalization while minimizing competition. Certainly from 1947 onward the merged Pathé-Gaumont company, under the tradename of Franstudio, dominated the industrial scene, with a range of production facilities that included St. Maurice, Joinville, Marseilles, Francoeur, and Clichy, the whole serviced by a merged laboratory system known as G.T.C.

A parallel impulse to renovate and concentrate studio facilities in a single major Hollywood-type complex came from the Commission Supérieure Technique, which had been set up at the liberation to plan the reconstruction of the film industry. It rapidly produced a program that would have seen a gigantic renovation and extension of existing facilities. Known as the Plan Monnet, this project noted that, as a result of a decade of what was now seen as "stagnation," the existing facilities were aging and inadequate. To increase production to the desired level of 150 films per year from the current 80, another 45 studio stages would be needed. It programmed their introduction in three groups of 15 stages and costed out both them and the related equipment. Writing six years later, Autant-Lara, then president of the filmworkers union, noted wryly that none of the proposed facilities had been created. On the contrary, in that decade, 25 stages had been lost to the industry.[58]

THE DECLINE OF THE STUDIO 1948–1960

The turning point in the availability of plant and equipment to the industry undoubtedly lies in the years 1945–1950. The economy was performing badly in the immediate postwar years, shortages and rationings were still common, and funds were not available as might have been hoped, to realize all the ambitions. Angry protests concerning the decrepit state of the studios and the outmoded nature of the equipment with which they had to work are once again frequently voiced in these years by the filmmakers and by their representatives. Courtade quotes three industrial representatives on the subject. For Charles Chazeau, speaking on behalf of the Film Workers Union, "For 20 years nothing has been done in France to develop our technical facilities, and we are still in the age of the makeshift. Our equipment in the studios is insufficient and often outdated."[59] For Louis Daquin, speaking for the Technicians' Union, "We lack studios; equipment and material are 15 years behind those of other countries, we depend on foreign sources for color and sound, we have only one filmstock factory, and that's in the hands of the American capitalists."[60] For Claude Jaeger of the Office Professionnel du Cinéma, "The one big problem is the *lack of any real equipment available to production firms to produce films that are up to date and of a superior technical quality. Our studios are full of outmoded equipment.*"[61]

This generally accepted deterioration in quality, due in part to the war years, was not helped by the Franstudio decision to pay off its studio-based workers and maintain only a skeleton staff. From 1948 on, production companies not only had to bring in key technical and aesthetic personnel when renting studios, they had to hire for each film a basic labor force with the necessary mechanical, electrical, and carpentering skills. In the lack of permanent staffing, no ongoing maintenance of studios and equipment took place, and the facilities deteriorated to the point where various parties, admittedly not entirely disinterested, spoke of them as sordid, grubby, and outdated. The increasing sense of anxiety pervading the film workers concerning the level of equipment of the studios can be measured by the titles of some relevant articles appearing in trade and critical journals between 1953 and 1962:

"If our studios continue to be ignored . . . ," *La Technique Cinématographique* 131, April 1953.

"Equipment problems in the French cinema," *La Technique Cinématographique* 151, February 1955.

"The degradation of our studios," *Objectif* 123, 22 November 1955.

"All the studios are packing up," France Film International 10, October 1955.
"The great shame of our studios," Le Technicien du Film, number 9, September, 1955, and at least two other journals.
"Crisis in the studios," Les Lettres Françaises 711, 27 February 1958.
"Disappearance of three studios," Le Film Français 808, 27 November 1959.
"Against the disappearance of our studios," La Cinématographie Française 1907, 4 March 1961.
"Disquiet in the profession, about the disappearance of several studios," Le Film Français 873, 17 February 1961.
"The studio crisis," Les Lettres Françaises 911, 25 January 1962.
"Protest of the cinema branch of the Fédération Nationale du Spectacle against the occupation of our film studios by French television," Le Film Français 918, 5 February 1962.

The sense of crisis found its most violent expression in an interchange in 1955–1956 between Autant-Lara, then president of the Filmworkers' Union, and representatives of the Chambers of Studio Managers and of Technical Industries. Autant-Lara lists the failure of the Plan Monnet, the filthiness of the studios ("coal for last winter's heating still scattered around the floor six months later"), the age of the studios ("many date from the silent film and suffered a conversion to sound even then considered temporary"), makeshift facilities, the constant intrusion of sound and vibrations on recording, the shoddy electrification. "The state of the studios inhibits the recording both of image and of sound; the lack of maintenance has generated an omnipresent dust-haze which interferes with shooting, and sprinklers must be used to settle the dust before most takes."[62] Security was largely nonexistent, walkways were too narrow, cluttered, and overloaded, fire risk was high and had already destroyed many stages, no studios were air-conditioned (temperatures often of 55°C, and a record of 63°C), and workers' facilities were outdated or nonexistent. Until that point, studios had been excluded from the subsidized funding provided to the industry by the Loi d'aide.[63] Autant-Lara called for its extension to studios on a grand scale, such that French studios might become competitive with those of neighboring countries.

The reply from the proprietors effectively acknowledged the justice of these statements but attributed the conditions to two factors inherent in the system: studios were rented on credit, and that credit was frequently not made good. Often when a film did not make money, the producer could not pay his debts; and often the producer reneged on his rental contract and refused to compensate the studio. An attempt to challenge Autant-Lara's figures on investment in modernization turned into a farce when it was revealed that Autant-Lara had been given the figures by the studio proprietors themselves.[64]

Tactically, at least, Autant-Lara had won. In fact, the debate merely underlined the fact that the whole system was running down, that everyone in the industry was anxious about it, and that they were attempting to blame one another.

That the industry had reason to be worried is shown by the rate at which studio facilities decreased between 1948 and 1961. By the latter date there were only 55 studios left, compared to 67 in 1948. By comparison, Italy had 58, and even Germany had 50 stages, of a far larger overall surface area and with a far greater extent of exterior terrain. One very evident factor in the contraction of French facilities had been the encroachment of television on what had previously been exclusively filmmaking facilities. The first clear sign of this had been the appropriation by the RTF of the Cité Elgé at the Buttes Chaumont in 1953 with a loss of nine stages, and in subsequent years they had expanded into the Francoeur studio. Tele Luxembourg had bought the studio in the rue du Fief at Billancourt, and the François I studio had been taken over in 1955 by Europe 1 Télécompagnie. Even American television companies had encroached. In 1955 they were occupying three stages at Epinay, all the stages at Neuilly for a period of eight months, and two stages at Billancourt.[65] Worse still, the whole of the Boulogne studios had been bought for the production of advertising clips.

The sense that an era was drawing to a close and that cinema was being displaced by television as it had itself quite abruptly displaced the theater pervades the industry's pessimistic self-evaluations of this period. If not the cinema as a whole, then at least a certain cinema—the studio cinema, then seen as synonymous with the classic cinema—was drawing to an end. Subsequent years were to confirm this evaluation. From fully occupying 67 studio stages in 1948, the industry had contracted its studio use to under 30% of the remaining 15 stages in 1976. From constituting 24% of a film's costs in 1933,[66] 21% in 1956,[67] and 18% of production costs in 1959, they constituted only 1.56% in 1976.

Television was far from solely to blame. Many of the studios were built on inner-city land, or at least on inner-suburban land rapidly overtaken by the urban expansion of the fifties and sixties. Property values increased dramatically, providing an acute incentive to proprietors not to renew leases. Even where those proprietors were local or state authorities, there were insistent reasons why alternative community utilization of such attractive terrain might be desirable and electorally popular. Several studios were demolished, to be replaced by apartment buildings—François I, Clichy, Neuilly, then in 1961 as part of the la Défense development, the Photosonor studios at Courbevoie. At the same time, several others were threatened with demolition, notably the Joinville studios, which Levinsky (who had first built a studio there in 1923) still owned, and La Victorine at Nice. The threatened disappearance of this latter studio became for a year a cause célèbre in the French film world, mobilizing a wide range of supporters in its defense. The studio itself became a symbol of the classic cinema, and its threatened demolition had to be fought to the limit.

Again, a selection of titles of articles appearing in the trade papers over this period is peculiarly evocative:

"No, the studios at La Victorine will not close," *France Film International* 1, January 1959.

"La Victorine studios evicted from their site," *Cinématographie Française* 1898, 31 December 1960.

"Respite for La Victorine till the end of 1961," *Film Français* 865, 13 January 1961.

"La Victorine will continue its activities but at Colle sur Loup," *Film Français* 911, 17 November 1961.

"Has the projected move to Colle sur Loup been abandoned?" *Film Français* 980, 8 March 1963.

"Still no sign of a transfer to Colle sur Loup," *Film Français* 1030, 7 February 1964.

"La Victorine back on its feet," *Le Technicien du Film* 116, 15 May 1965.

"Important modernization at La Victorine," *Film Français* 1100, 18 June 1965.

"A completely renovated complex," *La Technique Cinématographique* 282, February 1967.

These titles resume a drama that had arisen because the Banque Nationale de Crédit, which, as a result of wartime maneuvering, owned the site, was unwilling to renew the lease, seeing the site as a valuable development prospect. A similar attempt to evict the lessee company (André Paulvé's CIMEX) in 1952 had trailed off into legal debates, but a second attempt in 1958 saw the BNC successful against CIMEX's successors (André Paulvé's SOVIC and UGC). Union meetings formulated clamorous demands, and finally the sell-off was thwarted or at least delayed when the liquidator favored the City of Nice with an option on the land. The municipality built a sportsground on some of it and gave the studios until March 1961 to find another site.

At that point the salvation scheme became enmeshed with a final attempt to develop a Riviera Hollywood. The local member deputed to study the matter noted the closeness of the Nice airport to La Victorine, the limited "back lot" and the encircling development, and recommended to the ministry of culture that a site be chosen where "a Cinema City could be built similar to those near Rome and near Madrid."[68] An appropriate terrain was bought at Colle sur Loup, in the interior between Cannes and Nice, with a view not simply to transferring La Victorine but to revitalizing the whole studio-based classic cinema in a gigantic new complex. There was talk of combining with a Swiss foundation's project for a Cité scientifique international devoted to modern audiovisual techniques for third world countries, to be subsidized by UNESCO, and with a predicted output of 300,000 educational films.[69] "Administrative complications" delayed work, and in early 1965 the City of Nice agreed to a new long-term lease for La Victorine on its existing site. Major renovations revitalized the studio, and an enlightened proprietor—a textile manufacturer with a passion for the cinema—bought it in 1975, ensuring further expansion.

It was a victory, but a misleading victory. It was neither television nor the property developer that caused the abandonment of studio production, but new technology and a new ideology: a psychological realism based on location shooting gradually displaced that tradition of quality which had come to signify artifice, authenticity, a servility to mass markets and to capital. The move to filming in "natural" interiors and exteriors was to increase throughout the fifties till it became the norm in the 1960s.

The war's end had seen a move in that direction already. The film of the liberation of Paris, shot clandestinely, was perhaps technically lacking in quality, but rather than reading this lack of quality as incompetence, the audiences read it in the best convention of the newsreel as signifying truthfulness. Clément's reconstruction of the same period, *La Bataille du rail* (1945–1946), made soon after, appealed to the same set of conventions with its extensive use of location work. This conventionalized reading of the antinomies [studio/location] as [artifice but quality/clumsiness but authenticity] was confirmed by the Italian neorealist wave of films that so impressed French filmmakers in the years 1946–1950, as they did the whole world. The destruction of Italian studios was seen as having been a source of regeneration for the industry.

In the long term, however, and indirectly, the fact that the majority of French studios were *not* destroyed was a factor contributing both to the move in France to natural locations and to a regeneration of the industry. The aging studios, several originally built before World War I, all needed to be re-equipped. The new generation of Debrie Super Parvos and Eclair Caméréflex cameras were installed in most studios by the early fifties, but then the studios found themselves faced with two further technical "revolutions"—the introduction of magnetic sound and of color. Magnetic sound offered superior quality, at least at the point of recording, and over the years 1950–1953 the industry invested about a half million francs in that conversion alone. As with sound, the economic conditions of the time led to these conversions being slower in France than elsewhere,[70] and they required a rapid return on investment to the studio proprietors. The studio proprietors conspired to obtain that return by raising studio rental prices relative to the cost of living.[71] Immediately, production companies looked to ways of reducing studio time. Already by 1953 this move to maximize location shooting was so pronounced that the trade journal *La Technique Cinématographique* published the results of a survey of the effects on studio occupancy. The extent of the inquiry indicates the intensity of the anxiety, both on the part of studio proprietors and on the part of employees and unions, concerning the trend. The proprietor of the Boulogne studio asserted that, created partly at the request of elements of the profession, who needed a tool worthy of the French film industry, these most modern of French studios had been underused to the point where costs were only just being covered. "Personally, I get the impression that the notion 'studio' is becoming more and more alien to our producers."[72] The manager of Franstudio attempted to represent the increase in location shooting as a craze, a fad that would pass.

The role of devil's advocate was taken by the director, Maurice Cloche. Listing his own experiments with location shooting since 1940, Cloche noted that they "had such an air of truth to them that I decided from then on to abandon the studio. On my return to France, I perfected this technique by shooting *Domenica* in Corsica, where all the interiors were shot between real walls, producing a distinctly more real and living effect than the fragile plaster partitions of the studio. The stone has a *presence*—a soul, you might say—which the camera can bring out and set off to the advantage of the atmosphere and of the actors, whose work becomes more 'right,' more directly human. The studio offers a solution for the lazy, readymade for those who like an easy life. . . . " And speaking of some recent filming in the Faubourg St. Antoine: "No reconstructed setting could have evoked the poignant realism of these places of misery, scorned by the sun. We recorded our sound live, with the noise of machines, of the city; in a word—of *Life*—as a backing. To sum up: a gain in veracity, in time, and in money. From now on, all my modern films with social themes will be shot between real walls."[73]

The case for studios was compiled from the responses of directors like Christian-Jacque, René Clément, Carné, and René Clair. The terms of the defense are clear:

> A good set designer will always manage . . . to create in the studio impeccable interiors "*as real as reality*. . . . " Actors, if they are convinced of the character they are playing, will act with an equal sincerity whatever the setting provided, be it natural or reconstructed. . . . The case of Carné demonstrates that it is not necessary to leave the studio to produce films of international standard. Such is also the view of René Clair, who has long shown that the quality which pays off is only obtained at a cost.
> From what has been said above it is clear that if some of our filmmakers— and not the least of them—are seduced from time to time by the escape to nature, all recognize that it's in the studio that working conditions are best.[74]

But the studios were fighting a losing battle. Location shooting was not a fad that would pass. New techniques deriving directly or indirectly from wartime developments were ensuring that the various disadvantages and difficulties experienced by those undertaking location shooting were progressively reduced and eliminated. Camera technology became more sophisticated and lighter as a result of wartime "location" battle reporting. The lightweight German Arriflex, originally developed in 1937, became part of America's war loot and was taken over by Hollywood, where its use was generalized from 1947. In 1947 Eclair developed the lightweight (6 kg) Caméflex, which like the Arriflex had a reflex system for continuous through-the-lens viewing.

In fact the design of the Caméflex was such as to render hand-held shooting much simpler and reloading almost instantaneous;[75] and, though this potential was not to be fully realized till the 1960s, it was used extensively for location shooting during the fifties. In addition, faster filmstocks were generalized throughout the industry in the early fifties with ASA speeds of 100 and 200. This decreased any residual dependence on well-lit studio sets, since it permitted filming to be carried out more readily in the prevailing light conditions of an average home or office. The move was further facilitated by the development of tungsten photoflood bulbs, which over-run (at the cost of shortening their life to a few hours) produced an even floodlighting suitable for those location interiors still out of reach of the faster filmstock. Finally, toward the end of the fifties, the development of lighter, portable tape recorders made shooting of synchronous recordings much easier. The Swiss Nagra and the French Perfectone, respectively about 6 kg and 7 kg, fed into the increasingly common practice of location shooting with lightweight cameras, such that by the end of the fifties, except for fantasy films or historical films where settings needed to be (re)constructed or special effects realized, studios had become strictly superfluous. By 1960, of the 124 French films and majority coproductions, 47 were made *entirely* without the use of studios,[76] and large sections of most of the others were likewise shot on location. From then on, with influential members of the New Wave ideologically opposed to a studio-based cinema which it persisted in viewing as industrial, literary, artificial, and irrelevant, the use of studios decreased still further.

In view of these correlations, it is scarcely possible to see, as Barry Salt does, either the New Wave or the late classic cinema's move to location shooting as primarily "an aesthetic choice."[77] Production companies were incited to look for alternatives to studio production by the degraded condition of outmoded studios in the postwar years, by union antagonism to studios following the firing of nearly all permanent staff, by the further degradation of conditions caused by lack of maintenance, by the organizational difficulties they faced in hiring a whole production crew anew for each shoot, and by the studio proprietors' united bid to raise charges steeply when they finally did begin to update certain aspects of studio equipment. This steady incitement to leave the studios coincided with the coming on stream of a succession of technological developments that facilitated the move.

Of course an aesthetic of location shooting developed as the practice itself developed, but it was not the primary motivation for the move. As technology became lighter, more powerful, yet more affordable—more within the ability of one or a few people to buy and manipulate—the possibilities of "independence" and of something closer to an aesthetic of personal self-expression were opened up—possibilities which the idealists of the New Wave were more than willing to seize upon.

THE "NEW TECHNOLOGIES"

After the conversion to sound and the move toward location shooting, the introduction of color was the third major technological transformation of conditions of film production to affect the classic cinema and its practices and debates. It too was a development that came late to the French industry, not having a significant impact on production practices until 1953, and it was always associated in discussion with another technological development—the move toward a wide-screen format. Like the technology of sound, both of these new technologies were to be controlled by foreign corporations and patents, and as in the case of sound, there is a certain irony in this, since the French film industry had had an opportunity to develop each of them at an earlier stage but had sacrificed that opportunity through a lack of corporate entrepreneurship.

Strictly, the question of wide-screen formats covers three separate technologies—the use of several cameras to produce a wider (and/or higher) than normal image, the use of filmstock wider (and/or higher) than normal, projected through a single specially designed projector, and the use of an anamorphic lens to compress a larger than normal image onto a normal-sized film, which is then opened out again on projection by attaching a similar lens to the projector. Most of these possibilities had been developed and exploited in France long before the arrival of sound, yet the commercialization of them came from America in the 1950s, sometimes using French patents.

The idea of expanding the screen size to provide a spectacle approximating a total visual environment had appeared early in the cinema's history. Grimoin-Samson, at the Paris Exhibition of 1900, demonstrated his Cinerama, in which an audience standing in the center of a cylindrical theater was surrounded by a 360° visual image created by means of ten projectors. Many variants appeared, less ambitious in scope, including Lumière's Photorama of 1903. The first use in a fictional narrative was probably that of Gance, whose 1926–1927 experiments with the triple screen in *Napoléon* are well known. He established a 1926 Three-Screen patent for the process, specifying three synchronized cameras producing a single extra-large image (Panoramic) or three counterpointed normal-sized images (Polyvision), on an enormous (15 m × 4 m) and slightly curved screen. Discussions with Debrie led to the development of appropriate technology, but Gance and Debrie failed to interest Paramount in the commercialization of the design, the American representatives apparently considering it at the time to be "utopian."[78] Consequently, despite audience enthusiasm for *Napoléon*, the system remained an exotic phenomenon, with few cinemas equipped to cope with its demands—ten cinemas in France, and one each in a scattering of overseas capitals. Partly the difficulty lay in the junctions between the images. In counterpoint this provided no difficulty, but when the three screens were unified into a single image there was always a visible line at their junction.

The identical format was reintroduced in the mid-fifties as Cinerama and Cinémiracle using three projectors electrically locked together; but again it failed to take off commercially. There was, indeed, still a problem of blurring at the junction of the three screens.[79]

The second wide-screen format, involving wider filmstock than the standard 35 mm and recording a single image in which the width is up to twice the height, was likewise explored early on. The Lumière brothers had tried out 72-mm film in their early years, and in 1928 Debrie developed a camera for recording a wider image onto 65-mm filmstock. Barry Salt refers to "various wide films [which] had been unsuccessfully tried before around 1930, some of them even using 70-mm film."[80] Whether or not they were technically adequate is unclear; French accounts suggest they were well worth pursuing but that the advent of sound technology overwhelmed all nonessential technical developments of the time. A trade journal in August 1931 announced that the wide-screen format was being abandoned, despite the fact that several cinemas were already equipped for it, "because the cost of production and of equipping cinemas is not justified by the low level of public interest."[81] No industrial development of the format occurred until it reappeared in America in 1955 as Todd-AO (first films *Oklahoma* and *Around the World in 80 Days*), then Super Panavision, MGM65, Technorama, Fox 85, Panavision, Vistavision, etc. (the latter with the images sideways on the film reel). In France these were screened in the standard 35-mm format, and it was not till *South Pacific* (1958) that the necessary projection equipment was installed. Other wide-screen formats such as those promoted in the fifties by Universal (2 × 1), Columbia (1.85 × 1), MGM (1.75 × 1) and Paramount (1.66 × 1) were actually normal 35-mm images with the top and bottom masked.[82] They therefore did not involve any new technology and required no special camera equipment, but cinemas wishing to screen them to effect would have to fit an extra wide screen. One late arrival, Warnerscope (2.55 × 1) did require a specially designed lens, patented in Germany.

The masked formats had all appeared in 1953 in response to the introduction by Twentieth Century Fox of Cinemascope, which likewise involved the use of "new" technology—an anamorphic lens which squeezed a wider image in distorted form onto an ordinary 35-mm film, then expanded it again to normal proportions on projection. This was achieved by means of a cylindrical lens placed in front of normal camera and projector lenses. It had been patented in 1928 under the name Hypergonar by Professor Henri Chrétien, who claimed to have been inspired by a viewing of Gance's *Napoléon* in 1927. It was based on principles he had developed when working on antiaircraft defense during World War I. This innovation was exploited by Autant-Lara in his *Construire un feu* (1928–1930), which was screened from December 1930 to February 1931 in the *Studio de Paris* in Montparnasse. According to Courtade it included "images extended horizontally and vertically, grouped in pairs horizontally and vertically, and even four in a cross";[83] but it was a silent film, which made it seem outmoded as soon as screened, a residue of the avant-garde experiments of the twenties. The invention seems to have encountered industrial trouble, also: other exhibitors in the suburb claimed that it constituted unfair competition, to the point where the president of their union threatened the proprietor of the *Studio de Paris* with exclusion. It is probable that the union of exhibitors, traditionally conservative at the best of times, was more worried at the possibility of having to re-equip all its cinemas with an expensive new technology at a time when it was still attempting to cope with the conversion to sound. Autant-Lara travelled to America to try to interest the research services of MGM in the invention, but they did not take it up. A lens which must have been based on similar principles, the Brachyscope, was developed by Gance and the director of photography Kruger, the former using it for *La Fin du monde* (1929); but subsequent to this the only trace of either the Brachyscope or the Hypergonar was at the 1937 Exhibition, when two short 60-mm anamorphosed films were screened.

Certainly, French commercial film production showed no further interest in the concept, and it was only when Twentieth Century Fox was looking for an innovation that might reestablish the cinema in the face of competition from television that it bought up the rights to Professor Chrétien's Hypergonar. Early productions such as *The Robe* and *How to Marry a Millionaire* were prestigious productions with stereophonic sound and color, and they exported back to France within a matter of months both the anamorphic principle and the pressure to re-equip all major cinemas for wide format films. It was another costly lesson for the French industry, and to underline it, the *Technique Cinématographique* of March 1953 sardonically reprinted its own November 1931 article promoting the process.

Thenceforth, for each film in Cinemascope which they wished to make, French production companies had to pay 2,000,000 francs to Twentieth Century Fox (three million if there was to be a second language version) for the hire of what had originally been a French development. And even this was seen as a "cut-price deal" arranged by Fox precisely because the Hypergonar had originated in France; half of the amount paid was to go to a special fund set up by Professor Chrétien for research in France into optical technology. The returns to Fox from cinema conversions were even more startling. Each cinema had to buy two lenses from Fox at a flat rate, initially of a half million francs per pair. Against this had to be weighed the very positive audience response to Cinemascope films, with its promise of rapid returns. A first demonstration in France of Cinemascope, in June of 1953, generated an enthusiastic press response. On 4 December 1953, two months after its New York première, the first Cinemascope fiction film, which had beaten all previous records despite a very high entry price, *The Robe*, was premièred together with a French documentary short (*Nouveaux Horizons*, Ichac, 1953); already in October, *La Cinématographie Française* had been able to report that "four Paris cinemas and eight provincial cinemas were equipped for it, and 23 others were equipped for the wide-screen format." As a point of comparison, by the same date, 420 cinemas had been equipped for wide screen in England, and 350 others were being equipped for it. In America some 1,000 were already equipped. The journal again notes the slow response of the French industry. This lag was to continue throughout the decade. By the end of 1958, 84.5% of American cinemas were equipped for Cinemascope, 83% of British cinemas were equipped, but only 45.4% of French cinemas—marginally better than Latin America. As always, exhibitors were caught between the significant investment needed for conversion and the fear of diminishing box office returns if they failed to do so.

The pressure to equip, however, was less in France than in America or England, since the French production system was equally slow to invest, and the rate of production was slow. Given the French public's long-standing preference for French-language films, exhibitors could rely on a built-in prejudice in favor of the local product whatever the format. The first French film in Cinemascope was *Fortune carrée* (Borderie, 1954). In 1955, 12 were produced, 5 in Cinemascope and 7 in Cinepanoramic (wide screen from masked 35-mm film)—13%, compared to 80% of Hollywood production in the same year. Use of the wide-screen format peaked in 1956 and became less and less common throughout the rest of the decade (1956, 34%; 1957, 21%; 1958, 12%; 1959, 7%). By 1959, when 7% of French productions were wide screen, 5% were Cinemascope; by comparison, 33% of Italian films were in Cinemascope.[84] The discrepancy between French and Italian film industries, so alike in many respects, is here striking. No separate figures for box offices and profits related to wide-screen formats are available, so it is not clear why this dramatic diminution of usage occurred. It does not seem to be related to the New Wave directors, if only because the diminution occurs too soon; the displacement of traditional filmmaking teams was not that marked in 1957–1958. Moreover, usage begins to *increase* again as the New Wave gets underway (15% in 1960)—perhaps due to the availability of cheaper and more compact alternatives to Cinemascope technology, such as the Dyaliscope used by Truffaut, which had first come on the market in 1955.

The cost of introducing wide-screen formats was considerably increased by the adjunction of stereophonic sound. This too was a principle, and a technology, which had been developed in France over 20 years previously but never industrialized. Again it was Gance who patented the idea in 1929, intending to use it in *Le Vaisseau fantôme*. In 1932 Gance and Debrie extended this patent under the title "Sound Projection through Multiple

Speakers," and used the principle in certain sequences of the sound version of *Napoléon Bonaparte* (1935).

> The aim is to draw the spectators into the action of the film, by creating a sound environment that enriches the film's quality. This is achieved by placing several speakers at different sites around the cinema—for instance behind the screen, on the sidewalls of the cinema, on the back wall, on the ceiling, on the floor, etc. These speakers can work either separately, in series, or simultaneously. Take the case of a plane appearing in the distance on the screen and making as if to pass over the audience. The sound of the motors, at first scarcely perceptible, will increase as the plane moves into close-up; then the speaker on the ceiling will take over from that behind the screen, and finally the speaker in the back wall will take over from that in the ceiling. The aural impression of a plane passing over the spectators will thus be achieved.[85]

The principle was used again by Gance in 1935 when he made *Un Grand Amour de Beethoven* for the screening in the Salle Pleyel.[86] It then disappeared from sight till the fifties, except for an isolated use by Disney for some screenings of *Fantasia*.

The lack of French entrepreneurial capital is partly responsible for all these failures to exploit French patents; but more centrally, it was next to impossible for any national industry to introduce a technological innovation which was going to require a world-wide restructuring of production or exhibition facilities. The export potential for even the most successful of French films was not such as to be able to generate such a change. Within France, given the lack of industry-wide corporations, no individual producer could afford to risk having returns on a film depend on the possibility that enough exhibitors would switch to the necessary new technology. Only in America, where the links between production and exhibition were still strong and where ready amortizing on the home market was a real possibility, could such a risk seem possible. It could even seem necessary, in the face of the challenge from television. In France, no such challenge existed to frighten producers and exhibitors into new technologies. Effectively, backwardness in television technology had a knock-on effect, delaying the moment when the French film industry would feel pressure to introduce such competitive technologies as wide screen, stereophony, or even color. Once the American industry had committed itself, however, the French industry saw the desirability of equipping at least enough French cinemas to screen the more successful American films; and this in turn opened the way for French production to explore the new technologies. In the case of stereophonic sound (or, more accurately, wrap-around sound) the delay in industrialization is even doubly explicable. It wasn't until magnetic sound tracks were commercialized in 1949 that multitrack recording became readily practicable. Early Cinemascope films had multiple magnetic sound-

FIGURE 3.1   **Costs of Conversion to New Technologies, per Cinema**

3D	projection room metallized screen spectacles	340–478,000 fr. 10,500 fr. per m^2 28–32 fr. each.	For 1000 seats: 850,000 fr.
Wide screen	lens and windows metallized screen metal frame	48,000–148,000 fr. 7,500–11,500 fr. per m^2 450,000–2 million fr.	870,000–2.7 million fr.
Cinemascope	two anamorphic lenses special screen metal frame	362,000 fr. 8,000 fr. per m^2 (+ customs) as above	1–2.6 million fr.
Stereophonic sound	500 seats: over 1500 seats: with cinemascope:	1.7–2.3 million fr. 2.9–4.8 million fr. add 40%	1.7–6.7 million fr.
Total			4.5–12 million fr.

Source: Figures provided by *La Cinématographie Française* 1538, 17 October 1953.

tracks on a separate synchronized reel, but already by 1954 room had been found on the image track reel for the four soundtracks, one on either side of the image track itself and another one outside each set of sprocket holes.

Once the initial drive to equip a necessary minimum of cinemas in the main centers for Cinemascope and wide screen had been achieved, French exhibitors ceased the installation of stereophonic or wrap-around sound. Most wide-screen formats using masked images ceased to use it in their commercial films, and the only brands still regularly requiring multiple speakers for screening were Cinérama, Todd-AO, and Disney. It is not hard to see why the system was slow to extend beyond this minimum of cinemas. Figure 3.1 gives the price to exhibitors of converting a single cinema to Cinemascope, or masked wide-screen formats, and to stereophonic sound, in 1953 francs.

Figure 3.1 also mentions 3D films, another technology introduced in the early fifties to play on the disadvantages of television. An even shorter period of favor was experienced by 3D than by wide screen and stereophony. The exhibitors could not know that in advance, however, and again a necessary minimum of cinemas in main centers were adapted. Aside from the costs listed, this might involve doubling the number of projectors, or else enduring a three-minute reloading period, politely called an "entr'acte," between reels. Films requiring 3D equipment began to be produced in America between 1952 and 1954, and by October 1953 11 Parisian cinemas and 36 provincial cinemas were equipped to screen them. The same issue of the *Cinématographie Française* that investigated costs of the new technology listed 32 American films shot in 3D by the end of 1953, and 28 in process, out of a total of about 200 such films made during the fifties. At that time, four had been screened in France. Perhaps the only French film made in 3D was *Soirs de Paris* (Laviron, 1953).

The technology used for achieving the 3D effect was the anaglyph method, which again had a long technical history in France. Lumière had worked on it in the years 1932–1934 and arrived at the same level of reproduction as was to be achieved in the fifties by the American productions. Indeed, a number of French patents by C. Louis (1931), Lassus, St Géniès, G. Rochard (both 1934), J. Aubert et al., E. Noaillon, G. Rizard, F. Savoye (all 1936), and J. Bastien and R. Augé (1937) dealt with the reproduction of stereoscopic images.[87] Courtade suggests that the reason no further development took place was that audience response to the short films exploiting these 3D effects in the thirties was not enthusiastic. Among critical reviews, however, Alexandre Arnoux recorded an enthusiastic appreciation of Lumière's *Riviera* (1936), speaking of it as heralding a revolution of the scale of Lumière's original films and of sound film—"an invention at once admirable and awkward," that "will subvert our practices of découpage, editing, and acting."[88] He also states that audience reaction to the screenings was most enthusiastic, "The cinema is undergoing a new transformation: we are forced to rethink once again." Arnoux was wrong: the process faded from view, perhaps condemned as it was to be 15 years later, by the special glasses that had to be worn. For once, French industry can be excused for allowing a set of experimental advances to drop from sight, since the much more concerted effort by American concerns to diffuse identical technologies some twenty years later met with a similar fate.

Perhaps partly because of the limited employment of wide screen and stereophony, very little debate took place within the trade concerning the development of an appropriate aesthetic for the "new technologies." In critical journals of the time, they fed into realist debates conducted by Arnoux and later Bazin, Rohmer, and their acolytes, but these never impinged significantly on practice until the end of the classic cinema. Nor has any study yet produced objective evidence of stylistic changes that could be credited to their usage. Barry Salt's analyses, however (of American films employing Cinemascope), suggest that the effects of wide screen were minimal and transitory on editing practice, and even on mise en scène.[89]

COLOR

The same cannot be said of color. This was, for France, the last major technological development to confront the classic cinema with aesthetic decisions central to its self-understanding. The way in which it was introduced confirms a number of the elements typical of other technological developments. First of all, it came late to France: color films had been produced in America from the late teens using two-color additive processes, and from 1928 onward the Technicolor exhibition process had provided a technology suitable to the industry's needs. From 1934 onward, when its three-color process came on the market, it proved capable of a color quality and definition that left little to be desired. In France, although two prewar color films were made, further color productions were rare even in postwar years and did not have a significant impact on the industry till 1953.

As well as being delayed in France, color film when introduced was typically based on technology which had been developed in France long before but not effectively industrialized. Again typically, as in the case of Petersen-Poulson sound, the one concerted national attempt to commercialize a distinctive color process, Rouxcolour, did not receive the corporate financial support it needed to compete, so arrived in the market too late and in a nonviable form. Finally, when color did come to the industry as part of the package of innovations in 1953–1955, it proved a relatively transitory phenomenon, and by 1959 an industrial observer could have been forgiven for thinking that like 3D, stereophony, and wide screen, it was already a thing of the past. Nevertheless, in those five years from 1953 until 1958 it had generated a degree of reflection in the industry among producers, directors, set designers, and especially, of course, directors of photography, that exceeded the aesthetic debates on any other technological topic except sound.

When color became common in the mid-fifties, it was a German color process (various Agfa derivatives) and two American processes (Technicolor, then Eastman color) that were to dominate the market; but French experimental work dated back to the early years of the century. Of course, various minor color technologies had existed in the earlier cinema. Already in 1910 Pathé had employed a workshop of 400 hands for color stencilling, and tinting and toning were as widely used in France as elsewhere. The processes of tinting and toning were doomed, however, by the introduction of sound—partly because the chemistry of tinting in its current form was incompatible with the sound reproduction cells, but more importantly, as Steve Neale has underlined, because the practices of tinting and toning belonged to a rhetoric of signification which was incompatible with the concealment of signification that developed with the introduction of direct sound recording.[90] But more complex and forward-looking technologies had also been explored, and the idea for a bipack color film was formulated by Ducos du Hauron in 1895, and subsequent development by Lumière (1905 onward), Berthon (1908 onward), Keller-Dorian (1908 onward), and others solved theoretically all the problems of color film. Most of their proposals involved two- or three-color additive processes, which split the light and filtered it through different-colored filters to obtain two or three black and white versions of each image. When projected again using similar filters, the black and white versions recombined to produce the original color. At least one patent (Dascolour), however, used a subtractive process which produced a single-color negative image instead of multiple black and white ones. The patents of Berthon and of Keller-Dorian were bought up by American and German interests, and both worked with Kodak in the late twenties.[91] In 1930 there were some nine different color processes competing for market interest, of which at least four were French—the Keller-Dorian, Berthon, Nordmann, and Hérault processes.[92] Gaumont had also been working on an additive process since 1921, and Francita was to develop a similar system to a practical level based on 1933 patents.

It was the Francita-Realita process that was to be used for the only two French color films to appear before the war—*Jeunes Filles à marier* (Vallée, 1935) and *La Terre qui meurt* (Vallée, 1936). *La Cinématographie Française*[93] reviewed the first of these favorably, concentrating on technical aspects, and it is not clear why no further work was carried out on the process. Arnoux, speaking in general of the use to which color had been put to that point, notes that a few of the better productions avoid garish or vulgar colors and reproduce with some subtlety and accuracy, but he is scornful of the banality of the narratives and the lack of imagination shown in the uses found for color (sunsets, seascapes, etc.).[94] Banality and lack of imagination are, however, scarcely adequate explanations for the failure of a new technology, and some combination of technical difficulties and lack of venture capital might be hypothesized.

Four other color processes were in use in France for short films or publicity clips in the late thirties—Ondiacolor, the Combes system, Gasparcolor, and Dufaycolor, but Salt notes that Gasparcolor could only be used for cartoons, and that Dufaycolor was technically suspect and markedly inferior to Technicolor.[95] Basically, the latter process had a technical quality which outshone all other processes, due largely to its patented gelatine-mould printing procedures, but the French were permanently reluctant to use it, right through the fifties, because of concomitant disadvantages. For a start, the beam-splitting camera distributed the light to three separate reels of film, one for each primary color, and this required special, costly, and more cumbrous technology. The projector suffered from similar problems and imposed the need for costly equipment on exhibitors. But also, Technicolor processing had to be done until the mid-fifties in Britain or America, because it required a special machine to produce the three-color prints corresponding to the three dyes used. The delays in feedback on the day's takes were therefore very long, and the term "rushes" totally inappropriate. Perhaps most difficult for the French filmmakers to accept was the "color consultant" imposed on any production company by Technicolor as a condition of using the process. Perhaps initially justified by the peculiar nature of the process, the color consultant came subsequently to stand for the prestige of a company that would not let incompetent practitioners mishandle its sophisticated product. The implication was that to see a Technicolor film was to be guaranteed a quality product. In effect, however, the filmmakers were being required to abdicate aesthetic control over the uses of color in their film. There was one correct color balance, imposed by Technicolor on all films using its patents, and any variant effect was characterized as defective. Barsacq wryly likens the tyranny of the color consultant to the tyranny of sound technicians in the early thirties, likewise charged with the task of exploiting their technology with a blind devotion to the rulebook.[96] "Color assistants intervened at all stages of the production, from découpage through to the final edit, and had right of say over the colors, the materials, the make-up, the lighting, the succession of shots and sequence. The most obvious consequence of these interventions was to banalize and homogenize all films shot in Technicolor."[97] For Claude Renoir, too, "Technicolor was monitored by consultants who didn't permit certain levels of lighting, certain colors. . . . It was channelled into norms which were faulty. My first Technicolor film was *Le Fleuve* for Jean Renoir, filmed in India. Happily, I was far away, beyond their reach, and had little experience, which allowed me to do amazing things outside the laws they had laid down for us."

In conjunction with the extra cost and the delays, this aesthetic tyranny to which they would have to defer deterred most French filmmakers from using the process. Yet in the immediate postwar years the industry was under pressure to move to color if only because "foreign" imports (i.e., American production, of which 25% was then in color) were in danger of usurping the prestige market to the exclusion of the local product. "It's an undoubted fact," proclaimed the OPC in 1946, "that before long black and white productions will seem as outmoded as, 16 years ago, silent films seemed. We must produce French films in color, as much to dominate our foreign competitors as to respond to any desire of the public in our cinemas. But we simply don't have the filmstock to make those films."[98]

At the time in France there were five firms still working on additive color processes—Gaumont, Francita, Keller-Dorian, Pincharts, and the Roux Brothers.[99] Only the last was to result in postwar commercial color production. Called Rouxcolor, it was a four-color additive process using red, yellow, blue, and green filters to produce four small black and white images. The Roux brothers had been working on it for some 15 years at the time and talked Marcel Pagnol into trying it out on *La Belle Meunière* (1948), based on the life of Schubert. The experiment was not a success. The process required two synchronized cameras (and projectors), whence problems of coordination; the smaller size of the four images inevitably reduced the clarity of the resultant combined image; and to make matters worse, defective filmstock disrupted the shooting.[100] No reports speak highly of the resultant film, and a 1949 account of the Rouxcolor process announcing its use in a documentary speaks of further industrialization which is taking place with a view to eliminating faulty technology.[101] Either the technical problems proved recalcitrant, or capital was lacking, or limitations inherent in the process deterred its backers from continuing in the face of alternatives and then coming on the market with a proven technology. Speaking in general of French attempts to commercialize color film patents, *La Cinématographie Française* was to say that "though the Keller-Dorian, Chimicolor, Rouxcolor, Dugramacolor, Gasparcolor, Mondiacolor and Thomsoncolor, etc., formulas had all proved promising, the perfecting of them had proved delicate [*sic*] and costly."[102]

Rouxcolor's main advantage over Technicolor had been the reduced cost to producers. Of course there were built-in cost increases in any color production—some indirect (a greatly increased demand on lighting) and other more direct (more attention to the color and matching of décors and costumes). But as regards the actual costs of the filmstock, a color film could be produced by the Roux Brothers' additive process for about 1% of the cost of Technicolor. The new foreign alternatives to Technicolor also exploited this weakness. All were variants of the Agfa color process, first used for 16-mm film in 1936 and developed to a greater level of sophistication during the war.

At war's end, the Agfa process became de facto war loot, turning up as Gevacolor in Belgium, Fuji in Japan, Ferrania in Italy, and Sovcolor in the USSR, not to mention the original Agfa in both East and West Germany. By 1947, a former German subsidiary of Agfa in America, Ansco, produced its own derivative. While it had problems in reproducing certain ranges of colors, this family of color films was cheaper than Technicolor if only because it could be used in normal cameras, without the cost of a color consultant, and could be developed by commonly available processing techniques. As figure 3.2 indicates, the first French film to use Agfa color stock—*Le Mariage de Ramuntcho* (Vaucorbeil)—was made in 1946, but no other was produced until 1954. Import restrictions prevented its use before that time, and only in 1953 did the accredited company (Société Stavie) get permission to import the necessary filmstock. It was the Belgian firm Gevaert which in 1949 first began a trickle of its Agfa-derived filmstock onto the French market. In 1953 they expanded production enormously, from 150,000 meters per month to 2,000,000 meters per month, partly in response to a growing demand from France. Ready availability of the cheaper film in turn encouraged French producers to shoot in color, and the 1953–1956 boom in color production was under way.

The year 1953 saw the arrival on the French market of another Agfa derivative, Ferraniacolor, hitherto unavailable because the limited production of the Italian company was not even adequate to the needs of that nation's production. Moreover, none of the color-processing firms in France were set up to develop it, and the first films shot in any of these formats would have to be processed abroad, with consequent feedback delays. There is strong evidence that lack of initiative by French laboratories inhibited the introduction of color in France. Until they installed the appropriate developing vats, production firms could scarcely risk using a given color film;

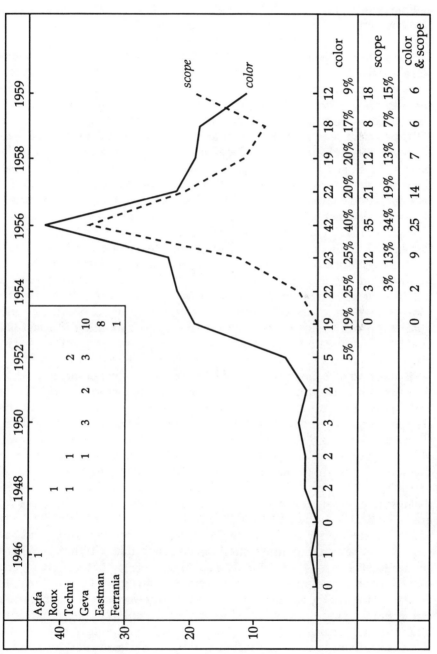

FIGURE 3.2 **Color and Widescreen Production in France**

Source: *Le Film Français* 500/501.

but they were reluctant to install them before they had strong evidence that the cost would be justified by ongoing production. The Eclair laboratories at Epinay had been prepared for Agfa color-processing in 1942, and early work on Agfa derivatives had thus been possible in France; the largest laboratory in France, G.T.C. at Joinville, had only begun equipping itself in 1950 and by 1953 could treat Geva and Eastmancolor film; but, though closely related to Geva, the Agfa and Ferrania film would have required extra equipment which G.T.C. did not feel justified in purchasing at the time. In Italy, however, Ferrania had been used for about twenty productions by 1953, winning awards for the quality of the color.[103]

A principal reason for the expansion of color production in 1953 was, however, the appearance from Kodak of Eastmancolor, an Agfa-type color process first used in America in 1951. According to Barry Salt, the color response, definition, and speed of Eastmancolor were superior to those of its Agfa-based competitors, though still inferior to Technicolor.[104] A further series of refinements in 1953 made it the natural choice of color filmstocks, and quite rapidly even Technicolor switched to using it for filming, maintaining the tradename solely to distinguish the unique and high quality gelatine-mold printing process. Demand for Eastmancolor in France was intense from 1953 onward, and the Vincennes Kodak factory produced positive stock in early 1953 and negative by the end of the year, though for some years production was limited by Kodak's inability to provide an adequate supply of negative—enough for one film per month in the last half of 1953, when the first six films to use it were put into production, beginning with Guitry's *Si Versailles m'était conté* and *Le Grand Jeu* (Siodmak).

By the end of 1953 it was possible to estimate the cost of making a color film—by any means other than Technicolor—as at most 25%, perhaps only 15%, above that of a black and white film. It was when faced with this cheaper competition that Technicolor took steps to make itself more attractive while retaining the prestige associated with its quality printing process. Hitherto Technicolor's regulations had made it necessary in effect for a production company to commit a minimum of 17 million francs payable in advance in foreign currency to use Technicolor. This had been a significant disincentive. When, for instance, Harispuru acquired the rights to the operetta *Andalousie* (Vernay 1950),[105] his first thoughts had been that it was an admirable subject for Technicolor. "But faced with the necessity to pay all costs in dollars and pounds sterling, currency that I didn't have and couldn't get, I chose Gevacolor. The advantage of that brand, which, employed by an experienced director of photography, gives excellent results, is that one pays in French currency, the laboratory work can be easily carried out in France, and delivery of exhibition copies doesn't take significantly longer than for black and white. The Technicolor laboratory requires 4–5 months."[106] Now, with the possibility of using Eastmancolor to shoot, all the early costs (special film from the US, special cameras from London, color consultant) were eliminated, and in addition the feedback did not have to depend on sending the rushes to an overworked London plant. Moreover, the cost in foreign currency was largely eliminated. *Les Révoltés de Lomanach* (Pottier, 1953–1954) was perhaps the first French film to exploit the new facility. Nevertheless, delays were still being caused by the need to have final copies printed at the Technicolor plant in Britain. In 1954, noting that production in color seemed to be expanding rapidly in France and would probably soon standardize itself, as it already had in the United States, at 75–80% of all films, Technicolor constructed a plant on vacant ground at Joinville to supplement the London facility. It was ready to begin production in January 1955.

Their calculations were faulty. Before the end of 1959 they had closed the plant because of lack of demand for its services. Figure 3.2 indicates the dramatic disaffection for color production that set in after the boom years of 1953–1956. The disaffection was not confined to Technicolor, but general to all color production. It is difficult to identify the source of that disaffection, which lasted for some ten years. (In 1965, color films exceeded 25% of production again for the first time since 1956; in 1966 they exceeded 70%, and from 1967 standardized at between 90 and 98%.)[107] Trade journals speculated that it was because of the arrival of a generation of New Wave director-producers anxious at all cost to minimize budgets. As with widescreen, it is hard to see why this would have had an effect as early as 1957, when New Wave production did not really get under way until 1959, and when large numbers of classic film productions continued behind the New Wave throughout the sixties. Nevertheless, it is true that color production had early been associated with epic and spectacular films, particularly with historical reconstructions. It was such "prestige" films, representing already a significant investment in studio rental for their set design and construction that could afford an extra investment in color if that extra was going to guarantee them the standing and thus the returns they needed. Technicolor, as the first brand on the scene, had played to this need. Moreover, under their rules, a minimum of eighty copies of any film using their process had to be printed; and later on when competing brands entered the market, a run of 100 copies or over was needed to reduce Technicolor costs at that end to roughly those of competing firms. But runs of 80–120 copies were reserved for prestige productions of a spectacular nature. Thus, among the first to use Technicolor were *Un Caprice de Caroline chérie* (Devaivre, 1952–1953) and *Lucrèce Borgia* (Christian-Jacque, 1952–1953). The same tendency can be seen in Gevacolor films: *Les Trois Mousquetaires* (Hunebelle, 1953), *La Dame aux camélias* (Bernard, 1952–1953), *Violettes impériales* (Pottier, 1952), *La belle de Cadiz* (Bernard, 1953); and in Eastmancolor: *Si Versailles m'était conté* (Guitry, 1953), *Les Révoltés de Lomanach* (Pottier 1953–1954).

In other words, color was only felt appropriate for certain subjects and certain genres—for international coproductions (18 of the first 24, primarily with Italy, where color was much more the norm than in France), historical

reconstructions, spectacles, musicals; for studio production rather than location; for the exotic, for the foreign, for fantasy, escapism, and entertainment. It came rapidly to distinguish itself from black and white films that
focused rather on the seamy side of reality, on routine, and on pessimism.
This is in line with the trade's initial impetus to define itself as different
from and superior to television: color, wide screen, and stereophonic sound
signified the same thing and were commonly used in conjunction. "Obviously, not all subjects lend themselves to color," said Pierre Robin in 1953.
"Psychological dramas, murder mysteries, intensely dramatic subjects
probably gain from being in black and white. But there are some subjects
whose very nature calls for the use of color: those in which the action takes
place in exteriors, for example, or those musical comedies that are only too
rare in our studios."[108] Thus, Harispuru, who was the most prolific producer of early French color films, reverted to black and white for the Jean
Gabin vehicle *Une chambre pour la nuit*, which became *Leur dernière nuit* (Lacombe, 1953) "because the subject wasn't appropriate for color."[109]

Pierre Autré in the *Film Français* noted the same distinction in 1955: "In
the United States and in Great Britain, as in France, there exist certain subjects particularly suited to black and white, and we might cite as examples
among recent French productions (or coproductions) Cayatte's *Le Dossier
noir*, Ralph Habib's *Les Hommes en blanc*, Alexandre Astruc's *Les Mauvaises
Rencontres*, Jean Delannoy's *Chiens perdus sans collier*, and Yves Ciampi's *Les
Héros sont fatigués*."[110]

It is not the case, therefore, that the introduction of color was a logical
or even necessary step in the steady progression of cinema from recording
images in movement, to recording sound, to recording in color, stereophony, Cinemascope, and relief—toward, that is, some idealized Bazinian
aesthetic of reality. In theory, there were numerous people who, like Bazin,
speculated that technological developments were motivated by some drive
toward an ever greater realism (Rohmer, Chartier, and Desplanques); but
in practice, on the contrary, within the profession "reality" was firmly
equated with black and white. From its beginnings in France, color was
equated with an aesthetic of antireality, of fantasy, escape, and optimism.
This opposition between the aesthetics of color and of black and white was
by no means peculiar to France. Steve Neale has described at length the
development of just such an opposition in the use of Technicolor in America
as early as the twenties, and subsequently during the boom in color film
production through the forties and early fifties.[111] Typical films for which
color was felt to be appropriate in America were *Pinocchio*, *The Thief of
Baghdad*, *Arabian Nights*, *The Bandit of Sherwood Forest*, and *The Pirate*, along
with innumerable musical comedies. But the linkage was not just generic,
with spectacle and the exotic. It involved a denial of domestic reality and
of the reportage genres, with which the black and white small screen of
television was irrevocably associated in the America of the fifties. Once
American television itself moved into color production, around 1965, color

ceased to be a distinctive feature of spectacle and the exotic. Genres such as the news, documentaries, and live broadcasts were thereafter also in color. At that point, an aesthetic of color as intensified realism could begin to take over; and this carried through to film production, where after 1965 it was primarily in the more rarefied world of the burgeoning art film genre that the black and white/color opposition continues to function as a signifier of realism/fantasy.

In France as in America, then, the return to color film production from 1960 onward can be credibly ascribed to the introduction of color TV and of the new set of realistic connotations consequently accreting around the use of color.[112] In the period 1953–1956, that is, color film was exploited to *compete with* television and to offer an escape from the domestic realities of the family living room; in the next decade it was reintroduced to *capitalize on* television's introduction into that same domestic living room of a colored representation of the everyday. The period 1957–1965 can thus be seen as an interval between two contrasting aesthetics of color, during which one had waned and the other had not yet waxed.

This hiatus was no more peculiar to France than were the two aesthetics that marked its beginning and its end. When in 1959 the French color production had bottomed out at 9%, that of Italy had retreated to 10%, that of Britain to 13%, and even that of America itself had retreated from 80% in 1955 to a low of 14%.[113] Most of these countries experienced nothing resembling the influx of new young filmmakers aiming to produce films on a small budget, which was so frequently invoked by French commentators as an explanation for the French retreat from new technologies—a fact which further invalidates that explanation. The economic factors implicit in that explanation were, on the other hand, at least partly responsible. Noting the beginnings of the retreat in the late 1956 production, the *Film Français* attributed it to the higher production cost of color.[114] Though not great, this additional cost may have been enough to deter producers in the face of the declining public market of 1958 and later; and the effect can only have begun in late 1956 and in 1957 if the actual returns on 1954 and 1955 color productions had proved unsatisfactory. While not authoritative, Barsacq's remarks about the retreat from color point in that direction: "Color costs a lot; and anyway the public got blasé and wasn't particularly attracted to color any longer; and statistics proved that there was as much likelihood of success with black and white as with color."[115] Complementing this economic hypothesis is the possibility that as television expanded it was ceasing to be purely and simply a rival medium and beginning to demonstrate the potential to become a new market for cinematic products. As starved for material as the early sound cinema, it looked to films as a logical complement to its own drama programs. As soon as acceptable mechanisms for remunerating the production companies had been developed, producers began to see a television screening as the natural sequel to a film's theatrical release. They could thus "recuperate" the spectators progressively being stolen from the cinema by television. But to exploit this potential, their products had to be compatible with the television format, or else suffer cropping and color distortion in the course of small-screen black and white transmission. Where color and wide screen (etc.) had been introduced partially as an attempt to counter the new format, as the latter expanded, color and wide screen were sacrificed for the sake of compatibility with the new format. In support of this logic is the fact that when television itself moved to color, film production moved back to color, whereas there was no concomitant return to the wide-screen format in the mid-sixties. Indeed, after 1964, production in black and white scope was to fall steadily from 20 (1963) to 15 (1964) to 8 to 1 to none after 1967; and color scope followed the same trend, from 40 in 1966 to 17 in 1967 to 7 in 1968 and 1969, after which 99% of French production was in the "normal" format, and thus compatible with television rescreenings.

As a final hypothesis concerning the odd shift in views about color production in the Western world, it is worth considering the very general sociological transformations that were taking place over this period. By the sixties, capitalism had transformed itself into a consumption-based economy which had begun to provide its citizens with a significantly greater quantity of domestic industrial goods. For the working classes, it is doubtful if the quality of life had ever before transformed itself so radically in so short a time. Information, mobility, comfort, control of one's destiny, were significantly more within each citizen's control. Reality was no longer a thing to be endured, self-denial and delayed gratification were no longer such necessary elements of mass ideology. Fantasy and escape were realizable, rather than a compensation for reality. The representation of reality as colored could more readily be accepted than in the early fifties (let alone the Depression or war years), when the residual morale of delayed gratification and of endurance was still powerful. While this hypothesis would be risky as an isolated explanation of such a fundamental media phenomenon, it might take its place beside others as a supplementary factor, rendering the shift (from color as fantasy to color as realism) that much more appropriate.

But if the earlier prestige productions of the 1953–1956 period that used color were committed in certain respects to an aesthetic of fantasy and of escape, this aesthetic had nevertheless to be married with that immovable substratum of realism which is a definitional characteristic of classic cinema. Thus any discussion of the way color was to be actually used in these prestige spectacles necessarily involved a rejection of "artifice," a rejection of extreme effects. Except in musical comedies, color must not be foregrounded or used "for its own sake," for that would be to indulge in a formalism that was not to be tolerated until the New Wave art films of the sixties. For the exponents of the fifties, true art lay in discretion, in that heightening of effects through a use of the available technologies so subtle as to remain just below the threshold of awareness of the spectators. To overstep that line would be to engage in "that barbarous abuse of 'smearing' (*barbouillage*) to which we are too often treated. . . . Color in sets must be discrete. . . . If there are still a few young Turks who advocate color at any cost, and as pure and aggressive as possible . . . nevertheless most practitioners, people of taste, opt for dove greys, . . . and only a trace of color."[116] "For the color film I realized [*sic*] that for sets, costumes, and exteriors it was necessary to avoid too great a contrast of colors. You can use all colors, but on condition they're of the same intensity. A bright red must be matched with a yellow of the same intensity, but you mustn't juxtapose somber colors and bright colors."[117] As in so many other technical areas, one of the few French color films of the time which broke, however modestly, with these practices was directed by René Clair. Still true to his modernist past, always willing to break with realism in the name of art, he earned nervous recognition from his colleagues for the structural use of color in *Les Grandes Manoeuvres* (1955). All colors were suppressed except red and gold, and all the neutral tones were treated to avoid the colorstock introducing accidental tonings. Consequently, the splashes of red and gold which occur, related primarily to the soldiers' uniforms, do serve to isolate and foreground certain objects in an aggressive manner. Tati was to use color in a similar structural manner a few years later in *Mon oncle*.

Apart from these rare instances, a delicate balancing act was everywhere maintained in which reality must be aestheticized, but not formalized. Certainly the visionary, indeed apocalyptic appeal uttered by René Barjavel in 1944 regarding the possibilities opened up by new technologies was to remain unanswered. "With peace," he had prophesied, "the reign of color will begin. . . . Like a new drug, color will invade the screens. The grey film will not be long in dying. It'll drag out a sad old age in the provincial circuits and the poorest houses of the more leprous suburbs. But finally even the kids there will reject it. . . . Colour will devastate the whole aesthetics of film, as it will the techniques of film. [Sooner or later] we'll be able to reproduce exactly all colors, whatever their intensity, and to modify and transform them at will. . . . Color will become solid, appear in blocks, in swirls, in veils, in volumes, in explosions. All the blue of the sky will condense into the eye of a maiden."[118] But already he feared the worst, recognizing and regretting the pressures toward realism which were in fact to win out: "It's to be feared that our directors will not exploit these prodigious possibilities. . . . They'll think they've done enough in dressing the star in ten different dresses and having their characters stroll through a field of tulips in the sunset. . . . They'll fall back on realism, painting the screen with pictures from calendars. Already the publicity thunders on about 'great films in natural colours.' [But] we don't need a camera to tell us the sky is blue, the field green, the dress pink. The cinema must use color less as a descriptive means than as a dramatic and poetic element."

His worst fears were to be realized. In the accounts of fifties practitioners the justification for this discretion is related not just to the essential criterion of a credible and unified diegesis, but to the centrality of characters. Fleshtones are the focus and reference point of any color system they discuss, and the "rules" formulated for set and costume design relate as much to the need to set off and not overshadow those fleshtones as they do to the fear of formalism. "More than ever now [i.e., with color] we must pay careful attention to the lighting of the face and not descend below 2,500 lux for fear of reddening the skin surface," says the director of photography, Pierre Montazel.[119] The flesh tones must not be too lurid, or too "cooked ham." "Shiny clothing is inadvisable, because of the risk of distorting the color of the face," says Barsacq; and for Robert Gys, "it is very important to dull all the color hues for Technicolor, for too bright a color provokes inevitably a set of dominants which affect . . . the faces. . . . " In discussions of French practitioners, this focus on fleshtones is less tied to the representation of femaleness than it seems to have been in American discussions;[120] it related rather to the face in general. Only the occasional reference to the expanses of flesh revealed by low necklines makes it clear that the female may implicitly be more central to the discussion than the male.

In all other respects, French discourses on the use of color in the classic cinema echo those of America, as chronicled by Neale. In terms of lighting technology, however, the French seem to have diverged slightly, preferring to retain tungsten incandescent lighting rather than the arc lighting for which the Technicolor system was designed. Arc lighting had been displaced by incandescent with the introduction of sound for a number of reasons, but not least because of the noise it made; and even when this difficulty had been overcome,[121] French studios seem not to have returned to arc lighting. The introduction of color, and more particularly Technicolor, required the use of high-intensity arc lighting of a sort not available in France. For some years, use of color automatically meant the hire of specially designed Mole Richardson straw-filtered arc lighting from England, at a cost to the budget of some 3–4 million francs. It was in these conditions that the puppet film *Alice au pays des merveilles* (Bonin and Maurette, 1948–1949), *La Taverne de la Nouvelle-Orléans* (Maurette and Marshall, 1951, United States) and *L'Homme de la Tour Eiffel* were shot at the Billancourt studios. On the instigation of the Billancourt studio director, a French company developed in the short space of six weeks an incandescent lighting system for color film (3,200° K) which could replace the arc lighting and incidentally reduce delays and costs to French producers.[122] First used on *Lucrèce Borgia* (Christian-Jacque, 1952–1953) it performed above expectations and consumed 40–50% less power. The incident is worth mentioning if only because it is one of those rare occasions on which the normal technological backwardness of French studios was made good by an exclusively French initiative. It was, however, only of short-term benefit, since once Technicolor began to accept that filming should take place with the more responsive and flexible Eastmancolor stock, the problem largely disappeared.

FOUR

PERSONNEL

"You'll be OK here, sir—Everyone in the world has two
homelands—his own, and Paris."

> Night porter, to Max Ophüls,
> in the thirties

Those that settled in Paris were essentially the worst sort
of scum, the lowest grade of con men, money-grubbing
parasites, cold-shouldered even by their fellow Jews of
any standing.

> Lucien Rebatet,
> *Les Tribus du cinéma et du théâtre*

THE CINEMA AS CULTURAL CROSSROADS

The classic French cinema served as a focus for the activities of people from
a wide range of different backgrounds and with a wide range of different
knowledges. It could do this—indeed it could not help doing it—because
by the thirties filmmaking had become a complex collaborative activity requiring a number of specialist skills. Already in the twenties, however, the
more visionary theorists of cinema had seen it as having the potential to
realize the old aesthetic dream of synthesizing and mobilizing in a single
project all the different forms of artistic activity. In the late nineteenth century, Baudelaire, Verlaine, and Mallarmé had speculated about the unity of
music and poetry, about a system of correspondences between all the
senses. The twenties saw a variety of multimedia experiments involving
such aesthetic interactions, not least in the sphere of abstract cinema, where
painterly forms and musical rhythms were mobilized in the search for a
specifically cinematic language. It was in this vein that Canudo called cinema "this sort of total synthesis, this fabulous newborn child of the Machine and of feeling. . . . We need the cinema to create the total art toward

which all the others have always tended. . . . The cinema, which subsumes these other arts, is plastic art in movement, partaking of the Immobile Arts at the same time as the Mobile . . . in Schopenhauer's terms, of the Arts of Time and the Arts of Space, or again of the Plastic Arts and the Rhythmic Arts."[1]

Cinema not only linked the static spatial arts and the narrative temporal arts, it linked the visual and the verbal arts, the performance arts and the recorded arts, the spoken and the written, the arts of the eye and the arts of the ear. It is not surprising in view of this that the cinema should have reawakened dreams of synesthesia, that it should have been seen as the ultimate integrated multisensory medium, bringing together creative artists from widely disparate fields. Moreover, it had the additional and rather improbable feature of bringing together in a common undertaking people with widely different social and cultural backgrounds: it bridged the culture gap between popular forms such as music hall and vaudeville, and high cultural forms such as classical theater and classical music. In it alone of all the arts collaborated people trained by established schools in techniques requiring years of practice, people drawing on folk culture whose only training was in copying those they admired, and people totally untrained, who had entered the film world through the humblest doors and worked their way up to positions of importance.

To take a more negative view, cinema could equally well be seen as *competing with* these various existing cultural activities and by the force of its apparently relentless success, displacing if not destroying them. The data in chapter 1 vividly evoke the inverse trends in cultural activity, as sound cinema draws audiences away from music hall, from caf'conc, and from legitimate theater. In the light of these trends, cinema was not just calling on the skills and knowledge of artists from these distinct spheres, it was calling upon them with an insistence which they were scarcely in a position to ignore. In a shrinking employment scene and depression conditions, performers from other popular cultural forms were happy to exploit the supplementary salary it provided, while those from high culture, if occasionally more disdainful of the cinema, were nonetheless pragmatic enough to recognize that they could subsidize their elitist extracinematic activities by an occasional concession to the higher salaries offered by the film world.

For several categories of work, it was clear where the sound cinema would look for its personnel. Its actors were drawn largely from legitimate theater—from the leading companies performing the classical repertoire, but also from the Boulevard theater, vaudeville, and music hall. Its authors came largely from the same arenas, but also from literature and from journalism, where they had been working either as critics or reporters. The theatrical actors and authors already knew well many of the set designers, who had long bridged the gap between the theatrical and cinematic world. Many of the designers had also done set design for opera and operetta and were known to the composers. The composers themselves were drawn primarily from the classical music scene, but some also came from light opera or the music hall world and were known for their popular songs. Certain of the directors had a musical background (Grémillon, for instance), others came from the world of set design (Autant-Lara, for instance), while still others had a fine arts training or had begun behind the camera.

All those directors, musicians, and cinematographers with a training in the beaux arts (art or architecture) or the conservatoires (actors and musicians), or the popular forms were acquainted with one another either directly through having met during their training or indirectly because the French cultural scene was and is intensely concentrated in Paris. Of all the categories of personnel, the musicians alone originated and were trained most commonly in provincial centers; but even they, once launched on a career, were almost of necessity forced to seek entry into the Parisian cultural scene. The cinema was, not accidentally, well placed to exploit this centralization of creative personnel in Paris, since some nine-tenths of its activity was also focused on Paris. The only region partially to resist this centripetal movement was the Midi, where a residual activity based on distinctive cultural and linguistic origins focused on the southern studios (notably La Victorine) and the local producers (notably Pagnol and Richebé). The thirties, however, was when this southern activity was at its lowest. Not till the war introduced a set of anomalous pressures did the South become a genuine alternative focus strong enough to attract large concentrations of personnel.

Because its principal activities were located in and around Paris, the cinema was in a position to draw at will on all the adjacent cultural activities already mentioned. That it drew on them, rather than capturing them, is due to the distinctive structure of the French industry. In the absence of a contract system, only limited categories of personnel (and those mainly of the laboring or maintenance categories rather than the so-called creative workers) could rely on any continuity of employment in the cinema. Essentially, everyone except for a few set designers permanently employed by Pathé-Gaumont was working freelance, dependent on reputation, word-of-mouth, and friendships for their next job. In these conditions it was only a few of the most reputable individuals who could afford entirely to abandon work outside the cinema.

This situation was at the origin of one of the most distinctive and beneficial features of the classic French cinema: there was a constant interchange of personnel between it and all other arenas. There was no real possibility of a specifically cinematic community of actors, directors, and technicians establishing itself in a geographic location remote from cultural centers, as in the United States, and isolated from other aspects of the nation's artistic activity. In these circumstances, a ready traffic in ideas, styles, and techniques occurred among all these media, and this precisely at a time when that aesthetic activity was at its most intense and exhilarating. Dadaism and surrealism, all forms of modernist art and architecture, realist and expressionist acting, were the common currency of the creative personnel called on by the early classic cinema: they constituted a gigantic artistic ferment of inventiveness which invested all forms of artistic activity with a certain wild unpredictability. The cinema benefited from this limitless inventiveness, and the central consequence of it was a constant tension between the pressures of a set of realist conventions originating elsewhere and the restless exploratory pressures of that central core of personnel working in the cinema—but simultaneously working in less constrained stylistic arenas.

The memoirs of those involved in this early classic cinema provide a vivid indication of this exhilarating interchange and of the chaotic cultural life from which the classic cinema emerged. Numerous studies have been devoted to the artistic activity of Paris in the twenties and early thirties, and it would be futile to attempt, even briefly, to recapitulate their account; but it may be worth giving some indication of the participation by certain filmmaking personnel in that cultural ferment. Certain key silent or transitional sound texts such as *Paris qui dort, L'Age d'or, Un chien andalou,* and *Le Sang d'un poète* constitute the tip of the artistic iceberg, pointing to a complex of (occasionally improbable) conjunctions of personnel: Dali and Buñuel and their surrealist background with Aragon, Breton and the Prévert brothers; René Clair's links to dada, to Satie, Picabia, and Tristan Tzara; Cocteau's circle, with its N.R.F. connections, which spread to the young Jean Aurenche (whose early scenarios he had published), set decorators such as Bérard and d'Eaubonne, and actors such as Jean Marais, not to mention Gide and his circle—notably his protégé, the young Marc Allégret, and Pierre Bost, for whose brother he had a platonic affection;[2] Jean Wiener, the musician friend of the Six and entrepreneur who frequently put on concerts of the recently composed works of Schoenberg, Stravinski, Prokofiev, Berg, and Webern, and who with Milhaud and Cocteau opened around 1920 the club called La Gaya, and later *Le Boeuf sur le Toit.* Regularly here one would see all the above groups, Diaghelev and Picasso, Mistinguett and Maurice Chevalier, Anna de Noailles, Raymond Radiguet of course, Auric and Fernand Léger; "Rubinstein would stop in after a concert and play us some Chopin."[3] Kosma too had come from dadaism and futurism; both he and Eisler were well acquainted with Brecht. Gaston Modot, so notable a presence in *L'Age d'or* and later thirties films, had been a painter on Montmartre with Picasso and Modigliani.

All of these groups and movements had their connections with particular journals and publishing houses; each had its ritual rendezvous in a bistro at Montparnasse or at St Germain des Prés; each had its cloud of critics—men such as Jean George Auriol, Nino Frank, Alexandre Arnoux, who could also be called on to act minor roles or walk-on parts in any film their group managed to produce. Between them, the circles, journals, and cafés acted not only as interconnecting vessels disseminating ideas, styles, and techniques, but as reservoirs of talent, like the conservatoires and private drama courses into which producers would dip as necessary, depending on the nature of the project. And the film producers themselves tied this loose agglomeration of artistic subcommunities into a financial world with which it was for the most part largely unacquainted, toward which it continued to maintain at best an ambivalent attitude, yet which was, as later events were to demonstrate, almost as chaotic an environment as the artistic community itself.

One of the more evocative ways of illustrating the complexity of this cultural life within which the cinema was enmeshed is to trace those links of career and friendship outlined in the innumerable memoirs of the period. Typical in this respect is Carlo Rim, who was to move through journalism to literary and film criticism to writing scripts or dialogues for some ninety-seven films and directing some seven films (1948–1959). Tutored at school by Marcel Pagnol, he is shown by his journal[4] having lunch with Bost and Marcel Aymé in 1926, friendly with Blaise Cendrars in 1927 and Gide in 1928; starting a review in 1927 with columns contributed by Bost, Desnos, Scize, Max Jacob, Charensol, and Man Ray; beginning the notorious magazine *Jazz* in 1928 with MacOrlan, Man Ray, Prévost, Nadar, Pagnol, and Jacob, with articles by le Corbusier and Montherlant; attending soirées of the Comtesse de Noailles with Poulenc, Léger, Malraux, Cocteau, and Moussinac; attending the filming of René Clair's *Sous les toits de Paris* in 1930 with Marcel Achard and Charensol; interviewing Sacha Guitry; attending a dinner with René Clair, Gide, and Vaillant-Couturier, or an Annales gathering where he is between Mauriac and Carco; chatting with Colette; and in 1932 visiting Arletty as she is having her picture painted naked by Kiesling "to remind me when I'm old and ugly that I didn't always look that way."

Many of these interlocking friendships started in 1923 with the formation of the "Group of Under-Thirties" begun by Marcel Achard, Henri Jeanson, Robert Desnos, and others to affirm the values of youth and irreverence and joined within the year by Carlo Rim, Bost, Fayard, Auric, Duvivier, Steve Passeur, Fresnay, Boyer, Epstein, Carette, Marcel Aymé, Salacrou, Kessel, and a dozen others. Achard's career, which included numerous scripts and the direction of three films, intersects frequently with Carlo Rim's but is closer to the theater, where it impinges on the deep friendship that linked Jouvet and Henri Jeanson. Acquainted with all the theatrical greats of the postwar, writing early for Dullin's troup (and virtually saving his theater with *Voulez-vous jouer avec Moa*); taking bit parts with Charensol, Mamy, and Scize in René Clair's *Entr'acte* (which Jeanson missed, typically, by sleeping in); writing for Jouvet and for Michel Simon, who like Dalio acts in his plays; writing bit parts for Jules Berry; friendly with Auric, who writes the music for one of his filmscripts; friendly with Rubinstein through his own pianist wife; mounting a show with Cocteau,

Pitoeff, and Michel Simon, dining with the Gallimards at their country house and with Henry Bernstein at Maxim's.

The dadaist and surrealist connections brought both into contact with Jacques Prévert, who had met Tanguy in 1920 during his military service in France, and Marcel Duhamel in Constantinople on service the next year; they set up house together from 1925 at 5 rue du Chateau, with constant visitors from that center of surrealism, Breton's house in the rue Fontaine, including Breton himself, Aurenche, Batcheff, Grimault, Benjamin, Aragon, Queneau, Max Ernst, Unik. Georges Sadoul recalls enigmatic graffiti on the walls, an altar for a black mass, a chaotic sequence of lodgers and visitors who never saw the daylight, but lived off boiled potatoes and smoked fish during the long periods without money.[5] This whole community seems to have idled its days away in Les Deux Magots, living off journalistic articles and bit parts in the cinema, but mainly Marcel Duhamel's job as director of the Ambassador Hotel. "Nous nous laissions vivre," as Prévert said of the life there. Georges Sadoul took over the house when, exiled from the surrealist circle, they moved on to the rue Dauphine to set up a rival artistic focus in St. Germain des Prés. Le Chanois recalls life there in the following terms: "The various rooms were always more or less rented out to members of the team. . . . Almost every evening we did a little number. . . . Depending on how in form we were, the sketch would last for one hour or two—an hour of crazy harangues, word play, witty dialogue, bringing out all the poetic genius of Jacques Prévert."[6] This was the period of the first series of the *Revue du Cinema*, which served as the focus for their writing. Its editor, Auriol, passed through the rue Dauphine, as did all the crew, together with Bataille, Leiris, Ribemont-Dessaignes, and many others.

Finally, as well as uniting these various artistic communities with one another and with the world of finance, cinema went some way toward uniting them all with the world of science and the world of tradesmen. Numerous cinematographers had backgrounds in optics or in chemistry and had come to photography through laboratory work; numerous set decorators had begun as handymen, nailing together or painting the theatrical flats in the days before three-dimensional sets became the norm. Many of the costume designers and makeup artists had begun in such trades outside the cinema, gradually moving across as demand for their services increased. One of the most startling things about the early classical cinema is the demotic nature of its personnel, drawing together skills and knowledges that had never before been juxtaposed; and this miscellany of backgrounds momentarily made the cinema at once one of the most democratic artistic arenas, where people of relatively humble background could find themselves in demand for highly paid jobs, and one of the most tense arenas, where people of radically different backgrounds had to struggle to work alongside others who didn't understand or even necessarily respect their talents but nevertheless depended on them.

THE LACK OF INSTITUTIONALIZED TRAINING

In the fluid and unregulated circumstances outlined so far it must be apparent that, insofar as the various key members of the filmmaking team received any preparation for a cinematic career, it was haphazard and extremely informal. A training establishment existed for cinematographers, and its courses were held in high regard within the profession, but no other category of personnel was catered to at all reliably. Such training as they received was either formal preparation for an artistic career outside but related to the cinema (as painter, architect, musician, or actor), informal training as novelist or playwright (which might equip them for the role of scriptwriter), a journalistic background as critic, reporter, or press photographer (which incidentally provided usable skills for the jobs of scriptwriter or cinematographer), or a tradesman's job as carpenter, electrician, or laboratory technician (that might permit backdoor entry to the job of set designer). Many were totally untrained, such as film actresses who had been models, had won beauty contests, or had answered newspaper advertisements. The few women other than actresses who managed to gain entry to the early classic cinema did so largely without qualifications, accepting those tasks with the least status, such as editor or scriptgirl.

Most actors had trained for the classic theater rather than for the cinema, and the official establishment for providing their training was the Conservatoire National d'Art Dramatique. Entry to it was by competition, and the number accepted was small—15 per year in the thirties, perhaps 25 after the war. Aside from individual and group classes, it provided classes in theater history, in diction, and in fencing. After two years a selection process resulted in a contract with the Comédie Française for the elect. Others had a good chance with one of the less regarded companies. The teaching was undertaken by a permanent staff of five appointed by the minister, usually from the Comédie Française (but exceptionally, as with Jouvet in the thirties, from another theatrical company). The initial selection process was more safely faced if the candidate had already acquired a certain theatrical baggage, and to this effect the Centre d'Apprentissage Dramatique in the rue Blanche provided a preparation for about 20 drama students each year (the best of which would go on to the Conservatoire) and 15 technicians. The work was primarily in the classical authors and might last from one to three years. In addition, the provincial Conservatoires or Ecoles Nationales provided training for another 130 or so students a year.

Most of the leading theatrical actors who worked in the cinema had come through this system—Pierre Fresnay, Marcelle Derrien, Jacques Charrier, Edwige Feuillère, Pierre Blanchar, Orane Demazis, Fernand Ledoux, Pierre Renoir, Madeleine Renaud. Once in such an institution, courses were free but were full-time, not allowing for the students to support themselves by outside work. For this reason (or because like Carette they had failed the entry requirements for the Conservatoire), a large number of aspirant actors took private drama courses (cours d'art dramatique). Before 1940, there were about six of these; immediately after the war there were an estimated twenty; estimates in the late fifties vary from twenty to fifty in Paris; many more existed in provincial cities, not counting the established actors who gave private classes outside any institutional framework.[7] One estimate puts at 250 the number of courses of one sort or another which were available in 1958 in Paris alone.[8]

The overwhelming proportion of them provided (or claimed to provide) a preparation exclusively in theatrical acting practices, ignoring the cinematic aspects of the profession. Certain of them, daringly, had a camera sitting in the room through which students could examine the framing of a given performance, but the number that took the cinema seriously was extremely small. On the whole, both the theatrical and the cinematic establishments were extremely critical of these private drama courses, counselling aspirant actors emphatically against joining them.

Nevertheless, certain of them were recognized as being useful pools of talent for filmmakers seeking to complete a cast. The oldest of the existing courses, begun in 1918, were run respectively by Mme Bauer-Thérond (Anouk Aimé went through this school, as did Michel Piccoli and Jacques Dumesnil); and by Mme Mercédès Brare. The Ecole Charles Dullin, founded by Dullin in 1921, was the seedbed of a lot of theatrical and thence cinematic talent (Jean-Louis Barrault, Jean Vilar, Raymond Rouleau, Madeleine Robinson, Jean Marais, Marcel Marceau, Vadim, etc.). But during the thirties and particularly the forties, it was the Cours René Simon that was most prestigious. Simon himself was by all accounts a most charismatic teacher. He had himself come through the Bauer-Thérond course and the Conservatoire and had been a successful actor in the Comédie Française and with Pagnol before concentrating more exclusively on teaching. His students included an astonishing percentage of the leading ladies of the period 1935–1955: Edwige Feuillère, Micheline Presle, Madeleine Ozeray, Marie Déa, Nicole Courcel, Cécile Aubry, Josette Day, Nathalie Nattier, Jacqueline Laurent, Marcelle Derrien, Maria Casarès, and Michèle Morgan, as well as Louis Jourdan, Jean-Pierre Aumont, François Périer, Daniel Gélin, and many others. He was appreciated by his students not so much for the inspirational teaching as for the good relations he maintained with both theatrical and cinematic directors. His class was always the first port of call when a casting problem arose.

When one adds to the 120 or more students undergoing at any one time a Conservatoire training, the enormous numbers of students in these private courses—230–250 in the Bauer-Thérond, 30–40 in the Henry Bosc (including Annie Girardot), 50 in the Escande Dussane (Serge Reggiani, Michel Bouquet, Jacques Charon, Robert Hirsch), 40–50 in the Raymond Girard (Belmondo), 30–40 in the Mercédès Brare, 40 in the Ecole Artistique du Cinéma (Maurice Ronet), 50 at Solange Sicard (Juliette Greco, Raymond Bussières, Suzanne Flon), 60 with Françoise Rosay, 50 with the Institut Moderne, 20 or so with the Centre d'Education par le jeu dramatique, begun by Barrault, Vilar, Mme Dasté, and others and later to become the Barrault/Renaud school, and the unspecified numbers with private teachers such as Tania Balachova (Danièle Delorme), Raymond Gérôme, Robert Manuel (Martine Carol) and Julia Bertheau (Madeleine Sologne)—there can have been in the fifties no fewer than 3,000 in training at any one time in Paris alone; and perhaps as many again in the provinces.

Among these aspirant actors, a certain number proceeded directly to the cinema without any practical theatrical work; this number increased as the number of private courses itself increased in the postwar period and as the amount of theatrical work available for the graduates steadily decreased. Relatively few of these actors who proceeded directly to the cinema rose to the leading roles. Michèle Morgan and Danielle Darrieux are perhaps alone in this. Most moved directly into the classical theater, making occasional forays into cinematic acting when the opportunity offered.

The theater had been particularly vital in France since 1887, when Antoine founded the Théâtre Libre, and for the following fifty years there was to be a flux of forming and reforming theatrical companies in relations of alliance or of rivalry. A number of figures emerged as dominant animators of this theatrical world, influential in forming a large proportion of the actors of the classic cinema. Antoine himself, after directing the Théâtre Libre from 1887 for twenty years, took over the Odéon in 1906. Among film actors to have acted in his productions, we might list Jules Berry, Pierre Blanchar, and Victor Francen, who joined him at the Odéon before World War I. Gémier took over from Antoine at the Odéon, and several of his troupe were to work extensively in cinema—Charpin, Annie Ducaux, and especially Pierre Richard-Willm. Antoine's real inheritor, however, was Gaston Baty, in the théâtre de Montparnasse. Inclined like Antoine to treat actors as rather recalcitrant elements of the mise en scène, he was against the notion of star roles; nevertheless some of his troupe formed a recurrent set of second-role faces—Roger Legris, Georges Vitray, Lucien Nat, Lucas Gridoux. In opposition to the Odéon and the Théâtre Libre in the prewar years (1913–1914) Copeau founded the Vieux Colombier. During the war he took over the Garrick in New York, revitalizing it, and returned to the Vieux Colombier from 1920 to 1924. From 1924 this was taken over by his nephew, Michel St.-Denis, as the Copiaux and then the Compagnie des Quinze; Jean Dasté, Copeau's son-in-law, who was to appear memorably in Vigo's films, was in this company, as was Pierre Fresnay. So also was Marcel Herrand, before founding the Rideau de Paris, later the Théâtre des Mathurins, with Jean Marchat in 1929. Both were to become leading actors in the cinema—Marchat not noticeably until 1941 with *Remorques*, Herrand frequently, though he is best remembered as Renaud in *Les Visiteurs du soir* and as Lacenaire in *Les Enfants du paradis*. In their troupe was Maria

Casarès, who was to make a name in cinema with *Les Enfants du paradis, Les Dames du Bois de Boulogne,* and *Orphée.*

In 1922, Charles Dullin, after having worked with Antoine at the Odéon and Copeau at the Vieux Colombier, founded his own troupe at L'Atelier. Always regardless of finances, he finally went bankrupt (twice, 1941 and 1947); but his passion for the theater and for acting as a profession had infected among others Orane Demazis, later to marry Pagnol and appear in his films, and Jean-Louis Barrault, who had also worked with Copeau and whose readily recognizable face recurs in the French classic cinema from 1935 onward (*Jenny, Drôle de drame, Les Enfants du paradis, La Ronde,* etc.). With Madeleine Renaud, whom he married in 1940, and who had herself come through the Conservatoire and the Comédie Française, he founded in 1946 the Compagnie Barrault-Renaud, which was to dominate postwar theatrical productions.

The other figure of note in the twenties is Louis Jouvet. Engaged by Copeau in 1913 at the Vieux Colombier, where he acted with Valentine Tessier (who was to appear in films directed by Renoir, Gance, Duvivier, Decoin, Cayatte, and Delannoy, among others), instrumental with Copeau in reviving the Garrick in New York, Jouvet founded his own company at the Théâtre des Champs Elysées in 1922, later taking over the Athénée. His troupe included Valentine Tessier, Michel Simon, Pierre Renoir, Jean-Pierre Aumont, Robert Le Vigan, and Odette Joyeux. These actors appear and reappear in film after film of the thirties and forties, while Jouvet himself was to appear in a limited number, notably in *Drôle de drame, Hôtel du Nord,* and in those two thirties homages to the acting life, *Entrée des artistes* and *La Fin du jour.*

This brief summary of several of the principal companies scarcely does justice to the shifting networks of influence and friendship which took various of these actors in and out of the companies, in and out of the Comédie Française. It omits the Pitoëffs, whose productions of Russian and French plays from 1913 on were such a powerful influence on French theatrical life, and who shared the Théâtre des Champs Elysées with Jouvet, founding the "Cartel" with him, Baty, and Dullin in 1927 in an attempt to put their various marginally viable companies on a sounder footing. It also omits the powerful Boulevard troupes—Guitry, with his succession of wives and attendant troupe (Pauline Carton, Marguerite Moreno, Robert Seller); Verneuil (Elvire Popesco, Gaby Morlay, Victor Boucher, André Lefaur); Yves Mirande (Jules Berry, Lucien Baroux, Marcel Vallée). If it omits a lot, however, this account does give some indication of the limitless and complex influence on the French classic cinema of these dynamic theatrical troupes of the period 1900–1930. With the decline of theater receipts, there was a tendency for the relatively fixed array of troupes to dissolve. By 1935 fixed troupes had already disappeared from all Parisian theaters except those of the Cartel; in particular the fixed troupes of the Boulevard theaters no longer existed and the provincial theaters were also failing.

In its heyday, however, the boulevard, music hall, vaudeville, and the caf'conc circuit provided a vital source of talent for the classic French cinema. To mention only those who were to establish themselves firmly in the cinema, Maurice Chevalier, who already with a large following in operetta and revues, after a few nondescript silent roles, was an enormous hit in early American sound cinema before moving back to France in 1936; Raimu had been in caf'conc and revue since the turn of the century, several times with Chevalier, but only came to the cinema in 1931; Georges Milton had worked in music hall and cabaret with Chevalier and was introduced by him to operetta, taking his fans with him to the cinema in 1931–1932 with the Bouboule series; Gabin, whose parents were in music hall and operetta, joined Mistinguett at the Folies Bergères from 1928 to 1930, at which time he got a contract with Pathé; Florelle inherited a caf'conc at Montmartre and was in revues at the Moulin Rouge and with Gabin at the Folies Bergères before singing the Weill songs in *L'Opéra de 4 sous* with Albert Préjean; Henri Garat was in Mistinguett's troupe at the Casino, taking over from Chevalier and making several of the early sound musicals (*Le Chemin du paradis* and *Le Congrès s'amuse*); Yvonne Printemps (Guitry's second wife and later Fresnay's third) was in the Folies Bergères with Chevalier and became one of the diva of the operetta world before moving into cinema in 1934; Gaby Morlay came from the Bouffes Parisiennes where she performed with Guitry; Fernandel's diverse early career included music hall and revues, before being recommended to Marc Allégret by Guitry and starting in cinema in 1930; Viviane Romance was in music hall and was a chorus girl at the Moulin Rouge before moving into bit parts in cinema and leads from 1936; Marie Déa came from the Pigalle, Noël-Noël and Ginette Leclere from music hall. Some of the greatest names in music hall tried their hands at cinema over the same period, though not always with success— Mistinguett herself, who had been an important actress for SCAGL and Pathé in the early 1910s and who made one sound film, *Rigolboche* (Christian Jacque, 1936); Josephine Baker, who starred in an amazing film called *Zouzou* (M. Allégret, 1934); Fréhel, who appeared in 17 films including the unforgettable song in *Pépé le Moko*; Edith Piaf, who appeared in seven (rather nondescript) films between 1936 and 1959; and in the next two decades the generation of Tino Rossi, Trénet, Mouloudji, Luis Mariano, Bourvil, Juliette Greco, and Yves Montand. Even Eddy Constantine came from music hall: in France from 1949 he performed with Edith Piaf before moving into cinema and making some fifty films.[9]

As well as for its actors, the classic cinema drew on these theatrical and musical spectacles for its composers. Jaubert had composed the music for Barca's *Magicien prodigieux* (1925) before coming to the cinema and produced music for six theatrical performances in all as well as two tableaus for *Liberté*. Eisler likewise had composed the music for Brecht's plays. Kosma was to produce the music for *Les Mouches, Huis clos*, and *Orvet*. Maurice Yvain, after leaving the Conservatoire and before turning to the cinema, had composed a series of elegant operettas, as had van Parys, who was thoroughly acquainted with the lyric theater of the *belle époque* and had, by 1949, composed some six operettas himself. Vincent Scotto was one of the mainstays of the Marseilles operetta. Jaubert was to conduct a season of *opérette-bouffe* in 1937. If none seem to have aspired to grand opera, Kosma had been assistant conductor for the Budapest Opera before leaving Hungary, and all would have been well versed in its conventions.

So, of course, were the directors, particularly Grémillon, Renoir, and René Clair. Renoir always dreamed of producing a cinematic opera and nearly did so literally in the case of *Tosca*. At least retrospectively he saw the operatic potential of *Le Crime de Monsieur Lange*, speaking in terms of "the song of the print-workers, the song of the washerwomen, the grand aria of the concierge amidst the rubbish bins . . . "

Most French film composers had had classical training, which was overwhelmingly avant-garde in its orientation. Jean Wiener, for instance, was a friend of Darius Milhaud from childhood.[10] They studied with Ibert and Honegger at the Conservatoire. Auric mentions meeting them there in 1913–1914, during his own time at the Conservatoire. Wiener's entrepreneurship was evident in putting on concerts of the recently composed works of Schoenberg, Stravinski, Prokofiev, Berg, and Webern (not to mention his own and those of his friends), and those concerts were regularly reviewed by Auric and Roland Manuel in the course of their critical activity. Wiener, who had been to the Conservatoires of Paris and of Liège and was to become professor at the Conservatoire of Paris in 1949, speaks of the long hours he spent discussing film music as a medium with his friends Roland Manuel and Maurice Jaubert. He met Maurice Yvain (who had also had a classical musical training, at the Paris Conservatoire) in the late 1920s, playing the piano in the silent cinema. Jaubert also attended the Conservatoire, but at Nice, and after doing a law degree returned to composing in the twenties. His first work was favorably reviewed by Roland Manuel; other reviews by Honegger and Auric followed.

Not only is there a continuity of training and personal friendship among those members of The Six who composed for film and those more marginal to contemporary "pure" music, but there was continuity between them and the previous generation of contemporary composers: Wiener met them through his entrepreneurial work, but Fauré was already a friend of the family; Roland Manuel was a friend and collaborator of Stravinsky, de Falla, and Satie; Ravel was best man for Maurice Jaubert; Auric had written an article on Satie at the age of 14, by which Satie had been sufficiently impressed for him to seek out the boy, thereafter becoming a weekly dinner guest at the Aurics. Later Auric and Poulenc played two of the four pianos at the première of Stravinsky's *Les Noces*. These film musicians were trained in and saw themselves as still participating in and perpetuating through their work in the cinema the high cultural tradition of French music.

If Kosma came from a different national musical culture, it was nevertheless an avant-garde twelve-tone training that he had had in Hungary.[11] Going to Berlin on a scholarship in the early thirties, he met Hanns Eisler, who had studied under Schoenberg at the Vienna Conservatorium. He left Berlin at the same time as Eisler, on Hitler's accession to power.[12]

The only exceptions to that heady cultural training are van Parys, who, though in other respects fitting the mould, later became oriented rather toward operetta, the lyric theater, and the belle époque;[13] and Vincent Scotto, who alone of these film musicians had no formal training. Well known to most of them and even more prolific, he nevertheless could not write music and thus could not write down the thousands of songs he composed, depending on neighbors or friends to transcribe them as he played.

For the most part, however, the musicians moved in the same intellectual and artistic circles as the directors, or even "higher." A chain of friendship linked the musicians not only one to another but to directors such as Renoir, whom Jaubert had known since their childhood in Provence, and Allégret, whom Wiener had known since his days as a nightclub proprietor, and to the scriptwriters, who like Prévert were often men of letters issued from dadaism and surrealism. Jaubert's first film was for his friend Renoir, Kosma's for his friends Renoir and Prévert; Thiriet was introduced into the milieu by his friend Jaubert; Roland Manuel's first film was for his friend Grémillon; van Parys was introduced to René Clair and thus to film music by a mutual friend.

Among the directors themselves, few had foreseen a career in the cinema. Certain of them had artistic backgrounds that are well known and which contributed from an early age to orienting them toward an ambitious artistic career. Renoir was the son of the painter; Autant-Lara had a well-known architect as father and the famous actress Mme Lara as mother. He made the acquaintance of L'Herbier and René Clair when those young poets published poems dedicated to his mother. Sacha Guitry was the son of a famous playwright father, Lucien Guitry. Raymond Bernard was the son of the famous playwright, Tristan Bernard, and mixed with theatrical celebrities like Sarah Bernhardt from childhood. Others were from the wealthy commercial and industrial middle class, such as Feyder, whose parents were of the Belgian grande bourgeoisie and well-known patrons of the arts, or Jacques Becker, whose family were rich industrialists. Ophüls was from the Jewish bourgeoisie, Malle and L'Herbier both came from wealthy middle-class families, Le Chanois's family was in medicine, and Jacqueline Audry was from the family of the French president Gaston Doumergue. Many were clearly from the intelligentsia of the nation, involved in literature, press, and publishing: Carlo-Rim's father was a press magnate, Pagnol's family were teachers, Clouzot's family were in the book trade as printers and publishers.

It was natural for such families to educate their sons well. An overwhelming percentage of the directors had fine arts or university training, usually with a view to entering one of the better-paid professions. Becker studied engineering, Chenal studied science, Lacombe was an agronomics engineer, Ciampi studied medicine, Verneuil studied engineering at the Arts et Métiers. A very large number studied law or arts/law: Astruc (law and engineering), both Marc and Yves Allégret (law and political science, arts/law), Cayatte (arts/law), Cavalcanti (law and architecture, in Switzerland), Clouzot (law and political science), Louis Daquin (law and economics), Lampin and Moguy (both studied law in Russia), Joannon (law), Le Chanois (law and philosophy, then psychiatry), L'Herbier (arts/law). Many of the others either took a straight arts degree—Delannoy, Malle (political science), Ophüls, Vadim (political science), Claude Vermorel (who became a lecturer in literature), and of course Jean Vigo, forced to leave university because of his tuberculosis. But a great number had had artistic aspirations from early on and had attended either the Beaux Arts or the Arts Décoratifs courses (sometimes both) with a view to realizing those aspirations— Autant-Lara, Borderie, Bresson, Devaivre, Carlo-Rim, with an orientation toward painting and design, Christian-Jacque and René Clément with an architectural orientation. Grémillon studied music at the Schola Cantorum Vincent d'Indy, came to film as violinist in a film orchestra, and was accustomed to writing out his découpage technique in the form of an orchestral score; Ophuls studied music and annotated his découpage with musical tempi, indicating the equivalent of slow movements, scherzi, and allegri; Raymond Rouleau studied music and painting; and Clouzot, who took up painting as a hobby, was encouraged to specialize in it by his friends Picasso and Braque. The Beckers were close acquaintances with the Renoirs and with Cézanne, and Becker had both painting and musical training in the Schola Cantorum but was seduced from classical piano to jazz, playing with a jazz orchestra (as did Christian-Jacque).

The Beaux Arts and Arts Décoratifs backgrounds of these directors made for ready understanding with those set decorators who came from Eastern Europe. These had nearly all trained as painters and had become interested in the ways in which that training could be applied to ballet, to opera, to theater, and to cinema—in short could become dynamic and spectacular. Those who were of the appropriate age on arrival in Paris, such as Wahkevitch and Barsacq, undertook the same sort of training in the Paris of the twenties, either at the Ecole Nationale Supérieure des Beaux Arts, the Ecole Nationale Supérieure des Arts Décoratifs, or the Ecole Boulle. They saw the cinema as a form of architecturalized painting and established the practice of producing preparatory wash or watercolor sketches of projected sets. It is clear that it was these Russians working for Albatros Films who first made French set design an ambitious and rigorous aesthetic undertaking. Their projects were uniformly grandiose, extravagant, elaborate.

A distinctive French "school" had already existed in the early years of the century, with groups in the Pathé, Gaumont, Eclair, and Montreuil studios. Of those who were to influence the classic cinema, Hugues Laurent joined Pathé as assistant in 1904, before moving to Eclair, then Tobis in

1929–1930 and Eclair again until the war; Robert-Jules Garnier took over at Gaumont in 1906 and was chief decorator there till 1938, and Perrier also worked there from 1906; Colombier worked as assistant at Pathé, later becoming with Guy de Gastyne chief decorator for that firm; Douy worked as assistant to Colombier and to Perrier; Aguettand likewise worked as assistant at Pathé-Natan, before taking over there from 1941 to 1948; and Krauss worked there as assistant to him and to Colombier. At Gaumont, Renoux worked under Garnier and Perrier and then at the Paramount St. Maurice studios. Jean André, who was to be prominent in the fifties, worked as assistant to Douy. Gys and Wahkevitch were the two set designers working on yearly contracts for Lauer, who held the set design contract for the Billancourt studio. At the Eclair studios, Pierre Linzbach and Trauner were on yearly contracts along with Meerson. D'Eaubonne worked as set painter at Epinay, before becoming assistant decorator to Perrier at Gaumont and finally chief decorator at the Haïk studio.

The qualifications of these French decorators had not always been as intensely artistic as those of the Russian school, nor had they been so specifically painterly. Several had trained and sometimes practiced as architects rather than painters, but many had done neither, beginning as carpenters or painters in theatrical set construction. Most had been trained in one of the numerous workshops around Paris that specialized in providing sets for the Paris theaters—Rubé et Moisson, Chaperon, Carpezat, Amable, Butel et Valton, Bailly, etc. These workshops would execute the cunning perspectives and trompe l'oeils for which there was a constant demand in the theater, and until the early twenties the provision of similar perspectives and trompe l'oeils in the cinemas was a natural extension of their work. Workshop friendships tended to carry over into studio recruitment policy.[14] Fabrège, from the Butel et Valton workshop, was an early employee of Pathé, and when he needed help he called in others from that workshop—Vasseur, Colas, Dumesnil. Charmois, from the Moisson workshop, was the initial organizer of Gaumont set construction. When Garnier and Perrier took over, they brought in a series of painter-decorators from the Bailly workshop. When the Laffite brothers inaugurated the Film d'Art, they called not only on actors from the Comédie Française, but on one of its set designers, Emile Bertin.

Aguettand had worked for Copeau and Jouvet in the Vieux Colombier and Théâtre des Champs Elysées; d'Eaubonne's first contact with filmmaking was as a simple set-painter; Perrier too seems simply to have worked in the theater, and Renoux had no recorded qualifications. Of those with beaux arts training, several came to the theater and cinema through publicity work, such as poster design (d'Eaubonne, Bertrand).

The relatively "deprived" cultural background of French set decorators by comparison with immigrant practitioners was echoed in the field of cinematography. Early French cinematographers had been expected to bring to their job a baggage of technical, optical, and chemical knowledge, and their background was more often scientific, technical, or industrial than artistic. Burel himself (who was to film some 113 films, of which 67 were in the period 1930–1960) emerged from the Eclair darkroom to take over the camera; Le Febvre (101/100)* had been a chemist for Kodak; Julliard (44/43) had worked as a lab technician; Thomas (38 films, all between 1930 and 1960) as an electrotechnician; and Bachelet moved from being cameraman to working in a lab, then managing it while filming part-time, until finally becoming full-time cinematographer. The detailed instruction in optics, chemistry, and other scientific fields contained in the early courses for cinematographers makes such moves readily comprehensible.

But equally, it was possible for people to move fluidly between radically different categories of work within the film industry when the opportunity arose or when the industrial need became urgent. Lucien (39 films) had been a producer before taking over the camera, Montazet (39/38) had been a projectionist, as had Raulet; and Kruger had been a projectionist for a travelling circus. Camera and projector were of course initially the same instrument, and rudimentary mechanical knowledge was a minimum requirement for a cinematographer. Fossard (79/64) had worked in Pathé's property department, as had Franchi (33/32); and both Weiss (33/16) and Périnal (Clair's cameraman of the early thirties) had worked in unspecific menial jobs before taking over the camera. The myth of cinema was sufficiently strong to incite young men such as these to take on any job to get a foot in the door, as a route to one of the more magical activities. Many of them, such as Bachelet and Alekan, reminiscing in later years about their start in film, talk simply of "haunting the studios" and plaguing anyone who would listen to take them on as assistant, free of charge. Sooner or later, someone would weaken, or an emergency would make an extra pair of hands necessary. [15]

But a large number of cinematographers had worked in a field which *had* prepared them in a more or less practical way for the position of cinematographer—as journalist, press photographer, or occasionally newsreel reporter. Many had begun in the first decade of the century, when Lumière and Pathé were sending out what could loosely be described as newsreel reporters to all parts of the globe, particularly Russia. Bachelet began in Russia as a newsreel reporter when his family moved there, and two of the newsreel reporters sent by Pathé to Russia—Mundwiller and Forestier—were to become cinematographers of influence. The Russian connection was strong, once again through Albatros Films—Bourgassoff (45/35), Toporkoff (74/58), and Roudakoff were all to come to France with that firm, and both Willy (81/63) and Kaufman (19) began work in Russia (the latter being the brother of Dziga Vertov). But the importance of press and newsreel photography as a basis for early work in the cinema industry extends

---

*Throughout this paragraph and the next two, the first number in parentheses represents the total number of films produced, and the second the number produced between 1930 and 1960.

beyond Russia. Bac (48/43) was a press photographer, as were Coteret (69/65), Kruger (60/45) (for Le Matin), and Maillols (30/29); Barry (36/35) was an art photographer; and both Hayer (77/72) and Matras (95/86) worked as newsreel cameramen, the former for 12 years, in Indochina and then for MGM. It is clear that, at the point when sound was introduced, the significant increase in the number of films being made, together with the sudden increase in the size of the camera team, generated an urgent demand for experienced or semiexperienced labor, and anyone with a reporting background who had ever held a camera—still or movie—was in a strong position to get the job.

It was likewise by working in the press that many scriptwriters had earned their living before venturing into the cinema, and many continued to do so between jobs. From 1919 on, Henri Jeanson was a journalist on *L'Oeuvre*, on *Paris Soir*, and on the *Canard Enchaîné* and a close friend of Vaillant-Couturier, editor of *Humanité*. For him, this period of journalism was clearly formative, exhilarating, ennobling. "At that time the press was the true parliament of the real nation. From *Libertaire* to *Action Française* by way of the *Canard Enchaîné* and *Le Temps*, it uncontestably exercised an influence on the intellectual, political, and social life of the country."[16] Among his many acquaintances on the staff was Marcel Achard, exercising parallel jobs as reporter and critic.[17]

Carlo-Rim's father was a newspaper proprietor; he himself worked as a drama critic in Nîmes from 1922 before going on to found his own magazines, *Jazz* and *Vu*. Early columns were allocated to several people who were to become scriptwriters—Pierre Bost, Robert Desnos, Charensol, as well as Man Ray and Max Jacob. In Belgium, at this time, Spaak was writing for newspapers and writing plays on the side while doing a law degree. When he moved to Paris he became chief of publicity for Armor Films before becoming secretary to Feyder. Involvement in publicity was a natural extension of their journalism for many writers. Journalism was just one of the many jobs that Prévert had undertaken—as little as was financially possible, which was fortunately very little indeed—during the twenties; but his first real sense of commitment to writing seems to have developed when he got involved in the slightly hysterical publicity production for the Etienne Damor agency. Coincidentally, it was in that same agency that Jean Aurenche began his writing career, producing in conjunction with Prévert, with Jean Anouilh, and with Paul Grimault a series of surrealist-inspired advertisements for the Galéries Barbès, Les Vins Nicolas, and Lévitan.[18]

The gatherings of film enthusiasts in Prévert's various lodgings were constantly treated to, and participated in, elaborate impromptu construction of far-fetched surrealist scenarios. Talking about the cinema and its possibilities, writing about the cinema, and writing for the cinema were indeed for most of this first generation of scriptwriters parallel and complementary tasks. Jean George Auriol, editor of *La Revue du Cinéma* and often a member of the Prévert group's impromptu scenarios, was to work on a number of scripts, as was his colleague on *La Revue*, Louis Chavance, as was Alexandre Arnoux. Yves Mirande was a journalist for the daily *Le Journal* before becoming with Guitry the leading Boulevard dramatist of the thirties.

But if it is relatively easy to identify the categories of work which had provided, in however unsystematic a way, the training for most of the key members of the filmmaking team, it is much harder in the case of the directors. With their background in high social and cultural circles, they had ready access to any of the jobs listed so far. Most classic directors began their artistic career in literature, advertising and design, the theater, or journalism, and only moved into cinema as an accidental result of their extra-cinematic artistic activities.

Like those silent-film directors whom they survived (Delluc, Epstein, Dulac) many of the "first generation" classic directors were versatile aesthetes who had dabbled in a variety of literary forms and who came to the cinema either through theater or through their reviewing activities, which extended to take in film-reviewing. Gance published poems, plays, and a novel and had acted in the theater before coming to the cinema through film acting and scriptwriting (1908–1909). L'Herbier likewise had published plays, poetry, and essays before becoming interested in film through a liaison with Musidora; his first scripts date from 1917. Maurice Tourneur was a theater decorator, actor, and director with Antoine from 1903 to 1909 before moving to film (1910). Duvivier followed him as theater actor and director with Antoine and at the Odéon before moving over to films. Feyder was a drama critic in Belgium with an interest in acting before moving to Paris (1912) and marrying Françoise Rosay. Gréville was, like several of his colleagues, a journalist on *Comoedia* and published novels and plays before moving into films via advertising films and then joining with Auriol and others on *Jabiru* and the *Revue du Cinéma*. Ophuls was a theater critic and directed some 150 plays before working for UFA. Nearly all would have seen themselves as writers initially, and this may be a factor in explaining the strong tendency toward retention of the scriptwriter/director figure in the classic cinema. This would certainly be true of all the filmed-theater directors such as Guitry (142 plays and operettas from 1902 on) and René Clair (theater and poetry, songwriter and reporter like many others on *L'Intransigeant*), Clouzot (who wrote plays from childhood and became a journalist with Henri Jeanson), Decoin (who wrote novels, plays, and operettas and was likewise a journalist on *L'Intransigeant*), Leenhardt (literary critic, novelist, and film critic on *Esprit* and later *Les Lettres Françaises*), Carlo-Rim (novelist, journalist, illustrator, and editor of literary magazines), and of course Cocteau. As this list makes clear, certain newspapers and magazines acted as foci for their developing interest in film in the twenties and early thirties—*L'Intransigeant*, *Comoedia*, *Paris Soir*, *Ciné-Magazine*, *Pour Vous*, and of course Auriol's *La Revue du Cinéma*. Remarkably few classic directors entered the profession other than by way of this generalized cultural ferment of the twenties, and those that did were often extremely sensitive about their status. Carné came from a furniture-making family and had himself been an apprentice cabinet-maker. He took up film courses at the Arts et Métiers and at the Ecole Technique de la Photographie et du Cinéma, emerging with qualifications to be a laboratory technician and assistant cameraman. This "backdoor" entry might well have seemed to him that of a poor relation and might go some way to explaining his obsessively meticulous approach to direction and his notorious rages on set. Duvivier, whose background was nearer to Carné's than to that of his literary colleagues, was likewise notorious. Melville also belonged to a different class from his colleagues—a travelling salesman before the war, he had to break into directing at the end of it by radically unconventional means.

If most had primarily a literary or theatrical background which allied them with writers and actors, some entered the cinema in ways which gave them a more extensive knowledge of some specific aspects of the technology of the cinema. Delannoy, a theatrical actor, decorator, and journalist before moving into film, nevertheless spent his early years in the cinema at the editing bench. He edited over seventy-five films for Paramount between 1930 and 1935 and was subsequently to see such a training in montage as the best possible background for a director.[19] Among other editors only René Le Henaff directed a significant number of films (16, from 1933 to 1951), Yves Allégret acquired a knowledge of sound and editing with the Braunberger Billancourt studios, and Clément, who had earlier dabbled in amateur filmmaking and cartoons, forced by his father's death to earn a living, did so as a film editor and short film cameraman. Joannon was also a cameraman, among many other roles, and Le Chanois was everything at some time or other, including film editor. Jacqueline Audry had been gender-typed as scriptgirl for years before being able to break into the ranks of directors.

Gender typing was most marked in the case of the editors, who had mostly come to the cinema as a result of chance encounters and friendships. Marguerite Renoir had been hand-painting silent film, frame by frame, before the opening which allowed her to move over to another (equally subordinate) role at the editing table. She in turn introduced Suzanne de Troyes to the job, as she introduced Marinette Cadix later.[20] Editing was seen as a mechanical skill which could be picked up practically instantaneously, by watching a friend at work.

Given the apparently random recruitment to the ranks of editors, it is interesting that it should have been almost exclusively women who came to fill the post in France.[21] This seems not to have been the case elsewhere. Diverse reports in French reviews and articles contrast the French situation with that in the United States and Italy,[22] where it was allocated to men, and in Britain where it was considered "physically tough work, and usually reserved for men."[23] The French tradition was partly due to the fact that the editor's job could be assimilated to the role of "the little woman." Contemporary accounts frequently link female editors and seamstresses, snipping away with their scissors, or mending and tidying up after the men.[24] The image is already used in 1929 by Coissac,[25] for whom they are simply cheery souls, working away with a will, and humming to themselves the while. Forty-five years later, in "Les femmes et le cinema"[26] the same image appears, this time as a bitter and ironic protest: "The editress is often reduced to the role of an underling, a machine minder, under the control of the director. . . . She cuts, glues, starts and stops her machine. The editing table is no more complicated, after all, than a sewing machine." It is noticeable that the only other role in the production crew regularly allocated to women was that of the scriptgirl, or production assistant, likewise subservient to a traditionally male role, and involving the tidying-up of loose ends, the taking of notes and entering up of production diaries, the discrete and supportive advice in little details as opposed to decisions of principle. Clearly this role could be assimilated to that of a secretary. Both, interestingly enough, were crucial in assuring the effective continuity of the narrative, the preservation of its unbroken realistic surface.

Once in the ranks, the editor's progress was dependent on a chain of assistantships, from which she could expect ultimately to emerge as chief editor. The same was true of directors, set designers, and cinematographers, all of whom could expect to spend several years in informal training as assistants. As a typical instance, Yves Allégret was assistant to his brother Marc, to Cavalcanti, to Augusto Genina, to Paul Fejos, and to Renoir, then "artistic director" for numerous other directors (notably L'Herbier). After writing scripts from 1931 to 1932, Clouzot was director of dubbing in Berlin between 1932 and 1938, then assistant for Litvak, Dupont, de Baroncelli, L'Herbier, Fresnay, Pettier, Decoin, and Lacombe before directing his first film in 1942. Louis Daquin was assistant for Duvivier, Chenal, Gance, Czep, and Grémillon before directing his own first film in 1941.

MIGRATION

The artistic, theatrical and musical world on which the cinema drew so heavily was already the focus of enormous international attention, attracting practitioners from all over Europe and from the Americas. It was inevitable, therefore, that the French cinema would have an internationalist aspect to it. In fact the degree to which foreigners—mostly, but not entirely, immigrants permanently resident in France—collaborated in the development of the classic cinema has caused some commentators to question its Frenchness. Of all those collaborators, three groups stand out as preeminent—the Russians, the Germans, and the Americans. That it should have been these three nations that were most influential is not surprising, since during the period following World War I it was these three cinema industries which had established the dominant national stylistic traditions, though the reasons for these filmmakers coming to work in France were always more directly political or economic than aesthetic. Nevertheless, as a result of the interaction between industries, the successive waves of visitors and immigrants flowing into and through the French cinema effectively introduced into it a wide range of technical, stylistic, and organizational possibilities, and this cross-fertilization was the more effective in that, for a variety of reasons, all three countries (but most particularly Germany and America) experienced the need for French personnel at various times in the thirties and forties. Any of the more successful technical and creative personnel in the French cinema would have had the opportunity to work in either the Neubabelsburg complex in Germany or in a Hollywood studio. Because the filmmaking conditions prevailing in these two countries were so radically different from those prevailing in France, the experience was often a revelation, even traumatic, and relatively seldom resulted in films of which the French personnel could feel proud.

Chronologically, the first nation thus to affect French filmmaking practices was Russia; the influence of Russian immigrants was enormous in the twenties and had lasting effects in a number of areas of production. Fleeing the Russian Revolution, they arrived in Paris via Berlin, or in Marseilles via Odessa in 1920. The focus of their activity was Ermolieff Films, founded by Joseph Ermolieff, who had been the director of Pathé's film-hire in Russia and a producer in his own right. He brought with him to France the bulk of that production troup, including directors (Volkoff, Tourjansky), cinematographers (Toporkoff, Bourgassoff, Roudakoff), set designers (Lochakoff, Bilinsky), and actors (notably Mosjoukine) and set up shop in Pathé's old Montreuil studio. In 1922 he decided to switch to Berlin and handed over French operations to Alexandre Kamenka and Noë Bloch, who renamed the enterprise Les Films Albatros.[27] Over the next seven years, from 1920 to 1927, their activities constituted one of the most exhilarating aspects of French silent film production. The Russian film community, with its center in Montparnasse, served as a channel for numerous other Russian exiles to make contact with French cultural life. Lazare Meerson, the finest of the early classic set decorators and a Polish-Russian working for Les Films Albatros, had been trained as a painter and was constantly surrounded by impoverished Russian painters like Ivan Puni and Pikelny,[28] not to mention Kiesling and Chirico, for whom his wife served as a model, and writers like Ilya Ehrenbourg. In 1924, the main body of Russian filmmakers left Albatros with Noë Bloch to found Ciné-France-Film, a subsidiary of the German company Westi, making several of the famous French silent films including *Napoléon*. Volkoff and Tourjansky were assistants to Gance as director, and most of the crew were Russian. Kevin Brownlow notes the irony of a community itself uprooted by one revolution committing such time and energy to glorifying another.[29]

Language problems prevented the Russian actors from having any significant impact on the sound film, but there were at least three areas where the Russian community's influence continued to be felt not just in the thirties but right through until 1960 and beyond. Certain of the directors continued to work in the classic cinema—Volkoff until 1934, Tourjansky making ten films between 1931 and 1937, and Starevitch, whose full-length marionette film *Le Roman de Renart* was finally completed in 1941. Strijewsky made three films in France in the thirties; Rimsky and Ermeineff directed one; and Fédor Ozep directed five, notably *La Dame de pique* (1927) and *Tarakanowa* (1937–1938), after working in Germany on French versions. Granowsky directed three films in the early thirties and Victor Trivas two; Léonide Moguy directed eleven between 1935 and 1961, with a decade's exile in between caused by the war. Perhaps the most important was Anatole Litvak, who made five films in France in the thirties and another five coproductions in the fifties and sixties.

But it has to be admitted that these directors did not, either individually or as a group, constitute a significant force within the industry. It is in the areas of set design and production that the Russian presence was most insistent. Ermolieff returned to France to take over production for GFFA at the end of the silent period; Albatros films remained in existence, run by Kamenka and Vladimir Zederbaum, and produced two or three films per year throughout the thirties, including Renoir's *Les Bas-fonds*. Joseph Bercholz set up Les Films Gibé with a French partner in 1928 and produced seven films in the thirties, including two directed by Decoin, one by Guitry, and then, after producing in America during the war, returned to produce most of Delannoy's postwar films, as well as Renoir's *Elena et les hommes*. Serge Sandberg, who had, like Kamenka, worked for Pathé in Russia, was instrumental in building the La Victorine studios in Nice and produced most of Guitry's films in the thirties. Michel Safra, after working in Germany for a decade, founded a production company with André Paulvé and produced some thirty films over the next thirty years, directed by Siodmak, Christian-Jacque, Becker, and Cayatte, among others. In the postwar years the Russian contingent was reinforced by the influential figure of Alexandre Mnouchkine who, with Georges Dancigers, founded Les Films Ariane, producing films by Decoin, Duvivier, Cocteau, Rossellini, and Gérard Philipe, along with many more commercial films by directors such as Christian-Jacque and Gilles Grangier. Again, Jacques Roitveld, after working like Safra in Germany for a period en route, produced films in the postwar period directed by Bernard, Decoin, Christian-Jacque, and others. In addition, it's to Gregor Rabinovitch, arriving in France from Germany, where he had produced films for UFA, that we owe the production of *Quai des brumes*, to Joseph Lucacevitch that we owe *Hotel du Nord*, and to Michel Kagansky that we owe both *Crime et chatiment* and *L'Homme de nulle part*, directed by Pierre Chenal.

When one adds to these Russian-born producers the other East European immigrants—Anatole Daufman from Poland, Henry Deutschmeister from Romania (60 films between 1949 and 1969, including René Clair, Ophüls, René Clément, Autant-Lara, Becker, and Guitry's extraordinarily successful *Si Paris m'était conté* [1955]), and the Czech producer, Eugène Tucherer (32 films from 1932 to 1974, including Ophüls, Ozep, Feyder, and Decoin)—the importance of this immigrant community in determining the direction of French classic cinema can be better evaluated. As producers, they were notably less committed to the making of profits than their French colleagues, tending to choose projects which appealed to them as worth making for their artistic or thematic value rather than their commercial viability. For them, as for Pierre Braunberger, their best-known French counterpart, film production was a passion before being a business.

The same can be said of the Russian set designers whose contribution was enormously important in determining the style of the profilmic reality in French classic cinema. A list of the films to which they contributed, especially if one adds in those designed by the Hungarian Alexandre Trauner, would cover three-quarters of those classic French films known outside France. Lochakoff and Bilinsky, who worked with Albatros, were instrumental in determining the direction of French set design in the twenties, moving it away from painted backdrops and toward constructed sets, influenced by the exotic, elaborate, and fantastic aspects of the Ballets Russes and Russian folk art. Their emphasis on film design as a transposition or poeticization of reality was taken up by Lazare Meerson, who worked with them, and thence by two generations of successors—Andrejew, who had worked with Stanislavsky in Moscow and Reinhardt in Berlin, and who worked in France from 1932 onward for immigrant directors and later for Clouzot, Cayatte, and Duvivier; Serge Rumenoff, who designed sets for three films a year on average throughout the period 1930–1960; Alexandre Trauner, who worked on most of the films directed by Carné and by Grémillon and several by the Allégret brothers before leaving for America in 1957 to work with his compatriot Billy Wilder; Eugène Lourié, chief decorator for some twenty-eight films in the thirties, including some by Ophüls, Clair, Becker, and most of Renoir's, before leaving for America in 1941 to continue designing for Renoir there; Georges Wahkevitch, whose work of chief decorator from 1943 onward includes all of Clair's postwar films; and Léon Barsacq, who worked on about eighty-seven films in the classic period alone.

If most of these set designers were also responsible for the costume design in their films, we might nevertheless add in Georges Annenkov, whose Beaux Arts training led to an invitation to design the costumes for Granowsky's *Les Nuits muscovites* in 1934, and who worked constantly thereafter with Cocteau, Ophüls, and many compatriots. Indeed, while not a ghetto, the Russian community, based in Montparnasse, would tend to cohere into recurrent partnerships, Russian producers employing Russian set designers and costumers, especially for films directed by Russian directors, and this corporate continuity tended to concentrate and perpetuate a stylistic contribution which might otherwise have been "diluted" by more French artistic traditions.

Many of these Russian immigrants were Jewish, and their numbers were increased as the rise of fascism in Germany and the threat of German expansionism incited Jews of neighboring Eastern European countries to seek refuge westward, often making France a more or less permanent base. As Marcel L'Herbier noted in *La Tête qui tourne*, "A Balkan Jewish contingent had infiltrated our film production. Strongly based in the Champs Elysées, people called Rabinovitch, Lucacevitch, Deutschmeister, and other conquering heroes whose names ended in 'gneff' and 'kruck' and in 'sky' (and whom François Vinneuil was to pillory unforgivably in his disgusting book) were occupying the terrain abandoned all too readily by our fellow countrymen. I had nothing against them . . . except that they brought along with them in their suitcases a mass of scripts full of white and red Russian stories, little adapted to our more subtly shaded dramatic style."[30] Despite his insistence that some of his best friends were Jews, L'Herbier betrays more than a little irritation at the extent of the Russian influence, going so far as to say that "from their arrival until the Second World War it too often seemed to us that France had been dispossessed of *her* cinema."[31] His rather unsubtle (and in fact unjust) suggestion that their sole aim (unlike that of French producers) was to extort as much money as possible out of the system is in fact well in tune with precisely that book which he purports to spurn, *Les Tribus du cinéma et du théâtre*, in which François Vinneuil castigated the performing arts for being corrupted by the sinister virus of Jewishness.[32]

Most of the Jews to travel to or pass through France were German (or Austrian) and arrived around 1933 when Hitler came to power. They formed just a small segment of the human flood that jammed all trains travelling west at that time. Not all, of course, were Jews—German communists had as much reason to move out as the Jews—and not all stopped in Paris; but given the haste with which many had left Germany, it was necessary for many to work in the French industry for one or more films before moving on to a final destination in England, or more often Hollywood. Lang, offered control over the German cinema by Goebbels, thought it prudent to leave Germany the next day and arrived in Paris penniless. The one (somewhat grotesque) film, *Liliom*, which he directed in France allowed him to continue on to the United States.

His case was typical of many artists and technicians from all areas of filmmaking. They were greeted in France with enormous professional respect, if only because the well-oiled and unified German film industry had achieved a level of technological and organizational sophistication envied by the French. Their own memoirs are united in the astonishment they felt at the underdeveloped and inchoate state of the French industry, with all its built-in inefficiencies. Pommer's unsuccessful attempts to transfer German production methods to his two French productions and Lang's problems during the making of *Liliom* are often-cited instances of this clash of production systems.[33]

German sound technicians were held in particular respect; so were composers such as Hanns Eisler (whose work with Brecht made him suspect in Germany) and Paul Dessau (who was also to work with Brecht), producers like Pommer himself, who had a high reputation in France for his work with UFA in the twenties, who had produced a dozen or so French-language versions in Germany, and who produced a Lang and Ophüls film in France for Fox-Europa (*Liliom* and *On a volé un homme*), but also Noë Bloch, Karl Froelich, and more durably Seymour Nebenzahl, who transferred Nero Films from Berlin to Paris in 1932 and produced a dozen or so films (four directed by Siodmak—*Le Sexe faible*, 1932; *La Crise est finie*, 1935; *La Vie parisienne*, 1935; and *Le Chemin de Rio*, 1936). And among the directors who passed through France were a number of men who had an established reputation in Germany—Victor Trivas, whose pacifist orientation had been expressed in *Niemansland* (1931) and who was to make a single remarkable film in France, *Dans les rues* (1933); Ludwig Berger; Kurt Bernhardt, who was to make two films before leaving for America (*L'Or dans la rue*, 1934, and *Carrefour*, 1938); Wilhelm Thiele, Robert Wiene, Max Nosseck, Kurt Gerron, Marc Sorkin, and Karl Anton, who directed 16 films in France between 1931 and 1936; Pabst, and Ophüls. To these we might add Robert Siodmak himself, who was American by birth but who had begun his career in Germany; arriving in France in 1933, he made eight films, perhaps the best of which are *La Crise est finie* (1935); *Mollenard* (1938–1939); and *Pièges* (1939) before leaving for the United States.

Of all of them, only two—Pabst and Ophüls—were to have any substantial French output, and even Pabst was to direct films which fell below expectations. Ophüls, however, while directing films wherever he could in Western Europe, returned repeatedly to France, where he made eight films before the war and the well-known sequence of four after it (*La Ronde*, 1950; *Le Plaisir*, 1951–1952; *Madame de . . .* , 1953; *Lola Montès*, 1955). Qualitatively, it is in the films by these latter directors that one should look for the German presence in French classic film; but even more importantly, one should look to the impact of such German cinematographers as Eugen Shüfftan and Kurt Courant, both Jews, and Rudolph Maté.[34]

Entering an industry in which few cinematographers had any real artistic training or background, they and fellow cinematographers Hans Androschin and Georg Kraus brought with them a solid Beaux Arts training and a decade of working in one of the most efficient and most experimental film industries in the world. Their effect on their French colleagues was of an initiation into a realm of infinite possibilities. They and their French disciples (including set designers and directors) perpetuated in the classic cinema—not universally, but recurrently, from 1930 to 1950—the theatrical forms of lighting, the odd angles, and the virtuoso camera work so typical of their expressionist heritage. Even discounting the enormous indirect influence effected by their prestige and by the master/disciple system then operative in the industry, the direct effect of Kurant and Schüfftan alone was enormous. Aside from working, like the Russians, in close cooperation with others of their emigrant contingent (notably for Ophüls and Pabst) and for the Russians, they worked for Renoir on *La Bête humaine*, for Gance, and for Carné on all of the films he directed in the thirties (Courant doing *Le Jour se lève*, Schüfftan the others).

Certain of the techniques they introduced had distinct thematic importance: the refusal to privilege the actor, noted by Kelber[35] as typical of the German contingent, was taken on occasion to extremes, such that it was objects and formal patternings that emerged as dominant from the mise en scène. Schüfftan had been cinematographer for *Metropolis*, and his work with its echoes of cubism and of futurism tends to produce a representation of human beings as themselves no more than objects, driven by inexorable forces. Thomas Elsaesser has noted a range of other technique-related themes which appear to be due to the influence of German personnel and which he finds in *Carrefour* (Bernhardt, 1938) and *La Mauvaise Graine* (Billy Wilder, 1933–1934).[36] Again, the typically cluttered and overcharged mise en scène often produces an impression of confusion or even claustrophobia. The circus and associated fairground scenes, which so often served as the site of such haunted representations of humanity, also tend to appear frequently, at least in the thirties French cinema, though it is not clear why the scriptwriters, primarily French in origin, should thus translate expressionist narratives to a French setting. As Ginette Vincendeau notes, however, one aspect of French and German narrative plotting that would have meshed perfectly is the "myth of departure," the dream of escape from a harsh reality to an idealized otherwhere.[37] It can scarcely be denied that the massive emigrant populations of refugees flowing to and through France in quest of a new sense of belonging must have given sinew to the characteristic thirties (and necessarily more oblique wartime) theme of escape to an idealized New World, "over there." For Elsaesser, these films seem to be saying farewell to a past which has been exposed as "morally or socially false, [and] to whose insufficiency the objects of everyday use bear mute but obstinate witness. One finds a corresponding pathos in Ophüls's films, and it gives resonance to Siodmak's French films, especially *Pièges* (1939) and *Mollenard* (1937)."[38]

While the East European and German contingents formed the bulk of this migrant population, others are worth noting in passing: Buñuel, whose *Un chien andalou* (with Dali) and *L'Age d'or* are the visible results of several years of mixing and working with French filmmakers and who was to return in the fifties for a further series of films (*Cela s'appelle l'aurore*, 1955; *La Mort en ce jardin*, 1956; *La Fièvre monte à El Pao*, 1959); and the various Italian directors who worked in France in the thirties. Cavalcanti, who directed seven films between 1930 and 1933, is only the best known of several— Mario Bonnard, Mario Camerini, Carmine Gallone, and in particular

Augusto Genina, whose eight early sound films included the delightful *Prix de beauté*, which René Clair had scripted and prepared before coming into conflict with the producer.

But "the Italian presence in France . . . is relatively limited," as Jean Gili notes: "most of the displaced Italian personnel headed for Berlin rather than Paris."[39] And even among the personnel from the principal nations, the immigrant population was by no means stable. A large number only stayed to make between one and five films. Some commentators find this difficult to explain, especially in view of the respect with which their professionalism was regarded. In fact it is not difficult to see why both Communists and Jews should find France still too close for comfort to the forces they were fleeing, especially as the threat of another Europe-wide war developed. Not least, the Jews among them had to cope with a French anti-Semitism which, if not as virulent as that which they had fled, had been a powerful constituent of French cultural and political life since the end of the previous century, and to which the employment pressures of the depression gave added force. François Vinneuil in the extreme right-wing *Action Française* never ceased his attacks on them. Sarcastic remarks about the heterogeneous populations of uncertain nationalities in the cinema became a cliché of thirties literary life. In Pagnol's satire of the profession, *Le Schpountz*, we find one character described as "A German or a Turk . . . anyway he's taken a Russian name and speaks with an Italian accent—all he needed to become a great French director."[40]

This is indeed some (exaggerated) indication of the extent to which foreign personnel had moved into the industry, but it is also an indication of the unhealthy racist atmosphere that this "foreign invasion" had generated, particularly in the case of the Jews, and makes their anxiety to move on to a less stridently anti-Semitic society more comprehensible.

MULTILINGUAL VERSIONS

Alongside these fluid and unstable migrant communities, not always distinct from them, but adding intensity to the cosmopolitan nature of the "so-called French cinema," was the two-way flow of personnel caused by the commitment of several companies and several nations to filming multilingual versions of all their key productions. Italy and Britain were both involved in this multiple-language production, though the principal nations involved were France, the United States, and Germany. As noted earlier, Paramount had already established a massive production unit at St. Maurice by the middle of 1930 with the specific intention of centralizing in Paris all its European productions. Its first film was produced in 13 different languages, and none was to be produced in fewer than two (French and German). To make these various multilingual versions, massive numbers of actors and a large number of artistic and technical personnel had to be mobilized from among the immigrant populations or imported specifically for the task. The resultant linguistic chaos, with several different directors and a dozen different casts all working in different languages and alternating in identical scenes on an identical set, earned for the studio the title Babel-sur-Seine.

A mixture of awe and cynicism infused the French press's reporting of this activity. On the one hand, the very existence of such a center in Paris tended to make France "the artistic and geographical center of European cinema," with foreign film personnel competing for a chance to participate in French productions and "French" films overcoming the language barrier erected by sound. On the other hand it was difficult for the French filmmaking establishment to reconcile itself to the alien production system imported by the American producers. The displacement of aesthetic decision making toward the producer and the dominance of commercial considerations soured their enthusiasm for the initiative. Accounts by French personnel of their participation in the American experiment are therefore at best ambivalent. They speak of an atmosphere of intense activity, but also of long periods of inactivity—of receiving astonishing amounts of money, often for doing practically nothing.

Something of the mocking tone infusing many such accounts emerges from Nino Frank's memoirs:

> At St. Maurice, in the new studios of a Californian firm, with palm trees and swimming pools, they're filming night and day, 12 films a week, 20 days per film, 80 stars on the set, and they're advertising for actors, directors, and technicians who can work in all languages. . . . The bosses are American, the administration Hungarian, the writers French, the directors Russian, the technicians German, the assistants Italian, the laborers from the Balkans. They film while eating, while sleeping, while swimming, while arguing. The great river of dollars flows endlessly. Millions are nothing; they build not even on chalk and on sand, but on champagne and on caviar. Alfred Savoir with his tight smiles, Marcel Achard with his lighthouse-spectacles, Yves Mirande and his puns, Marcel Pagnol and his wonderful accent, Henri Jeanson and his rapid-fire digs, Jacques Deval and his women, Steve Passeur and his irritability, the Café de Paris, Fouquet's, the Franco-Italians, they're all there. . . . A film on the circus, a film on the Société des Nations, a film on continental aviation, a film on television; in short, a cut price cosmopolitanism. It's Babel. . . . They bring in stars from all countries of the world: Vladimir Sokoloff, Dito Parlo, Buster Keaton, Inkijinoff, to have them speak in all languages they know, or if necessary with gestures and onomatopoiea.[41]

If the films generated by all this activity were generally regarded as of inferior quality, their production was nevertheless the occasion for a series of international encounters and exchanges which were to echo on long after Paramount shut up shop some two years later. The French personnel who worked there (or at least sat in a coffee room there, chatting with people from other filmmaking communities) were extremely numerous. Osso, then Alfred Savoir, was in charge of French-language production: scripts were vetted by a committee including Sacha Guitry and Pierre Benoit; scriptwriters employed by Paramount included Achard, Tristan Bernard, Paul Colline, Pierre Dac, André Dahl, Yves Mirande, Noël-Noël, Poulbot, Rip, Saint-Granier, Pierre Wolff, and Henri Jeanson—the bulk of contemporary French dramatists.[42]

Christian-Jacque directed 12 films there in two years; L'Herbier made *Le Mystère de la chambre jaune* and *Le Parfum de la dame en noir*; Renoir finished off *Boudu sauvé des eaux* there. While there they could meet Cavalcanti, who had come to film four films for Paramount, or Korda, directing *Marius*, and dozens of other international figures. Most of the recognized French actors passed through Babel-sur-Seine in the course of the three years, frequently with the unaccustomed luxury of a "long-term" contract—Marguerite Moréno, Jeanne Fusier-Gir, Dalio, Jean Murat, Pierre Brasseur, Henri Garat, Michel Simon, Madeleine Renaud, Jean-Pierre Aumont.

Other American companies adopted the reverse policy, of attracting French personnel to Hollywood to make French-language versions. MGM had begun this policy earlier but now proceeded to establish a special foreign-language unit to compete with the French Paramount undertaking. On the whole it did not consider French directors necessary for these French-language versions. Robert Florey, notionally French in origin, had established himself in Hollywood in the early twenties; both he and Jacques Tourneur made a few early sound films in France, but the bulk of their career was American. Jacques Feyder and Autant-Lara were the only French directors to have been invited to Hollywood, but in the case of Feyder it had happened in 1928, and in the case of Autant-Lara was due to his work with the early cinemascope lens which MGM agreed to test. In 1931 he directed Buster Keaton and Françoise Rosay in the French version of *Parlor, Bedroom and Bath*, subsequently filming the French version of Le Roy's *Local Boy Makes Good* for Warner Brothers. Neither had been brought over specifically to direct French versions. For those, MGM (and later the other companies, on a smaller scale) brought in primarily French actors together with a few scriptwriters to provide appropriate dialogues for the French-language versions. Thus Marcel Achard, Yves Mirande, and Jacques Deval managed to establish themselves in Hollywood in this period even scripting some complete films—notably *The Merry Widow* and *Folies Bergères* for Achard, and Keaton films for the other two, Deval staying through the war and scripting a film for Cukor, *Café Métropole*, with Tyrone Power and Loretta Young.

But naturally enough, given the task in hand, the Hollywood studios were primarily interested in French actors. MGM and Paramount competed for Maurice Chevalier, Paramount finally winning out; Françoise Rosay was already there with her husband Feyder, and while on a trip back to France chose André Luguet from the Comédie Française for one of Feyder's films in America; MGM invited Charles Boyer and Mona Goya, Lya Lys and André Berley; Suzy Vernon was attracted over by Warners, before acting for First National and MGM; Jeanne Helbling went to Warners. The traffic in stars became constant, later in the thirties, even after the vogue for foreign-language versions had been undermined by dubbing methods. Fernand Gravey was attracted in the late thirties and acted in three successful films, Danielle Darrieux went to Universal, Gravat to Fox, and Balin to MGM. Anabella did *Caravane* in 1934 and three films in the late thirties, marrying Tyrone Power. The salaries offered, together with the opportunity to visit such a mythic location, were difficult to resist. Edwige Feuillère turned down an offer by MGM, as did Simone Simon, assiduously pursued after her success in *Lac aux dames* (M. Allégret, 1933–1934). She refused $500 a week from MGM and later $700 a week from Fox, finally falling for Zanuck's offer of $2,000 a week.

Cumulatively, then, Hollywood in the thirties attracted a considerable proportion of the lead actors available to French production companies. It constituted a significant French community in Hollywood, centering now on the Feyder/Rosay household, where one might find Helbling, Chevalier, Mirande, Dekobra, Deval, and Arlette Marchal at a house party (not to mention other immigrants—Murnau, Garbo, Jennings), now on Charles Boyer, Maurice Chevalier, or Robert Florey's establishment. Considered "the French ambassador to Hollywood," Florey represented for visiting French personnel a sort of half-way house and safety net. Involved in the French cinema with Delbic, Max Linder, Canudo, and Charles Vanel, friend in America to Buster Keaton, Douglas Fairbanks, and Mary Pickford, codirector with Chaplin, confidante of Valentino, director in their first film of Edward G. Robinson, Claudette Colbert, Kay Francis, Louise Brooks, and the Marx Brothers, he could provide his compatriots with an entrée to whatever circles they desired. At his place they could eat authentic French meals, listen to French music, lounge in blue, white, and red garden chairs, admire his Napoleon room packed with marble, bronze, and porcelain effigies of the emperor, in a house designed according to Napoleon's own plans.[43]

But though the internationalism provided by Hollywood production companies may have enriched those who experienced it, both literally and figuratively, it was a serious threat to the French cinema as an industry, depriving it of many of its principal artists for much of the decade. That this may have in some instances been a conscious strategy is suggested by the sinister statement made by a Hollywood producer in 1930 and cited earlier. He concludes by saying, "Another part of our plan consists in luring to Hollywood all European artists of any renown. . . . What European producer will vie with us when we have captured their greatest actors with our money."[44]

Whether deliberate or not, the policy was effective because of the distance between Paris and Hollywood, because of the means of transport available, and because of the American contract system: one did not make the journey to Hollywood casually, and once there one could not return to Paris simply on impulse. The British and German studios cannot be suspected of any such long-term devious strategies, and the intense exchange of personnel which took place was often on the basis of contracts lasting no more than a few weeks. Britain was of less importance than Germany, attracting filmmakers primarily in the early days of sound before the French studios were equipped. French-language versions of British films were made prior to the development of dubbing, but the practice soon ceased, and René Clair is the only leading French filmmaker to have established himself in Britain in the thirties.

The internationalism fostered by German production was, however, on the same scale as that fostered by Hollywood. The Tobis studios at Epinay were widely respected by French filmmakers, both generally for the quality of the technology and of the productions, and specifically for the quality of certain films, filmmakers, and set designers. Whenever Duvivier or René Clair or Feyder were at work there, a stream of visitors would come to admire their work or the scale and detail of Meerson's sets. Duvivier's *Allô Berlin, ici Paris,* made in Epinay, was one of a small number of films in those early sound years to explore the possibility of the multilingual film as a way of overcoming language barriers while reducing production time and costs. Stars of different nationalities each spoke their own language within the context of a plot which could be understood by audiences of any nationality. Few plots lent themselves to such a strategy, however. Most of Tobis's French production consisted of straight French-language films rather than multilingual versions. Germany's French versions were made in Germany itself, at UFA's (beautifully named) Neubabelsburg studios. UFA employed Raoul Ploquin as head of its French production, and right up until the outbreak of war he continued to bring in French directors, actors, and technicians. At first the purpose was primarily to produce French-language versions of German films. Begun in 1929, the system was producing 40 such versions in 1931. Serge de Poligny worked in Berlin from 1932 to 1936; Clouzot scripted several films there in 1931 and 1932, then directed three French versions; Henri Decoin directed *Le Domino vert* in 1935. Jeancolas lists six films that Henry Chomette (brother to René Clair) "sub-directed" in Berlin between 1929 and 1936 and notes that Roger Le Bon filmed a few between 1930 and 1935.[45] If Courtade is right, Tobis in Berlin tended to specialize in light comedies, especially musical comedies, interpreted by Lilian Harvey and Henri Garat (*Le Chemin du paradis,* v.f. of *Die Drei von der Tankstelle,* 1930; *Le Congrès s'amuse, La Fille et le garçon,* and *Princesse à vos ordres, Un rêve blond,* and *Les Gais Lurons*). But in addition, UFA produced more ambitious French-language versions, such as *L'Opéra de quat'sous,* a French version of Pabot's *Dreigroschenoper,* with Albert Préjean, Florelle, and Margo Lion. "UFA had under contract at that time a good number of the best-known actresses and actors—Annabella, Arletty,

Annie Ducaux, Florelle, Jules Berry, Charles Boyer, Marie Bell, Pierre Brasseur, Fernandel, Fernand Gravey, Jean Murat, Albert Préjean, Pierre-Richard Willm, to cite only lead actors."[46] Indeed, Courtade's lists of lead actors who made at least one film in Germany is astonishing. It includes Raimu, Madeleine Renaud, Yvonne Printemps, Edwige Feuillère, Danielle Darrieux, Michele Morgan, Françoise Rosay, Simone Simon, Pierre Fresnay, Charles Vanel, Pierre Renoir, Jean Gabin—as he says, most of the French leads of the period. The qualitative distinction between these actors and those employed by Paramount was clear, and UFA also attracted favorable comment by allowing French directors a much freer hand than was possible within the American production system.

Not all such films were mere French-language versions of German originals: some twenty or thirty were produced from French scenarios, of which the best known are the three directed by Jean Grémillon between 1936 and 1939 (*Pattes de mouche*, 1936; *Gueule d'amour*, 1937; *L'Etrange M. Victor*, 1937–1938), but which also include films by Marcel L'Herbier (*Adrienne Lecouvreur*, 1938) and by Albert Valentin (*L'Entraîneuse*, 1938–1940; and *L'Héritier de Mondésir*, 1939–1940). Raoul Ploquin was particularly proud of these films: "They were 100% French, that's the right phrase to describe them, since I was in charge of production and had the choice of scenarios, of French directors, and of actors."[47]

This ongoing interchange of personnel with the German film industry throughout the thirties must be reckoned another important source of the expressionist elements that became incorporated into French production. Lucien Aguettand, the set designer, considered his period in Germany as "the solidest form of training I ever had: you met in Berlin people from all countries—Hungarians, French, English, but few Americans. German production was international. There was still a lot of evidence of expressionism (right up to Hitler's time, indeed)—a violent lighting setup that you find in France with cinematographers like Kruger, Hubert, Hayer. German sets were schematic. They were in a sense realistic, but a German form of realism."[48] It was an influence that was to infuse many of the best-known films of the poetic realist period and to outlast the thirties in France despite the occupier's wartime condemnation of precisely those expressionist elements, seen then as they had been eight years before in Germany as a symptom of national decadence and defeatism.

But if French attitudes toward Franco-German cooperation were generally more positive than toward American cooperation, there were nevertheless signs of that same apprehension mentioned earlier concerning an invasion of foreigners into a film industry already enduring an unacceptable level of unemployment. Among many warning voices in the thirties, L'Herbier expressed anxiety that "French literature should exercise so powerful an attraction on foreign directors that a Tourjansky should direct *L'Aiglon*, Korda *Marius*, Litvak *Coeur de lilas*, Lachman *Mistigri*, Czinner *Ariane*, Fejos *Fantomas*, Pabst *L'Atlantide*."[49] French personnel were being put out of work and French culture appropriated and spoliated. Likewise, mistrust of German motives is frequently voiced, most aggressively so in a propaganda pamphlet of 1934 entitled *Les Dessous du cinéma allemand*, in which the author attributes to German producers the same sinister program as that voiced by an American:

> France will never make fine films. The French government doesn't support it in any way. They don't have any idea of the effect a film can have abroad, or the influence it can exercise. So it's up to us Germans to make the French people's films for them. They will serve two ends: (1) counter French influence abroad, (2) replace it little by little by ours. . . . We'll beat the French on their own ground so that, discouraged, they finally give up. These great films will serve our propaganda and spread our ideas around the world. . . . With (our limitless) money, we will seduce and keep in Germany *all the good French film personnel*, Boyer, Garat, Lemonnier, Blanchar, Murat, Gabin, Rosine, Deréan, Ferny, Françoise Rosay, and others whom we'll pay highly. And the French producers, deprived of stars, will have to make do with the meager residue we leave them until their industry packs up and French culture dies out.[50]

The aspect of these international interchanges that is least well documented is this French presence in Berlin, since French filmmaking personnel, retrospectively self-conscious about their contributions to the enemy's economy, were understandably reluctant in later years to elaborate on their work there. For that reason, a contemporary account such as André Beucler's in 1935 is invaluable. He underlines the technical sophistication of the German industry, which impressed the French workers: "The Berlin workshops do things well: the photography is clever and precise, the sound excellent, the editing sophisticated. . . . In all technical matters, our neighbors make no compromises; near enough is not good enough. It's the substance that's most lacking in their work." He also contrasts the amicable internationalism of the film personnel with the potentially intrusive nationalism pressing upon it:

> You hear the German language marry with French, which shocks no one, since [UFA] is still a center of Franco-German collaboration where a bilingual murmur is part of the house style. . . . The atmosphere of camaraderie that reigns in this world of *cousins germains* is undeniable. It is based on a thousand little details of shared professional understanding; international—an understanding that allows a Danish actor to feel at ease with a Portuguese director, but which unquestionably creates deep bonds each year between 400 French and 400 Germans—sincere bonds, broken of course with the rapidity of cinematic images, but which recall wartime friendships and University relationships. To become a close friend with the Germans—whether they're secret liberals, Hitlerians, monarchists, or militants—all you have to do is confine yourself to a fictional world and not take too close an interest in the Third Reich. . . . If as Frenchmen you

commit the heresy of noticing what's happening not in the studio but in the nearby arsenals or military camps . . . you immediately become an enemy of art, of the cinema, and of Germany.

Describing the cinema as a sort of no-man's-land not altogether assimilated as yet to the Hitlerian ethic, he speaks of listening to Hitler's broadcasts alongside German personnel—themselves Nazi—who nevertheless observed quietly at the end, "That too is just cinema."[51]

POLITICAL ORIENTATIONS: LE GROUPE OCTOBRE

It is normal to represent French cinema of the thirties as a hotbed of leftwing radicalism. This misunderstanding is due to the selective survival of a limited number of films which allow of such an interpretation. In fact the great bulk of films and filmmakers were "apolitical," in the sense that they did not concern themselves directly with political issues. That said, it is inevitable that, given the highly charged nature of the political scene at the time, those filmmakers who *were* politically committed should have been, both at the time and retrospectively, singled out for particular attention. The period 1929–1939 saw the development of a large number of loose groupings of politically active culture workers. Within the cinema, there was one such group which survived long enough to have a consistent input into the political orientation of a large number of films, and that was the Groupe Octobre. Members of it were influential from the early thirties, and their political orientations were still apparent in classic French films produced in the late forties. The period of its most effective input into the cinema was from 1935 to 1939, and unquestionably the most influential of the members of the group was Jacques Prévert.

The group grew out of the surrealist movement, and all its most effective cinematic products retain an air of inspired lunacy. Aside from Vigo's *Zéro de Conduite*, those few French films from the classic period retaining authentically surrealist characteristics were all produced by members of the Groupe Octobre who had emerged from the surrealist movement of the twenties: *L'Affaire est dans le sac*, scripted by Jacques Prévert, acted by the group, and directed by his brother in the sets constructed for *La Merveilleuse Journée* during the nocturnal hours when the Braunberger studios were free; *Drôle de drame*, scripted by Jacques Prévert and directed by Carné; *Adieu Léonard*, written by Jacques Prévert in 1932 and finally filmed in 1943; and *Voyage Surprise*, adapted by Jacques Prévert from an operetta called *Paris Paris* and directed by his brother in 1946.

In the late twenties there had been no clear division between those members of the fluctuating population in the rue du Chateau who were apolitical in their poetic or cinematic commitments and those who were political. Only with the feud between Breton and Aragon in 1930 did the issue become crucial, and in the aftermath of that feud most of those who were to work in the Groupe Octobre defined themselves against Breton, and moved progressively leftward, coinciding for certain purposes and at certain moments with those who were already committed Communists, such as Léon Moussinac and Georges Sadoul.

The group consisted of a number of actors, one principal director—Lou Tchimoukow, and one principal writer—Jacques Prévert himself. The group's activities can be traced back to an amateur dramatic group called Prémices, which was formed in June 1929 and which performed wherever space was available—in the street, at parties, in café spectacles, or in union meetings. Caught up in the same debate as the surrealists concerning the politicization of culture—is a revolution in consciousness possible without a social revolution, and if not which must come first?—the Prémices group split in 1932 into a more aesthetically oriented group later called Masses and a more socially active group which styled itself the Prémices Shock troops (Groupe de choc Prémices). Consisting, among others, of Raymond Bussières, Lazare Fuchsmann, and Guy Decomble, this group had the support of Léon Moussinac and Paul Vaillant-Couturier. Through the agency of one of these,[52] Jacques Prévert, his brother Pierre, and Lou Tchimoukow attached themselves to the group. It changed its name in early 1933 to the Groupe Octobre, and over the next three to four years that group's activities became progressively more visible. Their agit-prop happenings resembled Piscator's Russian work and were based on poems and dramatic pieces, acted, mimed and danced, chanted and sung, within the loosest of overall frameworks. The tone was resolutely provocative, indeed iconoclastic, combining irony, satire, parody, and outright attack. As befitted a postsurrealist group, all forms of hierarchical and traditional authority were targeted: the group was anticlerical, antimilitarist, and anticapitalist, dramatizing all the forces of order as repressively destructive. In uncomplicated opposition to them, the group's work championed the poor, the weak, the disinherited, all those who were excluded from or who opted out of the official values and institutions of society. Notionally, it proposed for these groups a countersociety based on mutual respect and support. Love was opposed to hate, brotherhood to greed and selfishness, life to death, day to night, beauty to ugliness. This Manichaean representation of social relationships militated against any complex psychology, which fitted in with the group's emphasis in the cinema and elsewhere on the social rather than the psychological, the external rather than the internal.

It was a collection of these performances that the group took to Moscow late in 1933, where in competition with politically active drama groups from many nations their "montage-review" won first prize. Membership of the group fluctuated over the years. Those members who were to be influential in filmmaking circles included, in addition to the Prévert brothers, Bussières and Tchimoukow; Paul Grimault, whose animation work, often in conjunction with Prévert, had begun in twenties film advertisements; J.-B. Brunius, critic on the *Revue du Cinéma*, scriptwriter and assistant director who worked in collaboration with Buñuel and with Renoir, actor in many thirties films, but most notably in *Une partie de campagne*; Yves Allégret, who acted in the group's "chef d'oeuvre," *La Bataille de Fontenay* (1933), who like Pierre Prévert was already making short films, and whose subsequent career as director of some twenty-five films between 1940 and 1975 is well known; Jean-Paul Le Chanois, one of the more politically committed of the group, who scripted or directed a series of often aggressively committed films between 1937 and 1966; and actors such as Jean Ferry, Roger Blin, Sylvia Bataille, Maurice Baquet, Marcel Duhamel, Sylvain Itkine.

On the fringes of the group, drawn into its activities occasionally but more often themselves exploiting sporadic outbursts of the group's activities, were other influential directors such as Autant-Lara, Renoir, and Becker, whose political orientation was not so marked but whose work was inflected toward the left by comradely involvement with members of the group or simply by the atmosphere of excitement and intellectual creativity that it gave off. Autant-Lara's collaboration with Prévert on the operetta *Ciboulette* (1932–1933) is well documented, though their efforts to subvert the work were largely frustrated. Renoir, whose previous films showed no more than humanist sympathies for the outsider or mildly anarchic pleasure in poking fun at the bourgeoisie, produced in collaboration with Prévert (and indeed with most of the other members of the group) a much more subversive film, *Le Crime de M. Lange*—one of the finest films of the decade, and one of which Bernard Chardère has queried, "should we rewrite the credits as 'film of the Groupe Octobre, with technical assistance from Jean Renoir'?"[53] Largely under the influence of the group, Renoir was commissioned by the Communist Party to produce *La Vie est à nous* and subsequently worked with a collective of filmmakers funded by popular subscription to produce *La Marseillaise*; but a more fundamental apoliticism still shows through in most films of the time, such as *La Grande Illusion* and *La Règle du jeu*.

Although *Lange* had been sketched out by Renoir and Castanier before Prévert took a hand, Jeancolas has indicated the extent to which the scenario's populist and cooperativist potential was brought out by the group's collaboration.[54] It was as a result of seeing *Lange* that one of the secretaries of the PCF proposed the collaboration that was to become *La Vie est à nous*. At least four people contributed to the script of this film besides Renoir—Le Chanois, Vaillant-Couturier, Zwobada, and Unik—Jacques Becker was involved in filming some of the sequences, as were the photographer Cartier-Bresson, Maurice Lime, Brunius, and Marc Maurette. For this reason it could be said that *La Vie est à nous* represents a move to introduce into filmmaking some of the cooperative principles proposed in *Lange*. Its budget was about one-tenth of the average for the time; it was financed by donations from PCF members, collected during electoral meetings, distributed without any *visa de censure*, and it promoted a social and political line very close to that being outlined at the time by the PCF.[55]

The links between Renoir and the Communist Party established by the Groupe Octobre were to produce two further films—*Les Bas-fonds* and *La Marseillaise*. The former, based on a novel by Gorki (who just before his death gave his blessing to the script), was at least monitored by the party. Spaak, who adapted it, has described how his version, set in France and fairly radically modified, had to be revised at the last minute under direction from the party, in favor of a greater respect for Gorki's original.[56]

La Marseillaise, even more than *La Vie est à nous*, was an attempt to introduce collectivist principles into the film industry. Funded by partial presale of tickets to spectators, subsidized by the CGT and the Union des Syndicats, administered by a production cooperative and a distribution cooperative, it was intended to demonstrate "that the people can create an important work of this sort without the aid of 'capitalism.' This demonstration film represents the start of a new age in film production, in which employers and finance will have no place."[57] The promotional material took up the same theme:

THE FILM OF FRENCH NATIONAL UNITY

against an oppressive minority

THE FILM OF THE RIGHTS OF MAN AND OF THE CITIZEN

For the first time a film is to be commissioned by the people themselves,
in a vast . . .

POPULAR SUBSCRIPTION

LET'S SEE TO IT

that the people of France have their own film on the
French Revolution of 1789

LET'S MAKE

the first film ever produced by the people, for the people

Trainloads of workers on holiday went to Fontainebleau to watch the shooting and act as unpaid extras. A promotional meeting drew supportive statements from all parties in the Front Populaire, as well as Germaine Dulac and the anarchist Henri Jeanson. But by the time it was made and screened, the Front Populaire had begun to collapse. The years in which its support had been strongest—between the hopes of late 1935 and the collapse in 1937—had, not surprisingly, also marked the apogee and decline of the Groupe Octobre. Already by the end of 1935 the group was having financial troubles and was putting on screenings of *Zéro de Conduite* and *L'Affaire est dans le sac* to raise funds. In January 1936 the group put on its last major item, *Le Tableau des merveilles*, adapted by Prévert from Cervantès, drawing Jean-Louis Barrault, Jean Dasté, and the young Mouloudji into their sphere of influence; and in April it combined with the numerous other small theatrical troupes and the more formal independent companies to form the Union des Théâtres Indépendants de la France (or Theater of Liberty: president, Charles Vildrac; secretary, J.-P. Le Chanois [then still called J.-P. Dreyfus], council members including Henry Jeanson, Léon Moussinac, Aragon, Gaston Modot, Pierre Renoir, Harry Baur, Gaston Baty, Charles Dullin, Louis Jouvet, Marcel Herrand, Jean-Louis Barrault, Fernand Léger, Georges Sadoul, Jean Wiener, Jean Renoir, Charles Spaak). But already the big strikes of May and June were spelling the end of the period of leftwing hopes and convictions. In the course of the year, the Groupe Octobre's activities died away, though its work was briefly (1936–1937) perpetuated by Ciné-Liberté, a filmmaking collective grouping much the same body of people which grew out of the 1936 electoral campaigns. Ciné-Liberté has been likened to Radio-Liberté, established by Vaillant-Couturier in the context of developing enthusiasm for the idea of a Front Populaire.

Ciné-Liberté devoted its efforts primarily to the production of short activist films and political documentaries and only remained in existence for about a year; but it was involved directly or indirectly in the production of *La Marseillaise* and subsequently in the equally militant *Le Temps des cerises*. To a script by J.-P. Le Chanois, *Le Temps des cerises* proclaims itself a film committed to promoting the PCF's views on old-age pensioners. It looks twenty years later at a number of aged peasants and workers who had experienced the fraternity of the First World War; having suffered and often been mutilated for their native land, they find themselves largely ignored by it, until the PCF and the Front Populaire restore their faith. One of the reasons this and other similar thirties films are sometimes difficult to read nowadays is the lack of individual heroes: like many of the Russian films of the twenties, it is collective problems that are at stake and collective solutions that are proposed.

This is the sum total of classic fiction films produced by activist political collectives. It is not a large body of work, but there is of course an enormous body of secondary films produced by one or another of these politically committed scriptwriters or directors, heavily influenced by their commitment and by the political color of the period. Among the better-known of these are several scripted by Charles Spaak. From a strongly leftwing Belgian family, Spaak himself tended toward liberal humanism and pacifism in his orientation, but influenced partly by the times and partly by his powerful admiration for Jacques Prévert,[58] he produced between 1936 and 1938 a series of scripts which bear directly on the political aspirations of the working class. Aside from *Les Bas-fonds* for Renoir, he produced *La Belle*

Equipe (Duvivier, 1936) and *Mollenard* (Siodmak, 1937–1938). The first of these again focuses on a "collective hero"—five unemployed men of working-class origins who win a lottery and set about renovating and running a café-restaurant with the money, on the banks of the Marne. Like the more centrally political films, this one suffers from the difficulty experienced by scriptwriter and director in organizing a narrative line around a disparate collective group. By contrast, *Mollenard* borrows the strategy of *Le Crime de M. Lange* in organizing a working-class ethic around the narrative of an individual hero, whose activities show up and subvert the hypocrisies and collusions of the middle class, the church, and the state.

In addition to Spaak's scripts, those of Prévert for the films directed by Carné perpetuate most effectively in the late thirties the political orientations of the Groupe Octobre—*Drôle de Drame* (1937), *Quai des brumes* (1938), and *Le Jour se lève* (1939). But already in 1936 it was apparent that the scripts produced and directed by this group were moving from the optimistic, even visionary, toward the pessimistic, even tragic. *La Belle Equipe* can be seen as marking the turning point, if only because of its notorious double ending. Spaak and Duvivier had planned an ending in which, through a blend of persecution, chance, and internal dissension caused by a woman, the group progressively self-destructed; on the very day of the official opening of the restaurant, Jean (Jean Gabin) killed Charles (Charles Vanel) and observed, "It was a great idea, a beautiful idea we had. . . . Too beautiful, of course, to succeed." With a view to the popular myth of the happy ending, the producer insisted on a modification, in which the group's project did in fact succeed: instead of fighting over the woman, Jean remonstrates with Charles, "There are things between us worth more than any woman"; Charles chases the woman away, and the opening celebrations proceed unclouded by tragedy. In the spirit of the times, Duvivier organized a referendum among suburban spectators concerning their preference; 83% favored the happy ending. Both were filmed, but the version normally screened still has the upbeat ending.

Essentially, however, even as the Front Populaire was coming to power, those for whom it represented a political triumph were producing films foreshadowing disillusionment. The fate in these films of the working class hero, played more often than not by Jean Gabin, is well-known: from *Hotel du Nord* (Spaak/Jeanson/Carné, 1937) through *Pépé le Moko* (Duvivier/Jeanson, 1936–1937), *Gueule d'amour* (Grémillon/Spaak, 1937), *La Bête humaine* (Renoir, 1938), *La Fin du jour* (Duvivier/Spaak, 1938), *Quai des brumes* and *Le Jour se lève*, *La Règle du jeu* (Renoir, 1939) and *Remorques* (Grémillon/Cayatte/Prévert, 1939–1940), his dreams of escape into a finer, more just world were systematically thwarted and his destiny sealed by agents of a fatality defined in social rather more than in universal terms. As Jeancolas says, "One doesn't need to be an intellectual to establish the link between the multiple deaths imposed on Jean Gabin by his scriptwriters from the autumn of 1936 onward . . . and contemporary disappointment at the reverses and internal dissensions of the Front. The fantastic realism of 1938 was born out of the death of the great hopes of spring 1936."[59]

WARTIME CHANGES IN PERSONNEL

The invasion of France by the German army, the rapid collapse of the French defense, and the demarcation of France into an occupied and an unoccupied zone had a number of consequences for the French cinema, as for every other aspect of French society. Of the two million inhabitants of Paris, 1.3 million retreated south and west before the advancing Germans, leaving Paris momentarily depopulated. Indeed, for the duration of the war, a large percentage of the Parisian population decided for strategic reasons not to return, and a country that had been for centuries accustomed to think of itself in centralized terms as Paris and the provinces had to reconceive itself as not just double but multiple (Paris and the provinces, French and German, occupied and "free"). Moreover, administratively and culturally, the population was fractured and dispersed among a number of distinct regional centers, or even overseas. The refugee population ended up in an arc from Bordeaux through the south of the Massif Central to the Rhône and Côte d'Azur—Aragon in the Dordogne, Jean Marais in the Gers, Trénet in the Midi, Paul Eluard in the Tarn, Barrault in the Quercy, Sacha Guitry and Gide on the Côte d'Azur, Mistinguett at Biarritz.[60] Since Paris had been the focus of most filmmaking in the prewar years, this exodus radically disrupted production and had permanent effects on the distribution of personnel. In addition, the laws introduced by the occupying forces relating not just to Jews but to all those who had been antagonistic to fascism led to a different and even more urgent exodus toward more tolerant nations, or into a clandestinity which significantly hampered any professional activity. More generally, the Germans were for obvious reasons disposed to monitor and control all the main forms of journalistic and cultural expression in order to ensure that no unfavorable representation of their activities should eventuate. Regulations concerning Jews and other antifascist elements were to be applied with particular stringency to such media.

The Jewish statutes were introduced in October 1940, and Rebatet's attack on the Semitic control of French cinema was published in 1941. Rebatet records the names of German Jews involved in the cinema and specifies those that had passed through or taken up residence in France. Speaking of them collectively as "this incredible plague," he says, "the cinema is essentially international. The Jews who have pillaged it belong to the most shifty lot, always moving on." Of Natan: "Is this him we see in photos of lank-haired Jewish lads, in rags, slimy, puddling about in the sewers of their native ghetto?" Of Osso: "Legend paints him as receiving bankers and men of letters perched on a sort of throne, where he sprawls in gold-embroidered pajamas, while a Chinese pedicure trims his nails." Paramount's French agency is run by "a mafia of American Jews." "When they pullulate thus in christian organisms, it is only to make of them dead branches. If a healthy axe doesn't hack off this rotten wood, if the vermin aren't eliminated in time, the whole tree dies." And, echoing L'Herbier, "The very names I have been transcribing aptly depict this seething mass—all these yids with names ending in 'sky' and in 'off' and in 'eff' are wanderers vomited out of the ghettos of the East. . . . Their ugly faces reveal all varieties of baseness and hideousness—hook-nosed, jowled, frizzy, bald, oily; their eyes blinking and bloodshot behind opaque spectacles, or globulously sunk into puffy flesh, speaking at once of slyness and cocksureness." Having pillaged all the riches of France they move on to the cinema and the theater because "when you've got nothing left to steal, they set about rotting your mind."[61]

To indicate the extent to which this insidious corruption had overtaken the French cinema, Vinneuil lists the credits of five films of the thirties (*L'Esclave blanche*, Sorkin, 1939; *Le Dernier Tournant*, Chenal, 1939; *Les Otages*, Bernard, 1939; *De Mayerling à Sarajevo*, Ophüls, 1939–1940; and *Conflit*, Moguy, 1938), noting that out of the 60 personnel involved, only ten are Christians and five of those French: he lists 82 Jewish producers behind the 110 so-called French films in 1938, compared to twelve "Frenchmen"; he lists the Jewish directors—Leonide Moguy, Siodmak, Ophüls, L. Berger, Jean Benoît-Lévy, Marie Epstein, Anatole Litvak, Marc Sorkin, "Cohen, known as Pierre Chenal," Raymond Bernard, Kurt Bernhardt; he lists the Jewish distributors and exhibitors by name; he lists the musicians—"Wiener, disgusting rheumy yid, always looking as if he had some purulent abscess hidden away in his sordid nether regions," and Misraki, Ray Ventura, and "the Jew from Aix," Darius Milhaud. Only the actors are allowed by Rebatet to be mainly French, though even here Dalio and Jean-Pierre Aumont have infiltrated the ranks of the French patriots. Duvivier is noted as having been corrupted by his Jewish wife, and Carné, though Aryan, "has become impregnated by Jewish influences, owing his successes to Jews"; he is "the most accomplished representative of that Marxist aestheticism which everywhere is a fruit of the proliferation of Jews and which spontaneously engenders political, financial, and spiritual degeneration. . . . "[62] Carné and his Jews are blamed for the fatalism of this prewar cinema, as for its politically suspect promotion of leftwing values. "Eighty percent of all film personnel are Jewish, 10% émigrés without papers, and 10% French, but with Marxist or masonic links; and that's not counting the actors, of whom half are of foreign extraction—Russian, Romanian, Italian, American, Swiss, Belgian—the exact statistical state of the cinema we speak of as 'French.' "[63]

He can even quote Gide's criticism of the Jewish presence: " . . . they don't so much bring new material to [French] literature, they don't so much enrich it, as cut short and silence the slow self-definition of our race and seriously, intolerably, distort its meaning. . . . They speak more fluently than us because they have fewer scruples. They speak louder than us because they don't have the same reasons as we do to speak sometimes in hushed tones, out of respect for certain things."[64]

Of all those he mentions, only Carné was able to keep working more or less normally during the war years. Most, and indeed most of those who had worked closely with these suspect filmmakers, sought to emigrate to America or Britain. The French community in Hollywood, still centered on the "Americanized Frenchmen," Charles Boyer and Robert Florey, acquired a number of new and prestigious adherents. Dalio arrived, to begin a new and successful career in America, making 41 films between 1941 and 1970; Duvivier returned to make four films between 1941 and 1943, none as successful as *The Great Waltz* of 1938; one of them, *The Imposter*, scripted by Duvivier himself, starred Jean Gabin, who had refused a contract with Continental in favor of Hollywood, where he rejoined his companion of the time, Marlene Dietrich; Renoir, demobilized from his curious job in fascist but noncombatant Rome, found himself in the same cabin as St.-Exupéry, bound for America; René Clair, in England since 1934 and officially divested of French nationality by the Vichy government, was invited by Giraudoux (first commissioner in the recently established ministry of information) to set up a center for French film production in the United States with Duvivier and joined the Hollywood community in 1941, directing four films for four different studios between then and 1945; Louis Verneuil and a few lesser scenarists arrived (Théry, Pozner). Jean-Pierre Aumont, whose Jewish background was well known, fortuitously made the acquaintance of the Honduran consul and was able to set off in 1942 to take up a seven-year contract with MGM, which was to lead to a sequence of 15 films in America; Simone Simon, who had already established a reputation in Hollywood, returned like Duvivier in 1940; Michèle Morgan took up an RKO contract in June 1940; Victor Francen arrived to begin what was to be a permanent career in Hollywood. A dozen lesser-known actors joined these, as did numerous journalists and critics; Eugène Lourié, the set designer, arrived to work for Renoir and eventually to turn director himself. The credits of Renoir's and René Clair's wartime films give some indication of the size of this community and of the mutual support they extended to one another. Clair's films are mostly shot by Schüfftan, Maté, or Andriot, with Lourié as his architect-decorator.

This film community was only part, if a major part, of a much larger French refugee community in America, including Joseph Kessel, St.-Exupéry, Maurice Dekobra, Breton, Dali, Chagall, and St. John Perse. But not all French emigrants made for the United States. In June 1941, Jouvet got together a touring company and left Paris abruptly for Latin America (with 34 tons of costumes, sets, and archives) and stayed on tour until the liberation. Certain of them—St.-Exupéry and Gabin, for example—were to join up in the Free French forces, the former dying in the last days of the war in a plane crash, the latter returning to France as a tank commander in the allied invasion. For most of the rest, the exile was an ambivalent period.

Leaving France was not difficult, at first. In 1941, Gabin and Jouvet were still able to leave for America, having acquired the necessary papers through normal Vichy channels and sailed from Lisbon. In fact, "even if the holder of a passport was Jewish or Marxist, the Spanish and Portuguese authorities did not hinder their passage. As for the Vichy authorities, they made no effort to retain people opposed to their line . . . especially if they were famous."[65] Moreover, the American representative in Marseilles had established regular channels for antifascist intellectuals to be evacuated to America and was responsible for the departure of several hundred (most particularly Germans such as Thomas Mann, Arthur Koestler and Leon Furchtwangler).

It is widely stated that once in Hollywood, the French filmmakers had considerable difficulty in adapting to the American production machine and that the films they made while there are generally below their best. There is some truth in this, but the generalization results from too narrow a focus on directors, and specifically on Renoir. Certainly the role allocated to directors in Hollywood was unwontedly restrictive for Renoir, given his customary working habits; and more surprisingly, Duvivier didn't manage to work easily at Hollywood during the war; but after a disastrous start with *The Flame of New Orleans*, René Clair managed to reestablish his credibility and work to his own and the companies' satisfaction. More generally, the set designers, costume designers, and technicians found working conditions little different from France, yet technologically and organizationally more favorable. Inevitably, actors without fluent English were restricted to "quaint foreigner" roles, but those who, like Victor Francen and Françoise Rosay, spoke fluent English, made the transition without difficulty. The most constant complaint from actors and directors, however, whether working for majors or, like Clair, struggling to retain a certain independence, was the lack of autonomy in initiating projects—the long periods of paid inactivity were almost more irritating than the programmed nature of the periods of activity.

It is customary to suppose that this relatively large-scale emigration of film personnel left a gap in France which, on the resumption of film production, allowed a new generation of filmmakers to enter the system. The Ragaches, for instance, note that "among the 81 directors of films under the occupation, 19 were newcomers, and not insignificant, either, since among their number we find Jacques Becker, Yves Allégret, Robert Bresson, André Cayatte, Claude Autant-Lara, and Henri-Georges Clouzot, for whom the departure of Jean Renoir, René Clair, Julien Duvivier, and Jacques Feyder had left the way clear."[66] As usual, then, this generalization originates in a focus on directors, as if they alone constitute the category of filmmakers; but even here it is difficult to see how any precise ecological gap had opened up, or what specific qualities allowed the newcomers to "replace" the numerically fewer emigrants. Rather than speaking in terms of replacement, it is more useful to note the radically different conditions under which film production took place during the occupation: it became more heavily regulated and more corporative; longer-term contracts were for some years again explored, especially by Continental, which with its German background found such contracts normal. Consequently, a new type of filmmaker was required, who was more of an organization man, more able to work in a system involving preplanning, regulated production, and carefully observed time schedules. When the industrial kaleidoscope was shaken up and the pieces settled in a new order, it was such individuals who tended to shine.

A crucial element of the shake-up was the disappearance of key producers who had been responsible for some 80% of prewar production, rather than replacement of key directors who had been responsible for some 2%. With the loss of that prewar majority of Jewish producers, decade-long working relationships and friendships were disrupted. Not just directors, but technicians of all sorts found themselves effectively disenfranchised. The relatively small number of producers authorized to work between 1940 and 1944 thus had a disproportionate influence in decreeing which new personnel would be introduced into the industry. In particular, Continental had no established relationships except with those filmmakers who had worked in Germany in the thirties. Raoul Ploquin, head of French production in Germany in the thirties, was entrusted with the direction of the whole industry, and it is through Continental that much of the renovation of the personnel happens. Again, to confine discussion to directors (though, since directors usually had a decisive say in selecting the rest of the crew, there is a knock-on effect): Clouzot, who cooperated with Maurice Gleize on *Le Club des soupirants* (1941) and scripted *Le Dernier des six* (Lacombe, 1941), both produced by Continental, was given his first chance to direct by that firm (*L'Assassin habite au 21*, 1942; *Le Corbeau*, 1943); Carlo-Rim and Fernandel got their first opportunity to direct with Continental (co-directing *Simplet*, 1942; then *Adrien*, Fernandel, 1943); André Cayatte was given his first chance at direction by Continental (*La Fausse Maîtresse*, 1942; then *Au bonheur des dames*, 1943; *Pierre et Jean*, 1943; *Le Dernier Sou*, 1943). It was the Italian firm Scalera, expanding its activities greatly in the Midi, that produced Yves Allégret's *Boîte aux rêves* (1943–1945). Jacques Becker was given his opportunity to direct by a friend with no previous background in production, André Halley des Fontaines, who created a company specifically to produce *Le Dernier Atout* (1942) and later *Falbalas* (1944); the same company (Essor Cinématographique Française) later gave Pierre Prévert another chance at breaking into the ranks of directors with *Adieu Léonard* (1943). It was Synops Films, set up by Roland Tual largely to allow himself to begin directing films (*Le Lit à colonnes*, 1942; *Bonsoir Mesdames, bonsoir Messieurs*, 1943–1944), which gave Bresson his first chance to direct (*Les Anges du péché*, 1943) and Raoul Ploquin setting up his own production company in France for the first time, who gave him his second (*Les Dames du Bois de Boulogne*, 1944–1945). There is therefore a credible case for saying that it was the prohibition against Jewish film production which, by generating a new set of production companies run by individuals with a different range of contacts (and, no doubt, different ideological orientations), generated in turn a certain renovation of filmmaking personnel in these years.

A secondary factor in this renovation was the fact that a large proportion of those filmmakers who did not flee France during the war preferred to live in the so-called free territory in the South, which obliged Parisian studios and production companies to promote or induct new personnel when they began to resume production. In the Midi, the same factor produced a dramatic revival in the fortunes of La Victorine studios, which had been in danger of falling into disuse. By the middle of 1940, refugees and demobilized film personnel had begun to aggregate in Provence and reorganize with a view to resuming film production. Accounts of the succeeding four years all describe this period as paradoxical—the difficult living conditions and the constant political risks being counterbalanced by exhilarating cooperative projects within a cohesive and committed filmmaking community. Wahkevitch's description is typical:

> In the period immediately following the armistice, it was occupation time and Paris emptied itself of its vital component, its intellectual life. The free zone saw an incredible assembly of the country's artistic wealth. The Prévert brothers, Pierre Brasseur, Claude Dauphin, Odette Joyeux, Jean-Pierre Aumont, Sylvain Itkine, and numerous other friends met on the Croisette or at St. Paul de Vence. Impossible to list them all. In Aix, on the Cours Mirabeau, the terrace of the Deux Garçons café became that of the Deux Magots, of Lipp, of the Café Flore, of Foucquet's, and of Chez Francis all at once. Max Ophüls, Marc Allégret, Léo Joannon, Louis Jouvet, Jean Renoir, and a host of actors, musicians, and filmmakers, demobilized or refugee, grouped on the Côte d'Azur around two studio complexes, two filmmaking instruments that remained intact. In Aix, the painters, famous writers, academicians, great mathematicians, members of the Collège de France, the St Cyriens, all met under the century-old plane trees of the cours Mirabeau."[67]

If some subsequently moved on to America, many stayed. Trauner decided not to leave with Wilder, Lang, Lourié, and Ophüls, but to stay with the prewar team to which he had become so attached—Carné, Prévert (who had ridden south with retreating artillery to Pau), and Kosma. Hearing from Langlois that Prévert was now in Cannes, Trauner headed there too, setting up with Brabai, Kosma, and finally some twenty others. There was little food in the South to cope with the influx, and little work. Trauner talks of them all living sparsely, and mostly on credit, until Prévert managed to get work adapting or dialoguing a film (*Le Soleil a toujours raison*, Pierre

Billon, 1941, with Tino Rossi, *Une femme dans la nuit*, E. Gréville, 1941), which kept them in food for a while. Apart from this, "We did little jobs right and left, and were given credit. When Jacques had work, there was money for everyone. When the money dried up, everyone suffered. Then we waited. People said if we survived, we could pay them; if not, tough luck. And I must admit that it's thanks to Prévert that we did survive, ultimately, me and many others."[68]

Many of that group, like Trauner himself and Kosma, were Jews, so their existence was complicated by a semiclandestinity which required others (Wahkevitch, Barsacq, or Douy) to take official credit for the work that gradually began to flow their way. It was an existence not without risks, since a network of informers existed on the margins of the film community; but equally, the existence of the community, in the hills behind the coast, at Tourrette-sur-Loup, was an open secret. Raoul Ploquin wrote saying he knew of their existence there and would try to stop any denunciations before they reached the German authorities. But those authorities probably already knew, if only because on one slightly hallucinatory occasion Dr Greven dined in the same restaurant as they in company with Arletty, who was on particularly intimate terms with one German officer. As the Ragaches say when discussing the analogous community (living in distinctly more luxurious circumstances) at Bel Air—the Bretons, Victor Serge (a Russian political refugee), and others, not to mention visitors Max Ernst and St.-Exupéry's wife—"This noisy life could scarcely be termed clandestine, or even discrete; contrary to general belief in postwar years, such people did not have to hide out. . . . Although perfectly aware of the identity of those living in the villa, the Marseilles police closed their eyes."[69] Despite his ambivalent position, Trauner confirms the relatively benign atmosphere that prevailed until 1943: "On the square, there were big bistros where we met. Everything was sunny, a genial atmosphere that we tried to maintain because it just felt good. Time passed, people dropped in on us and moved on, friends came up to our village to see us. It was the Italian occupation, and, oddly, it was like a great reconciliation between Italians and French, after a long period of misunderstanding. . . . For an occupying army, they were distinctly benign. When Italy surrendered in September 1943, and the Germans arrived, then obviously things changed completely."[70] Gréville also talks of the Italians as sympathetic, and even implies they sabotaged their German allies' projects.[71] Gili too mentions the belief that the Italians saved various Jews from deportation by providing papers certifying that they were needed full-time at the studio.[72] It was in these ambiguous conditions that *Les Visiteurs du soir* and *Lumière d'été* were developed, and later, when Jean-Louis Barrault arrived on the coast in search of a role for a mime, *Les Enfants du paradis*.

Nearby at Cap d'Antibes, another community centered on the actor René Lefèvre: "Day by day, the world of Parisian arts and letters turned up down on the coast: Lucienne and Armand Salacrou, Juliette and Marcel

Achard, Madeleine and Fernand Pouy, Paul Weill and Suzanne Blum, Jean Effel and Madame 'Pachon,' Hélène and Roger Martin du Gard, Roger Chancel (the painter), Cécile and Pierre Laroche (the scriptwriter), Jacques and Pierre Prévert, Marcel Duhamel (of série noire fame), and several others I was to meet later, such as Simone Signoret and Yves Allégret. Roger Martin du Gard brought André Gide and Georges Simenon to meet us."[73] Lefèvre was to become head of the local resistance group centered at Puget-Théniers, responsible for the coastal section from Menton to la Siagne; in this capacity, he organized fellow film personnel and others in the tasks of information-gathering, liberating prisoners, and smuggling resistance and allied personnel into and out of France (notably Jean Moulin).[74]

At Nice, the La Victorine studios were functioning continually. Marc and Yves Allégret, Gance, and Carné all directed films of importance there. Edmond Gréville, who collaborated with Gance, Allégret, and Prévert, provides a more acidulous view of the Tourrette community: "[Prévert] had retired there with half the fauna of the Café Flore, who had followed him to the green zone. . . . It was a curious gathering. There was Pierre, his inseparable brother, Kosma, that talented musician, and a whole bevy of ill-kempt women and escapees from St. Germain des Prés. . . . Translated to the isolated aerial countryside of Tourrette which so contrasted with it, this Parisian mafia left a rather painful impression."[75] Himself prevented from official participation in filmmaking because of past articles ridiculing Hitler, and perhaps suspected by the Vichy government as a possible English agent, Gréville is understandably sour at those who managed to continue working; he implies that they were all in the pay of the Nazis. Unable to work, living like so many others on credit or the help of friends (Viviane Romance and Georges Flamant, also refugees on the coast), he too sought the not unpleasant seclusion of a hilltop villa at Cagnes to wait out the war and turned to writing for his actor friends. Claude Dauphin's company, now established at Nice, put on one of his plays, and he met the young Gérard Philipe being auditioned there. Claude Dauphin himself had to leave hurriedly for Britain soon after, following the filming of *Félicie Nanteuil* (Marc Allégret, 1942–1945), and the film itself was subsequently banned until the liberation because of his presence in it.

The interaction between a surface tranquility, continuing professional involvements, and the ever-present possibility of death is well illustrated by L.-H. Burel's account of the shooting of *La Belle Aventure* (M. Allégret, 1942–1944) with Louis Jourdan and Micheline Presle in the lead roles:

> I remember that the sound man, Jo de Bretagne, used his sound truck at night to pick up London's broadcasts and transmit back to them; and one evening he was arrested and taken to Cimiez by the gestapo, where he was thrown in prison. But with a few mates from the studios we managed to free him, and as I lived at Cap Ferrat—very isolated, in those days—I hid him for a week, as I had occasion to hide many other friends in diffi-

culties. In fact I had two villas and could conceal them while they prepared to head for Spain. My work put me above suspicion. Thus I permitted André Paul Antoine to hide out when he had a few little problems
over the Marseilles radio, and also Schüfftan for a few days before Duvivier managed to organize his passage to America. Allégret himself, with
the stage manager, was looking after the London connection.[76]

Given the size of the filmmaking community on the Côte d'Azur during
this period, the breakdown of existing organizational structures, and the
peculiar conditions of work, it is not surprising that those involved should
try to create a new organizational structure adapted as far as possible to the
situation. In the autumn of 1940 the Amicale des techniciens du cinéma
repliés sur la Côte d'Azur was created to produce an annuary of technicians
available on the coast for work, to help those in material need, and generally to liaise between the members of "this heterogeneous population of
temporary refugees."[77] It also organized benefits to support prisoners deported to Germany. Presided over by the journalist Pierre Gafferé and
funded largely by Léonide Moguy, until his departure for America, the
Amicale was itself often involved in resistance activities, many of its members being strongly militant. In 1942, Jacques Becker organized the pretext
of shooting some exteriors of *Le Dernier Atout* on the Côte d'Azur in order
to liaise between this group and the Parisian resistance. Jacques Lemare,
the cinematographer who had established a list of anti-Nazi militants for
the Amicale, worked with him there and returned to Paris as his cameraman. In an obituary for Nicolas Hayer, cinematographer on *Le Dernier
Atout*, he recalls the work undertaken by that Paris resistance group as the
German retreat signalled the approaching victory. Addressing the dead
Hayer, he says,

As soon as our group was formed, I introduced you to Jean-Paul Le
Chanois, a long-time friend with whom I had made many militant films
before the war. In the exhilarating period that followed, we formed with
Le Chanois, Max Douy, Faurez, and [the scientific documentarist and
communist] Painlevé the first resistance center of the cinema which, in
1943, became the Comité de Libération du Cinéma Français. Remember
how, in addition to the roneotyped circulars we distributed among our
colleagues, and your work helping Jews escape the Gestapo, it was in a
little Normandy hotel where we had gone to film the exteriors of *Graine
au vent* that we laid down the basis of that future ideal of a Collective
Convention, so as to be prepared when the moment came.[78]

As the Germans retreated, the more militant of the Amicale's members,
mostly of strong leftwing sympathies (Louis Daquin, Le Chanois, Nicolas
Hayer, Max Douy, Jacques Lemare, and Houdet) in the name of the Liberation Committee, beseiged and took over the Paris headquarters of film
administration—a symbolic rather than effective act, associating film per-

sonnel with those other categories of workers then resuming national (and, as they supposed, collective) responsibility for their own professional destiny.

Undoubtedly the liberation made retrospective resistants of many French people, but equally clearly there was widespread resistance activity by leftwing elements within the industry—latent and cautious early on, but more active, explicit, and effective as the war drew to an end. Even in his more vindictive moments, Gréville can put few concrete names to his implications of collaboration among film personnel. He talks of Suzy Delair "arriving from the capital to resume her rousing performances at the Cintra of that stultifying fascist song *Merde pour la reine d'Angleterre.*"[79] A very few directors made extended propaganda films for the fascist cause (*Les Corrupteurs*, Ramelot, 1941; *Forces occultes*, Mamy, 1942–1943). The best-known collaborator among the acting fraternity was Robert Le Vigan. Openly favorable to Nazism, he was obliged to depart abruptly as the Allied armies advanced through Italy, interrupting the shooting of *Les Enfants du paradis* (Pierre Renoir replaced him in the role of the rag and bone merchant, and the relevant scenes were refilmed). He was to be condemned to ten years forced labor, the confiscation of his property, and "national shame," and after several years of imprisonment to depart for Argentina. Arletty, whose involvement had been sexual rather than ideological, was arrested and placed under surveillance for eighteen months. Maurice Chevalier, without collaborating, had at least believed that Pétain and Vichy might represent a viable solution and had made imprudent contacts which got him into trouble at the liberation. Indeed, rumors that he had been lynched by patriots or executed by the maquis were widespread for some time and officially announced on the radio. As he acknowledged to René Lefèvre, "I'm an utter idiot, I was taken in by the old dodderer."[80] So was Pierre Fresnay: his rightwing sympathies for hierarchical structures, control by an elite, a strong leader, were well known, and he remained a convinced supporter of Pétain long after the war. This brought him considerable attention at war's end, including a six-week detention nominally for presiding over the Actor's Union during the war, but perhaps to save his skin during the most violent weeks of the purges.

But as Jeancolas rightly observes, it's as difficult now as it was in the immediate postwar years to know how to pose the question of collaboration. Since 1929, film magazines had been enthusing about Franco-German collaboration, and throughout the thirties that collaboration had been extremely fruitful, even prestigious for an actor or director. "In 1939, Fernandel and Jules Berry were filming *L'Héritier de Mondésir* in Berlin—a French-language film, financed by the Germans. In 1941 and 1942 they were to film more French-language films financed by the Germans; but in Paris and the Midi—under the auspices of Continental. When Greven, the boss, received Henri Decoin, Henri-Georges Clouzot, and Raoul Ploquin in his office on the Champs-Elysées, they had a lot of memories in common to discuss."[81] Greven, after all, had been director of production for Decoin in Germany. All those who had had such contacts and who had worked too consistently for Continental during the occupation (three times was somewhat arbitrarily fixed as the acceptable maximum) were to be investigated in the postwar purges—notably Clouzot and his scriptwriter, Louis Chavance, because of the contrasting readings allowed by his film *Le Corbeau.* Both were banned from the profession for life—a ban that was subsequently reversed. André Paulvé, who had managed the La Victorine studios during the occupation, was also investigated. Like Chevalier and Fresnay, Sacha Guitry was imprisoned for two months for his support for Pétain, and then released.

Of particular concern were those who had participated in the official visits to Germany during 1941 and 1942 intended to foster Franco-German cultural relations; along with Drieu la Rochelle, André Bonnard, Vlaminck, van Dongen, and many others, these included film personnel such as Danielle Darrieux, Viviane Romance, Albert Préjean, Junie Astor—and Suzy Delair. But then, Préjean and Darrieux had often been there before the war, notably to work in films directed by Clouzot. They had many friends there. "Habit and friendship counted for a lot. They may not excuse, but they certainly explain."[82] Préjean was imprisoned a while at the liberation, as were Giono, Pierre Benoit, and various editors and journalists. Among film journalists, Rebatet, Bardèche, and Brasillach are the best known. Bardèche was arrested and imprisoned, but Rebatet joined the many collaborators retreating with the Vichy government to Baden Baden, then Sigmaringen in the Black Forest—collaborators such as Céline and his close friend Le Vigan, the pianist Lucienne Delforge, and Jean Luchaire, director of *Les Nouveaux Temps.* Most later returned to France when the desire for a rigorous justice had somewhat abated, escaping with prison sentences. In the heat of liberation, a more violent judgment resulted in some 10,000 deaths of supposed collaborators throughout France, of which about 800 were the result of a proper trial. Among the latter, Robert Brasillach was executed on 6 February 1945 for his pro-Nazi propaganda in *Je Suis Partout* and for his many denunciations of compatriots, which on occasion led to their deaths.[83] Had he too absented himself for a discrete period, he would probably have survived. He surrendered to save his mother from persecution; but also, as he said, because he acknowledged responsibility for his acts, "I am willing to be judged, even executed; but they won't be able to say of me: the bastard got away with it."[84]

UNIONIZATION

The most significant institutional development within the postwar French cinema was the tendency toward the formalization of institutional structures, a tendency that contributed to moving the classic cinema out of an era of amateurism and organizational incoherence and making it a regulated body of people confident in their own professionalism. This development was twin-pronged: on the one hand there was a marked increase in emphasis on the need for formal training programs, providing qualifications which in some areas became essential prerequisites for entry into the industry. And on the other hand there was a marked increase in the degree to which the industry had become unionized, subject to the possession of a work card, and therefore effectively a closed shop.

This progressive formalization of the industry had an important secondary effect on gender distribution within certain job categories, notably in the editing area, where it contributed to reducing the number of women employed—a factor on which the French classic cinema had never had much cause to pride itself. These last sections of the chapter on personnel will look at these tendencies; they will also explore the fact that the tendency toward professionalization can, at least retrospectively, seem somewhat paradoxical, given the multiplicity of factors at work over the same period within the industry which were tending in precisely the opposite direction, toward its deprofessionalization. To that extent, the period is one of internal contradictions; arguably it was those contradictions, flowering in certain aspects of the New Wave practices of the late fifties, which were to bring about the demise of the classic cinema, or rather the more insistent division of French production between a classic and an auteurist cinema, based respectively on the producer and on the director.

In the course of the ten years from 1932 on, French filmmaking personnel had had to face a number of severe industrial pressures, including competition from foreign refugee and immigrant workers, unemployment, and political turmoil. It is precisely in these circumstances that the value of organized collective action becomes most apparent, and this was particularly the case in the thirties, given the fiercely populist and collectivist ideology espoused by a militant core of the filmmakers. Then in 1940 the occupation by a fascist power at once occasioned the dissolution of all such activist bodies and their reformation into other collectivities with a more hierarchical and instrumental role. This decade saw, then, the gradual development within the industry of a recognizable industrial organization, transforming it from an anarchic and atomized artisanat into a more systematically representative structure. The liberation revised this structure once again, leaving the postwar French cinema with a normally unionized personnel for the first time in its existence.

On the whole, loose federations of the four main employer groups (producers, distributors, exhibitors, and technical industries) had organized earlier and more effectively than the salaried workers, if only because they had had to represent the interests of a hitherto nonexistent "industry" in political and administrative circles. From 1908, a Chambre syndicale des éditeurs (i.e., producers) founded by Méliès had been succeeded by a variety of organizations grouping employers with different industrial and political interests. These diverse chambers, unions, and federations had made occasional attempts to unite into a coherent pressure group, focusing primarily on the reduction of taxes, the normalization of equipment standards, and the prevention of government intervention in private enterprise. Roger Weil-Lorac, who was active in these attempts and became secretary-general of the Chambre syndicale française de la cinématographie in the late twenties, recently noted that "the film establishment suffered in those distant days from chronic discord, and divisions disappeared uniquely when faced with the tax office."[85] All attempts at unity had, however, met with at best only momentary success, and throughout the early thirties fundamental organizational disagreements subsided. Paul Léglise has chronicled these disagreements[86] and the various bodies to which they gave rise—notably in 1935 an industry-wide division between those unions affiliated with the Fédération des chambres syndicales and those affiliated with the Comité du film.

Employee organizations were little better situated. From 1917 a Société des auteurs de films had been set up under Feuillade's presidency, which in 1929 united with composers to form the Association des auteurs de films, and there were groupings of a few other categories of workers. Actors had had associations of various sorts since 1840, which evolved into a Chambre syndicale in 1890, which in turn gave way to the Union des artistes, including film personnel in 1917. It was, however, the Confédération générale des travailleurs (CGT) which most nearly spoke on behalf of the industry's groupings, though these were not integrated systematically into its organizational structure. As with employers, employee associations proliferated in the early thirties. One of these, the Syndicat des chefs cinéastes français, founded in August 1933, had as its administrators André Berthomieu, Julien Duvivier, and Jean Renoir.[87]

As soon as the impact of immigrant workers was felt on the film industry, the salaried workers began agitating for a regulation of personnel which would protect French nationals. They were successful in obtaining a decree (23 April 1933) which was to remain in force throughout the three decades under study. This decree affected all forms of spectacle; its main effect in the cinema was to limit the foreign "artists" (lead actors) to 10% and technical personnel (notably foreign sound engineers and cinematographers) to 50%. The latter figure offers a vivid illustration of the impact of German technicians in the relevant latter fields. The text of the decree called for the reduction of this percentage at six-month intervals to 25% at the end of 1934.[88] Dissatisfaction continued, however, and in May 1934 the *Cinématographie Française* published statistics indicating the extent of the problem. Fifty percent of French workers were unemployed, whereas if French personnel had not been displaced by foreigners, up to two-thirds of the unemployed would have been working. It could easily seem as if, both globally in economic terms and locally in employment terms, France was losing out by being more generous in welcoming foreigners than were rival nations.

FIGURE 4.1   **Unemployment Rates in the Cinema 1934**

Personnel	Total French Personnel	Out of Work French Personnel	Working Foreigners
Directors	38	21	8
Cameramen	95	47	26
Cinematographers	30	3	17
Production Assistants	85	54	over 30
Musicians	21	18	5
Editors	27	8	over 15
Set Designers	39	10	6

It is in this context that the Fédération nationale des artisans français du film organized in March 1935 a gigantic demonstration, hiring ten buses to take protesting workers up the Champs-Elysées and around the boulevards, waving banners proclaiming "French workers are starving," and "Frenchmen, save your country's cinema."[89] Retrospectively, it resembled a rehearsal for the larger national strikes triggered by the CGT in June 1936, heralding the advent of the Popular Front and resulting in the 40-hour week, paid leave, and the principle of social contracts regulating working conditions. During the strikes which led up to these agreements, and which lasted from February to June, film personnel massively supported the other workers: for some weeks, studios and most laboratories ceased to function, most cinemas ceased to screen films, work places were occupied. The employers' federations, through P.-A. Harlé, editor of the *Cinématographie Française*, pleaded for an apolitical cinema, at times likening the film industry to one big family which could only be divided against itself by the virus of union agitations, at other times claiming that its artisanal nature meant that everyone was both boss and worker, so class interests did not apply to the film industry.[90] In fact, their principal anxiety was that Paul Faure, close ally of Léon Blum in the Socialist Party (SF10) would be effective in implementing his announced intention to nationalize the industry.

The CGT had played a leading role in the events of June 1936, and this incited the film workers to affiliate their organizations more formally with that union. Within the CGT there were two factions, led by Cebron and by Jarville respectively, the latter being the more militant. Cebron proposed a binary industry, with a nationalized core constituted by the former GFFA company, taken over and "sanitized" by the state, competing with a private sector. More intransigent, Jarville pursued a total nationalization of the film industry and in February 1937 outlined in the CGT's journal *Le Peuple* an elaborate plan for such a cinema.

Not surprisingly, the floating of this proposal, especially in such credible detail, disturbed the employer groups. Throughout the year they had been engaged in a campaign to ward off the threat. In an open letter to the minister they had warned him "to see that the industry was not subjected to regulation likely to hinder the free expression of the thought and art of our nation."[91] Now they united as they had not been able to before, forming a single *Confédération générale du cinéma* grouping all four employer sectors, through which their interests could be expressed rather more forcefully than in the past. For a brief period (1937–1939) the industry therefore functioned in a fairly classic unionized structure, with the CGT negotiating on behalf of the majority of workers and the CGC representing the united employer groups. Under the auspices of these two groupings, a number of collective conventions were agreed concerning conditions of work within the cinema: union membership itself was acknowledged as a right, and delegates were to be elected the day before each shoot; paid leave was to depend on period of work; model contracts were drawn up, etc.[92] These collective conventions acquired force of law and were applicable to all those working in the industry, not just to union members.

But that the organizational structure of the industrial personnel had not by any means completely emerged from its atomistic past is apparent from an attempt made by *La Technique Cinématographique* in January 1938 to describe the various representative organizations that had emerged from this process and their relations with one another. The list of organizations and relationships covers a page of print and mentions 34 different bodies.[93] Even this degree of coherence did not last long: in May 1939 the employer groups had already broken up, under pressure of internal dissension. The occupation saw the remaining sectors, together with all employee groupings, disbanded by the Germans.

What replaced them was a series of industrial groupings sufficiently few in number yet sufficiently closely related to work practices that the Propagandaabteilung could summon representatives rapidly and expect their instructions to be implemented efficiently: cinema proprietors, distributors, technical industries, producers, creative personnel, actors. As Léglise notes, "without wishing to judge the actions of these corporative organisms, it must be acknowledged that they seem to have answered to the needs of the profession in the circumstances of the day."[94] Instrumental in resuscitating the wartime cinema, they were subsequently integrated into a Vichy administration and continued to function throughout the war.

Alongside them, and frequently grouping the same personnel, a series of clandestine organizations developed. Around a Front national organized by René Blech, five other groupings developed: the Union des syndicats du film, which was affiliated with the CGT, now functioning illegally; the Comités populaires d'entreprise du cinéma; the Employeurs patriotes du cinéma; the Mouvement des prisonniers et déportés du cinema; and the Communistes du cinéma. Less related to the industrial structure and more to the political circumstances of the resistance movements, these groupings nevertheless established an effective liaison which lasted until the liberation. They were then united as the Comité de libération du cinéma français under the presidency of Pierre Blanchar, with the active assistance of Jean Painlevé, Louis Daquin, Jean Grémillon, André Zwobada, Jacques Becker, and Pierre Renoir, among others.[95]

The spirit of collective action and of fraternity that accompanied the liberation, but which drew heavily on the leftwing and particularly Communist element in the wartime film union movement, is evident in the "spontaneous" collaborations that marked the years 1945–1949. A sense of collaborating on nationally crucial tasks gave an intensity to existence: "there were a heap of clandestine organizations in the cinema and the theater—the unions, the PC—and things were really jumping. You could have three clandestine meetings in the one week."[96] As Lucien Aguettand has said, contrasting the spirit of the later classic cinema with the thirties and immediate postwar years, "We worked as friends, very close to one another. . . . Now, when a film's finished, you go home and you sit there on your own. Even after the liberation, we would still meet, forty or so of us from all the groupings, every Monday. We exchanged information. But little by little the studios became jealous of their techniques, and those technicians who 'talked too much' were blackballed. The industrials destroyed all that was living in the industry."[97]

Certainly the process of industrialization transformed the industry in the postwar years into an archetypal employer/employee confrontation, in which the CGT assembled and spoke for all ten worker unions, and the four leading employer groups united as they had before the war, this time into a Confédération nationale du cinéma français. Signs of this typically industrial struggle were apparent already in 1948, when the studios fired all technical staff in order to minimize overhead. For the worker, contract employment no longer existed thereafter, and work became dependent on being hired for a particular shoot. Deprived of personnel to undertake regular maintenance work, studio equipment deteriorated and decor storage and construction declined. But from the employers' point of view, "the modifications . . . proved excellent. Personally I was against the idea," said the director of Paris-Studios Cinema in 1953, "which I saw as a desertion of patronal responsibility. Regrettably, experience has proved me wrong since, anxious to get hired for a shoot, the workers promptly achieved a much greater productivity. From then on, the work got done normally with crews some 40% smaller than previously, and in the same time. This practice moreover permitted personnel to be selected such that only the best of them remained in the profession. So we can say that currently the film crews available to us are hardworking and highly qualified."[98] In sum it is clear that the French cinema in postwar years began to think of itself in industrial terms. For the bosses, cost efficiency and productivity overrode the considerations of fraternal and communal involvement. For the workers, improving working conditions began to assume as great an importance as their vocation for an intoxicating medium of expression. It is equally clear that the employers' emphasis on productivity ties in neatly with the union's own emphasis during this period on professional standards and qualifications.

During the fifties it became the case that union action could itself attract the wrath of employers, to the extent that the highest professional qualifications could not save a worker from being blackballed. Henri Alekan was widely recognized as the leading practitioner and theoretician among cinematographers of the fifties, yet he was forced out of work, "overlooked" by directors of production because his union activities had led him to take strong public stands on industrial matters. Finally, he was obliged to spend a long period overseas. The necessity for unions to affiliate with the Communist CGT in order to achieve any effective action also caused problems within the ranks of such a disparate "industry," riddled with anarchists and libertarians. Henri Jeanson, president of the scriptwriters' union, found at one stage that the ideological compromises required of him were too great, and he resigned to join a breakaway group. Charles Spaak took over until the split healed. In the actors' union, Gérard Philipe succeeded André Luguet, and his powerful leftwing convictions were perfectly compatible with the union's militancy throughout the fifties.

In general terms, then, the idealistic propositions formulated at the time of the liberation for a collectively administered cinema based on democratic institutions quite rapidly gave way to a largely capitalist industrial structure in which the power of finance was more determining than ideals. But though this postwar capitalism incorporated certain values and attitudes typical of other postwar capitalist industries—efficiency, productivity, specialization, profit—it incorporated also a minority nationalized element, and it retained its prewar industrial structure, characterized by a multitude of relatively small-scale production companies.

THE FORMALIZATION OF TRAINING

For all effective purposes the formal training of film personnel can be traced back to the founding of the Institut des hautes études cinématographiques (IDHEC) late in 1943, though that origin itself rapidly became enshrouded in mythology. IDHEC was not strictly the first institution to orient its courses toward the cinema. Certain categories of film personnel had always had extracinematic training of a professional nature. Most composers who worked in the industry had been trained in the network of conservatoires throughout France, and many actors had either been trained in the state-run courses or had enrolled in the private dramatic art courses. Certain of these latter had for tactical purposes oriented some of their teaching toward the cinema, though the main body of all such courses was oriented toward the theater, at least until the war. But one institution in particular had been founded with the needs of the cinema specifically in mind—the Ecole technique de photographie et de cinématographie (ETPC).

The ETPC was founded in 1925 by Paul Montel, a publisher who was to bring out a large number of the more technical film books of the next decades. The courses were inaugurated in 1926 by Louis Lumière himself, and the school was directed by M. Montel until 1946. Initially a private institution, in 1937 it became officially recognized as an Ecole des métiers, and in 1951 it was integrated financially into the state education system, though only in 1964 was it accorded the title of a Lycée technique d'etat and dedicated to the memory of Louis Lumière. Installed in a former primary school in the rue Vaugirard, it was usually known as either the ETPC or Vaugirard film school; but also, confusingly, the ENPC (Ecole nationale) and the Louis Lumière school. Initially, there were, as the school's formal title implies, two main sets of courses, directed respectively toward photography and the cinema, though to these was added in 1947 a section for electro-technicians, which was intended to develop the skills necessary for the design, exploitation, and installation of the new technologies (sound, color, projection equipment, etc.). As the director noted, "the vocation of our establishment is primarily technical,"[99] and the film courses were oriented toward the more technical aspects of the cinema. They were particularly effective in training sound engineers and film cameramen, and a large percentage of two generations of classic French cinematographers and camera operators (fiction films, newsreel, and documentary) went through their courses. In addition, they produced laboratory technicians skilled in developing and printing. Although they included the mention of "directors" in their publicity material, and although certain of the courses treated "the grammar of film," the history of art and costume, and "film criticism," the primarily technical and practical orientation of the courses was never effective in providing that theoretical, administrative, and artistic knowledge which both the industry and the individuals concerned considered essential to the formation of a director. Nevertheless, several directors of the New Wave (Demy, de Broca) were students at the ETPC.[100]

For the record, two further sets of courses in film existed before the establishment of IDHEC, both of them correspondence courses. The Ecole universelle par correspondance had existed since 1907 and aimed as its name implies to cover all aspects of human understanding. The extant film courses date from about 1930 and may have been initiated as a result of the theoretical and stylistic debates concerning film in the twenties or because of the demand for new personnel in the industry at the time of the introduction of sound. The other set of courses was produced by a correspondence school specifically oriented toward the cinema, the Ecole technique du cinema par correspondance. Founded by Ivan Noë around 1943 and based in Nice, the school offered a series of 24 courses in all aspects of film production and exploitation. Neither of the correspondence schools managed to deal effectively with the problems involved in treating such a practical and often technical subject without the availability of technology or practical classes. There is no evidence of their having had any significant effect on the training of film personnel; the main value of the courses is as a record of the state of certain debates at their time of writing.

The foundation of IDHEC is indissolubly linked to the name of Marcel L'Herbier, its first director, who had from at least 1938 called for the establishment of a more artistically oriented institution devoted to forming film personnel, as part of a "University of the New Arts."[101] He was by no means alone, however, in recognizing the desirability of such an institution: those in favor of nationalization in 1936 had foreshadowed it, and when he appeared before the Renaitour commission in March 1937, Jarville, secretary-general of the filmworkers union affiliated with the CGT, had spelled out the need for an "Institut d'etat de la technique cinématographique," combining theoretical and practical studies and associated with a laboratory and a production studio. His detailed account of the management of such an institute, of the scholarship system needed to support the students, and of its relation with the film industry outlined precisely the functioning of IDHEC. "There can be no question of constructing a genuinely national cinema," he said, "without a training establishment for forming expert personnel and for retraining existing personnel."[102]

But in fact the minister, Jean Zay, had himself acknowledged to the inquiry the previous month the need for such an institute. He ascribed the problems of the French cinema largely to the fact that recent advances in technique had been dramatic and that civil authorities had been indifferent to the pressures these placed on an already chaotic industry. "Since the cinematic professions have recruited up till now in a purely empirical fashion and no professional training has been involved . . . the industry has attracted a good number of well-meaning people who are totally incompetent and inexperienced. Aside from a certain Cinematographers School, which, whatever its interest, is not particularly influential, there is no professional training at all."[103]

The inquiry also heard from the director of an association called Ciné-photo-radio, which claimed to have begun to remedy this situation by establishing three schools in each of those three areas and a fourth in dramatic art (for actors), to be currently employing 18 teachers, and to be training some 650 students;[104] but no trace of its effect on the industry's personnel is on record. Effectively, therefore, when it appeared in 1944, IDHEC was filling a long-recognized and widely discussed need.

Accounts of its origins differ widely, perhaps because the prestige which it was later to acquire tempted various of the individuals concerned to appropriate to themselves prime responsibility for its existence. All accounts agree that it can be traced back to the exodus of film personnel from Paris in 1940 and their regrouping in the Midi. Alongside the Amicale des techniciens du cinéma repliés sur la Côte d'Azur, an organization called the Centre des jeunes (or Centre des jeunes du cinéma français) was developed for the dissemination among the young of film culture, knowledge, and skills. Responsibility for its establishment is allocated variously to the short-film director Louis Cuny (by Gili), to the feature director Maurice Cloche (by himself), to four cinematographers (Alekan, Agostini, Claude Renoir, and Page, by Dudley Andrews), or perhaps more securely to a vague but extensive cooperative involving most of those in the Amicale.[105] In Wahkevitch's account, in mid-1940, "Under the name of the Centre des jeunes du cinéma français we founded a grouping of cinema professionals and got the subsidies necessary to organize and install it in the Château de Castellaras, recently restored. Much later this Centre des jeunes was to transform itself into IDHEC . . . ; but who remembers now that this very important organization for the training of filmmakers grew out of an idea that germinated in that committed group of ours, that group that resisted throughout the occupation . . . the conformists and the blinkered civil servants of Vichy?"[106]

Certainly, before the year's end, a number of influential individuals were involved—Henri Alékan, Jacqueline Audry, Yves Baudrier, Jean Lods, René Clément, Paul Gilson, Maurice Labro, Claude Renoir, Roger Leenhardt, Agostini, Louis Page, Wahkevitch, and Maurice Cloche. In March 1941, the focus of activities switched from Castellaras (just north of Cannes) to Nice, where, perhaps at the instigation of Paul Legros,[107] the Centre installed itself in the villa El Patio on the boulevard Tzarewitch and became the Centre artistique et technique des jeunes du cinéma (CATJC). The main activity of the two successive centers was the screening of films (even banned films such as *Quai des brumes* and *L'Atalante*) accompanied by talks and discussions. They can therefore be seen as foreshadowing the postwar revival of the cine-club movement in France and oriented rather toward the formation of audiences than the formation of filmmakers. However, there is evidence to suggest that discussion at the Centres was also angled (perhaps inevitably, given the staff) toward practical aspects of filming, with a view to interesting the students in a career in filmmaking. According to Lods, one aim was the "formation of young film technicians."[108] Moreover, alongside the screening of short films, which were the mainstay of the course, some practical filmmaking took place: for instance, René Clément undertook in 1942 and 1943 the production of two short films, respectively on the railways (*Ceux du rail*, which was to lead to *La Bataille du rail*, 1945) and on the winter pasturing of sheep (*La Grande Pastorale*, of which some elements can be found in *Les Jeux interdits*, 1951).

The CATJC was an official organization subsidized at least partially by the government (the Secrétariat d'Etat à la Jeunesse). It put on public screenings (e.g., the Journées du cinéma et des arts, in March 1942) and began to establish the specialized library oriented toward the techniques of filmmaking which was later to become the basis of the IDHEC library. It seems likely there were other less formally organized groups involved in disseminating film culture, perhaps including that of Ivan Noë, which evolved into the correspondence school. Toward the end of 1943, the Nice groupings decided to amalgamate with a drama school in Paris oriented toward producing film actors (the Centre de formation artistique de Paris, directed by Henri Fescourt) and to transfer all activities to Paris. At a general assembly of the Centre's members on 4 September 1943 IDHEC was thus formed; it moved to Paris the following month and began teaching in January of 1944. Marcel L'Herbier was its first president, and in his inaugural address he represents himself as having struggled for 18 months (i.e., since mid-1942), with the active help of the government authorities, to get the project off the ground. He describes its triple aim as follows:

> We must hope that it will form a phalanx of artists and technicians who when peace returns will be able to work not only in France, but in all the new film production centers abroad. They will constitute a spiritual export of inestimable value. [Our aim is] to create creators of film, in the required numbers, and endowed with profound human values. Our second aim [is] to foster pure artistic and technical research. . . . Our third aim is to spread cinematographic culture.[109]

This third aim, the formation of public taste, involved the projection of films in various youth centers, accompanied by discussion sessions, and the publication of a number of brochures, bulletins, and film data cards. It never constituted a central aim and soon faded from sight. The second aim led to the establishment of the IDHEC library—an enormously successful enterprise, without which much recent research, including this present work, would have been unthinkable.

However, the core of the institute's work was from the beginning its commitment to providing systematic training in the arts and techniques of the cinema. The courses covered eight filmmaking activities at various times—direction, production, cinematography, sound, editing, scripting, decor, and costume. They lasted two or three years, depending on the areas of specialization, and were completed by an obligatory year's assistantship in the industry. At the end of this period, successful students received a diploma and the professional card which was now a prerequisite to working in the industry. From 1945, evening courses for upgrading the qualifications of existing industrial personnel were instituted at the request of the unions, and in 1948, with the benevolent support of the school head, Henri Agel turned the school cine-club screenings at the lycée Voltaire into a full preparatory class for secondary school students wishing to orient their studies toward directing or editing.[110] Successful completion of that course gave statistically a 40% chance of entry to IDHEC in the early years, when other candidates had no better than an 8–12% chance, because of the demand. The cinematography and sound courses were (or rapidly became) one-year postgraduate aesthetic supplements to the ETPC courses, which thus became essential prerequisites for entry to those IDHEC courses. In the fifties, the standard career path for a cinematographer was to graduate from one (or both) of these, then work up through the ranks of assistants to cadreur. The path was not linear and might well depend on whether the aspirant was more technically or more aesthetically oriented. In the former case, first assistant was a logical step, or even an endpoint to the career. In the latter, second assistant and then cadreur were more logical. By 1947 Leprohon could assert in *Les 1001 Métiers du Cinéma* that

> You can scarcely expect to become cinematographer without having passed successively through the various secondary positions in the team. Certainly, camera work can't be an ad hoc affair. The knowledges required in this trade of a purely technical nature are becoming more and more important. Incessant progress in the fields of chemistry and of optics, and incessant advances in technology don't allow one to approach the job as an amateur; you have to acquire the ABC of the trade, and it's not in the studio that the beginner will learn that. . . . The ETPC was until recently the seedbed of our cinematographers. Agostini and others came through it. To acquire the fundamentals of the job, the aspirant does two years' work there, completed if possible by a year at IDHEC. After that, he will be looking for a job as second assistant on the set; and after working on three films, whether paid or not, the apprentice will be able to begin his career as second assistant. . . . But if there exists a school to prepare one for the basic career grade, there's none to get one in to the next. It's up to the individual to provide those credentials on the job which will allow him to pass from second to first assistant or from first to cadreur.[111]

Not only Agostini, but Charoy, Grignon, Levent, Robin, Thiquet, Villard and many others followed this path. Early on, you had to be lucky to receive such a systematic formation; later on you had to be lucky to enter the profession without it.

But it was in the field of set design that this formalization of training was most striking. The décor section of the industry manifested a marked coherence and solidarity in the face of postwar threats to the profession, emphasizing regular career paths and essential qualifications. In this respect, the décor sector contrasts markedly with the directorial and script-writing sectors, which were never able to reconcile themselves to the idea that their job might be teachable. Perhaps because of the significant technical and trade aspect of the décor sector, which involved obviously teachable practices and techniques, but also because of the long history of Beaux Arts and Arts Décoratifs courses which many of the profession had themselves graduated from (and which also involved the techniques of painting and sculpture as well as art history), the décor sector at IDHEC found the design of an appropriate curriculum unproblematic.

It was overseen by Hugues Laurent from 1947 (by which time he had himself been in the trade for 43 years) till retirement in 1967 and by Léon Barsacq for two years thereafter till his death; but it attracted the commitment of all leading members of the sector. This commitment manifested itself in lectures, in comments on assignments, in "stages" for the students, and in a guarantee of work on graduation. Douy, Barsacq, Trauner, Wahkevitch, and others would regularly be involved in the students' projects. Indeed, so close was the link between IDHEC and the profession that it rapidly became necessary to have the IDHEC diploma to enter the profession. In this, the architect-decorators were distinct from other areas of the industry, all of which while recognizing that the courses at IDHEC were willing to accept other forms of qualification. In effect, in conjunction with the work-card required across the industry, the décor segment of the industry used the IDHEC diploma to regulate numbers qualified to work as decorators. Having passed through the IDHEC course, students were expected to spend 5–10 years as assistant decorator to one of the masters, whereupon the more talented ones would be offered the possibility of working as chief decorator themselves. At one international congress to discuss the teaching of architecture/decoration in the cinema, organized by IDHEC in 1955, the Italian contingent expressed astonishment at the high degree of regulation which resulted. For them, there was no oversight over those working in the trade, no work card, and no necessary qualifications. As the French representative explained to them, "the set of rules is not only formally written down, it is applied. We architect-decorators are highly unionized in France, but it is nevertheless not that which is the critical factor; what is critical is our profound professional solidarity, which translates notably as an intense awareness of the need for professional training in order to practice the trade. In the French cinema, decoration is certainly the most highly organized of all the professional specializations."[112]

It is hard to summarize the achievements of these training establishments, more particularly of IDHEC, and their impact on classic French filmmaking. They certainly constituted a useful contribution to France's international prestige, since about 273 of the 617 students who had graduated by 1960 were foreign students. One estimate suggests that the 344 French graduates from those fifteen cohorts constituted one-third of the film personnel in the relevant sections of the industry by 1960 and that two-thirds of French personnel had passed through IDHEC or the ETPC by 1965, only one-third being "self-made men."[113] A large number had gone into television—notably the bulk of the sixth cohort, which graduated in 1950, when the demand for production staff in television was increasing rapidly. In promotional material and articles much was made of certain significant figures who had emerged from its courses, notably Alain Resnais and the writer François Boyer from the first cohort, but also Henri Colpi and Sacha Vierney from the second, Claude Sautet from the fourth, Jacques Rozier from the fifth, Averty, Serge Bourguignon, and Bernard Evein from the sixth, Roberto Enrico from the seventh, Louis Malle from the eighth, and Costa Gavras from the thirteenth. Defending its record, the staff also claimed that close links with "the profession" (as it was now regularly called) had led to higher standards of technical competence and an informed personnel able to articulate arguments in defense of their practices. The French "quality product" of the fifties was seen as due in large part to the professionalism of IDHEC graduates.

Much of this is true. Announcing in 1954 that "the age of empiricism is over," and noting that IDHEC now formed the broad approach road to the technical branches of the profession, the then minister asserted that it was essential to systematize as far as possible in conjunction with the profession the integration of graduates into the ranks of filmmakers.[114] Qualifications had totally replaced the spontaneous and informal recruitment processes of the thirties. ETPC qualifications or a lycée Voltaire course were becoming essential to enter IDHEC, an IDHEC qualification was necessary in many cases to acquire a work card and thus to become an assistant on the set, and a fixed number or period of assistantships was needed before one could take an organizational role on a major shoot. But whether this formalization of recruitment and articulation of existing technical practices as professional codes had been entirely beneficial was by no means so clear. There are two obvious senses in which the professionalization of recruitment proved counterproductive. One is the progressive elimination of women from the single major role they had managed to appropriate for themselves in the French cinema—the task of editing. Certain minor roles, such as the script-girl (who could be assimilated to a director's secretary) were and continued to be considered appropriate for females. From all the major filmmaking roles, women were effectively excluded. This contrasts to some extent with the preclassic cinema, where female directors such as Germaine Dulac and Marie Epstein could play a leading role, and with the New Wave, where Marguerite Duras, Nina Companeez and Agnès Varda could play leading roles. The emphasis on technology and finance had rapidly excluded women from such roles in the classic cinema, and Jacqueline Audry is alone in scripting and directing a significant number of films. Editing was therefore all the more important as the sole remaining avenue for women to enter the profession. But the job of editing a film, which had fallen almost exclusively to women in the thirties and forties, underwent a reevaluation in the late forties and fifties, partially as a result of IDHEC's work. Both directly, because it became an intellectually respectable and even central task, and indirectly, because of the professionalization of all filmmaking tasks, editing began to attract male students. The role of both teacher and taught, both authority and future professional, tended to be male. Interviewed in the mid-fifties, Henri Colpi notes that the percentage of men occupying the post of editor in France is increasing,[115] and if in 1957 the IDHEC literature is still assuming that the editor in each production team is female,[116] subsequent graduation rates were a guarantee that this would not long remain the case. The one crucial avenue for women to enter the profession has been closed off.

The other way in which professionalization can be considered counterproductive is the conservative impact it had. For one thing, it destroyed the initially democratic and even populist nature of IDHEC. In the context of its founding, IDHEC was inevitably intensely leftwing in its orientation, and the postliberation aspirations of "the people" to a new society perpetuated this "equal chances for all" attitude. Originally, therefore, IDHEC went out of its way to generate applications from young workers. In addition to teachers and technically qualified applicants, IDHEC accepted likely applicants from the P.T.T., from the railways, from all walks of life. The growing emphasis on preparatory qualifications and on a costly extended period of study worked against this policy, producing a progressive bourgeoisification of the intake which paralleled the progressive conservatism of the 1950s Western world as whole. Calling for a return to more democratic criteria, the head of the ETPC was to note that this process had pushed a cinema which had still in 1950 been intensely influenced both positively and negatively by the aspirations of the Popular Front, toward a more sedate unproblematized view of society: "as a result of all this, the French cinema is far from representative of the multiple realities of the nation: most often it plays on the contrary the role of a deforming mirror. . . . It's only by widening the recruitment procedures for film, radio, and TV personnel that new and original talent will be discovered."[117]

Moreover, one of L'Herbier's central aims in creating new generations of creators had been to initiate an ongoing artistic revolution. In his inaugural address to the first students he proclaimed the glorification of the cinema as art and the need for perpetual reflection on and rethinking of the aesthetic basis of film.

> Shout it out loud: In what we see today *Everything is awful!!* Or almost. . . . Everything needs rethinking! Justify your youth by attacking these injustices. Or at least by revolt! Impose your views. Open your eyes and proclaim out loud: The image today is poorly proportioned. . . . Sound projection is a betrayal. . . . The quality of the image screams out its inadequacy. . . . The choice of subjects is locked into the old sentimental triangle. . . . Why not colors? And not a natural color, but a pictural color, transposed, composed? And why not relief? And why not a virtual image? And why not large screen? And why not variable focal length? And why not other miracles? This song of *Dissatisfaction* the institute is ready to accept; it will collaborate in all that might [lead to] pushing back the boundaries of the possible.[118]

In fact the institute rapidly found itself caught in the paradox generated by trying to teach a creativity which its teachers saw as transcending rules and indeed human understanding. At best IDHEC could foster the conditions for creativity (but could not, according to the myth, an attic or a tragic love affair do that as well?) while teaching history (the history of art, of the theater, of music, of film itself) and technique. In the end, it was a conscious appreciation of the potential of various technical practices and a sense of the propriety of certain usages that constituted the main instructional output of the institute. So one of its students could observe in 1960, "IDHEC doesn't claim to form people of talent, but merely professional personnel. As in medicine or painting, there is a cinema of genius, and there is a cinema of professionals."[119]

In the course of those fifteen years, then, there seems to have been a slow move away from revolution and radicalism toward system, technique, and competence. Indeed, in many respects IDHEC never made the slightest attempt to be inspirational and revolutionary. From the beginning it aimed rather to insert the cinema into an established range of humanities fields worthy of the respect and prestige associated with an institute of higher study, and to do this it adopted most of the fossilized educational strategies of French university education. Its early students have recorded sardonic, not to say insulting accounts of the pompousness and formality of the transcendental topics and discourses presented to them,[120] and the May 1968 insurrections were aimed precisely at the targets of irrelevant curricula and condescending formal lectures. Arguably, however, it was not only these establishment aspirations that doomed IDHEC to conservatism: the formalization, articulation, and regulation of technical practices itself worked against "a cinema of genius" to produce a conservative effect rather than the ongoing revolution initially foreshadowed. In the course of the ten years or so of specialist training which personnel now obligatorily underwent, from Vaugirard or Voltaire to IDHEC to assistantship, any initial aspirations to produce aberrant or innovative work were necessarily repressed and erased, while industrial norms and expectations were reinforced. This was certainly the view adopted by Truffaut who (ignoring the fact that Resnais, Malle, and Averty had attended IDHEC) saw all such schools as inherently conservative and needing to be abolished if the French cinema was to regain its creativity. Partly, however, this was symptomatic of Truffaut's fear that the singularity of the mythic artist-director might be threatened by the IDHEC-inspired ideas of other members of the filmmaking team. As another IDHEC student acknowledged, "established directors prefer to work with IDHEC graduates, but New Wave directors prefer the simple technicians from Vaugirard. They see us as thinking too much, and badly; they prefer to be the only ones doing any thinking on the set."[121] Significantly, by 1960 IDHEC was no longer defending itself on grounds of creativity and revolution, but on grounds of standards and professionalism. The "rank amateurism" of those who had not learned the ropes made for inefficiency and this wasted time and money. The most incisive defense of this position can be found in the corporate monthly *Le Technicien du film* during 1959. A typical editorial in the October issue asserted in its headline that "the struggle against amateurism has begun."

To struggle against amateurism is first of all, for a professional publication, to defend quality and to showcase the work of those who count among the true professionals. . . . Needless to say, our best *auteurs* put their trust in our best technicians. . . . As we know, a bunch of amateurs going under the title of the New Wave is these days claiming to be reinventing a cinema that they know nothing about. To shore up their unfounded notoriety, they don't hesitate to associate themselves with the names of young professionals who have gone through the *normal* training channels and who of course have nothing in common with these amateurs. So our advice to young technicians, graduating from IDHEC or from assistantships and trying to establish themselves, is to avoid these upstarts whose *arrivisme* must be embarrassingly apparent to everyone.[122]

If the New Wave can be seen as, in some limited sense, an artistic revolution in the cinema, and thus in line with the romantic myth appealed to by IDHEC's founder in his opening address, it nevertheless had to be made in the face of the IDHEC-inspired professionalization of the postwar personnel.

FIVE

THE FORMATION OF AUDIENCES

> "I am not totally convinced of the usefulness of censor-
> ship. It raises two questions. The first is the sexual ques-
> tion. Well, allow me to remind you that there are naked
> women elsewhere than in films. The second question is
> juvenile delinquency. . . . Here, what we need is a great
> cinémathèque . . . , great cultural centers. When young
> men can see the hundred finest films ever made, they
> won't tolerate mediocre films."
>
> André Malraux

> "I was once asked if I thought the cinema was an artform.
> I replied that I attached little importance to the term.
> Painting is an artform, but there's an awful lot of lousy
> painting, of which it matters little whether or not you call
> it art."
>
> Paul Valéry

AUDIENCES, JOURNALS, DISCOURSES

As earlier chapters have indicated, one of the principal factors inhibiting
the financial viability of the industry was the small size of the national
filmgoing population. In 1929 *Pour Vous* had proclaimed in bold type the
melancholy fact that "in France, 7% of the population goes to the cinema,
whereas in the United States, 75% of the population goes."[1] With the introduction of sound, attendances increased to 220 million per year, but this
figure was still far lower than that of other film-producing nations, and the
attendance average of 5–6 times per year per head of population was only
one-fifth that of Britain, one-seventh that of America. The war provided a
momentarily captive audience for the local product, and the postwar period
saw an attendance averaging 390 million or nine entries per year per head
of population, but this was still well behind that of other Western nations.[2]

The discrepancy was partly due to demographic factors and to the existence of a large rural population beyond the reach of the cinema, but these factors could never adequately account for the low attendance figures; so it is not surprising that a central preoccupation of the industry throughout this period was the maximization of national (and later, international) audiences.

These attempts at audience formation can be divided into two main categories: attempts by producers to construct an ongoing mass audience for films seen as commercial products, which needed larger national markets if they were to guarantee a return within the country of origin; and attempts by critics and enthusiasts to construct an informed audience for films seen as cultural products, which needed a larger audience if they were to survive within a production system where commercial pressures were so much greater than for most cultural products. There were, that is, attempts from inside the production system to construct a mass market and attempts from outside to form an elite market. The former process followed much the same procedures in France as it did elsewhere, but the formation (and indeed self-formation) of an informed intellectual audience for the film product was, from the 1920s onward, much more active in France than elsewhere and served to establish institutional forms which were to serve as a model for those of other countries. In the process French film criticism was to develop a range of critical discourses which likewise served as a model for other countries.

It is these two relatively distinct processes of audience formation that will be explored in the present chapter. Both of them centrally involve a discussion of the press and its relations to the cinema as an institution. While the self-formation of an intellectual audience could take other forms as well—the development of a ciné-club movement, the foundation of film libraries, film courses, and a cinémathèque—even these depended to a certain degree on the specialist press which developed to promote film as a cultural product. In more direct ways, the formation of a mass audience, while it might take other forms—such as posters, trailers, and festivals—depended to some extent on those essentials of the Hollywood system, the generic replication of successes, and "stars" who could attract recurrent audiences; and these in turn required a proliferation of fan magazines and "photo-romans" to promote the industry's products as objects of desire. More generally the industry required a complacent press willing to recycle its publicity handouts in a barely modified form.

The specialized press, which played such an important role in both these processes of audience formation, was of course subject to certain political and economic pressures common to the whole of the French press during this period, such as a rigorous political control during the war, which severely circumscribed the number of authorized journals, paper shortages in the wake of the victory, and a postwar expansion in leftwing publications between 1945 and the early fifties, which gave way to a more reactionary press during the rest of the decade. It was also, however, subject to certain pressures deriving from its relationship with the film industry. Various authorities, concerned over the potential impact of the cinema on the moral, religious, and political attitudes of its audience, adopted a paternalist role toward those sectors of it for which they felt responsible—attempting to channel them toward appropriate films, to minimize audiences for films they considered undesirable, or to modify production in ways they considered desirable. This activity produced various modes of formal and informal censorship and generated further journals aiming to inform and direct the various political and religious constituencies. It also, under the guise of cultural nationalism, generated a quota system, which tentatively circumscribed the number of foreign films available for national audiences.

In general, then, there were four main interest groups: the commercial, the aesthetic, the political, and the religious, institutionalized respectively in the production companies and finance houses, the intelligentsia, the government, and the church; and these four interest groups served as the focus for four recognizably distinct discourses on the cinema—the discourses of pleasure, of art, of politics, and of morality. Although theoretically distinct, these discourses could often be found in combination within the critical output of a single writer, and though certain journals were nominally devoted to the promotion of one or the other of them—though indeed, certain of them were momentarily dominant (pleasure in the thirties, politics in the forties, art in the fifties)—there is no case of a journal maintaining totally watertight barriers to all other discourses. The discourse of art, in particular, crossed most institutional boundaries at one time or another.

But alongside these four discourses, two others developed with a less powerful institutional base—the discourse of the real, which occurred in combination with both that of politics and that of morality, and the discourse of science, which saw in the cinema simply another sphere of human activity to which it might extend its practices of description, analysis, and interpretation. It is these discourses, the journals in which they found their most permanent expression, and the institutional mechanisms of promotion and regulation to which they gave rise that are the subject of this chapter.

If they have their own autonomous validity as cultural phenomena and a sociological validity as manifestations of specific social and political institutions, they also have an abstract conceptual validity deriving from their relation to the functions of communication, as outlined by Jacobson. From the six aspects of any communication act—a sender, sending a message, about something, through a channel, in a particular code, to a receiver—he deduced that any communication act, any text, might have a range of up to six related functions—expressive, poetic, referential, phatic, metalinguistic, and directive—according as it foregrounded one or another of these aspects.

message (poetic)
context (referential)
sender (expressive)   receiver (directive)
medium (phatic)
code (metalinguistic)

The various forms of critical discourse outlined in this chapter can likewise be categorized according as they foreground one or another aspect of communication at the expense of the others. Thus the discourse of entertainment, focusing solely on maintaining the reader/viewer in contact, is primarily phatic in nature; the realist discourse is primarily referential; the auteurist discourse is expressive; and the political and moral discourses are directive. The discourse of science, insofar as it focused on rhetoric and textual analysis, aimed at producing a poetics of the text. While the bulk of the chapter is devoted to the first four of these functions and their related discourses, the final pages will note the rise in the fifties, alongside the better-known literary poetics of Barthes and Robbe-Grillet, of the first traces of renewed interest in a poetics of the film, largely marginalized since the twenties.

MASS AUDIENCES AND THE DISCOURSE OF PLEASURE

The processes for forming mass audiences for the cinema were developed first and most systematically in America. Essentially, they involved two mechanisms for guaranteeing in advance that the film product would attract the necessary clientèle to make it financially viable. Those two mechanisms were the genre system and the star system. The former developed out of an attempt to replicate financially successful films, by identifying those elements of a given film which are responsible for its success and incorporating them in subsequent films. Those elements are then made the focus of the advertising campaign. Trailers, posters, press publicity, and press handouts will condense those motifs in a form that will appeal to the same desires that generated the original success; and as the number of films which incorporate these motifs increases, they solidify into a set of recognizable conventions that guide both film production and audience expectations. Before long, the existence of such generic conventions provides the conditions of legibility, of comprehensibility, of the film output of a production system, and the audience has effectively been trained into reading practices which it expects to exercise on future films.

The star system, on the other hand, serves to construct specific actors and actresses as cult objects, usually though not always of an erotic nature. These cult objects condense audience fantasies. In its most celebrated form—the screen goddess—the star system constructs of specific actresses the embodiment of audience desires. The desire to reexperience the affective sensations produced by a "star" in one film thus reproduces the audience for the star's future films. A high degree of generic stereotyping in these images further serves to form audience expectations and thus to recycle an audience from one successful film to another.

These procedures for forming mass audiences developed early in the century in both American and French film industries. As the French industry shrank under the impact of World War I, America came to definitively displace France as the leading film-producing nation, and by 1919 the French share of the world market had fallen to approximately 15%. Even in France, American promotional material dominated. American production companies distributed regular handouts on the activities of their stars and details of the shooting of their current films which played up the genre motifs. French companies did their best, in different industries, to follow suit.[3] Throughout the twenties, a rapid expansion in the volume of press publicity developed, with expeditions organized for press personnel to the site of shooting, interviews organized with stars and other production members, anecdotes fabricated and circulated among the specialist press. These practices were to continue largely unchanged for the whole of the period 1930–1960.

Nevertheless, French production and distribution houses could never commit the sums to such publicity campaigns that were available to their American counterparts. Without any ongoing production program, and without a permanent contracted "stable" of film stars, the French producer had only the one film with which to break even on any investment in publicity on the actors and actresses, and lacking an extensive financial base he could not justify the expenditure of large sums. Between 50% and 75% of this small sum would be allocated to publicity in the national and specialist presses, while the remaining 25–50% would be allocated principally to a poster campaign. About forty or so artists were available for the design work, including some fifteen specialists (notably Rojac, Lancy, and Péron).[4]

Most of the press budget was spent on the large-circulation press, such as *Figaro, France-Soir, Le Parisien Libéré* and *Paris-Presse-Intransigeant*, but a significant secondary part of it went to advertising in trade papers and in the specialist press. Although small by overall standards, this injection of funding was the lifeblood of most such specialist publications, with subscriptions from readers coming far behind. Those few magazines, such as Auriol's *Revue du Cinéma*, series 1 and 2, or the *Ecran Français*, which attempted to adopt a hard-line independent stand, untainted by publicity funding from the industry, doomed themselves thereby to eventual failure.

The material supplied by the production and distribution firms was dominated by the discourse of pleasure which it had borrowed from America. Representing the industry's product as "entertainment," it aimed to create in its target audience an irresistible impulse to view the film. Implicit in it is an assumption that the prime function of cinema is the enjoyment of the audience and that this pleasure is an unproblematic and innocent experience involving straightforward, natural, and universal responses to certain inherently pleasurable aspects of the film text—primarily the stars and generic elements such as adventure, spectacle, romance, and suspense. Pleasure is thus defined in purely affective ways. It is to the emotions that film is assumed to appeal, and the discourse tends to reproduce that affective appeal: it does not present any overall conceptual framework or aim at any intellectual analysis or "depth." Magazines through which it speaks tend therefore to be fragmentary, consisting of the juxtaposition of a series of brief segments of text. These fragments aim to maintain interest by the appearance of diversity. Different type formats will characterize the different segments, and the "affective" orientation of the genre will be present in the form of large headlines of a sensationalist nature and in the expressive and impressionistic use of language.

An allied characteristic of the discourse is its personalization of response. The text will focus on the personal experience both of stars and of writers. Anecdotes will be a dominant format, involving as they do the characteristics of brevity and personalized experience. Interviews will be another format much used in the genre, since they personalize the star and present the writer as an intermediary whose own personalized contact with the glamorous world of filmmaking can be shared by the reader who can thus find out "what it's like to be a star," "what it's like to make films." Readers are often addressed in the first person and in a chatty way: interviews will take the form, "I talked to Gérard Philipe." This personalization of experience serves as a guarantee of authenticity, a guarantee of the "truth" of the material presented. The anecdotal material thus conveyed will be recognizably related to the existing range of film genres. The stars' lives will likewise be organized around *dramas* of poverty and riches, of chance encounters, of being discovered, of trials and triumph; *sentimental romances* involving love at first sight, impending tragedy, and reconciliation; *adventure stories* related to the process of film production; evocations of *spectacle* and magnificence involving vast sets, casts of thousands, and exotic locations in which the stars encounter quaint customs. Typically, these genre stories, episodic in nature but picking up on elements of the stars' lives remembered from past issues, will be one of the few factors binding succeeding issues of such a magazine together into a cursory narrative form.

An important element in the fragmentation of each issue is the presence of numerous stills or pinup photographs, "corroborating" and reinforcing these generic—that is, mythic—elements. But alongside the mythologizing of the stars and of the process of filmmaking, there exists an apparently more trivial process of "gossip," which, presenting to the reader the trivia of a star's day and of a star's likes and dislikes, serves to construct an air of intimacy and of familiarity, which is in continual tension with the distancing effect of the glamorization process. The reader can "get to know" a star, can come to feel that in some ways he/she "is just like me." The pleasure on which this discourse plays is therefore double—treating the film world and stars as glamorous, mythic, objects to be adored, revered, and desired; yet also as familiar, all-too-understandable, subjects with whom the reader can identify. In this play of desire and identification, the discourse works in ways that are recognizably similar to those of the commercial cinema itself. Indeed, the publicity material directly advertising the films speaks in such a discourse of desire, identification, novelty, spectacle, and drama, such that, placed as it is alongside the articles, the boundary between direct promotional material and articles, themselves largely based on promotional material, is by no means clearly defined.

The entertainment discourse is relatively stable throughout the period 1930–1960. It totally dominates many magazines, either in its chaotic entirety or in a more focused way. Elsewhere, it exists alongside other largely incompatible discourses, such as those of art, realism, politics, or the academy. Despite protestations to the contrary, the *Revue du Cinéma* which became legendary as a repository of all that was most ambitious in French film criticism of the thirties and forties was itself initially dominated by aspects of this discourse and never entirely freed itself from them. While with the editor Corti, *La Revue* was fragmentary in format, with few articles extending beyond 500 words, and interspersed with pinup photographs which were largely unmotivated by any relevance to the "articles," but gratuitously inserted for their mythic value. The articles themselves were marked by affective vocabulary and were openly enthusiastic and impressionistic in orientation, consisting largely of passionate advocacy of films that had intoxicated the writer. Even in the later series (1946–1949), hagiographic eulogies of American female stars, usually authored by the editor himself, form a surprisingly incongruous element in juxtaposition to a now quite different set of discourses. Over time, however, these materials are rendered more respectable by being partially integrated into the more literary tradition of the biography of the great man/woman. This involved the incorporation of the fragmentary anecdotal material into a sequential formulaic narrative, "the life of the star," which was perfectly compatible with the highly personalized view of the world promoted by the discourse of pleasure. The same strong residue of this discourse is present in the early issues of *Cahiers du Cinéma*, which are prefaced by about ten unmotivated publicity stills and are marked by a fascination with the glamour of the industry and the Cannes Festival. Indeed, the only publications totally free of it during the period 1930–1960 are the *Revue Internationale de Filmologie*, published by the Presses Universitaires on behalf of an academic institute, and the *Revue Internationale du Cinéma*, published by the Office Catholique.

Within the specialist press there were three subcategories of film journal which voiced the same discourse—the fan magazine, the "film raconté," or magazine of the film, and the homage to the star. All are "mass" publications, in the sense that they had large publication runs and were oriented toward constructing mass audiences.

The earliest of the fan magazines or "illustrated magazines," as Pierre Mouliniers categorizes them,[5] were *Ciné Pour Tous* (founded 1919), *Ciné Magazine* (1920), *Mon Ciné* (1921), *Ciné Revue*, and *Ciné Miroir* (1922).[6] Two of the best known and longest-lasting—*Cinémonde* and *Pour Vous*—were founded almost together, in October and November 1928, respectively.

Most of these magazines were weekly, in order to orient the audience toward the week's releases of films, and this contrasted with the monthly press which in general was marginally more reflective and more critical. As *Ciné Magazine* moved from being a weekly to becoming a monthly, in 1929, it became more glossy and moved out of the former category and into the latter. The weekly fan magazines lived in a state of symbiosis not only with the production companies but with the mass daily press of the time. *Cinémonde* was founded by Gaston Thierry from *Paris-Soir*, and *Ciné-Miroir* came into being under the wing of *Le Petit Parisien*. It had reached a print-run of 100,000 copies by 1930.[7] *Pour Vous* was founded by Léon Bailby, director of the *Intransigeant*, whose passion for the cinema was well known. "He had even opened in the newspaper's headquarters at 100 rue Réaumur a cinema—Les Miracles—then on the Champs-Elysées an even more important cinema—Les Miracles-Lord Byron. At the same time he had launched *Pour Vous*, of which the core of the editorial team came from the film reporters of the *Intransigeant*, with Alexandre Arnoux at their head. . . . It was likewise in the shadow of a daily—the *Action Française* of Charles Maurras—but without any official ties, that the two publications directed by Paul Pavaux lived, namely *Ciné-France* and *Ciné-Combat*."[8]

The *Cahiers du Film*, on the other hand, was a brief-lived offshoot of Marcel Pagnol's production company, and one of its functions was to promote the products of that company. Likewise, *L'Image* was produced under the wing of the Pathé production company and was little more than a shop front for that company, despite the significant figures on its payroll, headed by Roland Dorgelès. Inevitably the degree of independence available to staff writing for such journals was minimal.

Much of the rest of the illustrated press was scarcely less dependent, since the dailies to which they were linked were themselves tied closely to other business enterprises and were always anxious to mollify corporate advertisers such as the film companies. Nevertheless, there were certain publications which were held in more respect than the others. Writing in 1931, Auriol notes that

> *L'Ami du Peuple* and its evening colleague were for a long time (till about a year ago) the only French news dailies where the critics were not slaves to a publicity contract; which explains why . . . one could publish tranquilly in those pages whatever one wanted. . . . Among specialist journals, we can cite *Pour Vous* and *Mon Ciné* as not being the servants of particular production houses.
>
> As for the dailies, the most independent of film writers in them are Léon Moussinac (*L'Humanité*), Alexandre Arnoux (*Intran*), François Vinneuil (*L'Action Française*), Gaston Thierry (*Paris-Midi*), Lucien Wahl (*L'Oeuvre*), and finally those strong, brave articles by Germaine Decaris in *Le Soir*.[9]

Developing parallel to the illustrated fan magazines in the twenties and thirties were two more focused sub-types—the "magazine-of-the-film" and the "homage-to-the-star."

The "magazine-of-the-film" consisted essentially of a condensed plot summary, concentrating on the generic elements of the film and illustrated by a series of stills which foregrounded the stars and inserted them into the appropriate generic roles. The best known of these was *Le Film Complet*, which was founded in 1922 and appeared throughout the period of the "classic" French cinema, to disappear in 1958. During that time, no less than 3300 issues appeared, each dealing with a recently released film. Almost as prolific were *Romans-Cinéma* and *Cinéma-Bibliothèque*, the latter running to over one thousand titles, and the former including serials, each of which, collected into a single volume, would have run to some 240 pages.[10] *Ciné-Miroir* itself had initially been a publication of this sort, devoted to a single film, but rapidly diversified into the format of a more general fan magazine. *Mon Film*, founded in 1924, competed with *Le Film Complet* till 1958 when they merged briefly before disappearing.

In all, over one hundred journals in this genre appeared in France between the twenties and the early sixties, among them *La Collection du Film, Enfin Film, Le Film Vécu, Le Film Chez Soi, Stars et Films, Les Grands Films* (1923), and *Films et Romans* (1937). A large number of these were devoted to films in specific genres, such as *Amor Film, Jungle Film, Star Ciné Cosmos, Star Ciné Aventures, Star Ciné Vaillance,* and *Star Films Bravoure.* Despite their similarities, these publications appeared in a range of formats, with an appropriate pricing structure. When *Le Cinéma Bibliothèque*, for instance, which was at the top of the range, was selling for 4 francs (or 5 fr. in the case of epics), *Ciné-Magazine* cost 1 franc, *Ciné-Miroir* .60 francs, *Mon Ciné* .50 francs and *Le Film Complet* .30 francs. The popularity of the genre was such that, while fundamentally weekly in their production, several were encouraged to appear twice or even three times weekly at certain periods.

The third subtype, the magazine-of-the-star, was essentially a form of hagiography, which had as its function the mythologization of the actor or actress concerned. It was therefore formulaic in its structure, adapting where necessary real-life elements to a mythic biography which included such phases as the deprived childhood, premonitions of a vocation, sentimental dalliance, triumphs and disappointments both in love and in work, and finally recognition and celebration on a world-wide scale. These narratives were frequently marked by destiny—say, in the form of an astrologer's prediction, a miraculous escape, or simply a chance encounter. Almost uniformly eulogistic and sanctimonious in tone, they were largely compiled from studio handouts and a knowledge of the appropriate biographic conventions. The earliest examples were series such as *Vedettes Françaises, Hollywood* (1932–33), *Les Grandes Artistes de l'Ecran* (which accompanied *Ciné Magazine* every two months), *Leur Vie Romanesque,* and *Visages et Contes du Cinéma* (which appeared between 1936 and 1939). The genre flourished mainly in fortnightly to two-monthly editions but produced a number of longer (book-length) publications, such as Ivan Noë's life of Clara Bow.[11]

Among them, these three genres constituted an instrument for constructing and recycling a committed mass audience. Proliferating in the 1920s and 1930s, they were severely reduced in number during the occupation. All that remained in Paris were *Ciné Mondial*, *Vedettes* (which had a production run of 50,000), and *Le Film Complet*; while in the unoccupied zone *Ciné Spectacles* resurfaced, and Pagnol's local *Cahiers du Film* continued to appear.

The end of the war saw a resurgence of all three categories. It was at this time that the *Star Ciné* magazines appeared, together with *Ciné Pour Tous*, *Nous Deux Cinéma*, and *Festival Ciné Révélation*; though in the fifties the magazine-of-the-film tended to become a "photo-roman"—a suite of stills from the film with captions or balloons, more like an upmarket cartoon than the illustrated prose story of the prewar years. Among postwar magazines devoted to stars, one might list *FilmsAr* (1944–1945), *Nos Vedettes*, *Stars et Films d'Aujourd'hui* (1945–1946), *Dans l'Intimité de . . .* (1946), *Vie et Souvenirs*, *Le Miroir des Vedettes* (1948), and *La Vie Heureuse*.

The most widely read of the diversified fan magazines was *Cinémonde*, which reappeared on 19 March 1946. Another magazine which, despite the claims of those involved in its production, was predominantly a fan magazine was *L'Ecran Français*. Its subsequent prestige owed more to its creation in the heroic circumstances of the resistance and to its doomed political stance than to its format or content, though it did distinguish itself by repudiating all publicity in the name of independence. Published clandestinely from December 1943 onward, in conjunction with *Les Lettres Françaises*, it had been first roneotyped, then printed as a section of *Les Lettres Françaises*, then finally produced as a publication in its own right from 4 July 1945. Infused with the leftist spirit of the resistance, committed to renovating the French cultural scene, *L'Ecran Français* nevertheless was sufficiently a fan magazine to feel itself severely threatened by the appearance of *Cinémonde*, as indeed both felt threatened by the proliferation within a matter of months of journals such as *Cinévogue*, *Cinévie*, *Ciné Pour Tous*, *Votre Cinéma*, *Filmagazine*, *Jeudi-Cinéma*, *Paris-Cinéma*, and (if only briefly) the resuscitated *Ciné-Miroir*.[12]

THE CANNES FILM-FESTIVAL AND THE STAR SYSTEM

But the postwar years witnessed the appearance of a phenomenon even more effective than these mass publications for "working" the public and generating an audience for the product, namely the Cannes Film Festival. The Cannes Film Festival was born of a reaction against its predecessor, the Venice Film Festival, which in turn had been introduced as a mere sideline to the longstanding Venice Biennale of contemporary art. Initially, the

Venice Festival was a small-scale event, involving 29 films, chosen informally. Somewhat to the surprise of the organizers, it was an enormous success and was repeated with each Biennale thereafter. From 1934 onward there was a cup for the best Italian film and a cup for the best foreign film, but the selection of the films for entry in the festival was largely left to chance, such that at one stage France found itself represented solely by *Bouboule 1er, roi nègre*[13] (Mathot, 1933–1934). Philippe Erlanger, who was a senior public servant in the Association française d'action artistique, saw the national advantage to be gained from introducing a little more order into the selection process and proposed national selection committees to sift the year's production and forward those most suitable to represent the nation. When the new system was introduced in 1937, France won two major prizes with *Un carnet de bal* (Duvivier, 1937) and *La Grande Illusion* (Renoir, 1936–1937). As it turned out, however, to put national prestige at stake in the period 1937–1939 proved to have been a dubious strategy. Accounts of what happened at the 1938 Venice Film Festival vary considerably, but it would appear that Hitler intervened on behalf of the German entry— Leni Riefenstahl's film of the Berlin Olympics—just as an American film was to be crowned. Although prizes ultimately went to both, the American and British contingents departed, refusing to return. Erlanger saw the opportunity for a rival "nonpolitical" French film festival, grouping "the free world" against the "totalitarian" festival of Venice. The minister, Jean Zay, approved the project and managed to get the government's agreement to "a festival of cinematographic art, from which all extracinematic preoccupations would be excluded."[14] America gave its support, and after much hesitation Cannes was selected in preference to Biarritz; but just as the festival was about to open under the patronage of Louis Lumière himself, war was declared.

With the liberation, Erlanger again proposed the festival and, despite Cannes' apprehensions about the cost of the exercise, pushed ahead with minimal financial support from a ministry slush fund.[15] Short timelines made the first festival a somewhat chaotic occasion, but it gradually developed an international visibility. From 1951 onward, and particularly after 1953, when Jean Cocteau was president of the jury for some years, the festival became the prestigious international showcase to which its founders had aspired.

From the beginning it was clear that four distinct sets of interests were involved in such festivals: the cultural interests, which were oriented toward film as an artform; the financial interests, which saw festivals as a showcase for products; local businessmen, who saw the festival as an influx of wealthy foreigners; and government interests which, while not at all averse to foregrounding the national product and earning much-needed export income, also saw festivals in terms of a prestigious political event on the international calendar. Cannes and its rival postwar festivals gradually differentiated themselves according to the emphasis they accorded these different criteria, and particularly as they focused on the cultural aspects of film as an artform, or the commercial aspects of film as a mass medium. Cannes, of course, despite opting for the camouflage of prestigious literary figures on its juries, early opted for that glamour and sensationalism which were to make it the complement of the fan magazine press as an instrument for the production of mass audiences. It became the big market for films in Europe and to this end concentrated on foregrounding stars as a prime attraction for publicity photographs—particularly the female star and the erotic fantasies of naked flesh so readily associated with a Mediterranean seaside resort. This distinctive feature of the Cannes Festival was already sufficiently apparent by 1949 for commentators to remark on it,[16] and neither Venice nor Berlin has ever challenged it. The main problem requiring delicate handling at Cannes has been the need to balance on the one hand the promotion of the national product above that of other nations, and on the other the provision of incentives to other national cinemas to continue attending. This balancing act was particularly apparent in the first year, when a prize was allocated to the best film of each nation attending, while attributing the prize for best director to René Clément for *La Bataille du rail*—as an index of the *real* winner, according to Erlanger;[17] and indeed the categories of prizes varied radically from year to year, in a search for the appropriate balance in marketing strategies.[18]

But if these strategies for the formation of a mass audience seem markedly similar to those implemented by the American production system, commentators have been in agreement that, with few exceptions, they were less effective than in the case of the American system. The statistics confirm that no mass audience was created, and a central reason seems to have been the lack of any continuity and coherence in the construction of the necessary mythic image around French stars.

In 1927 Coissac noted the absence in France of anything equivalent to the cult of the star so characteristic of the American film industry of the period.[19] Twenty years later, Charles Ford voiced a similar observation: "If France can boast of internationally acknowledged stars, their popularity is solely due to their talent, since the French cinema has never practiced the star system in any systematic way."[20] Such remarks became commonplace in the frequent comparisons made between the French film industry and that which it saw as its arch rival, Hollywood. Edgar Morin's monograph, *Les Stars*, seen as a definitive statement on the subject when published in 1957, devotes 90% of its space to American aspects of the phenomenon,[21] and looking back on the classic cinema just as the Nouvelle Vague was breaking, René Jeanne and Charles Ford regret that, though French actors and actresses are the focus of publicity campaigns on poster, in trailer, and in the press, "it is with a certain discretion"; "French journalists would erect altars to Hollywood stars, whereas they would speak of French stars in terms that made them seem close to the readers."[22]

This relative absence of a star system in France is due primarily to the distinctive nature of its production system and to the less developed form of capitalism of which that in turn was a symptom. A fully developed star system requires a conjunction of textual, industrial, and socioeconomic factors which simply did not exist in France. The surface phenomenon of a large segment of spectators expressing a sustained admiration, little short of adulation, for an actor or actress is dependent on their recognizing him/ her as a recurrent and essential factor behind a series of filmic roles, on those roles having something in common, and on that consistent element being of mythic significance for the audience. The actor or actress must, as Malraux says, have acted as a focus for a number of convergent scenarios, and those scenarios must speak to the audience of something intensely important to their identity. And the actor or actress in real life must be seen to embody those mythic elements; a correspondence must be conceived as existing between screen and reality.

It requires a considerable degree of industrial organization to fabricate and sustain such a situation: there must be a well-organized publicity machine to feed the audience the necessary "information" about the actor or actress; there must be established channels through which the audience can express its admiration, such as fan mail, fan clubs, and fan magazines; and these in turn require a secretariat to respond to mail. More centrally, the generation of a series of convergent scenarios and the casting of a given actor or actress in the recurrent mythic roles requires a high degree of continuity in the production system: it must be able to respond rapidly to audience approval of a film or of an actor or actress; it must have on call that actor or actress, and it must have on call scriptwriters who will accept its instructions concerning the form their next several scripts should take.

These preconditions could not be met in France. The fragmented production system had, except in odd instances and briefly, no contract basis to it such as would have tied actors and actresses and scriptwriters to a given production company. In these circumstances, responding to an audience's expressions of approval could not happen rapidly, and it could not happen on a scale sufficiently large to keep the star in front of the public eye in a given type of role. More importantly, the production companies had no vested interest in the merchandising of actors and actresses as stars, as did their Hollywood counterparts; the star was not their property, so his or her value would not reflect directly on the company's profits; any increase in the exchange value of an actor would benefit other companies. Indeed, the small production companies, run of necessity with an eye to short-term profitability, had a vested interest in *not* increasing the value of actors and actresses, since to do so would directly increase their own costs next time they brought in such a star. Moreover, without a studio base and associated support staff it was difficult for an actor or actress to become the focus of a fan system. Fans had no identifiable address to which to write; the administrative and secretarial work of answering letters and feeding "information" to fans about the star's lifestyle, tastes, romantic disposition, and movements, both directly by letter and indirectly through fan magazines, was a practical impossibility. Consequently, French actors and actresses tended to preserve a private life quite separate from their screen roles and professional career. Many—Charles Vanel, for instance—systematically refused to allow any public falsification and glamorization of that private life to take place, preferring to maintain it as an inviolable retreat from professional tasks. Finally, with production too low and contracts too uncertain, a leading actor could not justify committing him/herself exclusively to a cinematic future, as did (of necessity) U.S. stars; instead, they moved back and forth between various performance media, notably the theater, operetta, and music hall. Essentially, all these points can be summarized by saying that the French studio system was frozen in an artisanal mode of production, and it is arguable that a full-fledged industrial capitalism such as existed in Hollywood is necessary to support the merchandising of actors central to the star system. Certainly, there was none of that exploitation of an actor's or actress's exchange value in the merchandising of other goods, which is a sure sign of the achievement of star status. As J.-M. Monnier, director of publicity for Discina, put it in 1947: "[Stars] in America belong to a production house. In France they are successively in the service of this or that producer, such that each one has only one film to make good his publicity budget on. . . . It would be possible, certainly, to unite these efforts instead of dispersing them, if producers agreed to get together. A common budget for launching and promoting our stars would produce a greater impact on the audience."

Recognizing the disadvantages under which their own actors were laboring, certain fan magazines, in the aftermath of World War II—a time when sections of the industry held intensely anti-American attitudes—attempted to construct the necessary networks of information and correspondence to "stellarize" national actors and actresses. By 1950, clubs existed for Edwige Feuillère, Jean Marais, Tino Rossi, Renée St. Cyr, and Charles Trenet, and efforts were being made to form others around Martine Carol, Danielle Darrieux, and Viviane Romance.[23] But reporters continued to note the readier availability of information on American stars and the readier approachability of those stars: without the studio base, these isolated superstructural phenomena could not survive. Moreover, by that time, under the influence of the rapidly evolving transformation of capitalism that took place in the fifties, the star system was beginning to disappear even in America; and the most effective element of it to have been transplanted to France—the fan magazines themselves—likewise disappeared.

ART-HOUSE AUDIENCES:
CINÉ-CLUBS AND THE CINÉMATHÈQUE

But if the classic French cinema never succeeded in fashioning the mass audience it aspired to, it was extremely effective in developing mechanisms for fashioning an art-house audience. This process began much earlier and was much more systematic in France than elsewhere. Basically the audience concerned was the middle-class intellectual and cultural elite; they saw themselves as working for the defense of French cinema and of cinema as a cultural form; and their means of operation were the ciné-club, congresses and study groups, the concept of the cinémathèque, a separate theater circuit committed to art films, and critical journals of a more reflective kind.

Ciné-clubs originated in a series of discussion groups on the cinema held by an intensely cultivated and articulate group of people in 1921. The group included filmmakers such as Germaine Dulac, Louis Delluc, Léon Poirier, Jean Epstein, Marcel L'Herbier, and Cavalcanti, critics such as Léon Moussinac, Lucien Wahl, Lionel Landry, René Jeanne, and Pierre Scize, painters such as Mallet-Stevens and Fernand Léger, actors such as Eve Francis, Jacques Catelain, Harry Baur, the actor-painter Gaston Modot, musicians, and others of the intelligentsia.[24] Their main meeting place was the Club des Amis du Septième Art (CASA), founded by Ricciotto Canudo, whose *Gazette des Sept Arts* already had a film review column written by Moussinac. Louis Delluc simultaneously founded an ephemeral revue called the *Ciné-club* ("we have touring clubs, why not ciné-clubs?") where the name was reputedly first coined. Both these groupings organized film screenings in the course of the next twelve months, to focus their discussions and to keep the group up-to-date with interesting films being made elsewhere. Priority is usually given to Delluc, whose first program included *The Cabinet of Dr Caligari*. Gradually the meetings moved toward the tripartite format which was to dominate for the foreseeable future—the verbal presentation of a film, the projection of that film, then general debate and discussion.

Later that same year Moussinac founded the Club Français du Cinéma, "for the defense, the development, and the progress of cinematic art,"[25] but in 1924, with the untimely death of both Canudo and Delluc, the groups merged to form a new Club Français du Cinéma, directed by Germaine Dulac, Feyder, and Moussinac, and grouping those mentioned earlier with people such as H.-G. Clouzot, René Clair, Abel Gance, Charles Vanel, and Vuillermoz. The names themselves sufficiently identify the orientation of the club. It was designed precisely to combat the mass cinema by fostering a different audience, which would demand a different cinema, with an international vision.

The first ciné-club of the contemporary sort developed out of the Decorative Arts Exhibition of 1924–1925, where Charles Léger presented films—again primarily of the German expressionist school—and organized discussions of them. The Tribune Libre du Cinéma, as it was known, grouped other devotees who were to contribute to film criticism or filmmaking over the next 50 years—Marcel Carné, Jean Dréville, Jean George Auriol, J.-B. Brunius, and Jean Mitry. By the time of the talkie, then, ciné-clubs formed a coherent and committed movement, capable of holding in 1929 an International Congress at Sarraz in Switzerland, attended by various independent directors, presidents of ciné-clubs from France, Holland, Britain, Switzerland, and Spain, as well as representatives from German, Austrian, and Japanese organizations.[26] Eisenstein was invited to speak to the congress. Out of it grew a League of Ciné-Clubs, whose purpose was to coordinate and facilitate the activities of the clubs, but also to create an "international cooperative of independent filmmakers," based in Paris, to produce films for ciné-club circuits. "Thus the congress will permit in a pragmatic way, those directors who believe in the human and lyrical value of the cinema to express themselves in complete independence. The spiritual consequences of this move can and must be considerable."[27]

Throughout the 1930s, a total of about twenty such clubs, centered mostly in Paris, continued to focus on such avant-garde works as were available, or nostalgically to rescreen silent films (e.g., Les Amis du film muet). In the face of the increased industrialization and commercialization of the cinema brought about by sound, such clubs tended to take on the air of sanctuaries of snobbism, where aesthetes bemoaned the trends of the day and rescreened the artistic triumphs of the past.[28] But from the late twenties on an alternative usage of the ciné-club had been explored which was to compete with this elitist strategy, as it competed with the producers' strategies to form a mass audience—namely, the attempt to use ciné-clubs to redirect mass audiences toward more ambitious films by "educating" their tastes. Two particular clubs became renowned for their success in this area—Les Amis de Spartacus, founded in 1928 by Moussinac and therefore Communist in orientation, and Ciné-Liberté, founded in 1936 with Jean Renoir as president, also with a strong representation of Communists in the organizing committee.

The former arose out of an unusual experiment to develop an alternative exhibition network for mass audiences. The first such cinema, La Belle-villoise, was founded by a workers' cooperative, with the sole purpose of screening outstanding films of social importance which had been rejected as "uncommercial" by the normal exhibition circuit. It was so successful that Moussinac, Jean Lods, and two others decided to extend it into a ciné-club, whence Les Amis de Spartacus. The initial screening, in the Casino de Grenelle, saw an audience of 4,000 squeezed into a theater with seating for 2,500. Its success continued, not least because it screened Russian films currently banned by the censor from the normal circuit—Mother, Potemkin, The End of St Petersburg. The association spread rapidly to the outer suburbs and the provinces, generating a membership of 80,000 within five months.[29]

While the screenings were legal, in that the censor's ban did not extend to private organizations, the spirit of the ban and, indeed, the whole purpose of censorship, was clearly being thwarted by this success. Representatives of the normal exhibition circuit also complained, seeing their audiences diverted elsewhere. The préfet de police summoned Jean Lods and informed him that if the club continued with its present policy, disruptions would break out in the audience which would inevitably lead to police intervention to restore calm and thence to the closing of the club. Les Amis de Spartacus was obliged to restrict itself to a more cautious and conventional policy; but as Pinel notes, "the experience, though brief, was fruitful: it proved that the larger public was eager to seek other forms of cinema than the opium provided by the normal circuits."[30]

It was also fruitful in more concrete ways, leaving a heritage of small suburban and provincial clubs behind it. Its specific task, of initiating a mass audience into more ambitious films, was taken up by Ciné-liberté, in 1936. Ciné-liberté had grown out of Les amis du cinéma indépendant, founded in 1934 by technicians, and it benefited from the spirit of the Popular Front—within a few months it had achieved a membership of 100,000[31] and had spawned many subsidiaries throughout France. It was this club which, through a production arm, shot three short films for trade unions[32] and organized the public subscription to produce Renoir's *La Marseillaise.* It lasted till the war but was never able to live up to its promise because starved of appropriate films and lacking the organization to circulate the films efficiently throughout the country.

The ciné-club movement was tolerated by the various authorities only as long as it was not making inroads into the mass market and thus refashioning the mass audience, either in political or aesthetic terms; provided, that is, that it was fashioning only an aesthetic elite. During the war, even this limited function was considered excessive; or rather the potential for screenings to develop beyond that point into mass (especially political) gatherings was unacceptable. Ciné-clubs as such were totally forbidden. The few private screenings which were held in clandestinity—by such as Jacques Marel, Jean Pleury, and Henri Langlois[33]—constituted acts of bravura which no doubt had an intense private and symbolic value, but no wider significance.

As soon as the liberation permitted, ciné-clubs reappeared. Their numbers increased dramatically from 1 in November 1944 (Pierre Kast's Ciné club universitaire) to 6 in March 1945, 12 in June 1945, 83 in June 1946, 130 in June 1947 and 185 in June 1948.

Throughout the 1950s there were about 200, and by 1960, 235. The fifties saw a regular audience of about 60,000–80,000, with 100,000 by 1960. By that stage, it is clear that they saw their mission as cultural and aesthetic rather than sociopolitical: in a survey to which 130 clubs replied the central objective is "to give the public a taste for good cinema . . . , so that it will reject sensationalist publicity, star worship, and vulgarity."[34] Only one of the 130 indicates as an objective the desire "to seek in the cinema values which relate to the problems of the masses and the workers." The films which they screen are uniformly art movies, or where they have social implications, are represented primarily in aesthetic terms. No popular cinema is screened, and, no doubt because of the relative absence of provocative or contentious material, clubs note with some dismay the total collapse of the "debate" element of screenings. The audience generated is not, in the postwar period, a mass or working-class audience: only 13% are categorized as workers, as against 80% liberal or bourgeois categories (businessmen 15%, liberal/professional 18%, public service 22%, school or university 25%). At the war's end, it had been possible for Sadoul to see the rebirth of the ciné-club movement as "recruiting audiences for cinema as a whole. They fulfil this function well, and it's because, far from diverting audiences from cinema, they bring them to it, that producers, distributors, and exhibitors encourage them. . . . Ciné-clubs recruit spectators, but they also orient them. It's not a question . . . of combatting lousy films: . . . they actively aid the success of films which have a high artistic quality whose commercial success is not always sure."[35] By the end of the fifties, however, it was clear that they had had little impact on the commercial cinema. What they had done was to form an audience (not to mention filmmakers) for the art cinema of the sixties, when for totally extraneous reasons the commercial cinema lost much of its regular audience. If the size of that audience is fairly accurately known from attendance and membership records, its commitment can be measured by the growth in the ciné-club magazine, by which such clubs kept their members informed. Numbers of long-running publications of this sort occur in main cities in the fifties, but each provincial town has its own as well, at some time—Angers (1947–1959), Metz (1956–1961), Rouen has two (1949–1955 and 1952–1953), as does Toulouse (1953–1954 and 1955–1960), Valence (1950–1951), Villeurbane (1958–60), Grenoble, Moutiers, Poitiers, and Oullins.

An important byproduct of the ciné-club movement was the Cinémathèque française. Although not by any means one of the first cinémathèques to be developed, and although run idiosyncratically and incompetently for much of its existence, the Cinémathèque française was clearly central, if one is to judge by reminiscences, to the formation of a whole generation of art-film audiences. One of the twenty or so ciné-clubs of the prewar period was Le Cercle du cinéma, organized by Georges Franju and Henri Langlois. It was one of the less elitist clubs, in that no aesthetic criteria intervened in the selection of films to be screened: the whole repertoire of the cinema was screened, not just avant-garde or "ambitious" films. This was a principle that Langlois was to promote tirelessly when he became director of the cinémathèque which subsequently developed out of the Cercle du cinéma. The central aim of a cinémathèque was to be defined as the conservation of an entire cultural heritage, not just that part of it which measured up to the aesthetic criteria of a given age.

Although the first acquisitions for this collection date from 1936, innumerable opportunities had been missed to develop such a collection earlier on. Any of the commercial stockpiles of the more important production companies could have formed the basis of such a collection. As early as 1906, a Paris councillor suggested the development of a cinema archive relating to Paris, and the project was taken up again in 1911 by Emile Massard and in 1920 by Victor Perrot.[36] The focus was on a filmic record of social and political history rather than on film as cultural product, but had the opportunity been taken, innumerable fiction films would have been saved. In 1920, the Paris Municipal Council approved the plan but never implemented it. In 1925 Henri Clouzot, conservator at the Musée Galliera, in a speech to Moussinac's ciné-club, suggested a cinémathèque as an extension of that museum, with himself as director;[37] and in 1927 Mitry talked J.-P. Mauclaire into sponsoring such a project and got the agreement of various directors to contribute their works; but Mauclaire changed his mind, deciding to found an art cinema (Studio 28) instead. It was nevertheless Mauclaire who, hearing that a stock of films was lying deteriorating in the Normandy chateau of a businessman who had organized children's screenings in his shop, rescued them and classified them. They included early Griffith, Max Linder, Léonce Perret, and a large number of Méliès films. Having restored them, he organized in conjunction with the magazine *Revue du Cinéma* a gala screening, and thus began the "rediscovery" of Méliès.

Throughout the thirties, calls to rescue this national heritage from oblivion continued, without any official action or any efficient private action. The nearest approach to such an undertaking occurred in 1932–1933 when a critic, Lucienne Escoubé, wrote an impassioned article in *Pour Vous*, evoking the imminent destruction of the silent film heritage: "This state of things cannot continue. We must act, get together. What imaginative, generous man will take up such a task? Who will save the cinematic art by ensuring that it lasts as it should? . . . Time is terribly short. We must hurry if we wish to save all that from mutilation and destruction. . . . "[38]

Her proposal was taken up the same year by a producer, André Haguet, who in an address to his colleagues, said, "It is inadmissible that in our trade, where we have so many interesting documents to conserve, we haven't yet managed to create a national cinémathèque. All producers should combine to form one. . . . The conservation of these films would be undertaken by technicians whose job was to make new copies when needed. This cinémathèque . . . would organize regular public screenings."[39] In a 1933 article for *Pour Vous* headlined "Will we soon have a national cinémathèque?"[40] Nino Frank wrote, "Periodically every 6–12 months there's talk (and not only in France) of developing a cinémathèque. Over and over again, the topic comes up, and inevitably it must come to fruition sooner or later." On 10 January 1933 the Direction générale des Beaux-Arts went so far as to formally create such an organism, located in the Trocadero, and in an appeal headlined "Friends of the National Cinémathèque" announced that "from now on the works, the masterpieces of French cinematic production will be preserved from their three great enemies—wear and tear, destruction, oblivion. We must now breathe life into this project—that's to say capitalize on existing collections, class them, catalogue them, ensure their preservation."[41] Apparently because of inadequate administration, nothing came of the project.

Meanwhile, the Soviets had since 1926 been storing their films in an archive, Sweden began a cinémathèque in 1933, Berlin in 1934, London and New York in 1935. When Langlois and Franju began their private small-scale initiative on 9 September 1936 then, they were trying belatedly to make good the lost opportunities of decades and to catch up with the achievements of other nations. The delays in undertaking the task resulted in permanent loss of a large part of their French silent and early sound heritage. Karr estimates that 25% of U.S. production from the thirties has been lost and 10% from the forties.[42] The situation is much worse in France, where the most optimistic estimates see 50–55% of films from the thirties as lost, and 35% from the wartime period. Those losses arise from the fact that the films were subject to a purely commercial regime, which saw them thrown out once audiences lost interest, or processed to salvage reusable materials. By about 1920, the earliest films had all begun to seem "outdated": Pathé had stripped the gelatine off all his early production to recuperate the base, and Méliès burned all his copies in 1923, giving away the negatives to a salvage merchant.[43] Again after 1930, silent films came to seem "outdated" and suffered the same fate. Toward 1950, the switch from nitrate to celluloid caused past production to be abandoned for a third time.

A cinémathèque could have saved most if not all of these. Even the legal obligation to deposit a copy of each film, as editors must deposit books, would have saved them. Legislation requiring this was actually passed in 1943 but never signed into law by the minister. Consequently, another 200 nitrate films—one-third of the production of the late forties—have disappeared.

The Langlois-Franju enterprise did little to rectify this situation. It had no proper funding,[44] had collected only 200 films by 1939, and only through the benevolence of a German archivist colleague during the war, president of FIAF, (Fédération internationale des archives du film, founded 17 June 1938),[45] when Langlois and Franju were secretary-general and secretary, lifted this number to a respectable 3,500. After the war, Langlois was to remain in charge of the collection—indeed was to dominate the international film archive scene till his death. His unpredictable, paranoiac, disorderly but charismatic personality was to cause enormous losses as well as enormous gains to the collection. What cannot be denied is the intense enthusiasm he radiated and disseminated amid a whole 1950s generation on behalf of the cinema. His catholic policies provided one of the major impulses for that large-scale reevaluation of French filmmaking practices undertaken during the fifties by the critics of *Cahiers* and other magazines and by the growing populations of the ciné-club movement to whom (to its cost) he freely loaned the collection.

A measure of the scale of the audience being thus formed is available in the degree to which specialist critical magazines could be supported over these three decades and in the number of "art et essai" cinemas that existed to cater to that audience. It has to be acknowledged that, on these criteria, the audience was, for much of that time, very small indeed, even within the context of a national audience which was small.

Art cinemas had developed early in the twenties, alongside ciné-clubs and often in close coordination with them. The first was the Vieux Colombier, founded in 1924 by Jean Tedesco, followed by the Studio des Ursulines, which Armand Tellier founded in 1926 and ran till his death in 1958. Then came Studio 28, which Mauclaire founded in 1928, L'Oeil de Paris which Jean Vallée founded in 1929, and the Panthéon, which the producer Pierre Braunberger founded in 1930.[46] But the public for such art cinemas clearly ceased expanding with the advent of the talkie: no more such studios opened thereafter; by 1934 the Vieux Colombier had been obliged to revert to theatrical productions, and a year later the Ursulines was screening the standard repertoire again, with occasional more ambitious programs.[47]

But not only did the public cease to grow, the supply of films available to construct ongoing programs for such audiences was lacking. As Jeander observes perhaps somewhat too categorically, "the spirit of experiment disappears, [and] it's thanks to this death of the avant-garde that those living in the rue des Ursulines were able to get a decent night's sleep again."[48] Diminishing audiences and competition for the available programs were already so severe a problem in 1930 that when Armand Tellier attempted to develop a cooperative involving the five art cinemas, he met with strong resistance, "individual interests rapidly taking precedence over their common interests."[49]

CRITICAL JOURNALS AND THE DISCOURSE OF ART

This trend away from an avant-garde and an art cinema circuit in the years 1934–1935 is reflected in the critical journals of the period. The one ambitious critical journal to have been launched at the end of the twenties, the *Revue du Cinéma*, collapsed at the end of 1931 after 28 issues. Admittedly the prime reason for this was the editor Jean George Auriol's refusal to seek production company advertising, in an attempt to remain independent of industrial pressure. After a chaotic period with the publisher Corti, it had been taken over by Gallimard;[50] but even such a publisher, with prestigious literary journals and no lack of funding, could see no future in continuing to support a film journal which could not generate enough subscribers to buy the print-run of 2,000 copies a month. Those who did read it saw it as providing commentaries on the cinema which were neither conventional nor promotional nor banal nor sordidly commercial[51]—commentaries by Auriol himself (under various pseudonyms), by Brunius, by Mitry, Paul Gilson, Louis Chavance, Georges Altman, Denis Marion, and such literary figures as Desnos, Leiris, Aymé, Arnoux, Ehrenburg, and Pirandello; or again Darius Milhaud, Louis Page, and Roger Leenhardt. But the audience to which it spoke was small and decreasing.

Toward the end there was talk of its merging with *Cinea*, the journal founded by Delluc and revived by Tedesco and L'Herbier (despite its violent condemnation of L'Herbier in earlier issues); but that journal itself disappeared in 1932, and the more upmarket version of *Ciné Magazine*, launched as a monthly in 1929, likewise died in 1935. Though neither of these matched the critical tone of the Gallimard version of *La Revue du Cinéma*, they had provided an interim forum for occasional critical articles of a more serious kind, written by those who had contributed to *La Revue*, as did *Pour Vous*, which had once, under Arnoux, had some claims to critical authority and independence,[52] or more literary journals such as Antonin Artaud's *Cahiers Jaunes*, which published a special issue in 1933 stigmatizing "the precocious dotage of the cinema."[53] From 1932 onward, however, the main forum for such critics was the film column of the daily press, from which many of them had anyway originally come. Throughout the thirties, they published wherever they could—Léon Moussinac in *L'Humanité*, Alexandre Arnoux in *L'Intransigeant*, François Vinneuil in *L'Action Française*, Gaston Thierry in *Paris-Midi*, Lucien Wahl in *L'Oeuvre*, Roger Leenhardt in *L'Esprit*.

Needless to say, the discourse which marks out these critics and these journals as "serious" is the well-known romantic discourse of the author as creative artist. This discourse is most clearly associated with *Cahiers du Cinéma* and with Truffaut's passionate 1954 article on "Une certaine tendance du cinéma français." In it he attacks the "scriptwriters films" that he saw as having dominated the French cinema since the coming of sound, producing a "psychological realism" and a "quality product" which are abjectly artificial. His particular targets were the scriptwriters Jean Aurenche and Pierre Bost, but also Spaak, Sigurd, and Jeanson. The classic cinema's baseness he sees as due primarily to the fragmentation of the filmmaking process under such a production system and to the lack of a single guiding mind behind each film which might have produced a work that was at once coherent in form and authentic, passionate, sincere in its account of the author's experience. The scenarist's cinema of the past ten years seemed to him on the contrary to have produced nothing but stilted and artificial worlds inhabited by grotesque and abject puppets.

> These abject characters, who mouth abject phrases, I know a handful of men in France who would be *incapable* of conceiving of them—filmmakers whose vision of the world is at least as valid as that of Aurenche and Bost, Sigurd and Jeanson. I mean Jean Renoir, Robert Bresson, Jean Cocteau, Jaques Becker, Abel Gance, Max Ophüls, Jacques Tati, Roger Leenhardt. These too, however, are French filmmakers, as it happens, by a curious coincidence—*authors* ["*des auteurs*"] who often write their own dialogue and in some cases themselves invent their own stories, which they then go on to direct. . . . I cannot see any possibility of peaceful coexistence

between the *Quality Tradition* and an *auteur cinema*. . . . It is the unreasonably drawn-out existence of that *psychological realism* which has produced the public's inability to understand works so fresh in their conception as *Le Carosse d'or, Casque d'or*, indeed *Les Dames du Bois de Boulogne* and *Orphée*.[54]

This article was subsequently to be represented as a turning-point in French critical writing, a visionary moment of breakthrough when a rebellious younger generation ripped the veils from a nation's critical gaze and articulated truths about the cinema which no one had hitherto dared to voice. A major step in this mythologization of the Truffaut article was Doniol-Valcroze's review, in issue number 100 of *Cahiers du Cinéma*, of that journal's origins and critical standpoints. He sees the review as having had no fixed or coherent critical position up to 1954. Only when, after much hesitation, he and Bazin agreed to publish the Truffaut article, did it acquire one. Truffaut's article became a manifesto, auteurism a rallying cry, the young Turks of Cahiers the advance guard of the New Wave. "An idea had been set in motion which was to lead irrevocably to the accession of almost all its supporters to the status of director."[55]

This is to accept too readily the rhetoric of authorial discourse itself. As has already been implied, the discourse was far from new to French critical journals in 1954, and all of the elements of the *"auteur theory"* had been expressed as explicitly, and at least as forcefully, at intervals over the previous forty years or more.

The promotion of film as an artform goes back to the well-known Société Le Film d'Art, founded by the financier Lafitte in 1908, the most famous production of which was the *Assassinat du duc de Guise*, written by a member of the Academy, acted by members of the Comédie Française, with a special musical score by Saint-Saens. That the French filmmakers of the impressionist school of the twenties conceived of themselves as artists in the romantic sense, expressing their personal conceptions of the world in their works, is equally apparent. In 1919, Louis Delluc observed that "We are witnessing the birth of an extraordinary art. The sole contemporary art, perhaps, with a place set apart for it already, and its day of glory to come. . . . "[56] It was widely seen to be the supreme art, which would synthesize all the previous ones. "We need the cinema," wrote Canudo, "so as to develop that total artform toward which all the other arts have been tending."[57] Such comments were a commonplace, even, of French film criticism in the 1920s. "The cinema of yesterday was certainly not an art," wrote Claude Farrère in 1922, "but in all probability that of tomorrow will be so."[58]

That the discourse is fully formed by 1930 is apparent from the extent to which it infuses many of the articles in the *Revue du Cinéma* (series 1). Already in the slightly chaotic early issues it is becoming explicit in a review of an article by Germaine Dulac published in *Le Monde*. Her view that "Art is simply Sincerity" whereas "Industry is simply Calculation" is quoted favorably: the two are poles apart, irreconcilable.[59] As the *Revue du Cinéma* comes under Gallimard's control and the articles acquire substance, Auriol becomes more explicit on the subject: disparaging the talkie for the constraints it was imposing on filmmakers (100% sound films "are 100% frightful"), he asserts that "what is important above all else is to know whether the director was going to be ever more roundly betrayed than before, whether his vision, his hallucination, reaching the screen after such a large number of stages, was going to be inevitably distorted. Was the poet going to be obliged to follow well-worn tracks, have a style imposed on him which was determined by the richnesses and weaknesses inherent in the cinephonic machinery?"[60] In the same issue Denis Marion identifies the genius of the director as the source of value in films, as surely as Truffaut was to do 25 years later: "Certain Russian films are admirable because directed by Eisenstein, Pudovkin, Dziga Vertov; and others are execrable or mediocre according as they are made by Protozanoff or by Taritsch."[61] In view of this, it is not surprising that Claude Beylie, looking back on these articles 50 years later, should exclaim in surprise, "the auteur theory, already!"[62] Russian and German directors are most frequently allocated this authorial status, but certain American directors are credited with it also: Charlie Chaplin (issues 8 and 20), King Vidor (three articles in issue 11), Griffith (issue 19), and particularly Harry Langdon (issues 3 and 9). Stroheim (issues 5 and 8) "has a genius as authentic as Chaplin."[63] Extended biographies appear, not unlike the hagiographic eulogies of stars (of Stroheim, Chaplin, Langdon, Lubitsch, Sternberg, and Griffith). Typically, these depict the artist's struggles to overcome the ignominy of the Hollywood machine and of the repressive censorship apparatus, in order to impose his vision. Anecdotal but reverential accounts of the artist at work (Lubitsch, issue 5; Clarence Brown, issue 6; Vidor, issue 11) are juxtaposed with personality sketches (even where this is acknowledged as irrelevant).[64]

This status of auteur is by no means so readily accorded to French directors: René Clair and his brother Henri Chomette are acknowledged (issues 5 and 13) for their avant-garde work (though L'Herbier is systematically vilified for his), and in an interview with Feyder, his trials, including his struggles to impose his vision on actors and actresses, are explored.[65] But Auriol and the other commentators of *La Revue du Cinéma* were perfectly ready to acknowledge their preference for foreign directors, especially Americans. Already in issue 3, *Pour Vous* is scorned for its inexplicable promotion of French films,[66] and this preference was to become more marked in subsequent years. In a review of *Maman Colibri* (Duvivier, 1929), we read, "The French cinema: the people in charge need blowing up, the directors are hypocritical, jesuitical, impotent."[67] But it was not only through the pages of *La Revue du Cinéma* that this auteurist discourse spoke: in the pages of *Pour Vous* the word "auteur" often had its contemporary sense as in the 1929 argument in favor of author's rights, as opposed to producer's rights: "The author, who has brought forth the fruit of his genius in pain, does not give up [his rights] without much anguish: what matters to him is the expression of his thought and the fullness of its development. . . . It was I who conceived the work, he protests, you have no right over my legitimate child."[68] In its editorial page, this discourse frequently found expression in praise of such directors as Pudovkin,[69] Gance, or Murnau.[70] In later pages such assumptions about film were voiced by or about René Clair.[71]

It is undeniable, however, that the discourse is by the mid-thirties much less frequently heard. It disappears as the few specialist magazines in which it found a natural home disappear, and as the conditions under which films were being made render it a less "natural" way of conceptualizing their production. When Bardèche and Brasillach publish their *History of Cinema* in 1935, they reaffirm it powerfully; but it has clearly become by then a discourse from the past, beleaguered and strident. For them the great poets of the cinema are Chaplin and Eisenstein. "Abstraction and sensuality blend in Eisenstein as in the greatest of creative spirits. A creator he would have been anywhere—in America, in Germany. In Russia, he found his climate and his time. . . . Like all arts, cinema is a question of style, that is to say an individually produced work, expressed in a variety of individual ways."[72]

By 1936, when Clair writes a preface to the English edition of his novel *Adams*, the aesthetic discourse has become, as he himself notes, "morose" and ironic—so much so that many readers took him to be recanting on his belief in film as an artform. Certainly this is the period of the discourse's least visibility, and it coincides both with the stagnation of ciné-clubs and art-house cinemas and with the disappearance of those magazines which had been its most visible vehicles. Artist-directors of the twenties no longer had an outlet for their articles. René Clair's articles cease in 1935 with his departure for England. Epstein publishes nothing between early 1936 and 1946. The articles written by Renoir for *Ce Soir* during this period steadfastly avoid reference to the cinema as art. Marcel L'Herbier's invaluable collection of excerpts of such writers[73] only underlines the ten-year lapse in this artistic discourse. Nevertheless, it does not disappear entirely. Alexandre Arnoux maintained it in a scattering of articles in the late thirties.[74] Roger Leenhardt renewed it in his column in *L'Esprit* between 1935 and 1939, insisting that "the personal responsibility of the creator is fundamental to any work of art"[75] and that "whatever they might produce, we should always expect a lot from a René Clair, a Feyder, a Renoir, or a Chenal—nothing of a Duvivier. I find completely ridiculous the garbage spoken of this worthy craftsman, this honest workhorse of the French cinema."[76] These were, however, isolated instances of articles appearing in publications of "general" cultural import. Even the film books, which had appeared with remarkable frequency in the late twenties and early thirties, tail off with Charensol's *40 ans du Cinéma* (1935) and Bardèche and Brasillach's *Histoire du Cinéma* (1935), not to reappear in any number until the immediate postwar period.

Nevertheless, though they only rarely found their way into print during this period, in this circle of cultured but now marginalized figures, assumptions concerning the aesthetic status of the cinema were sufficiently common that both Auriol, in his introduction to *La Technique du film* in 1939,[77] and the young André Bazin, writing in 1943, can feel it is too readily accepted as the natural discourse of intelligent criticism, and that it needs qualification: "The problem of film authorship is not resolved and cannot be so, a priori. The facts of production are just too variable from work to work for one to be able to accept the director as invariably the unique creator. The cinema is a team art. Each film requires of the critic an individual judgment concerning its authorship."[78]

This eminently reasonable position, classic rather than romantic and more or less identical to that reached by Arnoux in a major article that same year entitled *L'Auteur d'un film, cet inconnu . . .* ,[79] was, however, to be rapidly swept aside. Immediately after the war ended the artistic discourse occupied the high ground of critical writing. *La Revue du Cinéma*, series 2, is much more explicit in its articulation of the position. "Is cinema an art?" asks Lo Duca dramatically in issue 3 of the *Revue*; but the question is largely rhetorical, since in that same issue Jacques Bourgeois has already likened Orson Welles to Proust: such authors "do the work of God," "bring to birth new being."[80] Indeed, Doniol-Valcroze had effectively answered Lo Duca in the very first issue of the *Revue*, first by devoting an article to "Two operas of Eisenstein," and second in writing of *Citizen Kane* that "Orson Welles always puts himself into his films. His private and public lives coincide with his work."[81]

Eisenstein and Welles were to become fixtures in the canon of master filmic artists that the *Revue* team of critics were to construct over the next few years. Major articles were to be organized around the work of Eisenstein (issue 7), Welles (5), Rosselini (17), Flaherty (4 and 12), Fritz Lang (5), Dreyer (8), Chaplin (9 and 11), John Ford (10), William Wyler (10 and 11), Jean Grémillon (16), and Lubitsch (17). Review articles were to extend this pantheon to include Hitchcock, Hawks, Leenhardt, David Lean, Pudovkin, Dovzhenko, Renoir, René Clair, René Clément, Preston Sturges, John Houston, and (on the basis of *Le Diable au corps*) a little improbably, Claude Autant-Lara.

The terms in which these articles are written are unequivocally authorial: film can only be an art when the work is dominated by an individual creative spirit. The editor, Jean George Auriol, himself publishes a six-part manifesto which explicitly accepts a division between routine cinematic production and daring improvizations, the former produced for the masses by routine corporate procedures, the latter produced for an elite audience out of dreams, sensitivity, and intuitive genius.[82] The term "auteur," later to acquire such discursive force, was early the subject of debate in the *Revue du Cinéma*. Recognized as appropriate primarily to describe the writer of the script, it is nevertheless soon linked by a hyphen to the term *metteur en scène*, to designate those directors who write their own scripts, and subsequently supersedes that clumsy phrase to stand alone as the term used to designate all true filmic artists.

But the *Revue du Cinéma* was not alone at this time in giving voice to this discourse: in its very first numbers, as it emerges from clandestinity in 1945, *L'Ecran Français* uses analogous terms. Articles by Georges Sadoul, Alexandre Arnoux, and Georges Altman all speak thus of John Ford and of Chaplin,[83] as does Astruc on Preston Sturges's *Christmas in July* and Jacques Becker on Bresson's *Les Dames du Bois de Boulogne*.[84] It is in this magazine that Astruc's coining of the term caméra-stylo occurs:

> The cinema is quite simply in the process of becoming a means of expression, as the other arts did before it, particularly painting and the novel. After having been successively a fairground attraction, an amusement analogous to the Boulevard theater, and a means of preserving the images of an age, it is little by little becoming a language—that's to say a form in which and by which an artist can express his thoughts, however abstract, or translate his obsessions exactly as is the case nowadays with the essay and the novel. That's why I call this new age of the cinema that of the Caméra-stylo. . . . Which implies, of course, that the scriptwriter himself shoot his films. Or rather, that there should no longer *be* scriptwriters, for in such a cinema that distinction between writer (auteur) and director is meaningless. Directing is no longer merely a means of illustrating or presenting a scene, but a genuine writing. The author writes with his camera as a writer writes with a pen.[85]

The discourse had become such a commonplace by 1947 that the *Ecran Français* could skittishly reply to an imaginary letter from Nino Frank as follows: "Entirely in agreement with you, old fellow: the author of a film is neither the scriptwriter nor even less the director, it's the projectionist."[86] When *Positif* began publishing in 1952, its critical standpoint as set out in the opening issue is resolutely auteurist: the cinema is an *art*, with timeless masterpieces that it is the critic's job to identify and revere. They are the product of "the *auteurs*" (original emphasis) who created them. True to this declaration, its early issues consist almost entirely of articles devoted to such films as *Los Olvidados*, *Orphée*, *Miracolo a Milano*, *Die blaue Engel*, and *Rashomon*, all treated in authorial terms. The quarrel with the Cahiers line, which they retrospectively inflated into a battle of giants, was simply over whether this auteurism should be extended from the independent cinema to the commercial cinema, as Cahiers was subsequently to do.

In view of this long history of authorial writing, even in its most extreme forms, it may be a little hard to understand why the Truffaut article in 1954 should have seemed to mark a new discursive departure. Our earlier discussion about audience formation and the critical orientation of the various journals can help here: *La Revue du Cinéma* had been addressing an audience which did not yet exist, and it had done little or nothing to construct that audience itself. When Doniol-Valcroze founded *Cahiers du Cinéma*, that earlier experience had clearly marked him: *Cahiers* attempts to address a larger audience by including extensive elements of a discourse of pleasure in its early issues; it does not disdain to attract advertising, thus requiring a much smaller audience to be viable; but most particularly it comes at a moment when a multiplicity of other mechanisms of audience-formation are beginning to have their effect. The Cinémathèque, the ciné-clubs, the art et essai circuit, the amateur filmmaking societies have by then begun to show signs of that geometric expansion which was to be particularly apparent after 1960. When the Truffaut article was published, it fell therefore on receptive ears, for which it had the appearance of a revelation, but also of a revolution, a romantic revolution attuned to the nature of the myth of the artist itself. The discourse was to be dominant in the reflective press thereafter, until the critical revolutions of the sixties.

THE DISCOURSE OF THE REAL

Its only real competitor was the realist discourse, with which the name of André Bazin is most readily identified. From 1945 until 1955, this discourse was as widespread in the journalistic forums we have been discussing as was the discourse of art, only being decisively swept aside by the latter in the debate that followed Truffaut's article, but present nevertheless even then in that it inflected the direction taken by that debate and the choice of critical canon that the artistic discourse was to erect.

Central to the discourse is a claim that certain texts, perhaps even the medium as a whole, have an intimate relation to "the real," bear a privileged witness to the true state of things. Such a discourse speaks through the writings not just of Bazin, but of Eric Rohmer, of Georges Sadoul, of Lo Duca, of J.-B. Brunius, of Jean Desternes, of Doniol-Valcroze, and of Auriol himself.

Its most focused expression occurs in 1946–1948 in *La Revue du Cinéma*, alongside the other two discourses, as that journal attempts to find an adequate way of talking and thinking about the postwar influx of foreign films—and particularly of those Italian films now dubbed "neo-realist"—and later in the series of articles which Bazin and Rohmer contributed to *Cahiers du Cinéma* between 1950 and 1955.

The discourse itself is not a coherent one. With the benefit of a further thirty years of analysis of these matters it is possible to group these variant forms of "realism" into three main categories, each with several subtypes: there are discourses of the real related to the nature of the medium, discourses of the real related to different notions of the real, and discourses of the real which attempt to correlate these two by focusing on the perceiving subject, spectator at once of the real and of the medium.[87]

Within the first category we can identify two main subtypes: ontological realism and technological realism. According to the first, film as a medium is inherently realistic, or at least inherently more realistic than other media. Focusing on the photographic aspect of the film as record, this subtype sees the relatively objective and impersonal character of the recording process as a guarantee that the filmic text is realistic to a degree that no literary or painterly text could be.

According to the second subtype, film was inherently realistic in some of these ways from its very beginnings, but has become more so over the decades, and its vocation is to become ever more so until ultimately it can be conceived of as simulating perfectly that reality which it represents. Under the sign of "progress" this subtype marks out a series of technological developments such as the addition of sound to image in the late twenties, the spread of commercially viable color in the fifties, the expansion of the screen size with the advent of cinemascope, and the postwar potential for depth of field which resulted from improved filmstock as so many steps toward the holographic perfectability of the filmic illusion.

The second category of realisms, consisting of subtypes which vary insofar as their proponents have different conceptions of the real, is potentially limitless but for schematic purposes can be reduced to three subtypes: humanist realism, social realism, and transcendental realism.

The first of these assumes implicitly an unmediated reality offering itself to human experience. This experience, often termed "life," is conceived as universal and is immediately recognizable when viewed on film (or any other medium). Texts which manage to capture this authentic life have a "vitality" which other—stilted, artificial—texts lack. The apprehension and capture of this authentic human experience is inhibited by socially routinized processes such as cultural stereotypes, censorship, and industrial practices and thus is the enemy of convention. It is often spoken of as a "breaking away from" fossilized conventions and traditions of filmmaking, and the resultant text is "fresh," and "direct."

The second subtype, social realism, implicitly or explicitly rejects any notion of an unmediated and universal truth and sees reality as primarily social and ideological and therefore the site of struggle, of contestation. There are realities that *should* be shown, truths that need to be told, and the realist filmmaker's obligation is to speak out on those matters. The social realist text will normally though not necessarily be leftwing in its political orientation and often openly and outspokenly political in its message.

The third subtype of realism focusing on the real—transcendental realism—sees the real as neither social nor even human, but basically as spiritual. The task of the realist thus becomes to pierce through the material crust of things in order to capture that spiritual reality which subtends it, or perhaps to isolate those rare moments of human existence when glimpses of some greater reality illuminate it. Exemplary, here, are those nonhuman moments of filmic texts (which avoid the nasty implications of sociopolitical taint) when Nature, represented here as uncorrupted by the human, floods the screen and produces moments of lyric beauty. Because the real is inherently nonphysical, such realists see film, because of its "external" and behavioristic quality, as having to struggle harder than other media to achieve a valid realist stylistic.

In the third category of realisms that concern the perceiving subject, we can identify two relevant subtypes: psychological realism and representational realism. According to the first, human perception proceeds according to certain identifiable practices which can be simulated by filmic practices or, at least, by technical equivalents of perceptual phenomena. Such realists will focus on the glance of the perceiving subject, the motivated question-and-answer process by which data is sorted and arranged cognitively to produce an understanding of what is happening in the world. Within film practices, this will lead to a claim that continuity editing, involving the repeated reframing of elements within a visual field and the motivated tracking of moving objects and people, corresponds closely to human perception and constructs the diegetic reality in ways that correspond to the apprehension of an anonymous or perhaps an "ideal" observer.

The final subtype—which might be called representational realism—sees a correlation between ways of conceptualizing both the physical world and its filmic counterpart, which leads to conventional and stereotypic representations on film of material and social reality. It is precisely these conventions which register as realistic with the viewing subject, since they are at once a grid of conventional representations through which he/she views the world, and analogous to the conventions of representation mobilized by other media. Because they correspond to *viewer expectations* as to how the world, or a world, will be constructed on film, they register as *plausible*, and are *accepted* as realistic. Emphasis on plausibility and credibility can lead to even the most extreme fantasy texts being deemed realistic if they conform to existing social conventions of representation and/or to the operative generic conventions of representation. This emphasis on conformity to convention distances this subtype significantly from others which see convention as inherently inimical to realism.

This categorization of the various realist stances brings out clearly the potential for confusion and contradiction in any exploratory discussion of the issue, such as that which *La Revue du Cinéma* undertook. Was film an inherently realistic medium, or was it merely possible for it to be so under certain specified conditions? Or, indeed, was it inherently unrealistic in its emphasis on the superficial "materialist" aspects of the world? Was convention essential to any realism, or was it the principal barrier to realism? Was realism neutral, politically, or did it have significant political implications? Was it dependent on reproducing the perception of a viewing subject, or was it the product of aspiring to eliminate that subject? On these difficult theoretical debates, another related issue was to intrude as a result of the uneasy coexistence between the realist and auteuristic discourses in the *Revue*: was realism incompatible with the promotion of directors as artists, or was it only such artists who could aspire to true realism?

Bazin's exploration of these positions between 1945 and his death in 1958 is well known. He is most often associated with the ontological and technological positions, if only because two of his essays focus directly on those;[88] but his views evolved considerably between 1943 when an early article entitled "Pour une esthétique réaliste"[89] argued for a basically contextual realism, incorporating elements of social, technological, and psychological realism, and his later contributions to *Cahiers du Cinéma, Le Parisien Libéré,* and *France-Observateur.*

In articles such as those that he contributed to *La Revue du Cinéma* on William Wyler, he recognized psychological realism as a valid set of practices which captures a way of viewing the world that he was willing to deem natural and universal: "Realism does not consist only in showing us a body, but rather in certain aspects of the showing which respect basic physiological or mental factors of natural perception, or more exactly of finding [cinematic] equivalents for them. Classical editing . . . corresponds implicitly to a certain natural mental process."[90] If he prefers other forms of realism, notably the realism of Renoir, Malraux, Welles, Rosselini, and Wyler, it is because the long take and depth of field privilege the real rather than the perceiving subject, and Bazin's ideological orientation was toward a transcendental view of the real seen as ambiguous, rich, and inexhaustible rather than toward a subjective and relativized real.

This same transcendental realism was more consistently expressed by his fellow Jansenist Eric Rohmer, first in the *Revue du Cinéma*[91] in 1948 and then in an extensive serialized manifesto appearing in *Cahiers du Cinéma* during 1955. Rohmer's transcendental realism is most emphatically apparent in his early article for *Cahiers* entitled "Vanité que la peinture." Beginning with a quotation from Pascal ("How vain an art is painting, which attracts our admiration for representations of objects which we do not admire in the original"), Rohmer agrees that "Art doesn't change Nature. . . . Things are what they are, and can get by perfectly well without us to look at them. . . . The task of art is not to confine us in a hermetic world of its own making. Born of things, it brings us back to things." It can thus be the instrument for

curing the artist of that self-love which everywhere is destroying him. A long familiarity with art has made us only the more sensitive to the brute beauty of things; an irresistible longing seizes us, to look at the world with our everyday eyes, to preserve for ourselves this tree, this stream, this face creased in a smile or a frown—just as they are, *in spite of us*. . . . The primary aim of art is to reproduce . . . not the object, let's say, but its *beauty*. What we call realism is merely the most scrupulous striving to ensnare this beauty. . . . The images of *Tabou* glow with this same beauty, which they convey without intervention; and the whole care of the cameraman is, by his supreme art, to better disguise his own presence. He cheats only in that he *perfects* a transcript of reality which, if lackluster, would have betrayed the original. . . . Fascinated by his model, the artist forgets the order he had intended in his arrogance to impose on it and, in so doing, reveals the true harmony of nature, its essential unity. The song becomes a hymn, a prayer. The song, transfigured, reveals that transcendent reality which gave it life.

Rohmer's commitment to this particularly realist discourse was unrelenting, whereas Bazin was always aware of the pluralism of realist discourses: "There is not one, but many realisms. Each age seeks its own—that's to say the techniques and the aesthetic which can best capture, retain, and restore those elements of reality one wants to capture."[92] Bazin, moreover, was always aware that such realist discourses could not in themselves adequately cope with the full complexity of film as language or film as social and industrial product.[93]

But the use of these realist discourses extended far beyond Bazin and Rohmer. It was, as with the aesthetic discourse, the sudden influx of a variety of diverse texts in the immediate postwar years that triggered the debate on realism, since in their various ways many of these could make some claim to an intimate relation with the real. Thus *Lady in the Lake* provokes a discussion oriented toward subjective realism because of its permanent first-person narrator. Excited though they are by the novelty and the extremism of this procedure, critics tended to find it ultimately unsatisfactory. This position is put most strongly by Chartier in an article entitled "Films in the first person: the illusion of reality in the cinema."[94] Realism in the cinema, he concludes, can best be achieved by other means, such as the psychological realism of classic découpage; the first person camera of *Lady in the Lake* is incompatible with those other forms and likely therefore to detract from rather then to enhance the reality-effect of the text.

Farrebique triggered a documentary realist discourse. In an interview, Rouquier himself said of it that "*Farrebique* is a true film, because it was filmed in a real village in the Rouergue, with real peasants as characters. My aim is to be true and simple."[95] *Brief Encounter* allows this documentary discourse to make contact with a humanist realist discourse. The film is praised for the authentic effect it achieves by rejecting the conventions of dramatic narrative and stereotyped characters. We might meet such people in the street; "it could happen to me or you; and if it did, we'd react like that."[96]

But it was particularly the Italian films of Rosselini and De Sica that provoked this particular alliance of realist discourses. They involve "production procedures analogous to those of silent filmmaking: shooting wherever possible outside studios, in real locations [these directors] have rediscovered a tone of integrity which is peculiar to them alone. . . . *Roma, citta aperta* gives the impression of being shot when it actually happened."[97] "As for the actors, they are never that . . . they manifest a divine gift—that of not acting in front of the camera, that of being themselves. They seem to deliver themselves up to us. Of course they are acting. But we forget it."[98] "Life is beginning to inundate our screens again, not just a simulacrum animated by cunning lighting effects—the life of a street, which is not just constructed out of stage flats. . . . The director tells a story [but] the great quality of the film is to inject the maximum of truth into the plot, to surprise life in action, to authenticate every last detail. . . . Because of its commitment to truth, we are nearer to a newsreel on the liberation of Paris than to *Jericho*."[99] "What is striking in Rosselini's procedures is their resemblance to those of all the best directors of recent years, in all countries. It's thus that the documentarists Basil Wright and Paul Rotha operate in England, the great Flaherty in America, Youtkevitch and Zgourdi in the USSR, Leopold Lindtberg in Switzerland in his *La Dernière Chance*, René Clement in France in his *Bataille du rail*, or Georges Rouquier in *Farrebique*."[100]

But it is not always the most obvious films that are the subject of realist discourse. Cocteau's *Les Parents Terribles* is discussed by André Bazin in terms of psychological realism.[101] Even a dramatic historical reconstruction could receive such a treatment: Donskoi's *Life of Gorki* is "fully realist": "the artistic technique of the cinema is invisible because the cinéaste wants us to forget it; because what counts is the story, is Gorki. . . . He reconstructs as faithfully as possible the setting and the characters, the attitudes and situations of the novel; he restores to life its authenticity; he observes . . . that life, that 'manufactured' reality, recording the body then seeking the spirit behind the sets, the soul within the body, substituting for his gaze a camera neither more nor less agile than that gaze."[102]

Clearly, for a period of some 5–8 years after the war, incorporating elements of one or another realist discourse into any critical commentary on a film was essential. For that brief period of time, critics feel obliged to be realist, in some sense, as well as auteurist, in some sense, if their criticism was to be taken seriously. Despite the existence of a realist discourse in critical writings of the twenties, there is no significant tradition of realist film criticism extending back through the thirties, out of which this debate can be seen as emerging. The first series of *La Revue du Cinéma* had shown no equivalent interest, and Auriol himself had been at that time actively hostile to the realist pressures of the talkie. In this he was echoing the widespread 1930s reaction against sound film, seen not as an advance in technological realism but as stultifying in its limitation of aesthetic experimentation.

All that one finds in prewar criticism are traces of the various realist positions that play on the (essentially aesthetic) opposition between "life" and "convention," "life" and "artifice," or the more politically oriented social realism. Léon Moussinac had been the only critical figure in the France of the twenties to have consistently employed such a discourse; he at least might have had the motive and the authority to continue so to do in the thirties. His promotion of the Soviet cinema as a true people's cinema had been insistent both before and after his visit to the Soviet Union. In the early thirties he was instrumental in organizing in France the Association of Revolutionary Writers and Artists, and the Theatre of Independent Action; but then, bankrupt and jobless, he left France for two crucial years to represent Aragon in the Soviet Union at the International Union of Writers. On his return, although he was able to get editing jobs, including one where he gave his young Communist colleague, Georges Sadoul, an opportunity to write on film for the first time, there does not seem to have been an audience for the sort of discourse one might have expected of him. Speeches which he gave at the time in working class areas talk of capitalist conspiracies, the complicity of state and big business, and the monopolistic aspirations of sound film patent-holders. Such tactics are seen as aiming to destroy the artistic independence that twenties cinema had known: "all that is in the order of things—the capitalists' order of things."[103] He regrets the paucity of nonconformist films in the sound period, criticizes the star system, the implicit colonialist propaganda of many thirties films, the censorship which prevents the screening of Soviet masterpieces, and the ideological support given to bourgeois institutions of repression.

But the occasions when this discourse is voiced are rare in the thirties. Inevitably, the war saw a total ban on it. From the start of hostilities, the totality of the leftwing press was banned or censored out of existence, and those who were suspected of having waged Communist propaganda were arrested and interned. The decree of April 1940 saw them subject to the death penalty. Ironically, Moussinac himself was saved by Hitler's breakthrough, which saw him evacuated to a Vichy concentration camp ("an extermination camp"—Sadoul).[104] He was released in November 1941 when the USSR entered the war on Hitler's side and Communists began to be viewed more favorably by the authorities.

It was not to be until the period 1944–1948 that this discourse came into its own, when an intensely politicized audience provided a large and receptive readership for a leftwing press.

Emerging as it did from clandestinity and sponsored as it was by a range of leftwing political parties, the *Ecran Français* enjoyed considerable professional prestige in the period 1945–1950. Alongside the discourse of pleasure that paid the journal's way and the discourse of art that had not yet fully found its audience, the social realist discourse flourishes in its clearest form. Central to the discourse was a debate as to what form a true people's cinema should take. Essentially, the problem was to produce an alternative mass cinema, dominated not by, or not only by, notions of pleasure and entertainment, but by notions of social responsibility.[105]

To this debate, Bazin contributes a definition of the true political film which sees *La Règle du jeu* and *Le Crime de M. Lange* as "truly popular films" despite the minimal audiences they attracted.[106] But the definition which attracts most support is that which sees a politically correct film as one which privileges the public over the private. J.-P. Sartre had early spoken of the peculiar ease with which film, as opposed to the theater, or even to literature, could do justice to crowds, to the masses, representing them to themselves as central to any social action. He called for large-scale public subjects to complement the psychological dramas of individual lives which formed the stock material of most films.[107] This line soon became the authorized critical viewpoint of the journal:

> *Taras Bulba*, taken by Marc Donskoi from a novel by Boris Gorbatov which was extremely popular in the USSR, is precisely such a work of great significance, expressing the moral climate of Soviet life with a striking sincerity. . . . The structure of the scenario may be a little negligent at times; aesthetically, it may lack unity; but there are some things which sweep such considerations aside and make any faults readily acceptable: the nobility of the sentiments; the tone of profound conviction exuded by the author and the cast; above all, the Soviet humanism which bathes the work from start to finish . . . such films are neither didactic nor naive; but as true as *Potemkin*. Quite simply they emerge from the realities of Soviet life.[108]

Such a discourse frequently involved the promotion of one national cinema over another—most often the Soviet over the American. The HUAC activities within America were followed closely, and that minority of American films which could be seen as conforming to socialist realist tendencies, and which were the subject of political repression in America, were praised for their courage, for daring to speak out, for daring to tell unpalatable truths about American society.[109]

Perhaps the most outspoken statement of this position can be found in the series of articles in which Georges Magnane explored the distance between the social reality of America and its representation on the screen. The working class is either invisible or present in certain stereotyped representations involving acts of violence and limited intelligence. "In fact American workers—they are not hard to find and to talk to—are the first to laugh at such falsely naive images. Like their European counterparts, they are learning and organizing themselves. At meetings, which are models of order and discipline, they discuss their responsibilities with a seriousness which shows that they at least consider themselves adult. They even go to the cinema but wonder how long they'll continue to appear in it as accessories in sensational plots. . . . "[110]

The representation of the worker, of strikes, and more generally of class interests, was a constant criterion of worth within this discourse. Thus the *Ecran Français* would support the view of workers in le Havre, on strike at the time over a refusal to unload arms, who considered themselves calumnied by their representation in Marcel Pagliero's *Un homme marche dans la ville*, which the director had attempted to present in terms of "a good story," of mere entertainment.[111] Films were closely scrutinized for ideological correctness, particularly in the immediate aftermath of the war, when the representation of the French nation as a whole was an intensely political fact. The classic instance was Clouzot's *Le Corbeau*, produced during the occupation. Accusing Clouzot and the scriptwriter Chavance of treason, of collaboration, the *Ecran Français* had interpreted this story of scandal and gossip in a provincial town as confirming the German's view that the French people were "degenerate, ripe for slavery, and that our ancestral qualities are mere historical relics. . . . This is the image of ourselves that we must be shown in order to convince us of our unworthiness."[112] *Le Corbeau* is contrasted in this respect with Grémillon's *Le Ciel est à vous*: "To the dirty-minded little girls, born vicious and devious, which the servile imagination of M. Clouzot has fabricated, as if to Nazi orders, [Grémillon] has replied 'No! These are all false! The true French of today are like this. . . . ' Here then are two films, one produced and implicitly encouraged by the Boches, nourishing anti-French propaganda, and the other refuting that propaganda, affirming . . . our confidence in ourselves."[113]

In his history of the French cinema written in 1962, the Communist George Sadoul still sees *Le Corbeau* at least as having lent itself to such a usage by the Germans. "Continental decided to use it for propaganda purposes," he says, "and screened it in various occupied countries where French prestige remained high. The ends pursued by Dr. Goebbels were not, however, attained," and neither Swiss nor Czechoslovaks saw anything but a quality French product.[114] By contrast, Courtade reports claims that Clouzot lost his position at Continental "because the high command complained that the film discouraged anonymous letters: this was the moment when they were becoming particularly useful to the Germans."[115] Rather than attempt to reconcile the diverse claims concerning the film or identify degrees of veracity in the various critics' assertions, it is useful to record the intensity of the ideological discourse surrounding all aspects of the occupation, resistance, and collaboration.

As these examples demonstrate clearly, this discourse was intensely aware of the cinema as a social instrument, an ideological tool, having political effects on the consciousness of the masses, on their self-representation. And these political effects were merely disguised by the discourse of pleasure, which served as an ideological smokescreen. Here it is the political formation of an audience that was central, as is made explicit in a number of articles: "Filmmakers, like all artists, play a historic role in the formation and transformation of mankind: more than writers even, because their audience is larger and their message, perhaps, more readily assimilated. It is of importance, then—above all—that they should be aware of what they can and might express."[116]

Whereas in the immediate postwar years *L'Ecran Français* had been able to exploit the large public support for leftwing positions and had been able to see itself as in the mainstream of cinematic discourse, by 1950 the war in Indochina and the Cold War had transformed the political orientation of the French populace. Instead of forming its audience, the *Ecran* was losing it to other more effective and contradictory mechanisms of political formation; it was becoming totally isolated in its critical support for leftwing positions. Rather than move with the times, preserve an audience, and retain its ability to affect the political climate of the fifties, the *Ecran Français* became more entrenched, more and more radicalized. Its strident support for Communism, its hard-line Stalinism were at odds with the government's positioning of France in the Western Alliance. Despite an attempt to mobilize notions of nationalism in its cause,[117] despite an even stronger emphasis on the entertainment elements[118] in its later issues, this magazine, which represented the last relic of a once vibrant political discourse, disappeared in 1953—indeed, effectively it had ceased to exist at least a year earlier.[119]

No subsequent publication provided a significant forum for this discourse. *Positif,* appearing in 1952, was subsequently to represent itself as fighting a leftwing political action against the conservative pro-American faction in *Cahiers du Cinéma,* and there is some evidence in its early issues to support this. Aggressive articles by the principal contributors manifest leftwing, anticlerical, and libertarian sympathies. There is a greater interest in Latin American cinemas than is apparent in any other film magazine of the fifties, and that subcontinent is consistently represented as subject to American cultural colonialism. There are also several references to political conditions in Spain under Franco, and a marked sympathy is apparent for the liberating anticlericalism of surrealism as manifested in the films of Buñuel. But progressively in the discursive struggle as to whether films should be seen as sociopolitical texts or whether films should be seen as timeless works of art, the latter wins out. Significantly, it is only when this happens that the magazine becomes financially viable. During its initial years its frequent changes of address as it sought protectors willing to shore up its financial status are sufficient evidence of the lack of a continuing public for its leftwing political discourse.

It is not hard to see how the war would have served to valorize such a discourse, and more generally the discourse of the real. The French, and not only the French, had been subject to an extraordinary and gruelling social experience which had marked all aspects of their life. They had endured four years in which an occupying nation had prevented any public expression of certain passionately held truths. This in itself would have been enough to guarantee the centrality of "truth" and "the real" in any discursive struggle, including that of art. Not only was the urge to speak of that experience insistent, but indeed not to speak of it could seem treacherous, almost blasphemous. When films did appear which spoke of it passionately, or which in any way seemed to aspire toward a closer relation with such recent experience, it was natural to mobilize a realist discourse to defend them.

The audience for such films and for such a discourse was large at the time of the liberation, but it disintegrated as the political complexities of the Cold War proceeded to confuse what had seemed clear-cut positions. When Michel Mourlet reiterates certain basic elements of the realist position in a 1959 issue of Cahiers, it is framed by an editorial introduction which effectively apologizes for it as an eccentric and extremist viewpoint; only the well-known intellectual liberality of the editors could have allowed them to publish it.[120]

CENSORSHIP

But if the critical discourse which focused on film as a social instrument for fashioning the mentality of the people knew only a short period of widespread acceptability, the political authorities whose job it was to govern that people were never less than intensely aware of the cinema's potential for the politicization of the people. The various forms of censorship and precensorship, together with the self-censorship which these engendered, can all be seen as working throughout this period to condition the consciousness of the people to "form the audience." At times, this formation is not only political but moral, the two paternalist discourses complementing one another to the same end.

Throughout the 1930s, these paternalist discourses were operative behind the scenes, conditioning in very concrete ways the sorts of film the populace could see and the sorts of themes that could be treated, and this despite the existence of extremely liberal regulations governing the granting of visas which, if properly applied, should have guaranteed a greater freedom to producers and importers of film.[121] Passed in 1928 by the then minister, Edouard Herriot, these regulations appointed a commission to oversee the granting of visas, on which there were only four government members out of 32, later to be reduced to three out of 44. It is clear, however, that despite their minority voice, the representatives of the government departments had a power of absolute veto over certain sorts of film whenever they wished to exercise it. As the president of the commission, Edmond Sée, confided in an interview with Pour Vous,[122] "In all questions of aesthetics or morality, our opinion is preponderant. . . . But as for films that might cause disruption or might harm the preservation of order, the opinion of the representatives of the ministry of the interior and of foreign affairs has the force of law. Their veto is, in sum, beyond appeal." Thus it was that the Soviet films (Mother, Potemkin, The General Line, and at least ten others) were banned, or heavily cut, as was All Quiet on the Western Front, despite strong support in some cases, even from the president of the commission himself.[123]

A list of the headings under which the commission banned films from screening in 1933 is revealing: licentious films (3), Communist or antimilitarist propaganda (3), Hitlerian propaganda (1), slight on the prestige of the teaching profession (1—*Zéro de conduite*),[124] likely to cause insult to a foreign power (1), succession of terrifying scenes (1—*The Mask of Fu Manchu*), miscellaneous (1). The secretary of the commission summed up its criteria in an interview as follows: "the predominant question is decency. After that, 'consideration of foreign relations, the prestige of our army and air force, the defense of religious convictions and private sensibilities—in a word, anything that might disrupt public order and cause disturbances.' " Thus *L'Age d'or* and *Le Rosier de Mme Husson* had their visas withdrawn when disruptions occurred at their screening. *Ecstasy*, although granted a visa, was subject to significant cuts when protests followed its screening. Ignoring this ruling, the exhibitor screened it in full.

The potential for political intervention in screenings was markedly strengthened in 1936, when "drastic" transformation of the commission of control saw the membership altered to include ten public servants from relevant government departments and ten members appointed personally by the minister for education, from outside the profession. In fact, representation from the cinema was now totally eliminated, and political considerations inevitably predominated. This potential found forceful expression in a circular letter sent out by Edmond See to producers, distributors, and exhibitors on 25 October 1937. It stated that

A. A visa would be rigorously refused to
   1. all films tending to bring the army into ridicule or to diminish its prestige
   2. all films tending to cause distress to the national susceptibilities of foreign peoples and consequently to provoke diplomatic incidents
   3. all films representing armed violence, breaking and entering, and similar criminal actions, such as might have a pernicious influence on young people

B. A visa will only in unusual circumstances be granted to
   1. war or spy films, which in recent times have tended to multiply
   2. films based on military or police incidents of any sort, other than those covered by the preceding condition.

"In the case of these latter categories of film," the letter said, "of films relating to matters of national defense, the high institutions of the state, and important French or foreign personalities, and of all others that you think relevant, would you be so good as to *consult me before proceeding to shoot the film*, and pass on to me for checking the detailed scenario of the projected film."[125]

On the one hand, it is interesting to note how the political discourse has completely won out over the moral discourse: by this time there is no mention of public decency or of blasphemy as a central criterion for censorship. On the other hand it is clear that this circular announced the explicit introduction of precensorship into the regulatory process and constituted an irresistible pressure on the producers toward self-censorship. More, it constituted an incitement to produce films that would represent France, French political and social institutions, and French and allied figures in a favorable light. It is most probable that this informal (since not legislated) censorship was instrumental in determining the direction taken by many scenarios in the following years. It can thus be seen as a factor determining the production of genres such as the military/foreign legion genre.

Undoubtedly, pressure of this sort was itself generated by growing apprehension about the possibility of another world war. The year 1938 was to see the attachment of Austria to Germany and the Munich agreement allocating Sudetenland to Germany. As Francis Courtade notes, in these circumstances it is not surprising if 1938 sees over one-third of the total French production related to the glories and duties of military life.[126]

Aside from films dealing unfavorably with military life, all films calling into question national institutions were banned, or, as with *Prison sans barreaux* to a scenario by Spaak, only released because of foreign recognition.[127] Carné recounts his relief when *Quai des brumes* was granted a visa with only minor changes.[128] But where the political censorship had its most serious effects was in the area of newsreels: contemporary accounts list innumerable instances of the tactical suppression of events with political and social implications and of the strategic representation of foreign dignitaries.[129]

Conditions on the expression of political and social matters were further tightened when war broke out. Restrictions targeted those passages of war films, in particular, which were thought "difficult, and as a result of the war, painful or giving a derisory view of the civilian populace during the invasion. . . . Films that are depressing, morbid, immoral. . . . As for export visas, we aim to avoid representing, in those foreign lands which are friendly but also subject to officious and insinuating German propaganda, our country and our race in a light which would be unfaithful, deformed by the prism of an artistic individuality which may be original but is not always healthy."[130] Under this political régime, 56 films were banned, including *J'accuse*, *La Grande Illusion*, *La Bête humaine*, *Les Bas-fonds*, *Le Dernier Tournant*, *Gueule d'amour*, *Hôtel du Nord*, *La Règle du jeu* (judged demoralizing), and most particularly *Quai des brumes*.

Inevitably, the degree of censorship increased even further under German occupation, not least because of the Jewish problem. The series of decrees[131] placing all film production and screening under tight political control, ultimately by the head of the military administration in France, have already been outlined in chapter 2. Every aspect of production, from the supply of carefully monitored quotas of film, through the precensorship of scenarios, to the distribution and exhibition of the resultant product, was regulated and monitored. An indication of the degree to which political censorship began to operate is apparent in the examples of its operations cited by Léglise:

> *Goupi Mains-Rouges*: visa granted subject to the introduction of a few optimistic elements.
> *Voyageur sans bagages*: subject to an indication at the end that the protagonist is facing a new and purified existence.
> *Les Malheurs de Sophie*: subject to the suppression of all riot scenes or scenes judged to have an inappropriate political orientation given current conditions.
> *L'Aventure est au coin de la rue*: subject to
>   (1) the role of the police inspectors not being treated crudely and the appearance of uniformed police being treated with care/precision.
>   (2) the scene of the singer's torn dress being treated delicately.[132]

All films of Anglo-Saxon origin were banned, as of 23 October 1942, even in the unoccupied zone, as they had been since the occupation in the North. All 16-mm production was banned, and the screening of all existing prints limited,[133] all normal format films dating from before 1 October 1937 were banned as "not responding to current needs, and technically inadequate."[134] Again, this measure was applied with particular stringency to films relating to military activities or to films with a tendency to represent the nation in nihilistic terms. The sense of an invasive political presence concerned to determine the nature of the totality of French film production and thus to condition, in the long term, the political orientation of the populace, was unmistakable.

Given these circumstances, critics have frequently been astonished at the nature and quality of French film production between 1940 and 1944. Nevertheless, it has to be acknowledged that this relatively liberal régime conceals a high degree of self-censorship. French producers were under no illusions about the fate of any impolitic script and had effectively internalized the political injunctions of the occupying forces, as witness the singular lack of films dealing to any extent with contemporary social life and the tendency to cloak any reference to sociopolitical conditions in heavy allegory (e.g., *Les Visiteurs du soir*), particularly with a historical base (e.g., *Pontcarral*), or in hallucinatory fantasy (e.g., *La Nuit fantastique*).

After the war, an intense sense of the need for continuing censorship persisted: from 1945–1950 it was exercised by a commission balanced, as the prewar commission had been, between representatives of government and representatives of the profession. When in 1950, at the height of colonial and Cold War anxieties, this balance was decisively altered in favor of the government, professional representatives went on strike. Effectively, however, this left the censorship of films totally in government hands. On their return to work 18 months later, the government retained effective control, as the selected list of political bannings cited by Francis Courtade from that decade clearly shows:

> *Afrique 50*, produced by the Ligue de l'Enseignement, and dealing with decolonization—banned, and the director (René Vautier) condemned to one year's prison.
> *L'Affaire Seznec*, dealing with a criminal case from 1923—banned by the minister for justice.
> *Le Rendez-vous des quais*, dealing with dockers' demonstrations in Marseilles, hostile to the Indochina war—banned.
> *Les Statues meurent aussi*, an anticolonial short by Resnais—banned until 1965 and then only released after cuts.
> *Avant le déluge*, dealing with a criminal case—approved only after cuts and subject to local bans.
> *Bel-ami*—banned, then released with cuts, then banned again, "because produced by a Viennese company functioning under Soviet control"; and finally released three years later, after major reworking of the (anticolonial) dialogues.
> *Nuit et brouillard*—released only after the soldier's cap of a French gendarme guarding a concentration camp during the German occupation had been obliterated.[135]

Nevertheless, however insistent the censorship provisions, they did not entirely prevent the cinema from critical reflection on French politics. Perhaps the most contentious political filmmaker in the fifties was André Cayatte, whose critical trilogy, *Justice est faite*, *Nous sommes tous des assassins* and *Avant le déluge*, all to scripts by Spaak, focused on notorious judicial cases. Political discourses and attendant strategies were particularly triggered by the virulent criticism which they levelled at the workings of justice. It was Cayatte who was to direct *L'Affaire Seznec*, but for a period of three years the producer was refused authorization to shoot it, without explanation and without receiving a reply to his protests. Finally in 1955 he published an open letter to the new minister for the arts, protesting the multiple forms of indirect pressure which deflected producers from tackling tendentious topics and which, in the face of his continued persistence, had conspired to put him out of business altogether.[136] On this occasion, the whole cinematic establishment backed him, signing a petition published in *Arts* requesting that he be allowed to resume his trade and offering their services absolutely free, for whatever film he would choose to make:[137] signatories included, among many others, Carné, Yves Allégret, Simone Signoret, Yves Montand, Barrault, Gérard Philipe, Trauner, Wahkevitch, d'Eaubonne, Alekan, Agostini, Auric, Kosma, Jeanson, Prévert, Aurenche and Bost, Marcel Achard, Spaak, Carlo Rim, Ophüls, Becker, Tati, René Clément, and Cayatte himself.

In fact, stonewalling tactics rather than explicit legislation seem to have been the form of censorship preferred in the fifties, because they were less controversial than a rigid political code of censorship formally enforced. Given the industrial and economic structure of the industry, producers could simply not afford to contemplate initiating a project which might meet objections and delays lasting several years—their funding base was not adequate to cope with it. So effective was the strategy that no cinematic representation of the Indochinese war occurred until *Patrouille sans espoir* (Bernard-Aubert, 1956), screened in 1957, three years after the war was over (and 11 years after it had begun). *L'Objecteur*, Autant-Lara's film to a script dealing with conscientious objection, begun in 1956, did not get screened until 1963. Soon after shooting began, the military refused to allow the original title to be used, and foreseeing trouble, the producer withdrew his funds. The film was finally made with Yugoslav backing but banned in France (as it was in Italy and Germany). It was only given authorization to be screened under a different title (*Tu ne tueras point*) and in a severely cut form when the Algerian war was safely over.[138]

In these circumstances, it is scarcely valid to speak of a political discourse surrounding films in the fifties, since the fundamental aim of the official strategy was to eliminate all political debate. No public policy was declared, no decisions announced, no explanations provided, and the end result was the suppression of any controversial representation of political material. A conservative government had devised perhaps the most effective form of political discourse—a silence which seemed like ignorance, or boredom, with the very stuff of politics.

A DISCOURSE OF MORALITY

Well before the war an index had been developed by the Church from tentative beginnings in the late twenties into an elaborate, well-organized and well-publicized system. In view of this, it is surprising that it should have been so relatively ineffectual throughout the prewar period, only beginning to have concrete effects on the formation of audiences after the war.

In 1927, following the urging of Pius XI, Canon Reymond had instituted the Comité Catholique du Cinéma (CCC) to focus the French Church's activities on the media. This published a series of film notes, *Dossiers du Cinéma*, which subsequently became *Les Fiches du Cinéma* and which were intended to keep the clergy up to date with film production. The film notes described each film in general terms and outlined its moral tenor. In addition, for the cinema-going public, a Catholic film weekly called *Choisir* was published.

This action was necessarily small-scale because dependent largely on the initiative of one individual with limited resources. In other Catholic countries, attempts at coordinating religious action in the sphere of the cinema proceeded much faster, resulting in the formation of an international organization of Catholic media groups (OCIC). At its first conference in

1933, this body implicitly reproached France for not doing enough to monitor and safeguard the moral welfare of its congregations.[139] This led to the setting up of the Centrale Catholique du Cinéma under the abbé Caffarel, and after July 1936 under the abbé Stourm.

Action was now coordinated under two broad headings: (1) the classification of films and diffusion of information about them, and (2) pressure on the production, distribution, and exhibition of networks.

The classification of films at first based on a letter system was subsequently carried out on a six-point numerical scale, from (1) "suitable for general viewing," through (3b) "suitable for adults only," to (6) "a fundamentally pernicious film."[140] The classification criteria were not of course artistic or technical: the evaluation was based purely on the morality implicit in the fictional film world and in the behavior of the characters, with particular attention to the narrative outcome. Of course, the representation of the Church and its representatives—indeed, of the whole religious sphere, including the devil—was of critical importance.

Sexuality was the focus of most reproaches, either because it was suggested that sexual relations and a happy relationship could occur outside marriage, or simply because gowns disclosed a sensuous female shoulder.

> *Accusé, levez-vous* (Tourneur, 1930): The theme would be acceptable. But the protagonists are *two people in an irregular relationship*, who affirm this insistently, calling one another "my husband" and "my wife." And as a setting we have once again a music hall, as a pretext to exhibit women in brief costumes. Clearly R [reserved for adults].
>
> *Troika*: The theme is instructive, but numerous scenes are distinctly reprehensible—scenes of extensive seductions, numerous déshabillés. From the social point of view, note the insistent opposition between the rich and the poor. Strictly R, if not D [dangerous].
>
> *All Quiet on the Western Front* is condemned for showing only the horrible aspects of reality.[141]

By 1937, some 7,000 films from the talkie period had been so classified and described. Diffusion of the resultant information took place by way of sermons, church notice boards, poster campaigns, parish bulletins, the *Fiches du Cinéma* (which were collected and bound in annual volumes), and the weekly *Choisir*. To these was added a monthly, *Ciné Entre Nous*. In order to mobilize sufficient pressure to affect the production networks, the church organized open debates on its classifications and participated in the launching and promotion of those films which it viewed favorably. An Agence de documentation et d'information cinématographiques (ADIC) was set up to monitor the course of production, wherever possible, "in order that [films] should be better adapted to the family viewing to which they would subsequently be subject. In particular, [ADIC] generated advice for producers who showed an interest, concerning the specific segments of the films which they should handle carefully, or the modifications necessary if their film was to achieve the required moral grading."[142]

At the point of distribution and exhibition specialized circuits of parish and family ciné-clubs were developed, and cinemas with a Catholic management were linked into commercial circuits. These were grouped regionally from 1935, and by July 1936 there were 350 cinemas thus associated, together with another 1,000 outlets in 16-mm or 17.5-mm format. In all, some 50% of the small-format market was thus tied into the campaign,[143] and in some regions 25% of the standard commercial market, including the largest cinemas.[144] Insofar as was commercially feasible, these circuits were required to program their cinemas exclusively with films favorably graded by ADIC, though in many years this might have meant depriving themselves of about half of the national output of films. As *Choisir* proclaimed, "Once we have grouped together and federated into vast and broad-based associations all those parish cinemas which are currently functioning in ignorance of one another's activities, we will have created a pressure group which can bring all its weight to bear on the production of films and thus ensure the production of good films."[145]

A separate programming body, the Cinématographe Paroissial, provided appropriate films for the circuits. From these it was a natural step to consider producing those films themselves. *Choisir* urged its Catholic readers to invest in the standard production circuit with an aim of ultimately achieving a position from which they could influence the nature of that production; and at least one attempt was made to set up a separate production firm alongside the existing system. Fiat Films, founded in 1935 by the abbé Vachet, had a studio at la Garenne Colombes, with its own workshops, equipment, and costumes. All scripts were vetted by a Catholic censorship board. For a period it produced a number of short and medium-length films for the circuits, but very few feature-length productions.

The general direction of these efforts was confirmed in 1936, when the Pope's proclamation, *Vigilante Cura*, took up the theme of the distressing influence of the media, and particularly the cinema, on public morality. It urged action on the film industry, action on the public, and the creation of a permanent commission to ensure that this action was implemented effectively and on an international scale. "By a more systematic and more disciplined organization of Catholic film outlets, the Pope hopes to form a client group of significance in the eyes of the producers, which has on call sufficient market power to generate films answering the bishops' needs."[146]

It was not, however, the French model which the Pope selected for praise, but the American model, the Hays Code. Introduced in 1922 to answer public cynicism about moral standards within the industry, this voluntary code of behavior had been subject to several modifications without ever really having the teeth needed to determine industry policy. In the early thirties, however, U.S. Catholics had organized to pressure exhibitors and others into a more rigorous implementation of the Code. In early 1934, the League of Decency had been formed, and by July of that year the MPPDA had accepted its program. All films would be produced in conformity to its strict moral requirements, on pain of a penalty of $25,000. As one commentator remarked, from 1935 on, an industry dominated by Jews in a country where Protestants predominated, was supervised by a Catholic pressure group.

The abbé Stourm was given the task of bringing about a similar compact in France. Indeed, a campaign to do so had already begun: *Interciné* of January 1935 quotes an article entitled "Morality in the production of films," which echoes American anxieties about the dissolute life of filmmakers, contrasting them (and the moral tone of their products) with the salubrious moral climate of the rest of the nation. It urges the French industry to censor its products and to attempt to introduce into its personnel individuals of undoubted moral authority.[147] *Choisir* published an analogous appeal for a French Hays Code in the same year.[148] But despite using the American system as a model, French advocates of a moral code did not achieve in France anything remotely analogous to the moral control exercised over Hollywood by their American colleagues. Certainly, from time to time, distributors or exhibitors requested the CCC to view their films and "correct" them where necessary. Certainly, many distributors consulted Catholic organizations before agreeing to fund the production of given scripts. Locally, indeed, where the campaign was most intensively implemented, it had effects. "For twelve years already, [the Church's patronage of my rival] has amounted to a war waged on me behind the scenes by all possible means. Aggressive sermons against the cinema assert that only their own establishment is worth attending. Talks in schools to the children, family visits by the priests, saying, 'Don't send your children to the Majestic, you'll destroy them.' Threats not to give absolution or Easter mass if they frequent my cinema."[149] But ultimately, the abbé Stourm was obliged to acknowledge that, undermined perhaps by lack of finance, perhaps by an ignorance of pressure tactics, the French campaign had been largely ineffectual. An interesting index of this comparative failure of the French moral discourse to determine the moral content of films in the thirties is the following table, which distributes into three gross categories, by the center's criteria, the output of the French and American film industries, as screened in France between 1930 and 1935.

It follows from this table that a rigorously obedient Catholic circuit, observing the Church's injunctions to the letter, would have been screening American films for 85% of the time, despite the better returns from French-speaking films.[150]

The industry had clearly not seen itself as under serious pressure from this moral discourse to modify the nature of its product. One prime index of this is the representation of female sexuality. In such films as *Rigolboche* (Christian-Jacque, 1936), *Zouzou* (M. Allégret, 1934), and *Club de Femmes* (Deval, 1936), the naked or largely naked female form is casually displayed

FIGURE 5.1   **The Catholic Church's Evaluation of French and American Films 1930–1935**

	A (general exhibit)	B (adults only)	C (to be avoided)
U.S.	50%	40%	10%
French	20%	25%	55%

in nightclub scenes or in the privacy of bedrooms. In such scenes the cinema was merely drawing on native traditions of exotic or intimate nudity in nightclub entertainments, but the crucial fact is that it was able to draw on them for so long despite the markedly different audiences for the two types of spectacle. Nothing could more clearly underline the government's orientation of censorship laws toward the political rather than the moral, and the impotence of the Church's moral strictures.

Throughout the thirties, then, despite all the pressure that the Church could muster, the government refused to intervene in the moral arena. It even refused to institute a grading system which would designate certain films as appropriate to, or restricted to, certain age groups. Proposed time and again throughout the twenties and thirties,[151] this measure—like all measures to class films according to moral criteria—was greeted by appeals to liberal (or less commonly financial) principles. Indeed, throughout the thirties many Catholic authorities themselves were against such a system, seeing it as the place of the family rather than the state to decide what the young should see. "Shutting children out of cinemas is shutting out families. But the cinema is in its essence a family entertainment, and to restrict the number of spectators is to impede an industry which is a source of wealth."[152]

In the face of continuing failure on the national front, pressure was brought to bear on local municipal authorities, who proved much more amenable to persuasion. Indeed, it may have been precisely because this local (but, if we are to believe Paul Léglise, illegal)[153] censorship was so widespread that centralized political action based on moral criteria could be deferred for such a long time. A list of the better-known instances, given by Paul Léglise, indicates how common a practice it was. In 1931, for example, the mayor of La Rochelle took to himself the right to censor all local spectacles, considering "that for some years theatrical performances and film screenings have been exploiting immorality in a public way."[154] In 1932, the mayor of Valenciennes placed a local ban on *Le Rosier de Mme Husson*, with the vocal approval of the Catholic Federation of Valenciennes and the Ligue des Familles Nombreuses. In 1933 many municipalities, such as Nancy, banned *Ecstasy* and *La Marche au soleil* for the complete nudity there represented. *Choisir* wholeheartedly approved of mayors thus "cleaning up their cities": "Their duty is to see that morals are respected. In forbidding the screening of documentaries on brazen nudism like *La Marche au soleil*, *Au-delà du Rhin*, or obscene films like *Le Rosier de Mme Husson* and *La Chienne*, they show good sense and healthy authority. In terms of the powers conferred on them by law, they take over from a censorship that is simply too generous in all ways. Who would reproach them, save those whose financial greed is involved in these unhealthy and shameful spectacles."[155]

While the film exhibitors affected by these multiple local anomalies protested loudly at this "high-handed action," they too inevitably became anxious whenever they saw what might be characterized as excessive license in the representation of immoral situations, likely to cause disaffection in families of a sort to significantly reduce audiences. On several occasions they voiced to their union president their worries about such films, and in particular concerning the titillating publicity campaigns that usually surrounded them.[156]

The resolutely noninterventionist attitude of the state was abruptly reversed with the advent of war and with the generalized regulation of this and other industries that followed the occupation. On 29 July 1939, the state instituted a "Code de la famille" which established as a formal obligation the protection of the moral welfare of the young. This laid the groundwork for the Germans to introduce the categorization of films, including a separate category of film forbidden to those under 18.[157]

Censorship was now attached to the information services, which were instructed to forbid "depressing, morbid, immoral films, and those detrimental to youth, this wartime youth which more than at any other time will be left to its own devices and free to go to the cinema, that distraction so ready of access. For this very reason, fine works of art such as *Quai des brumes* and *Le Puritain* might well have to be prevented from open screening in France."[158] While the essence of censorship policy from this time to the end of the war was to be political and racial rather than moral, the distinction between the two was no longer easy to make, since for the occupying forces a principal political aim was the moral reeducation of a debilitated people. It was in the interests of the country's moral revitalization that its political and social institutions should not be represented unfavorably. The resolutely political de-jewification of the cinema, for instance, was no less a *moral* crusade, aiming to reverse the insidious corruption and debilitation which their control of the media was seen as having disseminated among the populace. Most of the 56 films banned by the French government remained banned by the Germans. *Le Film*, number 4 (1 December 1940), published the following communiqué: "Implementing the government's principles concerning the reorganization of film censorship, the CCC . . . has just cancelled the visas of 110 feature films, including 65 French films and 45 foreign films. If the cancellation was motivated in many cases by political and diplomatic considerations, the banning of most of the films in question was due above all to questions of morality."[159] The list appended cites under this heading *Les Bas-fonds, Club de femmes, La Rue sans nom, Le De:nier Tournant, Franco de port, Hôtel du Nord, Le Jour se lève, Quai des brumes, Pepe le Moko, Le Puritain, Le Rosier de Mme Husson, Anges aux figures sales, Le Maudit, Gueule d'amour,* and many others. Questions of morality became so inextricably intertwined with questions of politics, and these in turn were so omnipresent, that in the Christmas 1941 issue of *Ciné-Mondial* Michel Duran exclaimed:

> I defy any director to do anything new at the moment. . . . French film production depends on corvette captains, on fathers of large families, on men of the church. Scenarios come back from Vichy with such require-ments, annotations, prohibitions, and cuts that we might as well just go to confession and learn another trade. . . . I foresee for 1942 the introduc-tion of a cinema card, with cinemas specializing in films for under 18s, films for under 30s, films for over 40s, films for spinsters, and films for the military. This cinema card will be granted on presentation of a birth certificate, a certificate of good behavior countersigned by your landlady and validated by the commissioner after an inquiry, and will earn you tickets to the week's latest flops.[160]

In fact, however, direct religious influence on audiences was to decrease rather than increase during the war. Independent moral proclamations and interdictions by the Church were no longer acceptable; the government was now the sole authorized source of a moral discourse. *Choisir* and the *Fiches du Cinéma* were closed down, and the Church was forbidden to diffuse its moral evaluations of cinematic programs (as were the local mayors). Never-theless, it continued to do so, clandestinely, even when the CCC was closed down. The criteria which it employed had in no way changed, as the fol-lowing selection indicates:

> *L'Age d'or*: women in scanty costume, bar full of loose women. . . . Certain images present dubious social groups and allude to irregular situations—4 (strictly for adults).
> *L'Assassin habite au 21*: murder, free love. Frivolous liaisons, sexual innu-endo—4b (advised to avoid).
> *Le Corbeau*: a harsh and painful film, constantly morbid in its complexity. Free love, cynically engaged in, and with crude insistence by the woman. . . . Deleterious atmosphere. . . . Avowal of atheistic beliefs by a sympa-thetic character. Suicide, murder, cursing, swearing—6 (to be avoided: an essentially pernicious film).
> *Les Visiteurs du soir*: film in which the presence of the devil is a mere pre-text for witchery, without any real Christian basis. A girl, challenged by the devil, proclaims publicly her transgression. Apology for love as all-conquering—5 (to be avoided: a film to forbid absolutely).[161]

In all, during the occupation, of 250 films evaluated by the CCC, 105 were declared unacceptable, 132 were acceptable for adults only, and a mere 13 were graded for general exhibition, and thus suitable for parish circuits. Not a single film was considered suitable for children.

With the return to peace-time conditions, the state ceased to compete with the Church for this moral authority. The Commission de Contrôle des Films was headed by Georges Huisman, who professed a fervent belief in liberty of expression. "The new commission has strictly forbidden itself from undertaking any tendentious censorship . . . based on preconceived ideas. . . . In the country which gave the world the Declaration of Human Rights, all subjects, even the most daring, can be brought to the screen."[162] Rather than a moral discourse, it is an artistic discourse, which threads through his accounts of the commission's functioning. "One single preoccupation animates us: finding in these films some permanent element of the technical and artistic greatness of our country. . . . The attachment of the French people to liberty will not permit the proscription of certain subjects, as long as they are treated with art, for in art there are no forbidden fields."[163] Of every 20 scripts presented to the commission, 15 or 16 will be approved without question. In the other cases, if they seem "empty of intellectual and artistic interest and not endowed with a cast capable of making good this deficit, it's merely doing the producers a service to draw their attention to the inevitable mediocrity of the final result. Up to them to decide whether to go ahead; but if they do, they'll have no reason to be surprised or to complain if we . . . refuse them an export visa."[164] "The sanction of quality is the export visa . . . for each of our films must become on foreign screens the most persuasive of ambassadors."[165]

In effect, then, this artistic discourse is not exempt from the preoccupations with the representation of French moral health that marked the censorship of the occupation regime. Now, however, it is not the French whose vision of themselves must be restored, but the rest of the world who must be convinced of French moral vigor. Direct state censorship of French production in the fifties, on moral grounds, was therefore minimal. It was once again the Church which established itself as the public source of a moral discourse aiming at audience orientation. It set up an ambitious magazine, entitled *La Revue Internationale du Cinéma*, and a publication oriented more toward the general public, called *Radio-Cinéma*. Of the three federations uniting regular cine-clubs throughout France, one—the Fédération des Loisirs et de la Culture Cinématographique—was Catholic in its orientation and produced a widely-read publication called *Téléciné*. More generally, all state bodies related to popular education included within them representatives of the Catholic (and often also of the Protestant) Church. UFOLEIS, a section of the Ligue Française de l'Enseignement,[166] included both Catholic (FLEEC) and Protestant (*Film et Vie*) representation, as well as lay. That organization had from 1946 published a modest information bulletin which was later in the fifties to become the film monthly *Image et Son*, aimed primarily at a broad young audience. The Church influence is apparent in the strong moral discourse which, in its early issues, infiltrates the pedagogic discourse of that journal. It is the moral well-being of the young of France, as well as their cultural development, which is to be the focus of the league and of its publication.[167]

Production runs of the more directly Church-influenced film journals were very large in the fifties, the three principal ones reaching 600,000, 1,600,000, and 2,000,000,[168] so their impact on audiences must be assumed to have been considerable. Certainly, a recurrent theme of trade journals of that decade is the need to manage religious susceptibilities of this sort. The major cinema proprietor for the southwest of Paris, for instance, attributes his successful development of the circuit to the intensive cultivation of potential local political and religious audiences, mentioning particularly the importance of recommendations pronounced from the pulpit by local priests, given that 22,000 of the local clientele in Versailles alone were regular attenders of Sunday mass.[169] And in his account of the French cinema published in 1960, Daquin says

> When the découpage and the dialogue are finished, the producer and distributor suddenly get worried: this scene is too original, it'll not please the public; that one is too tendentious, it risks attracting trouble from the CCC or the censors. The president of the circuit which is to screen the film has "by chance" read the découpage and suggests certain cuts, so as not to "distress his clients," etc.
> The script is reworked.[170]

OTHER DISCOURSES

Alongside these various discourses serving to orientate larger or smaller audiences there exists a minority discourse which is worth chronicling for the importance it was to acquire in later decades—the academic discourse. The term "academic" is here used of the whole range of discourses mobilized by different academic disciplines in a university context. Their prime distinguishing characteristic is their common element of intellectual rigor: they aim to bring to an understanding of the phenomenon of the cinema a set of already well-developed theories and methodologies within which statements are subject to the need for defensible rational justification. Basically, the major disciplines which were to be thus mobilized were sociology, psychology, political economy (Marxism), and linguistics.

In the main, the major discourses already discussed were fundamentally antipathetic to such an intellectual and analytical approach to the cinema. Within the discourse of pleasure, the intellect is commonly seen as at best irrelevant, at worst destructive. Within that of art, such concepts as theory, system, reason, science, and method are usually represented as a cold approach to the passionate truths of art, death to their life, inevitably inadequate in their attempt to account for the power and intensity of the work of art, a crude iron cage in which to catch a bright butterfly. "You'll begin to think . . . that I intend to construct a theory," says Auriol in 1930. "No; I speak for my liberty, for the liberty of those for whom the cinema opens a window onto love, onto life, onto eternity;"[171] and eighteen years later, "Most theories are withering for the artist and vain for the spectator. Works like [Citizen Kane] are more fruitful and productive of ideas than four theories of 400 pages written by their authors. In fact, too many theories of cinema resemble theories of love: they are the fantasized constructions of the frustrated. . . . "[172] Those who can, do; those who can't, theorize.

Certainly, the two attempts made by Auriol's collaborators to introduce a little system into the theoretical position of the journal, while interesting, ended in self-contradiction and disarray.[173] In France, it was Marxists such as the historian Georges Sadoul and the Swiss political economist Peter Bächlin who first began to reflect and publish systematically on the cinema from within a secure methodological framework. Sadoul's Histoire générale du cinéma began to come out from 1946, and Bächlin's first significant study appeared in French in 1947.[174] Even as these works were appearing, however, an academic entrepreneur by the name of Gilbert Cohen-Séat was mobilizing a wide range of Paris academics in a campaign to develop a comprehensive interdisciplinary theory of the cinema. The movement he generated was to become known as the filmology movement, and the text which constituted its manifesto was his Essai sur les principes d'une philosophie du cinéma, published in 1946.[175] It distinguished two fields of study—the filmic and the cinematic. For the proper understanding of the former, Cohen-Séat invoked the need to apply to film the disciplines of linguistics and of aesthetics; for the latter, the disciplines of sociology, anthropology, psychoanalysis, and psycho-physiology. If the mention of sociology relates particularly, as Edward Lowry, the chronicler of the movement, supposes,[176] to the intensely political conjuncture at which the theory emerged, the call for an analysis of film structure in terms of quasi-autonomous syntagmatic units was particularly adventurous. But it seems from the stress laid on it that the field closest to Cohen-Séat's own interests was the testing of viewers' responses to filmic stimuli, extending to questionnaires concerning the effects of film viewing on different audiences.

A group of academicians rapidly gathered around Cohen-Séat, promoting his program in every available forum. A review was published under the auspices of Mario Roques, professor of the Collège de France, with an extremely prestigious editorial board, including professors representing all relevant disciplines, together with Léon Moussinac, then director of the Ecole Nationale des Arts Décoratifs, and a committee including well-known representatives of the profession and of the arts in general—Gaston Bachelard, Raymond Bernard, Pierre Bost, André Chamson, Georges Charensol, René Clair, Louis Daquin, Jean Guéhenno, etc. The journal's aim was explicitly to build up an established corpus of reliable scientific knowledge about the cinema. It continued to appear at irregular intervals throughout the fifties, publishing articles by Sadoul, Etienne Souriau, Edgar Morin, and Roland Barthes. In addition, the university established an Institute of Filmology, which produced its first students in 1951 and which organized international congresses throughout the fifties, attracting scholars from all of Western Europe. Between them, the congresses and the journal articles served to lay the ground rules for that series of debates on film and literary theory that was to characterize the later fifties and the sixties. Articles appeared with a markedly structuralist orientation,[177] with a markedly linguistic orientation,[178] and with a markedly psychoanalytic orientation,[179] foreshadowing later work by Lacan, Metz, Barthes, and Bellour.

Reactions to these attempts to apply or adapt existing academic discourses to the cinema were mostly negative. *Cahiers du Cinéma* published a sarcastic article on "The filmology of filmology,"[180] expressing a reluctant admiration that the movement should have been more successful than the many other attempts of the past twenty years to break down the doors of the Sorbonne and suggesting that it was a last desperate attempt by academics to make themselves and their work seem relevant to twentieth century concerns and to the young. In *La Revue du Cinéma*, Marc Soriano, while giving a more positive evaluation of the movement, worries that it "perhaps treats the cinema too much as a language and not enough as an art,"[181] a tendency which he attributes to an excess of fervor, which time will hopefully temper.

It cannot be said that this intellectual discourse contributed significantly to audience formation or orientation before 1960. Nor did the discourse of capital which dominated *Cinéopse* and *La Cinématographie Française* before the war, *Le Film* during it, *Le Film Français* and the reborn *Cinématographie Française* after it. Discourses of unionism and of technology, with their attendant vocabularies of struggle and of specialization, dominate others such as *La Technique Cinématographique* and *Le Technicien du Film*. While elements of these are mobilized momentarily, for contradictory purposes of reputability or of mystification, in those journals aiming at audiences outside the trade, those authorized to speak them never aspire to reach that popular audience in any systematic way or to construct or modify its viewing interests. The major discourses that did do so and which have not been mentioned here (though outlined in earlier chapters)—those of nation and of race—were relatively strong in the thirties and the forties, respectively, and deserve a more detailed investigation. But it was the four major critical discourses of the period which, by way of their institutional mechanisms and rhetorical strategies, were most widely mobilized with a view to forming the audience for classic French films, namely the discourses of pleasure, of art, of the real, and of the moral.

MODE OF PRODUCTION
AND AUTHORIAL CONTROL

Prévert wrote in a dubious French, for the more dubious
among the French.

> Obituary, *Nouvel Observateur*,
> 18 April 1977

The scriptwriter? A person of secondary importance.
One day he brings in this scenario. I'll buy it says the
producer. Then he suppresses the principal role, modi-
fies the end, adds two love scenes, a song, an episode in
Marseilles, and a role for this attractive young woman
who interests him.

> R. Beauvais

"Producers should be shot!" says my friend and colleague
Henri Jeanson. I myself have no desire to be a member of
the execution squad. Why should I shoot people with whom
I've drunk so often and eaten so agreeably. Besides, we
have only to wait a bit: they're committing suicide.

> Spaak, 1963

Carné? Just one of Prévert's quainter inventions.

> Henri Jeanson

Behind the screen, there are no authors any more; what
a relief.

> Claudel

In general, directors possess a filmic style consisting of
tics, obsessions, and faults. . . . Their styles are reminis-
cent of the smell of an apartment—an amalgam of toilet
soap, tobacco, favorite perfume, cooking oil, and caustic
soda. This is called a personality.

> R. M. Arland, 1945

Here we have a machine capable of devouring the universe
and all we're allowed to feed it is scraps and leftovers.

> Feyder, slightly misquoted by Chavance

THE PRODUCER-PACKAGE SYSTEM

The mode of production is that set of work practices which develops within a production system. The work practices themselves derive from the conditions under which work is undertaken within the industry, and particularly from the industrial structure. Indeed, where the industrial structure can be likened to a machine, the mode of production can be conceptualized as that machine in operation. Within the film industry, the interest in the mode of production is double: on the one hand, identifying its characteristic features allows the critic to specify those points in the production process where crucial decisions are taken and thus to develop a rational model of authorship within that industry; and on the other hand, identifying the extent to which the system constrains and standardizes work practices, or on the contrary allows for variation in them, provides a rational basis for discussion of classical filmmaking style.

The most systematic study of modes of production operative within the film industry has been made by Janet Staiger in the study which she undertook with David Bordwell and Kristin Thompson of the *Classic Hollywood Cinema*.[1] She sees American film production as having adopted six distinct modes of production in the course of its history, and she identifies the years during which each such mode was dominant. For comparative purposes, her account provides an invaluable point of reference.

Between 1896 and 1907, the *cameraman system* was operative. The cameraman "would select the subject matter and stage it as necessary by manipulating setting, lighting, and people; [he] would select options from available technological and photographic possibilities, . . . photograph the scene, and develop and edit it."[2]

This system was succeeded by the *director system*, which was operative from 1907 to 1909. Here "a separate worker began to take over parts of the direction [such that] one individual staged the action and another photographed it. Moreover, the director managed a set of workers including the craftsman cameraman."[3] The historical precedent for this system was the legitimate theater and its stage director, and its dominance coincided with the shift to fictional narratives of a theatrical kind. Like his stage counterpart, the film director controlled the choices of scenery, costumes, and acting, and used a script as a basis for his decisions. That script—little more than an outline—would probably have been prepared for him by another worker, but the director was at liberty to diverge from it extensively during shooting. Once the film was shot, the director/producer edited it. As an employee of a company, he did not have to worry about finances or marketing.

The move to the director system is attributed to a growing complexity in the technology and to a need for efficiency which produced a detailed division of labor. By 1909, the need to further increase production in order to provide a constant supply of film products to the distribution exchanges and to meet exhibitor demand led to a further transformation in the mode of production. The firms were becoming too large for a single person to cope with both production and direction, let alone to monitor in detail the work of the growing numbers of progressively more specialized craftsmen. The *director-unit system* which evolved saw upper-level management personnel making long-term production decisions and allocating a series of films to be made to each of several units. "The director of [each] unit remained in charge of the producing, rewriting, directing, and editing functions. Generally he retained the same production staff with him from film to film. . . . What changes significantly is that the workers in each unit only participated in the work of their unit or only for sections of many films rather than in the production of all the firm's films."[4]

This system still allocated prime organizational control of the film to the director, but without imposing strict budgeting requirements on him. Numerous inefficiencies remained, which became unacceptable as the supply of films began to exceed the demand. From 1914 onward, therefore, there arose a new system, the *central producer system*, which was to dominate the remainder of the silent film period. Control shifted to a business manager, with an extensive production department under him, whose job it was to evaluate possible scenarios and generate detailed budget estimates. For this, a more detailed script was necessary, indicating all details of shots, settings, and timings. Once these estimates had been made, all the director had to do was approve them and work within them. "[He] had no more worries. Crews worked at night; when he arrived to shoot, everything was prepared as he had approved."[5] Directors, working to blueprints, no longer had the organizational authority allocated to them by the previous systems, but rather became just another category of operative.

This central producer system involved a single manager in controlling the production of a firm's films. By 1930 a new system was evolving, analogous to the director-unit system, in which effective responsibility for the production of a group of the firm's films was delegated to one of a number of "associate-producers" nominally working under the control of a central production manager but in fact largely autonomous. The *producer-unit system* seems to have originated in the difficulty experienced by a single central producer in keeping tabs on the whole of a large firm's output and in the tendency for production personnel to become expert in different aspects of that output—notably, in different genres.[6] The trend is therefore toward specialization again, but this time at senior management level.

After about 1955, this producer-unit system, in which each producer still had a commitment to make six to eight films per year with a fairly identifiable staff, gave way to a sixth and final mode of production which Staiger terms the *package-unit system*. She describes it as follows: it was "a short-term film-by-film arrangement. Of course, often many subordinate members of the labor hierarchy worked time and again with the same people because of skills and work habits; workers' employment was, nonetheless, based on a film, not a firm. With the disappearance of the self-contained studio, the means of production was also a short-term combination. Instead of a filming unit owning its entire means of production for use in film after film, the unit leased or purchased the pieces for a particular project from an array of support firms. Costumes, cameras, special effects technology, lighting, and recording equipment were specialities of various support companies available for component packaging."[7] Instead of a production house being the sole initiator of projects which they then produced in-house, directors and occasionally stars might initiate projects for which they had to assemble the funding, the personnel, and the plant. Basically this last evolution in production practices was motivated by the attempts of large production firms to divest themselves of fixed costs in the face of stringent financial circumstances, which in turn resulted from changing recreational habits (notably competition from television) and from export limitations due to quotas in Britain and elsewhere. More importantly, the antitrust decision requiring majors to separate their exhibition holdings from their production/distribution sectors removed the need for mass production to deadlines set by circuit programming.

Thus while Staiger rightly emphasises the distinction between industrial structure and mode of production, she equally strongly demonstrates the intimate causal links between changes in industrial structure and changes in production practices. The progressive increase in the size of the major production companies was the prime factor constraining the development of that progressively more detailed division of labor (first within the filmmaking team, then between it and management, then within the management team) which characterizes this succession of models; and ultimately the move to the package-unit system was intimately related to the breakup of the majors, coinciding with a postwar growth in the number of smaller independent production companies. Given the radically distinct industrial structure exhibited by the cinema industry in France during the twenties and thirties, it will come as no surprise to find that French production practices were considerably at variance for most of this period with those operative in the United States. In fact, there is good reason to see the package unit system which developed in Hollywood in the fifties as a close approximation to the system which had dominated French production since the twenties; and the resemblance is due precisely to the fact that the industrial structure of the American cinema was at that time moving "back" toward that which had existed in France for over thirty years.

Up until the First World War there were significant parallels in the development of the two national film industries, but the partial collapse of the French majors at that time and their partial withdrawal from production left a complex and fragmented industry, which throughout the twenties and early thirties made sporadic attempts to organize itself into larger production units. In these circumstances, a variety of modes of production existed side by side, from residual traces of the director system through to the director-unit system and the central producer system. Gaumont, for instance, had explored the possibilities of the director-unit system in the early twenties.[8] The "Pax series" of films, made between 1920 and 1922, involved a central executive producer, Edgar Costil, in managing a group of three directorial teams, headed respectively by L'Herbier, Poirier, and Desfontaines. Each of these was allocated a group of films to make. Company reorganizations and changed policies saw an end to this practice in 1922, with Gaumont becoming little more than a distribution company, subsequently taken over by MGM as an outlet for their American production.

A move toward the central producer system was made by Jean Sapène when he took over the Société des Cinéromans in 1922, with Louis Nalpas as executive producer. The same seems to have been true of Louis Aubert's firm. By the late twenties, however, when Cinéromans had become the major production unit for Pathé, both of these had renounced long-term production planning with contracted staff, Aubert because of a disastrous 1925–1926 season, and Cinéromans because Sapène took over all production decisions from Nalpas and proved at once more cautious and less well-judged in his decisions.

Alongside this central producer system, and soon to emerge as the dominant mode of production, was the package-unit system, which had generated a large proportion of French films throughout the twenties. It existed, however, in two forms—a director-package and a producer-package—according to whether the director himself/herself assumed responsibility for the assembling of the package, or whether there was a separate producer responsible for funding and assembling the package.

As soon as their finances were on a reasonably secure footing, the director-package system was used by Gance, by Baroncelli, by Feyder, Poirier, L'Herbier, Duvivier, and by Germaine Dulac. They would establish themselves as company directors of a firm established uniquely to fund and to package a specific film or series of films directed by themselves. Soliciting funds from a variety of sources, including wealthy patrons of the arts, they would assemble the components of their project and hire a studio if finances permitted and the subject required it.[9] On occasion, and when time allowed, these director-managed companies were used as umbrella organizations for producing films by the director's friends and colleagues. Thus Gance's company produced a film directed by Robert Boudrioz, *L'Atre*, and L'Herbier's company produced films directed by Catelain, Autant-Lara, and Louis Delluc.

Already by 1929, however, it was unusual for the director to undertake personally the role of funding and packaging his/her own films, and the move to sound made the practice even less common. The cost and complexity of the package put personally funded productions beyond the means of most directors, independently wealthy patrons were becoming uncommon because of the Depression, and the time required to assemble and administer the funding, assemble the personnel, and hire the plant infringed significantly on the aesthetic tasks which the directors saw as their primary role. Writing in 1929 of the need for a scriptwriter/director to find a wealthy patron whom he can convince of the viability of his project, G.-M. Coissac says, "Let's admit right away that this hunt for a financier will soon be no more than a rare exception. The cinema is an industry that one can call organized: it has its own producers who, because of their underlying daring, the capital they can bring together, the risks they run, the general surveillance they exercise, their choice of which works to fund, etc., remain the proprietors of the work they bring out in their own name or through others."[10]

Coissac then goes on to cite approvingly the definition of a producer provided by M. Charles Delac: "The producer is the man who brings to-gether (either from his own resources or by calling on other financiers) the capital funds essential to the good execution of the film. The producer is the man who chooses and accepts the scenario, who directs and advises the scriptwriter, who manages and supervises the director, who collabo-rates in the production of intertitles and the perfecting of the final positive. The producer is, in sum, the man who directs all those successive elements from which the completed production of a cinematic work emerges, and he alone has the entire responsibility for that work."[11]

Writing two years before Coissac, in 1927, M. Delac had still allowed for the possibility of the director's assuming these functions, either inde-pendently or on behalf of the funder of his project, though he clearly con-siders it more normal for both scriptwriter and director to be hired by the producer, the latter either for a fixed salary or for a percentage of the profits. It is clear, however, that by 1929 the possibility of an independent director-producer is not taken seriously: the producer has become a standard figure in the production chain.

This mode of production continued to dominate the French film indus-try without major modifications for the next thirty years. Writing during the occupation, André Boll describes essentially the same procedures,[12] as do Leprohon, Chartier and Desplanques, and Raoul Ploquin between 1947 and 1950. Production for most of these years was in the hands of between 150 and 500 small to medium-sized firms, putting together packages on a film-by-film basis at an average rate of one film per firm per year.

In the prewar period the producer's principal task—raising the money to fund these packages—was less a financial than a public relations exer-cise. When the average cost of a French film in 1936–1937 was one million francs, the producer only had to find 25,000 of these, by law. The rest was usually provided by other financiers whom the producer managed to con-vince of the viability of the package, by distributors, who acted as the prin-cipal unofficial funding source, and by studios and laboratories (and often artistic and technical personnel) who worked on credit. For a large percentage of producers, floating a production meant being able to convince a sufficiently large number of such people that there was a tolerable possibility of ultimate profit to be gained from the package. Persisting unemployment forced many of these people to tread the risky path of working against a hypothetical future payment, which was problematic if only because of the high failure rate of productions (30–40%) and the consequent high bankruptcy rate of the undercapitalized production companies. The potential for fraud was omnipresent, and the producer might be either victim or perpetrator—cheated by the distributor whose version of the film's receipts he had no means of verifying, cheating in turn his creditors whom he may well never have had any intention of paying.[13] As the director Raymond Bernard put it to the 1937 Renaitour inquiry, "There are frauds in the production, frauds in exhibition, frauds everywhere in the cinema; it's certain that if these frauds could be restricted, the cinema . . . would immediately prosper. . . . You know all too well how most films are produced, since the crash of the big companies. . . . They are made with a mere 25,000 fr, only a quarter of which has to be up front; and with that they make a film costing two million francs. And when this system doesn't work they still get a chance to try again: they change the name on the door, found a new company, find another 6,000 fr or so, and produce another film costing two million."[14] He recommended state control of box office receipts as a remedy, while his colleague M. Chataignier recommended that producers should simply be required to demonstrate a more solid financial base: "Credit for film production will only be stable when each film producer is required to put up front not 10,000, 20,000, or 25,000 fr., or even 100,000 fr., but exactly the sum necessary to complete the film he proposes to produce. Without this fundamental mechanism, any edifice you try to build must collapse."[15]

In the postwar period, however, the financing of the package had become markedly simpler because of the wartime regulation of the industry. Legislation had required producers to put up a capital of five million francs and had reassured the banking sector concerning its prior claim on returns. The banks progressively organized themselves into six groups, acting through financial establishments specializing in film production. In order to spread their risks, however, those establishments still preferred to finance the distribution sector which dealt with large numbers of films, rather than producers who dealt with one or two per year. It was therefore still through the distribution sector that producers obtained a large part of their finance, the rest consisting not only of credit from studios, laboratories, etc., but now also of a significant amount of state aid. Receipts from the film's exhibition went first to the banks/distributors, next to the businesses which had provided credit, and finally to the producer.

The uncertain nature of the returns to the producer, in conjunction with the heavy commission charged by distributors (no less than 35%, often up to 50%), pushed more and more producers toward involvement in the more reliable profitability of the distribution sector. This had the additional advantage of ensuring direct negotiation with the exhibition chain, but it further complicated the producer's task, emphasizing rather the commercial aspects of the role than the aesthetic involvement, which often constituted his primary motivation. As Braunberger, who had already moved in that direction around 1930, explained it: "My films had to be screened somehow, and from *Nana* on . . . I became my own distributor. It was the only way I could get direct access to the cinemas, to the public. Films that I produced but didn't distribute are the exception. I had regional distributors for the provinces, but in Paris I have always distributed them myself. The job of distributor is one that I undertook without pleasure or passion. It never interested me, but I was forced into it. It was a necessity if I was to continue producing."[16] Many other small producers were similarly constrained, such that a list of 27 notable survivors among them, published in 1957, revealed that nearly half acted as their own distributor as well. Allowing for obvious gaps and some known errors in that list, it is probable that well over half of the production companies were acting as distributor for their own and, to different extents, others' films.

Although in the course of the fifties the system of coproductions was to cause some modification to this producer-package system, the changes were minor, because to some extent producers had been involved in coproduction with one another throughout the thirty years, and the move to internationalize coproductions was merely an extension of this practice beyond national boundaries in order to guarantee a larger audience. When Daquin reviews the state of the industry in 1960, therefore, his description of the way producers put together a package closely reproduces the description that Coissac had given in 1929 and Leprohon in 1947.

COMPANY PRODUCERS AND PRODUCER COMPANIES

Although the producer-package system remained the dominant mode of production throughout the classic period, a range of variation was possible within it and a number of alternatives to it were explored from time to time. The range of variation can best be demonstrated by taking two limit cases of production practices, while recognizing that any one particular producer would have worked somewhere within the range marked off by these limit cases. The cases in question are Alain Poiré, in charge of most production for Gaumont from the moment it resumed production in 1941, particularly after 1944, and Pierre Braunberger, whose activities as producer began in 1924 with Renoir's first films and continued beyond 1960. The poles which they can be used to represent can be defined as those of the corporation producer and the independent producer. The interests of the former, a senior administrative officer within a large company which might have an extensive circuit of cinemas, its own studio and laboratory facilities, and an enormous weekly turnover, were primarily financial and administrative.

Working to business hours, responsible to superiors for the efficiency of the production arm, he could not normally afford whimsical or sentimental gestures. Braunberger, on the other hand, working through a series of small production companies which he constituted and reconstituted for the purposes of new films, was responsible primarily to himself. His activities as producer were undertaken almost entirely out of personal commitment to a medium which obsessed him and to director friends whose projects, devised perhaps spontaneously in the early hours of a night-long spree, caught his imagination. To simplify, the opposition is between money and art, between a formal set of businesslike procedures and an informal set of activities due as often as not to hazard and to chance encounters. The two extremes might be characterized as "the company producer" and "the producer company."

This opposition is apparent in all aspects of the production process—indeed, in the manner in which they entered the ranks of producers. Alain Poiré, grandson of the proprietor of the Havas Agency which had just taken over the ailing Gaumont, was promoted at the age of 20 to become Gaumont's financial and commercial manager with a brief to put it on a sound commercial footing. His accounts of how he did this concentrate on the problems of obtaining exclusive runs for prestige films, the need to guarantee funding to small production companies to obtain these rights, the intense competition with the rival Siritzky chain, and his maneuvers to gain favorable tax concessions from the government. Gaumont's move back into production is a rational calculation, motivated partly by a wartime deficit of films for its exhibition arm, but primarily by a German decision to refuse production certificates to those companies not producing a given quota of films. For Alain Poiré, criteria as to which films he will encourage are straightforward: he will produce gay comedies, light-hearted films with popular stars in the lead roles.[17] Gaumont's finances will be restored by a policy of entertainment and spectacle appealing to a broad spectrum of the public. The *Caroline chérie* series (beginning in 1950) was to achieve just that. Already in 1933, Charles Delac, doyen of such company producers, had talked in terms of keeping in touch with the mass public and offending no section of the community.[18]

Pierre Braunberger's professional orientation in interviews, according to his colorful but not necessarily inaccurate autobiography, contrasts markedly with that of such company producers.[19] Early determined to be involved in the world of cinema, he talked his wealthy father into funding a trip around various national production systems, in the course of which he took on a series of minor responsibilities. Introduced to Jean Renoir by Pierre Lestringuez, a mutual friend, he was immediately attracted by Renoir's views and projects as expounded in the course of an all-night drinking session. They decided "to get married, cinematically speaking," and he produced most of Renoir's films till the war. His accounts of how he came to be involved in producing the films of other directors bear a similar stamp. It is his passion for the cinema, for discussion of cultural matters, for art that is central. He is exhilarated to be involved in an activity central to the twentieth century and to his country's cultural heritage. His relations with Marc Allégret, whom he met through Gide, and many of whose films he produced, involve a regular Sunday meal together every week for 40 years. His relationships with the other film personnel are equally informal, motivated by affection, admiration, or lust. He undertook to produce *Une partie de campagne* largely because he was obsessed by Sylvia Bataille. He met Truffaut and Rouch at the Festival du Film Maudit, of which he was an organizer, and so enjoyed their conversation and enthusiasm that he had to get involved in producing films for them. His account personalizes all processes. Writing in 1986, he is nostalgic for an age when producers were on intimate terms with the rich intellectual and cultural brew of the cinematic and theatrical worlds, where directors, musicians, great actors and actresses, men of letters, and decorators designed new futures for the world. "I don't know whether it was because I was younger or because we were a group of the same age, but we were all the time together. . . . It's a sad sign of the times we live in that producers sleep far less often with their stars."[20] The extremes of informality within which this production process developed can scarcely be better instanced than by his account of himself and a group of friends (Jean and Pierre Renoir, Lestringuez, Jouvet, Giraudoux) heading off to a nearby brothel to drink naked around a table and plan their next film, while the prostitutes crouched under the table working on them. Likewise, negotiations with Michel Simon were commonly conducted in that gentleman's favourite brothel, surrounded by "a selection of erotic objects."

For Poiré at Gaumont, a film's production usually began when an aspiring author submitted in more or less detailed form a script outline. Once he found one fitting his criteria, his role in assembling the package was largely organizational, and with the backing of an extensive organization behind his decision the financing of the package was not a problem. As he says, "In a sense I'm an American sort of producer: I don't have to worry much about problems of funding, hunting out money right and left, setting up the package bit by bit."[21] But this was largely true because the criteria for selection of a project were based on profitability. For Braunberger, on the other hand, precisely because profitability ranked low in his criteria, finding the necessary money to fund the project occupied a large part of his time. "I've always tried not to lose too much money, so as to be able to continue exercising my trade as long as possible. That said, if I had been uniquely inspired by questions of financial viability, I wouldn't have got involved in producing certain films and would have been a rich man today."[22]

Instead of receiving scripts submitted by authors, Braunberger describes scripts arising out of conversations with Renoir, Allégret, Raimu, Cavalcanti, Michel Simon, Langlois, or with fellow producers, and being developed piecemeal such that it would be inaccurate to see them as other than collaborative efforts. Quite often his own reading led him to buy up the rights of a book and commission a script of it. A forced recluse during the war because of his Jewish background, he spent his time reading a thousand or so books to get script ideas. On occasion he would write these up himself. He had written up a script of *Le Silence de la mer* before discovering that one Grumbach (later known by his resistance pseudonym of Melville) was trying to get funds to film it. A passionate bullfight enthusiast, he scripted himself and directed *La Course de taureaux*.

Being deprived of any reliable source of funding, however, he was by no means always at liberty to produce those scripts which appealed to him. Basically, aside from those moments when a production had been particularly successful (such as *Un chien andalou*) or when the production was small in scale (such as Rouch's fifties films) he was obliged to solicit funds from such sources as distributors' and exhibitors' networks (in return for the right to exploit the product), colleagues (in the form of a coproduction, perhaps with Gaumont), regular financial institutions lending risk capital, or independently wealthy individuals attracted by the glamour of the profession. Surprisingly often, such wealthy men seem to have been willing to fund or partly fund productions in which a mistress would feature. The wealthy "protector" of his cousin's mistress funded *Tire-au-flanc* to the tune of seven hundred thousand francs,[23] while another such funded *La Nuit du carrefour*.[24] A chance meeting with a wealthy friend in the Deauville casino allowed him to produce *La Route est belle*. His own inheritance disappeared into his productions, as did that of Renoir, who progressively sold off some of the 150 of his father's paintings he had inherited in order to fund his films.

On the whole, he was unwilling to put himself in the hands of corporate finance in any form: his reluctance to call on banks and other such agencies limited significantly the size of his productions. Early on, while in collaboration with Richebé, he had used a financier called Marcel Monteux, who, he claims, turned out to be a con man, juggling money between accounts. When the bubble burst, Braunberger had serious difficulties. Consequently, after bumper years in 1930 and 1931 on the American proceeds of *Un chien andalou*, he produced or coproduced only one film each year in 1932 and 1933. Indeed, his finances did not really flourish again till after his ten-year wartime absence from production. Another crisis largely excluded him from production between 1953 and 1958. Such unpredictable irregularities were a feature of his career and of many other independents, as was his focus on relatively small-scale works. Willing always to take a risk to launch new directors, he was often unable to follow them as their ambitions developed. He could not fund *La Grande Illusion* or other later films of Renoir, some of which never did get produced; he would have liked to fund Clouzot, but found him always too expensive. He was unable to fund the later Buñuels. The price of a relative independence, which left him free to produce only those scripts which appealed to him, was a constant financial marginality which prevented him from producing most of those scripts that appealed to him. In these circumstances, the government's postwar policy of fostering quality and short films was of enormous importance, significantly improving the funding base of his fundamentally undercapitalized firm. It brought him large returns while allowing him to fund stylistically experimental short films by those who were to form the Nouvelle Vague— Rouch, Reichenbach, Agnès Varda, Fabiani, Resnais, Godard, Truffaut, Doniol-Valcroze, and Rivette.

Braunberger divides his productions into two categories—those in which he can consider himself a collaborative initiator of the film project and those in which he has simply become attracted to a ready-formed subject developed by others.[25] In the latter case, as with *Salto mortale*, or later with Godard's films, he might act the company producer and content himself with providing the requisite administrative context; in the former case, however, he clearly sees it as not only a right but a duty to be intensely involved at each stage of shooting. Having cherished the project of *Paris 1900* for a long time, he shared in the editing of it. Having participated in the development of *La Chienne*, he watched the rushes with Renoir and made suggestions which on occasion led to Renoir's refilming scenes. His interventions at various stages were so essential to the nature and very existence of *Forfaiture* (L'Herbier, 1937) that he talks of it confidently as "his film."

That the distinction between company producer and producer company was widely recognized as obtaining within the industry is vouched for by many commentators. André Desfontaines defines it in 1947 in the following terms: "You can notionally designate two sorts of producers: on the one hand the director of a production house which he has set up himself and which he runs like any commercial firm, with the help of competent people. He is then a sort of publisher of films, accepting a subject, having it filmed, but not following its production at all closely. On the other hand, there is the producer who is a true artisan, bringing together his material, having the film made, and selling it."[26]

Contrasting these two limit cases of the French producer-package system, Braunberger several times indicates that there has been a move away from the personalized producer company toward the more finance-oriented company producer: "the disappearance of the producer as inspirer of the project is an extremely serious matter. It's important that the producer participate in the elaboration of the subject and in the filmmaking process itself."[27] While his view of the timing of the move varies from account to account, it is clear that he sees this participation of the producer, and indeed of all of the team, in a collaborative undertaking in which there are no clearly defined roles, as having become more and more difficult to realize in the postwar years. He is by no means the only producer to voice the view that the war years effectively divide production practices into two periods—the one in which spontaneity and an interchange or overlap of roles were still possible at all stages of the production process, and another in which the progressive regulation of the industry, together with the absolute need to ensure an export market if one was to obtain an adequate return on investment, and consequently the increasing role of international co-productions, enforced a greater degree of calculation, planning, and compartmentalization, such that the ethic of the company producer came to dominate.[28]

The case for such an evolution having taken place within the production practices of the French cinema was most forcefully put by Raoul Lévy, in 1959:

> In France at the moment there are some one hundred producers, but in fact only four are worthy of that name. . . . A producer is someone with an idea, a dream he wants to realize—his film—and who does it without money.
>
> In France before the war there were some very great producers. They were all Russian, completely mad, penniless, but full of ideas, and didn't think it necessary to have money to make a film. At three in the morning, an idea came to them. Anywhere, in a bar, they found a director and began to dream their film. Two hours later, without money, without support, the film was under way. For them, producing a film was a passion. During the war, they left for England or America. . . . Then with the creation of the loi d'aide au cinéma, a new class of producers was born. Everyone made money, but most of these new producers have no vision and turn out a film as they would turn out sausages, with an eye on the till.[29]

It is not surprising that it should be the heirs of these Russians who are most often heard voicing regrets at the passing of an age of joyous interactive creativity. "What's the use of taking on a project," asks Silberman, "if not with friends whose qualities, generosity, nobility one admires? . . . You can't work with people if you can't live with them. . . . I make films, not money. . . . The important thing is faith, and talent; and they have disappeared since the cinema sold itself to the banks."[30] Likewise Alex Mnouchkine and Georges Dancigers describe their production house as a "pension de famille," where a stable little community collaborates on each film. They see this situation as perpetuating the prewar conditions under which they entered the trade, when film production was artisanal in nature. "Scarcely 5% of the ideas for our productions come from other sources than ourselves. . . . We are not simply promoters, we participate in the writing of the script, the hunt for actors, and are present on the set from beginning to end. That's why we never manage more than two films a year. . . . The interest for us is not in being promoters, accountants, but in being initiators, midwives."[31]

That this was in fact becoming less common after the war, ironically at the very moment when in America the package-unit system was beginning to work in the opposite direction, is evidenced by Mitry's 1948 account of the typical producer. The producer is most often now an industrialist or a financier attracted to the cinema but not part of the milieu. In a pointed contrast with America, he notes that in France, "the producer is more simply a funder and has only limited knowledge about the cinema."[32] Acknowledging that he has tended toward this role, Robert Dorfmann in 1954 saw himself as having really only produced two films—*Justice est faite* and *Jeux interdits*—despite the fact that his companies had produced some twenty films at that stage, because only in those two had he participated at all stages in the development of the film.[33] Dorfmann had come to the cinema as a company administrator for Film Tobis in Bordeaux and had subsequently owned a regional distribution house and a cinema chain. When he moved into financing the coproduction of films, he preferred to leave the choice of subject, director, and cast to others. This is not untypical of producers formed in the French agencies of German and American firms, since it is the model that they were presented with there. Raoul Ploquin was chief of production in the thirties for French-language films made in UFA's German studio and took over the redressing of French film production under Greven's administration during 1940 and 1941. His subsequent corporate responsibilities speak well of his business and administrative sense, and he makes due obeisance to the more romantic producer company tendency, but his fifties investment in big-budget coproductions directed by Grangier, Borderie, and Verneuil place him toward the other extreme. André Paulvé is another such company producer, having begun in banking and risen to become director-general of a banking society bearing his name.

Instances of production firms working entirely outside the producer package system are few and far between. Those larger foreign companies which for relatively brief periods of time established themselves in France introduced into the French industry work practices that had developed within a state or capitalist corporative context. When Paramount bought out the Joinville St. Maurice studio, it introduced into the production system certain features typical of its operations in America. At the center of operations was Robert Kane, "a magnate with a big cigar and a little French."[34] Not himself a director, he had under his control the management of a studio and a laboratory. He hired artistic and technical staff on contract, read and approved scripts, allocated them to teams of directors working with regular personnel to produce French and foreign-language versions. In this case, however, it is clear that the degree of autonomy residing with the directors was not large and that Kane's criteria and opinions were decisive. Several of the directors who worked there recall the production-line procedures that were in force as allowing them no room for directorial control.

By contrast with this central producer system, the German firm Tobis, which had bought up the Epinay studios for its French-based productions, did not attempt to introduce the more intensive production-line practices of its American rival. Although upper management clearly was crucial in deciding who should be employed and which films were to be made, a high degree of autonomy remained with the directors (notably René Clair and Feyder) contracted to produce those films. We can identify Tobis as working within a model closer to Janet Staiger's director-unit system, and perhaps because this bore a closer resemblance to the package-unit system to which the French personnel were accustomed, the results were, and are, widely considered to have been superior to those of the Paramount initiative. The same procedures as Tobis introduced at Epinay seem to have been operative in Berlin, where Grémillon and Chomette worked, and the results likewise were of higher technical and aesthetic standard.

However, when the German occupying forces moved into film production under the aegis of Continental Films, their production practices were more clearly demarcated from the French practices. Greven, who assumed control of the German-instituted Continental Films on its inauguration in October 1940 (and indeed of much of the French industry as well), established himself effectively as a central producer, allocating groups of films to directorial teams employed on year-long contracts.

In the three years of his activity, Continental Films did clearly move toward the central producer system, with its main directors being Henri Decoin (three films), Maurice Tourneur (four), André Cayatte (four) and Richard Pottier (five). Accounts of the relationship between Greven (as central producer) and these directorial teams make it clear that both production programming and final control of the production process and the products rested with Greven.[35] "Continental Films was a very compartmentalized production house, with services employing French and German secretaries. Alfred Greven would read all reports on scenarios and shooting. He would listen to all advice and then take, alone, all decisions, which were beyond appeal. When he decided to replace Danielle Darrieux, by Louise Carletti, for the lead role in *Annette et la dame blonde*, the director Jean Dréville could not get him to change his mind. For refusing to retake a scene in *L'Assassin habite au 21*, which Alfred Greven considered not up to standard, Suzy Delair was shown the door within 24 hours. She left Continental after having completed the third film for which she was contracted, *Défense d'aimer*, never to return."[36] Siclier likens Greven's rule to that of Thalberg over Metro-Goldwyn-Mayer.

Alongside these various moves toward state and corporative modes of production, modelled largely on those of other countries, there was a novel instance of a peculiarly French system established by Marcel Pagnol in the Midi. Pagnol created his own production company specifically to produce his own films, as had many of his predecessors in the twenties; but what distinguished his enterprise was the scale on which he was able to undertake it, as a result of the immense success of his theatrical works and the even more remarkable success of his first film, *Marius*, produced by Paramount's French production arm. With almost limitless funds at his disposal, Pagnol was able to build his own film studio in the suburbs of Marseilles, hire his own technicians to staff it, hire artistic personnel on year-long contracts, purchase areas of Provence which served for location shooting, buy an advanced sound van to do his location recording, buy a laboratory to process and print his films, and buy a chain of cinemas in which to screen them. It is clear that his prime aim in developing this Marseilles-based cinema empire was the desire for independence. In this respect he was acting on precisely the same motivation as director-packagers of the twenties, such as Gance and Feyder, but was able to go much further because of the funds at his disposal. Indeed, such was his obsession with independence that he contemplated buying or building a plant to produce his own film-stock.[37] Again like Gance, he was happy to use this production company as an umbrella organization to producer-package occasional films by friends, on the side.

Some have seen in Pagnol's undertaking a preview of New Wave practices in the early sixties. Pagnol was, however, more radical than the New Wave directors in owning his own means of production. The New Wave, on the other hand, were merely returning to the director-package system of the twenties, which had been kept alive by a number of directors through the years 1930–1960, though never to the point where it challenged the producer-package. Less well known is the analogous instance of Roger Richebé, who directed 18 films from 1933 to 1960 and whose production/distribution company regularly produced films directed by him, for a while in conjunction with Pierre Braunberger, with whom he owned the Billancourt studio. Fernand Rivers (22 sound films from 1933 to 1951) also set up his own production house, as did Yvan Noë (16 films from 1933 to 1950). Maurice Cloche (38 films from 1937 to 1971), having directed films for a number of production companies, set up his own company in 1948 to produce *Docteur Laennec* (1948–1949), *La Cage aux filles* (1949), and others. Claude Vermorel, Barthomieu, Leenhardt, and Rouquier also produced some or all of their own films, the last two as an offshoot of their short film and documentary production companies. André Hunebelle was a producer of films before he directed his first film in 1948. Indeed, "he was artistic director of all the films his company produced and therefore somewhat closer to the American than the French model of producer."[38] Perhaps the most dramatic instance of this drive for economic autonomy is the establishment by Jean-Pierre Melville of his own production company in 1945 to make first a short film, then *Le Silence de la mer* (1947–1949). Unable to enter the industry on demobilization because he was refused an industry work card, Melville had decided to reject entirely the established procedures, with their built-in constraints. He made his first feature film "clandestinely"—outside the union rules, with unknown actors, and without obtaining the rights to the book on which it was based. Subsequent legal procedures delayed exhibition, but its success brought him into contact with Cocteau, who asked him to direct *Les Enfants terribles*. Thereafter, Melville Productions was an official company, and the success of *Quand tu liras cette lettre* (1953) allowed him to buy the small studios in the rue Jenner, where he directed his subsequent films. What the New Wave did was to expand this director-package system and establish it as a norm for the more ambitious art-film project, while the producer-package system continued as a norm in the more commercially oriented segment of the market.

While current mythology sees this director-package system as a breakthrough, a case can be made for the producer-package system, against which they were reacting, having all the advantages of the director-package system and no real disadvantages. By comparison with the more industrial models of the American system, the French system had always enjoyed the advantage of favoring diversity. A fragmented production system, in which the crucial go/no go decisions were taken by individuals ranging from colorful eccentric immigrants through cautious, thoughtful, cultivated intellectuals to conservative, money-minded entrepreneurs, and in which a large number of these individuals from across the range each contributed a few films per year, was guaranteed to ensure such a diversity. The criteria on which production decisions were taken were themselves wildly diverse.

The relative diversity which developed, moreover, allowed for the continuance of elements of the art cinema of the twenties in a way that other large national cinemas did not. Renoir was not an awkward outsider to the system, fighting desperately against the economics of productivity to be heard; he was himself a product of the system. Films by Grémillon, Vigo, and Feyder in the thirties, not to mention Astruc, Ophüls, and Melville in the postwar period—and René Clair in both decades—were not made despite the system but because of it.

Nor was it just the artist-oriented producer-company end of the scale that allowed for such projects. The output of the company-producer end of the scale was itself diverse, incorporating both artistically ambitious and experimental products for which the audience would clearly be small, and spectacles aimed at a mass audience. If Gaumont under Poiré produced many sentimental romances like *Caroline chérie*, it also produced (as Poiré repeatedly pointed out) Bresson's *Un condamné à mort s'est échappé*, as earlier Pathé-Natan had produced Vigo's films. Ploquin, who had worked in UFA throughout the thirties as company producer for French films, and who had been bureaucratic head of the French cinema in the early war years, might (as one would expect from this history) in the postwar years normally produce films directed by Grangier, Verneuil, Bernard, and Borderie, but he was also a highly cultivated man, much admired by scriptwriters and directors for his linguistic competence and literary knowledge; he also produced several of Grémillon's films and Bresson's *Les Dames du Bois de Boulogne*; Raymond Borderie, who tended toward the company producer, also produced Yves Allégret's *Une si jolie petite plage*, and Becker's *Edouard et Caroline*. As Raoul Ploquin put it, "I make two sorts of films; first those of which I'm certain, that's to say films with Brigitte Bardot for which I select subjects which allow her to be seen in an appropriate light. Then, films which shouldn't be made, but which it would be a shame not to make; those also which, thanks to the tact and talent of the director, incorporate some degree of experimentation."[39] Indeed, even since the development of the New Wave, traditional producer-packagers have been responsible for many of the experimental works that are included under the New Wave banner.

In effect, by preserving an artisanal and "intimate" mode of production, the fragmented industrial structure contributed to the maintenance of a consciousness among all concerned in making the films (and specifically in the producers who were the central decision makers) of being involved in an exhilarating enterprise with national cultural responsibilities. Their representation of cinema and of French cinema, not to mention their own self-representation, was markedly different from that of their American counterparts. In effect, the lack of ongoing contractual relationships engendered constant personal negotiations, such that filmmaking could not escape seeming a highly personalized and adventurous undertaking. They might minimize the risk by repeating formulae where possible, and work with known colleagues where possible, but neither was by any means always possible. Each film was an autonomous enterprise, the end product of a chain of personal relationships and risks. This explanation for the continuing diversity of French production can be looked at in another light: since there had never been a dominant set of majors using mass-production methods, no standard set of practices had arisen which might have been seen—as they were in America—as defining what constituted "a quality film"—indeed what constituted "a film." There was no national standard widely accepted against which the diverse practices of the different producer-packaged films might have been measured and found wanting, or surprising or eccentric.

In respect of "individuality," then, the director-package system of the New Wave did not provide significant advantages over this classic French mode of production. All it did was inflict on the director the administrative and financial responsibilities normally accruing to the producer. Given that many such New Wave directors also took on the role of scriptwriter, their output was probably significantly reduced by the move. It is salutary to note that by 1960 a real appreciation of the virtues of the producer-package system was being voiced. As Louis Daquin put it, when deploring the entrepreneurial capitalism of Hollywood and the state capitalism of the USSR, "the concentration of production and of the means of production . . . can only paralyze, sterilize, creation. It is to its artisanal mode of production that we in France, as in Italy, owe the overall diversity of our output, its nonconformism, which can in no way be explained solely by reference to the liberalism of the independent producers."[40] René Clair had noted as much some ten years earlier,[41] as had Peter Bächlin:[42] a greater diversity and flexibility in the product derives in fact from the production practices which in turn derive from the industrial structure.

A SCRIPTWRITERS' CINEMA: FILM AS RECORDED THEATER

While by its very nature the producer-package mode of production generated work practices marked by a high degree of variation, some norms did develop in the course of the classical period against which such variations could be measured. The producer might obtain the script in a number of different ways: he might buy a proven literary or theatrical work, he might receive a script or script idea from an experienced or aspirant scriptwriter, or he might commission a script based on an idea informally generated. Once he had decided to proceed with the project, however, the production process became more standardized: typically, the producer would hire one or more scriptwriters and supervise the script development process through several stages, covering perhaps three months; he would simultaneously hire a director, in collaboration with whom he would develop a production schedule and a definitive budget, select and hire the cast, set designer, and cinematographer; these latter two team members might begin work some two weeks before the film was due to go into production, at a point where the script was fully written out; in those final weeks the director supervised the whole team in the development of a shooting script with all dialogues, staging, and technical directions fully indicated; the shooting would take place in a studio hired in advance by the producer and might occupy two stages of the studio for about 30–45 days; it might typically involve the construction and dismantling of some 15 different sets; the cast would usually be hired exclusively for the period of shooting for which they were required—lead actors by the month or by the film, bit-part actors by the day or by the week; both musician and editor would begin work after shooting began, working with material to the planning of which they had not contributed. Typically, this whole process, from the moment the producer decided to proceed with the project till the moment he received the definitive copy for marketing, would take six months. Each of the principal operatives, like the labor force and the studio itself, would have been hired for the shortest possible period, to minimize costs.

In these circumstances there were three categories of personnel who could claim either to be at the origin of the film's thematic statements or to exercise decisive control over key aesthetic work practices—the producer, the scriptwriter(s), and the director. Consequently, in the debate over authorship it was these three who figured most prominently. In legislative terms, the composer who furnished the music was also recognized formally as "an author," no doubt because of the long-standing creative competence attributed to musical composers; but this recognition never impinged significantly on the decade-long debate over film authorship in the classic cinema which arose in the postwar period.

While only the producers themselves took seriously the claims that they as a group put forward to be authors, the debate between the other two groups was evenly balanced for much of the decade. Jeanson, as head of the writers' union, waged a vicious public campaign with all the truculence of which he was capable, and that was not a little, to get the scenarist recognized as the "auteur" of a film. Spaak, too, more mild-mannered and laying more emphasis on the need for a compatible authorial team, nevertheless joined in with several satirical references to the pitiful state of French filmmaking before writers ("auteurs") brought to it the necessary subtlety. René Wheeler was still fighting a rearguard battle in this lost cause in the late fifties. Directors, he claimed, were merely obedient technicians carrying out the aesthetic program prescribed by the scenarist. In sum, over the decade 1945–1955 it was at least as common to see the term *auteur* used globally to indicate the literary sector of a film's production. In 1954, the *Film Français*, official organ of the industry, still categorized cumulatively the members of the scriptwriting team as *auteurs* of the film and listed directors separately.

The case for the scriptwriter as author of a film had only become defensible in France with the introduction of sound. Before that time, contemporary commentators agree that the script as such scarcely existed—most films were based on adaptations of literary works, the job of adapting them to the screen was normally undertaken by the director, and the role of scriptwriter remained to be defined and created.[43] The personal recollections of critics and of the few early scriptwriters certainly underline, and perhaps exaggerate in order to contrast it with later procedures, the extremes of informality existing in the industry at that stage. Sadoul speaks of the directors normally working from a cursory schema: "Feuillade, for example, who was the author of his own scenarios, improvised the majority of his stories on the spot; he often used whatever facilities that location provided, where he had happened to take his team; he used at best a few notes—bits of paper with ideas scribbled on them, that he kept in his pocket. These methods continued almost right to the end of the silent era."[44] Writing in 1929, Moussinac describes a similar situation: "Chance and intuition, that's what takes the place of a system. The scenario is constructed in haste. The essential is to get on with the filming."[45] Charles Spaak, speaking of his early experiences as assistant to Feyder, then scriptwriter for Feyder's last silent film, says, "In those days . . . there *were* no scriptwriters. . . . Naturally, there was a script of sorts, which the director had drawn up himself, rather hastily. It was just a rough schema, which he rarely consulted. If he'd left his script at home that morning, it was no great worry: if he'd lost it in a taxi, it was no great drama; films mostly consisted of putting into images well-known novels or famous plays: all he had to do was buy another copy of the work in question and pick up where he'd left off. . . . "[46] He estimates at roughly 10% the number of directors—the "serious" ones—who established detailed découpages, but makes it clear that even these were not considered definitive blueprints: at the editing stage, radical reconstructions might take place. "The scriptwriter, nonexistent, was replaced by the director who had roughly put together the principal elements of the plot and by the editor who (under the director's guidance) completed this work by plugging up the gaps and establishing the links."[47]

For Spaak, this absence of "real authors" was the source of all that was inadequate in the French cinema of the twenties—banal and repetitive plots and unsubtle characterization. On the other hand, of course, it was also the source of that assumption, characteristic of the French cinema, that writer-directors were a normal aspect of filmmaking—an assumption which permitted the unproblematic importation of romantic, individualist notions of authorship into the cinema; and it is precisely with the evolution of a specialist category of scriptwriters around 1930 that the artistic nature of cinematic creativity comes to be a contested area.

The debate was fuelled by various provocative statements made by established dramatists such as Pagnol and Sacha Guitry to the effect that the talkies provided a magnificent opportunity to immortalize great theatrical productions by recording them on film. Filmed theater, canned theater, was the obvious destiny of sound cinema and would endow the lowly medium with some of the prestige and aesthetic sophistication of the theater.

In fact, Pagnol's views on the cinema were more complex than this, but such statements as the following were guaranteed to generate heated exchanges: "The talkie is the art of recording, of fixing, and of diffusing theater."[48] "In my view, a good dialogue is not the enemy of the talkie. . . . A good dialogue, a real dialogue, a theatrical one, with its agile interchanges linking and clashing in lively fashion, like two swords in trained hands, is not, cannot be a wrong move."[49] Presenting *Marius* to the public, he said, "The recording is perfect. It's a great success in the field of mechanized theater, one of the formulas of the talkie, with few partisans among filmmakers but apparently much appreciated by the public."[50] For Sacha Guitry, "the cinema had interested me little till now. But I think the arrival of the talkie is of enormous importance. . . . Important for actors, first of all, who, if they prove incapable of speaking the dialogues, can be replaced overnight by theatrical actors. Important for the public, too, who will get to hear and see those actors it would never have thought to go to the theater to hear."[51] Léonce Perret proudly announced in 1932 that his next production was to be a piece of filmed theater.[52] Michel Simon acknowledged that his film version of Achard's *Jean de la Lune* (1930) was "photographed theatre."[53] Renoir did no more with Feydeau's *On purge bébé*. "The cinema is now an ersatz of the theater," said a critic: "It is to the theater what a disk is to the Colonne orchestra."[54] "Whether we like it or not we will be obliged to adopt the theatrical formula, since the talkie will be fundamentally cinematic theater. Our current industrial practices will be totally transformed; . . . I can't understand all this opposition to a new formula, and I'm intimately persuaded that this will bring to the silent film a force which can only be beneficial to the artistic development of the filmic art."[55] "I am the first person," said Guitry, "to have dared to film plays from one end to the other without changing a word . . . , to bring to the screen texts conceived, written, and directed for the stage."[56] As Torok notes, proponents of this line of action were at least implicitly denying that the sound cinema had any specific aesthetic of its own—it could only be of worth in its role as a technological extension of a stage play, which it mediated for a wider public. The film shone if the verbal text shone and/or if the actors were capable of bringing out its qualities.[57]

Opposing this opportunistic imperialism of the dramatists for whom the scenario was now to be the creative focus of the filmmaking process, veterans of the silent period became locked into a reactionary stance, claiming that the cinema was inherently nonverbal and that the practices of the silent era must persist. Any interest in theatrically scripted films had no more than novelty value and would soon pass. René Clair's early antagonism is well known: The talkie is "a dreadful monster, against nature, thanks to which the cinema will become a depressed theater, the theater of the depressed."[58] "It is essential that, cost what it may, the cinema remain a visual art: the arrival of theatrical dialogues in the cinema would be the end of everything I hoped of it. The talkies have generated a devastating misunderstanding for which certain journalists and theatrical dramatists are responsible. It has been said: right, the reign of the director is over, since he'll need collaborators who will have their own autonomy. This is false, absurd. *I* am the director, *I* remain the author of all my films, sound or silent: *I* will decide the words, as *I* decide the action. The sound cinema must steer clear of the theater even more than the silent film."[59]

Others were no less forthright, as this collection of statements taken from Icart's excellent anthology clearly indicates: "If this new form of expression is to be a sort of photograph or record of the actors performing as in the theater, I don't know whether it has a commercial future, but it certainly has no artistic future."[60] "To try to make of sound cinema a sort of auditory and visual theater would be a heresy."[61] "We must progress, you say? Don't you see that it is in fact a regression to add words to the cinema, because that only makes of it—and irrevocably—a theater without depth, that's to say, a subtheater."[62] "I hope I may be forgiven the bitterness, the sense of justice. After so much effort, so much hope, to fall back at the end on such a worn-out formula as the theater, to accept the tyranny of the word and of sound, exacerbated further by a mechanical intermediary."[63] "But the . . . 100% talkie, which according to its prophets was to occupy effortlessly all the territory of the silent film, will not last. Already, scarcely born, it is giving signs of debility and impotence; the almost literal adaptation of plays into which unimaginative producers had launched so enthusiastically is a false and bastard genre, in decline before having really found its feet. . . . We'll see next winter a few more runts born of this dangerous half-caste mismarriage of screen and stage. They do not threaten the cinema."[64] "Surely the art of cinema is an art of visual beauty in the combination of movement and light. To add the word is to destroy it in its profoundest being. This is to regress, not to progress."[65] "In any case, the word must not dominate the image. The cinema must not become 'theater'; its dramaturgy is different and depends on shots, their form, light, and rhythm. The image alone suffices."[66] "It is certain that, thanks to the talkie, there will be lots of recordings of plays, of operettas, of music-hall revues, and this will lead to a sort of artistic vulgarization and diffusion of certain works. That may be of considerable commercial interest, but in my view the future of the talkie lies elsewhere. Just because we can now join word to image, let's not commit the error of abruptly relegating the image to the role of poor relation. A piece of filmed theater will only be 'words with images,' with everything sacrificed to the dialogue. This is to abandon cinema in favor of a sort of 'subtheater.' "[67] "Theorists of the cinematic art have struggled for years to distinguish their technique from that of the theater. They had a conception of cinematic art as *pure*—free of theatrical and literary influences, an art of images in movement, sufficiently powerful to engender beauty without recourse to the procedures of dramatists and novelists. . . . These theoreticians were right. Cinematic art has no future if not in an ever more ingenious work on the image."[68]

On its side, the theatrical fraternity was almost as apprehensive, and the Comédie Française imposed stringent restrictions on its members acting in films, for fear that the cinema might appropriate and bastardize the great theatrical repertoire. Indeed, that filmed theater involved an inevitable degradation and bastardization of those works it adapted was likewise a constant theme of reviewers.[69]

The debate was much more intense in France than in other countries, and notably America, perhaps because the cinema in France had been quite distinct in its artistic and theoretical orientation, and the more "artistic" and articulate filmmakers felt that they had more to lose than their foreign counterparts. But the sudden demand for large numbers of cinematic scripts that resulted from the introduction of sound guaranteed their defeat. The increase in production, taken in conjunction with the fact that the French industry had not yet generated a scriptwriting fraternity, ensured that producers would be *obliged* to turn to the ready-made repertoires of theater and operetta.

No detailed study of the early years of the French cinema exists to clarify the extent to which this "threat" was real. Subjective impressions of the time suggest invariably that 90% of the films being made between 1930 and 1939 were barely modified theater. But then, there are many similar statements from the twenties claiming that original scenarios were a small minority in France even during the silent era. "It's the adapters who have been dominant [over writers of original scenarios] both in quantity and in

quality," claimed José Germain;[70] and Coissac recalls the numerical dominance of direct theatrical transpositions from the earliest days of the cinema.[71] Those involved in the debate continued to make such claims
throughout the thirties, long after they could be demonstrated to be false.
Figure 6.1 draws on several sources to outline the percentage of original
scripts compared to adaptations over the period 1936–1959. They significantly undermine contemporary claims, such as that by René Clair in 1937
that 90% of films are theater more or less adequately filmed,[72] or the claim
to the Renaitour inquiry in the same year that "Out of ten films, there are
eight nowadays which constitute theatrical plays transposed to the cinema."[73] Even Claude Beylie, in his extremely valuable study of the *comédie
mondaine* genre, talks of the consequent mixed "theatro-cinematic" genre
"dominating the first ten years of the talkie, and even beyond."[74] In fact,
with only two anomalous years (1937 and 1958), the proportion of all adaptations to originals was uncommonly stable throughout the period, with
the ratio approximately even at the beginning and end of the period but
favoring originals rather than adaptations in the period 1940–1955.

Within these figures, however, it is clear that the tendency to adapt theatrical works was commoner in the mid-thirties and fell off steadily from
22% to 12% at the war's end, and then after recovering slightly fell off to
6% at the end of the fifties. Operettas and the like make up the "other"
category in the mid-thirties, and feature-length documentaries constitute
the 2% in 1959. This does indeed suggest that "filmed theater" may have
been more common in the early thirties, especially when combined with
filmed operettas and musicals, whereas by 1936–1937, and even more so
in the fifties, it was predominantly novels that were being adapted.

This is important for two reasons. First, the plays and operettas that
were transposed to the cinema in quantity in the thirties were already of
film length, and second, they were already endowed with a script. Little,
if any, additional treatment was required to produce a filmable script; only
the découpage technique was required, and that was the province of the
director. Most "adaptations" of such works seem to have involved the original dramatic author being commissioned to produce a slightly modified version of his stage play. But it was not only that major adaptations were
unnecessary: they would have been inimical to the success of the subsequent film. It was precisely the witty and somewhat salacious dialogue of
these Boulevard comedies that had made them famous, and which had interested the producers in them. It was this element which attracted the public who wanted to see in the cinema what they might not so easily be able
to afford in the theater. Large numbers of the plays of Feydeau, of his successors, Donnay and Capus, and their contemporaries such as Tristan Bernard, Robert de Flers, Gaston Arman de Caillavet, Pierre Wolff, Edouard
Bourdet, Jacques Deval, and André Roussin were introduced into the cinema. It was from this tradition that two of the most prolific scenarist-
directors of the thirties and forties derived—Sacha Guitry and Yves

FIGURE 6.1   Sources of Scripts for Classic French Films

Source of Script	1936	1937	1938	1939	1940	1941	1942	1943	1944	...	1951	1952	1953	1954	...	1957	1958	1959
plays	22	21	18	18		16	12	8	12		18	15	16	11				6
novels	26	34	27	24		24	30	30	30		22	23	28	31				41
other	5	7	6	4		5	3	4	5		-	-	-	-				2
Total Adapt. %	53	62	51	46		45	45	42	47		40	38	44	42		50	34	49
Originals %	47	38	49	54		55	55	58	53		60	62	56	58		50	66	51

Columns   *De Blum à Petain: Annexes*
1–9
11–14   *Film Fr. 567/568*
16–18   *Arts 751, Film Fr. 832/3*

Mirande—but also scriptwriters such as Bernard Zimmer, Louis Verneuil, Roger Ferdinant, and Michel Duran, and the multiple talents of scriptwriter/director Fernand Rivers. Of the core group of famous French scriptwriters, only Henri Jeanson owes anything to this tradition, having written three Boulevard plays around 1930, though reputedly without much success. While other men of the theater from different dramatic traditions did turn their hand to scriptwriting for the cinema—Achard, Anouilh, Cocteau, Giraudoux, Sartre, for instance—their production was insignificant compared to that of the *comédie mondaine* and was never suspect to the same extent of ignoring the specificity of the cinema. In general, the "serious theatre," represented by such figures as Jouvet, Pitoëff, Dullin, and Copeau, deeply distrusted the cinema and, however much they may individually have enjoyed the company of people involved in filmmaking, were reluctant themselves to become involved.

It was therefore the Boulevard *comédies mondaines* that constituted the bulk of filmed theater, and it was that genre which attracted the violent resentment of the cinematic fraternity. While its numerical dominance was to diminish over the years, the depth of the resentment it had engendered can be measured by the automatic recurrence in commentaries of the forties and fifties of homilies concerning the need to avoid such "direct transpositions." "Death to theatrical procedures," proclaimed Louis Daquin at the climax of his lecture to the first IDHEC intake. Devoting two pages to the subject, Charles Ford in 1947 observed that "A play is never, as long as it remains a play, an appropriate basis for a film. The theater is at the opposite pole from the film." He summarizes his position by describing filmed theater as "that recurrent hindrance to film's aspiration to be an art."[75]

Three years later Chartier and Desplanques are still talking of filmed theater as "a great danger: how many filmed plays give the impression of being too talkative, with actors shut in by four walls talking about things which the cinema could just as easily show."[76] The theatrical spectator can afford to be blind, they say, whereas the cinematic spectator can afford to be deaf, so different are the specificities of the two media.

This continuing anxiety about "a talkative cinema" was to help determine the way that new category of personnel, the dialoguists, understood their trade. The dialogues they wrote for the cinema must, to be compatible with the classic self-understanding of the cinematic profession, be radically distinct in kind from those written for the theater. They must not incorporate literary flourishes, they must be closer to everyday speech, and especially they must be concise, sparse, secondary to the image. "For me," said Marcel Achard, "film dialogue should be like the caption on a cartoon; . . . you should aim at brevity, use short, incisive phrases. . . . The cinema has a realist vocation. You should get your characters to speak as real people do, or as we believe they do."[77]

The qualification implicit in the last phrase is important but is drowned in the consensual approval of brevity and realism. "Literature is the worst enemy of the dialoguist. . . . If most current dialoguists have come from the theater and the novel, they've only learned there . . . what not to do. . . . The limited role here advocated for film dialogue does not suggest it is unimportant. It is crucial, but its effectiveness is unquestionably in direct proportion to its conciseness. On the screen, there must be no verbiage. The word must not reiterate the image."[78] "If we were able to follow someone around for a day, we would rapidly realize that the moments when a man speaks are much less numerous than those when he doesn't, however talkative he may be, and that the central moments of his existence, those where great events are unfolding, are often characterized by silence. . . . The influence of the theater has been extremely detrimental in this respect."[79] Both the IDHEC course and the *Ecole technique*'s correspondence course contained warnings against excessive verbiage. The aspiring dialoguist "must struggle against this incontinence,"[80] advises Ford. The word is the source of all evil, and the acquisition of speech brings with it sin and guilt. The theme of incontinence is taken up by other commentators, who advise all those collaborating with dialoguists to cut and cut again, as if one could ideally castrate filmed theater. Only Bost, perhaps the principal target of this campaign, demurred. "Films talk nowadays," he said mockingly, "and basically they [directors] regret it. They regret the silent days when they were sole master of the ship. These days they can't do without authors; they know it; and that's perhaps why they hold this vague grudge against them."[81] For Bost, both theatrical dialogue and film dialogue were necessarily unrealistic. Both transposed reality, but because of the different characteristics of the two media, they transposed reality in different ways. "The cinema is not a mechanism for reproducing the real . . . it is a mechanism for transposition; so film dialogue too must by stylized, if it is to seem plausible, convincingly real."

This apprehension about theater and the word is in sharp contrast to the profession's attitude toward the adaptation of novels. There could be no such thing as "filmed novels," in any simple sense, if only because of their length and the importance of the nondialogued psychological notations within them. The transformation which the prose text underwent, in terms of selection, rearrangement, and substitution, was much more radical, allowing the practitioners to claim as they often did that the end product was not just a pale imitation but a "new original" generated with due consideration for the specificity of the cinema. It could thus not be considered subject to the opprobrium of the "filmed theatre."

This may explain why, in contrast to the "hemorrhage" of theatrical personnel into the cinema, very few leading novelists adapted to the role of scenarist; and those that did were not the most competent novelists. Malraux's *Espoir* is almost alone in the category of films scripted by a "great" novelist. On the other hand, several authors of detective and mystery novels moved back and forth between literature and scriptwriting. Pierre Véry, having tried his hand at ambitious novels without much success, became an established figure in the world of suspense fiction, writing novels in which the everyday overbalanced frequently into the eerie and the supernatural. In 1938 Prévert adapted one of them—*Les Disparus de St. Agil*—for the cinema, bringing Véry into contact with various filmmakers. Thereafter he became an adept scriptwriter, adapting his own and other people's novels and writing a few works specifically for the screen. Pierre Bost likewise had written novels and short stories over a period of twenty years, one of which won the Prix Interallié in 1931; but his reputation in that field was as nothing compared to the recognition (and later notoriety) he was to earn once he began working with Aurenche on the adaptation of other people's novels for the cinema.

CONVENTION AND INVENTION IN SCRIPTWRITING

Because the debate as to whether writing a filmscript was a key creative activity in the filmmaking process became so hotly contested in the period 1945–1955, the question of whether scriptwriters could be professionally trained and taught according to a set of formulas and rules was likewise extremely controversial. At various times throughout the classic period critics or practitioners outlined protostructuralist programs involving narrative grammars, typical cast lists and generic conventions that could have constituted a course in scriptwriting. As Leprohon said, "in a sense all films are adaptations. . . . The idea of adapting earlier works is not peculiar to the cinema, nor is it to be condemned by definition. Our classics, for instance, and our modern dramatists—Anouilh, Cocteau, Giraudoux—have proved it. There are certain eternal themes, which are eternal precisely because of the successive *adaptations* which have put them within reach of new publics."[82]

Henriette Dujarric takes up these ideas later, talking of repetitive narrative patterns that link apparently dissimilar films,[83] and Nouet recapitulates it in 1958.[84] By that time, the subject was becoming entangled in the long-standing dispute about authors' rights, and for legal commentators it became important to distinguish the point at which script ideas became subject to copyright. "With ideas," say Sarraute and Gorline,

> it is the same as with the fire in our homes. We often borrow a brand from our neighbors to light our own fire; we pass it on to others and it belongs to everyone. Thought is fluid, its origin indeterminate, diffuse. . . . How can we possibly talk of ideas that are entirely new? Fifty years after an author's death, his temporary privileges disappear. His work falls in the common domain. That immense common fund which we can all draw on contains everything men have written, conceived, or carried out from the beginning of time to [fifty years ago]. Give or take a few variations, all possible dramatic situations have already been devised and expressed. These sources belong to humanity in general. All authors have drawn inspiration from it.

> What is the protected domain, then? What is the original aspect of a work of art which cannot be imitated without accusation of plagiarism? It's the form given to the idea, the manner in which it has been exploited, the personal expression, the style of the work. That alone is protected.[85]

For Sadoul, too, "scenarists, however numerous and however clever, could never invent each year the hundreds of original situations needed. They must, therefore, often turn to established subjects, or openly adapt. In this they follow a law common to the theater and literature as well. Numerous versions of *Don Juan* were written in Spain in the sixteenth century, and that same character has turned up, in other costumes and under other names, in numerous contemporary works."[86]

These ideas receive their fullest contemporary expression in Charles Ford's *On tourne lundi* (1947). He refers to the Goethe/Gozzi/Schiller debate which concluded that there were only 36 dramatic situations: a disaster, kidnapping, an enigma, madness, vengeance, salvation, pursuit, rebellion, crime, fatal imprudence, ambition, judicial error, jealousy, etc. Once these are recognized, they can be recombined over and over in new variations. He later lists seven "typical" (i.e., generic or archetypal) plots which organize these elements in regular ways, often involving a basis of opposition: the Western plot, the Cinderella story, the eternal triangle, the *Dame aux caméllias* story of a femme fatale who dies, the love versus duty story, the drama of mistaken identity, the tragic clown.

Whichever is chosen can be organized into an exposition, development, and climax. The exposition must establish a conflict, in which opposing values are brought into play. The main characters must embody these values, though preferably not in any simplistic good/evil fashion, "such as one finds in the U.S. cinema," but complicating the characters by introducing weaknesses. There are "types," but these are best avoided, since the French public seems to prefer psychologically complex characters. It is essential that the audience be brought to identify with these psychological characters, and Ford provides a rudimentary outline of techniques by which this can be achieved. Among other techniques, the different shot scales and their uses are described: "When the characters of a film only appear in more distant shots the film gives the impression of simply reproducing theater. Moreover [in such cases], we rapidly become indifferent to the characters."[87] The specific problems that cinema faces in constructing psychological "interiority" are contrasted with the novel's ease in this respect, and a number of techniques "which the public has learned to read" for attributing interiority to characters by way of lighting, editing, and acting are explored.[88] In particular, the importance of psychological motivation is underlined.

Formally, the possibilities of flashback form and the advisability of a second story, or subplot, are described, and advice is given on when it is and is not acceptable to introduce new characters. Finally, a list of commercially successful ideas is provided, incorporating some of the above, but also noting the use of "happy endings," verisimilitude, rapid expositions, dramatic finales, suspense and enigma mechanisms, clarity of narrative logic, and the importance of writing with specific stars in mind.

While this summary condenses and partially systematizes a series of observations spread over some fifty pages of the book, it does serve to underline the extent to which Ford provides in outline a teachable and learnable set of techniques. On the basis of that outline, it would not have been difficult to devise a detailed course program which would have heightened students' awareness of the standard procedures by which film narratives in particular, but implicitly all narratives, are constructed.

The two courses in scriptwriting that were in fact taught at this time, and with them the sections on scriptwriting in "how-it's-done" manuals, make no attempt to do such a thing. The correspondence course entitled "The birth of a film," after enjoining the aspirant scriptwriter to think in terms of action, talks in terms of the need for imagination, talent, and intelligence in the development of a "balanced" construction. The nearest it gets to practical advice is when it counsels the student to think in terms of key scenes, scenes that set these up and that develop them, transitional scenes, and multiple lines of action. The course is brief, vague, and singularly lacking in pragmatic advice; and the use of terms such as imagination and talent suggest a fundamental hopelessness in the whole project: a student will either already have these qualities or will never have them.

This pedagogic nihilism is even more apparent in such of the early IDHEC lectures as have survived. This may be due to the high aesthetic aspirations of the founder, Marcel L'Herbier, for whom creativity in the cinema was bound up with his own idea of himself as an artist. The opening program in 1944 was entitled "Cinematic creation," and the contributions from Aurenche on adaptation, and Daquin and Bost on dialogues, readily espouse the myths implicit in that title. Aurenche begins his lecture by announcing that "adaptation is not a job that can be learned. I can well believe there are among you some who will be adapters, but I can't give you a course in adaptation."[89] Two months later, Pierre Bost likewise advised, somewhat unhelpfully, that the job of dialoguist "is one that can't be learned, and which does not readily lend itself to becoming the substance of a course."[90] While his lecture is in many respects interesting, it is totally unhelpful as a pedagogic exercise. Advice comes in the form of generalizations, or epigrams: "Film dialogue is to theatrical dialogue as ping pong is to tennis. Film dialogue should be not so much concise, as *dense.*"

This mystification of the creative process is general among practitioners. Interviewed by *Cinema 56* on the nature of the scenarist's task, Jeanson asserts "that the job of scenarist is a job that can be learned. But only by exercising it. I can't say how one writes a good scenario."[91] Basically, for him, it's "a gift." For Jacques Viot, too, "instruction is of no use to you; you have to have a gift for it; scriptwriting is an unknown land, an exact science of which no one knows the laws."[92] The same line is promoted, somewhat belligerently, by Charles Spaak in his contribution to *Le Cinéma par ceux qui le font* (1949). Experience is vaunted as the sole valid route to mastery, and the antitheoretical irony is so all-pervasive as to register as anti-intellectualism.

> Today, God help us, the career of young cineastes is not governed by chance! You don't get into a studio these days without being equipped with a good dozen diplomas attesting that you have received from M. Marcel L'Herbier an education which assures a total initiation into the secrets of filmmaking at the same time as all the mysteries of dramaturgy. A grammar written by M. Berthomieu, which you only have to learn by heart, confers on the most obtuse a luminous, total, and instantaneous understanding of these same matters, such that the coming generation of filmmakers . . . will count among its numbers at least ten Grémillons and twenty Préverts. Perhaps even, who knows, another L'Herbier or a second Berthomieu. As I've said, I didn't have the luck to benefit from the teachings of such learned men. As circumstances allowed, I simply got to know Feyder, Renoir, Duvivier. They all have very different ideas; there's only one thing they all have in common: they don't profess any theory of directing or writing. They work by instinct. Feyder would often repeat Tristan Bernard's witticism, which amused him greatly: "Dramaturgy is an exact science of which no one knows the rules." Renoir claimed that "You could smell a good subject." . . . When you asked Duvivier about these serious matters he would invariably reply "Don't fuck me up." That's the training I got. And naturally I came to think, like all those who have received no solid education, that perhaps the right sort of instruction was not entirely indispensable. . . . There is no secret; there is no method.[93]

For him, all theory, all intellection is "so much rubbish." In what is very likely a direct reply to the protostructuralist attempts to identify how narratives are put together and characters constructed, he mentions mockingly the "script-generating machine" that Feyder had brought back from America. He describes the well-known dial and list game, where you spin the dial to choose at random the hero's job, spin it again for the heroine's, spin it again to decide where they'll meet, why their blossoming romance is thwarted and ultimately how they triumph over adversity. "Apprentice scriptwriters," he declaims ironically, "get hold of such a machine, or make one for yourself. You'll acquire thereby as much imagination as many professionals."[94]

These sarcastic comments clearly have as their effect the division of scriptwriters into two categories—the inferior, who construct their scripts according to generic rules, conventions, and formulas, and the superior, who depend on native inspiration and whose scripts are endowed with the necessary originality to attain the level of great art. "All great films break out of the strait-jacket in which theorists have tried to enclose the cinema," he concludes, committing himself to serve the cinema as chance, whim, humor, caprice, and his state of intoxication permit. Art transcends all attempts to define and understand it. If the scriptwriter was to establish his claim to authorship, he had to mystify the script-production process.

Breaking even their own single rule about there being no rules, however, all these leading scriptwriters propose from time to time some general principle around which their own practice cohered. In no case is this related to narrative, to action. By implication, action narratives belong to the realm of the inferior formulaic scriptwriters; the manuals that advocate them are worthy only of scorn. Telling a story is crucial, but it is also a trivial task, secondary either to the depiction of a milieu or to the exploration of character, and arising so automatically out of these that the scenarist does not have to work at it. Indeed, unlike the commentators and critics, these articulate scriptwriters tend to disdain narrative as "mere action," the stuff of the silent cinema before writers introduced into the trade a bare minimum of sophistication. "Proud of their technology for reproducing movement, silent filmmakers thought the cinema consisted of reproducing all that moved, ran, and galloped. Adapting a literary work was simply pointing up its exterior happening: fight scenes, and chases; dances, festivities, and parades; a dramatic accident, the turmoil of a shipwreck, a raging fire were not only the centrepiece of such films but their raison d'être." This was the "simplistic form" cinema took, according to Spaak, before authors came along to introduce "a few serious ideas, a little subtlety of feeling."[95]

The case for character-construction as the central task of the scriptwriter was most forcefully put by Pierre Bost. Discussing "brilliant" scripts with witty repartee as superficial and worthless, he saw complexity and subtlety in the characters as the main aim. "What counts is less the story than the characters. . . . This is one of the essential tasks of the dialoguist—telling a story is of minor interest. What is of interest is bringing characters to life. Only in this does the scenarist find himself on a level with the playwright and the novelist. Only in this does his job attain a certain worth, a certain nobility."[96] This was a frequently expressed position, often supported by the focus on particular actors and actresses. For character-centered scriptwriters it was essential to know for whom they were writing, and it was essential to feel a strong bond of sympathy with that star. Only then could they write him/her plausibly into the script. Aurenche and Jeanson both underline this,[97] Jeanson to the point of obsession in his autobiography:[98] Jouvet is an intimate friend, and with him the scripted character spontaneously takes on substance under Jeanson's pen and the narrative line evolves from this base. As soon as Arletty and Jouvet were accepted by the producer on *Hôtel du Nord*, their roles expanded and the storyline firmed up. For Raimu, Harry Baur, or Francen, on the other hand, he never felt able to write an appropriate role or a good script.

Similar views were put forward by Prévert, who loved writing for Jules

Berry, Michel Simon, Arletty, and Saturnin Fabre: "And actors, let's talk about them. . . . I've always written my stories for them alone . . . it's fantastic, acting . . . it's the only thing that interests me in the cinema . . . actors. I chose them . . . loved them . . . created characters for them."[99] Aurenche likewise notes that discussions with the director on the general direction of the script led to the fundamental question "will this suit Philippe Noiret, or do we have to rewrite the character and thus the story to fit him?" The same problem arose when writing for Gabin and Gérard Philipe, the former very sensitive about his screen image and anxious that character and plot accord with it, the latter more at ease with younger scriptwriters like Jacques Sigurd and René Wheeler than with someone twice his age. To some extent then, the focus on character as the primary consideration of the script arose from the fact that the industrial system often required the producer to engage a star if he was to ensure the distributor's financial support, and both distributor and star would only agree if the proposed role was appropriate to their (and the public's) expectations. But the prestige within the trade associated with credible psychological character construction was an equally powerful motive: in achieving it, scriptwriters saw themselves as matching other men of letters in plumbing the human heart and capturing great human truths. It made them filmic authors.

The alternative focus—on milieu—benefited from an analogous prestige. For Jeanson the only element of the original novel to have been retained in his script for *Hôtel du Nord* was the Canal St. Martin. It was a quarter of Paris with its own atmosphere, and what mattered was to exploit that atmosphere. Spaak puts the case for milieu most forcefully: reminiscing about his collaboration with Feyder he invariably returns to the map of France which they would use as a starting point for each script. "We both felt that the essential was not to tell a story . . . but to discover first of all the milieu in which [the narrative] would unfold. In every great film there is an element of the documentary which is absolutely crucial to it, and it's in this way that despite appearances the cinema is closely related to the novel and the theatre. . . . Filmmakers have produced their greatest works when depicting men and women of our time, coping with daily problems, in settings familiar to them."[100] To generate a script, Feyder and he would sit in front of a map, reviewing the sorts of stories that each region of France might be expected to generate. This is the way *Pension Mimosas* arose, he claims. In similar vein he recalls how, happening upon a famous retreat for superannuated actors, he said to himself, "There's a film in that!": "Without the least idea of what we were going to do with it, Duvivier and I went to visit the famous house . . . ,"[101] and the film that arose out of that particular setting was *La Fin du jour*.

Both of these principles—promoting character construction and documenting a milieu—are interesting in that they are so readily compatible with the myth of the artist at work—his superior perception, spontaneity, realism, human truths, and the gift of imagination which can recognize them. They thus correlate closely with debates in the forties about authorship and about documentary. But one unfortunate result of this tactic was the ridiculing of all systems of training which claimed to teach scriptwriting as a trade. This in turn led to a perpetuation of that lack regretted so often by commentators in the 1920s—no viable system of formation existed to produce a new generation of scriptwriters. Of the five major figures associated with the French classic cinema, all were born around the turn of the century, all acquired their initial and lasting cultural orientation in the cultural ferment of the 1920s and early 1930s, and all entered the cinema in an informal way, as an accidental byproduct of this broad cultural activity. Such schools as existed opted out of their responsibility, apparently convinced by the spokesmen of this clique that the task was impossible. Perhaps the only instance of a pragmatic alternative to these failed educational institutions was the master/apprentice approach developed by Jacques Companeez. At the time of his death in 1956, he was credited officially with some 360 scenarios written over 20 years. In fact, he had developed a "scenario factory" which functioned in much the same manner as a medieval craft workshop. His "apprentices" were numbers of young, indigent, aspirant scenarists. "[Companeez] furnished the primary material, the ideas, the links, the key situations, and his collaborators polished, wrote out, finished off. The young people learned their trade under his guidance. . . . He thus introduced into film circles a number of young people in whom no one would have had confidence; he protected them under his ensign, his experience, his solid working knowledge . . . when he felt they were sufficiently strong, he had them sign the script along with him; and when they had earned their wings, he sent them off to work independently."[102] Spaak's account makes clear the extent to which Companeez's productivity was linked to a protostructuralist approach to his craft:

> Companeez works all day and late into the night, at the center of a quite specific and typically filmic world. . . . Thirty-two cards repeatedly reshuffled and redistributed generate ever new surprises. . . . Here is the female international spy, always in quest of ultra-secret documents which diplomats and superior officers carry in their attaché cases; the female adventurer, always in search of a new piece of crookery to get hold of pearls and diamonds; the prostitute forced onto the streets out of love for her child, and the lovable young girl forced into the same trade by a deplorable set of circumstances. Here is the policeman . . . the disgusting drug trafficker; the forty-year-old, prey to a late affection; the worker who deserves a better lot [etc.]. These characters are written into the cinema's law of being. They are subject to a set of rules and laws which constitute the cinematic code. And all career about, exchanging kisses and gunfire, chasing one another by all known means of locomotion. . . . After these trials, the good are rewarded and the evil chastised. This whole ballet is acted out against a background of palaces and slums, snow and desert, backstage at the music hall or in the jungle. . . . It's a game. And why

should that not be entertaining when competently undertaken? All these characters have as much life as the Queen of Spades or the Jack of Hearts. They are the emblems of our time. And Companeez tirelessly shuffles and deals his thirty-two cards.[103]

Effective though this practice may have been, it categorized scriptwriting as a craft, consisting of techniques to be learned from an experienced master, rather than an art. As such it was unacceptable to the rest of the trade. Neither Spaak, Jeanson, Prévert, Aurenche, nor Bost acquired protégés in this fashion. For them, embattled independence was an essential element of the image of the author. They had themselves entered the cinema by the back door, and they expected others to have to do the same.

STAGES IN THE DEVELOPMENT OF A SCRIPT

It was no accident that claims concerning the preeminence of the scriptwriter should have been most forcibly voiced in the period 1945–1955. If sound had established theatrical script as a major source and thereby promoted the theatrical model of the scriptwriter as author, if Paramount's brief but forceful presence on the French scene had promoted the American mode of production in which the scriptwriter was as central as the director, it nevertheless remained the case throughout the thirties that most films were based on original scripts or on adaptations of novels that involved a radical modification of the original. Moreover, the genial anarchy that prevailed in much of the "industry" meant that the scriptwriter's task was by no means seen as the specialist competence of a specific category of cinematic personnel.

The war transformed this situation, when scripting procedures became incorporated in formal legislation during the German occupation. In 1942 to obtain a production visa and thus acquire the material wherewithal to proceed, a firm had to submit the completed *découpage* for censorship purposes to the Services du Cinéma. Although this soon became optional, its advisability was clear, since an exhibition visa was dependent on the completed film conforming to the criteria of the Services. At the beginning of 1944, a regulation required producers to submit to COIC, before even proceeding to the script development stage, 17 copies of the synopsis for the purposes of a precensorship on various criteria, notably "quality." The *découpage* and the dialogues were subsequently submitted for evaluation on criteria of morality.[104] These regulations ensured that each script necessarily had proceeded through clearly defined phases and had reached a fully dialogued form before filming began. They guaranteed that the generation of filmmaking personnel inducted into the profession during the war years would acquire the expectation that a script would pass through certain fixed stages, undergoing defined operations at the hands of distinct personnel.

That dramatic changes had taken place during the war years is evident from the radically different accounts of the scriptwriter's role provided in "how to do it" books of the period 1946–1950. Responding to the sudden increase in public interest in the cinema of the years 1946–1948, publishers produced a series of books in which commentators or scriptwriters themselves[105] explained the stages through which a script passed before being filmed. Magazines commissioned articles along the same lines, especially the *Ecran Français*. They are remarkably consistent in their accounts, and consistent also with accounts from ten years later.[106] The transformation in scriptwriting practices has been in the direction of systematization and specialization, with a regular series of stages of script development allocated to a range of specialized workers. In fact, during the sound period French scriptwriting practices moved steadily toward a more and more rigid, elaborate, and formalized set of procedures, precisely at a period when American practices were retreating from them.[107]

There were, characteristically, five stages listed in script development "manuals": the *synopsis*, the *traitement*, the *continuité*, the *dialogues* or *continuité dialoguée*, and the *découpage technique*. Frequently, mention is made of a prior "stage," the *idée de film* which might be an anecdote noted in a few lines or at most a few pages. Formally, the script came into existence when this was typed out as a 10–20-page synopsis. Since it was often in this form that it would reach the producer, the synopsis had to indicate sufficiently clearly what the dramatic possibilities of the subject were. It consisted essentially of a short narrative written in the present tense. Whether developed from an "original" idea or from a preexisting work— say, a novel of 300 pages—the first formal procedure in making it a script was to build up the idea or strip down the novel to this synopsis form.

Once the producer had "bought" the project, he commissioned the next stage, the *traitement*, which involved an elaboration of the synopsis into an extended prose narrative of some 30–50 typed pages. All major events in the narrative would be outlined by this stage, and the construction of the plot would be clearly defined. Little would have been done to indicate any of its specifically cinematic possibilities. French commentators speak of the American habit of commissioning several, perhaps many, treatments for a single film and choosing the most promising; but it is clear that in France only one such *traitement* was normally commissioned, a second or third being an admission that the first was judged inadequate.

The *continuité* was the moment when the specifically cinematic aspects of the plot began to be outlined. It involved the segmenting of the narrative events into "sequences," each with its dramatic center sketched in and its causal links defined, its mood outlined and its setting indicated. Rather than the American continuity script, it resembled the master-scene format. A norm of 9–13 sequences was expected (equivalent, as the commentators loved to say, to chapters in a book) and sometimes divided up into two or three larger plot units (acts), and 40–50 "scenes," each of two to three typed pages in length: the *continuité* might therefore look somewhat like a sketchy play, with bits of dialogue indicated, of some 80–100 pages in length.[108] It would contain as an introductory element a revised version of the synopsis, taking account of any modifications that had taken place, together with a list of the characters and of the décors. Sometimes the term *continuité* was distinguished from *découpage artistique*, where the latter term designated the presence of staging directions (mise en scène, décors) but not yet the technical directions.

At this stage the dialogue had to be elaborated more fully. A *continuité* with its dialogues completed might run to 100 or 125 pages. In the final stage, the *découpage technique*, technical indications (which had hitherto only been mentioned where they seemed essential to the sense of the film) were elaborated in some detail—camera positions, angles and movements, punctuation, lighting—the whole often accompanied by concise sketches of the overall setup for each individual shot. By this time, the script would be a minimum of 125 typed pages, and the various accounts (and surviving copies) suggest a norm of 150–200 pages.

As these accounts invariably underline, the complete five-stage process was not necessarily followed for every film. Sometimes there would be more like three stages—synopsis, *traitement* through *continuité dialoguée*, and *découpage technique*; and even if all five stages existed, they did not necessarily or even normally succeed one another temporally: each flowed into and overlapped with the next. The addition of dialogue in particular might well not be a separate stage, but an ongoing procedure beginning at the *traitement* stage and not being finally completed till shooting began (or even after). Consequently, the term for this fourth stage fluctuated more than did the others, from *adaptation* to *découpage artistique* to *continuité dialoguée*; many writers simply use a descriptive phrase such as "addition de dialogues." The term scenario itself was used for the whole process, but sometimes for the synopsis or *traitement* stages. The earliest of these postwar commentators, writing in the period 1944–1946, show particular uncertainty as to how to label the stages, as if the range of terms was still then being developed and had not yet firmed up. "Scenario, synopsis, adaptation," says *Style en France* in 1946, "continuity, dialogues, *découpage artistique, découpage technique*—this flurry of prestigious and recondite terms cluster around the work of that modest collaborator of the cinematic project, its creator. . . . Sometimes filmmakers themselves get confused by them, not to mention journalists and critics."[109] Bost (1946) labels the second stage indifferently *traitement, continuité, construction,* and *scénario,* while Daquin (1944) calls the third stage the *prédécoupage* and the IDHEC guide (1945) uses the term scenario for the third stage of the process. The correspondence course (1944) uses the vague term *deuxième ébauche* to describe that same stage.[110] By 1947, however, the vocabulary has acquired a considerable homogeneity.

Aside from the director, three distinct categories of personnel were involved in the five stages—the *scénariste*, the *adaptateur*, and the *dialoguiste*. These three categories of personnel corresponded to three distinct stages in the industrial process and were felt to involve three distinct sets of competences. In the first stage, the *scénariste* had to have the ability to recognize a potentially cinematic plot and to develop it in a concise but forceful way, so as to convince the producer to outlay money on it. The crucial central stage fell to the *adaptateur* who was commissioned by the producer to develop the *traitement* and the *continuité*—that is, to adapt what was still basically a literary work resembling a short story to the form of the *continuité*. The *dialoguiste* was required to expand the as yet rudimentary dialogue, in conjunction with scenarist and director, to the stage, where the director himself took over.

Because it represented the definitive blueprint of the final film, the production of the *découpage technique* itself was felt to be necessarily the responsibility of the director; and of the three other categories of worker it was the adapter (not the scenarist, where these are distinguished) who performed the crucial role. Talking of this triple specialization into scenarist, adapter, and dialoguist, the IDHEC guide to professional careers says, "A specialization for the diverse preliminary operations in the filmmaking process is sometimes advantageous and is often encountered in practice. Thus there exist *auteurs d'idées, scénaristes, adaptateurs, dialogueurs* and *découpeurs*." To this list it was later to add "gagmen,"[111] though the term was included largely in homage to the American industry, and few specialists in this category of work ever emerged in France. Maurice Henry is the only person mentioned as working almost exclusively at generating "gags," to liven up a script at its final (dialogue) stage.[112] The "auteurs d'idées" were not an industrial category as they were in America (the firm's readers) since the origin of the film idea might be indiscriminately the producer, a known or aspirant scenarist, a director, or an actor. It was fairly normal for a given film to credit the script to three to five individuals—for instance, two scenarists, of which one might have had the "original idea," an adapter, and two dialoguists. While the credits are of interest in indicating the scale of this collaborative work, however, they may well not provide an accurate account of who did what at what stage.

If it was normal to find multiple collaborations, it was also recognized that certain particularly talented scriptwriters might have the competence necessary to fulfill more than one of the three categories of work, and perhaps all of them. Jacques Prévert, Pierre Véry, Charles Spaak, and M. G. Sauvajon were known in the industry as being capable of this, but by 1947 it was considered a dangerous practice: "Often the two tasks [of adaptation and dialogues] are accorded to the one man, and very often this is a fault. Adaptations require technical competence. Dialogues require literary competence. There is, then, a priori, a fundamental antinomy between the two tasks." The duo of Aurenche and Bost regularly divided the task according to what they themselves recognized to be their quite distinct and compatible competences: Aurenche would concentrate on the adaptation, because of his ability to develop a confident narrative structure, and Bost would concentrate on the dialogues. Again, however, they developed a practice of constant consultation at all stages, so that rather than a sequential collaboration it was a question of one partner gradually phasing out as the other phased in. Nevertheless, it is clear that during the earlier years of their collaboration their roles were more distinct and sequential than they were later to become. "We used to write first of all the continuity, discussed with the director, the producer, and conceivably the actors, and only after that did we turn to the dialogues. Today [1979], once the 'novel' version is written [i.e., the *traitement*] I work by blocks, by scenes, by sequences."[113] Interviews with scriptwriters are full of such accounts of complicity and affinity, and they always underline in particular the need for a close collaboration with the director at all stages, so that he in turn does not simply receive a dialogued continuity totally developed by others, but rather supervises the whole process, participating to a greater extent as the script firms up, and taking over completely at the point where the *découpage technique* needs to be done. The extent of this collaboration was usually such that his name was included in the credits as sharing responsibility for the script development.

The accounts on which this summary is based can, however, be misleading, since even in mentioning it, they tend to understate the degree to which the division of labor was a reality in the French classic cinema. When the relevant interviews were recorded and the articles commissioned, it was principally that small group of 10–12 scriptwriters who had participated in the production of those films recognized as classics who were approached—indeed, most of the printed records relate to a very small côterie of writers—Prévert, Jeanson, Spaak, Aurenche, and Bost. There is every reason to see their practices as untypical, placing them at one extreme of a range of practices permitted by the system. At their end, as soon as a producer bought a subject and hired star(s), director, and writer(s), a core group (often including the producer and star(s)) would isolate themselves in some agreeable location to develop the script to continuity stage. Interaction and collaboration were so intimate as to make any subsequent allocation of credit a mere formality. At the other extreme, and probably far more common if less often described, lay the total division of labor in which a scenarist was commissioned to develop a treatment and delivered it to the producer, who commissioned him or another to adapt it; this in turn was delivered to the producer, at which point it passed to a dialoguist, and he in turn worked on it for the few weeks before shooting, or sometimes phoning in the day's dialogues the night before. In this more divided practice, producer, star(s), and even director would play little or no role, the producer merely retaining the right at each deadline to proceed or refuse to proceed with the process.

In his account of scriptwriting published in 1949, Spaak outlines clearly the two types of practices. He talks of

> the desirability that scriptwriter(s) and director should have a common point of view on the subject matter of the prospective film. It's at this point that they acquire communally their status as author, and I insist on this point: they undertake together a similar task. A stupid debate seeks to set them up as undertaking in the creative process activities which are complementary—which is to say, different—when they are of the same kind and exercised in parallel. In fact, two friends whose sensibilities and backgrounds are similar sit down at the same table; . . . *Mettre en scène* is just that: in continual material difficulties, continually defending the sense of a film, that intended meaning, planned patiently, developed by two people who are good friends. No worthwhile film could come of the association of a scriptwriter and a director who have no respect for one another. Anyway, how are all the best films born? Always of the simultaneous engagement of a scenarist and a director who at that point have no idea in the world what they are going to produce. They head off to some peaceful spot [suitable for their task]. . . . That this way of going about things is rare doesn't prevent it from being excellent, and the fact that it's rarely employed may well explain the number of execrable films. What usually happens, on the contrary? A producer buys the rights of a play or a novel for a given star. The director whom that star approves of as a result of having met him on the skifields or in a nightclub designates the scriptwriter he would like to work with. That happy author . . . accepts with joy, replies that he'll be free from 23 September at 10:20 till 28 October at 5:40. . . . He sets to work, all alone, and delivers on the due date a manuscript of 150 pages, written in two columns with 50 sequences harmoniously organized.[114]

Leprohon outlines the same extremes of practice as Spaak. He himself had been present at the preparation of a film directed by Christian-Jacque, to a scenario by Pierre MacOrlan adapted by Sauvajon for Simone Renart to star in. "One fine day in June, everyone [arrived at] St. Cyr sur Morin and set up in Pierre MacOrlan's little house bathed in sun and set in lush greenery. . . . Between boating parties and telling far-fetched stories they spoke of the film, discussing the characters (etc.) Everyone had their word to say: the scriptwriter, the director, the star. . . . A film is prepared far from Paris in the peace of the countryside. Marcel Carné, Jacques Prévert, and Pierre Laroche follow the same method. But alas, such a meticulous preparation doesn't take place for all films."[115] And he goes on to describe productions in which the division of labor, handled sequentially, has led to crises as one stage unfinished produces a domino effect, until "a dialoguist engaged at the last moment" desperately attempts to produce an adequate text for the impatient director.

Leprohon, likening one end of the range to the U.S. process where a director (described by Duvivier as usually being no more than an executant, an illustrator) simply follows an inflexibly programmed *découpage* provided by the script team, sees French cinema as best advised to look to the other extreme: "a fusion [needs to] be established, or at least an ever closer contact between the adapter of the scenario and the director. This is assuredly the best method for making a film a work of art."[116] If the one extreme could justify its procedures in terms of the coherence and integrity which was assumed desirable in a work of art, the other could defend its procedures in terms of cost efficiency. After all, the "desirable" collaboration locked all members of the script-development team—all the highest-paid members of the team, that is—into an extended period of communal work where each might otherwise have been able to work sequentially in the given time on several other films. Instead they were paid to go on boating parties and sunbathe on the grounds of country houses. Producers in a highly critical financial situation could not normally have condoned the development of such inefficient practices. Paradoxically, it was the anomalous and unpleasant circumstances of the war, and of a guaranteed profitability for all films, that produced the conditions permitting this idyllic set of practices for the elite among the scriptwriters.

To quote a final example, Chartier and Desplanques in 1950 likewise talk of the director as quitting Paris with its insistent telephoning and demands: "He heads off for some weeks to a peaceful little hotel, or some country house. He doesn't work there alone, but in a team with the scenarist who has written the story and with the dialoguist. These three collaborators are mutually complementary . . . the scenarist may sometimes write the dialogues; but it takes a very particular talent to find the right words for characters."[117]

At the more collaborative end of the range, where cooperation between scriptwriter(s) and director was so intense and interaction so continuous from an early stage that questions of individual authorship were totally inapplicable, the French cinema developed a series of "tandems," involving recurrent collaboration between scriptwriter and director over a number of films. These arose in the early thirties with the Spaak/Feyder collaboration, and the most celebrated of them was the Prévert/Carné collaboration between 1936 (*Jenny*) and 1950 (*La Marie du Port*), but which included at least two other such collaborations on the part of Spaak—with Grémillon in the forties and with Cayatte around 1950—and other lesser-known instances: Jeanson/Duvivier, Christian-Jacque/Pierre Véry, Jacques Becker/ Pierre Véry, Jacques Sigurd/Yves Allégret, Jean Ferry/H.-G. Clouzot. Perhaps the longest such collaboration was that between the Aurenche-Bost duo and Claude Autant-Lara. Beginning with the Aurenche/Autant-Lara tandem on *Le Mariage de Chiffon* (1942) and becoming a trio with *Douce* (1943), this collaboration had resulted in 24 films by 1969 at a steady rate of one per year.

But if practices fluctuated from the businesslike sequentiality of divided labor to the slightly orgiastic chaos of an interactive houseparty, such that people within the system could only repeat, "There are no fixed rules, nor well-defined methods in the current confection of films,"[118] retrospectively it is clear that a radical transformation had taken place in the French cinema's approach to this process: no one in 1947–1950 would have denied that it was a collaborative process, involving multiple competences, usually shared among many individuals, who contributed to the development of a clearly distinguishable series of stages in the production process, all or most of which severally fed into one another and were cumulatively an essential prerequisite of any actual filming process. None of those who thought of themselves as scriptwriters—even those who had proved themselves capable at one time or another of performing the whole sequence of roles, would have been surprised to be called on to write, or to help to write, just the dialogues; to adapt or to help to adapt a script synopsis. Indeed, the division of labor had become so specialized that it seemed reasonable to suppose it would proceed even further: "The cinema needs to produce even more specialist collaborators: a dialoguist is not identically excellent in all genres. If today we allot a peasant drama and a murder mystery to the same writer, it's because good dialoguists are rare. But their talents are not universal. We need to create dialoguists [for specific tasks]."[119] The French cinema was at this time at its nearest approach to the classic Hollywood model; and this makes more comprehensible Truffaut's outburst of critical spleen against a scriptwriter's cinema in the notorious *Cahiers* article of 1954.

A DIRECTOR'S CINEMA

The producer-package system as practiced in France allowed for a high degree of directorial control over the production process. Indeed, in the vast majority of cases and throughout the classic period, whenever the discourse of art is mobilized by film critics it has as its focus the person of the artist-director. As we have seen, in appropriating that status, the director had to defend his territory against the claims, whether explicit or implicit, of both producer and scriptwriter. He also had to demonstrate that he had indeed exercised effective control over the other key personnel—actors, set designer, cinematographer, editor, and musician—whose work cumulatively constructed the aesthetic style of the resultant film.

These territorial claims were particularly contentious for the director of the classic period precisely because it was the introduction of sound which constricted in certain key ways the hitherto omnipresent authority of the director. It was the pressure of increased finance that promoted the figure of the producer, the urgent need for detailed written scripts that promoted the scriptwriter, and the increase in specialist technological competences which began to lend autonomy to the work of various other key personnel.

It was also at this stage, during the early thirties, that an administrative and financial agent of the producer called the director of production was introduced into the production process in order to relieve the director of some of his administrative responsibilities and to look after the producer's financial interests. He assumed control over personnel such as floor managers and props personnel, who ensured that the objects, sets, and costumes were available when needed (previously the director's responsibility). In the twenties, the director had had an assistant whose ill-defined delegations had included the supervision of these processes. It was the director's assistant, therefore, who had drawn up the list of items and costumes needed, the shooting schedule and décors needed, had selected secondary actors, had organized transport and supply for location shooting, and often had monitored in a necessarily nonspecialist way the film's conformity to the budget. The floor manager and props department had merely implemented the practical aspects of these tasks.[120] But as sound production complicated budgets and schedules, it became more organizationally efficient to have a specialist administrator to perform the supervision. Cavalcanti noted the "markedly diminished role" of the director once the post of director of production had become established.[121] Effectively, in relieving him of all day-to-day practical responsibilities, the director of production contributed to etherealizing the director's own role, such that it once more became easiest to conceptualize it primarily in aesthetic terms.

Another factor tending in the same direction was the introduction of the scriptgirl. Only with the elaboration of scripts in the sound era—indeed, only with the increased emphasis on realism that developed at the same time—did the question of conformity to the written script and continuity between shots, filmed perhaps days apart, become crucial. By 1933, largely under the influence of the Paramount production system at St. Maurice,[122] the scriptgirl had become an indispensable assistant to the director, always at his side watching for factors that might create technical problems during editing and perhaps necessitate retakes.

Despite the reduction in his functions, the French director, like most of his European counterparts, retained a considerably greater degree of control over the production process than his contemporary in Hollywood, hired on a long-term contract by a firm whose producers retained the determining say over most of the operational decisions. As Cavalcanti noted, "In the American industry, the director for the most part simply receives a detailed *découpage technique*, and confines himself almost exclusively to the direction of actors; whereas in Europe the direction of actors represents a minute part of his work."[123] The same contrast was made by all French directors who had, for whatever reasons, attempted to work in Hollywood— Feyder in 1932, René Clair and Duvivier in the forties. Quoting them, Sadoul specifies the differences in terms borrowed from Frank Capra: "In the studio, 80–85% of [U.S.] directors are the slaves of a script they have not helped to develop, and they never modify the *découpage* delivered to them. The rehearsal of each scene is undertaken not by his assistants but by dialogue directors, whose responsibility is to the producer rather than to him. Specific types of scenes (battles, fights, chases) are left to specialists (second units) whose work he does not supervise. Moreover, he ceases to have any role after the last day of shooting: editing is not his responsibility. At best, he is permitted a few observations when the copy of the film considered satisfactory is screened for him."[124]

Because the limited role which most American directors were seen as playing likened them to theatrical directors, or *metteurs en scène*, French directors early attempted to impose a more ambitious term to describe their own more important role, extending from the hiring of personnel through to the final cut. Canudo had proposed *écraniste*, L'Herbier promoted *metteur en film*; the word *cinéaste* had some of the right connotations but acquired too general a meaning, referring to anyone passionately involved in film. Already promoted in the twenties, the term *réalisateur*, or bringer-into-being of the work, competed with the more current phrase *metteur en scène* for some decades and finally achieved normal currency in the late forties with the resurgence of an artistic discourse on the cinema which lent it credibility.

The debate as to whether French directors could be described as authors—and if so, which ones could be so described—was further complicated by the fact that in individual cases this normal range of directorial duties was considerably exceeded. Even when it was not, of course, the least regarded director in France enjoyed the degree of control and decision making enjoyed by the most favored 10–15% of directors in Hollywood. When it *was* exceeded, the increased control tended to lend weight to claims for individual authorship. Various anomalous instances, limited to specific films, are indicative of the possibilities. The producer Pierre Braunberger directed with the film editor Myriam a film on bullfighting (*La Course de taureaux*, 1951), a subject long dear to his heart; the actor Gérard Philipe directed a German coproduction of Till Eulenspiegel (*Les Aventures de Till l'espiègle*, 1956); Jean Mitry, better known as a critic, but frequently a film editor, directed one film; the scriptwriter Henri Jeanson directed one of his own scripts (*Lady Paname*, 1949–1950) as did Charles Spaak (*Le Mystère Barton*, 1948–1949), while René Wheeler directed three (notably *Premières armes*, 1949–1950), and Marc-Gilbert Sauvajon no less than five, between 1948 and 1951. Various theatrical playwrights and actors did likewise (Marcel Achard in 1935, 1948, and 1949; Jean Anouilh in 1943 and 1951; Pierre Blanchar in 1942 and 1943; Fernandel in 1942, 1943, and 1951; Pierre Fresnay in 1939; Louis Jouvet in 1933; René Lefèvre in 1941, codirecting with Claude Renoir; Noël-Noël in 1950). We might also remember André Malraux's venture into direction with *Sierra de Teruel* (1938–1945), usually known by the title of its novelistic version, *L'Espoir*. Such movement between roles and between media leading to the accumulation of functions became more common after 1960, but even in the classic period it often gave rise to claims for increased authorial status.

As isolated or occasional ventures, however, these examples are not in themselves sufficient evidence for a claim that the French classic cinema regularly allowed for extended directorial control over production. Such a claim is better founded on the careers of established directors who frequently, or usually, or always undertook the functions of other members of the core team.

The most contentious of these was scriptwriting, since most scriptwriters, being either playwrights or novelists, were already *auteurs* in the more conventional sense of the term, and since their script could be seen as determining the thematic organization of the resultant film. The director who was closest to his Hollywood counterpart in "merely illustrating" the script provided him by a professional author was regarded with great contempt. Most directors avoided the accusation in that they could claim to have appropriated the initial script when they carried out the *découpage technique*. This allowed them rather dubiously to claim shared authorship of it in the film's credits, which they regularly did. The obvious way to counter all such accusations, however, was for the director to write his own "original" scripts. It had been common throughout the twenties, as both Coissac and Arnoux note, for the director to be "his own translator, having himself conceived the idea and developed the appropriate form."[125] During the classic period, Cocteau was regularly acknowledged as belonging to this category of authorial directors. It was René Clair, however, who was most frequently referred to in these terms, for instance by Charles Ford in *On tourne lundi*: "The truly great authors have always been those directors who brought to the screen their own subjects (Méliès, Chaplin, Stroheim, Clair, Renoir, and soon no doubt Grémillon, Becker, Bresson) or perfect teams of scenarist and director (Carné/Prévert, Autant-Lara/Aurenche, Becker/Véry, Duvivier/Jeanson); but the future lies with the former."

In fact, although it was common to speak of Renoir and Grémillon in these terms, only the last of Renoir's prewar films—*La Règle du jeu*—was scripted by himself from largely original material, and Grémillon was never to be able to bring to the screen his own scripts. In the thirties and forties large numbers of theatrical writer/directors had moved into film directing (Yves Mirande, Jean Stelli, later Carlo-Rim, Jean Anouilh, Yvan Noë, Fernand Rivers, and Marcel Achard), and had thus technically qualified to a greater extent than Renoir or Grémillon for the title of author. Instead, they were usually attacked as too theatrical, only Marcel Pagnol and Sacha Guitry being accorded a somewhat ambivalent recognition. In the postwar years and long before the *Cahiers* call for such procedures, it was common enough to be unremarkable for directors to be working with a script which they had themselves written (or at least had themselves adapted from a novel or play). In the seven-year period 1945–1951 when about eighty directors were filming each year and the total number with work cards was about 180, a minimum of fifty of them had so worked, many of them never to be recognized as "authors"—François Campaux, Théophile Pathé, Alfred

Rode, Robert Dhéry, Maurice Boutel, Léopold Gomez, and innumerable others.[126] Several of the established directors had long been accustomed from time to time to write their own scripts and continued to do so during this period—Pierre Billon, André Berthomieu, Jean-Paul Le Chanois (notably *L'Ecole buissonnière*, 1948–1949), Henri Decoin, Pierre Chenal, Albert Valentin, Roger Richebé, Jean Boyer, Maurice Cloche, Serge de Poligny, as well as the theatrical group already mentioned; so had those directors who had begun in the silent era when such practices were normal—Gance, L'Herbier, Léon Poirier, and on occasion Julien Duvivier. Cumulatively, this amounts to about 25% of the directors working during those seven years. So when they began directing their own scripts at war's end, such directors as René Clément (*La Bataille du rail*, 1945), André Cayatte (*Le Dernier Sou*, 1943–1946; *Le Dessous des cartes*, 1947–1948; *Les Amants de Vérone*, 1948–1949, etc.), Becker (*Rendez-vous de juillet*, 1949), Rouquier (*Farrebique*, 1944–1946), Leenhardt (*Les Dernières Vacances*, 1947–1948), Boissol (*Toute la ville accuse*, 1955–1956), Jacqueline Audry, Jacques Tati, Nicole Védrès, André Zwobada (and later Astruc, Varda, and Vadim) were not breaking new ground at all. It has to be recognized, therefore, that while it was more common for nearly all of the above directors to work with scripts mostly or completely developed by others, the possibility of authorial production by this criterion of a single scriptwriter-director was very common throughout the classical period.

Once the French director's claim to have originated or appropriated the script had been established, however, he had still to establish himself like his Hollywood counterpart as responsible for its performance and for its recording. The performance of the actors was of course crucial to the representation of the theme and to the style and pace of the resultant narrative. The actors were also for most of the classic period more readily and widely acknowledged by the public than were the directors. The question of relations between director and actor were therefore extremely contentious. Accounts of the directors' relations with their actors are usually organized within one of two alternative paradigms—of cooperation or of domination/subordination. On the one hand there were directors who respected the professionalism of their actors, accepted their suggestions, allowed their performance to evolve with no more than tactful guidance, and then organized the technical practices of cinematography around the resultant performance; and on the other hand there were directors who had a meticulous, even dictatorial preconception as to what they wanted of the performance, avoided professional actors where possible because their opinionated arrogance might make them less malleable, then manipulated, even tortured, those actors until the desired performance and images had been attained.[127]

The names usually associated with these opposed positions were Renoir and Bresson. For Renoir, the job of the actor was to astonish him by what (s)he could bring to the role. Nothing was finally determined in advance: "[At the moment of filming] a terrifying phenomenon occurs: in the presence of the actors and the settings I realize that all I've done and written is worthless; I realize that a bit of dialogue I thought full of vitality, once said by an actor who brings it to his own personality, is meaningless; in fact, I realize I have to blend my own personality with that of the actor."[128] "What happens with great actors [is that] they bring to the surface dreams one has had but had never quite formulated. In reality, it's the eternal mystery of creation. There arrives a moment when one is no longer oneself responsible for this creation, when it escapes you, and the great actor is a great actor in proportion as (s)he escapes you and in escaping you, nevertheless brings into existence those dreams you had had, and reveals them to you."[129]

In thus respecting the input of the actors, Renoir saw himself as working in the tradition of Molière and Shakespeare, who wrote for their troupe.[130] He was always ready to modify at a late stage whole scripts to include an actor who had interested him. This willingness to "improvise" could readily be assimilated to the mythic spontaneity of the true artist, and further enhanced Renoir's authorial status. Directors of this persuasion, with the nerve to modify and adapt their plans up to and during the hour preceding shooting in order to exploit the personality and capacity of the actors, were necessarily rare in a cinema always uncomfortably aware of financial pressures and after 1940 required to conform to an officially approved synopsis; Simone Signoret speaks of Feyder as having a genius for it and of Jacques Becker as inheriting the understanding of his master Renoir.[131]

Bresson, on the other hand, typified the director for whom the actor was according to various accounts merely an object, "clay in the director's hands," just another element of mise en scène, an ingenious robot, a mannequin capable of speech, at best a child or animal to be patiently instructed. It was of such directors that Sadoul said (in a section entitled "actors and trained animals"), "They employ actors as musical instruments, requiring only that they produce—consciously or not—the right note, to be incorporated later as an element of the wider symphony."[132] Abroad, Leslie Howard, Hitchcock, and Pudovkin had all indicated a degree of adherence to such a policy, and Antonioni admired Bresson for taking it to extremes. Like Dreyer, torturing Falconetti into a performance as Jeanne d'Arc, but using the more malleable material of nonprofessional actors, Bresson implemented what could only seem an obsessive and dictatorial régime, imposing on the brute matter of his actors (or, as some would more generously assert, drawing out of them) a performance of which they were considered unable to comprehend the significance.[133]

Clouzot, likewise, was notorious for his determination to mold an actor into the desired performance at any cost, not stopping short of striking them. With "reputable" theatrical actors (especially males) like Jouvet and Fresnay, Clouzot was more discreet, relying on their professionalism. With less professional actors, especially females, whom he considered unable to achieve the required performance on their own, he would trick, cajole, and bully them until they achieved it. Describing his practices on the set of

Manon (1948–1949), Leprohon says, "the young girl was required to kneel in prayer and begin to sob. [Clouzot] took Cécile Aubry in his arms, spoke to her in a low voice, his nose buried in the blond hair tumbling about her shoulders. She listened, doubtless moved, her eyes dry. Clouzot stepped back a little, still holding her, but his voice was raised, intense, violent. . . . He struck her several times. Her arm raised to protect herself, she was now just a sobbing child—not Cécile Aubry acting, but Manon, in despair. . . . 'Right, start filming,' Clouzot said, and the machine recorded her. This example is far from unique. 'I haven't the time to muck about,' Clouzot told me. 'That character she's supposed to be acting, it's essential it come into being, whatever the cost.' "[134] At the cost, for instance, of reminding his Jewish actors about the way Hitler treated Jews or feeding real rotten fish to his actors in *Les Diaboliques.* As Leprohon said, "Where his actors are unable to simulate, he makes them experience." What mattered was the achievement of a minutely preconceived end, from which no variation could be permitted.

Partly because of the threat to acting as a profession, and partly to defend the dignity of the actor as an individual, the Actors' Union became involved in a campaign to oppose such practices. In a 1956 trade journal it inserted an announcement saying, "If certain actors want to become mere objects . . . that's their business; they represent a sort of robot whose use in the cinema is in the limit tolerable; but to try in the name of some naive vanity or crazy arrogance to impose on an actor . . . a tone, a gesture, a thought which he finds unacceptable, that is inadmissible. If an actor of talent must adapt to that unity indispensable to a work of art, in the measure that he adapts to it so must his art itself be respected. . . . Between director and actor there can only be one valid sort of relationship: mutual understanding."[135] For most actors, as for most directors, an amiable compromise was possible: between Renoir, who allowed his actors to develop their performance and then rethought his technique according to it, and Bresson or Clouzot, who tyrannized them into achieving a minutely predetermined performance, the more common if less dramatic norm was for the director to evoke the general context and tone of the scene, to have his assistant mark out the general area of movement, then monitor the actor's conformity to the intended text and gesture. Frequently, the director would mime the scene in advance and advise the actors between rehearsals of desired modifications. Rehearsals of the technical aspects (camera, lighting, sound) would follow those of the acting, finally being combined with them.

The degree to which the director took account of these technical aspects and of the editing which followed them also constituted a significant variation within the system, and one which fed into the definition of the artist-author. At one extreme, the more theatrical directors were inclined to see their role as largely concluded once the performance was satisfactory. The same story was told of both Pagnol and Guitry by those technicians who worked with them: once the actor's performance was acceptable, they would say to the technicians, "Now, record that for me." In such cases each scene would normally be recorded several times by the cameramen, from different distances and with different lenses. Suzanne de Troyes was left by Pagnol to undertake the editing of the numerous parallel recordings as she saw fit, with no input from the director.[136] It is easy to believe that the other "theatrical" directors—Yves Mirande, Berthomieu, Louis Verneuil, Roger Ferdinand, Bernard Zimmer, Michel Duran, Pierre Colombier, Maurice Cammage, René Guissart, Léo Joannon—were likewise normally or exclusively interested in the performance. It was this disinterest in the specifically cinematic aspects of filmmaking that alone inhibited commentators from according the title of "film author" to either Guitry or Pagnol, though Pagnol in particular qualified under every other criterion. Because neither was at all preoccupied by technical matters, neither worked to or even prepared a *découpage technique*. While it could scarcely be said that Renoir was disinterested in technique, he was at that end of the spectrum where the procedures specified on the *découpage technique* were sacrificed to the discovery of the moment. Where possible, he would avoid producing a *découpage technique*, preferring to work directly from the more schematic continuity script. Louis Page described Feyder's procedures in somewhat similar terms:

> I was a little disoriented by Feyder's way of filming. Of course there did exist a *découpage technique* like any other, but if while filming he referred to it, it was rather to check a bit of dialogue than to remind himself of the proposed techniques written down there. The numbered shots were just guidelines for him, and I rarely saw him in dialogued sequences follow his initial *découpage*.
>
> Without the least worry about the placing of the camera, and contrary to normal practice, which was to outline the limits of the scene of action, Feyder would have the actors rehearse a section of the sequence, and occasionally the whole sequence, without giving them any indication, but leaving them total freedom. If I asked him now and then to give me some idea what was going to happen, he would reply, "For the moment, all we know is that they're going to come in by that door.". . . During this first rehearsal, the actors, free to do as they wanted and without any predetermined movements, carried away by the action often ended up scattered about the set. Then Feyder would move in, and he was marvellous. Of this first outline he had noted not only what needed keeping but also what was latent in it, potentially. [So] on the second rehearsal he knew exactly where he would place the midshots, the closeups, the reverse shots; but he still didn't determine the place of the camera. Only in subsequent rehearsals, which he followed moving around the set, examining the action from different angles, did he decide on that.
>
> To see him working, you would have thought he was constantly improvising, and that he had arrived on the set without any clear idea of what he was going to do; but that was only in appearance.[137]

For such directors, the moment of creativity was seen as the performance itself. Most directors preferred to see the production of the *découpage technique* as the moment of creativity and the performance as merely its implementation. This was true in the thirties of Duvivier and of René Clair, whose practices were early contrasted with those of Renoir and Feyder, and it became progressively more and more the case in the subsequent two decades. Because it bespoke a preoccupation with planning, and because it was often defended in the name of economics and of efficiency, this domination of the *découpage technique* over the moment of performance was readily ascribed, pejoratively, to the mere technician, the workmanlike director who got things done but who lacked imagination. It was the source of much ambivalence about the authorial status of Duvivier, of Clouzot, of Becker, of Autant-Lara, of Daquin, and of René Clair himself, whose assertion that, "When I have finished writing the *découpage*, my film is made" foreshadowed Hitchcock's similar assertion. Clair would normally take about a year to work out and develop his scenario—as would Bresson when he began writing his own scenarios in the fifties—one year for *Un condamné*, six months for *Pickpocket*. By contrast, Melville claims to have written the *découpage technique* and dialogues of *Deux Hommes dans Manhattan* in some three hours, between 1.00 A.M. and 4.00 A.M. one morning.[138] Partly, the difference was between directors like Clair with a literary formation, who saw the scenario stage as an intrinsically aesthetic activity in itself, and those without such a formation.

From the end of the war onward, however, the detailed and prescriptive *découpage* was almost universal; the standard advice to aspiring directors, as purveyed both by practitioners and by IDHEC was that "you can't afford to improvise on the set."[139] Details might be modified, but changes were costly and the coherent "vision" possible when working in tranquillity on a *découpage* was likely to be lost in ad hoc improvizations. The air of "genial chaos" and "spontaneity" for which Renoir had been appreciated in the thirties now seemed suspect: a visitor can tell immediately when a director is no good by the "fairground atmosphere" prevailing during shooting.[140] Yves Allégret is praised for his customary precision, which is unvarying even in exteriors, whatever the contingencies of an unknown region. Clouzot is praised for preparing his films with "a watchmaker's meticulousness." Nothing is left to chance. "When he arrives on the set . . . he has visualized his film and predefined each image. This method is dictated by his drive for precision; it is possible because he knows exactly what he wants."[141] Speaking of problems with lighting, Michel Kelber contrasts L'Herbier unfavorably with Duvivier: "The problem was that certain directors kept changing their minds. Marcel L'Herbier, not to name anyone in particular, made a speciality of last-minute modifications. On the other hand, Duvivier showed an astonishing precision: even before placing his actors, he could tell you where he wanted the camera, the dimensions of the support and the type of lens . . . he had it all in his head."[142] He speaks of Autant-Lara as similarly meticulous and insistent about achieving predetermined ends.

Indeed, the case for such a course of action was put most emphatically (and most frequently) by Autant-Lara:

> A studio is not an appropriate place for creativity—it's where you implement your ideas. The text must be written in advance—the image too—and everything is conceived *before* the filming stage. The creation takes place beforehand. That avoids blind groping.
> But what about inspiration?
> Do you think a studio atmosphere, the feverish state of shooting, with 250 actors, orders, and counterorders and fatigue is propitious for inspiration? Don't you think that you'll do better, a few of you around a table, with a jug of fruit juice, some cigarettes, and time to explore ideas at leisure, on paper, and sleep on them, and discuss in the morning whether they need changing, without losing a day's work? Don't you think that's a better atmosphere for creativity? . . . There's no better inspiration than that which is long in preparation, especially for a film. A story like my present one involves hundreds of millions of francs. You realize what that means? Can you imagine an architect saying, "Right, send 800 m of beams, 3 tons of cement, 30 truckloads of timber, and I'll see what I can knock together for you. . . . Some geniuses can manage it on the spur of the moment, but they're few and far between; and with a little more method they'd be no less a genius; they'd just waste less money and sweat.[143]

The preceding observations allow a number of conclusions: the degree of control aimed for by different directors varied considerably; the degree of control achieved in individual films by any one director varied considerably; commonly made claims for authorship based on this degree of control are often indefensible; many directors for whom no such claims were ever made deserved mention. Of the 530 directors active between 1929 and 1958, some 100 were not content with just directing, but aimed to control most or all major decisions in the areas of scriptwriting, acting and/or the technical practices of filming (set design, cinematography, editing and music composition). A smaller number aimed at the even greater degree of independence permitted, at least in theory, by the director-package system.

THE EXPRESSIVE MYTH

The question of authorial control is often conflated, by way of naive assumptions concerning the enduring unity and coherence of the self, creatively expressed in the author's *oeuvre*, with an assumption concerning the thematic and/or stylistic coherence of the author's output. Yet, while the classic French cinema allowed of a relatively high degree of directorial control, most attempts to identify the expected textual coherence that should result from that degree of control are characterized by an embarrassing bad faith. It would be futile to attempt to recapitulate the literature devoted to such studies of directors, their lives, personalities, and intentions as realized in their works. On the whole, this expressivity has been sought only in texts deemed of superior quality, which has further confused the debate, since there is no necessary connection between expressivity and quality. A director in total control of production may still express trivial views with a high degree of incompetence. Nevertheless, the correlations have been attempted primarily at the art-cinema end of the French classic cinema spectrum and have been contrasted with the more popular commercial end of the spectrum, seen as employing conventional technical means in order to recycle conventional views of the world. In Jakobson's terms, little attempt at correlation has been made in the case of texts where the phatic has been dominant (entertainment), or where the referential has been dominant (in the sense of standard representations of the world which allow the audience to read the diegesis in an unproblematic way). Correlations have been attempted primarily in cases where the expressive was dominant (or its adjunct the directive) or where the poetic was dominant (or its adjunct the metalinguistic).

Such attempted correlations have many difficulties to overcome. The fact that Grémillon was a passionately committed socialist is largely invisible in the films he managed to direct; very little of Daquin's aggressive social commitment comes through in his films; the passion to see justice done which is often represented as at the origin of several films directed by Cayatte in the fifties is largely invisible in his other films; and to claim that René Clair was attempting to express anything at all in his films is to misunderstand them. Similarly, no thematic or stylistic unity is apparent in the films directed by Renoir: some but not all of his films between 1935 and 1939 relate to the Popular Front; most of his postwar films promote a vaguely reactionary pantheism; others from throughout the classic period are totally apolitical, implying support either for an anarchistic amoralism or a romantic glorification of the artist. All of these themes are common to many other texts of the period, where they are sometimes attributed to directorial self-expression and sometimes to social and political determinants.

Often the expressivity of a text can more confidently be connected to the scriptwriter than to the director, or at least to collective authorship dominated by the scriptwriter. Yves Allégret was widely credited with an absurdist and existentialist outlook on the basis of four postwar films (*Dédée*, 1948; *Une si jolie petite plage*, 1948; *Manèges*, 1949; *Les Orgueilleux*, 1953), but all these were scripted by Jacques Sigurd, and their subsequent work suggests that Sigurd's worldview was dominant. *L'Air de Paris*, directed by Carné in 1954 to a script by Sigurd, is full of existentialist references of a sort not found elsewhere in Carné's work. Indeed, Carné is likewise credited on occasion with an expressive role, but the sets of ideas and attitudes structuring his films are so radically different once he ceases to collaborate with Prévert that again it seems likely that the scriptwriters were dominant. And while it is true that Cayatte's legal background is important to the casebook films of the fifties, it is also true that they are all scripted by Charles Spaak, whose humanist outlook had been consistently present in his scripts for many other directors before Cayatte. The specifically legal aspect of these films, however, would seem to call for a correlation with the lawyer-director Cayatte, making him an authentic 'auteur.' Interestingly enough, *Cahiers du Cinéma* categorically refused him this status, summarizing the films as "a lawyer's special pleading rather than works of art, [they] escape aesthetic judgment and critical appreciation as objects of beauty. Cayatte defended these ideas as he defended his clients— by addressing the gallery. Hence a series of procedures and eccentricities which perhaps have a polemic value but have no relevance to the art of film. [His next film] *Oeil pour oeil*, filmed entirely on location and without any such thesis, will be devilishly revealing: are we to learn at last who Cayatte is, now that like all authentic creators he is speaking *first of all* for himself?"[144] Perhaps, for the *Cahiers* of the 1950s, Cayatte's ideas were uncomfortably leftwing; but it is also true that too evident a social commitment was incompatible with the myth of the transcendent artist.

No director was promoted to the canon for strong and consistent political commitment. Le Chanois, for instance, was disregarded, despite the fact that his films manifest a constant preoccupation with the day-to-day problems encountered by workers and the poor. Such a claim cannot be made of any other French classic director with the exception of Claude Autant-Lara. The films to which his name is attached are consistently provocative and anti-authoritarian, attacking the established values of church and state. His anarchism was most often thought of as leftwing during the classic period because of the frequency of his attacks on the hypocrisy of the bourgeoisie, though the adaptation of *La Traversée de Paris* (1956) and *La Jument verte* (1959), based on the work of that right-wing anarchist Marcel Aymé, foreshadowed his much later alliance with the National Front. Again, all or nearly all of the films directed by Autant-Lara were based on scripts by Aurenche and Bost, whose anti-establishment orientations coincided with his own. While this further supports an argument for expressivity's being related more directly to scriptwriters than to directors in the classic period, it is nevertheless the case that certain directors with sufficient status were able, if they wished the films they directed to remain true to a consistent worldview, to impose on often unwilling producers the choice of appropriate texts and appropriate scriptwriters.

Autant-Lara is also exceptional in that, of all those directors whose work emphasizes the expressive function, he alone worked regularly and successfully. It is clear that the main reason for this was the tactic which he and his scriptwriters adopted of adapting (and appropriating) literary works by established men of letters. Other directors, who opted for original scripts (especially written by themselves) had extreme difficulty in realizing such expressive texts. The problems experienced by Gance and L'Herbier, whose compromises are often painful, or by Grémillon and Feyder, whose reluctance to compromise resulted in an effective silencing, are well known. Even where relatively successful, as in the cases of René Clair, Bresson, Renoir, Cocteau, or Ophüls (whose "success" resulted in the bankrupting of a series of producers), the result was a sparse output. In a system which, because of the extended involvement of directors in all stages of production, already guaranteed that an output of more than one film every nine months would be unusual, such directors sign significantly fewer works— Clair, having been constrained to self-exile in 1934, averaged on his return no more than one film every three years; Bresson averaged one every five years, and Tati one every six years.

It is perhaps surprising in a Catholic country that so few directors are associated with a strong religious commitment. Bresson stands out as the only consistent explorer of moral and religious themes. Of all those directors from a strongly protestant background (the Allégret brothers, whose father was a clergyman, Becker, Clouzot, and Delannoy) only Delannoy consistently returns to an examination of religious subjects. If the resultant films form a minority of his output (*La Symphonie pastorale*, 1946; *Dieu a besoin des hommes*, 1949–1950; *Le Miracle de Jeanne d'Arc*, 1953–1954), the general prevalence of propriety, order and moral rectitude which marks this mainstream director might well be interpreted as the expression of at least his "temperament." References to temperament are often the recourse of authorial critics failing to find clear evidence of expressivity. Thus, Becker is credited with "delicacy," Clouzot with "pessimism," Guitry with "megalomania."

Where correlation between a director's name and an expressive view of the world could not be substantiated, correlation might still be attempted on the basis of consistent style alone; though, divorced from content, this was always considered a little suspect, a little frivolous, as the following discussion from a 1957 *Cahiers* demonstrates:

Doniol-Valcroze: In 1946 and 1947 we could be understandably optimistic that as far as style was concerned, MM Bresson, Becker, Clouzot, and Clément were going to create a new movement within the French cinema. And that has not happened, I think, because there was no unity of views underlying it, no common inspiration.

Rivette: We can certainly say that despite their great successes Clouzot, Clément, and Becker failed because they thought that style alone was enough to save the cinema's soul. . . . I defy anyone to find the tiniest idea in a film by Clouzot, Becker, or Clément. Or if there is one it's banal, literary, and 20 or 30 years out of date. . . . There's still one filmmaker with integrity, namely Bresson. He's the only one. And then there are some young ones.[145]

One style that had come to the fore in those immediate postwar years was a set of documentary techniques which, in a way analogous to Italian neorealism, broke with conventional fictional techniques to the point where paradoxically a heightened realism could lead to the director's canonization as a poet. A small number of such films appeared in France in the years 1944–1948—*Le 4 juin à l'aube*, directed by Grémillon, reconstructing the recent Normandy landings; *La Bataille du rail*, directed by Clément, reconstructing the recent resistance work of railway workers; the communally filmed direct reportage of the liberation of Paris; and in a slightly different register *Farrebique*, directed by Rouquier, "recording" the seasonal life of a farm. It is clear that no close functional correlation exists between these films directed by Grémillon and Clément and their other work, and the same can be said for the first film of Louis Malle—*Le Monde du silence*, a documentary filmed with Jacques Cousteau. Equally clearly, however, Rouquier and later Jean Rouch continued to focus on films with a high if variable use of documentary techniques, thus serving as a model for many of the New Wave directors whose training at that time was principally focused on the production of short documentaries (notably Franju and Resnais), and others for whom realism or autobiography were important.

The prewar years had seen various directors' names associated with films of this sort. *Toni* (Renoir, 1934) is an isolated instance, dealing with the plight of immigrant workers in ways which reconciled fictional and documentary conventions; *La Vie est à nous* (which Renoir directed for the Communist party in 1936) largely consisted of documentary material, and *Le Temps des cerises*, directed by Le Chanois in 1937 for the same "syndicate" that commissioned *La Marseillaise*, is also heavily documentary in its techniques.

This form of realism could be seen as poetic in breaking with standard ways of representing the real and thus could inspire attempts to correlate it with a poet-director's name. The term "poetic realism" itself is of course usually reserved for a quite distinct set of films, made between 1935 and 1939. The sense in which that group of films is poetic is not difficult to identify: the visual representation of reality is technically underlined in a number of ways—notably by set design and lighting and occasionally by camera angles—thus foregrounding its representational nature. To a lesser extent, the verbal text is poeticized by standard poetic techniques. In this, these films share with a large majority of their fellows of the years 1930–1950 a theoretically articulated and systematically implemented poeticization which aimed not to *capture* reality but to *transpose* it. It is easier to correlate this tendency, as the next chapter will show, with the names of set designers and cinematographers than with directors, though the latter as organizers and decision makers had overall responsibility for the poetic effects that resulted. Inheritors directly or indirectly of a range of techniques/styles calculated to poeticize reality (principal among which were surrealist pictorial and montage techniques and expressionist acting, lighting, and cinematography techniques), the leading classic directors of these two decades saw their films as being produced within those same artistic traditions and as sharing elements of those same techniques. At the very least, the representation of reality that emerged would be the result of selection and arrangement, simplification and clarification—in a word, of stylization. Among leading directors of the thirties and forties only Renoir resists this foregrounding of décors, camera, and lighting; though in other technical aspects (including several oddly claimed as "realistic") films directed by Renoir are as poetic as those of his fellows—the foregrounding of transitions through inventive punctuation and the structural use of music in *Le Crime de M. Lange* is a flagrant example, but the virtuosity involved in long fluent takes with extreme depth of field and multiple planes of action, as in *La Règle du jeu*, is equally poetic.

Relatively few direct borrowings from surrealism emerge in the classic cinema—*L'Age d'or* (Buñuel, 1930), *Zéro de conduite* (Vigo, 1932–1945), and to a lesser extent *L'Atalante* (Vigo, 1933–1934) are well-known examples, and certain films directed by L'Herbier (notably *La Nuit fantastique*, 1941–1942) manifest it, as do the final images of *Une si jolie petite plage* (Yves Allégret, 1948) and of *Le Plaisir* (Ophüls, 1951–1952). Expressionism is much more common as a poetic device, inflecting the representation of reality in dozens of films of the period 1930–1950. It occurs frequently in conjunction with films directed by Raymond Bernard in the thirties, in several films directed by Christian-Jacque (notably *Rigolboche*, 1936, and *Sortilèges*, 1944–1945), and several of L'Herbier's films (*La Vie de Bohème*, 1942; and blended with surrealist elements in *La Nuit fantastique*, 1942). Rather than a correlation with director's name, however, one can more readily detect a correlation with subject and thus with genre. Elements of a story involving despair, fear, suspicion, or oppression would regularly be treated with these poeticizing techniques by any of the leading directors, set designers, and cinematographers. Not only leading directors were associated with such poetic effects, but many lesser-known directors as well: appropriate sections of *Le Baron fantôme* (de Poligny, 1942–1943) are modulated toward such expressionistic effects, as are important sections of *Portrait d'un assassin* (Bernard-Roland, 1949).

As a generalization, veterans of the silent era were most persistent in attempting to introduce aggressive poetic effects into their classic productions, and this was the reason for producers' mistrust of them. Any films of Gance or L'Herbier will manifest some form of stylization, some form of technical ingenuity foregrounded at the expense of the credibility of the diegesis. Directors who had been formed in the twenties but became established in the thirties regularly did the same, though less aggressively, and the poetic function of their films often derives from localized effects rather than a globally poetic conception. In postwar years, the decline of studio production and of the set decorator coincided with the increased prominence of the informational function to minimize poetic effects. Even when directing films noirs, which experienced a resurgence of favor in the fifties, directors were less inclined to poeticize the diegesis. Instances of poeticization, therefore, are the more remarkable when they do occur. The films directed by René Clair are consistently poetic, foregrounding production by means of zip pans and radically unrealistic set design allowing for extraordinary transitions between locations. Ophüls is often characterized as a "baroque" director because of the elaborate patterning of his images in the four fine films he directed in the fifties (*La Ronde*, 1950; *Le Plaisir*, 1951–1952; *Madame de . . .*, 1953; *Lola Montès*, 1955). While the poetic aspect of these works is inescapable, there was little trace of any analogous poeticization of his thirties French films. Films directed by Cocteau, also, frequently have a baroque aspect contributed by his theatrical set designer, Christian Bérard, and are consistently poetic. The baroque image had been less frequently met in the thirties, though it is insistently present in *Dans les rues* (Trivas, 1933).

Stylization in the fifties was sometimes found in an unusual place—the systematic "distortion" of acting procedures, either in the austere and undemonstrative practices extorted from his actors by Bresson (*Journal d'un curé de campagne*, 1950–1951; *Un condamné à mort s'est échappé*, 1956; *Pickpocket*, 1959) or in the mime-derived performances of Tati (*Jour de fête*, 1947–1949; *Les Vacances du M. Hulot*, 1951–1953; *Mon oncle*, 1957–1958). Some older-generation directors such as Autant-Lara and Delannoy continued with the theatrical stylization of earlier years; Autant-Lara's *L'Auberge rouge* (1951) is a flagrant instance, and his *Marguerite de la nuit* (1955–1956) combines this with an isolated residue of expressionist techniques. In general, however, poetic elements were less apparent in the fifties, as psychological realism began to displace poeticized realism.

In the extreme, poetic texts often overflow into metalinguistic texts. Not content merely with stylizing reality, such texts totally rework the naturalized conventions by which that reality is typically represented, thus calling into question not just the conventions themselves but the ideology on which these were based. Films with a high degree of metalinguistic function will be rare in any "classic" cinema, but there are several instances in the French cinema. *Juliette, ou la clef des songes*, directed in 1950 by Carné from a script he had long wanted to film, takes surrealist techniques to the point where basic questions are raised about the nature of reality and how best to represent it. Both this film and L'Herbier's *La Nuit fantastique* foreshadow in various ways that ultimate metalinguistic film, *L'Année dernière à Marienbad*; and the allegorical and hermetic aspects of *Orphée* and *Le Testament d'Orphée* (Cocteau, 1949–1950 and 1959–1960) likewise demand interpretive competences in their audience. Certain of Renoir's early sound films (*La Chienne*, 1931; *Boudu sauvé des eaux*, 1932) incorporated a clumsy allegorical frame to the realist narrative, but these were less metalinguistic than poetic, complacently foregrounding like his postwar stage curtains the artistic aspirations of the films. Unquestionably, the metalinguistic was less present in the classic cinema than it was to be in the New Wave, where such metalinguistic novelists as Marguerite Duras and Alain Robbe-Grillet were to give it an improbable prominence.

To sum up, a correlation between director's name and either expressivity of content or poeticization of technique is not strong in the French classic cinema. A variety of slack auteurist strategies will allow for any filmic element's being correlated with an author's name, but if one resists such strategies, it is easier to correlate thematic aspects of the classic cinema with the scriptwriter's name or with social and political determinants, and to correlate the global tendency toward poeticization with the general cultural background of all key personnel, but particularly set designers and cinematographers. While it is true that the industry was structured to permit expressivity and a poeticized cinema, and that such an art cinema did in fact exist at one extreme of the range of filmmaking practices, very few instances of consistent directorial practices exist to suggest that it could be or ever was exploited to allow "free play" to a director's personality or that, where it was, that personality was manifested in consistent ways throughout the director's oeuvre. There is even less evidence that such instances of expressivity were peculiar to the films now considered qualitatively superior: they were as likely to occur among "middle-rank" directors like Delannoy or relative unknowns like Le Chanois and de Poligny as among directors like Bresson and Tati, whose names have acquired authorial resonance.

PHOTO SECTION

I. Some of the more grandiose and notorious of décors designed for the classic French cinema:

1. *A nous la liberté* (René Clair, 1931): Lazare Meerson constructed this modernist factory around the Epernay Studio building itself.

2. *La Kermesse héroïque* (Jacques Feyder, 1935): Set designers came from all the other studios to admire Meerson's reconstruction of Renaissance Flanders.

3. *Hôtel du Nord* (Marcel Carné, 1938): Trauner's famous reconstruction of the Canal St. Martin in the studio.

4. *Le Jour se lève* (Marcel Carné, 1939): The suburban working-class apartment block, built in false perspective to
   heighten the sense of isolation.

5. *Les Enfants du paradis* (Marcel Carné, 1943–1945): The colossal set of the Boulevard du Crime and the cast of thousands that inhabited it.

6. *Les Portes de la nuit* (Marcel Carné, 1946): The Barbès-Rochechouart métro under construction in the studio courtyard at Joinville, with a hangar-like roof constructed above it.

II.   Residues of twenties modernist movements inflect the realist tendencies of the classic French cinema:

7. *Zéro de conduite* (Jean Vigo, 1932–1945): The dream-like pillow-fight sequence, the music of which was played in reverse.

8. *Tarakanowa* (Fédor Ozep, 1937–1938): Russian immigrant set-designers brought with them to France their tradition of elaborate, monumental, and symbolic set design.

9. *La Belle et la bête* (Cocteau, 1945–1946): This poster for the film evokes the elaborate tracery of Christian Bérard's fairy-tale sets.

10. *Lola Montès* (Max Ophüls, 1955): All Ophüls's four last films tend toward a baroque staginess in costume and set design (as well as in camera work).

III. Expressionism was the most influential of the modernist movements:

11. *Les Mirages de Paris* (Fédor Ozep, 1932–1933): Stairways, night-time, and threatening patternings of light are typical of the expressionist heritage.

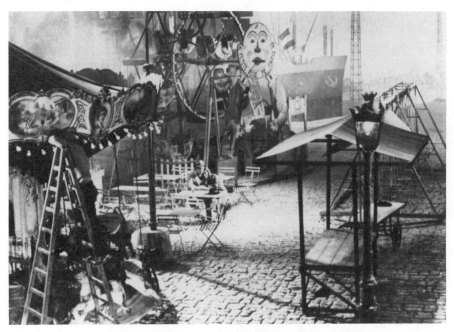

12. *Quai des brumes* (Marcel Carné, 1938): Fairgrounds and circuses, in expressionist iconography, constitute privileged sites for dark and weird forces.

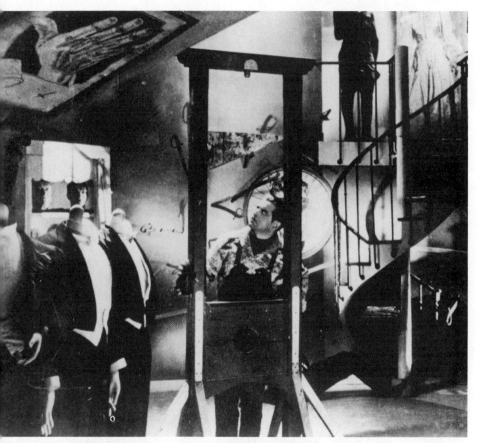

13. *La Nuit fantastique* (Marcel L'Herbier, 1941–1942): A world of
magicians and omens, where reality and nightmare are difficult
to distinguish one from the other.

14–16. *Sortilèges* (Christian-Jacque, 1944–1945): An unbalanced world, where grotesque figures inhabit remote nocturnal landscapes.

17. *La Môme vert-de-gris* (Bernard Borderie, 1952): The U.S. film noir,
    inheritor of this tradition, in turn inflected the French detective
    story of the fifties.

IV. René Clair, in particular, made insistent use of poetic effects to undermine classic realism:

18. *A nous la liberté* (René Clair, 1931): A veil of light isolates the characters from their background.

19. *Les Belles-de-nuit* (René Clair, 1952): The same effect, combined with musical comedy traditions.

20. *Porte des Lilas* (René Clair, 1956–1957): The little people of Paris, poeticized to universalize them.

21. *Le Silence est d'or* (René Clair, 1946–1947): One of the many classic French films to hark back nostalgically to the overt artifice of silent film sets.

V. Poetic Realism: Reconciling the poetic effects of expressionist lighting, vapor clouds, and night effects with the realist pressures of sound film production:

22–23. *Quai des brumes* (Marcel Carné, 1938): Gabin the deserter and doomed outsider.

24. *Le Jour se lève* (Marcel Carné, 1939): The worker as doomed outsider.

25. *Les Portes de la nuit* (Marcel Carné, 1946): The most overtly symbolic of the series of Carné-Prévert films, with destiny stalking the night streets.

26. *Touchez pas au grisbi* (Jacques Becker, 1953): Combining the film noir tradition with a character study full of nostalgia and melancholy.

27. *Le Mariage de Chiffon* (Claude Autant-Lara, 1941): Similar
techniques, but applied to a sentimental comedy.

VI. The theatrical aspects of poetic realism are apparent in effects of texture and structure that create an impression of exaggerated perspective.

28. *Pépé le Moko* (Julien Duvivier, 1936–1937): The strong forms of the Kasbah frame the action.

29. *La Citadelle du silence* (Marcel L'Herbier, 1937): The Russian set designer Andrejev contributed this massive design to a film on the Russian occupation of Poland.

30. *Drôle de drame* (Marcel Carné, 1937): False perspective and a painted backdrop make little pretense at recreating a realistic Britain.

31. *Le Jour se lève* (Marcel Carné, 1939): Man as machine, woman as flower—another form of poeticization of working-class realities.

32. *Les Portes de la nuit* (Marcel Carné, 1946): Stone and cobble, night and pools of light structure the image.

33. *L'Ombre* (André Berthomieu, 1948): Similar effects in a less well-known film indicate how pervasive were these set design and lighting strategies.

VII. Location shooting was always an option, but so was the elaborate reconstruction of nature in the studio:

34. *Toni* (Jean Renoir, 1934–1935): Filmed, like those of Pagnol who funded it, in natural locations, without make-up, and largely with nonprofessional actors.

35. *Lumière d'été* (Jean Grémillon, 1942–1943): Which likewise exploited the picturesque potential of Provence during the wartime expansion of activities around Nice.

36. *Une partie de campagne* (Jean Renoir, 1936–1946): The tranquillity of the river scenes is a little undermined by this production still.

37. *Les Misérables* (Raymond Bernard, 1933–1934): A tracery of wood-land branches, artistically constructed in the studio.

38. *Juliette ou la clé des songes* (Marcel Carné, 1950–1951): Trauner's studio forest, with real small trees and foliage interspersed with movable giant trunks on wheeled platforms.

VIII. Some characteristic aspects of Popular Front films:

39–40. *Le Crime de M. Lange* (Jean Renoir, 1935–1936): Jules Berry's
detestable clergyman, one of the many figures of moral and political authority to be satirized in Prévert's scripts; and the cooperative that transcends the individuals that make it up.

41. *La Belle Equipe* (Julien Duvivier, 1936): The transcendent group
at its moment of crisis.

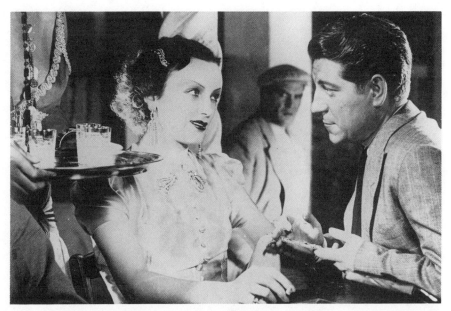

42. *Pépé le Moko* (Julien Duvivier, 1937): Gabin in the Kasbah—at once a refuge and a trap.

43. *La Bête humaine* (Jean Renoir, 1938): Gabin as worker, glorified yet doomed.

IX. Some characteristic and controversial films from wartime France:

44. *Les Visiteurs du soir* (Marcel Carné, 1942): Sometimes read as an allegory of the German occupation.

45. *Pontcarral* (Jean Delannoy, 1942): As French resistance hero, but safely distanced in time.

46. *La Nuit fantastique* (Marcel L'Herbier, 1941–1942): A dream figure
sometimes read as emblematic of a free France.

47. *Premier de cordée* (Louis Daquin, 1943–1944): Mountain films that reproduce the settings and sentiments of their German predecessors.

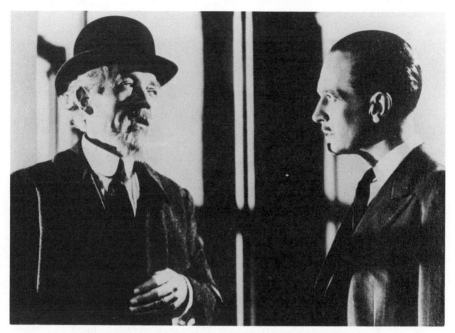

48. *Le Corbeau* (Henri-Georges Clouzot, 1943): The film which earned Clouzot the enmity of resistance fighters and a (short-lived) ban from filmmaking.

49. *Le Ciel est à vous* (Jean Grémillon, 1943–1944): Preferred by the resistance because it glorified the courage and endurance of the nation.

X. Some characteristic films from the fifties:

50. *Les Jeux interdits* (René Clément, 1951–1952): Set in 1940, using documentary footage, the film was boycotted and excluded from Cannes.

51. *Le Petit Monde de Don Camillo* (Julien Duvivier, 1951–1952): One of the increasing number of French-Italian coproductions from the fifties.

52. *Et Dieu créa la femme* (Roger Vadim, 1956): Bardot embodies the aspirations of an incipient youth culture and the morale of instant gratification generated by consumer capitalism.

53. *Mon oncle* (Jacques Tati, 1957–1958): Middle-class consumer capitalism and the mechanization of life, satirized.

XI. Classic film censorship was never successful in suppressing that long-standing nightclub tradition of exhibiting the female in a state of undress:

54. *Le Marchand de sable* (André Hugon, 1931): The exotic East was a ready pretext for nakedness.

55. *Quai des orfèvres* (Henri-Georges Clouzot, 1947): The world of the caf'conc singer provided an equally convenient pretext.

56. *Nana* (Christian-Jacque, 1954–1955): The Second Empire and the world of the cancan made this story a recurrent favorite for this purpose.

57. *Lola Montès* (Max Ophüls, 1955): Another performance, the same Martine Carole, displayed for the male gaze.

SEVEN

WORK PRACTICES AND STYLISTIC CHANGE

Anyone can be a director, anyone can be a scriptwriter, anyone can be an actor, only the job of director of photography requires a basic technological training.

Truffaut, *Arts* 619

The esthetic paradox of the cinema resides in a dialectic between the concrete and the abstract. . . . The cement forest of *Die Niberlungen* may well claim to extend infinitely; we don't believe in the reality of its space; whereas the merest shiver of a birch branch in the wind, on a sunny day, can suffice to evoke all the forests in the world.

If this analysis is valid, the primordial esthetic problem, as far as filmed theater is concerned, is that of the décor.

André Bazin, *Esprit*, July/August 1951

A theatrical actor is a little head in a big room; a cinematic actor is a big head in a little room.

André Malraux

It is natural that actors should prefer theater to cinema; in the theater we [authors] are in their hands, whereas in the cinema, they're in ours.

Jean Cocteau

Film music fulfills much the same rôle as the legendary orchestra bribed by assassins to play loudly, so as to drown their victims' screams. It is an accomplice, rather than an accompaniment.

Roland Manuel

MONSTRES SACRÉS AND CHARACTER ACTING

Despite the discourse of originality surrounding them, the expressive and poetic aspects of classic French films on which most claims for authorial status were based themselves involved an elaborate set of conventions. Nevertheless, those making such claims commonly contrasted "authored" films with conventional filmmaking, viewed as the more commercial and popular end of the spectrum of filmmaking practices permitted by the mode of production of the day. Authors were seen as unconventional insofar as they deviated from those contemporary norms of filmmaking which resulted from the recurrent and relatively routinized work practices of a cinema attempting to capitalize on successes. Since the genre and star systems were relatively underdeveloped within the classic French cinema, these norms were less coherent, less visible, and less articulated than in the case of the Hollywood cinema. Nevertheless, they can be shown to have existed by statistical style analysis and by reference to the more articulate observers and practitioners of the day.

Statistical style analysis can be most readily and convincingly applied to those aspects of filmmaking that involve large numbers of routinized procedures such as editing and camera work, where the repetitive nature of the activity largely precludes individual acts of conscious decision making. The norms that arose out of these practices often remained unrecognized and unarticulated throughout the period under study. Other norms of the day, in the area of set design, lighting, staging, and music composition were more systematically articulated; though, since those who articulated them were heavily implicated in the myths of artistic creativity, their observations should not be taken at face value.

The present chapter exploits these twin sources of information concerning the prevailing norms of the day in order to shed some light on the development and evolution of work practices in the classic French cinema. A central theme of the successive sections will be the claim that those practices evolved from what might broadly be described as a social cinema, based on the use of representative character types and a tradition of set design that foregrounded the influence of society and environment, toward a psychological cinema which dismissed those traditions in favor of a focus on individualized characters and the perceiving subject. Or rather, since that claim is not particularly revolutionary in itself, this chapter will aim to substantiate it in a number of methodologically defensible ways.

One field in which the evolution in work practices is particularly evident is acting. The early classic cinema drew heavily on actors trained in the various theatrical traditions, and these in turn conceptualized their personnel in terms of fixed character roles. The classic theater of the seventeenth and eighteenth centuries had had its recurrent categories of character, which were formalized in the early nineteenth century and supplemented slightly over the next century. They were known as *emplois*, and most of the theatrical actors coming to early classic cinema from the theater would have been trained in, and seen themselves as appropriate for, one or a limited range of such *emplois*. For tragedy, there were noble fathers, traitors, valets, kings, confidants; for comedy, there were first and second comics and peasants; women might be coquettes, soubrettes, lovers, and ingénues; and whatever the genre there were "young leads," subdivided into the lover, the young rake, etc.

Clearly the range of such *emplois* and the genres from which they derive correlate closely with the norms and structure of a given society and with its concept of human nature. Perhaps because of the greater degree of codification of these in France, the *emplois* themselves were more highly codified, and surveys of the drama courses through which such a large percentage of French cinema actors proceeded shows that they still constituted a reliable point of reference for drama teachers characterizing the talents and potential of their students.[1] The range of *emplois* common in operetta and on the Boulevard was transcribed bodily into the cinema in the thirties as these were filmed, and they tend to be more powerful as character-generators in the early than in the late classic cinema.

Clearly they are hardly compatible with common-sense notions of individualism and had already begun to break down in the post-Chekov theater. They had, however, the advantage of drawing on existing audience knowledge and thus obviating any need for elaborate character construction in the opening scenes of a play or film.

Because they had graduated through this system of character-typing, most leading and second-role actors of the classic French cinema were already heavily typecast before entering it; so whether they brought with them to the cinema the theatrical scripts in which they were accustomed to acting or whether they had scripts written around them, they tended to work within the fairly rigidly defined limits. This was particularly true if they had a distinctive physique appropriate only to one or a limited number of *emplois*, and leading actors so endowed tended more and more toward repetitive stereotypes somewhat analogous to Hollywood's generic roles. Such actors were known as *monstres sacrés*. They included Jules Berry, Michel Simon, Fernandel, Jean Gabin. Thus Renoir talks of organizing *Boudu* around Michel Simon, and Spaak had to rewrite *La Grande Illusion* when Stroheim decided he wanted to act both of the central roles for German officers, amalgamated into one. Gabin was constantly having roles written around him, and Yves Montand's film career was permanently set back when he had to step into the role in *Les Portes de la nuit*, written for Gabin.

Others, more physically neutral, could adapt to a wide range of radically different physical (and therefore moral) types, with the result that the actor's own extra-textual existence was not inherently foregrounded. Pierre

Fresnay is exemplary here: where material appeared in fan magazines concerning him, it was usually angled to emphasize his flexibility, his self-transformatory powers—accompanied for instance by 20 photographs of him in widely distinct roles.[2] The same flexibility was seen as characteristic of François Périer and Madeleine Renaud, and of Charles Vanel. It was around the former category of actor (the *monstre sacré*) rather than around the latter (the *acteur de composition*) that recurrent scenarios might most readily accrete; but the possibility of those recurrent roles acquiring a mythic dimension was in tension with the presence of the actor as person—Michel Simon might frequently play the uncoordinated anarchic disrupter of bourgeois order, but the performance was so baroque and eccentric as to become "Michel Simon's number" rather than a mythic amalgam of actor and role. The same was true of Jules Berry and of Fernandel—reinforced in the latter case by the difficult compatibility of myth and farce. Consequently, however highly paid and well known, such actors did not lend themselves to the mythic stature of a star. Perhaps the nearest to a true star in classic French cinema was Jean Gabin, whose physique and associated "number" lacked the baroque effusion of the others. It is instructive to observe how attentive Gabin was to the construction of his mythic persona, never accepting a role unless it contained those aspects of his past roles which had begun to emerge as mythic—the underprivileged origins, the social and legal marginality overlaying a fundamental goodness, the outburst of frustration at the constraints of his existence, the fatality that this attracts in the form of a tragic death. It is instructive as much as anything in that it serves as a reminder of the fact that no one else and no other agency or mechanism existed to organize such a construction if the actor did not undertake the task himself or herself.

Very few women figure among the *monstres sacrés* of leading French performers—indeed, Arletty is possibly the only one from the thirties and forties, and in her case, however feminine her physique, it is clear that her exaltation to that rank is due primarily to her raucous voice and hard-edged cynicism, which give the characters she embodies a competence and vitality in the face of adversity that make her an honorary man. Perhaps the only other actress to approach this level was Simone Signoret, likewise not categorizable as "a mere woman"—far outside the conventional canons of beauty, and therefore not suitable for romantic roles. Instead, she became one of the few leading women around for whom scripts were written allocating her an active narrative role.

By comparison with the *monstres sacrés*, those actors capable of modifying their appearance and performance to suit the role (the *acteurs de composition*) were widely regarded as the "real" actors, though the amorphous nature of their appearance and the uncertainty as to whether any continuous identifiable personality underlay their various roles made them less readily marketable in the currency of the fan magazines.

The same distinction, between character actors and composition actors, prevailed in second-role actors. Gaston Modot, Carette, Saturnin Fabre, Robert Le Vigan, Pauline Carton, Paulette Dubost, Noël Roquevert, Marcel Dalio, Jacques Dufilho, Louis Salou, and Raymond Bussières were seen as character-typed by physique and readily recognizable from film to film, but not eligible for the term of *monstre sacré* even when they played a lead role, as they occasionally did. Composition actors of the second roles, such as Bernard Blier, Albert Rémy, and Daniel Gélin, by definition remained relatively fluid and flexible in the roles they could play, and their main function was seen as a support function: in their blandness they set off the vitality and character of the lead roles. The same could be said for the innumerable young men and women introduced to provide a romantic interest that was seldom other than marginal. Summarizing the situation, Thierry Jousse says, "Today, with the necessary distance, we can distinguish two distinct categories of 'second role': the *obscure* and the *eccentric*. The obscure were there to set off the leads, in quasi-hierarchical relation with them and familiar without being famous." Of the eccentric, he says, "What was needed to become a good second-role player? A strong face, a voice, and it was in the bag. At that time . . . their job was to provide a noteworthy figure in the film, so as to give a little spice to the work . . . without for all that challenging the status of the lead actor."[3] Provincial actors often retained or developed their regional accent to provide an appropriate vocal interest for second-role parts.

There are indications that already in the thirties actors were conscious that this relatively stable set of character types was beginning to degenerate. In 1935 Fresnay, in an admittedly polemical context, could see "the profession of actor as losing its stability, its security, and its technique, the art of the actor as losing its rules."[4] This instability was only exacerbated in the forties, first by the departure of large numbers of the established actors to America or elsewhere, and then by the postwar impact of a neorealism which minimized the role of professional actors in favor of people drawn off the streets. This latter point of view had been explored much earlier: an article in *Interciné* in 1933 cites *Tabu*, *Mädchen in Uniform*, and Pabst (*Tragedy in a Mine*) as exemplary in their use of nonprofessional actors to avoid the mannered posturing of theater and achieve a simple unaffected sincerity.[5] Four years later an article entitled "A Cinema without Actors" recapitulated a whole range of acting theories which bypassed the professional actor by editing, by treating the actor as a mere puppet, or by preferring the authenticity of "unknown actors drawn from real life." The puppet notion was taken up by Bresson, whose manipulation of nonprofessional actors to achieve "neutral" de-dramatized nonexpressive performances drew on another French tradition—that of Lugné-Po, who had promoted Ibsen within a tradition of symbolist (antirealist) acting, and whose ideas were finding once more an echo in the modernist theater of Beckett and Ionesco.

More frequently, however, as the 1937 article made clear, nonprofessional actors were valued for the opposite reason—they might communicate a simple integrity and credibility through doing what they knew best. They "are indispensible in certain types of film like romanticized documentaries, or in specific milieus which require an authenticity of interpretation otherwise unobtainable—films set in tropical or polar regions, films involving working men, fishermen for example, especially where the narrative does not focus on a few protagonists but is a story with the masses as subject."[6] In the silent period, Antoine and Epstein had done this; Renoir had at times done likewise (in *Toni*, for instance); in the more industrialized postwar conditions, Becker did it for *Le Trou*, much to the wrath of the Actors' Union; Decoin could still in 1951 admire the effects to be achieved by it;[7] but once the momentary illusions of the liberation period were past, and as Italian neorealism itself faded from prominence, French gestures in the direction of fictional documentaries based on contemporary reality rapidly disappeared, and the debate died away. At no time did the practice of using nonprofessionals, either for the purposes of realism or of stylization, seem to have any significant impact on dramatic fiction production, though it could be cited by actors as an inspiration to draw on one's observation of real people, "regain contact with daily life, restore meaning to that life, and strip the veil of hypocrisy and lies" from a reactionary culture.[8] It thus became a rhetorical aid to the more subdued "composition" style of acting in the fifties.

A further support to that realist acting style, but emphasizing the importance of detailed psychological character construction rather than a neorealist credibility, came from the widespread interest aroused in France by the Actors' Studio. The "natural ease" of American actors had, from as early as 1910, been favorably contrasted with what was seen as inflated artifice in French acting; and the success of James Dean, Marlon Brando, Montgomery Clift, Anthony Perkins, Julie Harris, Carol Baker, Eva Marie Saint, and other adherents of the Strasberg Method Acting School revived an interest in Stanislavsky and the internal self-development that should go into creating a credible psychological portrait.[9] Concentration, an inward intensity of performance deriving from the actor's own total submersion in the role, and a credibility attracting identification again became the rhetorical norm in the late fifties. "Real actors" must observe "real life" and draw on it, forgetting they are actors.[10]

Meanwhile, through death or retirement the *monstres sacrés* had largely disappeared from the scene, and with them had gone the tradition of unashamed excess. What remained of this aggressively theatrical style in the period 1945–1960 was a degraded, formally self-conscious style, generally felt to be lacking in vitality. Perhaps it was degraded only in that it was now practiced by actors without the charisma and egotism of those who had established it and taught it in the preceding 50 years. Edwige Feuillère and Françoise Rosay were widely regarded as typical of this style, viewed as classical and admirable by some, stilted and affected by others. "You must have style," says André Luguet, attempting to define and defend this degraded theatrical acting in the mid-forties. "This means being able (1) to remain distinguished, without affectation; (2) to be vulgar, without crudeness; (3) to wear a coat with casual ease, overalls with conviction, a uniform without stiffness, a ball-gown without awkwardness, a short skirt with tact; (4) to know how to sit down, get up, walk, bow, kiss a hand; (5) to speak clearly, and above all, to listen."[11]

The favored terms ("distinguished," "casual ease," "tact") and the disfavored terms ("awkwardness," "crudeness," "stiffness") speak of a régime of good taste which was to come to seem the characteristic quality of the 1950s French cinema in many eyes. Its rise coincided with the increasing dominance of adaptations of classic novels, and consequently the increase in costume dramas drawing on a high cultural tradition analogous to that of classical theater. Unquestionably, this contributed to the validation of the criteria of formality, propriety, composure, and taste on which the actors drew. It is this "good taste," and the "cinema of quality" which it informed that was to be the principal target of Truffaut and Godard. The assumption that there was a special way of entering a room, walking across it, sitting down, and enunciating a phrase, which actors must acquire as part of their professional baggage, was anathema to them. The propriety that it invoked, the studied awareness of being watched that it implied, were contrasted by Godard to the grace and spontaneity of American and Italian actors.[12] In the same issue of *Arts*, Truffaut characterized the style more fully, contrasting it with the healthy unprofessional acting of Brigitte Bardot, who

> without realizing it is busy saving the French cinema. . . . I like Michel Boisrond, I like Annette Wademant and Charles Boyer, I tolerate Henri Vidal, but I know that *La Parisienne* will bring nothing new to the French cinema, no truth of any sort, only fine costumes, uniforms, evening dresses, probably a sumptuous ball and glittering decors. I'll be delighted if, thanks to the impermeability of Brigitte Bardot—her lack of sophistication and refusal of convention—a few false notes slip into this concert, a few words of dialogue are stripped bare, a few intonations raucous, the unity of tone destroyed, the homogeneity of the work destroyed. The film will delight me by bringing me some *surprises* and from time to time a second of truth—very little, a certain gesture, a glance, an emphasized syllable—because what use, I ask you, what interest is there in having an actress enunciate correctly a false text? Like Renoir, I prefer to hear a precise text spoken askew. I firmly believe that with Françoise Rosay and Edwige Feuillère will disappear a style of acting which has been typical of the French cinema since the arrival of the talkies—much batting of eyelashes, glances that speak volumes, an unctuously inflected diction, knowing looks, the face full of an intelligent appreciation of a text rich in undertones.

Of course, Truffaut's own critique, founded as it is on "glimpses of truth," foreshadows merely another metamorphosis of realism; but it is indicative of a growing impatience with the degraded theatrical style. With the victory of the New Wave, this tradition became received dogma, and the fifties cinema of quality became snidely dismissible: "You can still find, not so far from this very spot, films (so to speak) in which André Luguet, Edwige Feuillère, and François Périer exercise their fearful and implacable craft."[13]

In fact, one of the principal criticisms levelled against postwar cinema by contemporary critics was its lack of vitality, of spice, of character, due to the disappearance of *monstres sacrés*. Along with the second-role character actors, fifties French cinema had lost an array of readily recognizable character types—the concierge, the postman, the garage mechanic, the café owner, the goodhearted prostitute, the southerner—which had been central to the representation of French society in the earlier years. Arguably, the loss is consistent with the general move away from typing in the scripting and acting of late classical films, as the cinema moves from a focus on social motivation (with characters representative of social roles and forces) toward psychological motivation (with characters individualized at the expense of any general statement about society). It is also consistent with a move from dramatic subjects in the earlier period toward adaptations of bourgeois literary masterpieces in the later period, with the concomitant shift from extrovert expressiveness to anguished interiority. In this context, a heavily character-typed film such as Autant-Lara's *L'Auberge rouge*, with its acid social satire embodied in the familiar figures of Fernandel, Françoise Rosay, and Carette, can already seem almost prehistoric in 1951.

In the broader sociological context the decay of the theatrical *emplois* and of the character actor corresponds to a modification of audience expectations and aspirations under the developing consumerist ethic, particularly because of its extension of buying power to the younger generation. A new range of models was needed, related to a new social structure, new family and generational relationships. It is worth noting that both *emplois* and *monstres sacrés* in the period 1930–1945 were most effective in imposing older character types in the age range of 35–50. A popularity poll taken in 1939 placed Jean Gabin at the head of masculine stars, followed by Fernandel, Jouvet, and Raimu.[14] As the commentator notes, the "jeune premier" of the twenties had been displaced by maturer male models. Assurance and authority, whether affirming or subverting, came in the form of bulky or incisive older men.

René Mandia noted the same thing in the late forties, attributing it to the need for years of commitment if that perfectioning of technique which we read as genius is to be developed.[15] The *jeune premiers* and *ingénues* did not cease to people the cast lists of this cinema, but such roles were for the most part inhabited by actors lacking in either training or charisma, and the roles they were given did not call for an authoritative or incisive edge. Indeed, they didn't call for any clear characterization at all. Despite repeated attempts[16] by commentators to categorize these young leads into types, no clear recurrent characteristics attached themselves to the role, and the characters often seem perfunctorily sketched, cardboard cut-outs, included purely to fulfil an outdated casting expectation. But the theme of love itself was relegated as often as not to a bland subplot or became such a subplot (as in *Hôtel du Nord*) because the *monstres sacrés* elsewhere in the cast list played it into insignificance. This situation contrasts markedly with the fifties, when certain of the younger actors, often backed by a theatrical training in the classical *emplois*, took over the lead in popularity polls and reinvigorated the role of jeune premier and ingénue. Gérard Philipe, Jean Marais, and Georges Marchal dominated the fifties, and the rising star of Brigitte Bardot began the displacement of established actresses. No better symptom of new audiences with new values could exist than the young Brigitte Bardot, at once voluptuous and naive, animal and (as her initials imply) babyish. Her rise parallels the growth of the pop music industry and of youth culture in general, as the most evident cultural manifestations of that ethic of instant gratification promoted by consumerism and now extended to the increasingly affluent younger generation.

Likewise, the decay of typecasting, character acting, and *monstres sacrés* parallels the developing "death of ideology" to which this consumerism gave birth: the society structured into politically opposed groups and classes with distinct cultures and interests was giving way to a relatively apolitical culture in which origins and jobs were no longer permanently determining of character, because the fluid movement of individuals, geographically as well as economically, called into question the fixed interests within an enduring social structure which it had been so easy to type in the period to 1950. Not least, the myth of unique individuals, fostered by the breakdown of types and by the development of psychological realism, served to disguise the pressures toward mass culture and homogeneity that are intrinsic to a consumer culture.

Various commentators noticed this trend in characterization away from myths, types, and conventional categories that took place around 1945–1950. Bazin, writing in 1949 of the aging and passing of the French cinema's one truly mythic role, incarnated by Gabin, acknowledged that the myths which Malraux had seen as fundamental were becoming less visible in the cinema then.[17] Edgar Morin talked of "the old archetypes becoming degraded and giving birth to multiple subarchetypes, more faithful to empiric observation."[18] In general it was in the more theatrical acting tradition, based on adaptations of earlier literature, that the archetypes lived on into the fifties; and it was in the contemporary dramas of personal relationships, acted in a more psychological-realist style, that the new types of relationships were explored. As Chevassu said, looking back on the development, "the modern cinema . . . cannot endure the actor-become-sign or the gesture-become-stereotyped. It requires denser characters, better fleshed out, not because they reflect reality better, but because it is in behaviorist terms that we have come to expect the essential aspects of filmic individuals to be presented."[19]

POETIC REALISM: THE ACTIVE ROLE OF THE DÉCOR

This evolution in acting practices has unexpected parallels with the evolution of set design practices. The central problematic of the architect-decorator in the classic French cinema was the same as that of the cinematographer, the editor and the composer: should their contribution be noticeable, striking in its aesthetic appeal, or invisible, merging imperceptibly into the communal contributions of their colleagues. Specifically, should the sets determine the visual style of the film and comment on the action, or should they constitute a neutral environment integrated into the action. The question was of importance for a number of reasons, but most of all because one set of coherent answers to it produced that most famous of French film styles, poetic realism. The set decorators' contribution to this style was crucial, and their rationalization of that contribution helps to clarify a "movement" which is notoriously difficult to define.

Perhaps the most straightforward point of entry into this complex set of questions is the ritual list of explanations produced by set designers in defense of their practice of reconstructing aspects of an existing reality in the studio. The list summarized commercial and technical problems facing various members of the film-production team: many aspects of reality were too remote to make transport to them a viable proposition; the costs, both direct and indirect, in transport, wages, and insurance for workers, equipment, and stars would be far larger than those of reconstructing in the studio; in the case of nearer and more accessible localities, traffic problems, clearing the public away for the period of shooting, isolating the set from undesirable noises (or in the case of historical films, from anachronistic features of the locality), still made the problems of location shooting impractical; where these didn't apply, the location seldom allowed for those camera angles or lighting setups considered as ideal; the available power to run the lighting, etc., was seldom adequate; control not only over technical aspects but also over actor movements, entries, and exits, had to be sacrificed to existing layouts; the acoustic properties of existing locations were seldom appropriate for direct recording. Rather than let the filming be determined by the vagaries of existing locations, it was preferable to reconstruct those locations in the studio to provide ideal conditions of filming. "The layout of a set which fulfils all these needs . . . ends up looking not a little odd," notes the 1956 summary of their trade by the French architect-decorators, "and has little in common with the rational house plan of an architect . . . who has obeyed in designing his structure quite other principles than those of cinematic mise en scène." Trauner agrees: "The lens that films a set is not the eye that looks at life. A bedroom in which one lives is not a bedroom in which one films. The sets are a function of the scenario and only exist for it. Any set that aimed to exist in its own right would be a bad set. The decorator creates for the director and must furnish an appropriate instrument, with no flaws. The layout of the set must follow faithfully the action of the plot. A bedroom in which the hero is required to walk from window to bed is not the same as a bedroom in which the hero, sitting at a desk, reads a tragic letter."[20] His designs for the Barbès metro of *Les Portes de la nuit* are frequently cited by himself and others as a classic instance where the vast expense involved in recreating in the studio a complex nearby location was totally justified by the technical and logistic problems associated with filming at the real metro station.[21]

But the factors pressuring filmmakers to construct décors in a studio were not totally determining. Some were merely desirable; and those that were necessary did not apply in all cases. They also varied historically, with technological change, so that there was in most films, and in most years, a blend of studio and location work. At times, that location work had been justified not just by cost considerations but by claims for a greater degree of "authenticity" which it brought to the profilmic reality. The debate between location filming and studio reconstruction had been going on long before the sound cinema period and was closely involved with that other debate about the specificity of cinema as distinct from theater. The intensity of it can be measured by an article by André Antoine published in *Le Film* in 1917, which curiously prefigures that of Truffaut in *Cahiers du Cinéma* in 1954: "Real progress would be to abandon the studio and work in nature, as the impressionists did. Instead of improvising a fictitious world for the camera, we should plant the cameraman and his instruments in front of *real* interiors and *true* buildings and set up mobile lighting plants to light them. . . . We continue to fabricate theatrical sets and theatrical costumes. . . . But a set or a piece of furniture that's right for stage lighting becomes unacceptable in a film studio. . . . We are going to have to eliminate absolutely all studio work, even (indeed, especially) for interiors. . . . So as not to have to get out and about, we've got used to building and painting at great cost, with enormous loss of time, interiors that are inevitably defective. Wouldn't it be more sensible to go out and find them where they actually exist? The eternal objection, so often repeated, that the light is insufficient and the room for maneuvering the camera is inadequate is surely inoperative now that modern electrical equipment permits all sorts of feats. By doing this, we'd be establishing the essential difference of cinema, which is a living, airy form of creation, from theater, which is based on the contrary on the *imitation* of nature."[22]

Antoine himself, in his Théâtre Libre productions, had been responsible for the move to a greater realism in acting and in theatrical stage design. Coincidentally with the development of the cinema, he was to see the theater steadily move away from realism toward the avant-garde stylistic innovations of the twenties and thirties. As theater moved steadily further away from realism, the cinema moved steadily toward an even greater realism. There was certainly an element of irony in this for that majority of early set designers who came from the theater, and perhaps an even greater element of irony for that majority of classic set decorators with a Beaux Arts painterly training. Aware of and trained in the techniques of impressionist and postimpressionist design, they chafed repeatedly at the limitations of cinematic set design, with its progressively restrictive realism. "The set decorator will be working as an *artist*," says Pimenoff, "that's to say working not only with his experience and tradecraft, but above all with taste and imagination. So we might as well note right away that the scope available for a film decorator's imagination is fairly limited. In the studio it's always a question—rightly or wrongly, I make no judgment—of a *realistic* décor . . . of a naturalistic setting, a more or less faithful copy of reality. It's pretty well out of the question for a film decorator to have a spiritual conception of the décor, as is possible in the theater."[23] This complaint was particularly strong from those still heavily involved in stage design as well, such as Christian Bérard. Speaking of the naturalism of Antoine's theater design he says, "We've got far beyond that nowadays; our researches into staging have transformed the theater in the last thirty years, thanks to the efforts of Copeau, Baty, Jouvet, Dullin, and certain painters: Picasso, Derain, Dufy, Brianchon, etc. In the cinema we haven't yet got past the earlier stage. With few exceptions, we always have to produce a realistic setting. Few films require . . . what you could really call a décor. Settings are seen as secondary, and there is scarcely a case where the help of a painter would be of use. The cinema suppresses the imagination of the decorator.[24] But it is not unthinkable that in the cinema, as in the theater, a quite different conception [of décor] should appear one day."[25]

But with their theatrical and spectacular background, not to mention their acquaintance with German expressionism, the Russian contingent had in the twenties for Albatros productions pushed set design in the direction of the extravagant, the exotic, the baroque, the poetic. A powerful residue of this existed still in the thirties. Like Lochakoff before him, Andrejew, who worked in several other countries as well as France, was notorious for his tendency toward antirealist settings. In the extreme, he produced sparse sets dominated by a few grandiloquent foregrounded elements with an overtly symbolic value. A single majestic column would signify "power" ("a column's not a column until it's at least two and a half meters in diameter"). "He pushed the grandiose to the colossal, to the cyclopean, and progressively reduced his décors to a few essential elements that recurred, scarcely modified, in one film after another. . . . Ozep's film *Tarakanowa* was literally crushed by its décors. . . . The critics denounced the 'imperialism' of the decorators in this film, and Andrejev was forced to modify his working practices to some extent thereafter. But symbolism persists in his work. . . . "[26] But Andrejev was only the most extreme case of a widespread "nostalgia" for modernist set design. Frequently decorators would do the rounds of the studios in order to discuss one another's more modernist film set designs.

Moreover, it wasn't only the Russian/German inheritance that inspired this interest. The French impressionist filmmakers of the twenties had emphasized modernist set design, and other more avant-garde filmmakers with artistic contacts, notably L'Herbier, had, like his theatrical counterparts, explored the possibilities of translating modernist art movements directly to cinematic set design. His *L'Inhumaine*, in particular, on which Mallet-Stevens and Fernand Léger collaborated, was notorious for this. For Mallet-Stevens, who in the late twenties wrote several forceful articles on film-set design, "the décor must play a *positive role*. Whether it's realist, expressionist, modern, or old-fashioned, it must play its part. The décor must present the characters even before they appear—indicate their social situation, taste, habits, way of life, personality."[27]

This positive and assertive role for the décor, based on a modernist and theatrical tradition, largely taken for granted in the twenties, was disclaimed strongly by most decorators during the classic period. For them and their coworkers, the role of the décor was, however reluctantly, acknowledged to be a secondary and supporting role, serving to establish the atmosphere and fill out the audience's knowledge of the characters. It must not be so assertive as to be noticed in its own right. The following quotations are representative of this tendency:

> The décor must remain discrete and create the atmosphere. . . . It must not assert itself as a décor.[28]

> It is an art of self-denial: the decorator must constantly efface himself so as to allow the other elements of the production to take center stage—the subject, the acting, the mise en scène. The setting must never intrude or dominate the work itself. The décor is an accompaniment, it fits in with the film; it is the décor that generates that "atmosphere" so dear to director and to actors. It is much more difficult to compose an atmospheric décor, which, passing unnoticed in the eyes of the public, reinforces the scene and confers on it its true value, than to execute a super-architecture before which all fall back amazed and admiring, but which totally distorts the sense and scope of the production.[29]

> On the screen, the best décor is that which is barely noticed.[30]

> A set must not be composed so as to promote the personality of its creator, but to establish the setting and orient the spectator's imagination. . . . It must not distract from the action, either by its richness or its austerity . . . it must serve to establish the atmosphere.[31]

> We must never lose sight of the fact that the décor of a film remains of secondary importance, the primary role belonging to the characters.[32]

For Robert Jourdan also, writing in 1931, the "excessive modernism" of certain recent avant-garde films (such as *L'Inhumaine*) had destroyed the credibility of the characters and of the filmworld.[33]

If one of the most frequent justifications for this realist tendency in cinema is the need to create plausible characters with whose existence the audience can identify, set decorators nevertheless recognized that their "realist shackles" could equally be seen as arising directly out of the technology of the cinema. Antoine's identification of cinema's "airy" nature as the source of this distinctive realism was taken up by Barsacq in particular. Several times, in accounts of the realist pressures on set decoration, he isolates the following statement in italics: *"The day when real exteriors were introduced into films, the future evolution of the film décor was effectively determined once and for all.* Under threat of becoming a discordant element in the film, the décor necessarily had to establish an equivalent sort of setting."[34] The existence of "real" exteriors—real streets, real houses, real fields, real trees—as an element of any film's setting, was seen as placing an enormous pressure on studio interiors and exteriors alike to be "real" in the sense of not disrupting the stylistic continuity, not disrupting the illusion that the film text was an ongoing photographed record of real people living out their (however adventurous) lives. Either one worked entirely in the studio, stylizing the whole film, exteriors as well as interiors, or the very existence of "naturalistic" photographed exteriors constrained films stylistically to the point where interiors must conform to realistic exteriors. "The settings of a film constitute an overall whole," says Trauner, "and you must respect the homogeneity of that whole. An interior setting must flow into the street setting which we see through the window."[35] Such "découvertes" were themselves frequently photographs of the location exteriors.

A further constraint was the use of close-ups, which inevitably revealed any "inadequacies" in the realistic surface of these sets. This pressure, to which theater was not subject, was felt as constraining set designers to a greater degree of detail in their realism. Moreover, the mobile camera, exploring the sets from all angles, would reveal any "dead areas" and any poorly finished details. One of the distinctive aspects of cinematic set design therefore was seen as its "finished" nature. There could be no reliance as in theatrical décor on the distance of the spectator; and the effects did not have to be so grandiose as to impress at a distance. "Present-day photography," says Barsacq, "is of a high degree of clarity and doesn't allow us to drown in a grandiose gesture any papier mâché aspects of hurriedly thrown together sets."[36]

Moreover, coincident with the introduction of sound, the commercialization of panchromatic film in place of the earlier orthochromatic film established the conditions for a far greater realism. Where orthochrome had favored brutal contrasts in lighting and a relative absence of textures or shading, the more subtle panchromatic film allowed for these possibilities. Expressionism could evolve into the textured surfaces, the gradations of grey, the rain-splashed nighttime pavements of poetic realism. Describing the process, Douy wisely rejects any direct determination between panchromatic film and poetic realism but nevertheless considers that it did have the effect of "unleashing the imagination of set designers, who at the time were after all the prisoners of a technique imposed by laboratories and by chemistry."

Set designers were faced therefore with a set of tensions, of contradictions. Trained as artists, and seeing themselves as engaged in an artistic undertaking, they were constrained to suppress any inclination to realize their artistic aspirations in the ways their fellow artists in other media realized them. Conditioned to an ideology of individual self-expression, they had to recognize the supremacy of a teamwork and collaboration in which, if there was a directive personality, it was not theirs. Given the supreme creative task of designing and building a world, they found themselves restricted to building one that would be a credible replica of the real world. The décor must pass unnoticed, yet determine the mood and atmosphere of the film. A décor which obtruded to the point of being symbolic would mean fewer spectators, financial crisis for the producer, and no more work for the set designer.

It was out of this tension that the set designs typical of poetic realism arose. The essential characteristic was a delicate balance between naturalism and stylization, between reproducing the lived world and heightening certain representative elements of that lived world to the point where they determined the spectator's reading of it without being so marked as to register as symbolic. The three or four set designers who were responsible for developing this style—Meerson, Wahkevitch, Barsacq, and Trauner—are remarkably consistent in their description of the principles involved. The crucial first step was to identify certain specific signifying elements which were "typical," "characteristic," "representative" of the locale, mood, or atmosphere and to modify the balance between these and other more anonymous elements in the setting so as to favor typicality. Again using italics, Barsacq describes the process as follows: "*Choose the most typical elements and dispose them in a rigorous order, such that each element participates in the plastic composition of the images and at the same time indicates the locale in which the action takes place.*"[37] Elsewhere he elaborates: "A transposition is necessary in order to obtain on the screen the equivalent of reality . . . ; that transposition is only possible if one designs a décor which recreates what is most essential in a particular locale. . . . To obtain the 'equivalent' reality it is necessary to bring out the rich or the sordid, the cluttered or the bare, the light or heavy aspect of a setting, by exaggerating the dominant character of the elements that go to make it up while suppressing the useless details."[38] The balance is one between information and poetry, between circumstantial detail and abstraction. As Trauner put it, "The important thing is to isolate in whatever locale one is representing its principal characteristic details and to bring them out at the expense of those which don't contribute to the atmosphere. These details will vary from case to case. Sometimes it's the shape of a window, of a door, of a roof which the spectators will register immediately as a Parisian house, or a northern one, or a Provençal one; or the paving of a street, the trolley of a tramway. We seek to awaken memories inscribed in the spectator's subconscious."[39]

The balance which determined the style was widely recognized by his colleagues as first having been realized by Meerson in his designs for René Clair's first sound films. "Meerson hated first-degree realism," says Trauner.[40] "It's by exaggerating the characteristic elements of what he is representing that Meerson gives us a more effective illusion of reality than do real countrysides," says Jourdan.[41] Indeed, the idea that such a "heightened" reality could be more effective, more "real" than reality itself was an important element in the set decorators' defense of the style; it allowed them to maintain their self-respect as creators, going beyond mere surface appearances, rather than being mere servile hacks, copying those appearances. "A servile copy of appearances," says Aguettand, "from which all imagination is eliminated, would logically be remote from any artistic or dramatic creativity, which can only exist when personalized by a subtle observation of life and a generous understanding of the human condition."[42] Lourié agrees. "My attitude toward 'reality' in settings dates back many years to my work as a painter and scene designer. While painting, the artist doesn't strive to achieve a photographic likeness in a portrait or to slavishly copy a landscape. He tries to express a deeper reality, a perception of the essence of his subject. . . . I approach film settings in the same way, and my attitude is shared by most of my art director friends. . . . We think in realistic terms, we use all real elements, but we eliminate useless details and compose the essential elements to underscore our idea of the setting. Our sets are true to life, often truer than the real settings."[43] "It is not a question of copying servilely a given locality—you might as well film on the spot—but rather of replacing that reality by another, more persuasive truth: the 'Truth of Art.' "[44]

Trauner, Barsacq, Wahkevitch, and Lourié all worked as assistant to Meerson at one time or another and assimilated the notion of a qualified realism based on the isolation and tactful foregrounding of "essential" characteristic details. While the emphasis might have been slightly different from one to another, the overall similarity in approach was sufficiently obvious to be articulated at the time. "Realism is the dominant of all our decorators," says Pierre Robin in 1950, "[but] they stylize, simplify, lighten, accentuate, or reduce the forms and contours of what is familiar to us."[45]

These notions of simplification and stylization recur in all accounts of the style: "It's essential always to simplify," says Trauner. "There's no point in overloading the screen with a load of boring things that attract the spectator's attention to useless details. Basically, what you don't do is almost as important as what you do. It's like the sculptor's task, which consists in chipping away."[46] Bazin summed up this balance neatly in his appreciation of *Le Jour se lève*: "We can see how Carné's realism, while still remaining true to the locale's credibility, transposes it poetically, modifying it by a formal and poetic transposition . . . ; symbolism never takes precedence over realism in this film, but it completes it as a sort of bonus."[47]

That the balance achieved was a dangerous and inherently unstable one is betrayed by the anxieties expressed from time to time by these key decorators concerning the danger of falling into "convention." In the aesthetic discourse, convention is of course opposed to invention, to originality. Yet by stylizing reality, by isolating and underlining those elements of reality which would immediately signify a particular locale to the spectator, the set designers were committed to working with conventions in the name of art. When Meerson attempts to exploit the characteristic details of Spain, Algeria, or Flanders,[48] when Trauner distinguishes the characteristic details of a Belleville street, or the beginning of the Grands Boulevards from the end of them,[49] they are appealing to spectatorial knowledge of these locales, or "conventional knowledge." But as soon as those publicly recognized characteristics become foregrounded as convention, they cease to be acceptable to the artistic discourse of the decorators. As Barsacq expresses this dilemma, "one must avoid at all costs the 'formulaic,' the known décor, and aim for the specific case; flee the facile picturesque, but choose the décor which is most characterful."[50] He complains about the false stereotype of France promoted by American films, nervously half aware that the poetic stylization which he himself promotes is just as much a "false stereotyping" of America, of Algeria, or of a Belleville street.

It is perhaps Anne Souriau, in her 1953 protosemiotic discussion of this problem, who most consciously identifies the dangerous ambivalence of poeticization and convention which underlay set design practices.[51] Having identified a number of such signifying/significant conventions widely exploited by costume designers and set decorators alike, she notes that, "The sort of information given thus by the costumes risks sometimes overflowing into artificial conventions—like the typical costumes of the commedia dell'arte. . . . There is here . . . a danger of excessive facility for the filmmaker. If a convention of color or detail is enough to indicate character, why bother having the character speak, gesticulate, act?" Like Barsacq, she sees the cinema of *other* nations as more subject to this excessive conventionalization than her own, not recognizing that perhaps the force of a convention is precisely its invisibility to the appropriately socialized spectator. Nevertheless, the very existence of such a debate underlines the tendentious nature of such a conventional system as that which underlay poetic realist set design practices. It also underlies its instability. Once recognized and foregrounded, the signifying system ceased to be acceptably "artistic" and had to be replaced by a new, more subtle set of conventions.

A retreat from stylization toward a realism based on the accumulation of circumstantial detail was perhaps inevitable. That such a move—from an abstract realism toward a more concrete realism—actually took place and that it was represented in fact by the foremost designers as "a retreat" is beyond dispute. Where in the thirties and early forties—for instance in respect of *Les Visiteurs du soir* and *Les Enfants du paradis*—Trauner claimed to be always interested to see "just how far he could push stylization," by 1946 the stylized sets of poetic realism in *Les Portes de la nuit* (among other stylized practices) already seem dated, belonging to a past era. "Detailed realism," characterized by sets cluttered with an accumulation of everyday items and facilitated by the move toward an ever greater use of location shooting, begins to become the norm. Several contemporary factors encouraged the move: Italian neorealism was admired for its use of preexisting (unstylized) sets; the postwar generation of decorators gradually introduced as a norm the modification of existing locations rather than the conceptualization and abstraction of specific signifying elements of them; postwar material difficulties, the decay of the studio system, the dismissal in 1948 of their permanent staff and dispersal of their stocks of preconstructed décors, the progressively lower status of set design and progressively lower percentage of film budgets allocated to set design and construction forced an increased use of location shooting; improvements in filmstock and camera technology made such a move easier. From a maximum of close to 100% studio shooting in the occupied zone (possibly because of a law requiring it, as Sadoul claims, though I have been unable to find any official record of such a law) and some 90% overall, the percentage of studio shooting rapidly decreased after the war. The increase in location shooting favored a "naturalism" based on "real" locales which had not experienced the stylization, simplification, or abstraction of a set designer's hand. Realism began to depend, in the field of set design, on an accumulation of redundant signifiers of reality, rather than an isolation of essential signifiers of it. Thus for Paul Bertrand in 1952, "The décor must be as natural as the sky or the sun and must serve the actor without being noticed. The true set designer must above all forget that he is a decorator. He will establish the atmosphere by a mass of little details [*sic*] which will render credible the reality of the tale."[52]

For the old hands whose ideology was one of essentialism and classical simplicity, this postwar move toward a location-based naturalism was the beginning of the end for set design. Aguettand complains that from the liberation onward, although in technical terms French set design had progressed, in aesthetic terms it "had lost its poetic feeling and its humanism and become no more than a mediocre copy of reality."[53] Trauner notes the same evolution.[54] Barsacq seems to be reconciled to this transformation of design practices when he lays down as a general rule the need to include in each image "the maximum of details—streetlights, balconies, signposts, chimney pots, and for modern films, neon signs, traffic lights, TV antennae, all that enriches the image, that moves, glitters, and casts shadows."[55] This is precisely the opposite of the ideology he elsewhere and earlier advocated. More typical is the bitter comment of the biographer of Hugues Laurent, regretting that the great architect-decorators of the past have been replaced by a school of *ensembliers-décorateurs* who simply rearrange preexisting locales.[56]

It is a development which should not be seen in isolation, but rather as one aspect of the more general move away from poetic realism toward a postwar psychological realism. Perhaps the most useful analogy is with scriptwriting and acting practices: the move there was from the creation of larger-than-life characters, acting out clearly representative roles, toward individualized characters meticulously and subtly created through a mass of detailed notations. The set design practices evolve in conjunction with these other practices, and by the 1950s the principal refuge for the stylized construction of conventionalized fictional worlds was the historical epic and the fantasy film. As the *Livre d'or* noted in 1950, "Since the war the task of decorators has been difficult. That great movement sweeping through the cinema all over the world, and tending to introduce into it a notion of reality unknown till then, has completely changed the spirit in which décors are conceived. Save for historical reconstructions—and it's by no means certain the new line has not influenced their design as well—all the axioms of the décor question have had to be rethought." In this light, as in many others, the New Wave does not represent a sharp break with past practices, but the culmination of a development which had been apparent to many within the profession ever since the war. "Directors no longer care about set design," complains Douy, "because they shoot their films in sixth-floor flats or the maid's room, and what can you do with those? Set design becomes little more than hanging up a pretty picture in the corner."[57]

A balance has shifted: at the beginning of the classic period it had been normal to see the social environment as a central factor in the shaping of events, itself a distinctive player in the drama and contributing crucially to the definition of that set of roles which the characters might inhabit; by the end, it was normal to see those characters as autonomous individuals, independent of social environment, and locked into that set of endlessly unique relationships with one another by which they defined themselves.

CINEMATOGRAPHY: AN AESTHETICS OF THE IMAGE

Cinematographers negotiated the tension between personal style and communal contribution in ways similar to the architect-decorators, since both were collaborating closely to produce a poetics of the image. They had mostly, however, entered the profession from menial or, at best, technical positions, and this lack of artistic baggage was unquestionably one reason for the reluctance of directors (and other more aesthetically oriented personnel) to rate the cinematographers as highly as they themselves would have wished. It is also the reason why those German cinematographers who came to France on Hitler's accession to power had such a profound impact on the profession. Around 1933, several key German cinematographers moved to France, chief among them Kurt Courant and Eugen Schufftan. They had been intensely involved in the expressionist cinema, filming between 1920 and 1933 for such directors as Lang, Siodmak, Ophüls, Lupu Pick, Pabst, Volkoff. They had a much clearer idea than most of their French colleagues of how light and framing could be used for expressive purposes, and therefore a stronger sense of the cinematographer's role in the creative process. Schüfftan in particular also had a Beaux Arts training which allowed him to articulate these ideas in traditional aesthetic terms. The effect this encounter had on a generation of French cinematographers echoes through all their reminiscences. Alekan, who was to become the most aggressive French proponent of the cinematographer's aesthetic role, has often acknowledged the importance of Schüfftan in his development: "Schüfftan initiated me into the secrets of his Art [sic], which consisted of two principles: observation of composition and light in the Old Masters; transposition and application to the cinema of the rules this reveals."[58] "For me, this experience was devastating, a revelation. The relationship between Schüfftan and his directors—Pabst, Carné—was astonishingly rich. At last I had the opportunity to escape from a milieu in which light was considered as a simple physical given, and to get to know a cameraman who had over many years meditated on the aesthetic and psychological problems of light."[59] Daquin was to echo these sentiments: "As for the French school of cinematographers, it owes its quality to the German cinematographers. All the assistants competed to work with them."[60] Wahkevitch, the set designer, was equally impressed: "I was lucky enough to know the great Germans, such as Courant and Planner, who formed the whole group of people like Matras, Kelber, etc. . . . Our cinematographers were practically all taught by those people. We decorators also had a lot to learn. . . . German expressionism was the whole of our youth: *Caligari, Siegfried*. . . . After the crap we had been making with Léonce Perret or Jean Boyer, suddenly films like *The Last Laugh, The Blue Angel*, burst upon us. . . . The lighting, the acting, the intelligence behind the scenarios was devastating. For us, it was a revelation."[61]

This expressionist heritage can be recognized in many films of the period 1933–1945. Kruger was known to favor the violent contrasts of lighting typical of the expressionist style, as witness *Les Misérables* (Bernard, 1933), or *La Bandera* (Duvivier, 1935). More generally, French cinematographers adopted expressionist lighting practices including the use of aggressive shadowing of bars, grills, and netting, projected onto objects and people in such a way as to distort and defamiliarize them, whenever a macabre or gothic incident seemed to call for it. The provincial gothic genre, involving hints of the weird, primitive, and magical, was always treated in expressionist style, not least because its gloomy interiors and sinister nocturnal ruins provided an appropriate basis for such lighting (for example *Sortilèges*, Christian Jacque, 1944–1945). It was normal practice to introduce isolated instances of such lighting effects in any film involving murder or violence—

for instance in *L'Etrange M. Victor* (Grémillon, 1937–1938), *Le Corbeau* (Clouzot, 1943), and *Le Jour se lève* (Carné, 1939). In *Les Portes de la nuit*, the lighting is inflected toward the expressionist when fate appears, as it is in *La Beauté du diable* (Clair, 1949–1950) when the pact is signed. Circuses and fairgrounds, treated in typically expressionist fashion as sites of chaos, violence, and unreason, constitute the opening images of *Zouzou* (Allégret, 1934), *Liliom* (Lang, 1934), and *Portrait d'un assassin* (Bernard-Roland, 1949); they also occur in *Rigolboche* (Christian-Jacque, 1936). Slums can expect a similarly expressionist lighting (*Vie de Bohème*, 1943 and *Monsieur Vincent*, 1947). But more generally, even in films where there was little or nothing of the sinister and the macabre, expressionist lighting effects would be mobilized for purely aesthetic motives whenever the site lent itself. This was particularly the case with stairways. Expressionist shadows of railings occur in films such as *Gueule d'amour*, *Hôtel du Nord*, *La Fin du jour*, and *Remorques*, with the almost exclusive function of creating an interesting image.

The use of expressionist gusts of light to contrast with these macabre shadow effects was also normal practice. When a train passes, it always extrudes such a cloud, which diffuses and seethes with the reflection of unseen lights (*Les Bas-fonds*, for instance, or *Lumière d'été*). Indeed, in sordid scenes, a totally gratuitous train can pass solely to permit such effects (*Le Jour se lève*). *Lumière d'été* takes these effects to extremes when the mine workings are being represented, using steam, smoke, and rhythmic machinery in a way that recalls *Metropolis*; and the chateau party uses night and snow to create a similar disorder.

The way in which this expressionist tradition was communicated to the French cinematographers can be read off from the strings of assistantships: Page was assistant to Périnal, Thirard, Stradling, Kelber, Isnard, Mundwiller, and Schüfftan before himself becoming director of photography; Alekan was assistant to Périnal and Schüfftan among others; Barry trained with Schüfftan and saw him as his master; Claude Renoir was assistant to Matras, Kauffman, Bachelet, and Courant; Juillard was assistant to Périnal, Kruger, Matras, and Burel; Fellous was assistant to Courant, Thirard, Kelber, and others; Fossard to Kruger, Hubert, and Schüfftan; Douarinou to Thirard and Matras.

Already by 1935, then, a generation of cinematographers had been formed with radically different aspirations from their silent predecessors, all but a relative few of whom they saw as unambitious executants. Ironically, as a somewhat more industrial cinema replaced the more art-oriented cinema of the twenties, the ideology of cinematographers travelled in the reverse direction. They came to look down on their predecessors as mere *éclairagistes*—interested only in the light levels, preoccupied with the technical necessities of recording the profilmic performance, and printing the resultant film, unable to conceive of the expressive function of their job. "[Lighting that] conveyed ideas only came late to us," says Alekan, "when people began thinking about the problem of expressive lighting which could help to construct the image, not only in its aesthetic aspects but in its psychological significance. In France there were three or four great cameramen who had picked this up. But most worked commercially: they provided the light; in the jargon of the trade, they "sprayed it" over everything. The image in that case didn't signify much. An image only becomes meaningful when it corresponds to the intimate conviction of the two creators of the image, namely the director and the cinematographer (I class them on the same level), and that implies a perfect relationship and understanding between them. Me, I was lucky enough to work with Schüfftan, and to discover the importance of the light/structure of an image and its graphic construction; because he was an artist; these are things which can't be learned, which must be felt."[62]

Rejecting the practices of their predecessors in toto, such cinematographers regularly proposed the study of engravers (particularly for black and white film) and of painters. Gustave Doré in particular is cited by Alekan and Burel as their artistic model; Claude Renoir refers to Manet and the impressionists, including of course Auguste Renoir, as the inspiration for certain effects he aimed at; Alekan refers also to Rembrandt and Léonardo da Vinci and Piranèse. "Knowledge of the classics of the cinema and of painting," says André Dumaître,"—in brief a pictorial training—seems to be indispensable. For centuries people have been studying the sort of problems we face today, and we can find in them a whole heritage of feeling, sensitivity, art."[63] It was this painterly heritage that the cinematographers of 1935–1950 saw themselves as perpetuating, but with the important complicating factor of dynamism: instead of a still image, cinematographers had to develop lighting setups to cope with the movement both of subject/camera and of object/actor. Innovation was necessary, therefore; the models provided by their artistic predecessors could only inspire with possibilities; they could not be copied directly.

Despite this developing aesthetic awareness, at no stage did the bulk of the French cinematographers of the classic period develop the more egocentric aspects of this romantic ideology of the creative artist; they had no opportunity to do so, given the artistic authority widely conceded to the director, and given the close artistic cooperation that existed between the cinematographer and the set designer, whose sets he was called on to light but whose artistic credentials were usually considerably stronger than his own. The artistic status that the cinematographer aspired to, then, tended to develop within an ideology of cooperation. The creative team was a unit, each contributing its necessary aesthetic expertise to an ideally unified work in which, if cooperation and mutual understanding were complete, the individual contributions would not be noticeable. Questions of personal style tend therefore to be dismissed as an irrelevance, or even rejected as undesirable. Subordination to the subject and to an aesthetic framework determined by the director are prime constraints limiting any "self-expression" on the part of the cinematographer. This frequently overflows into a morale of discretion, even of self-abnegation, in which the photography should not be remarked by the spectator, but should form part of a holistic aesthetic unity.

"My only question," says Alekan, "each time I have begun work on a film, has been 'How, as illustrator, can I create the images suggested by the theme and desired by the director?' "[64] and again, "Obviously one has a certain conception of the image in general, but our job being above all an art of understanding and sensitivity, we must absorb the subject in order to transpose it from the literary to the plastic form. That work has its own atmosphere; the cinematographer's job is to 'engrave' that climate on film."[65] "Every cinematographer must work with this idea present in his mind: it's not him that must stand out, it's not a question of promoting his own worth, but of promoting the story. There is a theme to express, and the director offers us the prodigious privilege of helping him express it."[66] For Agostini, "There must be no disjunction between photography and direction, but a total cohesion, the job of photography being to serve everything else. . . . Of course the cinematographer has a certain latitude for creativity, but it must not extend beyond the limit of his attributions as determined by the title Director of Photography. . . . It's a question not of photography for its own sake, but photography to serve the overarching idea, the direction, and which corresponds not to a personality or personal style, but to a style which with the director we have chosen according to the subject of the film."[67] For Barry, "The cinematographer's job—very difficult, for he changes directors constantly—consists essentially of underlining the idea behind the film. . . . The operator must not produce 'His' photo, but one appropriate to the film."[68] For Burel, "The photography must never intrude. If it is successful, it must so merge with the whole that it has no importance in itself. If it is well integrated, you don't notice it. . . . A film of which you say 'The photography's beautiful' is rarely a good film."[69] For Bac, "When the public 'notices' the photo, the technician [sic] has missed the point. The public must forget that it is at the cinema, not be stopped short by 'effects,' good or bad, not notice camera movements; in brief, the cinematographer's job is to suppress the presence of the camera between the actor and the spectator." "There will never be 'a Bac style' of filming," comments the interviewer; "Bac doesn't like capital letters or signatures." "I agree entirely with Bac," comments Lemare, "when he says 'that the cinematographer must produce *the* photo appropriate to the film, not *his* photo.' "[70] The most flattering thing Matras can say in homage to the late Thirard is that "his images were constantly balanced, totally in harmony with the requirements of the scenario, but without those self-important effects that force your attention. He always served the film, instead of serving his own ends by introducing spectacular eccentricities."[71]

This minimizing of the personal and expressive aspects of cinematography is typical of the qualified realism which organized the practices of the early classic cinema. In line with it, a principal preoccupation of the cinematographer was to organize his lighting so as to produce an impression of depth and perspective in the image. The development of panchromatic film was an essential element in this project. Where orthochromatic film had pushed all light effects in the direction of high contrast, panchromatic film, first introduced into France in 1927 for *La Petite Marchande d'allumettes*, registered different colors and tonings as highly inflected shades of grey. This allowed for the molding of people and objects in a way that could be read as three dimensions and thus allowed for the reproduction of those chiaroscuro effects common in engravings. From then on the subtle organization of light and shadow within the frame became the principal—indeed only—aesthetic preoccupation of the cinematographer. Composition, mass, depth, and the realism of the three-dimensional profilmic reality which these could generate were his claim to creative status. Consequently, where a few French cinematographers concentrated on the stark contrasts of expressionism, most proclaim an aesthetic that marries this expressionist "pooling" and shafting of light with the molding effects of panchromatic film to produce a representation of reality which, though monochrome, has a wealth of those clues to distance and the relationship between people and objects which we obtain in real life. This tendency was underlined by the French practice of playing down the overall floodlighting (especially compared to American cinematographers), allowing large sections of the image to fade away into darkness.

As Agostini put it, "In the black and white period the director's prime preoccupation was that the actors should be in relief. If I photographed you now, . . . I wouldn't be sure your head didn't merge with the wall, that the grey registered by the wall wasn't the same grey as your hair. So when there wasn't an absolute guarantee of this relief effect, we had to use a backlight to define the volume occupied in space by the actors. Because although the character appears on the screen in two dimensions, except in rare instances you want the spectator to believe there is a volume. This was the great obsession of all cinematographers during the black and white period: this depth, this impression of reality."[72] Even more explicit is the account given by Kelber. Asked to characterize the standard lighting practices of French cinematographers, he said, "The back light, above all, to detach characters from the wall behind; black and white accentuates the 2D aspect of cinema, so you absolutely have to have a light to detach the important elements, and the backlight served that purpose. Next you lit the set: a separate lighting setup different from that used for the characters, and which also had as its purpose the generation of a certain relief, especially through the use of shadows; you had to suggest depth as with those shadows that architects draw in on their plans. . . . If you look at the sets of the great decorators (Meerson, Trauner, Andrejev), you'll notice that they're in two parts: one part directly used for the actor, and another, in the background, where the actors seldom go; it's this back part that we used to light so as to get an effect of depth. . . . Finally, once the set was lit, you began to deal with the actors."[73]

Whether you began by lighting the set and then moved to the characters, or began by lighting the actors and then lit the set to fit them was a matter of some debate to the cinematographers. It encapsulated the opposition between on the one hand providing an appropriate atmosphere for the subject and on the other hand setting off the beauty or virility of the actors—between genre and star. It is significant that nearly all accounts emphasize the prior importance of genre, subject, and atmosphere over star, and that in specifying this priority the French cinematographers felt that they were distinguishing the European lighting style from that of their American colleagues. "The Germans," says Kelber, "in contrast to the Americans, never privileged the actors at the expense of the sets, and it's under Pabst's influence, doubtless, that I rather lost the obsession with setting off the faces of stars."[74] "For American cinematographers," says Alekan, "who have made it an actual *rule*, light must first of all underline the physical aspect of the actors, whatever may be happening and wherever they are, so as to show them in their most favorable light. . . . In such a system, the light must be conceived principally in terms of setting off the face. The body comes next. . . . This hierarchy has become codified in America, and a certain sclerosis has resulted from it. . . . To dissociate the actors by a lighting which privileges them at the expense of the overall look is a nonsense—it's sometimes *necessary*, but you can't set it up as a rule."[75]

The range of "atmospheres" or climates appropriate to different genres were never spelled out in detail, and the generalities which cinematographers did provide in interview or textbook were scarcely surprising—dramas required a sombre lighting with accentuated contrasts, comedies require a bright lighting with well-lit backgrounds, reflective glints and sheens, and sunny windows; melodramas call for dark backgrounds, deformed shadows, and violent back lighting. Standard connotations are invoked to justify these setups—connotations of light and dark, the visible and the invisible, the open and the closed, day and night, sun and moon, uniformity and contrast, the recognizable and the strange. Nevertheless, such general atmospheres, felt to derive from the overall mood or genre of the film, were so important as to need careful preservation throughout the film. Continuity and homogeneity were invoked as principles, consonant with the holistic unity of the film, the basic realism principle, that needed constant attention: no disjunctions or discrepancies between lighting setups must be apparent from shot to shot or scene to scene, and all perceptible light effects must be seen to have a realistic source in lamp, window, or sun. "It's not a question of perfecting a single image, but of conserving the photographic unity throughout the whole film," notes Geneviève Coste,[76] and Burel instructs his pupils likewise: "The homogeneity of the photography must be an absolute rule."[77] "For days, weeks on end," says Jacques Lemare, "he must ensure the 'photographic' continuity of the film.

He must maintain the degree of contrast in the image such that a hardedged scene doesn't succeed or precede a scene in shades of grey."[78] All repeat such remarks, whether in terms of homogeneity, consistency, or "plastic" continuity, which is "the most important thing in the film."[79]

To a certain extent this emphasis on the overall film, its atmosphere, and the primacy of the sets over the actors reflects the relatively lesser importance attributed to stars within the French cinema of 1930–1960, but also the relatively greater importance of the representation of society over the representation of the individual. The centrality of personal relationships which usually underlies any Western narration was for much of the classical period downplayed in France, relative to America. It was the structure and mood of the world in which the actors moved rather than the glamour or presence of the actors themselves which had priority. Nevertheless, certain gestures toward a star system did exist, and no cinematographer could afford entirely to make light of the techniques of setting off an actress's beauty or an actor's virility. It was sufficiently common for films to be written around a given star's persona and for that star to have a determining say in the choice of cinematographer, to ensure that such techniques were widely recognized and used. Jean Gabin and Gaby Morlay were known to prefer Kruger's way of lighting them; Danielle Darrieux would insist on being filmed by Armand Thirard.

The basic setups for lighting the actors were not unlike those used elsewhere—a panel of floods for general illumination, a three-quarter front spot as a key light, and a spot as a backlight. To this might be added a spot from above on the man to make his brow and jaw stand out ("without which he will lack virility").[80] The use of strong key light on the actor from above and in front had not been common in France in the twenties, but was brought to France by Paramount and its American cinematographers. Kelber, who worked with them there and picked up from Stradling the appropriate techniques, contrasts the French tradition typified by Pathé with this type of lighting. "The Paramount boss, Robert T. Kane, warned us, 'Gentlemen, we are in the business of selling voices, and actors. . . . ' As a result, we had to constantly hold on the actors, film them from in front, in full light, avoiding anything that might distract from the expression on their face. The Americans had developed a quite specific type of lighting setup for this purpose—a single spot from in front. . . . This single unidirectional light, falling from above, came as a revelation to us. . . . One of its advantages was that it set off the beauty of the women, and we were smack in the middle of the star system. But opposite Paramount there was Pathé, the rival house, striving to maintain its own photographic style. . . . "[81]

For Burel, the most effective way to set off the beauty of the female star was to suffuse her with a romantic glow and to use a "gentle" lens: "Anyway be sure not to use a harsh lens, because it isn't proper to inspect beautiful women through a magnifying glass. They gain nothing from it, nor do we, and the film still less."[82] Her face must be the most glowing element in the image; it must be filmed to disguise wrinkles and the inevitable asymmetries; nothing must move behind them so as to distract the spectator's gaze, and it must always be filmed from the most photogenic angle; "from long experience we have learned that it is rare for an actor, and even more an actress, to disregard such advice."[83] Such concessions to the star system inspired the violent condemnation of Roger Fellous, who felt that "some cinematographers have established their reputations solely by filming women; for often the cinema seems to consist simply of selling female flesh. It's a sort of photographic pimping."[84]

The question of glamour and photogenics was by no means disregarded, so the difficulties became even more acute with the advent of color film, as the quotations in chapter 3 indicate (see the final section, entitled "Color.") Whatever their rationalization, however, these strictures concerning discretion in the exploitation of color combined with the parallel strictures concerning discretion in the exploitation of lighting and of camera work to construct an aesthetics, shared by cinematographers and set designers (and indeed by editors and composers), which favored that qualified, or "poeticised," realism that has already been explored in the previous section.

During the late thirties and forties, then, and largely under the influence of the expressionists, French classic cinematography consistently reached a height of technical perfection that it had seldom attained to that point. The effect of exquisite artifice, of plastic beauty, of studied theatricality that resulted was readily compatible with the poeticized décors designed by the set designers. The style which these practices constructed was, however, relatively shortlived: in the immediate postwar years a series of technological developments intruded on the work of the cinematographer in a way that was to significantly detract from the status of the job and make the period 1935–1950 seem in retrospect a peak of respectability and achievement which they could never again expect to scale. Essentially, these technological factors grew out of wartime developments and are well-known: over a decade cameras became lighter, more portable, at once more sophisticated and easier to master. Filmstock became more sensitive; effects which had required years of experience to master could be achieved effortlessly. Night photography and a fortiori filming in the light available in natural interiors allowed a more ready "escape" from studio conditions. The hours of meticulous preparation within the hermetic and magical world of the studio could be, at whatever cost, dispensed with. An amateur without significant training could achieve effects by the mid-fifties that a professional would have found difficult a decade before. The deprofessionalization of the role of the cinematographer could begin.

Perhaps the most significant of the changes was not the greater sensitivity of the new filmstocks, but their greater predictability. Where it had been one of the profession's most difficult and therefore most prized tasks to achieve consistency across a whole film, given the fluctuation of filmstock emulsions within and between batches, this was now made easier by a totally reliable and consistent level of emulsion. No longer did the cinematographer need to liaise endlessly with the lab and advise on printing and developing procedures to reconcile light levels. Given the manufacturer's indications, he could count on certain effects resulting from certain settings. In addition, a barrage of measuring instruments became available for specifying the exact light values of the profilmic reality and for translating this to an appropriate setting for a given filmstock and a given effect. A science of the image was taking over, in which rationality replaced experience and intuition. Inevitably, a degree of demystification took place as this predictability became widely recognized. Where before the cinematographer's personal technical knowledge and experience had been all that stood between the success and failure of the image, and enormous respect ensued when it was acceptable, it now became the case that he was *expected* to produce an acceptable image, and enormous scorn would have ensued if he didn't. "When I began in this job," says Agostini, "we didn't know what a photoelectric cell was; we had no notion of measuring light. Experience taught us what to do. Today it's different. Previously, the cinematographer had been somewhat favored by circumstances. He alone on the set organized the lighting and was responsible for the film's development. That gave him a status and influence that he no longer has, a sort of conjuror side to him which has completely gone. . . . Now you always know, when you film, what the result's going to be."[85]

The potential deterioration in the job's status was, paradoxically, exacerbated by the introduction of color. Whatever the difficulties it posed, it undermined the profession's main claim to aesthetic status, the ability, by ingenious and time-consuming disposition of lighting, to ensure a realistic three-dimensional impression. Where, in the case of black and white photography, elaborate lighting setups were needed to generate the impression of relief, knowledge of which could be represented as being handed down from master to disciple and perfected over years of practice, color film achieved this effect effortlessly and more or less automatically. No longer did objects or figures risk disappearing into the background, no longer did the chiaroscuro have to be worked over to detach grey from grey; distinct colors of settings, objects, costumes, and hair colors stood out one against another in a way that provided a multitude of depth cues for the spectator. Knowledge, experience, and technique began to seem superfluous, and the claim to artistic status which these had supported now threatened to collapse. Where a sort of second-degree star system had once operated among cinematographers, they now reverted toward the status of technicians and servants. "Today the status of director of photography is less important than it was ten or fifteen years ago," says Deville in 1959. "Technique is no longer a problem. There are a lot more directors of photography than before the war, when a half dozen 'tenors' held the stage and laid down the law. This newfound modesty of technique is due also to the fact that directors know more and more about cinematography. The dialogue between director and cinematographer is simpler today, for the director knows what he can expect of the image."[86]

Most of those in the trade cited 1950 as the date of transition between these two states. "Until 1950 the great directors and great cinematographers had enough clout to force producers not to shoot until conditions were favorable. Nowadays, too often economic considerations outweigh aesthetic considerations; shooting goes on whatever the light, regardless of that essential factor, continuity."[87] For Fellous, there had been a period when the cinematographer "had pulled the blankets to his side of the bed," but the fifties had seen a reversal with the director reasserting his prerogatives.[88] For their decorator allies, even more savagely hit by the transition toward location shooting, the opposition was similarly characterized, and even the scenarist Jean Aurenche noted the move: "You can't imagine what a dictatorship the cinematographer exercised at that time [the late forties]; the most profound silence reigned on the set when he spoke; his influence was enormous. Fortunately lighting and filmstock have made great progress since then; but before the war you had to regulate the lighting endlessly (the more so as you were working with actresses very sensitive of their looks; I remember Mme Edwige Feuillère, she was really extraordinary . . .). Louis Page, young Renoir, Christian Matras . . . were people endowed with a terrible authority, and everyone else was struck dumb. Today the atmosphere on the sets is very different. . . . A man like Lara was terrified of his cinematographer, Michel Kelber. That really impressed me."[89]

If there was one single technological development that determined this change, it was television. Cinematographers were early called in to advise on and work in the new medium, and the radically different working conditions required in that position affected the thinking not just of cinematographers—indeed, not so much of cinematographers, who were for the most part reluctant converts—as of producers. Essentially, television production was cheaper than film production, though at a significant cost to the quality of the image. For the first decade after the war, magnetic recording was not available, so the norm for dramatic productions was direct broadcast. This made the performance a theatrical rather than a cinematic event, with a lengthy lead time for rehearsals climaxed by a single continuous shoot. The shoot itself was a complex event to film, because it had to be filmed with a number of cameras, usually four or five. In the silent days, French cinematographers had been accustomed to working with multiple camera setups, and some of Gance's films involved notoriously complex shoots, from which a final sequence of takes would be selected at the moment of editing. With the necessity for developing a preconceived and detailed *découpage technique* before shooting began, the classic cinema had rapidly reduced the norm from four through three and two cameras, till it became standard for each shot to be filmed separately, by a single camera placed in the "right" position. More than one camera might be used on occasion, as "insurance" in complex takes that were not readily repeatable, such as fight scenes or accident scenes in which part or all of a set was destroyed, and certain directors (such as Marc Allégret) who didn't preplan as much as was normal, might cover themselves by using more than one, but these were exceptions. In moving to television, a generation of cinematographers brought up on this tradition of perfecting separately the minute fragments of a giant narrative puzzle, each filmed separately with a single camera and meticulous preparation, had to adapt to a situation where they must think out in advance the positioning and movements of multiple cameras surrounding a continuous performance, editing from one to another as the event unrolled. Moreover, though they might rehearse mentally the technical procedures required by the coming performance, they could not rehearse them in practice till just before the shoot; and to make matters worse, the light levels of the television cameras were unreliable, and there was no possibility as with film of correcting levels at a later lab stage.[90] It seemed to most of them a disturbing, dangerous, and basically inadequate set of practices.

A large part of their worry arose from the knock-on effects on the lighting setups: unable to modify, regulate, or adjust between takes as had become the custom in the cinema, directors of photography were obliged to revert to some extent if not entirely to the generalized "cheesy" lighting which they had so despised in their predecessors. Given the diverse movements of cast and cameras, every aspect of the set had to be adequately lit at every moment, so the aesthetics of the image was bound in their view to suffer. Any modifications to the lighting during filming had to be minimal but hasty. A 90-minute film which might normally require eight weeks of shooting had to be technically rehearsed and filmed in two days.

It was this rapidity in the execution of their lighting setups that affected their film work. On the one hand, a fifties generation of cinematographers, trained as much in television as in cinema, acquired the practice of rapidity and of minimum modification to a general diffused lighting, and on the other hand an older generation found themselves defending an art of cinematography against the "perfunctory" practices of these new *éclairagistes*. Recalling the early days of television, Agostini remembers the difficulties he had in convincing the television technicians in the late forties that light could and should be organized and modulated. "When I said they should cut these lights and turn on those they thought I was mad. They said 'The image's OK.' And in a sense it was—a cheesy light across the whole screen. We had a terrible struggle with those we called, and rightly so, the [new] *éclairagistes*."[91] "The role of the director of photography is sacrificed more and more," says Claude Renoir in 1959. "Producers and directors both treat him badly; he is progressively confined into a role of *éclairagiste*."[92] This was to be a continuing complaint for him: in an article entitled "Cinematography Has Collapsed" he complains that "the only thing asked of us these days is to work quickly and with a minimum of material. . . . The days when producers and directors asked for a quality image—which cost a lot, I agree, which meant waiting for the right light—those days are past!"[93] Burel voices the same regrets, likewise blaming television.[94] More generally, on a psychological level, "the joy had gone out of filming" in the fifties. The feeling of being engaged in a communal, ambitious, and creative undertaking, of being at once privileged and dedicated, no longer infuses the accounts of fifties cinematographers.

The trouble was that the speed and cheapness of television shooting began to be expected in the cinema, but without translating the multiple-camera continuous performance that had encouraged and permitted it. Only Renoir, for *Déjeuner sur l'herbe*, attempted to explore and exploit the television practices for a cinematic shoot, and that only in 1959. Four Mitchell cameras and an unblimped mobile Caméflex were used to shoot, not a single continuous performance of the whole film, but at least long continuously staged sequences. Partly the aim was to return the emphasis to acting in continuity, such that the actors had a chance to work their way into their roles and interact as in a continuous theatrical performance. Leclerc, the cinematographer, recognizes that in a sense he was being asked to modulate cinematic practices via television back toward the long-abhorred practices of "filmed theater";[95] and it was indeed something more like filmed theater that was being forced on fifties cinematographers, simply to achieve the speed and cost savings required of them.

An equally compelling pressure toward rapidity and cheapness was the postwar documentary movement, with its neorealist fictional counterpart. The critical magazines of the period 1945–1948 chronicle the powerful impact on the French public and on French filmmakers of the Italian neorealists. Clément, in filming *La Bataille du rail* (1945–1946) saw himself as producing the first French equivalent. The transfer of actuality and documentary techniques to fiction, whether in the form of *Farrebique* or the communal *La Libération de Paris* (1945), represented a dramatic challenge to the existing highly aestheticized filming and lighting styles. Alekan talked of his split personality when filming both *La Bataille du rail* and *La Belle et la bête*, and at least for the record expressed regret at not having had the nerve to take the documentary aspect of the former as far as Clément would have liked—his aestheticist principles didn't allow him to produce an image that wasn't composed, pictorial, premeditated, fabricated. By comparison neorealism "suddenly presented us with images that looked free and easy! It was liberation time in several countries, and the liberation of the camera as well."[96]

The tendency to desert studios, to film on location and in natural interiors furthered this tendency toward a less studied image. The unreliable light levels and the lack of space in natural interiors to produce any studied depth effects pushed postwar films toward a more flattened image, a study in greys rather than an organization of masses, pools of lights, sculpting, and shafting. Cumulatively, the result was not just a further pressure toward cheapness and rapidity, then, but a pressure toward a new aesthetic of the image, based on flatness and grisaille rather than on depth. No less a form of realism, it involved the authentication of fiction by way of the documentary practices of natural interiors, natural lighting, and a direct-reporting camera. Although this new tendency did not entirely displace the earlier aesthetic, it is everywhere apparent in films evoking the underworld and the bleakness of the postwar world; it also served as an appropriate camera style for the more psychological realism of the late forties and the fifties, in which personal interrelationships displaced social roles as the center of interest; and in which everyday domestic reality and everyday human relationships became a common theme for black and white films. "The current tendency is to make every attempt to duplicate lived reality," says Grignon, in the late fifties.[97] Any subtlety was due to the infinite gradation of half-tones produced within a generally bleak and flat image. Certain cinematographers such as Roger Hubert were recognized within the trade as particularly adept at this effect, known as the "onion-peel" effect. Burel's account of his early collaboration with Bresson[98] makes it clear that he saw himself as imposing this grisaille look on Bresson, who had been looking for something much more like the high-contrast aesthetics of the 1935–1950 period. On the whole, however, this new realism contributed to the gradual decline of cinematography as a profession: directors of photography were being called on to work faster, with less material, in conditions that did not allow them to produce the studied compositions which had been their aesthetic claim to status.

One important reaction against this "decline of the cinematographer" was an attempt to redefine his aesthetic status by an appeal to the principles of certain forms of modernist painting. Since the achievement of relief, depth, and the consequent impression of realism had, largely because of color, now become relatively simple, the more status-conscious cinematographers began proposing as an alternative philosophy the achievement of precisely the opposite effect: large blocks and planes of color, used dramatically rather than realistically. As noted earlier, color cinematography was at first used primarily for exotic and fantasy subjects, and in that sense was unrealistic; but it was used in "prosaic" rather than poetic ways to increase the impression of realness of those escapist films. Drawing on the cubist and abstract heritage of modern painting, cinematographers such as Alekan and Renoir began a campaign to use color structurally, as a signifying element rather than a crutch for realism.

Briefly, having proclaimed for 15 years that their art consisted in producing an effect of relief and of reality, they switched to proclaiming that their art consisted in juxtaposing flat cubist surfaces which broke with the banality of real color. Not that they saw themselves as having at any time simply "reproduced" reality. Even during the period 1935–1950, it is clear that they saw their lighting as "poeticizing" reality, in the sense that the creation of a particular atmospheric effect constituted an "interpretation" or "representation" of reality, rather than a reproduction. Fog effects, glistening watered surfaces, sombre night effects were all part of their arsenal for thus poeticizing reality.[99] The normal term which they employed for this process was borrowed from their decorator allies—the "transposition" of reality. But in its new guise, art did not consist of transposing reality; it consisted of restructuring it.

The following series of quotations from different interviews given by Alekan after 1955 sufficiently indicates the change in aesthetic: "Not enough attention is paid to the great experience of painters. All the avenues opened up by modern painting are available to us: for example, instead of striving to create in the image a pseudo-relief, why not try to do a film entirely in flat surfaces?" "Ultimately, the problem is no one dares use color like a painter, that's the truth of it. . . . As for me, it's not the 'truth' of light I'm interested in, it's the truth of feeling. In other words, I'm for an 'interpreted' light. . . . You can work with natural light, but also with a 'supernatural' light, rethinking it, reworking it to give it 'something more.' And that's what Art is, that 'something more' . . . otherwise you might just as well plonk your camera down and film, like a reporter." "Let filmmakers express themselves according to their temperament; for some, realism, for others irrealism; for some, fidelity to nature, for others, infidelity to its forms and colors. . . . Myself, I am in favor of infidelity." "We were ill-prepared for color . . . we used color as it presented itself in life. Films became véristes again. Directors and scriptwriters were primarily responsible, because they didn't give this problem any thought. Imagination no longer had any place. We reproduced colors supposedly 'natural,' and cinematographers allowed themselves to be caught up in this movement. Thank goodness, things have changed. Directors began asking what color could contribute thematically; and cinematographers abandoned striving for the natural." He cites examples from the 1960s: Losey, Dassin, Godard; Topkapi, Pierrot le fou, and Deux hommes dans Manhattan.

Claude Renoir supports him strongly, likewise from the fifties onward: "I would like to do a film where, with respect to contemporary painting, for example, the photography was abstract." "For me the cinema must not resemble reality as the eye sees it, but must interpret that reality. The image must be reworked. I like to recompose light, play with shadows to make an image nothing less than a painting." "The most fulfilling moment in my career will be when I cease to be compared to some great painter, but am recognized as simply having my own style."[100] He reminisces on the one film by a "classic" director that nearly got made according to these principles—Clouzot's L'Enfer, in which "the guiding principle was to make a film half in black and white, half in color, alternately. Thus the man's life would appear in black and white, but his imagination, deformed by jealousy—"the other life"—would appear in color. We arranged to obtain a black and white that was very pure, neutral. The color Clouzot wanted had nothing to do with natural color. Clouzot is a painter, so he was seeking to represent things and people on the screen by way of a totally recomposed, recreated color, having no relation whatsoever with everyday reality."[101] But this was in 1965, when Godard and others had already put into practice such an aesthetic.

The tendency to distinguish between *"véristes"* and *"aestheticists"* in the use of color had been taken up by others already in the fifties—Agostini[102] and Fellous[103] both make the distinction, and Edmond Séchan talks of "lots of color films being made, but few really *using* color."[104] Indeed, aside from the structural use of red and gold in *Les Grandes Manoeuvres* (Clair, 1955), Tati's *Mon oncle* (1957–1958), and the use of red in *Le Ballon rouge*, no one can point to such a procedure's having yet been explored. To a certain extent, one of the virtues of this aesthetic was precisely to distance the cinematographer from current practice. They could occupy in theory the higher aesthetic ground of modern art, as yet unexplored in practice by any of their less artistically aware colleagues.

FRAMING AND CAMERAWORK

It is clear that throughout the classic period the normal situation was for the director, and not the cinematographer, to take primary responsibility for framing the image and deciding on camera angles and positions. While actual practices varied from the extreme disinterest of Pagnol and Guitry to the extreme precision of Duvivier, the standard procedure would see such factors specified in general terms in the *découpage technique* which the director produced in the two weeks or so before shooting. Of course this was normally done in conjunction with the cinematographer, who offered advice, and also with the decorator, since it tied in with the layout of the décors, the existence or not of a ceiling, the height of the walls, and the need or not for special effects (paintings on glass, models, etc.); nevertheless, it was primarily the director's decision, and any resultant stylistic features might be expected to correlate with directors' names rather than the cinematographers' (especially as the directors conferred directly with the camera operator for any last-minute variations, rather than with the cinematographer). As an aspect of cinematography, however, it is more logical to treat it in the present context.

All aspects of camera technique lend themselves to statistical style analysis, but little has been done except by Barry Salt. No reliable figures have ever been produced to substantiate the various wild generalizations about this aspect of directorial style in the French cinema. A number of sources make impressionistic assertions to the effect that the camera was relatively liberated in the twenties, was inhibited by the cumbrous blimping and heavier materials of sound cinema, began to be more agile again as these technological limitations were gradually overcome, and was somewhat inhibited again by the advent of color, which again involved heavier technology, though this may have been compensated by the simultaneous introduction of television practices. The only concrete estimate of camera movements in French cinema that I know of is that of Chardavoine, who asserts (without indicating her reason for believing this) that 20–30% of shots involved camera movement in 1920, and 50% in 1926 (whereas "now," in 1973, 70–80% did so).[105] This implies a progressive "liberation" of the camera over these five decades—an implication which recurs in Sadoul's *Histoire générale du cinéma*.[106]

Barry Salt notes a worldwide vogue for camera mobility in the wake of the Italian film *Cabiria* (1914) which lasted until about 1917, followed by "a new explosion of camera mobility in France and Germany" in 1923[107] which was more far-reaching in its effects, flowing on to America in 1926. He considers, though without giving evidence for it, that in all major filmmaking nations in the late twenties "those films which do use tracking shots still make do with only a handful, and they are still a minority among the total production"; though he thinks the delay in the advent of sound in France may have meant that the tendency toward camera movement went further there. Unlike most French commentators, he sees this tendency continuing unchanged into the sound period and being confirmed in the late thirties as better technology allows more readily mobile cameras.

That these generalities are less precise than most of his observations is due to the smallness of his sample. He tries to relate the data to directorial style, but with little success. Figure 7.1 is perhaps therefore the first attempt to explore on a reasonable statistical basis the evolution of camera movements, at least in the French cinema. It lists the number of (1) tracking shots (with or without crane), (2) simple camera-head movements such as pan or tilt, and (3) complex movements involving both camera and camera-head. It then totals these (4) and relates them to a standard 100-minute film (5). It also lists the number of shots with camera movements of any sort (6) and relates them to a standard 100-minute film (7).[108]

While more films need to be analyzed to produce reliable data, the existing analysis indicates that the introduction of sound did indeed inhibit camera mobility. From a low of 10% of shots in 1930, camera mobility increased rapidly, until by 1935 it had reached a level at which it was to remain for the next twenty years—an average of one shot in three, with a normal variation between 20% and 50%. Films directed by Carné and Grémillon tended to be at the bottom end of this normal range, whereas films directed by Duvivier, Christian-Jacque, and Delannoy tended to be at the top end, with an active camera in over 40% of shots.

The figures are deceptive, however, because the number of shots varied so dramatically from film to film; and it is for that reason that the standardizing to a 100-minute film is more reliably informative about the degree of activity of the camera. Column 7 shows that the number of shots with an active camera in such a standard film rose steadily throughout the thirties from about 50 shots per 100 minutes in 1930 to 160 by 1940, stabilizing at

FIGURE 7.1   Camera and Camera-Head Movements

	Track	Pan	Complex	Total	Per 100'	Shots with active camera	Per 100'	%
1930–1934	24.3	96.7	12.8	133.8	123	103.3	98.5	19.5
1935–1937	37.3	108.1	31.3	176.7	197	125.2	140.2	32.3
1938–1941	40.5	109.2	40.6	190.3	198	139.5	150.8	32.0
1942–1945	54.5	147.9	47.7	250.1	247	187.4	184.3	32.5
1946–1949	50.7	126.6	33.3	210.6	222	159.8	168.6	33.1
1950–1953	44.5	130.9	44.5	219.9	260	152.4	180.4	34.6
1954–1961	60.9	159.2	54.5	274.6	274	169.5	171.4	39.5

Source: Analysis of 10–12 films from each period

about 175 thereafter. After the war, the range of variation is greater than in the period 1930–1945, but no films record fewer than 110 such shots per 100 minutes. The same generalizations still hold about directorial tendencies, though it turns out that, after the war, films directed by Clément, Becker, and Clouzot also have a more active camera (over 200 active shots per 100 minutes) and that films directed by René Clair, which had in the thirties been low in camera activity but increasingly active (presumably as technology permitted) are after the war very active.

Consideration of the actual number of camera and camera-head movements (rather than just the number of shots with such movements), both raw and standardized, confirms these observations for the prewar period. The average number of camera movements, including pan and tilt, per 100 minutes shows a steady increase throughout the thirties, but it continues to increase right through the classical period, from a low of 50 in 1930 to 200 (1935–1940), 250 (1940–1955), and finally 275 (1955–1960); Duvivier's films stand out in the thirties as averaging 250 movements per 100 minutes at a time when the average was only creeping up from 50 toward 200.

A breakdown of the figures into camera movements and camera-head movements shows that, as might be expected, there were few of the former until 1935, the greater part of camera activity being due to pans (and occasionally tilts). Thereafter the proportions remain roughly the same, with an increase in both panning and tracking over the whole period; between 1935 and 1960 camera movements (tracking or complex) range between 25% and 50% of all activity, whereas camera-head movement ranges between 50% and 75%. It becomes clear that Grémillon and Carné used the normal amount of panning but relatively little actual camera movement, which is the reason for their overall low activity, whereas the highly active camera of Delannoy is largely due to an unusually large number of tracking shots.

Tentatively, then, such statistical data can provide a basis for observations concerning both directorial style and national norms in technical areas. One aspect of camera movement is hidden by these purely quantitative data, however, and that is the degree to which camera movements are relatively slight, gentle, and discrete, or on the contrary so aggressive and virtuoso as to foreground technique and register as poetic, or even formalist. Within the low figures for camera movements in René Clair's early films, for instance, there is typically at the beginning a long, complex, virtuoso camera movement which moves into and explores the whole set, orienting the audience within it and establishing right away the overall atmosphere as defined by set, costumes, and lighting. Such elaborate establishing shots, involving numbers of complex camera movements, became a regular feature of French films between 1935 and 1950 (see, for instance, the opening of *Jenny*, *La Belle Equipe*, *Hôtel du Nord*, *La Règle du jeu*, *De Mayerling à Sarajevo*, *Le Ciel est à vous*, *Les Portes de la nuit*, *Edouard et Caroline*, *Le Plaisir*). Such opening shots pale into insignificance, however, beside the extraordinarily complex establishing shot in *Poil de carotte*

(Duvivier, 1932), nearly two minutes long and containing eleven distinct movements. Apart from these establishing shots, themselves "motivated" in a way and rapidly conventionalized, nearly all camera movements are motivated in the sense that they form part of the "logic of presentation" of the fictional world developed by the classical cinema in America and since standardized throughout the world. While it is by no means a "natural" set of practices, it has come to seem so through long acquaintance, and some (or even most) early thirties films from France (and elsewhere) now seem "clumsy" because they were made before the system had standardized itself outside America. After 1935, however, the practices had been assimilated, and by 1950 French theoreticians had articulated fairly clearly the logic of this set of practices. Since it relates not just to camera movement but to camera angles and framing (and later to editing practices), it is worth quoting their observations at some length. Probably the most complete statement of these norms came from Marcel Martin in his *Langage cinématographique*, first published in 1955, but a more concise description occurs in Chartier and Desplanques's *Derrière l'écran* (1950).

What meaning do these camera movements give the image? Like shot changes, they correspond to characteristics of *normal vision*.[109] When we watch a tennis match, we turn our head from left to right to follow the ball. The camera gets a similar effect by "panning" from right to left. When we approach someone with our eyes fixed on him, that person's image enlarges in our visual field until it occupies it entirely. A forward tracking shot produces on the screen the same impression.

. . . Shot changes [too] correspond to the changing concentration of our normal vision: even when standing still in front of a café, I can see the whole café [long shot]; subsequently I focus on one of my friends who is talking to me [midshot]. *The change in shot scale translates the shift in attention of a stationary observer.* If instead of a shot change the director had used a tracking shot, the audience would have the impression of the observer walking toward his friend. *Camera movements correspond to the vision of an observer turning his head or moving.*

[. . . Early on] directors, struck by the novelty of these means of expression, abused them through excessive use. . . . In some films the use of extreme angles is totally gratuitous. . . . With some directors the camera seems obsessed by a constant frenzy of movement. The unjustified use of closeups, rare angles, and camera movements has a great disadvantage: it destroys the illusion of participating in the narrative: instead of believing in the film, the spectator focuses on the way it's put together. The author, by this abuse of technical procedures, constantly recalls his presence. . . . This is not the case where these procedures are *motivated*. In a duel scene, for example, one of the adversaries, wounded, falls to the ground; the following image is a steep upward shot of the victor from ground level; the vertical perspective of this unusual shot gives the victor a menacing look. This rare angle of the victor is not gratuitous; it is *motivated*, for it corresponds to the wounded man's view of the victor, as he lies on the

ground. The spectator, faced with this *rare angle* identifies with the wounded fighter. The rare angle is not a bit of technical virtuosity that attracts the spectator's attention. . . .
It is the same for camera movements. . . .
A systematic use of such motivated camera angles and movement is a sort of calculated risk (*gageure*); it limits considerably the expressive possibilities of the cinema, and when you think about it it doesn't actually correspond to real perception . . . ; in breaking with this motivation, cinema may in fact be more faithful to our psychological view of the world.
With contemporary directors, the use of emphatic expressive techniques, like the closeup or elaborate camera movements, is rarely due to a whim of the author. It is not, however, linked solely to the point of view of any one character: it permits the spectator to identify now with one, now with another. Nor is the choice of camera angle conditioned by the desire to "produce a pretty image." More or less consciously, though mostly by instinct, the director reconciles all these camera practices with the point of view of an *ideal observer*. [110, 111]

This description can stand in for the numerous corroborative remarks by critics (and directors of photography) between 1945 and 1960. If French critics were early to analyze the practices of "motivation," French filmmakers were relatively slow to adopt them. Needless to say, they have a number of important ideological implications, which were not at the time recognized. Basically, for contemporary filmmakers and critics there was a classical style, involving motivation and identification, which came to be seen as natural, and then there were occasional instances where the director foregrounded technique for artistic purposes which might be admired as virtuoso achievements but often was considered self-indulgent, imperilling the success of the film as entertainment. In the limit they could be regarded as simply meaningless. "If they are demonstrations of virtuosity," says Martin, "they have a merely anecdotal value."[112]

Instances of this "suspect virtuosity" had been extremely common in the twenties. During the classic period, certain examples became notorious—in particular, the camera movement in *Le Crime de M. Lange*, in which, during the scene where Lange kills Batala, the camera, beginning on Lange's getting the gun and descending the stairs, completes a circular pan totally without motivation to pick him up again at the point where he grabs Batala and shoots him. But this is only one of several "formalist" moments of camera virtuosity in *Lange*, complementary to the outrageously inventive punctuation and use of music, which contravene all realistic practices. Martin also mentions a long virtuoso movement in *Madame de . . .* (Ophüls, 1953), though for outrageous virtuosity there is no film of the period to match the sketches in *Le Plaisir* (Ophüls, 1952), in which several shots (including all three establishing shots), between one and two minutes in length, contain elaborate unmotivated camera movements—a circular pan, combined crane and tracking shots that foreground the set as set, and a notorious forward tracking shot out a window and down, simulating the subjectivity of a woman committing suicide. The baroque extravagance of these isolated films serves to set off the discretion of the motivated norms to which the directors were largely conforming. They were not, however, limited to films directed by people with known "artistic" tendencies. Certainly most films directed by Renoir have something of this sort—a long dizzy tracking shot in the dance scene of *La Chienne*, the complex pans and tracking as Boudu is rescued from the water, the swinging camera in *Une partie de campagne*, a completely circular pan in *La Bête humaine*, and an astonishing series of movements in *Les Bas-fonds* (gratuitously twisting, tracking movements in shot 150, the long retreating camera movement at the end, and the formalist circles of the camera in the opening shot)—but so do nearly all Duvivier's films, and those of many less well-known directors. *Poil de carotte* is full of elaborate and largely unmotivated movements, as is *La Bandera*; and *La Belle Equipe* has nearly circular pans and disconcertingly rapid slides, while very often a "handheld" effect produces the effect of stumbling, fighting (*La Bandera* and *Les Misérables*, Raymond Bernard, 1933) or being jostled (*Pépé le Moko*). A two-minute tracking and panning shot in *Le Bossu* (Delannoy, 1944) presents the chaos of the money market, and rapid bursts of disorienting camera movements occur in *Sortilèges* (Christian-Jacque, 1944). Admittedly, most of these are motivated in the very general sense that they contribute to the construction of a predefined "atmosphere," either of the film as a whole or of a particular scene; but there is no doubt that they register as technical foregrounding of the production process imperilling the realism of the diegesis. After the war Ophüls and Astruc use an unconventionally active camera, and Melville's astonishing *Le Silence de la mer* pushes this to formalist lengths: one of the many unconventional usages in this film involves a camera panning left and right between two people conversing in profile, in a way that foreshadows Godard's *Vivre sa vie*.

A particular threat to the diegesis is posed by that most aggressive form of the pan, the "zip-pan," which produces a visual blur momentarily wiping clean the image. Barry Salt notes the initial introduction of the zip-pan around 1926, its appropriation as a structural device in newsreels about 1930, and its brief vogue in Hollywood fiction films toward 1932.[113] It seems not to have been taken up till much later in France. Such zip-pans occur as one of the many disconcerting elements in *Sortilèges* (1944) and in *Le Silence de la mer* (1947); and in the postwar years René Clair adopted them as a favorite form of punctuation—they occur usually as liaisons, in *La Beauté du diable* (1949–1950), *Belles-de-nuit* (1952), *Les Grandes Manoeuvres* (1955), and no less than 42 times in *Tout l'or du monde* (1961).

Camera height and camera angle could be "motivated" in the same way as camera movement. In the silent period, a norm of eye-level camera height seems to have been established, though Salt mentioned Vitagraph films as varying from this in the United States by being filmed from chest height. He does not mention the subject again, so it is worth recording that most classic French films adopted the chest height of an anonymous observer as a normal camera height. This slightly lower camera takes in more of the actor's/actress's body in closer shots and gives him/her a certain "stature," which presumably was felt to justify the marginal break with eye-line motivation. When more closely involved in shot/reverse shot series, however, the camera would normally adopt the subjective eye-level or over-the-shoulder position; and in general the nearer to the actors, the nearer the camera came to head height. Despite this generalization, however, a range of variation was possible from film to film and even within a film, between waist height and head height. The variation becomes particularly pronounced after 1940. A series of films in 1942 use a head-high camera for many of the sequences (*La Duchesse de Langeais*, *Le Dernier Atout*, *Le Corbeau*); and from then on it is more common (often in *Les Enfants du paradis*, *La Bataille du rail*, *Les Jeux sont faits*, *Une si jolie petite plage*, *Gervaise*, *La Traversée de Paris*). A waist-high norm was less common but can be found in sections of *Le Silence est d'or*, *Monsieur Vincent*, *La Symphonie pastorale*, and *Les Grandes Manoeuvres*). There is no obvious motivation for these variations.

Markedly low or high camera angles were usually used only when motivated in the terms described by Chartier and Desplanques, but certain low and high angles register as expressionist by their gratuity, calling attention to themselves as technique. Some waist- or knee-high shots in *Poil de carotte* have this effect, and the general motivation of "drunkenness" produces odd near-vertical upward and downward shots in *La Kermesse héroïque* and a wobbly camera in *La Belle Equipe*, as does a fight in *Le Grand Jeu*, *Les Misérables*, and most particularly *La Bandera*. The chaos and violence associated with the mine in *Lumière d'été* produce vertical shots so hard to read that they are initially disorienting. Stairwells in various films are exploited for such odd technical practices (*Le Jour se lève*, *Le Rideau cramoisi*) and another initially unreadable shot, in *Hôtel du Nord*, turns out to be a vertical downward shot of a barge emerging from a lock.

In their initial unreadability, or at least in their break with convention, such relatively frequent images remind us that realism was by no means an overriding concern in this classic cinema and that technical virtuosity with a formalist effect, in camera work as elsewhere, could frequently not be resisted.

A more radical break with motivation is apparent in the strangely tilted image of several films. Salt calls this a "Dutch tilt," and notes that it developed in the expressionist cinemas of Russia and Germany during the twenties. He notes that it recurred on rare occasions in the thirties, notably in *Un carnet de bal* (Duvivier, 1937) and *Marthe Richard au service de la France* (Bernard, 1937), and that in the former case this is combined with pans. Indeed, Agostini has recorded a vivid account of the violence done to him as cameraman when trying to control the panning of a diagonally tilted camera in *Un carnet de bal*[114] (director of photography, Kelber) and implies it was the rediscovery of a hitherto lost silent film technique. In fact, however, Bernard had filmed much of *Les Misérables* (1933) with an aggressively diagonal camera. Most often the off-balance effect that this produces is totally unmotivated. It is, however, compatible with the other expressionist techniques, notably the lighting that recurs in that film (director of photography, Kruger), and it may be that such diagonal shots were regularly used when the subject called for expressionist effects. In this sense they always had a very general atmospheric motivation. Certainly in the strangely gothic *Sortilèges* (Christian-Jacque, 1944, director of photography, Louis Page), diagonal shots proliferate throughout the film, collaborating with expressionist lighting, steep camera angles, and abrupt camera movement to produce a particularly appropriate expressionist accompaniment to Prévert's script. Indeed, from 1942 onward, the use of a diagonally tilted camera became a standard procedure in any film with a remotely fantastic or baroque atmosphere, such as *Le Baron fantôme* (1942), *Le Plaisir* (Ophüls, 1951), *Le Rideau cramoisi* (Astruc, 1952), and occurs largely unmotivated in otherwise realistic films—*Le Corbeau* (Clouzot, 1943), *La Symphonie pastorale* (Delannoy, 1946), *Monsieur Vincent* (Cloche, 1947), *Paradis perdu* (Gance, 1939), and even *Nous les gosses* (Daquin, 1941).

One other aggressive technical practice that quite frequently foregrounded production in these films was the overt focus change. Normally, of course, the aim of the cinematographer, especially within conventional realist practices, is to focus so that the center of interest is seen in the desired degree of clarity, whether total or gently softened, and so that any subsequent movement of camera or actor can be accommodated either without a focus change, or without that change being noticeable. When the depth of field is such as not to cover all the center of interest in an image, but changes in the course of a shot so as to shift focus from one to another, the effect is of the spectator's attention forcibly being manipulated by technological means. This happens with sufficient frequency in the French classic cinema to be worth noting—in *Hôtel du Nord*, *La Fin du jour*, *De Mayerling à Sarajevo*, *La Symphonie pastorale*, *Les Jeux sont faits*, *Gervaise*; twice in *Sous les toits de Paris* and *Lumière d'été*; no less than five times in *Le Silence de la mer*.

To these heterodox camera practices can be added the startling moments in certain films when a character addresses the camera, either directly or in a complicitous aside (Michèle, in *Lumière d'été*, or various characters, for comic effect, in the comedy *Miquette et sa mère*). Cumulatively, and in conjunction with the expressionist or fantasy lighting practices mentioned earlier, they serve to remind us of the degree to which the classic French cinema resisted the conventional realism of classic Hollywood practices. It resisted them most particularly in certain specific genres—the provincial Gothic of *Goupi Mains-Rouges* and *Sortilèges*, which infuses sections of many other films (for instance, *Le Baron fantôme*); the fantasy of *La Kermesse héroïque*, *Les Visiteurs du soir*, and a cluster of films from the early fifties

(*Juliette, ou la clef des songes, Belles-de-nuit*), which sometimes extended to surrealist effects (*La Nuit fantastique, Une si jolie petite plage*); the baroque extravagance of Cocteau's films and of Ophüls's fifties films; and more generally the artistic aspirations of prewar directors formed in the twenties, such as L'Herbier, Gance, Clair, Renoir, Feyder, and Grémillon, and postwar directors such as Melville and Astruc, for most of whom conventional realism was incompatible with personal self-expression.

But this already large array of realist-resistant categories overlaps heavily into the standard production of the French classic cinema, and there is no watertight exclusion of such practices from films directed by Delannoy, Cloche, Clément, and Autant-Lara (himself formed in the silent period), let alone Carné. It was not only magic, fantasy, horror, comedy, violence, chaos, or powerful subliminal forces that attracted these "aberrant" camera and lighting practices—not only, that is, criteria related to expressionism, surrealism, the gothic, the baroque, or the allegorical. A perfectly realistic film might veer unpredictably toward them, because the site seemed compatible (a stairwell, a cliff-top, a fairground, or a forest) or for no perceptible diegetic motive. They formed, that is, part of an array of potential practices available to the industry, which might be mobilized according to genre, incident, or personal preference; and the lack of any fixed industrial structure or stable team structure meant that these preferences were diffused widely and unpredictably across the industry. Statistically, however, one or another of them was likely to occur in any given film, whatever the genre, narrative, or personnel. In these conditions they can scarcely be described as aberrant at all, but one more instance of the tension surrounding the production of a realist diegesis in the classic French cinema.

EDITING NORMS: EXPRESSIVE EDITING AND PSYCHOLOGICAL EDITING

Editing during the classic period was an area of filmmaking to which little attention was paid. Editors were seldom interviewed, and little direct evidence survives concerning their understanding of their job or of the ways in which it was evolving during the period. Fortunately, however, the editing of a film lends itself to a variety of quantitative analyses. The most simple and basic of these involves noting the number of shots in each film and correcting for the length of the film. The resultant editing rates can be compared either in the form of "shots per 100 minutes of film," or in the more common form of "average shot length" (ASL). Bearing in mind the provisional nature of any conclusions these can provide, given the nature of the sample, the resulting data (fig. 7.2) are nevertheless very suggestive. The films directed by Carné over the period 1936–1950 are characteristic of a major trend in the edit rate: beginning in the middle to late thirties with a quite slow rate (13.3 seconds, and indeed even slower in *Hôtel du Nord*),

FIGURE 7.2 Edit Rates in the Classic French Cinema

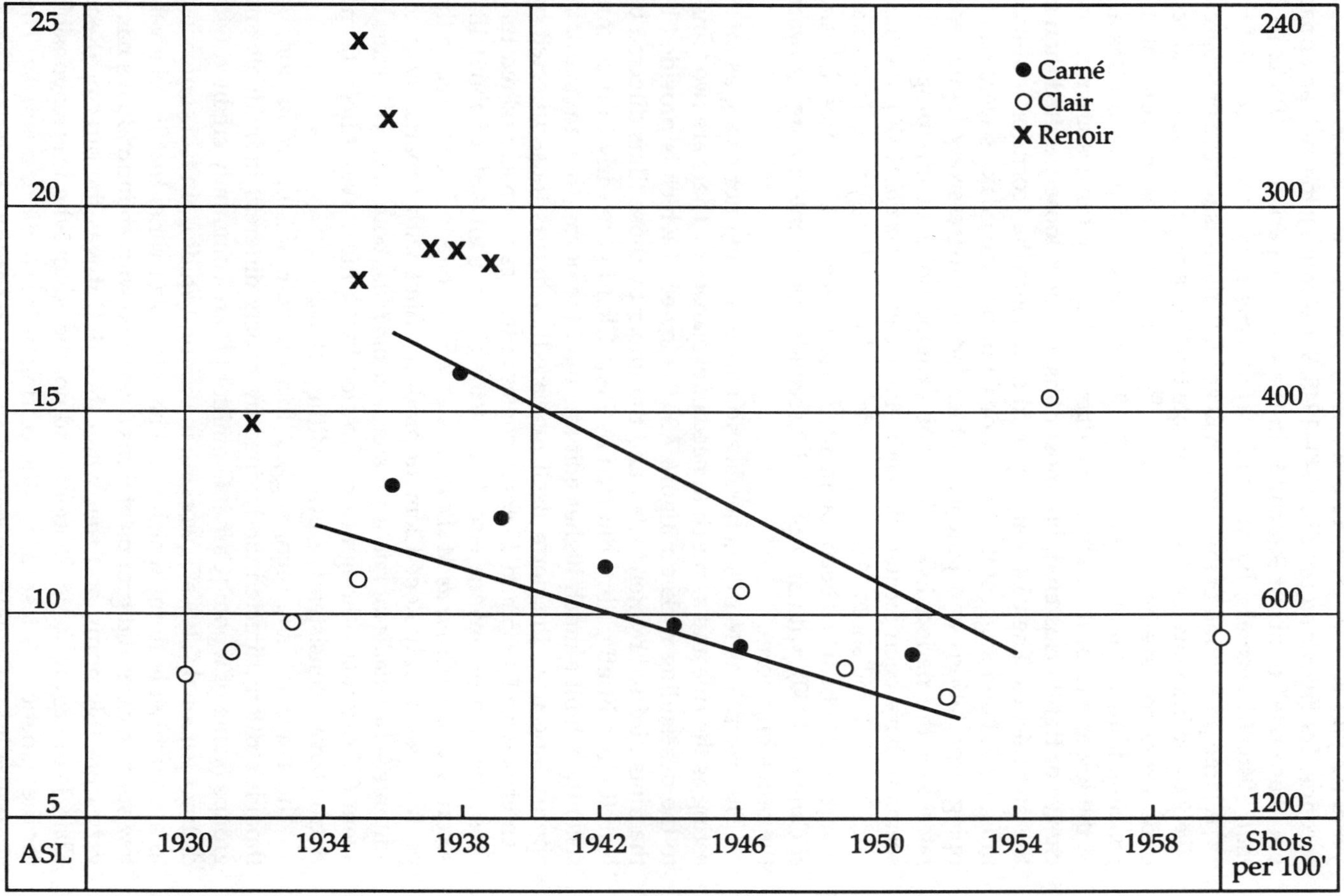
25
20
15
10
5
ASL
240
300
400
600
1200
Shots per 100'
1930
1934
1938
1942
1946
1950
1954
1958
Carné
Clair
Renoir

those films become progressively more intensely edited through the war years (*Le Jour se lève*, 1939: 12.5 seconds; *Les Visiteurs du soir*, 1942: 11.2 seconds; *Les Enfants du paradis*, 1943–1945: 9.7 seconds); to reach an apparent "base rate" of about 9 seconds in the postwar period (*Les Portes de la nuit*, 1946: 9.1 seconds; *Juliette, ou la clef des songes*, 1950: 9.05 seconds).

A large proportion of the films analyzed fall into this pattern of progressively more intensive editing. In the late thirties, a norm of about 12.5 seconds seems to have been established,[115] whereas the vast majority of the wartime films fall into the range 9.5–12.5 seconds, and postwar films are at the lower end of this range. The data for the early thirties are not conclusive or tightly clustered, but most films are more loosely edited than in the later thirties. The vast majority of films fall into the "corridor" outlined in figure 7.2 and suggest that, consciously or not, filmmakers were developing expectations and practices which led to progressively higher edit rates over the period 1935–1945. The extreme point of this progression seems to have been Jacques Becker's *Antoine et Antoinette* (1946), credited with 1,200–1,250 shots (ASL 5 seconds) and immediately notorious as an image-track which had been fragmented to an unacceptable degree. *Edouard et Caroline* (1950), with an ASL of 8.3 seconds, represents a retreat toward the prevailing norm.

The exceptions to this generalization about editing norms are as interesting as the rule and as much in need of explanation. There are two "fins" to the descending rocket in figure 7.3, the lower of which is provided by the films directed by René Clair and the upper by those films directed by Jean Renoir. Briefly, films directed by René Clair in the early thirties consistently exhibit a much higher edit rate than the norm (though gradually approaching it as the norm itself increased), whereas those directed by Renoir between 1935 and 1939 are consistently less intensely edited than those directed by anyone else: four of the six have an ASL of about 18.5 seconds, and *Le Crime de M. Lange* has an ASL of nearly 24 seconds. In the postwar years, only René Clément produces films with a markedly faster edit rate—*La Bataille du rail*, and later *Jeux interdits*, both with edit rates of about 6.7 seconds—though films directed by Ophüls, Yves Allégret, and Astruc have a consistently slower editing rate.

The available data, then, suggest that the bulk of film production, although written, directed, and edited by widely different individuals and groups (some of whom [Carné, Grémillon][116] are commonly credited with distinct personal "styles"), working in different studios, in fact conformed to a system-wide norm which was changing over time; that in relatively few specific cases did groups of films associated with an individual's name vary from this norm; and that when they did, it was the director (René Clair, Jean Renoir, René Clément) and not the editor who was responsible for the variation. A test case is the editing of *Une partie de campagne*. This short film was of course constructed from fragments of a projected feature film shot in 1936. Filming was never completed, and the fragments re-

FIGURE 7.3   Comparison of French & US Edit Rates

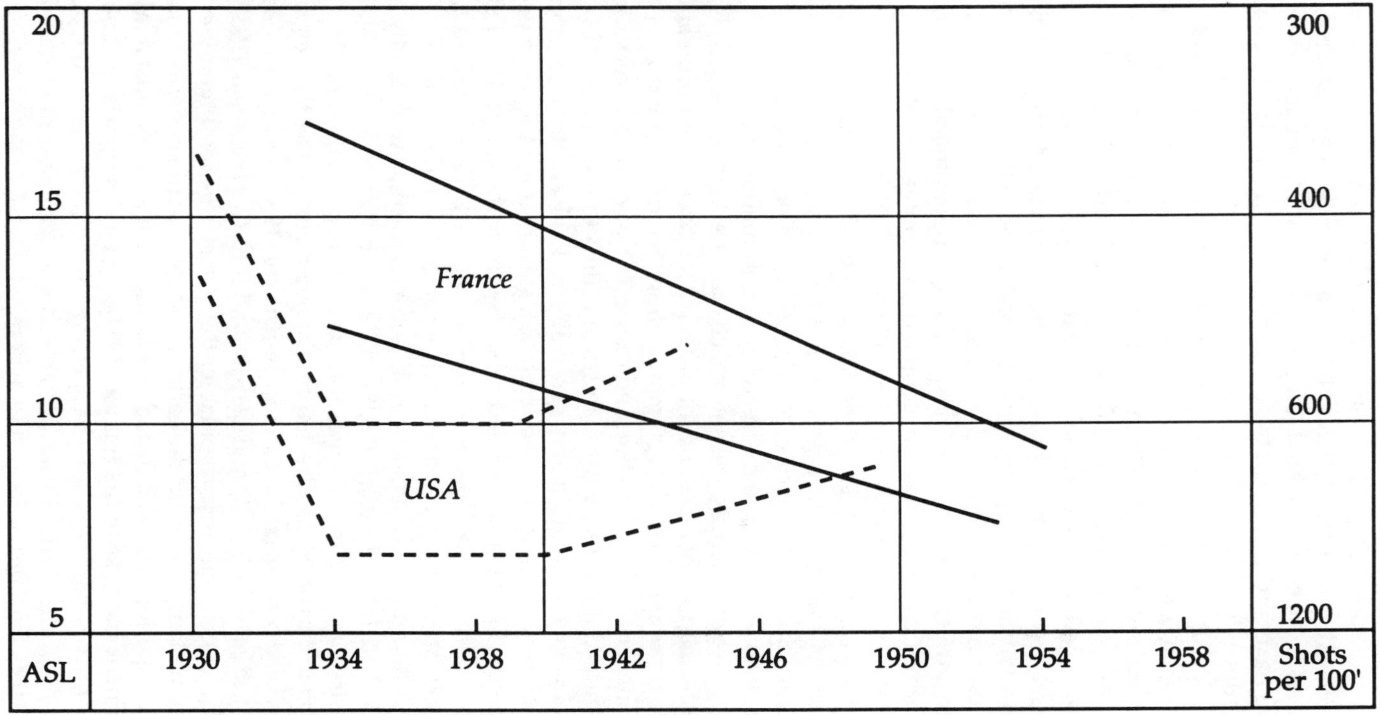

mained unedited until 1946, when Marguerite Renoir set about ordering them into something resembling a coherent narrative. Renoir himself was still absent from France at that time, so the film now screened under his name is at once a film edited long after it was shot, when editing practices, as we have already begun to see, had changed considerably, and also the sole film edited by Marguerite Renoir without the direct supervision or guidance of Renoir himself. The initial figures for it indicate the consequences: it is edited far more intensively than his other films, and perhaps more like those that Mme Renoir was editing for Becker at that time. Probably the film would have looked very much different had it been edited when filmed, and with Renoir present.

As a point of comparison with these French editing practices, Barry Salt's analysis of a very large number of American films[117] suggests that the ASL of American films, which had been about 5 seconds at the end of the twenties, rose like the French ASL to approximately 15 seconds with the introduction of sound but dropped much more rapidly than the French rate back to its previous level. From 1934 to 1939 it remained relatively stable at 7–10 seconds and then began to rise again during the war years. Figure 7.3 graphs the different practices of the two national cinemas. Any explanation of the regularity of evolution of French edit rates must clearly be of a sort to account for the discrepancy in national practices.

One way to identify the specific characteristics of editing in France is to analyze the number of shots of different lengths in each film and to standardize the results for a 100-minute film. Such a tabulated set of data is extremely rich in information and results in two reliable observations: there was indeed a tendency for mainstream films to use more and more shots of 0–5 seconds' duration between 1930 and 1950; and their number of shots over 45 seconds in length tended to fall steadily over the same period. The norms for brief shots (0–5 seconds) rise from the range 110–170 shots in the early thirties to 150–250 in the late thirties, 190–350 during the war, and 300–550 in the postwar period. As an index of the renunciation of long takes, the number of shots over 45 seconds in films directed by Carné fell from 33 in *Hôtel du Nord* (1938) to 22 in *Le Jour se lève* (1939), 11 in *Les Visiteurs du soir*, 7 in *Les Enfants du paradis* (1943–1945), and 9 in *Les Portes de la nuit*. In the films directed by Duvivier during the thirties it fell from 20 in *Poil de carotte* (1932) to 11 in *La Bandera* (1935) and 12 in *La Belle Equipe* (1936), then 4 in *Pepé le Moko* (1936) and 8 in *La Fin du jour* (1939).[118]

The conclusion is unavoidable: there was a general tendency to break down the longer takes of the early sound period into series of smaller shots over the period 1935–1950, and this tendency had as its most marked effect a dramatic increase in the number of shots of 0–5 seconds. It is not difficult to identify where this was happening in the narrative chain. A detailed analysis of the films shows that it was not occurring randomly along the narrative chain but at local sites where "clusters" of such brief shots occur more and more frequently as the years pass. Such clusters, from occupying

1–4% of the image track in the thirties frequently came to occupy 6–8% during the war and over 10% in the mid-forties. In *La Bataille du rail* they reached 14.5% and in *La Traversée de Paris*, 16.5%.

Attempts to account for changes in editing rate often look to technological change as a crucial causal factor. Barry Salt's thesis, for instance, is that the advent of sound interfered with and totally transformed editing practices in America, as in Europe, but that by 1934 the development of progressively more sophisticated technology permitted American filmmakers, trained in the silent period and frustrated by the constraints of sound, to return to their previous practices. This process, he implies, was facilitated by intense competition among the great studios, which were constantly vying with one another in the introduction of more flexible lenses and lighting, faster filmstock, more effective back-projection, more mobile sound cameras, etc. Two specific advances were relevant to editing practices: the sound Moviola, he notes, was introduced in 1930, "and from 1931 the ASL in Hollywood films started to drop. . . . The other development that facilitated this fast cutting (in both senses) of synch-sound shots occurred in 1932 with the introduction of 'rubber numbering' (or 'edge numbering') for sound and picture tracks. . . . After numbering has been carried out it is possible to shuffle the sections of picture and sound track about in the editing process with perfect freedom, secure in the knowledge that synchronism can be regained when necessary, purely 'by the numbers.' "[119]

A form of technical determinism is invoked, therefore, to account for the rapid decrease in ASL in America, qualified by his comment that "the trend toward faster cutting . . . can be easily explained as a desire on the part of many people to return to the sort of cutting that had been usual in the majority of American silent films made in the twenties, when ASLs were usually down around 5 seconds."[120]

Leaving for later consideration the question of whether in fact the fast cutting of the late thirties was in fact a return to the fast cutting of the twenties or something entirely different, let us note that neither technological nor biographical factors allow Salt to account for the subsequent move that he chronicles—away from faster cutting, in about 1940—since at that point he invokes a totally different criterion, namely "fashion."[121] This is disappointing, as his argument to that point had seemed to be an attempt precisely to demystify "fashion," in terms of various sorts of quite material determinants.

Nevertheless, his data are useful to our purposes: the Moviola (or its French equivalent, the Movitone) was available as early as in America, but even in 1949 no machine for rubber numbering the sound and image tracks seems to have been available. Speaking of the synchronization of these two tracks on the editing table, Jean Feyte says "A special machine allows the printing at regular intervals of a sequence of numbers on these tracks, such that when the film is segmented the appropriate piece of sound track can readily be located for any given piece of image track. In France, as no such machines exist, it's up to the editor's assistant to mark the appropriate points of synchronization in India ink."[122] Yvan Noë confirms this in his 1945 correspondence course on editing. Describing the operation of synchronization, he states that it can be obtained thanks to the clapperboard. "By beginning from there and unrolling simultaneously the two tracks on the double drum mechanism and inscribing from time to time points of reference with a soft pencil. . . . "[123] He does note, however, that the negative bears a footage number which is a help. It seems that the technology already available to American editors in 1932[124] was still not available in France 17 years later, where the equivalent work was still being done by hand. It is not till 1956 that we find a description of the editor's job which represents this mechanical numbering as a routine facility.[125]

To the structural reasons already adduced for the reluctance of the French film industry to redesign and update material, Alépée adds another: the women who had constituted the core of the editing personnel for thirty years had been constrained to timidity. A morale of self-abnegation, a professional inferiority complex, had led them to expect lack of recognition, low salaries—and bad working conditions. They had been expected to work with intuition, not sophisticated technology. It would, anyway, have been a brave editress who made a fuss about conditions in a period of structural unemployment, when there was an overabundance of editors and assistant editors eager to accept a job on any conditions.[126] All this would clearly militate against any rapid move in the direction of the faster ASLs such as American editors had been able to achieve relatively effortlessly by 1934. Moreover, in achieving an ASL of about 7 seconds by 1934 the American editors (etc.) were simply returning to a set of "classical" editing practices with which they were well acquainted as a result of implementing them for the previous 15 years. Because of its anomalous development in that period, the French industry had never developed in any coherent or industry-wide way a set of "classical" practices to which it might naturally expect to return, once technical factors permitted.

Editors, critics, and commentators give no sign of reflecting on these practices till the period 1944–1955. At that time, their analyses led them to identify three distinct sets of practices which might guide the editing of a film—expressive, psychological, and realist practices. It is worth dealing in some detail with at least the first two of these.

The clusters involving dramatic action are a specific instance of what has been called "expressive editing," in which a series of brief takes is felt appropriate to certain intensely dramatic experiences of the characters and is intended in turn to generate a corresponding emotional intensity in the spectator. Thus, such clusters occur when Poil de carotte leaps into a cart and whips the horse to a frenzied gallop; when Pierre in *Le Grand Jeu* gets involved in a fight in the Kasbah; when Toni is running away from the Carabinieri; when Monsieur Victor kills the gunman or Pierre "kills" Renée in *Hôtel du Nord*.

Clearly this practice cannot be separated from its opposite counterpart, the tendency to use long takes in moments of idyllic calm or tranquillity, such as when Poil de carotte is with his godfather and Mathilde in the fields, when he is reconciled with his father; when Monsieur Lange and Valentine are in bed together, or, in the same film, Charley and Estelle are reunited.

More generally, both these extremes draw their effectiveness from not-being-the-other, from being not-the-normal shot length for the film, from being part of a formal conventional system. But it is clearly not an entirely arbitrary system. The fact that brevity is equated with intensity of emotion is motivated by psychological factors. Already in 1946 Chartier was explaining that though the eye can assimilate a vast amount of information with great speed, work is nevertheless involved. To mention just the most obvious and necessary work, a shot change involves a peak of mental activity as the spectator identifies the content of the shot and relates it to the content of previous shots. Once that identification and interrelating has been done, everything else being equal, there will be a fall-off in mental activity. A series of rapid shot changes involves, therefore, the maintenance of a high level of mental activity, which translates as a tension, perfectly compatible with and appropriate to affective tensions, which it will generate or reinforce. But quite aside from this, the analogy between shot rate and heartbeat rate ensures that a faster "pulse" to the editing will be equated with the approach of danger, with excitement, with anxiety—especially as that rate approaches the true heartbeat rate.

This latter fact has long justified the identification of the various "movements" of a musical work with different moods and degrees of excitement, thereby establishing a long-standing cultural tradition of which expressive editing practices are simply one of the more recent manifestations. Once handbooks, manuals, and formal courses of training became common, some general statement of these principles could regularly be found in them. In his "Golden Rules of Editing" M. Jeandret[127] asserts that, "for a rapid movement, a rapid montage is appropriate; for a slow movement, a slow editing rate." For Henri Agel,[128] too, "A succession of lively and rapid shots carries us along in a joyous rush . . . a headlong dash," whereas "a cunningly contrived slowness" is equated with "a solemn or even awesome" diegesis. R. Bataille had already stated the same in 1944,[129] quoting approvingly in this respect P. Mouchon, whose little handbook was to come out 10 years later.[130] "The example of a stroll around a lake, contrasted with the descent of rapids, indicates that there will be [sic] a difference in shot length in each of the two cases, especially if you want to emphasize the sentimental aspect of the lake and the extreme rapidity of the torrent."

The effects to be obtained had been tabulated by Lo Duca,[131] and in his excellent appreciation of montage as it had been practiced and theorized to that time, Marcel Martin in 1955[132] spells out these possibilities in more detail (though subsequently he confuses a crucial issue by talking indiscriminately of expressive and psychological editing):

It is clear that beyond a given point the director [*sic*] doesn't decide on the length of his shots by considering what he needs to *show* (materially) but what he wants to *suggest*. . . .

Thus in the case of longish shots, a rhythm will result, giving the impression of languor (certain sequences in *La Red*), of sensual fusion with nature (*Earth*), of boredom and ennui (*Les Vacances de M. Hulot, Vitelloni*), of sinking into a mire (*Une si jolie petite plage*), of impotence before a blind fatality (the final sequence of *Greed, Les Orgueilleux*), of desperate bleakness in a search for human communication (*La Strada, L'Avventura*). On the other hand, shots mainly short or very short (flashes) will give a rapid rhythm—nervous, dynamic, very possibly tragic ("impressionist" editing), lending itself to anger (glimpses of indignant faces and clenched fists in *Potemkin*), to speed (glimpses of galloping horses in *Arsenal*), to strenuous activity (riveters working on the construction of a cargo ship in *The Deserter*), to effort (struggle between a woman and a young thief in *Le Chemin de la vie*), to violent shock (the crashing of the Republican's car against the enemy cannon in *L'Espoir*), to murderous brutality (machine-gun fire in *October*, bombs falling in *Jeux interdits*), to people driven to distraction (the suicide in *Le Fantôme qui ne revient pas*).

Martin then goes on to list the diegetic moments appropriate to progressively shorter shots, progressively longer shots, and abrupt changes of rhythm, while acknowledging that most series of shots in a film exhibit none of these clear patternings—a useful reminder that expressionist editing practices cannot themselves account for the majority of shot lengths and relationships in a film.

The standard way to express this determination of the editing by the dramatic/emotive content of the diegesis was in terms of a double rhythm. When Jeandret in his rules, or Bretoneiche[133] (who taught at IDHEC) affirm that the external rhythm must follow the internal one, must be subordinate to it, they mean that the pace of editing must be determined by the "pace" or "intensity" of the diegesis, the technical manipulation of the signifier be determined by the signified. It is the mechanical application of this rule and the consequent expectations developed in the spectator that Bretoneiche is regretting when he says that "it is almost impossible to accelerate the succession of shots without disrupting their interior movement. That's why the découpage acquires such an importance and must be considered as a sort of pre-montage." It is against this same aspect of the degradation of editing in the talkies that Colpi is railing when he says that "the rhythm is no longer imposed externally, by the editor, but internally, by the acting and directing. The internal rhythm of the image has come to dominate the external image constructed by the editor, who is obliged to obey that internal rhythm, producing supple, precise sequences determined by the director's style. . . . Length of shot is no longer left to judgment; it is dictated by the scenario."[134]

Their rage was understandable, because not only had these practices become mechanical in their application, but as has been mentioned, they were extremely crude in their signifying power. Indiscriminately, a series of long shots was called on to signify despair and tranquillity, boredom and a transcendent fusion with nature, while a series of brief shots likewise signified the exciting and the tragic, the angry and the terror-stricken, the triumphant, the agitated, and the suicidal. Such practices were not only an unwelcome constraint on ambitious editors, therefore; they could seem intellectually and technically stultifying to implement.

There are clear indications that the system was not stable. In particular, the use of markedly longer-than-average shots to represent tranquillity, bleakness, or transcendence fell progressively into disrepute with editors. By 1954 P. Mouchon,[135] in his guide to editing, can posit as "an essential principle" that "except in cases of absolute necessity" no shot should ever last longer than 20 seconds. "And even here we should note that shots of that length can only be justified by the exceptional interest of the subject and the cameraman's total inability to change the angle or distance. Even at the scenario stage it is wise to increase the number of shots by decomposing into two or more parts a scene which might become too long filmed in a single take." In particular he recommends the avoidance of long takes "even to suggest monotony, despair, and the like," preferring to see these evoked by a series of shorter shots linked by cross dissolves. R. Bataille is of like mind: "(3) an idea of slowness is to be suggested by an adequate series of shots of middling length, and not by a few long ones. . . . (4) An idea of calmness can be conveyed . . . by shots of moderate length." Like Mouchon, Bataille specifies the precise lengths: between 6 and 12 seconds for such shots. And again, "it is far better to use several shots from different angles to express what you intended to put in the 6–12 seconds. . . . Several short shots are worth more than a single over-long shot."[136]

This progressive disrepute into which the "longer half" of the expressive editing practices fell in the late forties and fifties corresponds precisely to the data described earlier. The norms for professionally made feature films never reached the point recommended by Mouchon and Bataille, since shots of 20–45 seconds continued to appear in films throughout the late classical period, but it is true that beyond that length there is a marked drop-off in the number of shots, "even to suggest monotony, calmness, or slowness." The expressive range available to an editor had in effect contracted greatly, from an initial state in the early thirties of about 3 seconds to 90 seconds, down to a state in 1945 of two-thirds of a second to 30 seconds, corresponding to the progressive drop in ASL over that time from 15 seconds to about 8 or 9 seconds. In the course of this contraction and acceleration of expressive editing practices, more and more of the series of shots at the rapid end of the scale come in the forties to fall within our definition of a "cluster." By 1947, clusters of expressively edited brief shots occupied five times more of the image track than they had fifteen years before. As Barry Salt has shown, the American cinema had also moved in this direction, at least in some respects, but much earlier than the French cinema; and a desire to emulate the narrative economy and efficiency there developed might well have been one of the motives behind similar developments in France. Certainly, since World War I and more particularly since the commercialization of the talkie, the American cinema had established itself as the dominant model in the Western world. In the period following World War II American films enjoyed an unprecedented critical and professional reputation in France. Of all the forms of training, formal and informal, undergone by the editors (and the directors themselves) during this period, probably the one most likely to have had an impact, however incalculable that may be, is the experience of sitting night after night in the cinema watching, with or without the conscious evaluation of the professional's eye, the editing practices of the dominant national cinema, the dominant nascent genres, the dominant narrative modes.

But cutting across these evolving "expressive editing practices," and based on an entirely different principle, we can discern another set of practices, which can best be described as "psychological editing practices." The clusters of brief takes formed by psychological editing are normally composed of a series of alternating shots, presenting the two (or sometimes more) conversants in the dialogue or other intense interaction. The French term for this alternation is champ/contre-champ (shot/reverse shot), and the fact that they had begun to proliferate in frame only after the introduction of the talkie was early recognized.

As was the case with the expressionist editing practices, these clusters of brief shots have a counterpart in the single long take, not here used for expressive purposes, to correspond to tranquility, serenity, reconciliation, or boredom, but rather to present a single individual in his psychological complexity and development. Thus near the beginning of a film it was common to find such a shot introducing the main character—establishing him/her as central to the drama by the very fact of dwelling on him/her, establishing his/her relationship with the social environment and milieu, revealing his/her place in the network of developing relationships. Monsieur Lepic is presented thus, in the first shot (115 seconds) of *Poil de carotte*, as is the eponymous hero himself (shot 13, 52 seconds; shot 79, 52 seconds) in circumstances which are far from tranquil or harmonious. Jean (Gabin) in *La Belle Equipe* is introduced thus (shot 18, 97 seconds) as is Monsieur Victor (shot 24, 100 seconds), Maréchal in *La Grande Illusion* (shot 1, 56 seconds) and François in *Le Jour se lève* (shot 27, 61 seconds), etc. In these long takes we "get to know them" intimately, integrally; uninterruptedly. The same phenomenon often occurs at moments of solitary psychological crisis for the central characters, later in the film—often, in *Le Jour se lève*; at the moment of attempted suicide in *Poil de carotte* (shot 349, 59 seconds), etc. It is to this practice that Agel is referring when he says that "any narrative involves moments of more violent dramatic intensity—in that case the shot can be either longer (if it is a psychological crisis) or much briefer (if it is a Western or action film)."[137] In effect he is contrasting psychological and expressive practices, the latter of which come into play normally in external, active, and public dramas, the former in internal, static, and solitary dramas; the latter of which aim at awakening an emotional reaction in the spectator, the former at introducing the spectator to (i.e., constructing) the psychological complexity of the central character.

While the two sets of practices are distinct in principle, in practice they could act in a complementary fashion. The development of shot/reverse shot clusters to structure dialogues, while basically psychological in origin (since it developed to reveal the multiple transitory reactions of speaker[s] and listener[s] to one another), introduced a pseudo-expressive "animation" into what threatened otherwise to be a distressingly static set of tableaus. It could be seen as "livening up" an otherwise theatrical and uncinematic script, as treating heightened psychological states in the same manner as heightened dramatic action. This is the most common explanation of it proposed (not always enthusiastically) by practitioners. For Louveau[138] the process was developed basically to "break up the monotony of the dialogues"; for Colpi, it seems to represent a sort of "editor's revenge" on the scenarist, whose tyranny he resents ("the length of a shot is no longer a matter for judgment; it is dictated by the text; so they resort to the good old shot/reverse shot to increase editing rate, hack up the film, provide 'variation' as they say").[139] Amengual,[140] in true Bazinian terms, sees the practice as a way of insidiously defeating the realistic subtleties of the word and transforming each conversation into a simulacrum of action, of simple physical exertion—a way of treating ideas as simple noises in a verbal tennis game.

Perhaps it is true that a primary impulse was simply to revitalize a theatrical script. Perhaps again it was largely to cope with the markedly more realistic acting style of the sound cinema, as the quietly spoken word replaced the extravagant and easily readable gesture or expression, and the camera needs to close in on the relatively understated acting if the spectators are to see and hear with the required accuracy and subtlety. Whatever the reason, as these editing practices spread toward the point where, by the mid-forties, many films consisted largely of a string of such highly edited interpersonal exchanges, connected by perfunctory narrative links, they proved to have consequences beyond the obvious.

Rather than transform the film into a pseudo-action film, they radically expanded the importance of the psychological element in the film—made the film a constantly changing force-field of psychological relationships. The repeated crosscutting that the procedure involved, if the camera was to provide information about the participants' attitudes and reactions, relied essentially on a waist-up view of each character—occasionally moving in from that to the close-up or out to the general view of the conversants—and that knee- or waist-up view allows the spectators the more intimate acquaintance with the characters that is acquired in any "real" conversation. It is known to the French as the *plan américain*, or American shot, so thoroughly is it associated with that country's cinema, and there is reason to link the development of these practices (originating in the United States and associated with the name of Griffith) with the ideology of individualism.

The growing recognition that such dialogued confrontations and interactions constituted a special and central feature of contemporary filmmaking, requiring quite distinctive technical treatment by cameraman and editor alike, corresponds to an equivalent recognition that the scripting of a film also involved several different skills and that a central one was the ability to write effective dialogues.

Indeed, in the 1945 correspondence school courses two "special cases" of editing are mentioned in some detail—pursuits and dialogues—and the latter are discussed in terms of shot/reverse shot and *plans américains*.[141] Perhaps the most important consequence of this is that the editing practices which resulted, and which dominate increasingly the structuring of the signifier in the forties, are not at all those of the twenties: they have their origins in a different set of problems and a different ideology; they are applied to different elements of the diegesis, which they construct to different effect. One of the results was "character"—psychologically complex ("rounded"), plausible, realistic figures. Another was a new form of identification mechanism. The two are closely interconnected, both as effects and as technical practices.

The theory behind these practices began to be formulated in France as soon as editing began to be the subject of formal teaching. Before the war, any references to them are phrased in very vague terms—the need for "sensitivity," "delicacy," a feel for "rightness" in the ordering and duration of shots—and much later, Sadoul (surprisingly enough) could still talk of "modern editing" as involving a succession of crosscutting "without anything legitimating these abrupt changes of viewpoint."[142] But already in 1946, in bulletin number 3 of IDHEC, J. P. Chartier had affirmed that

> the succession of edited shots corresponds to normal perception through a series of glances. In the same way as we have the impression of receiving a continuous and global vision of the visual field because our mind constructs that vision from the successive data received by our eyes, so, in well-constructed editing, the shots pass unnoticed because they correspond to the normal shifting of our attention and thus construct for the spectator an overall view which gives him the illusion of *real* perception.[143]

The following year Bretoneiche, another lecturer at IDHEC, expressed this in similar terms:

. . . the images which succeed one another on the screen obey a visual rhythm which would be that of an imaginary witness looking at each image, according to the interest he would accord each one, by virtue of a certain logic according to which the movement, the soundtrack, in any one image directs attention onto that immediately following it.[144]

Probably the most complete statement of these practices came from Marcel Martin in his *Langage cinématographique*, first published in 1955, but a more concise description is that already quoted from *Derrière l'écran*, which Chartier published with Desplanques in 1950. It has the advantage of linking editing and cinematography into a coherent set of work practices motivated by the psychology of the characters and the psychology of the spectator, both of which are of course being constructed by these practices.

The delusion that psychological editing and cinematography allowed for an "ideal" view of the events being represented was common to several commentators of the period. As Martin said, "In real life we only see of the world what is within our reach, and even of that we have most often only the most partial and narrow view, whereas on the contrary the director reconstructs reality in such a way as to give us the best and most complete vision possible."[145] Even twenty years later, in a footnote, he sees the logic so constructed as providing "a succession of [shots] *determined by the spectator's curiosity* concerning the unfolding of the story,"[146] whereas it is scarcely possible to maintain that the spectator is, in any useful sense of the phrase, in control of the psychology. While seeming to "respond to" a need for further information on the spectator's part, the film has of course also provoked that need. The consequent "psychology" is therefore a predetermined one which the spectator must accept or stop watching the film. A good editing job for Martin will construct a view of the world superior to that achievable by any single individual. It will be truer, it will be more instructive. In a word, it will be ideal, not ideological. In this he is surely mistaken. With these qualifications, it would seem that the late forties saw a remarkably rapid appreciation of the practices which had been slowly developing in France over the preceding fifteen years.

As in the case of expressive editing practices, the degree to which they affected any one film or any one director's films might vary considerably. Nevertheless, the general tendency to fragment the diegesis into a series of "glances" was a central factor in the steady reduction in ASL. In theory, of course, a change of focus of attention, a glance, or a sudden effort of concentration could be translated by camera movements rather than by editing, but to do so required a rapidity of pan or tracking which was visually disconcerting and which foregrounded technique. To edit such glances together proved less obtrusive than to reproduce them with a camera. Nevertheless, by the mid-forties, as each "scene" was broken down into a series of glances and each of the proliferating dialogues was broken down into multiple point-of-view shots, it was beginning to result in an editing intensity which, in its sheer technical virtuosity, resembled the editing intensity of Russian films of the twenties. Psychological "clusters" of brief takes were by that time four times as frequent as they had been in the early thirties. Becker's *Antoine et Antoinette*, already 850 shots at the découpage stage (which would have given an ASL of about 7 seconds) was further "fragmented" into 1250 shots at the editing stage precisely through the proliferation of champ/contrechamps. It immediately became a scandalous instance of technical excess, to be cited somewhat disapprovingly alongside Pabst and Pudovkin. At that stage, psychological editing practices were, like the camera movements which they to some extent replaced, beginning to foreground a technique they had initially served to naturalize and thus to come into contradiction with that psychological realism of which they had initially been one of the principal mechanisms.

As a generalization, where films of the thirties exhibit a rapid edit rate, it is because they constitute the early introduction into France of such psychological editing practices, often by personnel (such as Korda and Ophüls) trained in a foreign production system such as the American system, where they had been the norm since 1910. If the thirties French cinema was resistant to them, it was because it was resistant to the ideology of individualism implicit in them and because French technicians had never been conditioned to find them normal in the silent period, so experienced no need to "return to" them as soon as possible in the sound period, as did their American colleagues. The late forties saw the most widespread use of psychological editing practices. The total lack of any consistent pattern of edit rates in the fifties is due to the fact that many filmmakers in the postwar period rejected psychological editing procedures and returned to practices that are in some respects closer to those of Renoir in the thirties. Thus, the films directed in the fifties by Yves Allégret, Max Ophüls, and Alexandre Astruc lack such clusters of brief takes and have an ASL of approximately 15 seconds.

To sum up, both expressive and psychological editing experienced a gradual yet steady growth from 1930 to 1945, culminating in a set of practices which cohered well with the psychological elements of acting, set design, and cinematography which were likewise experiencing a peak of popularity at this point. They thus confirm the general trend of the classic French cinema's work practices away from a social cinema marked by typecasting and spectacle and toward a psychological cinema marked by individualized characters and identification mechanisms. In addition, the broader range of editing practices available to directors in the fifties serves once again to remind us that the well-known experimental aspects of New Wave editing did not constitute an abrupt reaction against classical style, but a logical extension of new-found technological possibilities that the classic directors themselves had already begun to explore.

THE CLASSIC FRENCH CINEMA
AND THE NEW WAVE

There are good arguments for seeing the classic French cinema as enjoying a certain global continuity and coherence over the thirty years under discussion. Throughout that period it was characterized by its fragmented nature: a large number of small-scale production firms, mostly with a negligible capital base and with no plant or contracted personnel, put together one-off packages for sale to circuits which they did not own. A distinction can be made within this system between those production firms which did not distribute their own films, owned no (or few) outlets of their own and no plant of their own, and on the contrary those firms with a more stable financial base due to their direct or indirect linkage with distribution firms, their profitable exhibition circuits, and, from time to time, their own production facilities. Because they themselves normally produced no more than five films a year, these latter firms hired out their facilities to the former and were obliged to contract with them for the resultant films if they were to fulfil the quota screening requirements in the circuits.

It was a system which required constant negotiation between sectors and between firms within a sector, and in which the slender financial resources of various negotiators made for extended credit and a constant threat of bankruptcy. Its origins can be traced primarily to the economic determinants of the move to sound and the Depression. These were succeeded by political determinants, which could have brought about a change, but which did not. These in turn gave way to a postwar industrial situation where neither economic determinants nor political determinants were decisive, but where the system had become part of the ideological taken-for-granted of those working within the industry—one of those aspects of Frenchness which it was essential to restore and perpetuate in the aftermath of the liberation. Regarded as anarchic and intolerable in the thirties and a flagrant symptom of the industry's lack of control over its own destiny, the system could rather come under the occupation to stand for French individualism, autonomy, and independence in the face of totalitarian hegemony, finally to become a norm, a set of routines within which the industry felt comfortable.

Within the continuity of this industrial structure and mode of production, however, a crucial breaking point was the year 1940, in which the German occupying forces introduced what were to prove lasting institutional changes, such that without too much exaggeration we can contrast the anarchic, unregulated, artisanal tendencies of the thirties with the progressively more regulated, monitored, state-subsidized, unionized, and professionalized industry of the fifties. In terms of work practices, a parallel evolution is identifiable at all stages of production, characterized by a move from a social cinema toward a psychological cinema, from social motivation, character typing, and an aesthetic of poetic transposition toward psychological motivation, individualized character construction, and a diegesis authenticated by more documentary forms of realism. If the transformation of the industrial structure took place quite abruptly in 1940, the transformation of work practices and thus of film style took significantly longer and was not complete until 1950.

In view of this demonstrable ability of the classic cinema not only to evolve but also to regenerate itself in the face of political crises and of American economic aggression, there is good reason to question standard accounts according to which, stultified by routine and convention, it must inevitably be displaced and superseded by a quite different system, the New Wave of the sixties. On the one hand there certainly were powerful socioeconomic factors pressuring the classic cinema to metamorphose or die. Triggered by changes in the nature of capitalism and consequent changes in domestic technology—notably, but not exclusively, television and the automobile—the unprecedented audience numbers of the period 1947–1957 began their rapid decline from nine attendances per year to four attendances per year. With declining returns, pressures on entry prices and on production costs must inevitably push the cinema of the sixties toward new types of film for new categories of audience. If the art-film, its existence validated by the middle-class intelligentsia, is the most widely acclaimed of these phenomena, it was by no means the most significant, numerically—the rise of pornography dominates French production statistics of the sixties.

But nor was it a question of a new system simply displacing and superseding an old one. There are three types of arguments that can be adduced for seeing the New Wave not as a displacement of the classic cinema but rather as a logical outcome and continuation of it. First, the New Wave constituted little more than the emphatic foregrounding of the art-film end of existing production practices. Not even the New Wave directors themselves denied that a powerful element of art cinema had existed throughout the period 1930–1960; nor could they have denied that a powerful element of commercial filmmaking continued to exist in parallel with their own efforts. If in the name of greater autonomy certain of the New Wave directors exploited the director-package mode of production, so had a certain number of directors in previous decades; and by no means all New Wave directors did so. Most worked within the long-established producer-package system like their predecessors, assuming like them that high degree of control over the aesthetics of filmmaking which the classic cinema had always been willing to accord. Within that system, in the sixties as in earlier decades, they could count on the presence of a large number of producers willing to take on board risky yet ambitious projects, while the bulk of producers continued to seek a more popular audience.

Secondly, not only had the New Wave always had its counterpart within the classic French cinema, it can be shown to have been generated by a set of processes and mechanisms orchestrated within the classic cinema. The audience itself had been formed during the classic period—not just a national audience, by way of the ciné-clubs, the cinémathèque, the art-house circuits, and that intensive promotion of an appropriate discourse within the film press, but an international audience, by way of the carefully nurtured coproduction system and of the Cannes Film Festival and its foreign analogues, where French films consistently won high awards.

On the production side, if a number of producers continued to invest in high-risk artistic ventures during the difficult postwar years and on into the sixties, it was not least because their risks were largely underwritten by a state subsidy aimed specifically at fostering ambitious artistic experiments. Introduced in 1941, reaffirmed in 1948, and revised in 1953 and 1959, these subsidies were ultimately ploughing half a billion francs each year into projects that foreshadowed the New Wave and indeed that nurtured it. In this they were complemented by that other legislative initiative of the wartime régime, the banning of the double program. The shorts and documentaries needed to supplement the single-feature program provided an ideal training-ground for young filmmakers to explore and demonstrate their competence in financially benign conditions. After a difficult decade from 1932 to 1942, a new generation could acquire its professional standing in the same way as had the filmmakers of the twenties and thirties.

These analogies between the two groups are easy to establish. Certain of the shorts and documentaries of the earlier group have become famous: Marc Allégret's *Voyage au Congo*, made on the 1926 expedition with his uncle, André Gide, the Vigo films *A propos de Nice* and *Taris, roi de l'eau*, René Clair's *Paris qui dort* and *Entr'acte*, and Cocteau's *Le Sang d'un poète*. But the auteurist approach which categorizes these with such directors' later works conceals the extent to which they represented a perfectly normal stage in the cinematic development of the twenties and early thirties. At least half of the 50 leading directors of the period made one or more short documentaries, film ads, or short fiction films, in order to develop their competence in less threatening and financially crippling circumstances.

Carné, Le Chanois, the Allégrets, Cavalcanti, Gréville, Ciampi, and Jacqueline Audry all did so; Grémillon made a series of industrial, professional, and tourist documentaries with his cameraman friend Périnal in the twenties, later editing together an avant-garde short from them; Autant-Lara made a short called *Fait-divers* (1925), a documentary (*Vittel*, 1926), and a series of shorts on his return to France in the early thirties.

During the thirties only Becker, who made shorts and documentaries for seven years from 1932 to 1938, and Leenhardt, who from 1934 concentrated on producing and directing short films, followed this career path. Once the conditions favored it again, however, it rapidly became the norm: Verneuil followed it; Astruc made two short films in 1948 and 1949 before the middle-length fiction *Le Rideau cramoisi*; Melville's first production was a short which gave him sufficient financial stability to make *Le Silence de la mer*; Albert Lamorisse's shorts are well known, notably *Crin blanc* and *Le Ballon rouge*; and between 1949 and 1959 Pierre Kast and Agnès Varda directed numerous shorts and documentaries. Those who were to figure among the leading New Wave directors acquired their formation in precisely the same way—Jean Rouch filmed a series of eight short documentaries from 1947 on; Chris Marker filmed a 16-mm documentary in 1952, then *Les Statues meurent aussi* with Alain Resnais, who himself directed and edited several shorts on art history as well as his notorious political essays in the twelve years preceding *Hiroshima, mon amour*. Then there was the well-known series of short fictions made between 1950 and 1958 by a group centered on Eric Rohmer and including Godard, Gégauff, Brialy, and Rivette; and again, there was the Truffaut/Godard collaboration of the late fifties.

What is not adequately emphasized, then, in most accounts of the origins of the New Wave is the debt owed by such directors to the industrial and financial mechanisms put in place during the classic period to foster just such filmmaking practices. This process had been complemented by that commercialization of wartime technological breakthroughs which transformed work practices in the cinema during the period 1945–1960 as it transformed them in many other arenas. The material available was lighter, faster, more flexible, and cheaper, and these characteristics interacted with the decline of the studio system and of set design to permit more extensive location shooting and a more dynamic camera style, while reducing the cost of that crucial first feature film for aspiring filmmakers.

This account sees the theory and practices of the New Wave as a logical and progressive extension of those of the classic French cinema, and thus calls into question the significance, indeed the very existence, of the supposed break between them. A third and final argument to the same effect would begin by refuting the standard New Wave propaganda of Truffaut et al. which represented the classic cinema as a closed shop, deprived of new blood and new ideas for so long that it could produce only desiccated and irrelevant films. Figure 8.1 shows the number of directors making their

FIGURE 8.1 **Recruitment of New Directors**

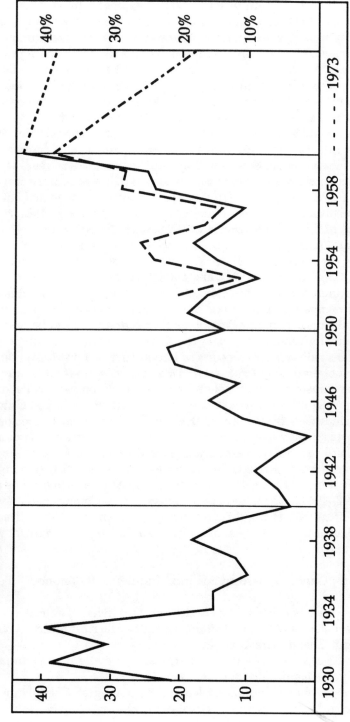

Sources: Numbers of new directors, derived from V. Pinel, *Filmographie des longs métrages sonores*, 1985 (solid line).
Percentage of new directors: *La Technique Cinématographique* 274, May 1966 (broken line).

first film in each year from 1930 to 1960 and expresses this for the fifties as a percentage of the total number of directors working in each year. Although it is true that the number of new directors increased dramatically in 1960, just as it had in 1931–1933, when demand for French sound films was intense, the rate of recruitment throughout the fifties was high and reasonably steady, at the same level as it had been during the period 1934–1939. It is the war years which are anomalous for their low level of recruitment. It seems that the normal rate of recruitment within the classic French cinema has always been about 20% per year and that the political circumstances of the war depressed this rate to an all-time low. If commentators judged otherwise at the time (and they did,[1] seeing the war years as bringing about a regeneration of cinematic personnel), it was because they identified as "newcomers" several of those prewar directors who had not made their name until the wartime—Christian-Jacque (first feature 1931, twenty-eight films of little interest except *Les Disparus de St. Agil* until 1941–1942), Autant-Lara (first feature 1932, no other solo direction until 1941), Delannoy (first feature 1933, next solo direction *Macao* 1939–1942), Le Henaff (1933), Gourguet (1934), and Daniel-Norman (1936).

This tendency to categorize directors according to when the films they directed first made an impact on the enlightened public or on enlightened critics, and thus when an aesthetic discourse first began to be applied to them, gradually came to supplant the literal statistics of recruitment as a criterion. It made thirties directors of Renoir (first feature 1924), Duvivier (1919), and Grémillon (1927), and it made Yves Allégret (first feature 1940) a resolutely postwar phenomenon because of his postwar collaboration with Jacques Sigurd on a series of notable existentialist subjects. Using this system, critics were by 1950 regularly dividing classic French directors into four cohorts (*promotions*): the *veterans*, who had established a name in the silent era and survived as best they could in the sound era; the *older generation*, who might have started in the twenties but had established themselves during the thirties; the *wartime generation*, who had come to the fore in the period 1940–1944; and the *postwar generation*, whose abilities had only been revealed after 1945. Using this classification system in the *Livre d'or 1950*, René Thévenet produces a list of which the following is a slightly supplemented version:

(1) *Veterans*: Gance, L'Herbier, Maurice Tourneur, de Baroncelli, Feyder, Epstein.
(2) *Older generation*: René Clair, Renoir, Duvivier, Grémillon, Marc Allégret, Decoin, Cloche, Billon, Lacombe, Pierre Prévert, Raymond Bernard, Chenal, Gréville.
(3) *Wartime generation*: Clouzot, Autant-Lara, Dréville, Christian-Jacque, Delannoy, Daquin, Bresson, Becker.
(4) *Postwar generation*: Rouquier, Clément, Yves Allégret, Calef, Hunebelle, Devaivre, Jacqueline Audry, Cayatte, Leenhardt, Melville, Tati.

While certain of these are debatable, the notion that at any given moment the French cinema's vitality depended primarily on an elite of some ten to twelve directors and that these could be expected to appear in "waves" was widely accepted.

For Thévenet, the first two of these four cohorts had not lived up to expectations in the postwar years. Only the two younger generations had "managed to adapt to the determinants of the economic crisis . . . and, moreover, the moral contingencies, the social and individual psychology, and the difficulties of the postwar period." This reflects the contemporary view that the classic French cinema was indeed capable of renewing itself, that it did so regularly, and that its postwar vitality had depended on that self-renewal. A series of annual reviews throughout the fifties recapitulated this theory and identified the significant numbers of new recruits each year—the fifth cohort—as a sign of vitality. Articles with titles such as "The Young French Cinema," "New Blood in the French Cinema," and "A Changing of the Guard? No! Entirely New Troops" were regularly to be seen in the mid to late fifties before any of the filmmakers normally classified as New Wave began their first feature.[2]

It is worth emphasizing that this "fifth cohort" of fifties classic directors was already widely recognized as having revitalized the classic cinema by endowing it with qualities of freedom, gaiety, exhilaration, intelligence, artistic integrity, and relevance well before 1959. Astruc (first feature 1955), Malle (1957–1958), Vadim (1956), Marcel Camus (1956–1957), Pierre Kast (1957), Agnès Varda (1954–1956), Brabant (1952), and Carbonnaux (1953–1954) had all been welcomed in these terms, as had several others. A particularly interesting retrospective on this group, appearing in *Cinéma 58*,[3] identified 40 such young hopefuls and, while acknowledging that they shared no common stylistic or thematic traits, spoke of them collectively as the "New Wave" [*sic*] on whom the future of the French cinema depended. The concluding summary by Pierre Billard perceptively described a series of industrial and social factors which had made entry into the profession more difficult for this fifth wave than for preceding waves—notably "a professional organization which multiplies barriers, compartmentalizes specialists, and prescribes hierarchies and career paths, thus inhibiting the promotion of the most capable," and the tendency for French production "to turn to large-scale international coproductions in color, with foreign stars and astronomical budgets, which leads producers to entrust them to proven directors rather than beginners." But the resultant statistics—these 40 young directors had made 100 films over the preceding 12 years—could easily be read as a continuing willingness to open doors to young talent, which is astonishing given the circumstances cited in the article.

Globally, the article evaluates the New Wave of 1950–1957 in negative terms, but its analysis of the social conditions underlying their failings is interesting. On the one hand this generation of directors is disenchanted and believes in nothing, not even its own revolt; and on the other the social evolution of the fifties has transformed society, generating new ways of talking and thinking, new values, new ways of representing and categorizing people. Few of the directors have managed to cope with this radically transformed reality. "Signs of it can, however, be recognized in the sensualism of Vadim and Brabant, the critical anarchism of Boissol and Carbonnaux, in Astruc's analysis of ambition, and in the freer, sincerer, and more modern study of male/female relationships undertaken by Astruc, Vadim, Kast, and Varda."[4]

Perceptive finally in recognizing that 1957 was in fact the trough of a wave, Billard and Sadoul both foresee another (sixth) such cohort acceding to the rank of director in the near future, coming from television, from the short film (Resnais, Fabiani), and from the Cahiers critics (Rivette, Truffaut, Chabrol). This group is seen, however, as merely the next in an ongoing series of renovatory waves, more able to cope with the transformed conditions of production and more able to represent the new social reality precisely because it will be building on the foundations established by the fifties wave. The career track of most of these foreshadowed directors is not seen as significantly different from that of their predecessors (scriptwriting, literature, journalism, short filmmaking), except that they have relatively infrequently acted as assistants to established directors and that a few have had the (somewhat suspect) benefit of an IDHEC formation.

Once again it is continuity and evolution that this "wave-theory" would support, rather than a radical paradigmatic break. The propagandists of the New Wave, obsessed with myths of rebellion, originality, and the uniqueness of the autonomous individual artist, could not afford to admit as much; and many classic filmmakers themselves, irked by the sixties filmmakers' bumptious arrogance and blinkered ingratitude to the system that had given them birth, reacted in ways that seemed to acknowledge as a reality this gulf between classic French cinema and New Wave; but thirty years later we no longer need be duped by such superficial phenomena: we can afford to recognize that, with no more than a necessary shift in the balance of production practices, a new adaptation to evolving conditions, the classic French cinema had survived yet another threat to its existence. In all its essential features, it is still with us today.

APPENDIX
PRIZES AND AWARDS

CANNES FILM FESTIVAL

1946: Eleven prizes, one to each of the participating countries. *Lost Weekend* (Wilder, U.S.A.); *La Symphonie pastorale* (Delannoy, France); *Brief Encounter* (Lean, England); *Roma, citta aperta* (Rosselini, Italy); *María Candelaria* (Fernandez, Mexico); *La Dernière Chance* (Lintberg, Switzerland); etc.
Special Jury Prize: *La Bataille du rail* (Clément, France)

Best direction:	René Clément
Best actor:	Ray Milland (*Lost Weekend*)
Best actress:	Michèle Morgan (*La Symphonie pastorale*)

1947: Six prizes, one to each of six genres.
Antoine et Antoinette (Becker, psychological)
Les Maudits (Clément, adventure/detective)
Crossfire (Dmytryk, social)
Ziegfield Follies (Minnelli, musical comedy)
Dumbo (Disney, cartoons)
Inondations en Pologne (documentary)

1948: Cancelled, for financial reasons.

1949: Grand prix: *The Third Man* (Reed)
Best direction: René Clément (*Au-delà des grilles*)
Best actress: Isa Miranda (*Au-delà des grilles*)
Best actor: Edward G. Robinson (*House of Strangers*)

1951: Grand prix: *Miracolo a Milano* (de Sica)
    Fröken Julie (Sjöberg)
Special Jury Prize: *All About Eve* (Mankiewicz)
Best direction: *Los Olvidados* (Buñuel)
Best actress: Bette Davis (*All About Eve*)
Best actor: Michael Redgrave (*The Browning Version*)

1952: Grand prix: *Due soldi di speranzi* (Castellani)
    Othello (Welles)
Special Jury Prize: *Nous sommes tous des assassins* (Cayatte)
Special prize (lyrical film):   *Le Médium* (Menotti)
Best direction: Christian-Jacque (*Fanfan la Tulipe*)
Best actress: Lee Grant (*Detective Story*)
Best actor: Marlon Brando (*Viva Zapata*)

1953: Special prize: Walt Disney
Grand prix: *Le Salaire de la peur* (Clouzot)

Best actor: Charles Vanel (*Le Salaire de la peur*)
Best actress: Shirley Booth (*Come Back Little Sheba*)
Seven prizes for distinct genres:
Adventure: *O Cangaceiro*
Comedy: *Bienvenudo, Mr Marshall*
Entertainment: *Lili*
Drama: *Come Back Little Sheba*
Legend: *Valkoinen Peura*
Exploration: *Magia Verde*
Visual narration: *La Red*

1954: Special prize: *From Here to Eternity* (Zimmerman)
       Grand prix: *Jigoku-mon* (Kinugasa)
       Special Jury Prize: *Monsieur Ripois* (Clément)
       and also nine national prizes and five genre prizes
       Best direction: René Clément

1955: Golden Palm: *Marty*, for script (Chayevski), direction
                               (Delbert Mann), actor (Ernest Borgnine),
                                 and actress (Betsy Blair)
       Best direction: Serge Vassiliev (*Geroite na Chipka*)
                                 Jules Dassin (*Du rififi chez les hommes*)
       Best actor: Spencer Tracey (*Bad Day at Black Rock*)
       Best team of actors: *Bolchaïa Semia*
       and two genre prizes

1956: Golden Palm: *Le Monde du silence* (Cousteau/Malle)
       Special Jury Prize: *Le Mystère Picasso* (Clouzot)
       Best direction: Youtkevich (*Otello*)
       Best actress: Susan Hayward (*I'll Cry Tomorrow*)
       and two genre prizes:
       Human document: *Pather Panchali* (Ray)
       Poetic comedy: *Smiles of a Summer Night* (Bergman)

1957: Golden Palm: *Friendly Persuasion* (Wyler)
       Special Jury Prize: *Kanal* (Wajda)
                                 The Seventh Seal (Bergman)
       Special prize: *Sorok Pervyi* (Tchoukrai)
       Best direction: Bresson (*Un condamné à mort s'est échappé*)
       Best actress: Giulietta Masina (*Le Notte di Cabiria*)
       Best actor: John Kitzmiller (*Dolina Miru*)
       and two genre prizes

1958: Golden Palm: *Letiat Jouravly* (Kalatozov)
       Special Jury Prize: *Mon oncle* (Tati)
       Best direction: Ingmar Bergman (*Nara Livet*)
       Best actress: the four leads of *Nara Livet*
       Best actor: Paul Newman (*The Long Hot Summer*)
       also two special prizes, and best scenario

1959: Golden Palm: *Orfeu negro* (Camus)
       Special Jury Prize: *Sterne* (Konrad Wolf)
       International prize: *Nazarin* (Buñuel)
       Best direction: François Truffaut (*Les 400 Coups*)
       Best actress: Simone Signoret (*Room at the Top*)
       Best actor: Dean Stockwell/Bradford Dillman/Orson
                                 Welles (*Compulsion*)
       and a prize for the best comedy

1960: Golden Palm: *La Dolce Vita* (Fellini)
      Special prizes: "best participation": *Ballada o soldatie* (Tchoukrai) and *Dama S. Sobatchkoi* (Kheifitz); "for the daring of its subject and for its plastic qualities": *Kagi* (Ichikawa); for his remarkable contribution to the search for a new cinematic language": Antonioni (*L'Avventura*)
      Best actress: Melina Mercouri (*Never on Sunday*) and Jeanne Moreau (*Moderato cantabile*)

PRIX LOUIS DELLUC (BEST FRENCH FEATURE FILM)

1937	*Les Bas-fonds* (Renoir)
1938	*Le Puritain* (Musso)
1939	*Quai des brumes* (Carné)
1940–1944	not awarded
1945	*L'Espoir* (Malraux)
1946	*La Belle et la bête* (Cocteau)
1947	*Paris 1900* (Védrès)
1948	*Les Casse-pieds* (Dréville and Noël-Noël)
1949	*Rendez-vous de juillet* (Becker)
1950	*Journal d'un curé de campagne* (Bresson)
1951	not awarded
1952	*Le Rideau cramoisi* (Astruc)
1953	*Les Vacances de M. Hulot* (Tati)
1954	*Les Diaboliques* (Clouzot)
1955	*Les Grandes Manoeuvres* (Clair)
1956	*Le Ballon rouge* (Lamorisse)
1957	*Ascenseur pour l'échafaud* (Malle)
1958	*Moi, un noir* (Rouch)
1959	*On n'enterre pas le dimanche* (Drach)
1960	*Une aussi longue absence* (Colpi)

PRIX LOUIS LUMIÈRE (BEST FRENCH SHORT FILM)

1948	*A l'assaut de la Tour Eiffel* (Pol)
1949	*1848* (Mercanton)
1950	*Utrillo* (Gaspard-Huit)
1951	not awarded
1952	*Images pour Debussy* (Mitry)
1953	*Aux frontières de l'homme* (Védrès)
1954	Awarded to Georges Franju for his work as a whole.

1955 *Paris la nuit* (Baratier and Valère)

1956 *La Crise du logement* (Dewewer)

1957 *Les Filles du feu*

1958 *Lettre de Sibérie* (Marker)

1959 *Corrida interdite* (de Daunant)

1960 *L'Amour existe* (Pialat)

PRIX JEAN VIGO (BEST FRENCH FILM ON A SOCIAL THEME)

1951 *La Montagne est verte* (Lehérissey)

1952 *La Grande Vie* (Schneider)

1953 *Crin-blanc* (Lamorisse)

1954 *Les Statues meurent aussi* (Resnais)

1955 *Emile Zola* (Vidal)

1956 *Nuit et brouillard* (Resnais)

1957 *Léon la lune* (Jessua)

1958 *Les Femmes de Stermetz* (Grospierre)

1959 *Le Beau Serge* (Chabrol)

1960 *A bout de souffle* (Godard)
     Les Enfants des courants d'air (Luntz)

PRIX EMILE COHL (BEST FRENCH CARTOON)

1955 *Le Voyage de Badabou* (Gruel)

1956 *Soir de fête* (Pierru)

1957 not awarded

1958 *Voyage en Boscavie* (Herman and Choublier)

1959 *Monsieur Tête* (Lénica and Gruel)

1960 Awarded to Arcady, for his work as a whole.

GRAND PRIX DU CINÉMA FRANÇAIS (FOUNDED IN 1934 BY THE SOCIÉTÉ D'ENCOURAGEMENT À L'ART ET À L'INDUSTRIE UNDER THE PATRONAGE OF LOUIS LUMIÈRE. AWARDED BY A PANEL PRESIDED OVER BY THE MINISTER)

1935 *La Kermesse héroique* (Feyder)

1938 *Quai des brumes* (Carné)

1946 *Farrebique* (Rouquier)

1947 *Monsieur Vincent* (Cloche)

1948 *Les Casse-pieds* (Dréville and Noël-Noël)

1949 not awarded

1950 *Jour de fête* (Tati)

1951 *Journal d'un curé de campagne* (Bresson)

1952 not awarded

1953 not awarded

1954 *Le Blé en herbe* (Autant-Lara)

1955 *Les Evadés* (Le Chanois)

1956 not awarded; medals to *Le Ballon rouge* and *Nuit et brouillard*

1957 *Porte des Lilas* (Clair)

1958 *Les Tricheurs* (Carné)

1959 *Les Etoiles de midi* (Ichac)

1960 *La Vérité* (Clouzot)

FOREIGN RECOGNITION OF FRENCH FILMS AND PERSONNEL

1937	Venice:	Grands Prix to *Un carnet de bal* (Duvivier) and *La Grande Illusion* (Renoir)	
1946	Venice:	Grand Prix to *The Southerner* (Renoir)	
	Locarno:	Grand Prix to *Ten Little Niggers* (Clair)	
1947	Venice:	Best direction:	*Quai des orfèvres* (Clouzot)
		Best actor:	Pierre Fresnay, in *Monsieur Vincent*
	Brussels:	Grand Prix:	*Le Silence est d'or* (Clair)
		Best actor:	Gérard Philipe in *Le Diable au corps*
		Best direction:	*Le Diable au corps* (Autant-Lara)
		Critics' prize:	*Le Diable au corps* (Autant-Lara)
	Locarno:	Grand Prix:	*Le Silence est d'or* (Clair)
1948	Hollywood:	Oscar for best foreign film, *Monsieur Vincent* (Cloche)	
1949	Venice:	Grand Prix International: *Manon* (Clouzot)	
		Best scenario: *Jour de fête* (Tati)	
1950	Venice:	Grand Prix:	*Justice est faite* (Cayatte)
		Critics' prize:	*Orphée* (Cocteau)
		Grand Prix International (ex aequo): *Dieu a besoin des hommes* (Delannoy)	
1951	New York:	Critics' prize for best foreign films: Une Partie de campagne (Renoir) Jofroi (Pagnol)	
	Venice:	Three different prizes to *Journal d'un curé de campagne* (Bresson)	
		Best actor:	Jean Gabin, in *La Nuit est mon royaume*
1952	Venice:	Golden Lion:	*Jeux interdits* (Clément)
		Critics' prize:	*Les Belles-de-nuit* (Clair)
	Hollywood:	Oscar, best foreign film: *Jeux interdits* (Clément)	

1954 Venice: Best actor: Jean Gabin, in *Touchez pas au grisbi* and in *L'Air de Paris*

1956 Venice: Critics' prize (ex aequo): *Gervaise* (Clément)
Best actor: Bourvil, in *La Traversée de Paris*
Best actress: Maria Schell, in *Gervaise*

1958 Hollywood: Oscar, best foreign film: *Mon oncle* (Tati)
Oscar in recognition of his contribution to acting:
Maurice Chevalier
Venice: *Les Amants* (Malle)

1959 Hollywood: Oscar, best foreign film: *Orfeu negro* (Camus)
Oscar, best actress: Simone Signoret
Venice: Best actress: Madeleine Robinson, in *A double tour*
Berlin: Golden Bear: *Les Cousins* (Chabrol)

1960 Venice: Golden Lion: *Le Passage du Rhin* (Cayatte)

ABBREVIATIONS

The following abbreviations for frequently cited journals have been used through-out the notes:

C 56	Cinéma 56 (etc.)
CC	Cahiers du Cinéma
CF	La Cinématographie Française
Cin	Cinématographe
CNC	Bulletin d'Information du Centre National de la Cinématographie
Com	Comoedia
EF	L'Ecran Français
FF	Le Film Français
FFI	France Film International
FO	France Observateur
Int	Interciné
IS	Image et Son
JC	Jeune Cinéma
LF	Les Lettres Françaises
Obj	Objectif
Pos	Positif
PV	Pour Vous
RC I & II	Revue du Cinéma, series 1 (1928–1931) and 2 (1946–1948)
RIC	Revue Internationale du Cinéma
TC	La Technique Cinématographique
TF	Le Technicien du Film

NOTES

INTRODUCTION

1. D. Bordwell, J. Staiger, and K. Thompson, *The Classical Hollywood Cinema* (London: Routledge, 1985).
2. P. Léglise, *Histoire de la politique du cinéma français*, vol. 1 (Paris: Librairie Générale de Droit et de Jurisprudence, 1970); vol. 2 (1940–1946) (Paris: Pierre Lherminier, 1977).
3. P. Bächlin, *Histoire économique du cinéma* (Paris: La Nouvelle Edition, 1947).
4. F. Courtade, *Les Malédictions du cinéma français* (Paris: Alain Moreau, 1978).
5. J.-P. Jeancolas, *15 ans d'années trente* (Paris: Stock, 1983).
6. G. Sadoul, *Le Cinéma français 1890–1962* (Paris: Flammarion, 1962).
7. R. Chirat, *Catalogue des films de long métrage*, vol. 1 (1929–1939), Cinémathèque Royale de Belgique, 1975; vol. 2 (1940–1950), Cinémathèque Municipale de Luxembourg, 1981.
8. V. Pinel, *Filmographie des longs métrages sonores du cinéma français* (Paris: La Cinémathèque Française, 1985).
9. B. Salt, *Film Style and Technology: History and Analysis* (London: Starword, 1983).

1. POLITICAL ECONOMY AND INDUSTRIAL STRUCTURE 1930–1940

1. See J.-Ch. Asselain, *Histoire économique de la France*, vol. 2: de 1919 à la fin des années 1970 (Paris: Ed. du Seuil, 1984) (for a brief account), and A. Sauvy, *Histoire économique de la France entre les deux guerres* (Paris: Fayard, 1965–1970) (for a fuller account).
2. Asselain, p. 42.
3. Ibid., p. 36.
4. Ibid., p. 47.
5. D. Leroy, *Economie des arts du spectacle vivant* (Paris, 1980), pp. 303, 306, 325 passim.
6. J. Durand, *Le Cinéma et son public* (Paris: Sirey, 1958).
7. Leroy, p. 8.
8. G. Sadoul, *Le Cinéma français* (Paris: Flammarion, 1962), p. 139.
9. Durand, p. 48.
10. Except in the immediate postwar years.
11. *Où va le cinéma français?* (Paris: Baudinière [1937?]), pp. 427, 433.
12. Durand, p. 154; see also G. Charensol, *Panorama du cinéma* (Paris: Ed. Jacques Melot, 1947), p. 146.
13. Durand, p. 157.
14. Sadoul, p. 144.

15. Durand, pp. 69, 70.
16. See Durand, p. 111, for examples from England, France, and the U.S.
17. G. Fain, "Finance et cinéma," in H. Fescourt, *Le Cinéma, des origines à nos jours* (Paris: Cygne, 1932).
18. Courtade, p. 44.
19. Coissac, *Les Coulisses du cinéma* (Paris: Les Editions Pittoresques, 1929), p. 216.
20. Bächlin, p. 60.
21. Coissac, p. 214.
22. A. Chevanne, *L'Industrie du cinéma: le film sonore* (Bordeaux: Delmas, 1933).
23. Fritz Bertran, cited in Léglise, vol. 1, p. 157.
24. Léglise, vol. 1, p. 158.
25. Ibid., p. 159.
26. Viviani, Minister of Education, in 1916; see Léglise, vol. 1, chap. 5.
27. Courtade, p. 114.
28. 803, 24 March 1934.
29. 1000, 31 December 1937.
30. Quoted in Léglise, vol. 1, p. 297.
31. *Le Cinéma des origines à nos jours.*
32. Léglise, vol. 1, p. 123.
33. Cited in Courtade, p. 129; see Léglise, vol. 1, pp. 123–125.
34. CF, 6 July 1927.
35. J. Cleynen, *La Politique du cinéma français: stratégies et réalisations 1929–1935*, vol. 1, chap. 1.
36. *Courrier Cinématographique* 18, 4 May 1929.
37. No. 650. Cited in Courtade, p. 64 (omitting English as a language).
38. See Jean Wahl, PV no. 12, June 1930.
39. *Catalogue des films français de long métrage: films sonores de fiction 1929–39.* Cinémathèque royale de Belgique, 1975.
40. Quoted in Jeancolas, pp. 24–25.
41. Bulletin of July 1930, cited in Courtade, p. 69.
42. *Ciné-Journal* 1134, 22 May 1931, cited in Courtade, p. 69.
43. *Lectures Pour Tous*, August 1931, cited in Courtade, pp. 69–70.
44. René Jeanne, cited in Courtade, pp. 71–72.
45. *L'Epicerie des rêves* (Paris: Ed. Baudinière, 1933).
46. Speech of 17 April 1930; cited in A. Poiré, *Gaumont: 90 ans de cinéma* (Paris: Ramsay, 1986), p. 80.
47. See R. Abel, *French Cinema: The First Wave 1915–1929*, section 1.
48. *Gaumont: 90 ans de cinéma*, pp. 81–82.
49. See Abel, pp. 33–34.
50. See Abel; also Chevanne, p. 73 et seq., and Cleynen.
51. Cleynen, vol. 1., pp. 126–127.
52. Ibid., pp. 164–172.
53. Jeancolas, p. 33. Cleynen gives April 1935 as the date of arraignment.
54. To Renaitour inquiry; cited in Jeancolas, p. 29.
55. Anatole de Monzie, in Parliament, 5 April 1933; cited in Léglise, vol. 1, p. 98.
56. See Cleynen, pp. 119–120.
57. In a speech to the Congrès de l'Union des Intérêts Economiques, Paris, 19 November 1930.
58. See Léglise, vol. 1, pp. 67–70, for a fuller account.
59. Ibid., p. 95.
60. See Léglise, vol. 1, pp. 105 et seq. for a fuller account.
61. See Léglise, vol. 1, chap. 13.
62. Published in *Cinémonde*; cited by Courtade without giving date.
63. See Courtade, pp. 147–149, for a fuller account.

64. *Où va le cinéma français*, pp. 388–399.
65. Ibid., p. 399.
66. CF 911, 18 April 1936.
67. Cited Cleynen, p. 80, from documents in the Arsenal Library.
68. He is probably referring to UFA and ACE.
69. To the Renaitour inquiry, 3 February 1937.
70. Jeancolas, p. 34.
71. See Léglise, vol. 1, pp. 190–195 and 301–315.
72. Asselain, p. 91.
73. Léglise, vol. 1, p. 192.
74. P. Braunberger, *Cinémamémoires* (Paris: Centre G. Pompidou, 1987), p. 100.
75. Bächlin, p. 100.

2. POLITICAL ECONOMY AND INDUSTRIAL STRUCTURE 1940–1960

1. Sadoul, pp. 139–146.
2. R. Régent, *Cinéma de France* (Paris: Ed. Bellefaye, 1948).
3. R. Bonnell, *Le Cinéma exploité* (Paris: Ed. du Seuil, 1978).
4. Paris: Ed. France-Empire, 1977.
5. Paris: Les Editions du Cerf, 1984. Coll. 7ᵉ Art.
6. *La France de Pétain et son cinéma* (Paris: Henri Veyrier, 1981), p. 21.
7. Léglise, Courtade, etc.
8. Léglise, vol. 2, pp. 32–33.
9. Siclier, p. 27.
10. For accounts of this period, see Léglise, vol. 2; also Siclier, p. 26, Jeancolas, p. 298 et seq., Courtade, pp. 186–188.
11. Philippe Amaury, *De l'information et de la propreté de l'etat*, p. 425, cited in Courtade, pp. 183–184.
12. In a note of May or June 1941; cited in Courtade, p. 185.
13. Jeancolas, pp. 345–346.
14. Cited in Courtade, p. 186.
15. Cited in Léglise, vol. 2, p. 17; cf. Sadoul, pp. 90–91.
16. Siclier, p. 29.
17. For instance, F. Garçon, "Un bien curieux bilan," in *De Blum à Pétain*, pp. 46–47, and Courtade, pp. 221–222.
18. I. Maine, *La Propaganda nazie par le cinéma, en France*, thèse de diplôme, Paris X; cited Courtade, p. 193.
19. Siclier, chap. 1.
20. Ibid., p. 44.
21. Ploquin, letter to Siclier, 8 December 1980, cited in Siclier, p. 46.
22. Jean-Paul Le Chanois (Jean-Paul Dreyfus).
23. Léglise, vol. 2, p. 56.
24. See Léglise, vol. 2, pp. 59–61, for a fuller account.
25. Sadoul, p. 89. See also vol. 6 of his *Histoire générale du cinéma* (Paris: Denoël, 1954).
26. Various sources give varying percentages, but all of the same order.
27. Siclier, p. 20.
28. Garçon, p. 45.
29. Jeancolas, p. 313, citing *Le Film*, no. 17, 7 June 1941.
30. Certain days were "alcohol-free."
31. G. Braucourt, *André Cayatte* (Paris: Seghers, 1969), p. 62.
32. See figure 2.3.

33. Cited in Courtade, p. 189.
34. Jeancolas, pp. 304–305.
35. Courtade, p. 188.
36. "Le Problème juif," a talk given in 1942; cited in Garçon, p. 35.
37. Courtade, pp. 189–190.
38. Article 5 of the legislation. See Garçon, p. 39.
39. *Ciné Mondial* 8, 26 September 1941.
40. Jeancolas, p. 308.
41. Garçon, p. 35.
42. *Le Cinéma: grande histoire illustrée* (Paris: Atlas, 1982), p. 383.
43. *L'Action française*, 29 April 1938.
44. Quoted by Truffaut in the preface to A. Bazin, *Le Cinéma de l'occupation et de la résistance*.
45. See also Siclier, p. 459.
46. *Le Film* 17, 7 June 1941.
47. Courtade, p. 201.
48. Ibid., p. 206.
49. Data extracted from Léglise, vol. 2, pp. 206–213.
50. Courtade, p. 213.
51. *Gaumont: 90 ans de cinéma*, pp. 85–100.
52. In *Il Cinema* (Roma: L'Arnia, 1949).
53. See *Filméchange* 38, 2, 1987, "Cinecitta au secours du cinéma français."
54. Pos 168, April 1975.
55. Léglise, vol. 2, p. 144.
56. R. Richebé, *Au-delà de l'écran* (Monte-Carlo: Ed. Pastorelly, 1977), p. 175.
57. G. Jesseb, "René Clair m'a dit," in *Vérités sur le cinéma français*, ed. Carlo-Rim, n.d. (1945).
58. For instance, 1,000,000 apartment buildings were destroyed.
59. Asselain, p. 109, and more generally, section 4.
60. Leroy, pp. 263–265.
61. Ibid., pp. 104–105; see also A. Bazin, "Situation économique du cinéma français," *France Observateur* 352, 7 February 1957.
62. FF 884–885, p. 114.
63. "Cinéma français: perspectives 1970," Paris, Ministère des Affaires Culturelles, 1965; published in CNC 91, February 1965.
64. See also C. Degand, in FF 884–885, p. 111.
65. FF 884–885, p. 119.
66. C. Degand, in TC 274, May 1966.
67. Ibid., p. 28.
68. CF 1154, 27 April 1946.
69. Fuller text cited in Courtade, pp. 244–245.
70. Léglise, vol. 2, p. 169.
71. See Courtade, p. 246.
72. Léglise, vol. 2, p. 171.
73. See Courtade, p. 247, for more details.
74. Courtade, p. 248.
75. Actually, by a committee chaired by the PDG of CNC and including representatives of government, finance, and the profession.
76. J. Quéval, "L'Economie du cinéma," in *Chronique Sociale de France* 4–5, 1954.
77. See Bonnell, p. 319.
78. Article 10, cited in Courtade, p. 251.
79. J.-C. Batz, *Action syndicale et politique européenne du film*, pp. 13–16.
80. See G. Comte, "La Coproduction: banc d'essai du Marché Commun," in FF 832–833, p. 123, for a fuller account of this matter.

81. CNC 28, February 1955. See also CF 1768, Festival Special 1958, p. 8 (etc.).
82. FF 884–885, p. 94.
83. Quéval, 1954, p. 337.
84. FF 869–870, p. 72.
85. G. Sadoul, "Bulletin de santé du cinéma français," in LF 657, 7 February 1957.
86. The films investigated do not correspond exactly to those listed by most sources for 1955.
87. LF 657, 7 February 1957.
88. CF 1768, p. 8.
89. FF 884–885.
90. Sadoul, *Le Cinéma Français* (Paris: Flammarion, 1962), p. 144.
91. *Arts*, no.751, 2 December 1959.
92. Fifteen to sixteen per year throughout the fifties. See TC 274, May 1966, p. 7.
93. See Bonnell, chap. 6, for more details.
94. "Alerte au cinéma," published by *La Vie Catholique* and cited in Quéval, *Chronique Sociale de France* 4–5, 1954.
95. See FF 884–885, p. 55.
96. See Bonnell, chap. 7 (especially for the period after 1960).
97. FF 611–612, Winter Special, 1956, p. 4.
98. See Durand, pp. 213–215, for the years 1938 and 1949, and TC 274, May 1966, for the fifties.

3. PLANT AND TECHNOLOGY

1. J. Kruger, quoted in RC I, 2, 1930; A. Trauner, *Décors de cinéma* (Paris: Jad-Flammarion, 1988), p. 25; R. Clavel, in *Le Livre d'or du cinéma français*, October 1950; M. Carné, in *Style de France* 4, 1946; L. Daquin, in *L'Ecran français* 31 March 1946; L. Derain, 1950.
2. J. Quéval, "L'Economie du cinéma," in *Chronique Sociale de France* 4/5, 1954.
3. See H. Laurent, *Evolution du décor cinématographique* (Paris: IDHEC, 1955), p. 17.
4. See R. Prédal, *80 ans de cinéma: Nice et le 7ᵉ art* (Serre, 1980), part 2.
5. R. Richebé, *Au-delà de l'écran* (Pastorelly, 1977), p. 48.
6. See Jeancolas, p. 51, for an account of this.
7. Courtade, pp. 29–31.
8. CF 27 October 1928. See R. Icart, *La Révolution du parlant* (Institut Jean Vigo, 1988), for a fuller account.
9. Quoted in Dudley Andrews, "Sound in France: The Origins of a Native School," *Yale French Studies* 60, 1980, pp. 97–98, and also in Icart, pp. 51–52, who gives the translation appearing in the *Courrier Cinématographique*, no. 11, March 1930.
10. Joseph Engl, Joseph Massole, and Hans Vogt. Massole may have been French.
11. RC I, 2, n.d. (ca. February 1930), p. 75.
12. Courtade, p. 41, and RC I, 9, 1 April 1930; Icart, p. 89, lists prices between 75,000 (German) and 480,000 (American) for optical systems; Sadoul, *Le Cinéma français*, p. 54, gives 800,000 for Western Electric; Courtade, pp. 39 and 41, gives 500,000 and "a millon, they say." Abel, p. 60, proposes 250,000 to 500,000 or even 600,000.
13. Courtade, p. 39; Icart, p. 104.
14. These and following figures come from Courtade and Jeancolas. Richebé claims that he and Aubert were already equipped in 1927.
15. Jeancolas, p. 64.
16. Gomery, "Economic Struggle and Hollywood Imperialism," *Yale French Studies* 60, 1980, p. 82.

17. Courtade, p. 44.
18. Richebé, *Au-delà de l'écran*, pp. 47–50.
19. Talking to Armand Panigel; cited in Courtade, p. 78.
20. See Jeancolas, pp. 97–102.
21. Jeancolas, pp. 98–99.
22. Jeancolas. Courtade gives October 1929.
23. A few weeks later to become GFFA.
24. RC I, 9, p. 46.
25. For more details on early sound productions, see Courtade, chap. 2, and Jeancolas, chap. 2.
26. For more details, see Barry Salt, *Film Style and Technology: History and Analysis*. See also RC I, 18, 1 January 1931, for a contemporary French view.
27. Pos 254/255, May 1982. Douy talks of it being generalized in France in 1930 (Pos 246).
28. L. H. Burel, interviewed by René Prédal; cited in Courtade, pp. 58–59.
29. A. Walker, *The Shattered Silents* (New York: Morrow, 1979), p. 97.
30. S. Neale, *Cinema and Technology*, p. 96.
31. Ibid.
32. Cited in René Clair, *Cinéma d'hier, cinéma d'aujourd'hui* (Gallimard, 1970), pp. 188–189.
33. René Clair, p. 190.
34. Cited in René Clair, p. 221.
35. In an interview recorded by Armand Panigel in 1974.
36. Armand Panigel interview, 1974.
37. L'Herbier, in *Mon Ciné* 361, 17 January 1929.
38. René Clair, pp. 205–206, writing in May 1929.
39. See chap. 6.
40. Armand Panigel interview, 1974; broadcast no. 2.
41. *Ciné-Journal* 1123, 6 March 1931.
42. *Ciné-Miroir* 217, 31 May 1929.
43. PV, 11 August 1932.
44. *Cinéa*, 15 December 1929.
45. *Ciné-Journal* 1123, 6 March 1931.
46. *Machines Parlantes et Radio* 133, 6 December 1930.
47. TC 43/44, p. 197.
48. Debrie: founded 1900; first Parvo 1908; automatic fade 1921; interview model 1922; 3,000 sold by 1923; L. Parvo and T. Parvo (300 meters) 1926–1928; reflex 300, 1941; color version for bipack films, 1950.
49. TC 43/44, July/August 1934, pp. 197 and 200.
50. By Claude Beylie, for instance.
51. But also in Pagnol's Marseilles studio.
52. Sadoul, probably erroneously, cites 1941 as the year of maximum capacity (18 studios, 52 stages) (*Le Cinéma français*, p. 146).
53. *Où va le cinéma français*, p. 151.
54. Ibid., pp. 159, 163, and 165.
55. See *Ciné-Magazine*, November 1930, "Un Hollywood français."
56. *80 ans du cinéma*, p. 78.
57. *Cours no. 8: Le studio vous ouvre ses portes* (Nice: *Ecole Technique du Cinéma par Correspondance*, 1944).
58. "La grande pitié de nos studios," published in various journals (for instance, *Le Monde*, 19 October 1955, and TF9, September 1955).
59. CF 1137, 29 December 1945.
60. Speaking at La Maison de la Chimie, 31 March 1946.
61. CF 1154, 27 April 1946.

62. "La grande pitié de nos studios," TF 9, September 1955.

63. Or rather included, but under terms which had precluded funding, because of legal technicalities.

64. See FF, 28 October 1955 and 2 December 1955; CF 1652, 21 January 1956.

65. C 55, no. 2, p. 3.

66. A. Chevanne, *L'Industrie du cinéma: Le cinéma sonore* (Bordeaux: Delmas, 1933).

67. CC 71, May 1957.

68. TF 69, 15 February 1961, p. 15.

69. CF 2082, 3 October 1964, p. 28. The project for a French Hollywood remained alive throughout the 1960s and 1970s.

70. Magnetic sound was a fait accompli in the U.S. by the end of 1949, according to Barry Salt.

71. See M. Gérardot, in TC 131, April 1953.

72. TC 131, April 1953, p. 103.

73. Ibid., p. 112.

74. Ibid., p. 112.

75. The magazine could be changed in two seconds; see Salt, pp. 290–291.

76. FF, 17 February 1961, p. 6.

77. Salt, chap. 17.

78. TF 9, September 1953, p. 18.

79. Salt, p. 315.

80. Ibid., p. 319.

81. TC 7, August 1931, p. 22. See also TC 130 and 131, March and April 1953.

82. Marey, incidentally, was filming in 2.66 × 1 in 1896.

83. See Courtade, p. 84.

84. FF 832/833, p. 135.

85. CF 850, 16 March 1935.

86. According to TF 9, September 1955.

87. See RC II, pp. 2957–2961.

88. *Du muet au parlant* (Paris: La Nouvelle Edition, 1946), pp. 137–141 (in a review dated 9 May 1936).

89. Salt, pp. 317–318.

90. Neale, pp. 118–119.

91. RC II, pp. 2957–2959.

92. See Courtade, p. 84.

93. CF 872, 20 July 1935.

94. Arnoux, pp. 142–145 (in a review dated 8 May 1937).

95. Salt, p. 278.

96. *Le Décor de film* (Paris: Seghers, 1970), p. 128.

97. Barsacq, p. 129; also Claude Renoir in TF 209, 15 November 1973.

98. CF 1154, 27 April 1946.

99. RC II, 8, Autumn 1947.

100. Courtade, p. 255.

101. "Naissance du Rouxcolor," *Ciné Digest*, no. 1, May 1949.

102. CF 1538, 17 October 1953, p. 24.

103. For more details, see CF 1538, 17 October 1953.

104. Salt, p. 310.

105. Harispuru speaks of it as having been in 1951. Pinel gives 1950 as the production date.

106. Interview in CF 1538, 17 October 1953.

107. Courtade, p. 298.

108. CF 1538, p. 25.

109. Ibid., p. 33.

110. FF 567/568, p. 41.
111. Neale, chaps. 8 and 9.
112. See the FF/CF Winter special issue 1228, 26 January 1968.
113. FF special issue 832/833.
114. FF 611/612, p. 17.
115. Barsacq, p. 130.
116. Barsacq, in CF 1538, 17 October 1953, p. 36.
117. Marcel Grignon, in CF 1538, p. 35.
118. René Barjavel, *Cinéma Total*, pp. 38–53.
119. This and following statements are from interviews in CF 1538.
120. See Neale, pp. 151–158.
121. See Salt, pp. 222–223, 265, 276, etc.
122. See the Matras interview in CF 1538 and G. Gérardot in TC 131, April 1953, p. 101.

4. PERSONNEL

1. Ricciotto Canudo in *Candide*, 14 April 1931.
2. Cin 53, December 1979, interview with Jean Aurenche.
3. Jean Wiener, *Allegro appassionato* (Belfond, 1979).
4. Carlo Rim, *Le Grenier d'Arlequin* (Paris: Denoël, 1981).
5. *Ciné Club*, January 1949, quoted in *Jacques Prévert, Premier Plan* 14, 1960, p. 49.
6. *Premier Plan* 14, 1960, p. 51.
7. See C 59, 35, April 1959; also *Etudes Cinématographiques* 14/15, 1962, pp. 90–92, and *Spectacles*, 3 December 1958, pp. 48–49.
8. P. Chesnais, *L'Acteur* (Paris: Librairie Technique, 1957), p. 24.
9. For further details see A. Sallée, *Les Acteurs français* (Bordas, 1988), pp. 37–48.
10. For these relationships see Porcile's biogaphy of Jaubert and the autobiographies of Wiener and Auric; also J. Chabannes, *Les Petits Enfants du siècle* (France-Empire, 1980).
11. M. Fleuret, "Bonjour M. Kosma," in *Journal Musical Français* 91, 17 October 1960.
12. Film Dope 2.
13. M. Fleuret, "Van Parys, notre Offenbach," JMF 95, 5 February 1961.
14. For details, see André Barsacq, *Le Décor de film*, pp. 17, 20, 21.
15. This section condenses a vast number of sources; see in particular the *International Directory of Cinematographers* . . . II, KG Saur, 1983, and René Prédal, *La Photo de Cinéma* (Paris: Cerf, 1985).
16. Henri Jeanson, *70 ans d'adolescence* (Stock, 1971), p. 116.
17. See J. Lorcey, *Marcel Achard* (France-Empire, 1977).
18. See examples in Cin 53, December 1979.
19. D. Marion (ed.), *Le Cinéma par ceux qui le font* (Arthème Fayard, 1949), p. 125.
20. TF 57, 15 January 1960.
21. Alongside the dozens of women, there were only four men—Jean Feyte, Henri Rust, Léonide Azar, René le Hennaf.
22. IS 283, April 1974, "Les Femmes et la technique du cinéma."
23. Stephen Watts (ed.), *La Technique du Film*, tr. G. Auriol (Paris: Payot, 1939), chap. on editing.
24. See Colpi, "Dégradation d'un art," *Cahiers du Cinéma* 65, December 1956, and Lo Duca, *Technique du cinéma* (Presses Universitaires de France, 1948), p. 48.
25. In *Les Coulisses du cinéma* (Editions Pittoresques, 1929).
26. IS 283, April 1974.

27. See Jeancolas, *15 ans d'années trente*, pp. 118–126, and also the dossier edited by him in Pos 323, January 1988.

28. See Alexander Trauner, *Décors de cinéma* (Paris: Jad-Flammarion, 1988), pp. 16–17.

29. In *Napoléon* (Jonathan Cape, 1983), p. 48.

30. *La Tête qui tourne* (Paris: Pierre Belfond, 1979), p. 204.

31. L'Herbier, p. 244.

32. Vol. 4 of *Les Juifs en France*, written by Lucien Rebatet under the pseudonym of François Vinneuil.

33. See "Les Cinéastes allemands en France pendant les années trente," in Pos 323, January 1988, p. 46. See also Thomas Elaesser, "Pathos and Leavetaking," in *Sight and Sound* 53, 4, 1984.

34. Born in Poland, Maté had trained in Hungary but had worked in Vienna and Poland before coming to France.

35. Cin, June 1981.

36. *Sight and Sound* 53, 4, 1984.

37. Pos 323, January 1988, p. 49.

38. *Sight and Sound* 53, 4, 1984.

39. Pos 323, January 1988, p. 43.

40. *Le Schpountz*, written and directed by Marcel Pagnol, 1937–1938.

41. *Petit Cinéma sentimental* (Paris: La Nouvelle Edition, 1950), pp. 66–68.

42. See Charles Ford, *Pierre Fresnay* (Paris: Editions France-Empire, 1981), pp. 31–32.

43. See Maurice Bessy, *Les Passagers du souvenir* (Paris: Albin Michel, 1977), pp. 83–87; Robert Florey, *Hollywood d'hier et d'aujourd'hui*; and D. Lebrun, *Paris-Hollywood* (Paris: Hazan, 1987).

44. Cited by Dudley Andrews in *Yale French Studies* 60, 1980, p. 98.

45. Jeancolas, pp. 24–25.

46. Courtade, p. 66.

47. Cited in Courtade, p. 107.

48. Cin 76, March 1982, p. 19.

49. *La Tête qui tourne*, pp. 208–209.

50. *Les Dessous du cinéma allemand* (Paris et Limoges: Courrier du Centre, n.d [1934]), pp. 9–10.

51. *La Revue de Paris* 1, 1935, pp. 572–573, 588.

52. Accounts differ: see Jeancolas, pp. 191–193, and *Premier Plan* 14, pp. 71–73.

53. In *Jean Renoir*, Lyon, *Premier Plan* 22–23–24, 1962.

54. Jeancolas, pp. 194–195.

55. See Courtade, pp. 134–136.

56. Courtade, p. 137.

57. CF 959, 19 March 1937.

58. See Janine Spaak: *Charles Spaak, mon mari* (Paris: Editions France-Empire, 1977).

59. Jeancolas, p. 225.

60. See G. Ragache and J. R. Ragache, *La Vie quotidienne des écrivains et des artistes sous l'occupation* (Paris: Hachette, 1988), especially chap. 1.

61. Lucien Rebatet, *Les Tribus du cinéma et du théâtre*, pp. 9, 20, 26, 30, 54, 65, 77.

62. Ibid., pp. 40–41, 56–61, 86–87.

63. Ibid., pp. 64–65.

64. Ibid., pp. 123–124.

65. G. Ragache and J. R. Ragache, p. 84. See also "Les Emigrés" in the *Ciné-Miroir Almanach* for 1945.

66. G. Ragache and J.-R. Ragache, p. 175.

67. *L'Envers des décors* (Paris: Robert Laffont, 1977), pp. 160–161.

68. *Décors de cinéma*, p. 57.

69. G. Ragache and J. R. Ragache, pp. 88–89.
70. *Décors de cinéma*, p. 57.
71. *80 ans de cinéma*, p. 87.
72. *La Vie cinématographique à Nice* (Nice: Faculté des Lettres, 1973).
73. *Le Film de ma vie* (Paris: Editions France-Empire, 1973), pp. 21–22.
74. See *Le Film de ma vie*, chaps. 20–33.
75. See his account in *80 ans de cinéma*.
76. *80 ans de cinéma*.
77. For an account of this population, see Gili, *La Vie cinématographique à Nice, 1939–1945*; Mauriche Cloche, in TC 181, November 1957; Dudley Andrews, in JUFVA 35, 1; and *80 ans de cinéma*, p. 87.
78. TF 266, 15 January 1979, p. 26.
79. *80 ans de cinéma*, p. 86.
80. *Le Film de ma vie*, p. 105.
81. See Jeancolas, pp. 316–318.
82. Jeancolas, p. 318.
83. See P. Pellissier, *Brasillach . . . le maudit* (Paris: Denoël, 1989); and P. Louvrier, *Brasillach: l'illusion fasciste* (Paris: Perrin, 1989).
84. Cited in *Le Monde*, 5 November 1989, p. 7.
85. *Histoire de la confédération national du cinéma français*, Bois d'Arcy, CNC, 1983.
86. *Histoire de la politique du cinéma français*, vol. 1, pp. 38–39, 82–93, 115–120, 129–130.
87. Léglise, vol. 1, pp. 39, 83, 87–88.
88. Ibid., pp. 136–137.
89. Ibid., p. 138.
90. See, for instance, CF 918, 6 June 1936, and CF 932, 12 September 1936.
91. CF 934, 26 September 1936.
92. Léglise, vol. 1, pp. 142–145.
93. TC 85, January 1938.
94. Léglise, vol. 2, p. 28.
95. Ibid., pp. 109–110.
96. Max Douy, in Pos 244–245, p. 9.
97. Cin 76, March 1982.
98. G. Gérardot, in TC 131, April 1953, III, p. 101.
99. CF 2099, 30 January 1965, p. 55.
100. See André Lang, *Le Tableau blanc* (Paris: Horizons de France, 1948), pp. 207–209, and Jean Lods, *La Formation professionnelle des techniciens du film* (Paris: UNESCO, 1951).
101. For instance, in "Formons les techniciens," in *Le Jour*, 18 October 1938.
102. *Où va le cinéma français*, pp. 394–396.
103. Ibid., pp. 115–116.
104. Ibid., pp. 232–234.
105. See Gili, *La Vie cinématographique à Nice, 1939–1945*; Cloche, in TC 181, November 1957; Andrews, in *Journal of the University Film and Video Association* 35, 1.
106. *L'Envers des décors*, p. 161.
107. *80 ans de cinéma*, p. 87.
108. *La Formation professionnelle des techniciens du film*, p. 31.
109. Speech of 10 January 1944, reprinted in *La Tête qui tourne*, pp. 319–324.
110. See *Cinémaction* 45, 1987, pp. 45–46.
111. *Les 1001 métiers du cinéma* (Paris: Jacques Melot, 1947), pp. 156–158.
112. Address to the 2nd International Congress of Film and TV Schools, Cannes, 1955.
113. CF 2099, 30 January 1965, p. 54.
114. Ministerial speech by J.-M. Louvel, reported in FF, 2 April 1954.

115. CC 65, December 1956, "Dégradation d'un art."
116. C 57, March 1957.
117. CF 2099, 30 January 1965.
118. *La Tête qui tourne*, pp. 322–323, Speech of 10 January 1944.
119. Collective interview in *Arts* 761, 109, February 1960.
120. See the Boyer Series in EF 249, 10 April 1950 et seq.
121. Collective interview in *Arts* 761.
122. TF 54, 15 October 1959. See also TF 55, "Les Non-professionnels resteront dans leur trou."

5. THE FORMATION OF AUDIENCES

1. PV 12, 7 February 1929.
2. See Barrot, p. 135.
3. See V. Volmane and Charles Ford, *Cinéma pour vous* (Paris: Juillard, 1974).
4. Pierre Leprohon, *Les 1001 métiers du cinéma* (Paris: Editions Jacques Melot, 1947), p. 305.
5. P. Mouliniers, *Catalogue des périodiques français et étrangers consacrés au cinéma* . . .
6. Ch. Bosseno, IS 341, July 1979.
7. *Le Cinéma et la presse*, pp. 80 and 86.
8. Ibid., p. 80.
9. RC I 24, "La Vie d'un film," footnote.
10. Ch. Bosseno, IS 342, September 1979.
11. For some wonderful quotations from this, see Bosseno, IS 343, October 1979.
12. O. Barrot, *L'Ecran français 1943–1953: histoire d'un journal* (Paris: Les Editeurs Français Réunis, 1979), p. 174.
13. See Philippe Erlanger, interviewed in *Ciné Revue* 21, 21 May 1981.
14. Volmane and Ford, p. 126.
15. *Ciné Revue* 21, May 1981.
16. "Il faut repenser la formule," in RIC 14, 1949.
17. In *Ciné Revue* 21.
18. See the appendix for a list of prizes awarded over the years.
19. *Les Coulisses du cinéma* (Les Editions Pittoresques, 1929), pp. 156–160.
20. "Firmament français," *Le Livre d'or du cinéma français* (1946).
21. Paris, Le Seuil, 1957.
22. Jeanne and Ford, pp. 142–143.
23. See the initial articles, for instance, in each issue of *Ciné Digest* during 1949 and 1950.
24. Jeander, "Les Ciné Clubs," in D. Marion, *Le Cinéma par ceux qui le font* (Paris: Librairie Arthème Fayard, 1949).
25. V. Pinel, *Introduction au ciné-club* (Paris: Edition Ouvrières, n.d. [ca. 1964]).
26. RC I 4, p. 80.
27. Ibid.
28. See Jeander, in Marion, p. 385.
29. See Jeander and Pinel (who gives the figure of 80,000 without specifying his source).
30. Pinel, p. 31.
31. Jeander, in Marion, p. 387.
32. For the railway workers, the builders, and the metalworkers.
33. Jeander, in Marion, p. 389. Pinel discusses this more fully.
34. *Arts* 772.
35. In *Synthèse* 2, 1947.

36. *Ciné Pour Tous* 59, 1921.
37. R. Borde, *Les Cinémathèques* (Lausanne: L'Age d'Homme, 1983); see particularly pp. 40–50.
38. PV, 31 March 1932.
39. Cited in Borde, p. 56.
40. PV 189, 3 June 1932.
41. *Arts et Cinéma* 1, March 1933; cited in Borde, pp. 56–57.
42. Cited in Borde, chap. 1, "A History of Destruction."
43. Borde, chap. 1.
44. 20,000 francs from P.-A. Harlé (Borde, p. 67).
45. An incalculable number were lost when the nitrate stock in one of his caches spontaneously caught fire and went up in flames.
46. See Volmane and Ford, pp. 51 et seq., and the monograph by P. Léglise, *Le Cinéma d'art et essai* (Paris: La Documentation française, 1980).
47. Jeander, *Armand Tallier et le studio des Ursulines* (Paris: AFCAE, 1963).
48. Ibid.
49. Ibid.
50. See Jean-Paul Le Chanois, in the introduction to the reprint of RC II.
51. Le Chanois, in the introduction to the reprint.
52. Nino Frank, *Petit Cinéma sentimental*.
53. Odette Virmaux and Alain Virmaux, in the introduction to the reprint of RC I.
54. CC 31, p. 26.
55. CC 100, October 1959, pp. 62–68.
56. Cited in Volmane and Ford, p. 218.
57. Volmane and Ford.
58. Ibid.
59. RC I 2, "Revue des revues."
60. RC I 4, p. 14.
61. RC I 4, Denis Marion.
62. Ecran 79, 86, 15 December 1979. See pp. 24–27.
63. RC I 8, Robert Desnos in "Revue des revues."
64. For instance on Sternberg, in issue 12.
65. RC I 12.
66. RC I 3, "Revue des revues."
67. RC I 9, p. 65. Written by J.-P. Le Chanois (Dreyfus).
68. PV 9, 17 January 1929.
69. PV 10, 24 January 1929.
70. PV 16, 7 March 1929.
71. PV 7, 3 January 1929.
72. *Histoire du cinéma* (Paris: Denoël and Steele, 1935).
73. *Intelligence du cinématographe* (Paris: Correa, 1946).
74. Republished in *Du muet au parlant* (Paris: La Nouvelle Edition, 1946).
75. *Esprit*, November 1935.
76. Ibid.
77. His translation of Stephen Watts's edited volume.
78. *L'Echo des Etudiants*, 23 October 1943 (student newspaper).
79. *Du muet au parlant*, pp. 161–180.
80. RC II 3, p. 19.
81. RC II 1.
82. RC II 1–4, 6–7.
83. EF 25, Christmas 1945, for instance.
84. See EF 12, 19 September 1945; EF 16, 17 October 1945; and EF 42 and 53.
85. EF 144, 30 March 1948.
86. EF 110–111.

87. See C. Williams (ed.), *Realism and the Cinema* (BF 1 Reader in Film Studies).

88. "The Ontology of the Photographic Image" and "The Evolution of Film Language," in *Qu'est-ce que le cinéma*.

89. *L'Echo des Etudiants*, 8 November 1943.

90. RC II 10, p. 45.

91. "Cinéma, art de l'espace," RC II 14.

92. CC 3, August 1951, p. 22.

93. RC II 10, p. 44.

94. RC II 4, p. 38.

95. RC II 10, p. 36.

96. RC II 3.

97. RC II 2, p. 66.

98. RC II 3, p. 66.

99. RC II 3, pp. 64–66 (Jean Desternes).

100. EF 72, November 1946 (Georges Sadoul). See also J.-P. Barrot, in EF 35.

101. EF 180, 7 December 1948.

102. RC II 3, p. 68.

103. In a speech at La Bellevilloise, 1933. See L. Moussinac, *L'Age ingrat du cinéma*, pp. 329–375, particularly pp. 345–350.

104. In the introduction to *L'Age ingrat du cinéma*.

105. See René Clément and Pierre Chenal, in EF 24, and Léon Moussinac, in EF 25 (both December 1945).

106. EF 196, 29 March 1949.

107. EF 15, April 1944.

108. EF 202, 8 May 1949.

109. See the review of Dmytryk's *Crossfire*, EF 122.

110. EF 18, 31 October 1945.

111. EF 247, 27 March 1950.

112. EF 14, 10 March 1944.

113. Ibid.

114. Sadoul, *Le Cinéma français*, pp. 99–100.

115. Courtade, p. 209, quoting the Armand Panigel TV broadcast no. 8, 5 May 1975.

116. EF 79, J.-P. Barrot, 31 December 1946.

117. See, for instance, EF 261, 3 July 1950.

118. For instance, borrowing the format of the sequence of stills retelling a film narrative.

119. When it "reamalgamated" with *Les Lettres Françaises*.

120. CC 98, August 1959.

121. See Léglise, vol. 1, pp. 238–259, for a fuller account.

122. PV 234, 11 May 1933.

123. Léglise, vol. 1, p. 248.

124. Reputedly banned without even being viewed.

125. Cited in Courtade, pp. 149–150.

126. Courtade, p. 155.

127. At the 6th Venice Film Festival.

128. The word "deserter" must not be pronounced, and the Gabin figure had to act with "a certain propriety."

129. See Léglise, vol. I, pp. 257–258, and Courtade, pp. 151–154.

130. Suzanne Borel of the Commission de l'Information, in CF 1093, 14 October 1939.

131. See Léglise, vol. 2, pp. 35–37, 61, and 77–79.

132. Cited in Léglise, vol. 2, p. 78.

133. Courtade suggests this may have been done to give Tobis an advantage over Pathé, which still had the 16-mm rural circuits.

134. Law of 21 May 1941.

135. Courtade, pp. 239–240.
136. TF 4, March 1955.
137. *Arts* 16–22, February 1955.
138. Courtade, p. 258.
139. Report of the Semaine d'étude internationale catholique du cinéma (Brussels, 1933). See also Georges Altman, *Ça, c'est du cinéma* (Paris: Les Revues, 1931), pp. 175–238.
140. See J. Cleynen, *La Politique du cinéma français, 1929–1935* (Paris: EHESS, 1983), p. 291.
141. Examples from Altman.
142. CF 1768, Festival Special, 1958.
143. See Cleynen, pp. 290–295.
144. CF 1768, Festival Special, 1958.
145. *Choisir*, 17 November 1935.
146. Cited in Cleynen, p. 310.
147. *Cinéopse*, 1934; cited in Int, January 1935.
148. *Choisir*, 15 July 1934.
149. The manager of the Majestic, St. Pol de Léon, reported in *Le Courrier Cinématographique*, 7 March 1931.
150. See the relevant discussion in chap. 1, the first section.
151. For instance by Benoît-Lévy in 1919, Raymond in 1930, Germaine Dulac in 1933.
152. CF, 8 November 1930, cited in Léglise, vol. 1, p. 250.
153. Léglise, vol. 1, p. 251.
154. See Léglise, vol. 1, pp. 250–252, and vol. 2, p. 152.
155. *Choisir*, 21 May 1933, quoting from *L'Aube*.
156. Léglise, vol. 1, p. 251.
157. Law of 20 December 1941.
158. Mlle Borel, cited in Courtade, p. 161.
159. Cited in Courtade, pp. 198–199.
160. Cited in Courtade, p. 201.
161. For further examples see Siclier, pp. 447–457.
162. "Le Censeur," in D. Marion (ed.), *Le Cinéma par ceux qui le font* (Arthème Fayard, 1949), pp. 341 and 348.
163. Ibid., p. 348.
164. Ibid., p. 352.
165. Ibid., p. 354.
166. Founded in 1953 to replace UFOCEL, itself founded in 1933.
167. Attachment to the first issue of the bulletin, announcing the formation of the league; May 1946.
168. CF 1768, Festival Special, 1958.
169. France Film International 2, February 1955 (Jean Edeline).
170. L. Daquin, *Le Cinéma, notre métier* (Paris: Les Editeurs Français Réunis, 1960), p. 189.
171. RC I 4, p. 46.
172. RC II, 18 October 1948, Document 3.
173. RC II 4, "A quoi sert la critique," by Jacques Bourgeois, and RC II 8, "Bucéphale bicéphale," by Nino Frank.
174. *Histoire économique du cinéma* (Paris, La Nouvelle Edition, 1947).
175. Paris, Presses Universitaires de France, 1946.
176. "Filmology: History of a Problematic," Quarterly Review of Film Studies, Winter 1985.
177. For instance, E. Souriau, "La Structure de l'univers filmique et la vocabulaire de la filmologie, RIF 7–8 (n.d.).
178. For instance, A. Souriau, "Succession et simultanéité dans le film" in *L'Uni-*

vers filmique (Paris: Flammarion, 1953); and Jacques Guicharnauld in *Revue Interna-tionale de Filmologie* 1.

179. For instance, Serge Lebovici, "Psychanalyse et cinéma" in RIF 5 (n.d.).
180. CC 5, September 1951, pp. 33–34.
181. RC II 4, p. 80.

6. MODE OF PRODUCTION AND AUTHORIAL CONTROL

1. London: Routledge, 1985.
2. Staiger, p. 116.
3. Ibid., p. 117.
4. Ibid., p. 123.
5. Ibid., p. 135.
6. Ibid., pp. 321–322.
7. Ibid., p. 330.
8. Richard Abel, *French Film: The First Wave*, pp. 22–23.
9. See Richard Abel, pp. 17–38, for a fuller account.
10. Coissac, p. 51.
11. Charles Delac was president of the Comité directeur de la Chambre Syndicale Française de la Cinématographie (Coissac, p. 51).
12. André Boll, *Le Cinéma et son histoire* (Paris: Sequana, 1941); Leprohon, *Les 1001 métiers du cinéma* (Jacques Melot, 1947); J. Chartier and R. Desplanques, *Derrière l'écran* (Paris: Spes, 1950).
13. *Où va le cinéma français?* p. 306.
14. Ibid., pp. 220–222.
15. Ibid., p. 239.
16. *Cinémamémoires* (Paris: Centre G. Pompidou, 1987), p. 149.
17. This set of oppositions is based on several sources, notably Yannick Flot, *Les Producteurs: les risques d'un métier*, and A. Poiré, *Gaumont: 90 ans de cinéma*; also "Alain Poiré: la liberté de produire," in FF 2118, 5 December 1986.
18. See "Le producteur: son rôle," in *Le Cinéma des origines à nos jours*.
19. See *Cinémamémoires* and "A quoi servent les producteurs?" in C 61, 54, March 1961.
20. *Cinémamémoires*, p. 83.
21. *Gaumont: 90 ans de cinéma*, p. 152.
22. *Cinémamémoires*, p. 55.
23. Ibid., p. 50. Braunberger reports that Renoir agreed to direct because he too became infatuated with her.
24. The same man later had an affair with Valentine Tessier, star of *Mme. Bovary* and tried to buy up and destroy all the negatives of that film.
25. "Au genérique les producteurs: Pierre Braunberger," in C 65, 94, March 1965, p. 77.
26. Leprohon, *Les 1001 métiers du cinéma*, p. 78.
27. *Cinémamémoires*, p. 48.
28. All those of East European descent felt the same way.
29. *France-Observateur* 46, 5 March 1959.
30. Flot, pp. 144–149.
31. Ibid., pp. 71–81.
32. *Stars et Films* 21, 1948.
33. Unifrance Film 31, August/September 1954.
34. Claude Beylie, *Marcel Pagnol*, p. 56.
35. See J. Siclier, *La France de Pétain et son cinéma*, pp. 41–67.

36. Siclier, p. 47.
37. According to Pierre Braunberger, in *Cinémamémoires*.
38. René Thévenet, in C. Ford, *Le Livre d'or du cinéma français 1950*, p. 76.
39. FF 722, 28 March 1958.
40. Louis Daquin, *Le Cinéma, notre métier*, pp. 195–196.
41. René Clair, *Cinéma d'hier, cinéma d'aujourd'hui*, pp. 242–243.
42. Peter Bächlin, *Histoire économique du cinéma*, pp. 198–199.
43. See Coissac, *Les Coulisses du cinéma*, pp. 35–58.
44. *Le Cinéma*, p. 56.
45. *Panoramique du cinéma* (Paris: Sans-Pareil, 1929).
46. "Le Scénario" in D. Marion (ed.), *Le Cinéma par ceux qui le font*.
47. D. Marion (ed.), p. 101.
48. Cited by Icart, *La Révolution du parlant*, p. 166.
49. Presentation of *Marius*, October 1931.
50. *Ciné-Journal* 1160, 27 November 1931.
51. *Ciné-Miroir* 213, 3 May 1929.
52. Probably referring to *Enlevez-moi*.
53. Freddy Buache, *Michel Simon*, cited in Jeancolas, p. 66.
54. A. Mortier, *Ciné Magazine*, March 1932.
55. G. Tavano, *Ciné-Journal* 1002, 9 November 1928.
56. In *Le Cinéma et moi* (Paris: Ramsay).
57. J. Torok, *Le Scénario: histoire, théorie, pratique* (Paris: Artefact, 1986), p. 54.
58. "Le Cinématographe contre l'esprit," 1927, in Icart, *La Révolution du parlant*, p. 155.
59. PV 57, 19 December 1929.
60. *Pour Tous*, 1 August 1929.
61. Marguet, cited in Icart, p. 186.
62. Francoz, in *Ciné Magazine* 32–33, 10 August 1928.
63. Arnoux, in PV, 22 November 1928.
64. Arnoux, in PV 81, 31 July 1930.
65. Germaine Dulac, in *Ciné-Journal* 983, 29 June 1928.
66. Germaine Dulac, in *Ciné-Journal* 1123, 6 March 1931.
67. Henri Chomette, in *Ciné-Miroir* 224, 19 July 1929.
68. Editorial in *Mon Ciné* 353, 22 November 1928.
69. See Icart, pp. 170, 246, 260, etc.
70. Cited in Coissac, p. 38.
71. Coissac, pp. 41–42.
72. Quoted by Claude Beylie in "Un prince de la comédie," but with unidentifiable source (Cin 102, July 1984).
73. *Où va le cinéma français?* p. 332 (M. Pietri).
74. Beylie, in Cin 102, July 1984.
75. *On tourne . . . lundi*, pp. 33–35; see also pp. 81 et seq.
76. *Derrière l'écran*, pp. 50–52.
77. Cited in Leprohon, *Les 1001 métiers du cinéma*, p. 96.
78. Leprohon, p. 98.
79. Chartier and Desplanques, *Derrière l'écran*, p. 158.
80. *On tourne . . . lundi*, p. 178.
81. Lecture to IDHEC, 26 April 1944.
82. *Les 1001 métiers du cinéma*, p. 56.
83. TF 22, 15 November 1956.
84. *Comment écrire pour le cinéma*, p. 24.
85. In *Droit de la cinématographie*; cited in Nouet, p. 24.
86. G. Sadoul, *Le Cinéma*, p. 58.
87. *On tourne . . . lundi*, p. 178.

88. Ibid., pp. 71 et seq.
89. Aurenche, lecture to IDHEC, 25 February 1944.
90. Bost, lecture to IDHEC, 26 April 1944.
91. C 56, 10, March 1956, pp. 4–9 and 93–95.
92. EF 244, 6 March 1950.
93. D. Marion (ed.), *Le Cinéma par ceux qui le font*, pp. 105–107.
94. Ibid., pp. 113–114.
95. Ibid., p. 102.
96. Lecture to IDHEC, 26 April 1944.
97. Unifrance Film 48, October-December 1958.
98. *70 ans d'adolescence*.
99. Guillot, *Les Préverts*, p. 85.
100. Marion, pp. 107–108.
101. Ibid., p. 109.
102. Death notice in CF 1686, 29 September 1956.
103. J. Spaak, *Charles Spaak, mon mari*, pp. 243–244.
104. Courtade, p. 197.
105. Nino Frank, 1946; Charles Spaak, 1949.
106. Nouet, 1957; Agel, 1957.
107. See Bordwell, Staiger, and Thompson, *The Classical Hollywood Cinema*, p. 322.
108. See, for instance, *Style en France* 4, 1946; p. 22.
109. *Style en France* 4, 1946, p. 20.
110. *Ecole Technique de Cinéma par Correspondance*, Cours 9, 1944.
111. Nouet, p. 3.
112. Leprohon, p. 101.
113. Cin 53, December 1979.
114. Marion (ed.), pp. 110–111.
115. Leprohon, p. 55.
116. Ibid., p. 64.
117. *Derrière l'écran*, pp. 42–43.
118. Charles Ford, *On tourne . . . lundi*, p. 98.
119. Leprohon, p. 97.
120. Coissac, *Les Coulisses du cinéma*.
121. RIC 22, 1955.
122. See Jeanne Witta, in D. Marion (ed.), p. 160.
123. Cavalcanti, in RIC 22, 1955.
124. *Le Cinéma*, p. 103.
125. Coissac, pp. 108–109.
126. Data derived from H. Agel (ed.), *Sept ans de cinéma français* (Paris: Cerf, 1953).
127. For this opposition see articles in TF 47, February 1959, and TF 17, May 1956.
128. *Arts*, 30 June 1954.
129. CC 78, about Michel Simon.
130. See Leprohon (ed.), *Présences contemporaines: Cinéma*, pp. 134–135.
131. C 59, 35, April 1959.
132. *Le Cinéma*, p. 132.
133. For the more generous view see V. Pinel in *Etudes cinématographiques* 14/15.
134. *Présences contemporaines*, p. 277.
135. TF 17, May 1956.
136. See CC 173, December 1965; interview, Suzanne de Troyes.
137. Louis Page, "Les Méthodes de travail du metteur en scène," in *Feyder, ou Le Cinéma Concret*, 1949.
138. These figures are from Sadoul, *Arts* 75, 2 December 1959.
139. Sadoul, *Le Cinéma*, p. 57; Leprohon, p. 43; etc.
140. Cavalcanti, RIC 22, 1955.

141. *Présences contemporaines*, p. 276; *Ciné-Revue* 68, February 1957; etc.
142. Cin, June 1981.
143. TC 39, May 1958.
144. CC 71, May 1957, p. 52.
145. CC 71, May 1957, p. 90.

7. WORK PRACTICES AND STYLISTIC CHANGE

1. See Duvignaud, *L'Acteur: statuts professionnels*, pp. 218–221.
2. See, for instance, *Ciné Revue* 35, 30 August 1957.
3. CC 407–408, May 1988.
4. *Encyclopédie française*, 1935 ed., section 17-88-5.
5. Int, February 1933; article by O'Hanlon.
6. U. Barbaro, "Le Cinéma sans acteurs," in *Le Rôle intellectual du cinéma*, (Paris: Société des nations, Institut International de Coopération Intellectuelle, 1937).
7. *Ciné Pour Tous* 8, 11 May 1951; see also Sadoul, *Les Merveilles du cinéma*, pp. 65–67.
8. Raf Vallone, in C 59, p. 33.
9. C 59, 33; C 61, 58; C 60, 48; *Spectacle* 2, 1958; TF 76, October 1961; *Théâtre Populaire* 32, 1958.
10. Decoin, in *Ciné Pour Tous* 8, 11 May 1951.
11. *Le Livre d'or du cinéma français, 1945*; see also "L'Acteur," in Marion (ed.), *Le Cinéma par ceux qui le font*.
12. *Arts* 619, 15 May 1957.
13. B. Dort, in *Etudes Cinématographiques* 14–15, Spring 1962.
14. CF, cited in C 69, 138, p. 96.
15. René Mandion, *Cinéma, reflet du monde* (Paris: Ed. Paul Montel, 1944), p. 70.
16. Cadars, *Les Séducteurs du cinéma français*, and Ducout, *Les Séductrices du cinéma français*, explore some categorizations; see also EF 908, 13 May 1947; C 63, 78; *Ciné Magazine* 4, April 1930.
17. *Ciné Digest* 1, May 1949.
18. *Les Stars*, p. 21.
19. *Cinéma d'aujourd'hui* 10: "L'Acteur, matière vivante du film."
20. *Etudes cinématographiques* 607, 1960, p. 103, which quotes Barsacq.
21. *Décors de cinéma*.
22. Pos 244–245, p. 5.
23. André Antoine, "Enquête sur la crise du cinéma," in *Le Film*, 1917.
24. Cited in Leprohon, p. 135.
25. Cited in Leprohon, p. 136.
26. Barsacq, *Le Décor de film*, p. 63.
27. *L'Art Cinématographique* 6, 1929.
28. Epstein, quoted in H. Chardavoine, *L'Evolution du décor dans le cinéma français*.
29. Meerson, quoted in Barsacq.
30. René Clair, quoted in Barsacq.
31. Hugues Laurent, *La Technologie du décor de film*, p. 30.
32. Barsacq, p. 104.
33. RC I 27, October 1931.
34. Barsacq, introduction.
35. Quoted in Chardavoine, p. 90.
36. CF, October 1950; Douy quote: Pos 246, p. 28.
37. Marion (ed.), p. 195; see also *Arts* 8, December 1954, and CF, October 1950.

38. *Le Décor de film*, pp. 102–103.
39. Quoted in Leprohon, p. 138.
40. *Décors de cinéma*, p. 20.
41. RC I 27, October 1931.
42. TC 264, May 1965, p. 55.
43. Lourié, *My Work in Films*, p. 116–117.
44. Barsacq, *Le Décor de film*, p. 104.
45. Pierre Robin, CF, October 1950.
46. Quoted in Guillot, *Architecture de film* (unpublished thesis).
47. *Regards neufs sur le cinéma*, fiche filmographique (Paris: Editions du Seuil, 1963).
48. Barsacq, p. 62.
49. Quoted in Chardavoine, p. 90.
50. *Le Décor de film*, p. 104.
51. *L'Univers filmique*, p. 92.
52. *Unifrance Film* 20, October 1952.
53. TC 264, May 1965.
54. *Décors de cinéma*, p. 23.
55. *Le Décor de film*, procedures section.
56. *Avant-scène Cinéma* 192, September 1977.
57. Pos 244–245, p. 5.
58. Prédal, in C 73, 173, February 1973, p. 93.
59. Alekan, in C 79, 246, June 1979.
60. Cin 38, May 1978.
61. Cin 76.
62. C 79, 246, June 1979, p. 12.
63. TF 50, June 1959.
64. C 79, 246, June 1979, pp. 16–17.
65. TF 50, June 1959.
66. Cin, June 1981.
67. *Photo Cinéma* 65, January 1956, p. 18.
68. C 72, 168, July 1972, pp. 103–104.
69. Ibid., p. 113.
70. *Ciné Digest* 9, January 1950, and EF 216, 22 August 1949.
71. TF 210, 15 December 1973.
72. Cin, June 1981, p. 36.
73. Ibid., pp. 30–31.
74. Ibid., p. 32.
75. *Des lumières et des ombres* (Paris: Le Sycamore, 1984), pp. 256–257.
76. IS 80, March 1955.
77. Correspondence course, lesson 5.
78. *Ciné Digest* 9, January 1950.
79. Alekan, in C 79, 246.
80. Correspondence course, lesson 5, chap. 8.
81. Cin, June 1981, p. 29.
82. Correspondence course, p. 46.
83. Ibid., p. 58.
84. TF 50, June 1959.
85. Cin, June 1981.
86. TF 48, April 1959.
87. Alekan, in C 79, 246, June 1979.
88. TF 49, May 1959.
89. Cin 53, December 1979, p. 47.
90. See Bac and Lemare, in TF 53, September 1959.
91. Cin, June 1981.

92. TF 48, April 1959.
93. TF 209, November 1973.
94. C 72, 168, July 1972, p. 112.
95. TF 55, November 1959.
96. Cin, June 1981, p. 24.
97. TF 49, May 1959.
98. *Sight and Sound* 1, Winter 1976–1977.
99. See, for instance, Alekan, in Cin, June 1981, p. 24. The following quotations are from TF 50, June 1959; Cin, June 1981; *Des Lumières et des ombres*, p. 296. See also LF 1343, 15 July 1970.
100. See TF 209, 15 November 1973; *Culture et Communication* 19, September 1979; C 57, 17 April 1957.
101. Clouzot references from FF 2099, 30 January 1965, and TF 209, 15 November 1973.
102. *Photo Cinéma* 651, January 1956.
103. TF 49, May 1959 (Fellous is in fact *against* the structuralist use of color).
104. TF 49, May 1959.
105. *L'Evolution du décor dans le cinéma français.* Unpublished thesis (Paris 1), chap. 1.
106. Vol. 2, pp. 172–174.
107. *Film Style and Technology*, pp. 153, 202–203, 228.
108. Barry Salt uses 500 shots rather than a 100-minute film.
109. See Bordwell, Staiger, and Thompson, *The Classical Hollywood Cinema* (especially part 1).
110. My emphasis. Elsewhere, original emphasis.
111. Chartier and Desplanques, *Derrière l'écran*, pp. 140–145.
112. *Le Langage cinématographique*, p. 60; see also chap. 2.
113. Salt, p. 262.
114. Cin, June 1981, p. 36.
115. See Crisp, "The Rediscovery of editing in the French cinema," in *Histoire et Mesure*, 1987, II 3–4, pp. 199–214.
116. Except *Remorques*, primarily because of multiple tank shots to simulate storm effects.
117. B. Salt, "Film Style and Technology in the Thirties," *Film Quarterly*, vol. 3, 1, Fall 1976.
118. See Crisp, *Histoire et Mesure*, 1987, II 3–4.
119. Salt, *Film Quarterly*, p. 28.
120. Ibid., p. 29.
121. Ibid., p. 29.
122. Jean Feyte, "Le Montage," in Marion (ed.), *Le Cinéma par ceux qui le font*.
123. Correspondence course: lesson 14, "Le Montage."
124. And assumed as standard in Britain in 1948—see Karel Reisz, *The Technique of Film Editing* (London and New York: Focal Press, 1953), p. 394.
125. M. Bridoux, in *Photo Ciné Revue*, July 1956.
126. In 1960 there were still 318 registered editors, but only enough continuous work for one-sixth of them.
127. *Le Cinéma Chez Soi* 9, December 1956.
128. *Le Cinéma*, Casterman, 1954.
129. Dr. R. Bataille, *Le Savoir filmer* (Taffin-Leffort, 1944).
130. *Ciné-Montage* (Paris: Paul Montel, 1954).
131. *Technique du cinéma*, p. 49.
132. *Le Langage cinématographique*, pp. 171–172.
133. EF 94, 15 April 1947.
134. "Dégradation d'un art," in CC 65, December 1956.

135. *Ciné-Montage.*
136. *Le Savoir filmer,* pp. 164 et seq.
137. H. Agel, *Le Cinéma,* chapter on editing (Paris: Casterman, 1954).
138. Report of the Congress of Vienna, on editing, May 1963.
139. CC 65, December 1956.
140. IS 5, March 1952, p. 7.
141. "We will return . . . to the plan américain whenever the conversational focus is on the (reactions of the) participants."
142. *Histoire générale du cinéma,* vol. 2, p. 172.
143. *Bulletin de l'IDHEC* 3, July 1946. See also *Bulletin* 4, on rhythm.
144. EF 94, 15 April 1947.
145. *Le Langage cinématographique,* pp. 157–158.
146. Ibid., footnote to p. 159.

CONCLUSION

1. See, for instance, *Le Livre d'or du cinéma français, 1945,* article by René Ginet.
2. E. Tranchant, in IS 106, November 1957; Lachenay, in *Arts* 652, 8 January 1958; Unifrance Film 38, January-February 1956; CF 1654, Special, January 1956.
3. C 58, 24 February 1958.
4. Pierre Billard, in C 58, 24, pp. 31–34.

BIBLIOGRAPHY

BOOKS

Abel, R. *French Cinema: The First Wave 1915–1929*. Princeton University Press, 1987.
———. *French Film Theory and Criticism: A History-Anthology, 1907–1939*. 2 vols. Princeton University Press, 1988.
Adorno, T., and H. Eisler. *Musique de cinéma*. Paris: L'Arche, 1972.
Agel, H. *Le Cinéma*. Paris: Casterman, 1954.
———. *Jean Grémillon*. Paris: Seghers, 1969.
———. *Les Grands Cinéastes que je propose*. Paris: Cerf, 1967.
———. (ed.). *Sept ans de cinéma français*. Paris: Editions du Cerf, 1953.
Agel, H., and G. Agel. *Précis d'initiation au cinéma*. Paris: Ed. de l'Ecole, 1957.
Aguettand, L., L. Barsacq, H. Laurent, et al. *Rapport concernant la décoration de film en France*. 2ᵉ Congrès International des Ecoles de Cinéma et de TV. Cannes: 1955.
Ajame, P. *Les Critiques de cinéma*. Paris: Flammarion, 1967.
Alekan, H. *Des Lumières et des ombres*. Paris: Le Sycamore/La Cinémathèque française, 1984.
Altman, G. *Ça, c'est du cinéma*. Paris: Les Révues, 1931.
Amengual, B. *Les Français et leur cinéma, 1930–39*. Créteil: Losfeld, 1973.
Andrews, D. *Film in the Aura of Art*. Princeton University Press, 1984.
Annenkov, G. *En habillant les vedettes*. Paris: Robert Marin, 1951.
Arlaud, R. *Cinéma bouffe*. Paris: Jacques Melot, 1945.
Armes, R. *French Cinema*. Oxford University Press, 1985.
Arnoux, A. *Du muet au parlant: souvenirs d'un témoin*. Paris: La Nouvelle Edition, 1946.
Asselain, J.-Ch. *Histoire économique de la France*. Vol. 2, de 1919 à la fin des années 1970. Paris: Editions du Seuil, 1984.
Aumont, J.-P. *Le Soleil et les ombres*. Paris: Robert Laffont, 1976.
Auric, G. *Quand j'étais là*. Paris: Grasset, 1979.
Autant-Lara, C. *La Rage au coeur*. Paris: Henri Veyrier, 1984.
Bächlin, P. *Histoire économique du cinéma* (tr. Müller-Strauss). Paris: La Nouvelle Edition, 1947.
Bandy, M. (ed.). *Rediscovering French Film*. New York: Bullfinch Press, 1983.
Barjavel, R. *Cinéma total*. Paris: Denoël, 1944.
Barrot, O. *L'Ecran Français, 1943–1953: histoire d'un journal*. Paris: Les Editeurs Français Réunis, 1979.
———. *Inoubliables! visages du cinéma français, 1930–1950*. Paris: Calmann-Lévy, 1986.
Barrot, O., and R. Chirat. *Les Excentriques du cinéma français*. Paris: Veyrier, 1983.
Barsacq, L. *Le Décor de film*. Paris: Seghers, 1970.
Bataille, Dr. R. *Le Grammaire cinégraphique*. Lille: Taffin-Lefort, 1947.
———. *Le Savoir filmer*. Lille and Paris: Taffin-Lefort, 1944.
Batz, J.-C. *Action syndicale et politique européenne du film*. Bruxelles: Université Libre, 1965.
Baudrier, Y. *Les Signes du visible et de l'audible*. IDHEC, 1964.

Bazin, A. *Le Cinéma français de l'occupation et de la résistance*. Paris: Union Générale d'Editions, 1975.

———. *Qu'est-ce que le cinéma?* Vols. 1–4. Paris: Editions du Cerf, 1969.

Bellanger, C. *Presse clandestine, 1940–44*. Paris: Armand Colin, 1961.

Bellanger, C., J. Godechot, P. Guiral, and F. Terrou. *Histoire générale de la presse française*. Vol. 4. Paris: Presses Universitaires de France.

Bernard, G. *L'Art de la musique*. Paris: Seghers, 1961.

Bertin-Maghit, J.-P. *Le Cinéma français sous Vichy: les films français de 1940 à 1944*. Paris: Revue du Cinéma/Albatros, 1980.

Bessy, M. *Les Passagers du souvenir*. Paris: Albin Michel, 1977.

———. *Les Truquages au cinéma*. Paris: Prisma, 1951.

Beylie, C. *Marcel Pagnol*. Paris: Seghers, 1974.

Billecocq, G. *Régime fiscal du cinéma en France*. Montpelier: Canne, 1930.

Blakeway, C. *Jacques Prévert: Popular French Theatre and Cinema*. Fairleigh Dickinson University Press, 1989.

Bonnell, R. *Le Cinéma exploité*. Paris: Seuil, 1978.

Borde, R. *Les Cinémathèques*. Lausanne: L'Age d'Homme, 1983.

Bordwell, D., J. Staiger, and K. Thompson. *The Classical Hollywood Cinema*. London: Routledge, 1985.

Boujut, M. (ed.). *Europe-Hollywood et retour*. Paris: Autrement, 1986.

Bourgeois, J. *René Clair*. Geneva and Paris: Roulet, 1949.

Braucourt, G. *André Cayatte*. Paris: Seghers, 1969.

Braunberger, P. *Cinémamémoires*. Paris: Centre G. Pompidou, 1987.

Brieu, Ch. *Joinville: le cinéma*. Paris: Ramsay, 1985.

Brunius, J. *En marge du cinéma français*. Paris: Arcanes, 1954.

Buchsbaum, J. *Cinéma engagé: Film in the Popular Front*. University of Illinois Press, 1988.

Burel, L.-H. *Cours d'opération de prise de vues*. Paris: Ecole Universelle de Cinéma par Correspondance, 1980.

Cadars, P. *Les Séducteurs du cinéma français, 1928–1958*. Paris: Veyrier, 1982.

Carné, M. *La Vie à belles dents*. Paris: Jean-Pierre Ollivier, 1975.

Catelain, J. *Marcel L'Herbier*. Paris: Jacques Vautrain, 1950.

Cavalcanti, A. *Etat du cinéma, 1927: le metteur en scène*. Bordeaux: La Revue Fédéraliste 103, Special Issue, 1927.

———. *Working for the Films*. London and New York: Focal, 1947.

Chardavoine, H. *L'Evolution du décor dans le cinéma français, des origines à nos jours*. Uni Paris I, thèse 399, 1973.

Charensol, G. *40 ans de cinéma, 1895–1935*. Paris: Sagittaire, 1935.

Charensol, G., and R. Régent. *Un maître du cinéma: René Clair*. Paris: La Table Ronde, 1952.

Chartier, J., and R. Desplanques. *Derrière l'écran: initiation au cinéma*. Paris: Spes, 1950.

Chesnais, P. *L'Acteur: statuts professionnels*. Paris: Librairie Technique, 1957.

Chevalier, J. *Cinéclub et action éducative*. Paris: Centre National de Documentation Pédagogique.

Chevanne, A. *L'Industrie du cinéma: le cinéma sonore*. Bordeaux: Delmas, 1933.

Chevassu, F. *Faire un film*. Paris: Edilig, 1987.

Chion, M. *Ecrire un scénario*. Paris: Cahiers du Cinéma/INA, 1985.

Chirat, R. *Catalogue des films de long métrage*. Vol. 1 (1929–1939), Cinémathèque Royale de Belgique, 1975. Vol. 2 (1940–1950), Cinémathèque Municipale de Luxembourg, 1981.

———. *Le Cinéma français des années 30*. Paris: Hatier, 1983.

Clair, R. *Cinéma d'hier, cinéma d'aujourd'hui*. Paris: Gallimard, 1970.

———. *Réflexion faite*. Paris: Gallimard, 1950.

Claude, R., et al. *Panoramique sur le 7ᵉ art*. Paris: Ed Universitaires, 1959.

Cleynen, J. *La Politique du cinéma français: stratégies et réalisations 1929–1935.* Paris: EHESS, 1983 (thèse d'état).

Cocteau, J. *Entretiens autour du cinématographe.* Paris: André Bonne, 1951.

Cohen-Séat, G. *Essai sur les principes d'une philosophie du cinéma.* Vol. 1. Paris: Presses Universitaires, 1946.

Coissac, G.-M. *Les Coulisses du cinéma.* Paris: Les Editions Pittoresques, 1929.

Colpi, H. *Défense et illustration de la musique dans le film.* Lyon: Serdoc, 1963.

Courtade, F. *Les Malédictions du cinéma français.* Paris: Ed. Alain Moreau, 1978.

Cuinet, R., and M. Grancher. *Pour faire du cinéma.* Paris: Publitout, 1927.

Dalio, M. *Mes années folles.* Paris: J.-C. Lattès.

Danel, I. *Des Etoiles sont nées.* Paris: L'Herminier, 1986.

Daquin, L. *Le Cinéma notre métier.* Paris: Les Editeurs Français Réunis, 1960.

David, P. *Le Cinéma et l'expansion économique* (report presented April-May 1929).

de Lauretis, T., and S. Heath. (eds.). *The Cinematic Apparatus.* London: Macmillan, 1980.

Degand, C. *Le Cinéma . . . cette industrie.* Paris: Ed. Techniques et Economiques, 1972.

Delluc, L. *Cinéma et cie.* Paris: Grasset, 1919.

Desfontaines, H. *Cours d'art dramatique appliqué au cinéma.* Paris: Edition Universelle par Correspondance, n.d. (ca. 1930).

Diamant-Berger, H. *Le Cinéma.* Paris: La Renaissance du livre, 1919.

Douin, J.-L. *Comédiennes d'aujourd'hui.* Paris: L'Herminier, 1980.

Ducout, F. *Les Séductrices du cinéma français, 1936–1956.* Paris: Henri Veyrier, 1978.

Dumesnil, R. *La Musique en France entre les deux guerres.* Geneva: Milieu du Monde, 1946.

Durand, J. *Le Cinéma et son public.* Paris: Sirey, 1958.

Duvignaud, J. *Esquisse d'une sociologie du comédien.* Paris: Gallimard, 1965.

Ehrlich, E. *Cinema of Paradox: French Filmmaking under the German Occupation.* Columbia University Press, 1985.

Eisler, H. *Composing for the films.* New York: OUP, 1947.

Elsaesser, T., and G. Vincendeau. *Cinéastes allemands en France: les années 30.* Paris: Institut Goethe, 1983.

Epstein, J. *Ecrits sur le cinéma.* Paris: Seghers, 1974 (vol. 1) and 1975 (vol. 2).

Fabre, S. *Douche Ecossaise.* Paris: Fournier Valdès, 1948.

Fain, G. *Une Industrie clé intellectuel.* Paris: Chambre syndicale française de la cinématographie, 1928.

Fescourt, H. *Le Cinéma, des origines à nos jours.* Paris: Cygne, 1932.

———. *La Foi et les montagnes.* Paris: Paul Montel, 1959.

Feyder, J., and F. Rosay. *Le Cinéma, notre métier.* Geneva: Skira, 1944.

Flitterman-Lewis, S. *To Desire Differently: Feminism and French Cinema.* University of Illinois Press, 1990.

Florey, R. *Hollywood d'hier et d'aujourd'hui.* Paris: Prisma, 1948.

Flot, Y. *Les Producteurs: les risques d'un métier.* Paris: Hatier, 1986.

Ford, Ch. *Le Breviaire du cinéma.* Paris: J. Melot, 1946.

———. *Histoire du cinéma français contemporain, 1945–1977.* Paris: France-Empire, 1977.

———. *On tourne . . . lundi.* Paris: Vigneau.

———. *Pierre Fresnay.* Paris: France-Empire, 1981.

Frank, N. *Henri Jeanson en verve.* Paris: Pierre Henri, 1971.

———. *Petit Cinéma sentimental.* Paris: La Nouvelle Edition, 1950.

Garçon, F. *De Blum à Pétain: cinéma et société française, 1936–1944.* Paris: Les Editions du Cerf, 1984.

Garnier, R. *Cours de technique de décors appliquée au cinéma.* Paris: Ecole Universelle, 1930.

Gili, J. *La Vie cinématographique à Nice, 1939–1945.* Nice: Faculté des Lettres, 1973.

Godard, J.-L. *Godard par Godard.* Paris: Cahiers du Cinéma, 1968.

Guback, T. *The International Film Industry: Western Europe and America since 1945.* Bloomington: Indiana University Press, 1969.

Guillaume-Grimaud, G. *Le Cinéma du front populaire*. Paris: Lherminier, 1986.
Guillot, G. *Les Préverts*. Paris: Seghers, 1966.
Guillot, Ph. *Architecture de film*. IDHEC, n.d., unpublished.
Guitry, S. *Quatre ans d'occupation*. Paris: L'Elan, 1947.
Hacquard, G. *La Musique et le cinéma*. Paris: Presses Universitaires de France, 1959.
Hamelin, H. *L'Industrie du cinéma*. Paris: Le Conseil National du Patronat Français, 1954.
Hayward, S., and G. Vincendeau. (eds.). *French Film: Texts and Contexts*. London: Routledge & Kegan Paul, 1989.
Henri-Robert, J. *De la prise de vues à la projection*. Paris: P. Montel, 1930.
Hillier, J. (ed.). *Cahiers du Cinéma*. Harvard University Press, 1986.
Icart, R. *La Révolution du parlant*. Institut Jean Vigo, 1988.
Jeancolas, J.-P. *15 ans d'années trente: Le Cinéma des français, 1929–1944*. Paris: Stock, 1983.
Jeander (ed.). *Armand Tallier et le studio des Ursulines*. Paris: AFCAE, 1963.
Jeanne, R., and Ch. Ford. *Le Cinéma et la presse*. Paris: Armand Colin, 1961.
Jeanson, H. *70 ans d'adolescence*. Paris: Stock, 1971.
Jouvet, L. *Le Comédien désincarné*. Paris: Flammarion, 1954.
Kossowsky, A. *ABC de la technique du cinéma*. Paris: Chiron, 1934.
Krautz, A. (ed.). *International Directory of Cinematographers, Set and Costume Designers in Film* (to 1980). Vol. 2 (France) and vol. 6 (Supplement 1980 *IN*). Munich, New York, London, Paris: K. G. Saur, 1983.
L'Herbier, M. *Intelligence du cinématographe*. Paris: Correa, 1946.
——. *La Tête qui tourne*. Paris: Pierre Belfond, 1979.
Lacombe, A., and C. Roche. *La Musique de film*. Paris: van de Velde, 1979.
Lagny, M., et al. *Générique de années 30*. St. Denis: Presses Universitaires de Vincennes, 1986.
Lang, A. *Le Tableau blanc*. Paris: Horizons de France, 1948.
Laulan, A.-M. *Cinéma presse et public*. Paris: Retz, 1978.
Laurent, H. *Notes sur l'organisation des studios*. Paris: IDHEC, 1965.
——. *La Technologie du décor de film*. Paris: IDHEC, n.d. (1955).
Lebrun, D. *Paris-Hollywood: Les Français dans le cinéma américain*. Paris: Hazan, 1987.
Leenhardt, R. *Chroniques de cinéma*. Paris: Cahiers du Cinéma, 1986.
Lefèvre, R. *Le Film de ma vie, 1939–73*. Paris: Editions France-Empire, 1973.
Léglise, P. *Le Cinéma d'art et essai*. Paris: La Documentation française, 1980.
——. *Histoire de la politique du cinéma français*. Vol. 1, *Le Cinéma et la IIIe république*. Paris: R. Pichon et R. Durand-Auzias, 1970. Vol. 2, *Entre deux républiques* (1940–1946). Paris: Pierre Lherminier, 1977.
Leprohon, P. *50 ans de cinéma français*. Paris: Editions du Cerf, 1954.
——. *Les 1001 métiers du cinéma*. Paris: Jacques Melot, 1947.
——. *Hommes et métiers du cinéma*. Paris: A. Bonne, 1967.
Leprohon, P. (ed.). *Présences contemporaines: Cinéma*. Paris: Nouvelles Editions Debresse, 1957.
Leroy, D. *Economie des arts du spectacle vivant*. Paris: 1980.
Lévy, J. *Etude et présentation de la revue* La Critique Cinématographique. Thèse, Sorbonne.
Lo Duca. *Technique du cinéma*. Paris: Presses Universitaires de France, 1948.
Lods, J. *La Formation professionnelle des techniciens de film*. Paris: UNESCO, 1951.
Lorcey, J. *Marcel Achard*. Paris: France-Empire, 1977.
Lourié, E. *My Work in Films*. San Diego, New York, London: Harcourt Brace Jovanovitch, 1984.
Louvrier, P. *Brasillach: l'illusion fasciste*. Paris: Perrin, 1989.
Lowry, E. *The Filmology Movement and Film Study in France*. UMI Research Press.
Mallet-Stevens, R. *Le Décor moderne au cinéma*. Paris: 1928.
Mandion, R. *Cinéma, reflet du monde*. Paris: Ed. Paul Montel, 1944.

Marais, J. *Histoires de ma vie*. Paris: Albin Michel, 1975.

Mareschal, G. *Les Techniques cinématographiques*. Vols. 1, 2, 3. IDHEC, 1963.

Marion, D. (ed.). *Le Cinéma par ceux qui le font*. Paris: Arthème Fayard, 1949.

Martin, J. *The Golden Age of French Cinema, 1929–1939*. London: Columbus Books, 1987.

Martin, M. *Le Langage cinématographique*. Paris: Ed. du Cerf, 1955.

Mathos, P. *Décors: du studio au plateau*. Paris: n.d. (1931).

Mazeau, J. *Les Grands Acteurs français*. Paris: P.U.F. (Coll Que sais-je), 1982.

Mazeau, J., and D. Thouart. *Les Grands Seconds Rôles du cinéma français*. Paris: P.A.C., 1984.

Metz, C. *Essais sur la signification au cinéma*. Paris: Klincksiek, 1968 and 1972.

Michalczyk, J. *The French Literary Filmmakers*. Philadelphia: Art Alliance Press, 1980.

Mitry, J. *Esthétique et psychologie du cinéma*. Paris: Ed. Universitaires, 1963.

Morin, E. *Les Stars*. Paris: Le Seuil, 1957.

Moris, R. *Le Cinéma: étude économique*. Montpelier: Canne, 1930.

Mouchon, P. *Ciné-Montage*. Paris: Paul Montel, 1954.

Mouliniers, P. *Catalogue des périodiques français et étrangers consacrés au cinéma et conservé au département des périodiques de la Bibliothèque Nationale*. Paris: IDHEC.

Moussinac, L. *L'Age ingrat du cinéma*. Paris: Sagittaire, 1946.

———. *Panoramique du cinema*. Paris: Sans-Pareil, 1929.

Nahon, C. *La Notion d'auteur de films*. Mémoire de fin d'études, IDHEC *XIᵉ* cohort, 1956–57.

Naumberg, N. (ed.) *Silence, on tourne* (tr. J.-G. Auriol). Paris: Payot.

Neale, S. *Cinema and Technology: Image, Sound, Colour*. Bloomington: BFI and Indiana University Press, 1985.

Noë, Y. *Cours no. 8: le studio ouvre ses portes*. Nice: Ecole Technique du Cinéma par Correspondance, 1944.

———. *L'Epicerie des rêves*. Paris: Ed. Baudinière, 1933.

Noë, Y., et al. *Cours no. 14: le montage*. Nice: Ecole Technique du Cinéma par Correspondance, 1945.

Nouet, M. *Pour Vous: contribution à l'étude d'un magazine de cinéma*. Institut Français des Presses et des Sciences de l'Information, 1974 (thèse).

Nouet, R. *Comment écrire pour le cinéma*. Paris: Agence Littéraire du Cinéma, 1957.

Pagnol, M. *Confidences*. Paris: Julliard, 1981.

Paris, J. *The Great French Films*. Secaucus, N.J.: Citadel Press, 1983.

Passek, J.-L. (ed.). *D'un cinéma l'autre: notes sur le cinéma français des années 50*. Paris: Centre Georges Pompidou, 1988.

Pathé, Ch. *De Pathé Frères à Pathé Cinéma*. Lyon: Premier Plan (SERDOC), 1970.

Pathé, T. *Le Cinéma*. Paris: Correa, 1942.

Pellissier, P. *Brasillach . . . le maudit*. Paris: Denoël, 1989.

Pinel, V. *Filmographie des longs métrages sonores du cinéma français*. Paris: La Cinémathèque française, 1985.

———. *Introduction au cinéclub*. Paris: Ed. Ouvrières, n.d. (ca. 1964).

———. *Le Réalisateur de films face à son interprète*. Mémoire de fin d'études, IDHEC, June 1961.

———. *Techniques du cinéma*. Que sais-je? Paris: PUF, 1981.

Pivasset, J. *Essai sur la signification politique: l'exemple français, de la libération aux événements de mai '68*. Paris: Cujas, 1971.

Poiré, A. *Gaumont: 90 ans de cinéma*. Paris: Ramsay, 1986.

Porcile, F. *Maurice Jaubert, musicien populaire ou maudit*. Paris: Editeurs Français Réunis, 1971.

———. *La Musique à l'écran*. Paris: Cerf, 1969.

Prédal, R. *80 ans de cinéma: Nice et le 7ᵉ art*. Serre, 1980.

———. *La Photo de cinéma*. Paris: Ed. du Cerf, 1985.

———. *La Société française à travers le cinéma, 1914–1945*. Paris: Armand Colin, 1972.

Quéval, J. *Marcel Carné*. Paris: Cerf, 1952.
Ragache, G., and J. R. Ragache. *La Vie quotidienne des écrivains et des artistes sous l'occupation, 1940–1944*. Paris: Hachette, 1988.
Rambaud, Ch., et al. *Initiation au Cinéma*. Paris: Ligel, Vol. 1, 1963; Vol. 2, 1965.
Rebatet, L. *Les Tribus du cinéma et du théâtre*. Vol. 4 of *Les Juifs en France*. Paris: N.E.F., 1941.
Régent, R. *Cinéma de France*. Paris: Bellefaye, 1948.
———. *Raimu*. Paris: Chavane, 1957.
Reisz, K. *The Technique of Film Editing*. London and New York, 1953.
Renoir, J. *Ecrits, 1926–1971*. Paris: Belfond, 1974.
Richard, A.-P. *Les Tendances modernes de la cinématographie: état du cinéma 1927*.
Richard-Willm, P. *Loin des étoiles*. Paris: Belfond, 1975.
Richebé, R. *Au-delà de l'écran: 70 ans de la vie d'un cinéaste*. Monaco: Pastorelly, 1977.
Rivers, F. *50 ans chez les fous*. Paris: G. Girard, 1945.
Roger, J. *Naissance d'un film*. Paris and Brussels: Ed. Universitaires, 1956.
Rohmer, E. *Le Goût de la beauté*. Paris: Cahiers du Cinéma, 1984.
Rosay, F. *La Traversée d'une vie*. Paris: Robert Laffont, 1974.
Rothschild, P. de. *Le Cinéma: les techniques au service de la pensée*. Paris: 1938.
Roux, J., and R. Thévenet. *Industrie et commerce du film en France*. Paris: Ed. Scientifiques et Juridiques, 1979.
Sabria, J.-C. *Cinéma français: les années 50*. Paris: Centre Georges Pompidou, 1989.
Sadoul, G. *Le Cinéma français, 1890–1962*. Paris: Flammarion, 1962.
———. *Le Cinéma: son art, sa technique, son économie*. Paris: La Bibliothèque Française, 1948.
———. *Histoire générale du cinéma*. Vol. 1, 1946; vol. 2, 1948; vol. 3, 1951; vol. 4, Sound in Europe, 1952; vol. 5, 1975; vol. 6, 1975. Paris: Denoël.
———. *French Film*. Edited by R. Manvell. London: Arno Press, 1972 (1953 ed.).
———. *Les Merveilles du cinéma*. Paris: Editeurs Français Réunis, 1957.
Sale, Ch. *Les Scénaristes au travail*. Renens: Hatier, 1981.
Salles-Gomes, P. *Jean Vigo*. Paris: Seuil, 1957.
Sallée, A. *Les acteurs français, depuis Sarah Bernhardt*. Paris: Bordas, 1988.
Salt, B. *Film Style and Technology: History and Analysis*. London: Starword, 1983.
Schlosberg, L. *Les Censures cinématographiques*. Paris: L'Union Rationaliste, 1955.
Servel, A. *Frenchie goes to Hollywood: la France et les Français dans le cinéma américain de 1929 à nos jours*. Paris: H. Veyrier, 1987.
Sesonske, A. *Jean Renoir: The French Years 1924–1939*. Harvard University Press, 1980.
Siclier, J. *Le Cinéma français, 1945–1985*. Paris: Ramsay, 1989.
———. *La France de Pétain et son cinéma*. Paris: Henri Veyrier, 1981.
———. *Le Mythe de la femme dans le cinéma français*. Paris: Cerf, 1957.
Souriau, E. (ed.). *L'Univers filmique*. Paris: Flammarion, 1953.
Spaak, J. *Charles Spaak, mon mari*. Paris: France-Empire, 1977.
Strebel, E. G. *French Social Cinema of the Nineteen Thirties* (doctoral thesis). Ayer, 1980.
Stromberg, H. *La Technique du film*. Paris: 1939.
Tabet, G. *Vivre deux fois*. Paris: Laffont, 1980.
Thiher, A. *The Cinematic Muse: Critical Studies in the History of French Cinema*. University of Missouri Press, 1979.
Torok, J. P. *Le Scénario: histoire, théorie, pratique*. Paris: Artefact, 1986.
Trauner, A. *Décors de cinéma*. Paris: Jad-Flammarion, 1988.
Trojani, C. *Henri Alekan: biofilmographie complète, 1929–1985*.
Truffaut, F. *Les Films de ma vie*. Paris: Flammarion, 1975.
van Parys, G. *Les Jours comme ils viennent*. Paris: Plon, 1969.
Vigneau, A. *Le Cinéma*. Cairo: Les Lettres Françaises, 1945.
Villiers, A. *La Prostitution de l'acteur*. Paris: Editions du Pavois, 1946.
———. *La Psychologie de l'art dramatique*. Paris: Armand Colin, 1951.

Villiers, M., and G. Gessard. *Stars d'aujourd'hui*. Paris: Ramsay, Vol. 1, 1985; vol. 2, 1986.
Vinaver, M. *La Fin et les moyens de l'acteur*. Paris: Théâtre Populaire, 1958.
Vincendeau, G., and K. Reader. *La Vie est à nous: French Cinema and the Popular Front*. London: BFI, 1986.
Volmane, V., and Ch. Ford. *Cinéma pour vous*. Paris: Juillard, 1974.
Wahkevitch, G. *L'Envers des décors*. Paris: Robert Laffont, 1977.
Watts, S. (ed.). *La Technique du Film* (tr. J.-G. Auriol). Paris: Payot, 1939.
Weil-Lorac, R. *Cinquante ans de cinéma actif*. Paris: Dujarric, 1977.
———. *Histoire de la confédération national du cinéma français*. Bois d'Arcy: CNC, 1983.
Wiener, J. *Allegro appassionato*. Paris: Belfond, 1979.
Winock, M. *Histoire politique de la revue* Esprit. Paris: le Seuil, 1975.
Wyn, M. *Initiation aux techniques du cinéma*. Paris: Eyrolles, 1956.
Zay, J. *Souvenirs et solitudes*. Paris: Juillard, 1945.

OTHER BOOKS

Aide-mémoire de construction standard. Paris, CST, n.d.
Annuaire de l'IDHEC, 1944–1960. Paris: IDHEC, 1961.
Annuaire des anciens élèves, 1944–64. Paris: IDHEC, 1965.
L'Architecture-décoration dans le film. Paris: IDHEC, 1955.
Les Catholiques parlent du cinéma. Paris: Editions Universitaires, 1948.
Le Cinéma, des origines à nos jours. Paris: Cygne, 1933.
Le Cinéma français, 1930–1960. Paris: Editions Atlas, 1984.
Cinquante ans au service de la presse cinématographique. Paris: FIPRESCI 2, 1981.
Cours no. 9: la naissance d'un film. Cannes: Ecole Technique du Cinéma par Correspondance, 1944.
Cours no. 12: le metteur en scène. Cannes: Ecole Technique de Cinéma par Correspondance (n.d., 1944?).
Les Dessous du cinéma allemand. Paris et Limoges: Courier du Centre (n.d.).
Dossiers du Cinéma: Cinéastes, no. 1. Paris: Casterman, 1974.
L'Expression cinématographique. Paris: L'Herminier, 1977.
L'Industrie du cinéma. Paris: Société Nouvelle Mercure, 1954.
Jacques Feyder, ou le cinéma concret. Bruxelles, 1949.
Jacques Prévert. Lyon: Premier Plan 14 (SERDOC), 1960.
Jean Renoir. Lyon: Premier Plan 22–24, 1962.
Le Livre d'or du cinéma français. 1945, 1946, 1947–48, 1950.
Le Montage de cinéma et de télévision. Paris: CILECT, 1965.
Organisation et équipement d'un studio de prise de vues. Paris: CST/IDHEC, 1958.
Où va le cinéma français (report of the Renaitour inquiry). Paris: Baudinière, n.d. (1937).
Revue du Cinéma I and II. Rev. ed., with introductory essays by Jean-Paul Le Chanois, Odette Virmaux, Alain Virmaux, and Jacques Doniol-Valcroze in 5 volumes. Paris: L'Herminier, 1979–1980.
Synthèse, no. 2, 1947: special issue.
Wahkevitch: décors et costumes. Marseilles: Musée Provençal du Cinéma, 1980.

ARTICLES IN BOOKS AND JOURNALS

L'Age Nouveau 51, June 1950.
Aguettand, L. In *Le Livre d'or du cinéma français*, 1950.

L'Amour de l'Art 37–39 n.d., 1949.

Andrews, D. "IDHEC," *Journal of the UFVA* 35, 1, Winter 1983.

———. "Sound in France: The Origins of a Native School," *Yale French Studies* 60, 1980.

Architecture d'Aujourd'hui 4, 1938.

Arland, R.-M. "Des histoires et des auteurs," *Le Livre d'or*, 1950.

Arts 423, 7 August 1953; 484, 6 October 1954; 487, 27 October 1954; 489, 10 November 1954; 495, 8 December 1954; 502, 2 February 1955; 503, 16 February 1955; 504, 16 February 1955; 540, 2 November 1955; 608, 27 February 1957; 619, 15 May 1957; 620, 22 May 1957; 627, 10 July 1957; 628, 17 July 1957; 632, 14 August 1957; 640, 16 October 1957; 652, 8 January 1958; 667, 23 April 1958; 670, 14 May 1958; 699, 3 December 1958; 700, 10 December 1958; 751, 2 December 1959; 761, 10 February 1960; 772, 27 April 1960; 797, 23 November 1960; 816, 5 April 1961; 826, 14 June 1961; 857, 21 February 1962; 863, 4 April 1962; 873, 13 June 1962.

Aurenche, J. "Création cinématographique," IDHEC lecture, 25 February 1944.

Auric, G. Entretiens, *L'Ecran Fantastique* 5, 1978.

———. "Musique et cinéma," *Unifrance Film* 50, July-September 1959.

Avant-Scène du Cinéma 297–298, December 1982.

Barbaro, U. "Le Cinéma sans acteurs," in *Le Rôle intellectuel du cinéma*. Paris: 1937.

Barjavel, R. "L'Age de la couleur," *Le Film* 86, 1 April 1944.

Barkan, R. "Qu'est-ce qu'un acteur de cinéma?" *Ciné Amateur* 277, August 1962.

Barry, M. "La Lumière," *Télécine* 121–122, 1965.

Barsacq, L. "Le Décor," in *Le Cinéma par ceux qui le font*. Ed. D. Marion.

Baudrier, Y. Cours de technique et d'esthétique de la musique de film, Cours de l'IDHEC, October-November 1944.

———. "Musique et cinéma," *Cahiers de l'IDHEC*, 1950.

Bazin, A. "Comment présenter et discuter un film," *Cinéclub*, April 1954.

Bernard, G. "Hollywood et les musiciens," *Formes et Couleurs* 6, 1946.

Bertrand, P. "Le Décorateur," *Unifrance Film* 20, October 1952.

Bessy, M. "Types et caractères des jeunes premiers," *Ciné Magazine* 4, April 1930.

Beucler, A. "Au studio," *Revue de Paris* 1, April 1935.

Beylie, C. "Il y a 50 ans: 1929, le grand tournant," *Ecran* 79, 86, 15 December 1979.

Blanchar, P. "Le jeu de l'acteur," IDHEC 1, December 1944.

Blemmech, O. "Tour d'horizon, 1957," *Cinéopse* 366, January 1958.

Borde, R. "La Cinémathèque française: recherche de la vérité," *Cahiers de la Cinémathèque* 22–24, 1977.

Borie, P. "La Grande Misère des artistes de cinéma," *Ciné Magazine* 2, February 1930.

Bost, P. "Le Cinéma devant la société," IDHEC lecture, 5 December 1944.

———. "Création cinématographique," lecture to IDHEC, 26 April 1944.

Bricon, R. "A propos du montage," *Photo-Revue*, November 1946.

Bridoux, M. "Le Montage du film," *Photo-Ciné-Revue*, July 1956.

Cahiers de la Cinémathèque, no. 23–24, Christmas 1977.

Cahiers du Cinéma, all issues.

Les Cahiers du Mois 16–17, 1925.

Carsalade du Pont, H. de. "Musique et cinéma," *Etudes* 7–8, July-August 1958.

Centre National de la Cinématographie, Bulletin d'Information: All issues, especially 31, February 1955.

Charensol, G. "Le Cinéma et la presse, 1946," *Le Livre d'or du cinéma français*, 1947.

Chazal, R. "Voici l'histoire du festival de Cannes . . . ," *Ciné Revue* 18, 2 May 1958.

Chevalier, J. "Une thèse sur les cinéclubs," *Education Nationale* 22, 14 June 1956.

Chevassu, F. "Mesures à prendre pour une meilleure musique de film," *Le Cinéma Chez Soi* 19, September 1958.

Choisir, all issues.

Christian-Jacque. "Notre métier," *Unifrance Film* 18, May-June 1952.
Cilane, J. "L'Enchaînement des plans," *Photo-Cinéma* 732, October 1962.
Ciné Digest, all issues from 1 May 1949.
Cinéclub 4, January-February 1951.
Cinema 56, all issues.
Cinéma d'Aujourd'hui 10, Christmas 1976.
Cinéma International 14, 1967.
Cinéma Pratique 131/132, 1974—history of Debrie firm.
Cinémaction 45, 1987 (Dossier).
Le Cinématographe 17, February 1976; 18 and 21 (Jean Gabin); 27, May 1977; 31, December 1977; 33, February 1959; 35 and 39 (Simone Signoret); 46 (Gérard Philipe); 53, December 1979; 55 (Florelle); 58 (Sylvie Bataille); 58, 1980; 61 (Modot); 61, October 1980; 68, June 1981; 69, July 1981; 75, February 1982; 76, March 1982; 78, July-August 1963; 86, February 1983; 94, November 1983; 100, May 1984; 102, July 1984; 103, September-October 1984; 119, May 1986.
La Cinématographie Française, all issues.
Coffet, A. "Possibilités et servitudes de l'évolution technique," *Le Livre d'or*, 1945.
Combes, M. "Les Studios: techniques du cinéma et de la télévision," *Photo Ciné Revue*, April 1965.
Comoedia 6, 30 December 1952; 7, 6 January 1953; 20, 7 April 1953; 41, 11 November 1953; 47, 23 December 1953; 52, 27 January 1954; 53, 3 February 1954; 56, 24 February 1954; 66, 5 May 1954; 96, 1 May 1943; 108, 24 July 1943; 131, 8 January 1944.
Coste, G. "Images et musique," *Education et Cinéma* 4, November 1955.
Cottom, J. "Cette crise d'imagination qui paralyse le cinéma," *Ciné Revue* 23, 8 June 1956.
———. "L'Evolution de goût cinématographique . . . ," *Ciné Revue* 19, 6 May 1960.
———. "Philippe Erlanger, son fondateur raconte . . . Cannes," *Ciné Revue* 21, 21 May 1981.
Cournot, M. "Prévert, comme l'espoir," *Nouvel Observateur* 649, 18 April 1977.
Cozarinsky, E. "Foreign filmmakers in France," in *Rediscovering French Cinema*. Ed. Bandy. New York: 1983.
Crisp, C. G. "The rediscovery of editing in the French cinema, 1930–1945," *Histoire et Mesure* II, 3–4, 1987.
Cuny, A. "Tragédie du comédien," *Psyché* 9–10, July-August 1947.
Dailly, R. "Les Cinéclubs," *Chronique Sociale de France* 4–5, 1954.
Damas, G. "Les Points et les virgules," *Stars et Films* 18, 15 January 1948.
Daquin, L. Lecture to IDHEC, 8 March 1944.
Debrix, J. "L'IDHEC de Paris," *Revue de la Pensée Française* 2, February 1947.
Degand, C., and D. Corbet. "Le Cinéma français," *La Documentation Française*. November 1966.
Delac, Ch. "Le Producteur: son rôle," in *Le Cinéma des origines à nos jours*. Paris: Cygne, 1932.
Derain, L. "L'Equipement des studios français," *Le Livre d'or du cinéma français*, 1950.
Douy, M. "L'Architecte-Décorateur," *Unifrance Film* 51, October 1959.
L'Ecran Français, all issues.
Elsaesser, T. "Pathos and Leavetaking," *Sight and Sound* 53, 4, 1984.
Etudes Cinématographiques, no. 14–15, 1962 (ed. C. Gauteur).
Fargier, J., et al. "La Notion de production," *Cinéthique* 4, 1969.
Feuillère, E. "La Vedette," in *Le Cinéma par ceux qui le font*. Ed. D. Marion.
Film et Vie 29, May 1966.
Le Film Français, all issues.
Filmdope 5, July 1976; 23, September 1981.

Films et Documents 141, June 1959.

Fougères. "Le Film reflète le tempérament de son créateur," *Ciné Revue* 6, 8 February 1957.

France Film International, 10 October 1955; 2, February 1955; 6, 20 April 1956; 8, 20 May 1956; 9, 5 June 1956; 9–10, May 1958; 1 January 1959; 28 January 1961.

France Observateur 297, 19 January 1956; 352, 7 February 1957; 461, 5 March 1959; 615, 15 February 1962.

Frank, N. "Petits Secrets du métier de scénariste," *Formes et Couleurs* 6, special issue, 1946.

Fresnay, P. "La Profession de comédien," *Encyclopédie Française*, vol. 17, 17.88, December 1935.

Frogerais, P. "Mission du producteur," *Le Livre d'or du cinéma français*, 1946.

Fronval, G. "Les émigrés," *Ciné Miroir Almanach*, 1945.

Gili, J. "Cinecitta au secours du cinéma français 1940–1943," *Filméchange* 38, 1987.

———. "Une société malade de moralité," *Ecran* 72, 8, September-October 1972.

Ginet, R. "Les Nouveaux Venus," *Le Livre d'or du cinéma français*, 1945.

Gomery, D. "Economic Struggle and Hollywood Imperialism: Europe Converts to Sound," *Yale French Studies* 60, 1980.

Grelier, R. "31e anniversaire de l'IDHEC," *Cinéma Pratique* 131–132, July-August 1974.

Grémillon, J. "A propos des cinémathèques," *Le Livre d'or du cinéma français*, 1945.

Hanoun, P. Philippe Agostini interview, *Photo Cinéma* 651, January 1956.

Honegger, A. "Du cinéma sonore à la musique réelle," *Plans* 1, January 191.

Huisman, G. "Le Censeur," in *Le Cinéma par ceux qui le font.* Ed. D. Marion. Paris: Arthème Fayard, 1949.

Ibert, J. "Musique et cinéma," *Le Livre d'or du cinema français*, 1945.

Image et Son 49, January 1952; 51, March 1952; 61, March 1953; 65, July 1953; 77, November-December 1954; 80, March 1955; 106, November 1957; 107, December 1957; 163, June 1963; 167–168, November-December 1963; 175, July 1964; 206, May 1967; 283, April 1974; 341–343, July-October 1979; 403, March 1985; 431, October 1987.

Interciné, February 1932, January 1935, April 1935, October 1935.

Jaubert, M. "Le Cinéma: petite école du spectateur: la musique," *Esprit* 43, 1 April 1936.

Jeander. "Les Cinéclubs," in *Le Cinéma par ceux qui le font.* Ed. D. Marion. Paris: Arthème Fayard, 1949.

Jeandret, J. "Voici les règles d'or du montage," *Le Cinéma Chez Soi* 9, December 1956.

Jeanson, H. "L'Auteur de film, c'est son scénariste," *Soirées de Paris*, 1945.

———. "Cinq semaines à la Paramount: choses vues," *Crapouillot*. Special issue, 1932.

Jeune Cinéma 126, April-May 1980; 131, December-January 1980–81; 133, March 1981.

Journal Musical Français, 1 December 1949 through 7 February 1950; 95, February 1961; 91, 17 October 1960; 110, 25 September 1962; 114, 5 January 1963; 55, January 1957; 26, September 1952;

Jouvet, L. "L'Art du comedien," *Encyclopédie Française*, vol. 17, 17.64, December 1935.

L'Herbier, M. "Ecole du film," *Style en France.*

———. "Sur une faculté du film," *Livre d'or du cinéma français*, 1945.

Legrand, H. "Le Cinéma connaît-il la musique?" *Ciné Digest* 1, May 1949.

Lemare, J. "Comment on éclaire les images d'un film," *Ciné Digest* 9, January 1950.

Les Lettres Françaises 353, 18 April 1952; 360, 6 June 1952; 545, 2 December 1954; 553, 27 January 1955; 576, 7 July 1955; 603, 19 January 1956; 611, 15 March 1956; 613, 29 March 1956; 621, 24 May 1956; 642, 25 October 1956; 653, 10 January 1957; 657, 7 February 1957; 708, 6 February 1958; 711, 27 February 1958; 712, 6 March 1958; 724, 29 May 1958; 734, 7 August 1958; 736, 28 August 1958; 780, 2 July 1959; 879, 8 June 1961; 911, 25 January 1962; 922, 12 April 1962; 1059, 17 December 1964; 1343, 15 July 1970.

London, K. "Musique et cinéma," *Interciné*, April 1934.
Lopez, R. Cours de musique appliquée, IDHEC.
Lowry, E. "Filmology: History of a Problematic," *Quarterly Review of Film Studies*, Winter 1985.
Luguet, A. "Le Métier d'acteur et l'art du comédien," in *Le Cinéma par ceux qui le font*. Ed. D. Marion.
Macke, C. "Le Décor est-il un acteur," *Ecrans de France* 154, November 1955.
Maigret, D. "Le festival de Cannes, c'était hier," *Cinémonde* 1834, 5 May 1970.
Manevy, R. "Cinquante ans de cinéma," *Almanach Ciné Miroir*, 1945.
Marion, D. "L'Economie du cinéma," in *Synthèse* 2, 1947.
Matras, C. "L'Opérateur, interprète de l'image," in *Le Livre d'or*, 1946.
Meyer, C. "La Télévision aux Buttes-Chaumont," *Télé* 58, 732.
Mirbel, J. "Un Hollywood français," *Ciné Magazine*, November 1930.
Mitry, J. "Les Carrières du cinéma," *Stars et Films* 21, 1948.
Morienval, J. "Quand aurions-nous la cinémathèque nationale?" *Cinéopse* 337, January 1955.
———. "Le Véritable Auteur du film," *Cinéopse* 355, October 1954.
Moussinac, L. "L'Age héroïque du cinéma," in *Cinéma: oeil ouvert sur le monde*. Lausanne: Clairefontaine, 1952.
Nogueira, R. "Burel and Bresson: An interview," *Sight and Sound* 1, Winter 1976–77.
Objectif 123, 22 November 1955; 125, 24 January 1966.
Pennec, C. "Le Règne des grands chef-opérateurs est fini", *Arts-Loisirs* 70, 25 January 1967.
Ploquin, R. "A propos des festivals," *Ecrans du Monde*, 1 October 1960.
———. "Le Producteur," in *Le Cinéma par ceux qui le font*. Ed. D. Marion.
Poitier, P. "De la musique filmée," *Interciné*, June 1935.
Pollet, A. "Qu'est-ce qu'un festival," *Ecrans de France* 152, September 1955.
Polyphonie 6, 1950.
Positif, all issues, especially 1, May 1952; 2, June 1952; 13, March-April 1955; 27, February 1958; 162, October 1974; 174, October 1975; 223–224; 244–245, July-August 1981; 246, September 1981; 254–255, May 1982; 261, November 1982; 286, December 1984; 293–294, July-August 1985; 323, January 1988; 327, May 1988; 329–330 and 331, July-August and September 1988.
Pour Vous 234, 11 May 1933.
Prédal, R. "Hugues Laurent," *Avant-Scène Cinéma* 192, September 1977.
Quéval, J. "L'Economie du cinéma," in *Chronique Sociale de France* 4/5, 1954.
Raccords 9, Autumn 1951.
Rambaud, P. "Musique française," *Le Livre d'or*, 1945.
Régnier, G. "Le Scénario," *Photo Cinéma* 655, May 1956.
Renoir, C. Dossier, *Culture et Communication* 19, September 1979.
———. "Soyez tranquille: il reviendra," *Cinéclub* 6.
Revue du Cinéma, all issues, notably I 3, 4 5, 8, 9, 11, 13, 16, 18, 20, 23, 27, 28 and II 1–6, 8, 9, 10, 12, 16, 17.
Revue Internationale du Cinéma 4, 1949; 7, 1951; 18, 1954; 22, 1955; 34, 15 September 1959.
Richmond, B. "La Musique nouvelle du film," *Ciné Magazine* 5, May 1930.
Robin, J.-F. "Les Cinémas d'art et essai, défenseurs des films hors série," *Ciné Presse* 1, 20 January 1960.
Roland-Manuel. "Rythme cinématographique et rythme musical," *Le Cinéma* 2, IDHEC, 1945.
Sadoul, G. "Les Cinéclubs en France et dans le monde," *Synthèse* 2, 1947.
Sengissen, P. "Enfin! De nouveaux réalisateurs," *Radio Cinéma IV* 415, 29 December 1957.
Sengissen, P. "Le Montage," *Radio Cinéma Télévision* 218, 21 March 1954.

Soriano, M. "Position de la filmologie," *Synthèse* 2, 1947.
Souillac, P. "A propos des festivals," *Cinéopse* 338–339, February-March 1955.
Spaak, Ch. "Des scénaristes et du scénario," *Synthèse* 2, 1947.
———. Interview, *Film Culture* 5, December 1957.
———. "Le Scénario," in *Le Cinéma par ceux qui le font*. Ed. D. Marion.
Spectacles, no. 3, December 1958.
Le Technicien du Film, all issues to 1960, and 92, March 1963; 104, April 1964; 234,
      February 1976; 236, March 1976; 379, April 1989.
La Technique Cinématographique, all issues.
Tessonneau, "The French Institute of Cinema," *Journal of the University Film Pro-
      ducers Association* 1, 1957.
Thévenet, R. "Les Réalisateurs français depuis la libération," *Le Livre d'or*, 1950.
Torok, J.-P. "L'Age du scénario," *Avant-Scène du Cinéma* 319–320, January 1984.
Trauner, A. Interview: *Culture et Communication* 19, September 1979.
Vagnon, F. "Les Cours pratiques de l'ATCT," *Cinéma Pratique* 151, April-May 1977.
van Parys, G. "Le Musicien," *Le Cinéma par ceux qui le font*. Ed. D. Marion.
———. "La Musique de film," *France-Illustration* 51, September 1946.
———. "Musique et cinéma," *Les Annales* 57, July 1955.
Véry, P. "A propos du scénario," *Ciné Digest* 1, May 1949.
Vignaud, J. "Le Problème du scénario," *Almanach Ciné Miroir*, 1936.
Wiener, J. "Le Rôle de la musique dans le film," IDHEC Conference, 17 April 1945.
———. "A Joinville et à St. Maurice," *Pathé Magazine* 20, Spécial Cannes, 1960.
———. "Abcédaire des paroles de maîtres," *Cinéma Pratique* 47, July-August 1963.
Yvoire, J.d'. "Allons-nous vers le cinéma sans montage?" *Radio Cinéma Télévision*
      230, 13 June 1954.
———. "Sept ans d'efforts," *Bulletin de la FLECC* 4–5, January 1954.

OTHER ARTICLES

Architecture d'Aujourd'hui, no. 4, 1938. Spécial cinéma.
"Le Baptême de la 1ere promotion de l'IDHEC," *Le Film* 86, 1 April 1944.
"Cannes: 35 ans de Festival-star," *Télé-Ciné-Vidéo* 7, May 1981.
"Les Cinéastes allemands en France pendant les années 30," *Positif* 323, January 1988.
Cinéma 2, IDHEC, 1945.
"Le Cinéma de Vichy, un cinéma d'acteurs," *Ecran* 72, 8, September-October 1972.
"Cinéma et culture populaire," *Education et Cinéma* 2, October 1954.
"Le Cinéma français du samedi soir," *Cahiers de la Cinémathèque* 23–24, Christmas 1977.
"Cinémas d'art et essai," *Cinéma Spectacle* 1461–1462, 18 July 1959.
"Le Comédien: cours d'initiation à l'usage des enseignants," CRDP 3 (Ministère de
      l'Education Nationale, Académie de Lyon), s.d.
"Comment ils sont devenus metteurs en scène," *Radio Cinema Télévision* 136, 24 Au-
      gust 1952.
"Comment on devient réalisateur," *L'Ecran et la Vie* 6, December 1961.
"Concours d'entrée," *Le Film* 88, 8 May 1946.
"La Dernière séance," *Monuments Historiques* 137, March, 1985.
"Dossier: studios," *Technicien du Film et de la Vidéo* 359, June 1987.
"L'ENSC," *France Illustration* 51, 21 September 1946.
Interview. *Cinémaction* 45, 1987.
"La Musique dans le film français," *Unifrance Film* 40, July-August 1956.
"Un million et demi de Français vont au cinéclub," *Radio Cinéma* 415, 29 December 1957.
"Naissance du Rouxcolor," *Ciné Digest* 1, May 1949.
"Onze réalisateurs français," *Unifrance Film* 38, January-February 1956.

"Le Parfait Cinéaste," *Style en France* 4, 1946.

"Paris-Studios-Cinéma," *Cinéopse* 266, April 1948.

"Un producteur: Robert Dorfmann," *Unifrance Film International* 31, August-September 1954.

"Quatre producteurs français," *Unifrance Film* 47, July-August 1958.

"Rendez-vous avec quatre écrivains du cinéma," *Unifrance Film* 48, October-December 1958.

"Le rôle des cinéclubs," *Revue des Spectacles* 5, September 1946.

"Studios Francoeur," *Pathé Magazine* 19, Special Cannes, 1959.

"Votre avenir à l'IDHEC," *Top* 73, 10 April 1960.

Colin Crisp is Associate Professor in Film Studies in the Faculty of Humanities, Griffith University and Acting Provost and Director of the Queensland College of Art. He is the author of *Eric Rohmer: Realist and Moralist*.